# British Multinational Banking
## 1830–1990

# British Multinational Banking

## 1830–1990

GEOFFREY JONES

CLARENDON PRESS · OXFORD
1993

*Oxford University Press, Walton Street, Oxford* OX2 6DP

*Oxford New York*
*Athens Auckland Bangkok Bombay*
*Calcutta Cape Town Dar es Salaam Delhi*
*Florence Hong Kong Istanbul Karachi*
*Kuala Lumpur Madras Madrid Melbourne*
*Mexico City Nairobi Paris Singapore*
*Taipei Tokyo Toronto*
*and associated companies in*
*Berlin Ibadan*

*Oxford is a trade mark of Oxford University Press*

*Published in the United States by*
*Oxford University Press Inc., New York*

© *Geoffrey Jones 1993*

*First published 1993*
*Clarendon Paperback first published 1995*

*British Library Cataloguing in Publication Data*
*Data available*

*Library of Congress Cataloging in Publication Data*
*Jones, Geoffrey.*
*British multinational banking, 1830–1990 : a history | Geoffrey*
*Jones.*
*p. cm.*
*Includes bibliographical references and index.*
*1. Banks and banking, International—History.  2. Banks and*
*banking, British—History.  I. Title.*
*HG2992.J66  1993*
*332.1'5'0941—dc20  92-23918*
*ISBN 0-19-820273-3*
*ISBN 0-19-820602-X Pbk*

*Printed in Great Britain*
*on acid-free paper by*
*Bookcraft Ltd., Midsomer Norton, Bath*

# Preface

This study of the development of British multinational banking over the last 150 years has been five years in the making. It grew out of my history of the British Bank of the Middle East, which was commissioned by the Hongkong Bank, and published in two volumes in 1986 and 1987. It became apparent as I wrote that work that the whole subject of the British overseas banking was badly in need of a modern general history. These British multinational banks were a set of important business institutions which had been unaccountably neglected.

This book is largely based on confidential banking archives. It is not a commissioned work and has not been sponsored by any bank. I do owe a large number of banks my gratitude for allowing me access to their archives and allowing me to publish the results of my research without restriction. I was privileged to see confidential material extending from the nineteenth century until the very recent past. I would like to thank the following institutions for allowing archival access: the Bank of England, ANZ Bank, Barclays Bank PLC, the Hongkong Bank, Ionian Securities Ltd., Lloyds Bank PLC, Midland Bank PLC, National Westminster Bank PLC, and Standard Chartered PLC. Sir Michael Sandberg, Will Bailey, and John Pank were most helpful regarding the archives of the Hongkong Bank, ANZ, and Standard Chartered respectively. This project made unusual demands on the time and patience of numerous archivists in the banks and elsewhere. I would particularly like to thank John Booker, Jessie Campbell, Damien Cash, Ron Dyke, Peter Emmerson, Henry Gillet, Edwin Green, Trevor Hart, Margaret Lee, Philip Winterbottom, Lily Sung, Angela Raspin, and Elaine Wong. Their collective help was indispensable.

Financial and other support was provided by a number of sources. The Nuffield Foundation gave me a one-year fellowship which enabled the first stages of the project to be planned and implemented free of the burdens of teaching. This was an immense help. At the same time the Leverhulme Trust provided two-year funding to enable me to employ Frankie Bostock as researcher on the project. Subsequently, both the Nuffield Foundation and the Economic and Social Research Council provided small grants to allow Mrs Bostock to explore in greater depth various specialized aspects of the history of British multinational banking.

Although the majority of surviving bank records are held in the United Kingdom, the extremely important collections of the Hongkong Bank and ANZ are now located in Hong Kong and Melbourne respectively. I had two immensely enjoyable research trips to explore these materials. In Hong

Kong, I stayed at Robert Black College in the University of Hong Kong in the spring of 1987. I would like to thank the Master for allowing me the privilege of being a part of this fine academic community. The friends I made at Robert Black College and the hospitality of Margaret Lee, her husband, W.T., and son, Shung Lok, helped to make my stay in Hong Kong one of the happiest periods of my life. In the summer of 1990 I was equally privileged to be appointed a visitor to the Economic History Department at the University of Melbourne. This enabled me both to research ANZ's archives and to meet an especially stimulating group of economic historians. I would like to thank C. B. Schedvin and David Merrett for this invitation, and for their hospitality.

The single greatest contribution to this book was made by Frankie Bostock. She undertook most of the archival research at Standard Chartered, and all of that of Ionian Bank, demonstrating an outstanding ability as a historical researcher. She took responsibility for the analysis of bank profitability and worth which is reported in Appendix 5, and in which she received much help from her husband, Mark. Each draft of the book was subjected to her critical comments, and she refined and developed the central arguments in countless ways. It represents no exaggeration at all to say that this book could not have been written without both the research of Frankie Bostock and her formidable understanding of British overseas banking. Her energy and devotion to this project was remarkable and she has made a major intellectual contribution to the arguments presented here.

A number of academic colleagues and bankers read all or part of the manuscript, and much improved it as a result. David Merrett made a seminal contribution at a stage when I had a great deal of material but less understanding about how to use it. Mark Casson, Leslie Pressnell, Stuart Muirhead, and Mira Wilkins have read the manuscript in its entirety, and helped me in many ways to see woods rather than trees. Frank H. H. King was an indispensable source of wisdom on the history of the Hongkong Bank, and Eastern Exchange banks generally. Charles Jones taught me much about Latin American banking while Maria Barbara Levy provided me with valuable information on Brazilian banking. Over the years, various embryonic ideas have been tried out on seminars and conferences, and participant comments have frequently exercised a considerable influence on the writing of this book. I would particularly like to thank participants at conferences and seminars held at Reading in 1989, Leeds, Leuven, Auckland, and Wellington in 1990, and Cambridge, South Bank Polytechnic London, Warwick, and Sandbjerg in 1991.

This project began when I was a Lecturer in the Economic History Department of the London School of Economics. LSE provided a good base for the initial research. My understanding of economic history was much enriched in this period. I would like to thank, in particular, Raj Brown and Malcolm Falkus, two former members of LSE's staff, for their intellectual stimulation. In 1988 I moved to the Economics Department of the University of Reading. The support there of Professor Mark Casson for business history in general, and my work in particular, has been critical for the completion of this book. Reading has provided the intellectual environment in which the interaction of business history, economics, and management can be explored in depth in a challenging academic environment. This book is one of the first fruits of this dialogue. It is hoped there will be others, by others.

Lynn Cornell typed and retyped the draft chapters of this book with good humour, despite my handwriting. However, her contribution to this book was much greater, for it could scarcely have been finished if she had not taken over many administrative tasks from the author, and managed the business history office with such efficiency. Finally, I should thank Fabienne for all her help and support.

G.J.

*Reading*
*November 1991*

# Contents

# List of Figures

# List of Graphs

# List of Tables

# List of Abbreviations

*In Text*

| | |
|---|---|
| ANZ | Australian and New Zealand Bank 1951–70. Australia and New Zealand Banking Group since 1970 |
| BBI | Barclays Bank International |
| BBME | British Bank of the Middle East |
| BBWA | Bank of British West Africa |
| Bolsa | Bank of London and South America |
| CEO | chief executive officer |
| DCO | Barclays Bank (Dominion, Colonial and Overseas) |
| E, S & A | English, Scottish & Australian Bank |
| IRR | internal rate of return |
| LBI | Lloyds Bank International |
| MAIBL | Midland and International Banks |
| NPV | net present value |

*Archives*

| | |
|---|---|
| ANZ | Australia and New Zealand Banking Group |
| B. of E. | Bank of England |
| BBA | Barclays Bank |
| Bolsa | Bank of London and South America and its predecessor banks |
| BT | Board of Trade |
| CO | Colonial Office |
| FO | Foreign Office |
| HSBC | Hongkong Bank Group |
| LB | Lloyds Bank |
| LSE | London School of Economics |
| PRO | Public Record Office |
| SC | Standard Chartered |
| T | Treasury |
| UCL | University College London |

# CHAPTER 1

# British Multinational Banking in Perspective

## 1.1. Issues

This book is a history of British multinational banking from its origins in the 1830s until 1990. The first British banks to establish branches outside the United Kingdom appeared in the 1830s. These pioneers built offices and businesses in Australia, Canada, the West Indies, and the Mediterranean, directed and controlled from corporate headquarters in London. In the following decades they pioneered modern banking in much of the world. By the eve of the First World War around thirty British banks owned over 1,000 branches in the British Empire and elsewhere. Until the 1960s Britain remained the world's largest multinational banker, the international activities of its banks far exceeding those of any other nation, including the United States.

The story of British multinational banking could be written in several ways, each of which would highlight different but important aspects of their history. The banks can be treated either as components of the British financial system, or through their roles and impact in the countries in which they operated. There would be a strong case for considering the British banks in their regional context. Arguably, the British banks which specialized in Australian business came to have far more in common with their fellow Australian banks than their British cousins active in, say, West Africa or Brazil. However, the approach of this book is to examine the activities of British multinational banks in the banking industry worldwide, and to follow their evolution over time. Banking is treated as an industry in the service sector. The focus is on the origins, strategies, and performance of the British banks, rather than on their impact on host economies. Five related themes have been chosen for particular investigation.

The first is why multinational banks exist. This question has been the central concern of economists. Since the publication in 1977 of Herbert Grubel's 'first attempt to develop a general theory of multinational banking',[1] a number of models have been put forward. The pattern of multinational banking has been related to differences between countries of the cost of capital.[2] Many writers have argued that banks often become

---

[1] H. G. Grubel, 'A Theory of Multinational Banking', *Banca Nazionale del Lavoro*, 123 (Dec. 1977).

[2] Robert Z. Aliber, 'International Banking: A Survey', *Journal of Money, Credit and Banking*, 16(4) (1984).

multinational by following their corporate clients over national borders.[3] More general theories have been put forward which seek to embrace such specific explanations. John H. Dunning's eclectic paradigm of international production has been applied to banking, and an attempt made to establish the ownership, location, and internalization factors behind the growth of multinational banks.[4] Product differentiation, economies of scale, imperfections in markets for information and technology, and government support have all been discussed as sources of advantage in this context.[5] More recently the evolution of multinational banking has been discussed using internalization theory.[6] The search for a satisfactory theory complicated by the existence of different types of multinational banking. Grubel distinguished between multinational retail, service, and wholesale banking, and argued—almost certainly correctly—that they required different explanations. This book presents a large amount of empirical data on a large group of banks which were active over a long period in multinational retail, service, and wholesale banking. The chapters which follow will attempt to explain why these banks came into and stayed in existence, and so to contribute to debates on the origins of multinational banks.

The second theme pursued here is the question why British-owned banks were so prominent in multinational banking for so long, and why—from the 1960s—they lost that prominence. The relative economic decline of the United States *vis-à-vis* Japan has resulted in a renewed interest in such questions of ownership and national competitiveness. Michael Porter's *The Competitive Advantage of Nations* explained at length why some countries were more 'competitive' than others, and—more exactly—why firms domiciled in some countries have been successful in penetrating foreign markets in some products but not in others.[7] This book offers a case study of national competitiveness in an industry over a long period.

The third theme is concerned with the internal management and organization of the multinational banks. Problems of the efficient organization of a firm's functions are particularly acute in the case of multinational enterprise. Controlling subsidiaries or individuals in foreign countries is a difficult task for a multinational, yet success in this area is likely to prove an essential prerequisite for overall success. As a result, organization theorists and international business researchers have been concerned with

[3] D. Channon, *Global Banking Strategy* (Chichester: Wiley, 1986), 3–4.

[4] Jean M. Gray and Peter H. Gray, 'The Multinational Bank: A Financial MNC?', *Journal of Banking and Finance*, 5 (1981).

[5] Adrian E. Tschoegl, 'International Retail Banking as a Strategy: An Assessment', *Journal of International Business Studies*, 19(2) (1987).

[6] Mark Casson, 'Evolution of Multinational Banks: A Theoretical Perspective', in Geoffrey Jones (ed.), *Banks as Multinationals* (London: Routledge, 1990).

[7] Michael Porter, *The Competitive Advantage of Nations* (London: Macmillan, 1990).

strategies of 'control'.[8] The problems of control were particularly acute in the history of British multinational banking. In the nineteenth century the banks faced the problem of managing extensive branch networks often thousands of miles away from their corporate headquarters. In some cases, such as for the British banks active in Latin America or Iran or Thailand, problems of geographical distance were compounded by operation in countries with alien languages, cultures, and legal systems. In an age before telephones, let alone jet aircraft, it is necessary to explore how the British banks were able to organize such extensive and far-flung international business activity.

A fourth theme pursued in this book is the response of the banks to changing environmental circumstances, a central concern of economic analysis. Some of the British multinational banks active in 1990—such as Hongkong Bank and Standard Chartered—were the direct descendants of banks founded in the mid-nineteenth century. In the course of their corporate careers, they were faced with tumultuous changes in markets and politics. World wars, economic depressions, the collapse of the British Empire, and the economic decline of the United Kingdom were only some of the changes they faced—and survived. How did the banks respond to change? What were the constraints on change? Did British banks change quickly enough?

These issues are particularly pertinent to a set of British business institutions. There is an extensive literature attempting to explain the relative economic decline of Britain over the last one hundred years.[9] Among the many explanations, it has been observed frequently that twentieth-century British business as a whole has been unable to change quickly or adequately enough to new circumstances. Such an allegation can be found in almost every writer on the subject, from the distinguished British economic historian Donald Coleman—who has noted 'an attitude of mind antipathetic to building change into the system'—through to Michael Porter —'British firms have, too often, a management culture that works against innovation and change.'[10] British multinational banks have, as already noted, been subjected to particularly dramatic changes, and an examination of

---

[8] C. Bartlett and S. Goshal, *Managing across Borders* (Boston, Mass.: Harvard Business School Press, 1989).

[9] Recent examples include M. W. Kirby, *The Decline of British Economic Power since 1870* (London: Allen and Unwin, 1981); B. Elbaum and W. Lazonick (eds.), *The Decline of the British Economy* (Oxford: Oxford University Press, 1986); Scott Newton and Dilwyn Porter, *Modernisation Frustrated* (London: Unwin Hyman, 1988); Geoffrey Jones and Maurice Kirby (eds.), *Competitiveness and the State* (Manchester: Manchester University Press, 1991).

[10] D. C. Coleman, 'Failings and Achievements: Some British Business, 1910–80', in R. P. T. Davenport-Hines and Geoffrey Jones (eds.), *Enterprise, Management and Innovation in British Business, 1914–1980* (London: Cass, 1988); Porter, *The Competitive Advantage of Nations*, 502.

their corporate responses over time offers a valuable opportunity to study change in British business.

A final theme pursued in this book is performance. It has been suggested that contemporary multinational banks perform better than domestic ones, partly because they can escape the systematic risk of any one national market, and partly because internalization strategies create advantages for multinational banks by overcoming imperfections in international financial markets.[11] This book investigates the performance of British multinational banks over the long term. For a sample of banks over the core period of 1890 to 1975, returns to shareholders have been calculated, and compared to what they could have earned from investing in the shares of two domestic banks or in British government stock. Profitability ratios using both published and unpublished information have also been calculated. This detailed financial information is presented in Appendix 5. Returns to shareholders and profitability, however, provide only one measure of business success, and other measures of performance will also be discussed, including market share.

The thematic approach means that this book does not provide a comprehensive history of each British bank. In different time periods, business strategies in some regions are examined more than in others. Individual banks are prominent in certain issues and periods, and not at other times. Appendices 1–4 provide a source of reference on individual banks, and on the overall structure of British multinational banking. Appendix 1 ranks the banks by total assets and market capitalization at various bench-mark dates between 1860 and 1990. Appendix 2 provides a brief corporate biography of each bank listed. Appendices 3 and 4 analyse the geographical distribution of branches and assets at the bench-mark dates. This data provides support for the generalizations in the main text.

## 1.2. Concepts and Context

Certain key concepts are used in this study and it is as well to make these clear at the beginning.

This book is a study of multinational banking. Multinational banks own and control branches and affiliates in more than one country. This may be distinguished from international banking, which includes foreign trade finance and lending to governments and corporations resident in foreign countries. While multinational banks are often engaged in international banking, cross-border lending and trade finance can be, and often is, conducted by banks which have no branches or affiliates outside their own country. Banks can export such services, appointing independent banks in

---

[11] Alan Rugman, *Inside the Multinationals* (London: Croom Helm, 1981), 89–103.

foreign countries as their 'correspondents'. Multinational banking is concerned with the location and ownership of banking facilities in different countries.[12]

International banking had been undertaken for hundreds of years before the nineteenth century. International trade had been financed, and national currencies exchanged. Sovereigns had frequently borrowed from beyond their borders. In the late Middle Ages, Italian banking houses such as the Bardi, the Peruzzi, and the Medici had been prominent in such activities. In the sixteenth century south German bankers, and subsequently Dutch bankers, became the industry leaders. This international banking had occasionally involved multinational activity—the early Italian bankers sometimes established branches outside Italy—but for the most part bankers sent members of their family or other staff to represent them abroad, or developed reciprocal agreements with their equivalents in foreign countries.[13] Multinational banking on a large scale began with the British banks of the 1830s.

The concern with banks which owned and operated branches abroad means that the British merchant banks, such as the Rothschilds, Barings, Schroders, and Morgan Grenfell, have not been studied in detail for this book. In the nineteenth century such houses were prominent figures in international banking. They handled much of the trade finance between Europe and the United States, and were the leading institutions in the issue of foreign loans in London, the financial centre of the world's largest capital-exporting country. For the most part, the merchant banks, like their Italian and German predecessors, undertook international banking without establishing branches abroad. Instead they built up large networks of 'correspondent' banks in foreign countries, for whom the merchant banks acted as London bankers for trade finance and payments in return for equivalent services in their countries. Family connections and related partnerships in foreign countries provided other important means to conduct international banking. The merchant banks were extremely important in the nineteenth century and later. Fortunately, a series of excellent studies of their growth and strategies have been published.[14]

A second point to emphasize is that this is a study of British-owned

[12] M. K. Lewis and K. T. Davis, *Domestic and International Banking* (Deddington: Allan, 1987), ch. 8.

[13] Rondo Cameron, 'Banks: The First Multinationals', in V. I. Bovykin and Rondo Cameron (eds.), *International Banking, Foreign Investment and Industrial Finance, 1870–1914* (New York: Oxford University Press, 1991); Charles P. Kindleberger, *Multinational Excursions* (Cambridge, Mass.: MIT Press, 1984), 155–70.

[14] Stanley Chapman, *The Rise of Merchant Banking* (London: Allen and Unwin, 1984); Vincent P. Carosso, *The Morgans: Private International Bankers, 1854–1913* (Cambridge, Mass.: Harvard University Press, 1987); Kathleen Burk, *Morgan Grenfell, 1838–1988* (Oxford: Oxford University Press, 1989); Stephanie Diaper, 'The History of Kleinwort, Sons & Co. in Merchant Banking, 1855–1961', Ph.D. thesis, University of Nottingham, 1983.

and -managed institutions. This may seem an obvious point, but for most of the period covered by this book contemporaries used the concept of 'British' in a way which now seems odd. This comes out in the work of A. S. J. Baster, who wrote the first—and last—general studies of British multinational banks, published in 1929 and 1935.[15] Baster's original and masterly studies mapped out the nineteenth-century origins of these banks so well that this present book has been able to take more of an overview of their first century, leaving those who want more detail on particular banks to refer to Baster, but his concept of nationality is different from the one used here. In his 1929 study, *The Imperial Banks*, he does not always distinguish between banks registered in the United Kingdom and operating branches in the British Empire and banks registered in Australia, Canada, and elsewhere in the Empire. They were all 'imperial banks'. This was in accordance with contemporary usage, until well beyond the inter-war years. As late as the 1970s British banking statistics included in the single category of 'British overseas banks' British banks with London head offices operating abroad, and banks with head offices elsewhere in the Commonwealth with London offices. In London, these banks were joined in a single representative body—the British Overseas Banks Association—which was completely separate from the Foreign Banks Association, the equivalent organization for banks headquartered outside the Commonwealth.[16] To further confuse matters, such was the importance of the British Empire to contemporaries that Baster distinguished between 'imperial' banks—which were active in the Empire—and 'international banks'—the subject of his 1935 study—which he defined as British banks active in foreign countries.

There is little sense in following such contemporary usage in a book written in the 1990s, when the British Empire is no more, and when modern economics has identified and defined concepts such as the multinational enterprise and foreign direct investment. This book is concerned with British banks which engaged in foreign direct investment. The local banks founded in Canada, Australia, and elsewhere in the Empire in the nineteenth century were for the most part owned in the colonies, where they had their headquarters and from where they drew their board of directors. Their business strategies resembled those of British-registered banks active in the Empire, but they are not examples of British multinational enterprise. The major exception to this rule is the Hongkong and Shanghai Banking Corporation, registered in the British colony of Hong

---

[15] A. S. J. Baster, *The Imperial Banks* (London: King, 1929) and id., *The International Banks* (London: King, 1935).

[16] 'British Banking Enterprise in the Colonies and Other Countries', *Bankers' Magazine*, 45 (1885); 'The Overseas Foreign Banks in London', *Bank of England Quarterly Bulletin*, 1(4) (1960–1); 'Overseas and Foreign Banks in London, 1962–68', *Bank of England Quarterly Bulletin*, 8(4) (1968).

Kong in 1865, which is included throughout as a British bank on the grounds that its senior management has, from the 1860s to the present day, consisted of United Kingdom citizens, that for long periods much of its shareholding was held in the United Kingdom. In 1991 the bank shifted its domicile to the United Kingdom. Appendix 1 contains a more extended discussion of the problems of defining a British multinational bank.

The approach taken in this book has been heavily influenced by a number of writers in business history and business strategy. Fundamentally this is a work of business history. Much of the discussion rests on material re-searched in the internal confidential records of British banks, which has combined with existing published sources.

Any researcher in business history owes an immense debt to Alfred D. Chandler, and his ideas permeate this volume. In three fundamental studies, Chandler traced and explained the rise of modern managerial capitalism.[17] From the late nineteenth century, and beginning in the United States, ownership and control were separated, as professional managers organized in hierarchies replaced owners. Key economic decisions were increasingly taken by such managers in large firms, who replaced the invisible hand of the market with the visible hand of managerial co-ordination. Changes in firm strategies and corporate structures were driven by changes in markets and technologies. Changes in structure followed the changes in strategy, usually with a lag.

Chandler has been fundamentally concerned with the modern industrial enterprise. Banks feature in his studies as influences on industrial com-panies, rather than as objects of attention themselves. His major criticism of British manufacturing industry—that its organizational capability was handicapped by the retention of family or personal capitalism—does not directly translate to the banking sector, where family ownership of banks was a rarity by the end of the nineteenth century. However, despite his own focus on manufacturing, his concepts are valuable for the student of business enterprise in any sector. Chandler's ideas pervade the discussions that follow about the internal organization of the British banks, and about the problems they faced in changing their structures as conditions—and business strategies—changed.

The work of a second business historian has also fundamentally influ-enced the writing of this book. Mira Wilkins virtually invented, and for over two decades has sustained, the historical study of multinationals. In three volumes she has traced the evolution of American multinationals and, more recently, the history of foreign-owned multinationals in the United

---

[17] Alfred D. Chandler, *Strategy and Structure* (Cambridge, Mass.: MIT Press, 1962); id., *The Visible Hand* (Cambridge, Mass.: Harvard University Press, 1977); id., *Scale and Scope* (Cambridge, Mass.: Harvard University Press, 1990).

States.[18] Wilkins has set the historical context in which this study is based. We now know that the multinational form of business enterprise was created and flourished in the nineteenth century, much earlier than had been thought when the concept of a multinational was first formulated in the 1960s. The building of a factory in Glasgow, by the Singer Sewing Machine Company in 1867—often taken as the first successful example of a multinational manufacturing investment—was followed by hundreds of similar investments. By 1914 a range of American firms such as Coca-Cola, Eastman Kodak, Ford, and Quaker Oats had established manufacturing plants in foreign countries. Germany and Britain were equally prolific in establishing multinational manufacturing operations. By the time of the First World War the level of foreign direct investment was small compared to the levels which would occur after 1945, but hundreds of multinational manufacturing companies were in existence, some with factories spread over a dozen or more countries.[19]

Until recently much research on the multinational enterprise concentrated on the manufacturing sector, and it was thus one of the most original features of Wilkins's work that from the beginning she took a wider view of her subject. Extractive and service industries feature strongly in her books. During the nineteenth century there was extensive foreign direct investment in minerals and extractive industries, in advertising and insurance, in commercial and communication services.

British multinational banks need to be seen in the context of their wider world of multinational business explored by Wilkins and others. Their multinational strategy was not unique in the nineteenth century, yet it had a number of distinguishing features. Beginning in the 1830s, British

[18] Mira Wilkins, *The Emergence of Multinational Enterprise* (Cambridge, Mass.: Harvard University Press, 1970); id., *The Making of Multinational Enterprise* (Cambridge, Mass.: Harvard University Press, 1974); id., *The History of Foreign Investment in the United States to 1914* (Cambridge, Mass.: Harvard University Press, 1989).

[19] The literature on the history of multinational business is now enormous. In addition to her three monographs, see the valuable literature survey and discussions in Mira Wilkins, 'The History of European Multinationals: A New Look', *Journal of European Economic History*, 15 (1986) and id., 'European and North American Multinationals, 1870–1914: Comparisons and Contrasts', in R. P. T. Davenport-Hines and Geoffrey Jones (eds.), *The End of Insularity* (London: Cass, 1988). The history of European multinational business can be approached in Peter Hertner and Geoffrey Jones (eds.), *Multinationals: Theory and History* (Aldershot: Gower, 1986); Alice Teichova, Maurice Lévy-Leboyer, and Helga Nussbaum (eds.), *Multinational Enterprise in Historical Perspective* (Cambridge: Cambridge University Press, 1986); Geoffrey Jones (ed.), *British Multinationals: Origins, Growth and Performance* (Aldershot: Gower, 1986); A. Teichova, M. Lévy-Leboyer, and H. Nussbaum (eds.), *Historical Studies in International Corporate Business* (Cambridge: Cambridge University Press, 1989). Mira Wilkins (ed.), *The Growth of Multinationals* (Aldershot: Elgar, 1991) contains an excellent selection of the most influential writings on the history of multinational business. J. H. Dunning, *Explaining International Production* (London: Unwin Hyman, 1988), ch. 3 contains the best estimates of the stock of foreign direct investment at various historical bench-mark dates.

multinational banking was an unusually early form of international business. By the time of the Singer investment in Glasgow, British multinational banks were already active on five continents. British multinational banking was also unusually extensive and geographically widespread. Pre-1914 American multinationals largely clustered in neighbouring Canada and Mexico, while few manufacturing multinationals of any nationality had more than a dozen foreign factories in operation. In contrast, by 1914 several banks headquartered in London were controlling networks of 100 or even 200 bank branches thousands of miles away. Finally, British-owned institutions were uniquely important in the history of multinational banking. In multinational manufacturing, both American and German firms have better claims to be the pioneers of the multinational firm, although by 1900 Britain, Germany, and the United States were all homes to many manufacturing multinationals. In contrast, British multinational banks appeared forty years before German banks took this route, while the American lag was very much larger.

A final feature of Wilkins's work merits attention here. Over the last decade and a half the traditional view that the huge flows of foreign investment seen in the nineteenth century were portfolio in nature has been radically revised. It is evident that a half at least of foreign investment in this period was direct—involving ownership and control.[20] The corporate form of this nineteenth-century direct investment was often quite different from that of the modern multinational. Wilkins explored this issue for Britain, devising the concept of the 'free-standing firm'. Britain was the world's largest foreign direct investor before 1914, and indeed before the Second World War, but Wilkins observed that much of this investment possessed—in contrast to American or other European investment—an unusual form. Typically, a company would be registered in the United Kingdom to do business in a single foreign country. There were Anglo-Australian, Anglo-American, and Anglo-Argentinian firms, usually operating in a single economic activity overseas. The same structure appeared in the whole spectrum of activities, from manufacturing to agriculture and services. Free-standing companies were a form of direct investment because real managerial control was exercised from British headquarters, even if the administrative structures were tiny and elementary.[21]

British multinational banking developed as a variant of this free-standing structure. Elsewhere in Europe and in the United States, multinational

[20] P. Svedberg, 'The Portfolio: Direct Composition of Private Foreign Investment in 1914 Revisited', *Economic Journal*, 88 (1978); I. Stone, 'British Direct and Portfolio Investment in Latin America before 1914', *Journal of Economic History*, 37 (1977).
[21] Mira Wilkins, 'Defining a Firm: History and Theory', in Hertner and Jones (eds.), *Multinationals: Theory and History*; idem, 'The Free-Standing Company, 1870–1914: An Important Type of British Foreign Direct Investment', *Economic History Review*, 2nd ser. 41 (1988).

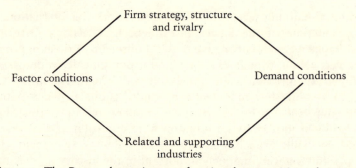

FIG. 1.1. The Porter determinants of national competitive advantage.
*Source*: Michael Porter, *The Competitive Advantage of Nations* (London:
Macmillan, 1990), 72

operations were begun by banks with an existing domestic banking business. In Britain, this was not the case. Nineteenth-century British multinational banks did not undertake domestic banking business inside the United Kingdom. They were established to undertake banking business outside the country, yet their London-based directors and executives took all major business decisions, and many minor ones. It was not until just before the First World War that domestic British banks established their first branches abroad. British multinational banks were atypical in the history of multinational banking, but typical in the context of British foreign direct investment.

Much of the discussion on the competitiveness of British multinational banks in this book draws on concepts developed by the economist and business strategist Michael Porter. In *The Competitive Advantage of Nations* Porter argued that a nation's competitiveness in a particular industry rests on the extent and quality of, and interaction between, four main sets of attributes, which as a system contribute the diamond of competitive advantage. Figure 1.1 illustrates Porter's diamond.

Porter's first determinant is the level and composition of natural and created factor endowments. These include human, physical, knowledge, and capital resources, and infrastructure. The ability of nations to create and upgrade factors is regarded as critical. Those countries with weak educational systems—such as contemporary Britain—are then handicapped in the 'factor creation mechanisms' compared to those who invest more in their human resources, such as Germany or Japan.[22]

Demand conditions concern the nature of home-market demand for an industry's product or service. Both the size and the character of home demand are important for Porter. A sophisticated and demanding home

---

[22] Porter, *The Competitive Advantage of Nations*, 368–71, 396–8, 497–8.

market (such as that of contemporary Switzerland) can pressure local firms to meet high standards in terms of product quality and service. A relatively poor and undemanding market (such as that of contemporary Britain) is a competitive handicap.[23] Domestic demand can be internationalized by, for example, political ties or cultural transfer.[24]

The third determinant is related and supporting industries. Porter suggests that firms benefit from agglomerative or external economies by being partially grouped in clusters of related activities. National success in an industry is particularly likely if a nation has competitive advantage in a number of related industries, which can create a challenging domestic environment and a network of suppliers and competitors.

Firm strategy, structure, and rivalry, the fourth of the determinants, concerns the conditions in a nation governing how companies are created, organized, and managed, as well as the nature of domestic rivalry. Porter emphasises, this final point, arguing that the presence of strong local rivals is a powerful stimulus to the creation and persistence of competitive advantage, as it creates a uniquely strong pressure on companies to innovate and improve.[25]

The Porter 'diamond' is not primarily concerned with multinational business, and indeed it might be legitimately argued that this is one of its defects. Porter does not explore why competitive advantages are sometimes exploited by exporting, and other times by foreign direct investment. Nevertheless, it provides a valuable tool for examining country-specific sources of competitive advantage.[26] In this book, an elementary version of the diamond is applied to each main chronological period to examine the sources of competitive advantage initially held by British multinational banks, and the decline in those advantages during the twentieth century.

One problem with the Porter model for this study is the role it allocates to public policy. Porter does not neglect government—indeed he allocates a whole chapter to it in his 1990 study—but he sees it as an influence on the four determinants of competitive advantage, rather than as a determinant in its own right. However, government policies have always had a considerable influence on banks, because governments have always felt a special need to intervene in that industry. Banking is not merely one economic sector among many. Banks have an impact on all other sectors through their lending policies; on large numbers of individuals through their deposit-taking function; and on the general financial and monetary conditions of economies. There is now a formidable theoretical and empirical literature which has demonstrated the importance of the regulatory

[23] Ibid., 321–4, 500–1.    [24] Ibid., 97–8.    [25] Ibid., 121.
[26] J. H. Dunning, *Dunning on Porter: Reshaping the Diamond of Competitive Advantage*, University of Reading Discussion Papers in International Investment and Business Studies, No. 152, 1991.

environment in explaining the development of multinational banking.[27] This book supports such a view, and the importance of public policy on the shape and fortunes of British multinational banking is examined throughout.

## 1.3. *Summary*

British banks pioneered multinational banking in the nineteenth century, and remained the predominant institutions in that industry until at least the 1960s. This book will examine the origins of British multinational banks, their sources of competitive advantage, their strategies of control, their response to changing environmental circumstances, and their performance over time. These subjects are explored using concepts developed in studies on the rise of managerial capitalism, the history of multinational enterprise, and the determinants of national competitive advantage.

The next chapter examines the origins of British multinational banking. The fifty years between the 1830s and 1890 were a critical period, for the strategies and structures put in place then were to exercise a fundamental influence on the later evolution of the British banks.

[27] Lawrence G. Goldberg and Denise Johnson, 'The Determinants of US Banking Activity Abroad', *Journal of International Money and Finance*, 9 (1990).

# CHAPTER 2

# Foundations, Markets, and Strategies

## 2.1. The Origins of British Multinational Banking

A British influence on the banking systems of other countries can be found well before the 1830s. British investors played an important role in the banks of the newly independent United States. By 1811 foreign investors, principally British, held 70 per cent of the stock of the Bank of the United States, America's largest business enterprise at the time. There was also a strong British shareholding in its successor, the Second Bank of the United States.[1] British migrants established the first banks in the Canadian and Australian colonies. The Bank of Montreal, founded in 1817 as the first full bank in British North America, had a prominent Scottish influence among its initial subscribers.[2] The first bank in Australia, the Bank of New South Wales, founded in 1817 or nearly thirty years after the first British penal settlement on that continent, was formed by British settlers, both free and ex-convicts.[3]

These were not multinational investments. The British investors in the Bank of the United States did not control that bank, whose management was firmly in American hands. The British migrants active in the Canadian and Australian banks managed them from the colonies, without reference to the United Kingdom. Their children would become Australian- and Canadian-born British subjects who, in all probability, would never even visit Britain. In the 1990s prominent financial institutions in the sovereign states of Canada and Australia—the Bank of Montreal and Westpac (as the Bank of New South Wales became in 1982)—were direct descendants of this first generation of colonial banks.

The first British overseas banks founded in the 1830s were quite different creations. They were multinational banks. Promoted and owned largely in the United Kingdom, they established branches overseas managed from headquarters in London. Until the 1850s these banks went almost exclusively to regions under British imperial control. The timing of the promotion of banks, and the region of their specialization, were intimately connected

---

[1] Mira Wilkins, *The History of Foreign Investment in the United States to 1914* (Cambridge, Mass.: Harvard University Press, 1989), 38–9, 61–2; id., 'Banks over borders: Some Evidence from their pre-1914 History', in Geoffrey Jones (ed.), *Banks as Multinationals* (London: Routledge, 1990), 222, 226–7.

[2] A. S. J. Baster, *The Imperial Banks* (London: King, 1929), 8.

[3] Ibid., 9–11; R. F. Holder, *Bank of New South Wales: A History* (Sydney: Angus and Robertson, 1970).

to patterns in British imperial expansion, in the incorporation of outlying regions into the world economy, and in the discovery or exploitation of precious metals and primary products. The first banks went to the British colonies in Australia, the West Indies, and Canada, as those regions boomed through high wool and sugar prices and flows of British migrants. The Bank of Australasia, the Bank of South Australia, and the Union Bank of Australia opened between 1835 and 1837 in the Australian colonies. The Colonial Bank and Bank of British North America, both founded in 1836, went to the British West Indies and British Guyana, and to Canada respectively. The Ionian Bank was established in 1839 to operate in the Ionian Islands in the Mediterranean, then a British protectorate.

These banks were primarily intended to finance foreign trade. They were multinational trade banks, although in most instances profitable opportunities in other types of banking business were at least in the back of their promoters' minds. Frequently the initiative for their foundation came from the intended region of operation, but banking and other commercial interests in the City of London were usually also well represented among the promoters of such banks. The idea of the Bank of Australasia, for example, may have originated from a colonist who sought to combine a whaling and banking venture, but the initiative soon passed to London interests.[4] The British banks transformed banking in the Australian colonies. The local banks were single-branch units, which did not seek deposits and generally relied on capital and the issue of banknotes. The British banks paid interest to attract deposits and established branches to follow the moving frontier of settlement. They took the lead in establishing a regularized foreign exchange market, which had previously been in the hands of a government agency.

The Colonial Bank was promoted by a combination of British banking interests and prominent merchants and planters at a time when the West Indies were experiencing a boom based on high sugar prices, the leading commodity produced in those colonies. The first chairman was a partner of a merchant firm with offices in London and Liverpool and a number of plantations in the West Indies. The Bank of British North America combined merchants concerned with trade between Britain and its Canadian colonies with those sensing that profits could be earned from domestic banking within Canada.[5] As with the British banks in Australia, the banking practices introduced by this institution had a long-term impact on the development of the Canadian banking system.[6]

The genesis of the Ionian Bank was somewhat different, for the initiative

[4] S. J. Butlin, *Australia and New Zealand Bank* (London: Longman, 1961), 20–2.
[5] Merrill Denison, *Canada's First Bank: A History of the Bank of Montreal* (Toronto: Dodd Mead, 1966), i. 313.
[6] Gordon Laxer, *Open for Business: The Roots of Foreign Ownership in Canada* (Toronto: Oxford University Press, 1989), 172–3.

came from the British colonial administration of the Islands. The local economy was dominated by currants and olive oil production, and the agriculturists were dependent for both selling their produce and obtaining credit on a powerful group of merchants. As a solution to this problem, the idea of an indigenously owned bank evolved, with up to a sixth of the shares held by the government. When it proved impossible to raise the capital in the Ionian Islands, bankers and merchants in London were approached, and by 1839 a bank had been formed in London to operate in the Ionian Islands.[7]

There was a considerable overlap among the promoters and directors of the first generation of overseas banks. Among the fourteen names who were the original promoters of the Bank of Australasia, five were also involved with the Ionian Bank and two with the Bank of British North America. One of the Bank of Australasia promoters was also amongst the promoters of the Union Bank of Australia, and two of the original promoters of the latter were also directors of the Bank of South Australia.[8] Merchants were the source of some of this overlap, but there was also a noteworthy connection with English and Irish provincial banking, and more especially the Provincial Bank of Ireland.

The organizational structure which the British overseas banks were to adopt to manage their colonial branches had been pioneered in Ireland. The Provincial Bank of Ireland was established in 1825, with a head office in London and a branch network in several Irish towns. It was modelled on the Scottish joint stock banks, which had extensive branch networks, issued notes, and paid interest on deposits. The Scottish banking system at this period was considerably different from that of England and Wales. English banks were normally single (or a few) branch institutions that (if they had note issues at all) could only issue large denominations. The location of the Provincial Bank's head office in London stemmed from the Bank of Ireland's monopoly of note-issuing banking in Dublin.[9]

The Provincial Bank of Ireland was a financial success. It demonstrated

---

[7] *Ionian Bank Ltd.: A History* (London 1953); A. S. J. Baster, *The International Banks* (London: King, 1935), 51–5; Colonial Office Correspondence 1833 to 1837, in Centenary File, Box 2, Ionian Bank Archives.

[8] The five Bank of Australasia promoters who were also involved with the Ionian Bank were Captain Sir Andrew Pellet Green, Richard Norman, Oliver Farrar, Charles Barry Baldwin, and John Wright. Farrar and Pellet Green were also among the promoters of the Bank of British North America. Jacob Montefiori promoted both the Bank of Australasia and the Union Bank of Australia, while George Fife Angas and Christopher Dawson were original promoters and directors of the Union Bank and directors of the South Australian Bank. See also Baster, *The Imperial Banks*, 120–1.

[9] Philip Ollerenshaw, *Banking in Nineteenth Century Ireland* (Manchester: Manchester University Press, 1987), 17–8; Charles W. Munn, 'The Emergence of Joint Stock Banking in the British Isles: A Comparative Approach', in R. Davenport-Hines and Geoffrey Jones (eds.), *The End of Insularity* (London: Cass, 1988), 73. Rondo Cameron *et al*, *Banking in the Early Stages of Industrialization* (New York: Oxford University Press, 1967), chs. 2 and 3 still provide a valuable comparison of the English and Scottish banking systems.

that a London head office could supervise a branch network in a geographically separate region, and its promoters were soon extending these principles elsewhere. In 1833 the Provincial Bank's founders promoted the National Provincial Bank in England 'which was untypical in having a large number of branches'.[10] Soon afterwards they perceived profitable opportunities further afield. Of the directors of the Provincial Bank of Ireland who were also promoters of the National Provincial Bank, one was in addition a director of the Ionian Bank, the Bank of Australasia and the Bank of British North America, another was a director of the Ionian Bank and the Bank of Australasia, and three others were directors of the Bank of Australasia. The Provincial Bank of Ireland's Deed of Settlement provided the model for that of the Bank of Australasia,[11] and almost certainly that of the Bank of British North America, which in turn provided the model for the Ionian Bank. It is scarcely an exaggeration to say that British overseas banking was modelled on Scottish banking practice, as tried and tested in the Provincial Bank of Ireland in the 1820s, and on the separation of head office and branches pioneered in that bank.

Like the Provincial Bank, the overseas banks were normally British-registered institutions with London-based boards of directors which presided over branches abroad. The British presence of the banks was normally confined to a single office in London, although very occasionally a further office was operated in a city such as Edinburgh or Liverpool.

This institutional structure was well suited to international trade finance. The London-based boards and offices provided essential contacts with, and information about, British mercantile interests, who imported the commodities and minerals produced in the colonial economies, and exported the manufactured goods needed by them. London had a large secondary market specializing in bills. Surplus sterling credits accumulated during the export seasons could be profitably employed on the London markets, while seasonal shortfalls could be covered in the same way. Meanwhile an overseas branch network could provide a British institution with valuable creditor information and a debt collection facility in overseas countries. Both functions could be undertaken using independent correspondents. This was how Britain's trade with the United States and continental Europe was largely handled by the merchant banks. However, in most of the territories in which the new overseas banks were interested from the 1830s, it was hard to find local banks which could be trusted to act as correspondents, for banking systems were non-existent or in their infancy. In other words, the transaction costs involved in the use of the market were likely to be high, and it was rational to internalize trade finance by establishing a multinational branch network.

[10] Munn, 'The Emergence of Joint Stock Banking in the British Isles', 79.
[11] Butlin, *Australia and New Zealand Bank*, 23.

The British overseas banks were highly specialized both functionally and geographically. In terms of their business activity, they did not have domestic banking business within Britain, nor did they have equity links with domestic banks. They were formed exclusively to undertake banking outside the United Kingdom, but with their ownership and control firmly based in that country. They were, as a result, an early example of what came to be a distinctively British form of foreign direct investment in the nineteenth century—the 'free-standing' company. However, the overseas banks were not entirely separate from the domestic financial system, for there were often links at director level. Quite apart from the exceptional influence of the Provincial Bank of Ireland on the first British overseas banks, London bankers were quite often involved in the foundation of overseas banks, and very often represented on boards in the nineteenth century and beyond. A study of the directors of British overseas banks between 1890 and 1914 found 44 per cent of them were also directors of other British banks, both domestic deposit banks and merchant banks.[12]

The most vivid illustration of this point was the activity of the London private bank Glyn, Mills in overseas banking from the 1850s. A Glyn became a member of the board of the Union Bank of Australia in 1854, and thereafter there was either a Glyn or a Mill on the board until it merged with another bank a century later. During the 1850s Glyn, Mills was involved in the promotion of two new British overseas banks, the Bank of Egypt and the Ottoman Bank. In the following decade it helped promote the London and Brazilian Bank and the Anglo-Austrian Bank, and in the 1880s the English Bank of the River Plate and the Imperial Bank of Persia. Usually members of the Glyn, Mills families were represented on the boards of these banks, as well as others which they had not themselves promoted. This London bank, therefore, served as a powerful promotional bloc which also provided senior management in the form of directorships, but its venture capitalist role does not seem to have extended to providing significant amounts of equity, nor to any attempt to co-ordinate the business strategies of the different overseas banks. In this sense, the latter remained fully 'free-standing' from domestic banking.[13]

As the names of the first banks demonstrated, each had its own geographical area of operation, although often several banks competed within the same region. This pattern continued, apart from a very few exceptions, as British overseas banks spread to Asia, Africa, and Latin America. Geographical specialization remained a characteristic feature of British multinational banking over the next 150 years.

[12] Youssef Cassis, *Les Banquiers de la City à l'époque edouardienne, 1890–1914* (Geneva: Librairie Droz, 1984), 96–7.
[13] P. L. Cottrell, 'The Coalescence of a Cluster of Corporate International Banks, 1855–1875', *Business History*, 33 (1991); Roger Fulford, *Glyn's, 1753–1953* (London: Macmillan, 1953), 159–60; David Merrett, *ANZ Bank* (Sydney: Allen and Unwin, 1985), 31–2.

A number of influences explain the functional and geographical specialization in British multinational banking. The British financial system as a whole was evolving by the early nineteenth century into a system of specialist institutions. The domestic banks in England and Wales—which were divided into London banks and country banks, both private and (after 1826) joint stock—had no overseas branches nor did they conduct foreign exchange business, though from the 1830s the London-based banks developed networks of reciprocal agreements with foreign correspondent banks. Retail banking was in the hands of a large number of institutions, especially in England and Wales, where single-unit banking prevailed. In 1825 there were over 700 banks in the United Kingdom, and in 1850 there were still over 450.[14] The smallness of these banks, and their narrow specialization on retail business, help to explain their lack of interest in multinational banking. Specialist discount houses, an institution unique to the London money market, sold, bought, and resold bills of exchange. Initially such bills were used to finance domestic trade, but after mid-century (when their use in inland trade finance declined) the discount houses became increasingly involved in purchasing ('discounting') international bills accepted by the merchant banks, specialists in finance of international trade and the issue of foreign government and railway stock on the London market. Given the general environment of the early nineteenth-century British financial system, it is not surprising that the overseas banks emerged as a further distinct institutional form.

The geographical location of the first multinational banking investment was influenced by the merchant banks, which held first-mover advantages in the finance of British trade with continental Europe and the United States. Equally important was the degree of receptivity to foreign banks. The United States had a variety of restrictions on foreign banks. In most states they could not operate at all, and almost everywhere they faced limitations on their activities. The British overseas banks went where they were permitted to go. Initially, this included the Australian colonies, which only strongly restricted entry by non-Australian banks after the First World War, and Canada, where they could evade requirements dating from 1821 that bank directors had to be British subjects.[15] Subsequently they were able to go to the East and to Southern Africa as barriers to entry imposed by the East India Company and colonial administrations gave way.

[14] On the structure of the British financial system in the early 19th century, see Michael Collins, *Money and Banking in the UK: A History* (Beckenham: Croom Helm, 1988), ch. 3. See also A. R. Holmes and Edwin Green, *Midland: 150 Years of Banking Business* (London: Batsford, 1986), 132–3.

[15] For receptivity in the United States see Wilkins, *The History of Foreign Investment in the United States*, 61–3, 455–6. For Australia, see David Merrett, 'Paradise Lost? British Banks in Australia', in Geoffrey Jones (ed.), *Banks as Multinationals*, 71, 73. For Canada, see Laxer, *Open for Business*, 216–18.

Geographical and functional specialization was much reinforced by the regulatory framework faced by the first overseas banks. The most important regulatory influence on the banks was the Colonial Banking Regulations, which were developed by the British Treasury during the 1830s, although later amended. These regulations were meant to be a set of rules applied universally throughout the Empire, and they were designed to influence the organization of banks, the kind of business they undertook, and their relations with shareholders. They aimed to prevent banking failures, by—for example—confining business to 'banking', broadly defined, and by limiting note-issuing powers to a ratio of paid-up capital. The regulations never had the force of law and were applied flexibly, but they had a strong influence on the structures adopted by both British-registered and colonial banks.

The principles of the Colonial Banking Regulations were incorporated into the Royal Charters, under which many of the British overseas banks operated. In the early nineteenth century English law did not confer the privilege of limited liability on companies, yet the risks of conducting a banking business overseas necessitated some kind of guarantee of this kind if equity funds were to be raised. The solution was a Royal Charter, which offered a kind of limited liability, and under which the Bank of England operated. Following the Colonial Banking Regulations, the Royal Charters limited the issue of banknotes to the size of paid-up capital; stipulated double liability for shareholders (i.e. in the event of default, shareholders were responsible for up to twice the amount of their subscribed shares); imposed requirements to publish annual accounts; imposed controls on the opening and closing of branches; limited business to 'banking'; and limited the period of operation so that banks were required periodically to renew their charters. Royal Charters did not confer monopoly rights on banks, but they did allow banks to issue notes and gave them authority to receive funds for British colonial government bodies without further authority. The provisions also implied—misleadingly—some kind of government approval of or guarantee to banks. They certainly awarded them a degree of respectability which was coveted.[16]

The Royal Charter system exercised a major influence on the geographical specialization of the early British overseas banks. All charters specified the geographical area in which a bank was allowed to operate, although the details varied with the pressures and circumstances of each particular case. The Treasury took the view that banks should confine their business to one region. It was particularly concerned about the security of the note issues of the banks, and fearful that multi-regional banks would be unstable and prone to failure.[17] The promoters of the Bank of Australasia,

---

[16] Baster, *The Imperial Banks*, ch. 2.

[17] F. H. H. King, 'Structural Alternatives and Constraints in the Evolution of Exchange Banking', in Geoffrey Jones (ed.), *Banks as Multinationals*, 87.

for example, originally conceived of their bank as the Royal Bank of Australasia and South Africa and there were even thoughts of extending it to Ceylon (Sri Lanka), Mauritius, and Singapore—in effect, all along the (pre-Suez Canal) trade route between Britain and Australia. However, during the charter negotiations the Board of Trade considered it 'inexpedient to connect under the same establishment banks in colonies at a great distance from and having no natural connection with each other'. A subsequent proposal that the same promoters should establish separate banks in Australia and South Africa was blocked by the Colonial Office on the grounds that government banks of deposit and discount already existed in South Africa.[18] The Bank of British North America was launched in 1836 without a Royal Charter, but found this prevented it from acting as a depository for colonial government funds. It applied for a Royal Charter, and received one in 1839, but this confined the bank's activity to that 'of carrying on the business of a banker in any cities, towns and places within any of the British Colonies or Settlements in North America, or adjacent to British North America'. These provisions excluded the bank from conducting business in London.[19]

Banks which did not seek a Royal Charter did not face such restrictions on their geographical area of operation. The most dynamic overseas bank in the 1840s did not at first have a Royal Charter. This was the Oriental Bank Corporation. The venture originated as the Bank of Western India, founded in Bombay in 1842, and grew out of the distinctive regulatory framework prevailing at that time in British India. A number of Western banking institutions were active in the Indian territory controlled by the East India Company in the opening decades of the nineteenth century. Foreign exchange banking was the preserve of the East India Company and a number of large British-owned 'agency houses', established in late eighteenth-century India. Government business, note issues, and certain commercial banking—but not exchange banking, from which they were prohibited—were conducted by the Presidency banks established at Bengal (1806), Bombay (1840), and Madras (1843). These banks had a government shareholding until 1876. In addition, following a major crisis in the agency house sector between 1829 and 1834, a number of new private banks were established by British expatriates, led by the Union Bank of Calcutta and the Bank of Agra in Bengal.[20]

During the 1840s the profitable opportunities available in exchange

[18] Butlin, *Australia and New Zealand Bank*, 27–8.
[19] Baster, *The Imperial Banks*, 82–3.
[20] A. K. Bagchi, 'Anglo-Indian Banking in British India: From the Paper Pound to the Gold Standard', *Journal of Imperial and Commonwealth History*, 13(3) (1985); id., *The Evolution of the State Bank of India* (Bombay: Oxford University Press, 1987), parts 1 and 2.

banking in India and the East began to attract new entrants. International trade in the region was booming because of expanding commodity production and improvements in sea and land transport. British business interests were proliferating following the abolition of the East India Company's monopoly of trade with India in 1813 and China in 1834, and the fast growth of trading entrepôts such as Singapore and Hong Kong, which became British colonies in 1819 and 1841 respectively. The Bank of Western India was established in Bombay to perform the exchange banking and other functions from which the Bank of Bombay was excluded.

This institution soon exhibited dynamic tendencies, establishing branches in Colombo, Calcutta, Hong Kong, and Singapore. In 1845 the bank moved its head office from Bombay to London and changed its name to the Oriental Bank. Four years later it took over a bank in Ceylon which had been established by British coffee planters, and which had a Royal Charter. By this means the Oriental Bank gained access to charter privileges and in 1851 the combined institution—to be called the Oriental Bank Corporation—was given a new charter. Through an administrative oversight, the Corporation became the first bank incorporated in England to obtain a Royal Charter to permit it to enter India. The Treasury failed to realize that a clause authorizing the bank to operate 'anywhere east of the Cape of Good Hope' would legally entitle it to operate in India, and as a result the charter application was agreed by the Treasury without following the usual procedure of first consulting the Indian authorities.[21]

The Oriental Bank became the first, and for a time the greatest, of the Eastern Exchange banks. It led the assault on the India foreign exchange market which became the preserve of the Exchange banks, to whom the Presidency banks came to function as a form of intermediary banker, supplying them with much of their working capital requirements in India. The Oriental Bank also constructed a multinational branch network extending from the major trading centres of the East to South Africa and Australia.

The 1850s saw a second surge in overseas bank promotion. Glyn, Mills were involved in the promotion of the Bank of Egypt, designed to finance Anglo-Egyptian trade. The three existing Anglo-Australian banks were joined by two new creations, the London Chartered Bank of Australia and the English, Scottish & Australian Chartered Bank. Rich gold discoveries had been made in the colony of New South Wales in 1851, followed by even richer discoveries in the newly separated colony of Victoria. Both new British banks opened branches in Sydney and Melbourne, the principal

[21] Baster, The Imperial Banks, 105–6; Compton Mackenzie, Realms of Silver (London: Routledge & Kegan Paul, 1954), chs. 1 and 2; F. H. H. King, 'The Mercantile Bank's Royal Charter', in F. H. H. King (ed.), Asian Policy, History and Development (Hong Kong: University of Hong Kong, 1979), 48.

cities of New South Wales and Victoria respectively. Gold led to an explosion of new bank branches, whose number grew in all the Australian colonies from 25 in 1851 to 197 in 1860, as local banks joined the British ones in multi-branch banking.[22]

Two new banks were also established with the aim of emulating the Oriental's wide geographical coverage, but in both instances regulatory considerations worked to constrain multi-regional ambitions and confine the new institutions to being Eastern Exchange banks. The Chartered Bank of India, Australia and China was incorporated in 1853. The moving spirit was the founder of *The Economist*, James Wilson, together with a small group of East India and Australian merchants and shipowners, who sought to provide banking facilities to finance trade in, and between, Asia and Australia.[23] Despite the precedent set by the Oriental, the acquisition of a Royal Charter proved to be extremely difficult because of opposition from the East India Company, but eventually was granted in 1853. Despite its name and original intention, Chartered never opened branches in Australia, for by the time the bank's charter had been granted a new rule of the Board of Trade was in operation requiring British banks to seek the sanction of the colonial legislatures before opening in Australia. Chartered duly applied to the Colonial Office for permission, but there was by then growing opposition towards English banks in Australasia from locally promoted colonial banks and its application was turned down. The bank could have renewed its application when this opposition had abated, but it chose not to.[24] Instead, Chartered concentrated on the East.

The origin of the Chartered Mercantile Bank of India, London and China lay in the Mercantile Bank of Bombay founded in Bombay in 1853 and almost immediately renamed the Mercantile Bank of India, London, and China. Mercantile Bank had been formed with the intent of acquiring a Royal Charter and an acknowledgement that this would mean a transfer of its head office from Bombay to London. A charter was eventually secured in 1857 and, to avoid delays, the bank excluded the Australian colonies from its agreed area of operations. In the following year the bank's head office moved from Bombay to London.[25]

The Eastern Exchange banks stood ready to take advantage of the expanding frontiers of Western influence in Asia. In 1853 Commodore Perry had ended Japan's 250-year period of exclusion from the rest of the world by demanding that country opened its doors to trade. Fifteen years later

---

[22] S. J. Butlin, *The Australian Monetary System, 1851–1914* (Sydney, 1986), 23.
[23] Prospectus of the Chartered Bank, SC.    [24] Mackenzie, *Realms of Silver*, 16–27.
[25] See the entry on this bank in Appendix 2. The account of its origins differs from many others, and is based on new research by S. W. Muirhead, who is writing a history of the bank.

the Meiji Restoration brought a new government to power committed to the modernization of the Japanese economy. However, British banks entered Japan even before the Meiji Restoration, and remained the only foreign banks active in that country until just before the turn of the century. Chartered Mercantile opened a branch in Yokohama in 1863, followed by the Oriental Bank and others in 1865. The Oriental Bank acquired a particularly important role as financial adviser to the Japanese government, and floated in London the Meiji government's first two foreign loans, in 1870 and 1873.[26]

Meanwhile, if 1860 is taken as a bench-mark date to assess the progress of the first three decades of British multinational banking, there were 15 banks active at that point. Collectively, they operated some 132 branches outside the United Kingdom. Almost half of these were located in Australia, with a handful in New Zealand. South Asia, the West Indies, and Canada were the next most important locations. The geographical distribution of assets, in so far as it can be estimated, was rather different. In 1860 probably just over half of British multinational banking assets were located in Asia, and just over one-third in Australasia. The operations elsewhere were modest in comparison.[27]

During the 1860s changes in British company legislation helped foster a speculative boom in the promotion of overseas banks. In 1862 Parliament codified two previous Company Acts of 1857 and 1858, which had introduced unrestricted creation of limited liability joint stock companies, including banking companies, and as a result there was a spurt of enthusiasm for organizing joint stock banks, both for domestic and overseas purposes. Between 1857 and 1866 nearly 30 new banks were founded to operate within the British Empire. They were mostly incorporated under the new limited liability legislation, and after 1864 the next Royal Charter granted to an overseas bank was in 1889. Many of these banks were fragile speculative enterprises which did not survive the major British banking crisis in 1866, associated with the failure of the leading London discount house, Overend Gurney.[28]

The suspension of one bank—the Agra and Masterman's—during this crisis deserves attention. Originating as one of the new private banks established in India in the 1830s, it had shifted its head office to London in 1857 following its incorporation under the Companies Act of that year. In 1864 it had broken through the institutional barrier between domestic and overseas banking by amalgamating with the London bankers Masterman, Peters, Mildred and Company. The bank extended its branch

[26] R. P. T. Davenport-Hines and Geoffrey Jones, 'British Business in Japan since 1868', in R. P. T. Davenport-Hines and Geoffrey Jones (eds.), *British Business in Asia since 1860* (Cambridge: Cambridge University Press, 1989), 222–4.

[27] See Appendices 1, 3, and 4.    [28] Baster, *The Imperial Banks*, 126–9.

network to include India, China, and even Paris. In 1862 it also opened in Sydney, and two years later a branch in Melbourne followed. By 1866 plans were also under way for a branch in Brisbane, in the colony of Queensland, and it successfully tendered for that government's business. The result was a very different model of multinational banking from the norm which had been established. Instead of an overseas bank specializing in a particular region, Agra and Masterman's combined domestic and overseas banking, and operated branches in three continents. This model was virtually stillborn. The City of London was suspicious of the heretical combination of overseas and domestic banking, while the geographical spread of branches made the bank vulnerable in the financial crisis in 1866. The result was collapse. Subsequently, the institution was reconstructed as the more modest Agra Bank, which limited its business to the East, and which survived until being liquidated in 1900.[29] Later generations of bankers were to spend much of the twentieth century trying to create multi-regional banks integrated into domestic British banking.

Leaving aside the many speculative ventures, the new waves of British overseas banks founded in the 1860s and 1870s went to the settler economies of the Southern Hemisphere, Latin America, South Africa, and New Zealand. They were frequently launched at times of booms in minerals or commodities.

In the first half of the 1860s British import and export merchants trading with Latin America, and others who scented profitable opportunities on that subcontinent, promoted a series of banks, including the London and River Plate Bank, the London and Brazilian Bank, the English Bank of Rio de Janeiro, and the London Bank of Mexico and South America. They established branches at the ports and in a few major inland trading centres, especially in the fast-growing River Plate region, where British mercantile interests were active in the export of wool, hides, and skins, and the import of British-manufactured textiles and other commodities. This economy boomed as immigration from southern Europe intensified and railway construction began in earnest. British-owned companies built and managed many of Argentina's railways—and those of Brazil and other Latin American countries—and were also active in public utilities, shipping companies, and mining ventures. The British banks serviced these ventures, lending them funds and receiving deposits from them. Throughout the nineteenth century and beyond, British banking activity in Latin America was confined to four countries, Argentina, Uruguay, Brazil, and Chile. Most British investment in the subcontinent was located there, and by the last

---

[29] Ibid., 129–30; F. H. H. King, *The History of the Hongkong and Shanghai Banking Corporation*, i (Cambridge: Cambridge University Press, 1987), 242; Butlin, *The Australian Monetary System*, 55.

decades of the century these countries had established a greater reputation for stability than the other republics.

The pioneer banks were soon joined by others. In the 1870s there was the ambitious, but short-lived, Mercantile Bank of the River Plate, promoted by Anglo-Argentine merchants who found the original British banks too conservative. In the following decade the English Bank of the River Plate and the Anglo-Argentine Bank were founded. Another creation of this period, which was to grow to be the largest British overseas bank before being overwhelmed in the Great Depression of the early 1930s, was the Bank of Tarapaca and London formed to operate in Chile in 1888. The moving force behind this latter venture was John Thomas North, who had obtained control of much of the Chilean nitrate industry and its related infrastructure, especially railways.[30]

The 1860s also saw the arrival of British overseas banks specializing in South Africa. As the economy of the Cape expanded in the 1850s the local banks, which the authorities had sought to protect since the 1830s, proved deficient in providing an adequate level of banking services. In 1857 a group of prominent merchants in Port Elizabeth (in the Eastern Cape), most of whom had close connections with London, proposed the setting up of a local Standard Bank of Port Elizabeth. It was eventually decided to raise British capital for the venture, and in 1862 the Standard Bank of British South Africa was incorporated in London. A rival, the London and South African Bank, was established in 1860 and gained a Royal Charter a year later, and had a chequered career before being acquired by the more successful Standard Bank in 1877. An economic boom based on relatively high wool, copper, and diamond prices led to the foundation of another British overseas bank, the Bank of Africa (1879), which acquired the South African business of the Oriental Bank.[31]

In New Zealand, the Union Bank of Australia had established the first bank branch in 1840, the year the first British settlers arrived. The enterprising Oriental Bank opened a branch for a few years before withdrawing in 1861, and the Bank of Australasia appeared in 1864. Meanwhile in 1861, following the discovery of large gold deposits, the colonists founded their own local institution, the Bank of New Zealand, which came to be that country's largest bank. This Auckland-based enterprise provoked the business community in the town of Otago to promote the rival Bank of Otago, which they registered in Britain in 1863. This bank had mixed

[30] David Joslin, *A Century of Banking in Latin America* (London: Oxford University Press, 1963), chs. 2–9. The career of the Mercantile Bank of the River Plate is discussed in Charles A. Jones, *International Business in the Nineteenth Century* (Brighton: Harvester, 1987), 129–33, 172–3. For British business activity in Latin America, see J. Fred Rippy, *British Investments in Latin America, 1822–1949* (Hamden: Archon, 1966).

[31] J. A. Henry, *The First Hundred Years of the Standard Bank* (London: Oxford University Press, 1963), chs. 1–7.

fortunes and by 1872 it was ready to sell its business to a new London-registered bank, the National Bank of New Zealand.[32]

Few new institutions were promoted to operate in North America. The Bank of British Columbia was formed to operate in Canada, while a number of banks were founded to operate in California, then a settler economy not unlike the Australian colonies. These included the London and San Francisco Bank, the Anglo-Californian Bank and the London, Paris and American Bank. They initially acquired an important role in Californian banking—the Anglo-Californian Bank 'became the largest dealer in the international exchange market of the Pacific coast'[33]—but over time their importance waned.

Although most attention was focused on the settler economies from the 1860s, the East continued to offer profitable opportunities. A second bank was formed to operate in Egypt, the Anglo-Egyptian Bank, and the Imperial Bank of Persia was established in 1889 on the basis of a concession appointing it as the state bank of Iran (as Persia became known in the 1930s).[34] Another Eastern Exchange bank emerged from the Calcutta City Banking Corporation formed in Calcutta in 1863 by expatriate British and Indian merchants, initially with a majority of Indians on the board of directors. The name was changed to the National Bank of India in the following year, and in 1866 the registration was moved to London.[35]

The most important new entrant into Eastern Exchange banking after 1860 was the Hongkong Bank, founded in 1865 by merchants of several nationalities trading in Hong Kong. It was chartered by the colonial government, but under the Colonial Banking Regulations the charter's provisions were similar to those of a Royal Charter. Eight of the fourteen members of the founding committee were not from Britain, and included Germans, Americans, and three representatives of Bombay interests, two of them Parsees and the other a member of the Jewish merchant house of David Sassoon. The purpose of the bank was to finance regional trade, and as a result the bank's initial focus was on the trading ports of China, Japan, and neighbouring countries. Although Hongkong Bank established a London office only four months after opening in Hong Kong, it did not

---

[32] Butlin, *Australia and New Zealand Bank*, ch. 9; G. R. Hawke and D. K. Sheppard, 'The Evolution of New Zealand Trading Banks mostly until 1934', Victoria University of Wellington Working Papers in Economic History, No. 84/2, Mar. 1984; Baster, *The Imperial Banks*, 141–2. The foundation of the Bank of New Zealand is discussed in Charles A. Jones, *International Business in the Nineteenth Century*, 133–4.

[33] Baster, *The International Banks*, 159; Wilkins, *The History of Foreign Investment in the United States*, 850 n. 43.

[34] *A Banking Centenary: Barclays Bank (Dominion, Colonial and Overseas), 1836–1936* (London: Barclays, 1936); Geoffrey Jones, *Banking and Empire in Iran* (Cambridge: Cambridge University Press, 1986), ch. 1.

[35] Geoffrey Tyson, *100 Years of Banking in Asia and Africa* (London: National and Grindlays, 1963), chs. 1–3.

follow the example of the banks founded in India and seek to transfer its domicile to Britain. Instead it flourished as a 'local' bank, albeit one managed by expatriate Britons, and by 1876 'was already established as the principal regional bank'.[36]

Eight years later came the most important exit from Eastern Exchange banking, when the Oriental Bank failed in 1884. The background to the demise of the greatest of the Exchange banks was the falling price of silver, in which most Asian currencies were dominated, against gold, to which sterling, and increasingly other developed countries' currencies, was linked on the gold standard. As explained later in this chapter (pp. 34–35), this depreciation had unfortunate consequences for British banks with assets denominated in Sterling. In 1878, as a result of this factor, Oriental virtually exhausted its reserves by writing down its holdings of short-term assets denominated in Eastern currencies.

Managerial failure and the wide spread of its branches greatly exacerbated the depreciation problem. Miscalculations on the future movement of the price of silver were combined with ill-judged lending policies which left the bank managing repossessed coffee estates in Ceylon and sugar estates in Mauritius. The over-exposure to coffee was particularly serious because a chronic leaf disease blighted the Ceylonese industry in the early 1880s, causing bad debts for all banks active on the island. Oriental's policy of continuing to pay dividends rather than rebuilding reserves left it vulnerable to the crisis of confidence which overwhelmed it in 1884.[37]

As in the case of Agra and Masterman's, this bank was reconstructed as the New Oriental Bank Corporation, but this too collapsed a mere eight years later. The Oriental also represented a different model of multinational banking than the norm seen in British overseas banking. It was the global bank *par excellence* of the nineteenth century, whose enterprise gave it a remarkable multi-continental branch network in the Eastern Hemisphere. Yet its global network appeared to provide insufficient knowledge of local business conditions, leaving the bank over-exposed to bad debts. Contemporaries could be forgiven for coming to the conclusion that regional specialization was a more prudent strategy.

By 1890 British multinational banking had grown considerably compared to thirty years earlier. The number of banks had more than doubled, to reach 33. There had been an enormous expansion in the number of British bank branches overseas, which had grown to exceed 700. The main thrust of this expansion had been in Australia and New Zealand, which by 1890 accounted for over 60 per cent of all British overseas branches.

[36] King, *The History of the Hongkong and Shanghai Banking Corporation*, i. 41–73.
[37] Baster, *The Imperial Banks*, 258–9; King, *The History of the Hongkong and Shanghai Banking Corporation*, i. 278–81; A. K. Bagchi, *The Presidency Banks and the Indian Economy, 1876–1914* (Calcutta: Oxford University Press, 1989), 205.

This thirty-year period had been one of sustained economic growth in the Australian colonies, during which many new colonial banks had been founded, and the total number of bank branches increased nearly eight-fold.[38] As in 1860, the asset distribution revealed a different picture from that of the branch distribution. British multinational banking had become centred on a 'Triad' of Australasia, Latin America, and Asia. In the first region the British banks operated an extensive branch network. In the other two regions the banks conducted their business with a handful of branches.

The reasons behind the prolific spread of British multinational banks will be explored later in this chapter, but it is evident immediately that their growth must be related to the development of the British Empire, British capital exports, and British foreign trade. The link with the Empire was the most obvious of the three. Although their operations in Latin America lay beyond the formal borders of the Empire, elsewhere the location of the branches of the British banks were overwhelmingly correlated with British imperial power. In Asia, they operated from either British colonies, or cities which had fallen under the *de facto* control of the Western powers.

The importance of British multinational banking in the nineteenth century also rested, fundamentally, on the overall importance of Britain in the world economy. The Industrial Revolution gave Britain the largest economy in the Western world, in terms of aggregate income, until passed by the United States in the middle of the nineteenth century. She remained the leading nation in terms of manufacturing per capita throughout the century. Britain was the pivot of international trade. Her exports of manufactured goods, her chief exports, were almost 40 per cent of the world's total in the decade 1876–85.[39] From the 1850s, British capital exports accelerated to make her by far the largest foreign investor in the world, a position retained until the First World War.[40]

The charts in Figure 2.1 show, however, that the correlation between British multinational banking and British trade and capital flows was less direct than with the borders of the Empire. The snapshot of British imports and exports in 1890 shows that British trade was heavily biased towards North America and the rest of Europe, the two regions in which British banks had the least direct investment. This trade pattern remained largely in place in the pre-war decades. Although the exact size and nature of

[38] Butlin, *The Australian Monetary System*, 297–8.

[39] C. K. Harley and Donald McCloskey, 'Foreign Trade: Competition and the Expanding International Economy', in Roderick Floud and Donald McCloskey (eds.), *The Economic History of Britain Since 1700* (Cambridge: Cambridge University Press, 1981).

[40] M. Edelstein, 'Foreign Investment and Empire, 1860–1914', in Floud and McCloskey (eds.), *The Economic History of Britain*; P. L. Cottrell, *British Overseas Investment in the Nineteenth Century* (London: Macmillan, 1975); Lance E. Davis and Robert A. Huttenback, *Mammon and the Pursuit of Empire* (Cambridge: Cambridge University Press, 1986), ch. 3.

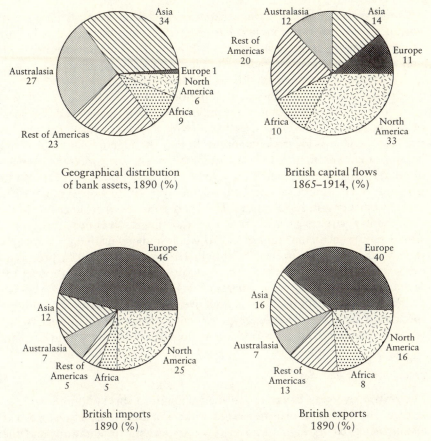

Geographical distribution
of bank assets, 1890 (%)

British capital flows
1865–1914, (%)

British imports
1890 (%)

British exports
1890 (%)

FIG. 2.1. Multinational banking, trade, and capital flows, c.1890.
*Sources*: Bank asset distribution in Appendix 4. Geographical distribution of
British capital calculated from Lance E. Davis and Robert A. Huttenback,
*Mammon and the Pursuit of Empire* (Cambridge: Cambridge University Press,
1986), 46 (minimum estimate). Import and export data from B. R. Mitchell,
*British Historical Statistics* (Cambridge: Cambridge University Press, 1988),
497–515, table 1.6; in these two charts 'Europe' includes North Africa and
'Africa' includes Turkey and the Middle East

British capital exports remain disputed, the estimate given in Figure 2.1 for
their geographical destination over the period from 1865 to 1914 provides
at least a crude approximation. It shows the disparity between the importance of the United States and Canada as recipients of British capital and
their unimportance in British multinational banking. However the three
'Triad' regions were the next most important hosts for British capital exports, although only just so in the cases of Asia and Australasia.

British multinational banking, therefore, rested on Britain's unique importance in the world economy, but the overseas banks formed only part of the international financial system of Britain. They were concerned with only part of the flows of trade and investment, leaving other institutions and contractual arrangements to service the rest of it.

Born in the 1830s, the British multinational banks had proliferated over many of the settler economies of the Southern Hemisphere and the ports of the East by 1890. Their origins lay with a desire among British and overseas merchants for trade finance facilities. Although foreign trade could be and often was financed through correspondent networks, the absence of reliable correspondents had provided an incentive to internalization and the creation of multinational banks with overseas branches run (in the main) from London head offices. They had gone to where there were no host country barriers to entry; to where trade finance was not already well served by the merchant banks; and to where indigenous banking systems were weak or undeveloped. The Provincial Bank of Ireland, a prototype overseas bank based on Scottish banking principles, provided a model for such banks. Regulatory requirements as well as the traditions of the British financial system had resulted in the overseas banks adopting a highly specialized structure. They were particularly distinguished by their focus on single regions, and by their lack of domestic business within Britain.

## 2.2. Products and Services

The British overseas banks raised their capital on the London Stock Exchange. By the late nineteenth century the London Stock Exchange was distinguished by its high turnover, its international orientation, and the sophistication of its services compared to capital markets elsewhere. Banks floated in London, therefore, were able to tap greater resources than those quoted in the small or even non-existent capital markets of the Australian and South African colonies, India, and the Latin American republics. A larger capital, in turn, allowed the building of a larger loan book and a larger note issue than most local banks could achieve. The attraction of the London Stock Exchange was a major factor leading the series of banks floated in the East in the 1850s and 1860s to 'migrate' to London. The Hongkong Bank was exceptional in being floated on a local stock exchange and not subsequently seeking to transfer domicile to London, although even this bank had its shares quoted on the London Stock Exchange and by the early 1890s over half its shares were registered there.[41]

It was certainly not the case that all of the capital of British overseas banks quoted in London was held by residents of the United Kingdom. It

[41] King, *The History of the Hongkong and Shanghai Banking Corporation*, i. 284–5, 436.

was not uncommon for a certain block of shares to be reserved for people in the intended country of operation, a device in major part to secure future business, as shareholders were potential customers. When the Colonial Bank was launched in 1837, three-quarters of the £2 million capital was raised in Britain and the rest was allocated to subscribers in the West Indian Colonies. One-third of the share issue of the National Bank of New Zealand in 1872 was reserved for residents of that Colony. The British banks in Australia had colonial share registers, and on occasion—such as in the early 1870s—sought to improve their colonial public relations by promoting colonial shareholding. Again, at least up to the 1880s, substantial portions of the share capital of the British banks in Latin America were held by residents of Latin America and various continental countries.[42]

The British overseas banks used their capital to finance their business, sometimes physically transporting it around the world, but once a bank was established the preference was to finance local lending by local (deposit) borrowing rather than by using sterling capital. The underlying reason for this policy was the problem of exchange risk. Although funds *were* often transferred abroad to start a new branch or buy fixed assets or to support a business with an insufficient level of local deposits, the search for deposits in the countries in which the overseas banks established branches was a distinctive feature of these institutions. The banks generally maintained their reserves in London in British and Empire securities. Even the Hongkong Bank's reserves were invested in British and Indian government securities, and largely domiciled in London.[43]

At least from the 1860s, many overseas banks began to seek British deposits for fixed periods extending from three months to five years. The banks obtained such funds through their London offices, through the appointment of independent agents, and even sometimes by establishing their own branches or agencies, especially in Scotland, which was a particularly fertile source of savings. Very soon after its foundation, for example, the Hongkong Bank sought British deposits to finance its bill operations, appointing agents in Edinburgh. London deposits contributed 36 per cent of Hongkong Bank's total deposits in 1888.[44] The banks in Australasia, both British and local, also actively sought British fixed deposits, especially from the mid-1870s. With very little exchange risk because of the parity between sterling and the local currencies, these British fixed deposits were used to fund lending in the colonies, especially illiquid advances to primary

---

[42] Butlin, *Australia and New Zealand Bank*, 195–6; Charles A. Jones, draft chapter for Colin M. Lewis and Rory Miller (ed.), *British Business in Latin America* (Cambridge: Cambridge University Press, forthcoming).

[43] King, *The History of the Hongkong and Shanghai Banking Corporation*, i. 311.

[44] Ibid., 154–5, 299–301. Chartered Mercantile had 61 per cent of its fixed deposits (of £2.8 m.) drawn from Britain as at 31 Dec. 1890. Information from S. W. Muirhead.

producers. The obvious incentive for the banks was interest rate differentials. Australian banks paid less for fixed deposits in Britain than in the colonies, while they attracted funds by paying higher interest rates to British investors than could be secured on other investments such as Consols. Considerable sums were collected. In 1892 Australian banks (both Australian and British-registered) held over £38 million of United Kingdom deposits, or 28 per cent of their total deposits. In that year, 20 per cent of the deposits of the Bank of Australasia and the Union Bank of Australia were from Britain, while the London Chartered Bank of Australia held British deposits larger than their colonial deposits.[45]

The finance of international trade was the core business of the overseas banks. By the late nineteenth century they handled much of the trade of the East. In Australia the British overseas banks were the dominant institutions financing that country's foreign trade, retaining their lead over local banks until at least the inter-war years.[46] In Latin America, the British banks in the 1860s took over from the merchant houses the role of foreign trade finance. As much of the trade financed by the overseas banks consisted of the exchange of manufactured goods usually from Britain, for raw materials and primary commodities produced by the countries in which they had branches, the institutions often became known by the names of the primary commodities produced in their regions. Thus Anglo-South American Bank was the 'nitrate bank'. The Ionian Bank was the 'currant bank'. The Bank of Mauritius was the 'sugar bank'.

The basic instrument of trade finance in the nineteenth century was the bill of exchange. An exporter, A, in Britain would send goods to a customer, B, in an overseas country, at the same time drawing a bill requiring payment after a given period, often sixty or ninety days. The bill would be presented to the overseas customer, B, who would 'accept' it, arranging payment before taking delivery of the shipping documents giving title to the goods (in the case of bills drawn on a 'Documents against Payment' basis) or taking immediate delivery of the shipping documents upon acceptance (in the case of bills drawn on a 'Documents against Acceptance' basis). B could ask a bank in Britain to pay A, and in turn pay this bank in local currency in his own country. In practice, the operation of bills of exchange often involved the granting of credit. A, instead of waiting for funds from B to arrive, might sell the bill to a bank, usually at a discount. A would then receive prompt payment for his goods, while B would have

---

[45] D. T. Merrett, 'Australian Banking Practice and the Crisis of 1893', *Australian Economic History Review*, 29(1) (1989), 75–6; Butlin, *Australia and New Zealand Bank*, 305–6; David Pope, *Bankers and Banking Business, 1860–1914*, Australian National University Working Paper in Economic History, No. 85, 1987; Baster, *The Imperial Banks*, 152–4; J. D. Bailey, 'Australian Borrowing in Scotland in the Nineteenth Century', *Economic History Review*, 2nd ser., 12(2) (1959), 268–79.   [46] Merrett, 'Paradise Lost?', 70–1.

a period of credit when he had a chance to sell the goods he had imported. Merchant banks were known as 'accepting houses' because so much of their business was accepting bills of exchange. In London, the bills of exchange were often sold on to the discounting houses. In the nineteenth century the London acceptance or 'bill on London' became an extremely common form of international credit even for transactions not involving Britain. From the 1860s an alternative method of payment, involving the use of the international telegraph to transfer funds, spread.

The essence of foreign trade finance was, or was meant to be, its short-term nature and high premium on security. It was held to be essential that credit was only made available for a short term. Long-term loans were 'lock-ups' to be avoided at all costs. Bills of exchange were expected to be 'self-liquidating' and to represent real trading transactions. Attempts by customers to borrow on the security of goods which did not exist were known as 'accommodation bills' and were also avoided at all costs. Credit was normally extended against the security of goods in transit, although local practice and customs led over time to a wide variation of practice in this respect. Accurate knowledge of customers and commodities was an essential part of the system. This helps to explain the regional specializations among the British financial institutions involved in trade finance. The managers of overseas banks became experts in the commodities they financed, for unless they knew with great accuracy the quality of, and market for, the goods they held as security, there was always the risk that a loan would become a 'lock-up'.[47]

The finance of foreign trade was intimately connected with exchange operations. The currencies of the British colonies in Australia, New Zealand, and South Africa were approximately at parity with the British pound, and exchange operations between Britain and those countries were limited to transferring funds, sometimes within the same institution. To take the example of Australia, before 1930 the Australian pound was not distinguished from the British pound, and British coin circulated freely in the Australian colonies. The exchange rate quoted by Australian banks was regarded merely as the rate for the same currency in another place (London), and was expressed by saying that Sterling in London stood at so many pence premium or discount. The banks enjoyed a virtual mono-poly of exchange dealings between Australia and London. The British banks initially dominated this market, but from the 1850s locally registered banks established London offices—beginning with the Bank of New South Wales in 1853—and acquired a share of the exchange market.[48]

---

[47] Tyson, *100 Years of Banking in Asia and Africa*, 79.
[48] H. W. Arndt, *The Australian Trading Banks* (Melbourne: Cheshire, 1957), 87–8, 102–3; Merrett, 'Paradise Lost?', 65–71; Butlin, *Australia and Zealand Bank*, 5–7.

In the absence of a central bank, the British and local banks in Australia together controlled the exchange rate. At the heart of the system were the 'London funds' held by all the banks in London. These were in effect Australia's international reserves as well as the working balances of the banks from foreign trade finance. The level of London funds of each bank regulated its domestic credit policy, and through this mechanism the banks contrived to maintain parity between the Australian and British currencies. Each bank closely watched its level of London funds and its domestic credit situation to ensure that its cash deposit and advance deposit ratios were maintained at levels considered safe. An increase in London funds would arise if Australian export receipts were high, or there was an increase in government borrowing abroad. This would improve the liquidity of a bank, and therefore its power to lend. It would as a result expand credit in Australia. Any increase in advances would tend to increase deposits, and result in a fall in cash ratios and liquidity ratios. It would also stimulate imports, which would in due course reduce London funds. The system successfully maintained exchange stability, but the reliance on individual banks to adjust their ratios was suboptimal. A slowness in reacting to sudden shifts in the trade balance was to lead to crisis and collapse at the end of the 1920s.[49]

The British multinational banks in Latin America and Asia faced more complicated exchange problems, for many of their host economies were not on the Gold Standard and the value of their currencies could fluctuate against sterling. The banks could cover exchange risks arising from daily operations through routine practices. Sterling drafts were bought locally from exporters, who received local currency in exchange, and the sterling represented by these drafts could be sold for local currency to importers and others who needed sterling to make remittances. Equilibrium could be achieved, if necessary, by changing the rates or shipping bullion. However, funds transferred on a more permanent basis were subject to an exchange risk. Exchange fluctuations created plentiful opportunities for arbitrage and pure speculation, activities condemned by British banking orthodoxy, but in practice an almost inevitable characteristic of banking in the period.

For the British banks operating in the East, the exchange problem became acute from the mid-1870s, when the value of silver began to depreciate against gold. Banks with London head offices and sterling capitals found the sterling value of their Eastern assets falling, as well as having to

---

[49] C. B. Schedvin, *Australia and the Great Depression* (Sydney: Sydney University Press, 1970), 76–8; *Report of the Royal Commission Appointed to Inquire into the Monetary and Banking Systems at Present in Operation in Australia* (Melbourne, 1936), 40–3. A similar system operated in New Zealand, and in the 19th century the 'London funds' of New Zealand and Australia were not separated in any systematic fashion. Hawke and Sheppard, 'The Evolution of New Zealand Trading Banks', 51–2.

contend with the problems of day-to-day fluctuations. The silver depreciation was not continuous, and there was room for considerable managerial discretion in judging the correct responses to market movements. The Hongkong Bank had an advantage in this respect that its accounts were in silver-based Hong Kong dollars, although as many of its shareholders were in Britain the bank still needed to make dividend payments in sterling. Hongkong Bank developed a set of policies known as 'keeping on an even keel'—the matching of sterling uses of funds by sterling sources of funds, and similarly with silver. Its Hong Kong head office, dollar balance sheet, and branches in the major Asian ports enabled the bank to accept silver deposits without arranging exchange cover against depreciation, and to find uses for them. As a result, it was in a position to compete strongly against the other Exchange banks, and often to outbid them for British and colonial government business.[50]

The finance of foreign trade led the British overseas banks into purely local lending in the countries in which they established branches. In the banks operating in areas of British colonial settlement, such a trend occurred very early in their histories. In Australia, banks lent to farmers, evading the restrictions embodied in Royal Charters against taking real property, livestock, and wool on the sheep's back as collateral. Some banks, such as the Bank of Australasia, made advances direct to pastoralists from the 1850s, while others—such as the Union Bank—preferred to 'on-lend' through intermediaries, either merchants or specialist mortgage companies.[51] Much of the lending to primary producers came to be, in fact, long-term credit for the purchase of land and construction of buildings and other improvements, a major deviation from British banking orthodoxy.[52] The banks followed the wool-growers and later the gold-miners inland, seeking their business and spurred on by the threat of competition.

At different speeds and to different extents, these processes occurred in every economy in which the British banks invested. The finance of international trade drew banks into the domestic economy as they financed the distribution, and sometimes the growing, of crops. Once established in a territory, few banks could resist lucrative banking opportunities of a purely local nature. The impossibility of separating 'local' and 'foreign' business, the search for profits, and the absence or inadequacy of local banking institutions all conspired to push the British banks in this direction. Similarly, the realities of the local currency and legal system in each country forced the overseas banks to take forms of security which their domestic British brethren would never have accepted.

---

[50] King, *The History of the Hongkong and Shanghai Banking Corporation*, i. 273–8; iv (Cambridge: Cambridge University Press, 1991), 11.

[51] Butlin, *Australia and New Zealand Bank*, 211–22, 250–2.

[52] Arndt, *The Australian Trading Banks*, 50–1.

In mid-nineteenth-century New Zealand, the European settlers needed credit to build up sheep flocks and develop grasslands from bush and swamp. Specialist mortgage companies appeared, as they did in other settler economies, but New Zealand was unusual in the development of close equity links between such companies and the banks. The locally registered Bank of New Zealand pioneered such a link, and the other banks under the threat of competition followed this trend. The National Bank of New Zealand originally intended to confine its activities to orthodox British banking, but within four years of its foundation it felt obliged to take a prominent role in the formation of a mortgage company, or 'stock and station agent' as they were known locally.[53]

The British banks established in Latin America in the 1860s followed a similar path, though more hesitantly. In the first decade of their foundation both the London and River Plate Bank and the London and Brazilian Bank made highly unorthodox loans, and lent against the security of mortgages, often despite the wishes of their London-based boards.[54] Such unorthodoxy, however, carried greater risks than in the British settler economies. Taking mortgages as security for loans which subsequently defaulted resulted in the London and Brazilian Bank acquiring in 1870 a huge coffee plantation in the interior of Brazil. The bank ran the plantation for the following fifteen years, a task which even involved trying to recruit immigrant workers in Germany.[55] The Mercantile Bank of the River Plate failed only five years after its foundation in 1872 after making loans which went 'bad' to local railway and waterworks companies.[56] Such painful learning curves pushed the British banks back towards more conventional commercial banking and trade finance after the mid-1870s,[57] and it was not until the two decades before the First World War that orthodox lending policies began to be modified.

The Ionian Bank in the eastern Mediterranean was an unusual instance of a British multinational bank obliged by law to engage in local lending. This situation arose because the Ionian Bank was established under a charter from the Ionian Islands as well as a Royal Charter (surrendered in 1883 when the bank became a limited liability company). In 1864 when

---

[53] Hawke and Sheppard, 'The Evolution of New Zealand Trading Banks', 55–7.

[54] Charles A. Jones, 'The State and Business Practice in Argentina, 1862–1914', in C. Abel and C. M. Lewis (eds.), *Latin America, Economic Imperialism and the State: The Political Economy of the External Connection from Independence to the Present* (London: Athlone, 1985), 187.

[55] Joslin, *A Century of Banking in Latin America*, 73, 76; Maria Barbara Levy and Flavio A. M. de Saes, 'Foreign Loans, Debt and Development: Brazil 1850–1913', unpublished paper, 1989.

[56] Charles A. Jones, 'British Financial Institutions in Argentine, 1860–1914', Ph.D. thesis, Cambridge University, 1973, ch. 1.

[57] Id., 'Commercial Banks and Mortgage Companies', in D. C. M. Platt (ed.), *Business Imperialism, 1840–1930* (Oxford: Clarendon Press, 1977), 40.

the Ionian Islands became part of Greece, the bank's Ionian charter was replaced by a Greek one. Ionian Bank soon came under pressure from the Greek government to make loans in what were considered socially desirable sectors. According to a convention signed by the bank in April 1880—acceptance of which underlay renewal of its charter privileges, including note issue, in Greece—the bank was obliged to employ in the Ionian Islands sums equivalent to 40 per cent of its paid-up capital in agricultural loans and 25 per cent of its paid-up capital in mortgage lending. The terms and conditions of the loans, including the interest rate, were fixed. The agreement had special provisions to protect the small agriculturists who were to get the loans: when crops failed or there was other due cause, there was to be no recourse to legal proceedings for at least three months after the due date of the bill.[58] These agricultural loans caused frequent bad-debt problems, and the bank's discomfort was accelerated by a moratorium declared in the 1890s which enabled small farmers to take advantage of their freedom from debt. Mortgage lending also frequently led to default, and the Ionian's end-year balance sheet regularly contained an item representing the value of mortgaged property owned (temporarily) by the bank.

In the East, the Exchange banks financed the movement of commodities: Ceylon tea; Malayan rubber and tin; the export of opium from India and its import into the major market, China. However, the Exchange banks, too, found that the finance of the trade in a commodity led them 'up-country' into the local economy, and also prompted the modification of conventional rules about the security taken for loans. In addition, the British banks used indigenous intermediaries to on-lend to the local economy. This complex process will be examined in greater detail in the following chapter, for these trends grew in strength towards the end of the nineteenth century.

If the lending policies of the British banks led them deeper into local economies than originally intended, their search for local deposits and their note issues had a similar effect. In the British settler economies large branch networks developed. Banks which were focused more on exchange banking and foreign trade finance had less of an insatiable appetite for funds. In the second half of the nineteenth century, the British banks in Latin America generally restricted themselves to attracting the deposits of the British-owned merchant houses and railway companies, although by the turn of the century many of these banks had begun to seek the funds of smaller depositors.[59] The Eastern Exchange banks in the nineteenth century sought

---

[58] Convention of 1880, File on Royal Charter and Subsequent Conventions, Box 1; Note on Agrarian Loans, Miscellaneous File, Box 5, Ionian Bank Archives.

[59] Joslin, *A Century of Banking in Latin America*, 132, 168, 171–3; Charles A. Jones, 'British Financial Institutions in Argentine', ch. 3.

deposits in the ports at which they established branches, although they made no attempt to penetrate the interiors of the Asian countries to find deposits on similar lines to the Anglo-Australian banks.

The circulation of banknotes provided a second source of funds alongside local deposits for the British banks. The desire to increase this circulation also served as a stimulus to branch expansion and to penetration 'inland'. The private issue of banknotes grew directly out of British banking traditions. When the first overseas banks were established in Britain in the 1830s, it was still common practice for domestic commercial banks outside London to issue their own banknotes, alongside those of the Bank of England. These notes of the commercial banks were not legal tender but depended upon public confidence for their circulation and, after a major banking crisis in 1825, the banks in England and Wales were not allowed to issue 'small' denomination notes under £5. The situation was different in Scotland and Ireland, where notes of 'small' denomination were not banned in 1826, and where Bank of England notes were not legal tender.[60] It was, therefore, not surprising that the overseas banks were note-issuing institutions; nor that their Royal Charters conferred neither a monopoly of note issue nor the status of legal tender on such note issues.

The British Treasury was always concerned about the note-issuing rights of the banks, because of the consequences if a bank failed, and this was a major reason for the insistence that banks should confine their activities to a single region familiar to them. The Colonial Banking Regulations of 1846 also specified that banks were not to issue notes under the value of £1. The Colonial Ordinance under which the Hongkong Bank was established in 1865 had limited the bank's note issue to the size of the paid-up capital, forbidden the issue of notes of less than $5 in value without special authorization, and required the bank to maintain a reserve *in specie* equivalent in value to one-third of the note issue. In 1872 the Hongkong Bank briefly secured the right to issue lower-denomination notes—of $1— but within fifteen years the Treasury had achieved the curtailment of this privilege.[61]

The failure of the Oriental Bank in 1884 confirmed the worst fears of the Treasury regulators. In Singapore, the other British banks had moved to maintain confidence by accepting the Oriental's banknotes, but in Ceylon the public sector had taken the initiative. The Governor of Ceylon acted, without reference to London, to guarantee Oriental's banknote issue in the colony in order to prevent a general financial crisis. This apparent acknowledgement of government liability for private note issues provoked a bitter

    [60] Collins, *Money and Banking in the UK*, 42–4; Munn, 'The Emergence of Joint Stock Banking in the British Isles', 77, 79.
    [61] Baster, *The Imperial Banks*, 22–4; King, *The History of the Hongkong and Shanghai Banking Corporation*, i. 119–20, 370–2.

TABLE 2.1. *Note issues of British multinational banks by region, 1890*

| Region | Notes issued (£ sterling) | No. of banks |
|---|---|---|
| The East | 2,284,870 | 3 |
| Australia and New Zealand | 1,591,458 | 6 |
| South Africa | 907,345 | 2 |
| South America | 781,365 | 2 |
| Canada | 475,709 | 2 |
| West Indies | 457,210 | 1 |
| Greece | 381,796 | 1 |
| Other[a] | 685 | 1 |
| TOTAL | 6,880,438 | 18 |

[a] This small issue was by the Anglo-Egyptian Bank in Egypt.

exchange of words among the different British government departments involved, and led to a determined Treasury resolve to phase out private note issues in the colonies.[62]

Table 2.1 shows the extent of the note issues by British multinational banks in 1890.

The largest note issues were in the East, mainly in British colonies, principally Hong Kong and the Straits Settlements (Singapore, Penang, and Malacca), together with small issues in China and Japan. In some cases, these banknotes circulated far beyond the territories of issue. Hong Kong notes, for example, were in widespread use in neighbouring provinces of China by the early twentieth century.[63] The British colonies in Australia, New Zealand, and South Africa also had substantial note issues by British banks, although coinage remained their chief form of currency in this period. Outside the Empire, there was quite a large note issue in South America, principally Uruguay, and in Greece, where the Ionian Bank was a bank of issue.

Whether, or to what extent, note issue was a 'profitable' exercise for the British banks is a moot point. Banknotes represented an interest-free loan for a bank. A note issue also gave a bank prestige and represented a form of advertising. In practice, the value of a note issue depended on the reserves required to support it, which were specified in Royal Charters and local banking regulation. The level of reserves was also influenced by the likelihood of 'runs' against a bank. In addition, taxation rates, which varied between countries, could affect considerably the profitability of a

[62] King, *The History of the Hongkong and Shanghai Banking Corporation*, i. 375–6, 391–3.   [63] Ibid., 84, 392, 485.

note issue. Before 1914 such taxation mainly took the form of duties levied on the number of notes issued, or, more usually, in circulation.

As a result, the 'profitability' of note issues varied widely between country and period. In Latin America, the London and River Plate Bank was already, by the 1870s, dubious about the merits of issuing notes because of 'the reserves they necessitate'.[64] However, the bank appears to have found its large note issue in Uruguay profitable, even after the banking crises of the early 1890s.[65] The Ionian Bank in the 1890s clearly considered that the privilege of note issue in Greece was worth having, and worth striving to keep. One calculation within the bank suggested that a '5 per cent profit' was made on the issue.[66] Such profitability estimates were clearly very rough-and-ready, but the importance of their note issues became a matter for investigation by the banks when governments began to seek control over paper currencies.

British overseas banks, therefore, evolved over the nineteenth century from their origins as multinational trade banks to institutions offering a wider range of financial products, even though international trade finance and exchange banking remained their core activities by the end of the century. A number of factors encouraged product diversification. Trade finance and exchange business led the banks inland as they followed crop production or the pastoral frontier. In the process they often had to modify their lending practices. The banks had sought to operate on the basis of deposits raised locally and the issue of banknotes. Both the search for deposits and the desire to increase note circulation stimulated branch expansion and penetration into local economies. Competition from other banks spurred on these developments. These processes occurred at very different paces in different regions. By 1890 the British banks in Australia had large branch networks and were engaged in retail banking in the domestic market. At the other end of the spectrum, the Eastern Exchange banks were still confined largely to the ports of Asia, and their business remained far more focused on trade finance and exchange banking.

## 2.3. Organizational Capability and Strategies of Control

The British overseas banks of the nineteenth century were extraordinary examples of multinational enterprise. They managed, in most cases from London, extensive branch networks in overseas countries. Those banks active outside the British Empire had to contend with alien political, legal,

[64] Charles A. Jones, 'The Transfer of Banking Techniques from Britain to Argentina, 1862–1914', *Revue Internationale d'Histoire de la Banque*, 26–7 (1983), 254.
[65] Manager's Letters from Montevideo, 21 Jan. 1892, Head Office Confidential Letters, Book 2, LB.
[66] Undated Note in Note Issue File, on Note Issue Profit, Box 3, Ionian Bank Archives.

and cultural systems. All the banks were faced with serious problems of communication in an era before aircraft and telephones, although there were remarkable advances in electronic communications as the century progressed. By 1865, for example, Ceylon was linked to London by cable. Seven years later the cable reached Darwin, and thereby the other major cities of Australia. In 1876 a cable link opened between Sydney and New Zealand. However, personal visits between London and overseas branches remained difficult and time-consuming affairs. The Provincial Bank of Ireland had provided an organizational model, but Ireland was a short sea journey from Britain. The problems of distance were magnified many times for British overseas banks controlling branches in Uruguay, or New South Wales, or Japan.

The success of the first generations of British overseas banks in overcoming such problems was considerable. There were failures, some of which, such as that of the Oriental Bank, were serious, but it is the number of banks which survived to build viable businesses that is most striking. This section explores in more detail the management structures which enabled these banks to co-ordinate business activities over distances on a large scale.

The British overseas banks were 'free-standing' business organizations, with none of their equity in the hands of domestic banks or any other institution. Unlike the merchant banks, which were usually owned by a small family circle, they were owned by a substantial number of individual shareholders, although in some cases founders or their descendants held blocks of shares. In 1890 the two largest Anglo-Australian banks, Bank of Australasia and Union Bank of Australia, had large shareholder registers, with 3,776 and 3,133 names respectively. Chartered Bank had only 929 shareholders in that year, while the much smaller Agra Bank had 2,250 and the newly founded Imperial Bank of Persia 2,085, although in the latter case one of the bank's founders (the Sassoon family) probably held around a third of the shares.[67] The Hongkong Bank limited the number of shares an individual could own: initially the maximum permitted holding was 10 per cent of the total outstanding, but this fell over time to 1.2 per cent by 1929.[68]

At the apex of the banks were their boards of directors, who were normally located in London. These boards usually consisted of three different types of men. First, there were merchants or other businessmen with connections with and experience of the bank's specialist geographical region. Secondly, there were bankers, and sometimes accountants and lawyers, with a London background, some of whom also had overseas connections.

[67] Geoffrey Jones, *Banking and Empire in Iran*, 31; Cassis, *Les Banquiers de la City*, 101.
[68] King, *The History of the Hongkong and Shanghai Banking Corporation*, i. 134.

Finally, there were usually one or more former British diplomats or colonial civil servants, with experience of the relevant region.

Inevitably there were variations in the weight given to the three groups between the different banks. A few illustrations will suffice to make the point. Chartered Bank's board (or court, as it was known in the tradition of the East India Company) in 1890 included a former high court judge in Calcutta; a partner of a merchant house based in Shanghai; a partner in a firm of London and Manchester merchants; a member of Jardine Matheson, one of the leading Far Eastern trading houses; and the bank's London manager. The chairman had been one of the founders of the Singapore-based merchant house of Paterson, Simons and Company. The board of the Ionian Bank in 1890 included three members of the Greek business and professional community resident in London; a member of a London firm of chartered accountants; a member of a London law firm and relative of an original founder; and a partner in Lloyds Bank. The London and River Plate Bank had begun in the 1860s with a board representing a strong combination of City bankers and River Plate merchants, but over the following three decades the River Plate connections grew stronger, with the bank's nine directors holding between them some twenty-five directorships of other River Plate companies by the mid-1890s.[69] Apart from descendants of founders, directors appear to have been elected on the basis of the firms they represented or, as in the case of former government officials, their experience of a region and network of contacts.

The degree of interlocking directorships became less concentrated over time than in the 1830s, when the same group of people associated with the Provincial Bank of Ireland and the National Provincial Bank appeared in most of the overseas banks. Nevertheless, by 1890 there were plenty of connections at director level between overseas banks and domestic banks, and between different overseas banks.[70] The case of Glyn, Mills has already been noted (see above, p. 17). By the beginning of the 1890s members of these two families sat on the boards of the London and Brazilian Bank, the Imperial Bank of Persia, the English Bank of the River Plate, the Bank of Egypt and the Bank of New Zealand, the Bank of British North America and the Union Bank of Australia. Directors did not, however, sit on the boards of banks which were in direct competition with one another because of their geographical area of operation. A decision of the English Bank of Rio de Janeiro in 1887 to open branches on the River Plate was followed by the resignation from its board of two directors who were also directors of the London and River Plate Bank.[71]

Some banks had family dynasties on their boards, giving them the

[69] Joslin, *A Century of Banking in Latin America*, 28; Charles A. Jones, 'British Financial Institutions in Argentine', 135.　　　　[70] Baster, *The International Banks*, 247–8.
[71] Joslin, *A Century of Banking in Latin America*, 169.

appearance, almost, of family businesses. Several members and generations of the Gibbs family sat on the board of the Bank of Australasia after 1887. This bank also had a Hamilton between 1860 and 1951 and a Sanderson for most of the period between 1873 and 1944, while a Flower sat on the board of the Union Bank between 1878 and 1951.[72]

Many chairmen served for long periods. The London and River Plate Bank had the same chairman between 1869 and 1899. Chartered had the same chairman from 1874 to 1896, and the National Bank of India from 1872 to 1898. Naturally such longevity was not a feature of all bank chairmen and, in some cases, institutional arrangements guaranteed a rapid 'turnover'. Standard Bank of South Africa had a weekly chairman, with each director taking his turn in the position. Hongkong Bank rotated its chairman and deputy chairman almost annually, a device to ensure the bank remained independent of any single trading company in Hong Kong. Until 1891, when the position became a permanent one, the chairmanship of the Ionian Board revolved on a one-monthly rota system.[73]

The duty of directors was to safeguard the interests of the share-holders. In the nineteenth century, this duty was interpreted as implying that boards needed to control many aspects of the institutions' operations. Nineteenth-century boards had many more executive functions than their late twentieth-century counterparts. Boards made executive decisions on corporate strategy matters, such as the opening of new branches. They made banking decisions, especially in the area of lending, where boards would often closely monitor facilities and make decisions on loans above a certain size. The investments policy of each bank was typically a matter for directors. Boards also directly controlled personnel matters, including the appointment of British staff intended for managerial positions, and even the granting of permission for staff to marry. Inevitably, such executive powers meant frequent—and lengthy—board meetings and a considerable time commitment from directors. At the Ionian Bank, there was a rota committee consisting of the chairman for the month plus one other director, who attended the bank twice a week. The chairman of the London and River Plate Bank in the late nineteenth century was in daily attendance at the head office of the bank for thirty years from his election to the post until a few weeks before his death.[74]

Boards had other functions than making executive decisions. They provided commercial intelligence, and they brought business with them through the firms they represented or through other contacts. The appointment of a London banker as a director would be followed by the addition of his

[72] Merrett, *ANZ Bank*, 30–2.
[73] King, *The History of the Hongkong and Shanghai Banking Corporation*, i. 338–9; Henry, *The First Hundred Years of the Standard Bank*, 317–18; Ionian Bank Archives.
[74] Joslin, *A Century of Banking in Latin America*, 39.

bank to the list of London banks of the overseas bank in question. An Eastern trading house would typically divert its business to the bank on which it had a representative on the board. A British railway company or merchant house in the Argentine might deposit funds with a bank with which it was connected at board level.[75]

The importance of local business information was so great that British banks often also appointed local directors or local boards to advise managers on lending decisions. The first Anglo-Australian banks formed local boards of directors in the major towns in which they operated.[76] Standard Bank of South Africa followed this pattern in the 1860s with a local board in Port Elizabeth, from where the initiative for its foundation had come. The bank grew subsequently by acquiring small local banks, and the norm was that it also acquired their directors, who were transformed into further local boards.[77] The pattern was widely followed elsewhere. Ionian Bank had a local council in Corfu and, after 1873, in Athens as well, while National Bank of New Zealand had local boards in various cities. In Latin America, the London and River Plate Bank opted for a system of local directors rather than boards.[78]

By the late nineteenth century, however, many banks were questioning the value of such local boards. Transport improvements had reduced the isolation from one another of, say, towns in Australia, while also speeding up communications with London. The London boards of a number of banks also clashed with their local boards, from whom they wanted advice but not rivals in executive decision-making. During the 1870s and 1880s Standard Bank began not to replace local directors when they retired, and the Bank of Australasia and the Union Bank followed this practice in the 1890s.[79] The system of local boards was not to reappear on a large scale until after the Second World War.

Hongkong Bank faced the reverse problem to the banks with London headquarters, because it had a board in Hong Kong and needed advice and a presence in London. The bank initiated a London Consultative Committee in 1875, a year of financial crisis for the institution. The committee was conceived as a group of experts with a role in the City who could advise a distant board, and it included a director of the London and County Bank, its London clearing bank. Hongkong Bank was continually alert to the threat that a London committee might pose to the control of the Hong Kong-based board, a magnified version of the worries of the London boards

[75] Charles A. Jones, 'British Financial Institutions in Argentine', 81–2.
[76] Butlin, *Australia and New Zealand Bank*, 89.
[77] Henry, *The First Hundred Years of the Standard Bank*, 5–8.
[78] Joslin, *A Century of Banking in Latin America*, 24.
[79] Butlin, *Australia and New Zealand Bank*, 317; G. T. Amphlett, *History of the Standard Bank of South Africa Ltd., 1862–1913* (Glasgow: Maclehose, 1914), 22ff.

about their overseas equivalents. The London Consultative Committee survived, but the Hongkong Bank appointed no other 'local' boards except for a brief experiment with one in Shanghai.[80]

Beneath the board, banks had a figure who can be identified as the predecessor of the modern chief executive officer (CEO). These men were known by various names, including chief or general manager, London manager, or superintendent. There were wide variations in the nineteenth century between banks on the power of such men *vis-à-vis* their boards, on their status, their location, and their authority. Even within institutions the influence of CEOs fluctuated over time with changing personalities.

One important distinction was between those banks whose CEOs were based in the region of operation, and those whose CEOs resided with the board in London. The former case included the British banks in Australasia and South Africa. From 1864 Standard Bank of South Africa had a general manager, residing first in Port Elizabeth and, after 1885, in Cape Town. The first occupant of the post, until 1876, was Robert Stewart. Such was Stewart's standing that when he returned to England in 1876 he was created chief manager in London, while he was succeeded in South Africa by two joint general managers. However, the London post died with him in 1885, and the bank reverted to having its CEO in South Africa, a post held either by a single person or jointly. In Australia the Union Bank had a general manager and the Bank of Australasia a superintendent, both based at Melbourne. These were powerful executive posts, whose occupants exercised a very tight control over branch managers.[81] The CEO posts in the Anglo-Australian banks were, by the later nineteenth century, usually held by locally born men, and the positions carried very considerable influence, even if the London boards could and did continue to have an important policy role. At the other extreme from these banks was the Imperial Bank of Persia, which had a chief office and a chief manager in Tehran, but whose London board exercised—or at least sought—a very tight control over almost every aspect of business. Managers of individual branches had direct access to the board and London office, who on occasion overruled their chief manager.[82]

The alternative organizational pattern was to have CEOs residing in the same location as the board. This arrangement reduced opportunities for tension between the two parties—indeed relations between them were usually much closer than in the first type—but it could mean that both the board and its CEO were deficient in up-to-date local knowledge. This was

[80] King, *The History of the Hongkong and Shanghai Banking Corporation*, i. 145–6, 211–12, 342–3, 420–2.
[81] Henry, *The First Hundred Years of the Standard Bank*, 8–9, 88; Butlin, *Australia and New Zealand Bank*, 146, 275–7.
[82] Geoffrey Jones, *Banking and Empire in Iran*, 37–8, 96–7, 100.

the normal pattern, in the second half of the nineteenth century, for the Eastern Exchange banks and the British banks in Latin America. In the Chartered Bank, the CEO function was performed by J. H. Gwyther, the London manager. He became managing director in 1887, and then chairman of the bank between 1896 and 1904. The National Bank of India also had a system of London-based general managers. Between 1877 and 1880 there had been two joint general managers. After 1880 one of these (Robert Campbell) became sole general manager, a position he held until 1902. He subsequently served as chairman of the bank from 1903 to 1924. A similar structure came to prevail in the South American banks. London and Brazilian Bank's London manager had evolved, by 1885, into a managing director. In the London and River Plate Bank the man appointed London manager in 1883 became managing director six years later. In both banks the managing directors of the period later became chairmen.[83]

The chief manager of the Hongkong Bank also resided in the same location as his board, but in this case it was Hong Kong. In the late nineteenth century the bank's chief manager was not a member of the board, but he held very considerable executive power, perhaps more so than in any of the British-registered banks. The power of the chief manager was reinforced, as in various other banks, by a long-serving and strong personality. Thomas Jackson, a man who combined strong leadership qualities with technical brilliance in exchange dealing, held the post from 1876 to 1902, except for two brief periods.[84]

The main physical presence in the United Kingdom for all the banks was their London offices. The functions of London office included the provision of support for the board and—where appropriate—the CEO. Typically, it would also undertake the 'London end' of trade finance with the bank's specialist region, and manage the investment portfolio. Staff for the overseas branches would be recruited in London and generally serve a number of years there, but the permanent London office staff would not be sent abroad, and could rarely expect to proceed to the higher levels of management within the banks. Despite the importance of their functions, the London offices of the banks were modest affairs, consisting of a handful of clerks working in what were almost invariably described as cramped conditions.[85]

The board and the general management of each bank presided over a network of branches, each headed by a manager. By the late nineteenth

[83] Joslin, *A Century of Banking in Latin America*, 161–2, 113.
[84] King, *The History of the Hongkong and Shanghai Banking Corporation*, i. 339–41, 563–4.
[85] Mackenzie, *Realms of Silver*, 163; Geoffrey Jones, *Banking and Empire in Iran*, 158–60.

century branch managers operated under an established system of standing orders and instruction manuals. They were expected to follow the general policy of their bank regarding the type of business conducted, and to refer all credit facilities beyond a certain amount for approval by superiors. Managerial hierarchies existed, but were very simple. Typically a branch manager would report directly to the CEO or, in some cases, the board. In addition, a kind of regional 'chief branch' emerged in some banks which represented another layer of management whose function was usually ill defined. In the late nineteenth century, Chartered Bank's Hong Kong branch performed such a role for that bank's Far Eastern branches, although not for its South Asian ones.

In the Eastern Exchange and Latin American banks, in particular, branches were virtually single-unit banks joined in a federation to a centre which laid down overall policy guide-lines and acted as a lender of last resort. Branches of these banks funded their lending from their local deposits and, in some cases, their local note issues. Transport problems often meant that even the lender-of-last-resort function of the centre was of little practical value, for a 'run' on a branch could overwhelm it before funds could reach it from elsewhere. Problems of distance and poor communications worked to increase the independence of branches, while fears at head office about imprudent policies of branch managers worked in the opposite direction.

Matters of information and control were at the centre of the organizational structures—and many of the organizational problems—of the overseas banks. The profitable and prudent operation of a bank required accurate information—about clients, commodities, likely movements in the exchanges, and credit conditions in the City of London. This information was dispersed within each bank between directors, CEOs, branch managers, and—as in the Eastern Exchange banks—intermediaries who linked the banks to indigenous credit networks. Decision-making powers were also dispersed among these groups. The assembly of the different layers of information needed to operate a successful bank was a complex matter, and inevitably many decisions had to be taken in conditions of great uncertainty. Meanwhile, there were constant tensions over who decided which information to 'trust', and what policies were to be followed as a result.

The most visible manifestation of such tensions came in the uneasy relationship between boards, CEOs, and branch managers which were a constant theme in the history of the nineteenth-century overseas banks. Economists will recognize the issue as an aspect of the agent-principal question. Branch managers acted as 'agents' for their principals, the boards. (The role of the CEOs will be, for the moment, ignored.) Within this relationship there was both asymmetry of information and conflicts of interest. Information asymmetry arose from the different geographical location of the board and managers. Typically, while a board would 'know' about conditions and norms in the City of London, a branch manager would 'know' about conditions and norms in his local market. Conflicts of interest arose in a number of ways. Directors, as representatives of British shareholders, usually desired that 'prudent' banking policies be pursued, with some resemblance to those followed by domestic British banks. Conversely, managers at overseas branches were often under pressure to meet the needs of the customers, with whom they were in regular contact. Alternatively, a manager seeking promotion might be willing to pursue 'unorthodox' policies in order to make the profits of his branch look impressive. London-based boards might be influenced by the political or regulatory authorities in Britain, while managers at overseas branches were inevitably subject to pressure from their host governments. The problem for the board was how to provide sufficient incentives to motivate the managers, and yet to prevent 'opportunistic' behaviour by them, which might include a range of possibilities from boosting branch profits by irregular practices to engaging in exchange speculation on their own accounts.

The starting-point for the board in controlling its 'agents' was the contract offered to staff when they joined as 'juniors' destined for executive posts. For the banks which recruited their executive staff in Britain—that is, all of them apart from those operating in the English-speaking settler economies which by 1890 generally recruited staff locally—a man would be offered a 'contract' or appointment overseas, usually after a short period in the London office of the institution. These contracts were normally renewable at intervals, although non-renewal was unusual after the first contract except for misdemeanours. They were rudimentary affairs, committing the person to abide by the bank's regulations, outlining conditions for leave, and often prescribing various forms of behaviour. Banks offered their staff a remuneration package—a salary, allowances, arrangements for medical assistance, and sick leave—which, if meagre by later standards, was superior to that obtainable in a domestic bank, and sufficient to convince men that they were not merely doing a job, but were members of a 'service'.

Non-renewal of a contract was the ultimate board sanction over any member of staff including a manager, but incentives to perform well and appropriately were more often contained in the career structure. In many areas the financial performance of a branch could be very materially influenced by the competence, or lack of competence, of a manager, and reward systems were necessary in order to try to encourage achievement. In most banks branches struck half-yearly profits. An outstandingly good result—or the reverse—would often merit a letter of thanks—or the reverse—from head office or the board. Career structures were elementary, the major positions being junior, accountant (or deputy manager) and branch manager, with salaries and conditions improving as a man rose in the hierarchy. In the twentieth century promotion would depend heavily on seniority, but in the more pioneering days of the nineteenth century exceptional performance might be rewarded by fast promotion. For the outstanding few in an Eastern or Latin American bank, there was the hope that after thirty years' service overseas, the call would come to join general management in head office. The career and reward structure in the British banks operating in the areas of British settlement were fairly similar. The major difference was that transfer back to and employment in London was not usually the highest reward, because the managerial cadre was—by 1890—generally recruited locally.[86]

Means of monitoring the performance and behaviour of branch managers grew slowly and on an *ad hoc* basis over the nineteenth century. In most banks by 1890 branch managers had to compile half-yearly reports, sometimes called Reports on Progress, which would detail every aspect of a branch's performance. These were avidly checked in head office and often went to the board, but few banks relied for long on such 'self-regulation' as a means of checking moral hazard. There were many ways a branch's true position could be disguised in a half-yearly report. Internal audit systems, therefore, evolved, beginning with the appointment of in-dividual 'inspectors', and, over time, developing full-scale inspection de-partments. The function of inspectors, who in many banks were branch managers on secondment, was to check all aspects of a branch's business, from the petty cash to the overall portfolio of loans. They would often descend with little warning on a branch, checking and questioning every-thing. The Bank of Australasia appointed a general inspector of branches as early as 1862. Twenty years later an arrangement was made whereby all the Australian branches of the banks were supervised by an inspector in Sydney, while the New Zealand branches had their own locally based inspector.[87] Hongkong Bank appointed its first full-time inspector in 1885.[88] Inspectors' reports were a major source of information to boards about their branches, though they were more effective in detecting failures of control than in positively asserting board control over their agents.

The primary technique used by the British banks to control their overseas branches was not hierarchy, but socialization. Each bank developed a specific corporate culture. This was based on the recruitment of a cultur-ally and socially homogeneous managerial corps, which enjoyed lifelong employment and was given on-the-job training. The British banks were not the first enterprises to use socialization strategies, which were evident in the operations of the great trading companies of earlier centuries, such as

---

[86] Butlin, *Australia and New Zealand Bank*, 226–8.    [87] Ibid., 197, 264.
[88] King, *The History of the Hongkong and Shanghai Banking Corporation*, i. 341.

the East India Company and the Hudson's Bay Company.[89] Nevertheless, the banks carefully refined such strategies, resulting in a management system quite similar to that seen in post-1945 Japan, and whose success provides the key to understanding how the early British multinational banks were able to control their far-flung branches.

The process of creating this corporate culture began at the 'port of entry' into the executive cadre. In the mid-nineteenth century there was some element of an external labour market for overseas bank managers. Men moved between banks, and newly founded banks often recruited their initial managers from other British banks.[90] The Oriental Bank seems to have been almost a training school for bankers who were then recruited by others. Its failure, and that of Agra and Masterman's, provided a useful source of manpower for competitors. Agra's collapse, for example, provided Thomas Jackson for the Hongkong Bank, while Oriental's demise gave the Union Bank of Australia a future general manager.[91]

As the century progressed, however, recruitment from other banks became a rarity, to be replaced by the employment of young men with a view to long-term service with the bank. For the banks active outside English-speaking colonies—primarily the Exchange banks and the Latin American specialists—future managers were recruited young, either directly after leaving secondary school or more usually after a few years' service with a domestic bank, very often a Scottish or Irish one, whose structure of note-issuing and multi-branch banking most closely resembled that of the overseas banks. A strong and long-term Scottish influence was noticeable in many of the South American and Exchange banks. The Mercantile Bank of India, for one, was sometimes referred to as the 'Mercantile Bank of Scotland'.[92] These banks recruited their future managers through their London office, a device which effectively limited staff to British subjects. Recruits were invariably middle class, and normally from the fee-paying public schools. Formal educational attainments were less important than the possession of social and sporting skills, which ensured that young recruits would conform to the corporate culture, be trusted, and perform a proper representational role for a British overseas bank.[93]

Once recruited, future managers followed similar career patterns,

---

[89] Ann M. Carlos and Stephen Nicholas, 'Giants of an Earlier Capitalism: The Early Chartered Companies as Modern Multinationals', *Business History Review*, 62 (1988), 398–419; id., 'Agency Problems in Early Chartered Companies: The Case of the Hudson's Bay Company', *Journal of Economic History*, 50 (1990).

[90] e.g. King, *The History of the Hongkong and Shanghai Banking Corporation*, i. 220–1.

[91] Ibid., 242; Butlin, *Australia and New Zealand Bank*, 235.

[92] Information from S. W. Muirhead. For the South American banks, see Joslin, *A Century of Banking in Latin America*, 23. The Imperial Bank of Persia preferred Scots, but often had to settle for Irish. Geoffrey Jones, *Banking and Empire in Iran*, 139, 268.

[93] King, *The History of the Hongkong and Shanghai Banking Corporation*, i. 575–8.

beginning with brief service as juniors in London office, before being dispatched abroad. The 'first tour' of three to five years overseas was often used to detect and remove unsuitable staff from the bank's service. Men were usually not allowed to marry until they reached a certain income level, which often meant until their mid-thirties. Juniors in the East lived, at least at the larger branches, with other bachelors in a chummery. There were equivalent arrangements in other regions. This system encouraged male bonding and strengthened corporate feeling. Young men living as well as working together got to know each other well. They would gain insights into their contemporaries' business abilities and general dependability which they could use for the rest of their careers, especially as—given transport problems—the paths of staff employed within even a small bank might not cross for decades. When men did marry, their wives were screened by the board to weed out disruptive elements.

From their foundation until at least the 1960s, the British banks used on-the-job training. This would begin as soon as a junior entered London office, when experience in the inward and outward bills departments would give him some idea of the bank's business, the kind of trade conducted between Britain and the specialist region of his bank, and the names of principal branches and customers. Such training would continue when he was transferred abroad. Job rotation systems were used to give junior staff as much experience as possible. Promotion was, as in modern Japanese corporations, essentially on a seniority system tempered by provision for the most able to reach the most important senior posts.

The upshot of these recruitment and career patterns was the creation of strong corporate cultures centred on small management élites of British nationals. Hongkong Bank had some 44 Eastern staff in 1876, rising to around 150 by the turn of the century. The Imperial Bank of Persia, a smaller bank, rarely had more than 50 British expatriates serving in Iran before the First World War. These men were imbued with Victorian public school values of service and loyalty, strengthened by years of service within an individual bank during which they were socialized with corporate traditions and standards.

The British banks active in English-speaking colonies operated very similar personnel policies, with the important exception of nationality of recruits. Until the 1860s the Anglo-Australian banks had recruited almost all their senior executives in Britain as well as many juniors, but as the population of the colonies grew, recruitment of staff in the United Kingdom became unusual.[94] A minor exception was the Union Bank of Australia, which continued up to the First World War (and beyond) to transfer some British juniors to Australia after five years' service in London office as a means of

---

[94] Butlin, *Australia and New Zealand Bank*, 226–8.

maintaining links between the British and Australian operations.[95] However, the general pattern in Australia, New Zealand, and South Africa came to be local recruitment into the managerial cadres, but otherwise these banks followed the socialization strategies of the Eastern Exchange and Latin American banks. They recruited middle-class boys who were given the expectation of lifetime employment and, in return, developed strong corporate loyalties.

The socialization strategies pursued by British overseas banks enabled them to effectively manage their branch networks, and to limit losses from bad debts and frauds. The geographical dispersion of their branches and the many idiosyncratic tasks involved in banking would have made a hierarchical control system ineffective in nineteenth-century conditions. The careful selection of staff with the same goals as management and the socialization of staff economized on information and monitoring costs and limited—if far from eradicated—agent–principal conflict. The system was also flexible. Managers at isolated branches could not constantly seek orders from superiors when faced with unexpected circumstances—in some countries circumstances were often 'unexpected' in the nineteenth century. The directors of the British overseas banks could have some confidence that their socialized staff could be trusted to follow the traditions of the bank, and not to cheat, although the tensions between different levels of each bank's hierarchy were seldom resolved.

Mira Wilkins has identified the elementary governance structures of nineteenth century British 'free-standing' companies as a major reason behind their ultimate decline. Their fragile head offices had little capacity beyond that of raising capital, and lacked the technology and knowledge to sustain their existence.[96] Alfred D. Chandler has, similarly, identified the weaknesses in British managerial structures before the First World War associated with 'personal capitalism', which led, among other things, to Britain's delayed entry into many new industries pioneered in the United States and Germany.[97]

The British overseas banks were of the same 'free-standing' genre as those enterprises criticized by Wilkins, while their managerial hierarchies were small and elementary, if not family-based. Yet this organizational form was much better suited for nineteenth-century multinational banking than for industry. The modest managerial hierarchy did not prevent considerable organizational capability. Socialization strategies were used to great

[95] Standing Committee to General Manager, 22 Sept. 1921, U/61/11; Standing Committee to General Manager, 21 July 1937, U/61/13, ANZ Archives; Butlin, *Australia and New Zealand Bank*, 334.

[96] Wilkins, *The History of Foreign Investment in the United States*, 613–14.

[97] A. D. Chandler, *Scale and Scope* (Cambridge, Mass.: Harvard University Press, 1990), ch. 7.

effect to control multinational operations and reduce agent–principal tensions. The London head offices were numerically small but they were also effective, both in overall control of business and—through the composition of boards—providing invaluable links with principal customers at home and overseas, and with other financial institutions. Unlike some of their 'free-standing' cousins in other sectors, the British multinational banks represented a well-organized and well-structured form of foreign direct investment.

## 2.4. Market Shares and Competitive Advantages

The British multinational banks were important business institutions in the nineteenth century, both within the British context and in many of the host economies in which they operated. In Britain, multi-branch banking spread from Scotland to England and Wales in the second half of the century, and mergers—especially in the late 1880s and early 1890s—led to a fall in the number of domestic banks, with the creation of nation-wide banks headquartered in London. This was a gradual process, however, with the number of banks falling from 380 in 1875 to 180 in 1900. The overseas banks were comparatively large compared to most domestic banks. In the early 1890s the biggest British overseas banks—Hongkong Bank, the Bank of Australasia, and the Union Bank—were larger in terms of assets and deposits than all but three or four of the sixteen large London joint stock banks which sat at the apex of English banking.[98]

Britain was the world's leading multinational banker. The United States had virtually no multinational banks by the time of the First World War. It was the world's principal debtor nation, but regulatory factors seem to provide the key to understanding the retardation of American multinational banking. Until 1913 America's largest banks, the national banks, were forbidden by law to branch abroad. Even the participation of national banks in international banking was discouraged by Federal law. They were not allowed to undertake acceptance business. Only at the very end of the century was there a glimmer of activity. In 1897 National City Bank of New York established a Foreign Department to take foreign deposits and deal in foreign exchange. Five years later the International Banking Corporation was formed somewhat on the lines of a British overseas bank,

---

[98] See the data on assets and deposits in Appendices 1 and 5. Balance sheet data of the London joint stock banks between 1891 and 1914 are given in C. A. E. Goodhart, *The Business of Banking, 1891–1914* (London: Weidenfeld and Nicolson, 1972), app. 3. A ranking of the fifty largest British companies by market value in 1904/5 suggests the Hongkong Bank might just have made it into this category in that year. See Peter Wardley, 'The Anatomy of Big Business: Aspects of Corporate Development in the Twentieth Century', *Business History*, 33 (1991), 100. The market values of the sample banks in this study are given in Table A5.1.

but it had a mere 16 foreign branches by 1913.[99] Japanese multinational banking was similarly in its infancy. Japanese multinational banking between 1880 and 1914 was confined to the Yokohama Specie Bank, predecessor of the Bank of Tokyo. This bank's 20 or so foreign branches, spreading from China to Europe and the United States, were a remarkable achievement for an Asian bank in this period, but its activities were of little significance beyond Japan.[100]

There was more multinational banking in Europe. From mid-century, and in France, Belgium, and Germany in particular, domestic banks began to establish foreign branches and specialist overseas banks. In France, five banks had been established by the government in the 1850s, each one allocated to an individual French colony. In 1874 a new generation of colonial banks began with the creation of the Banque de la Nouvelle-Calédonie, which was the initiative of Paris bankers. This only lasted three years, but in 1875, following this model, two French domestic banks established a private sector colonial bank, the Banque de l'Indochine. This bank was given—in contrast to British overseas banks—the exclusive right to issue banknotes for twenty years in the two French colonies of Cochinchine (part of modern Vietnam) and Pondicherry (in India), and it was also authorized to lend money and discount bills. It evolved as the bank for all the French colonial possessions in the East, and also established branches in Singapore, Bangkok, Hong Kong, and China. By 1914 it had 19 branches in Asia. In 1901 the Banque de l'Afrique Occidentale was created to operate in France's African colonies.[101] French multinational banking was also active beyond the French colonies. Domestic banks established branches in London in the late nineteenth century in order to participate in the business of Europe's leading international financial centre. In the 1900s French domestic banks also took substantial equity stakes in leading Russian banks, involving some exercise of management control.[102]

In some respects French multinational banking can be seen as a more modest version of British. The creation of specialist overseas banks and the importance of imperial links provide obvious parallels. The main differences were the greater official influence in French banking, even when privately owned, and the fact that French domestic banks were closely involved as shareholders in most multinational ventures before the First World War.

---

[99] Wilkins, *The History of Foreign Investment in the United States*, 454; Mira Wilkins, 'Banks over Borders: Some Evidence from their pre-1914 History', 232–3.

[100] Norio Tamaki, 'The Yokohama Specie Bank: A Multinational in the Japanese Interest 1879–1931', in Geoffrey Jones (ed.), *Banks as Multinationals*, 205.

[101] Marc Meuleau, *Des pionniers en Extrême-Orient* (Paris: Fayard, 1990), parts 1–3; Y. Gonjo, 'La Banque coloniale et l'etat: la Banque de l'Indochine devant l'interventionnisme, 1917–1931', *Le Mouvement Social*, 142 (1988), 45–73.

[102] Olga Crisp, *Studies in the Russian Economy before 1914* (London: Macmillan, 1976), 170–3.

The development of multinational banking in other continental economies followed similar lines. In Belgium, the largest domestic bank—Société Générale—acquired a French bank in 1890, and before the First World War founded a number of overseas banks, notably the Banque Sino-Belge, to operate in China, and the Banque Italo-Belge, to operate in South America. Belgian banks were also active in foreign direct investment outside the financial sector. In the 1900s the Banque d'Outremer, for example, owned and managed considerable mining, natural resource, and paper interests in Canada.[103]

The beginnings of German multinational banking were closely followed by German political unification. One of the first moves of the Deutsche Bank, established in 1870, was the foundation of a joint venture bank in London. In 1872 it established branches in Shanghai and Yokohama, followed by a wholly controlled operation in London in the following years. Several other German banks also established London branches, while Deutsche Bank opened further branches in Brussels and Istanbul. However, the general pattern became the establishment of specialist overseas banks, owned by one or more domestic banks. In the late 1880s and 1890s specialist banks for Latin America and the Far East were established. These included the Banco Alemán Transatlántico, the Brasilianische Bank für Deutschland, the Bank für Chile und Deutschland, and the Deutsch-Asiatische Bank. In the continental mixed-banking tradition, German banks also engaged in foreign direct investment in other sectors, Deutsche Bank, for example, acquiring large oil production interests in pre-war Romania.[104]

It was only in the two decades before the First World War that British overseas banks began to experience competition from multinational banks owned by other countries. In the Far East and Latin America, German banks became influential. Competitive pressures were felt even in the West Indies, a British colony where Canadian banks established branches. This competition will be explored in greater detail in the following chapter, but it can be asserted now that British enterprises continued to be the pre-eminent multinational banks in terms of their spread of interests and overall size of business activities, and this remained the case until the 1960s.

The main competition for the British banks came from other directions. In international banking, the merchant banks had an unrivalled business in trade acceptances in the nineteenth century. They were responsible for much of the finance of British trade with North America and the rest of

---

[103] G. Kurgen-van Hentenryk, *Leopold II et les groupes financiers belge en Chine* (Brussels: Palais des Académies, 1972); id. and J. Laureyssens, *Un siècle d'investissements belges au Canada* (Brussels: editions de l'Université de Bruxelles, 1986).

[104] Peter Hertner, 'German Banks Abroad before 1914', in Geoffrey Jones (ed.), *Banks as Multinationals*; Manfred Pohl, 'Deutsche Bank London Agency Founded 100 Years Ago', in Deutsche Bank (ed.), *Studies on Economic and Monetary Problems and on Banking History* (Mainz: Hase & Koehler 1988), 233–6.

Europe. They were also the leading institutions in the flotation of foreign government loans in the City of London, even for South American countries where the British banks had considerable business. Generally the merchant and overseas banks concentrated in different regions and different products, although where there was some competition—as in India and the Far East—the overseas banks prevailed over the course of the nineteenth century.[105] By the late nineteenth century, certain London domestic banks were also active in international acceptance business, using foreign and colonial banks as correspondents, but much international business—such as dealing in foreign exchange—remained beyond their concern.

As multinational retail banks, the British banks faced competition from domestic banks in the countries in which they operated. In some parts of Asia, Africa, and the Middle East, British overseas banks were the first modern banks. Only a few of these countries—notably Japan—had indigenously owned modern banks in the nineteenth century. In most of the settler economies, they entered a market in which local banks were already established. They had often rapidly gained market share, against single-unit banks (as in Australia) or unstable ones (as in South Africa and parts of South America). From the second half of the century, the trend was for local banks in such economies to gain in competitiveness and to challenge the British banks in domestic banking, and often in trade finance and exchange operations also. However, this trend progressed at very different speeds in different countries and regions.

The combination of lack of statistics and the problems of definition prevents more than a cursory estimate of the market shares achieved by British multinational banks by 1890, but it does seem that in the late nineteenth century much of the foreign trade finance and exchange business of Latin America, Asia, and the English-speaking settler economies was passed through the British overseas banks.

The British banks also held substantial shares of many domestic banking markets. In 1914 one estimate is that British banks controlled a third of the deposits of the Brazilian banking system, and over a quarter in Argentina and Chile. The proportions would have been higher in 1890.[106] In Southern Africa in the late nineteenth century, the Standard Bank of South Africa was the leading bank in the region which consisted of the British colonies of the Cape, Natal, and British Bechuanaland, together with the independent Boer states of the Orange Free State and the South African Republic. The British banks, led by the Standard Bank, were generally larger and better managed than their local counterparts, and between the 1860s

---

[105] Stanley Chapman, *The Rise of Merchant Banking* (London: Allen and Unwin, 1984), 172. The role of the overseas banks in foreign loans in the 19th century is discussed in ch. 4, below.     [106] Joslin, *A Century of Banking in Latin America*, 110.

and 1890 they came to dominate the market completely. At the end of 1890 Standard's current account deposits were more than three times those of all other banks in the region, and its loans and advances over twice as much. The bank's general manager considered it to be 'by far the largest institution in the land'.[107]

In Australia and New Zealand, locally established banks became more influential. In 1851 the three British banks held over two-thirds of the total commercial bank assets in Australia, but by 1890 the share of all the British banks had fallen to 40 per cent as local banks grew in importance. The small group of British banks established after 1850 to operate in Australia or setting up branches there failed to make the impact that their predecessors had done in the 1830s and 1840s. Local banks, especially the Bank of New South Wales, successfully emulated the multi-branch model, and opened offices in London in order to engage in trade finance and exchange business. In 1890, however, the Union Bank and the Bank of Australasia were still among the largest four commercial banks in Australia, with around 10 per cent each of deposits, and they—along with the Bank of New South Wales—were the only banks with branches covering almost all the Australian colonies.[108] In New Zealand, the Union Bank of Australia had almost monopolized the small colony's banking until the 1860s, apart from the intervention of the Oriental Bank in the second half of the previous decade. This era ended in the 1860s with the entry of the Bank of Australasia and the Bank of New South Wales, and the foundation of the Bank of New Zealand in 1861. The Bank of New Zealand rapidly acquired the largest share of banking business, not least because it received practically all government business, but British banks remained important. In 1887 (before a precipitous though temporary decline in the Bank of New Zealand's fortunes) the two Anglo-Australian banks and the National Bank of New Zealand together held 42 per cent of non-government deposits and 30 per cent of private sector advances in New Zealand.[109]

The reasons why British multinational banks were able to obtain such a prominent position can be understood in terms of Michael Porter's model of the determinants of national competitive advantage, outlined in the previous chapter. In the nineteenth century, all four elements of the 'diamond' were favourable to the competitiveness of multinational banks based

[107] Amphlett, *History of the Standard Bank of South Africa*, 124; GMO 3/2/1 'Special', 10 Feb. 1890, in A. Mabin and B. Conradie (eds.), *The Confidence of the Whole Country* (Johannesburg: Standard Bank Investment Corporation, 1987), 270; Stuart Jones, 'The Apogee of the Imperial Banks in South Africa: Standard and Barclays, 1919–1939', *English Historical Review*, 103 (1988), 892; Henry, *The First Hundred Years of the Standard Bank*, 111–12.

[108] Merrett, 'Paradise Lost?', 67; Butlin, *Australia and New Zealand Bank*, 232–9.

[109] Hawke and Sheppard, 'The Evolution of New Zealand Trading Banks'.

in the United Kingdom and engaged in international banking. The merchant banks exploited these competitive advantages by exporting from London, and by utilizing family partnerships as an alternative to full internalization. Similarly, some London banks used independent agents abroad as correspondents. The overseas banks, in contrast, exploited the competitive advantages by the international transfer of certain types of expertise by ownership links—in other words, by establishing multinational branches.

Factor conditions of various kinds were favourable for the development of multinational banking in Britain. Banks were able to raise capital on the highly developed London Stock Exchange. The well-established domestic banking system provided a flow of trained personnel. The British overseas banks often recruited bankers with a few years' training with domestic banks. At least initially, this helped to give British banks in countries such as Australia management skills superior to their local competitors.[110]

Demand conditions were exceptionally favourable and rested on the unique importance of British trade and investment in the world economy. The competitive advantages for banks engaged in international banking of possessing such a 'core market' are self-evident. The overseas banks were multinational trade banks servicing the world's leading trading economy. These advantages were enhanced because a considerable percentage of British trade and capital exports involved foreign direct investment. As noted in Chapter 1, Britain became the world's largest foreign direct investor before the First World War. Although some of this investment took the form of modern multinational enterprises, most consisted of the numerous British 'free-standing' companies and other corporate forms spread over different regions.[111] British companies, for example, ran the railways, the dock companies, and meat-packing factories in Argentina. British interests owned many of the exporting firms and shipping companies, although not the coffee plantations, of Brazil. The trade of South-east Asia, and many of that region's commodity and extractive industries, was in the hands of the powerful British agency houses based in Singapore.

The British multinational banks were part of this wider world of British overseas business in the nineteenth century, and they were intimately connected with it. The banks serviced the requirements of other British businesses, and often secured many of their deposits from them. The boards of the banks contained representatives of the British mercantile and other

---

[110] Merrett, 'Paradise Lost?', 65.

[111] Different modern perspectives on the complex world of British business overseas are provided in S. D. Chapman, 'British-based Investment Groups before 1914', *Economic History Review*, 2nd ser., 38 (1985); Jones, *International Business*; Mira Wilkins, 'The Free-Standing Company', *Economic History Review*, 2nd ser., 41 (1988); Davenport-Hines and Jones (eds.), *British Business in Asia*.

interests in each region. Such links made it unlikely that the business of the British trading firms, mining companies, and agency houses active overseas would go anywhere but to a British bank. In many cases these expatriate British business interests had been among the main promoters of the banks in the first place. Contrary to the writers who argue that multinational banks develop by following their corporate clients over national borders, in the case of the British overseas banks, they were often the creation of their corporate clients.

Porter suggests that a strong domestic demand for an industry can, by various mechanisms, be transmitted abroad.[112] The reputation enjoyed by British financial institutions for probity and security was important in this respect. Because of their reputation for security, British banks were able to attract local deposits to an extent which far surpassed Asian or African indigenous credit institutions or, initially, modern banks established in Latin America and the settler economies. Nineteenth-century banking markets, especially in developing economies, were characterized by asymmetric information, and the reputation of British banks was attractive to depositors who could reduce search and other costs by doing business with them. The mere fact of being British suggested stability. Political factors and the strength of the British Empire provided obvious advantages for the British overseas banks. Within the dependent Empire, colonial governments would usually only use British banks as bankers, though in the settler economies such as Australia and New Zealand there was a preference for local banks. In diplomatically sensitive countries such as Iran and China, British banks received support from the British Foreign Office.

All British banks involved in international banking benefited enormously from Britain's unique importance in world trade and investment, and from its international prestige. The regulatory barriers and strong indigenous banking systems of the United States and Europe, as well as family connections, favoured the exploitation of these advantages by strategies other than direct investment. The absence of such factors, initially at least, in much of the Southern Hemisphere and Asia favoured the multinational branch strategies of the overseas banks.

Porter's third determinant of national advantage is the presence of related or supplier industries that are internationally competitive. The agglomeration of financial services in the City of London provided a highly favourable environment for British banks in this respect also. By the opening decades of the nineteenth century London had replaced Amsterdam as the leading international financial centre in the world, a position retained until the First World War and beyond. In addition to a wide range of financial

[112] Michael Porter, *The Competitive Advantage of Nations* (London: Macmillan, 1990), 97–9.

markets, many of the world's most important commodity markets for raw materials and foodstuffs were based in London. The agglomeration of banking services enabled banks active in international banking to secure readily overdraft facilities from their London bankers. The overseas banks often borrowed large sums in this way, which played an important role in routine trade finance, and a vital role at times of crisis.

Sterling, fully convertible into gold, was the world's hardest currency, and the London financial system provided a large amount of finance for world trade. The use of sterling to finance two-thirds of world trade, by the end of the nineteenth century, and the prominence of the 'bill on London' gave British banks considerable cost advantages in trade finance. The working of the gold standard and the position of sterling gave British bankers enormous freedom for the switching of funds within countries. Surplus deposits collected abroad by the overseas banks could be transferred and invested with ease in the London money markets. There was a constant flow of funds inside these banks, reflecting seasonal movements in trade, rates of exchange, and other circumstances, a process which required constant skilful judgement.

The final determinant of national competitive advantage, according to Porter, is firm strategy and structures. This chapter has argued that the organizational capability of the British multinational banks was high. They had effective governance structures which enabled them to control branch networks over large distances. They developed reputations for honesty and integrity which represent major competitive advantages for financial institutions. Inadequate management and business strategies could, and did, lead to failure, as the collapse of Agra and Masterman's and the Oriental Bank demonstrated, but these were the exceptions rather than the rule. The British multinational banks were not merely 'free-riders' on British economic and political power, important as they were in explaining their success. They were the product of entrepreneurial initiatives which had perceived profitable opportunities, and they succeeded by devising business structures which contained the large risks of nineteenth-century multinational banking.

In the nineteenth century, although less so over time, British overseas banks benefited from the vigorous domestic rivalry stressed by Porter. While the geographical specialization of the overseas banks limited the degree of competition between banks, there was usually a group of competing British banks in each region. Although collusive agreements were already present before 1890, in most markets competition between rival British banks was still strong.

The strong internationally competitive position of British banks in the nineteenth century is, therefore, readily understandable in terms of factor and demand conditions, the strength of the City of London and the overall

British financial sector, and strong organizational capability. Beyond the United States and continental Europe, there were few host country regulatory controls over the activities of foreign banks, while indigenous banking systems were often underdeveloped. It was a near-perfect environment for the British overseas banks.

## 2.5. *Conclusion*

The first British multinational banks had been founded in the 1830s, and by 1890 there were over 30 of them operating over 700 branches. They had little importance in the United States or continental Europe, which had their own banks, and whose trade with Britain was financed by other types of bank, which used networks of correspondents and partnerships. The overseas banks had gone south and east, and in those regions of the world they had flourished. For a variety of reasons they developed as highly specialist enterprises. They were specialists in overseas banking, with no domestic British banking business, and they were specialists in particular regions or countries. Often, they were specialists in a single commodity.

The specialization of the British overseas banks grew naturally out of the British financial system. British regulators worked to enforce this structure on the grounds of the increased risks involved in multi-regional banking. The failure of Agra and Masterman's and the Oriental Bank helped confirm suspicions about alternative models of multinational banking, and nineteenth-century conditions did make branch banking in different regions a risky venture. The multinational banks of other European countries took the same view and specialized in particular regions. They differed from the British banks, however, in their strong links with domestic banks in their countries. In Britain there was only a fragile connection, largely confined—as seen in the case of the Glyn's promotional block—to interlocking directorships. The separation of overseas and domestic banking in Britain was to prove an enduring and troublesome legacy.

The banks originated as multinational trade banks, but various factors led them to seek to internalize trade finance and exchange operations by establishing branches, rather than using the correspondent or market relationships favoured by merchant banks. Almost everywhere, they also became involved in other activities. Financing the exports of primary products led them up-country. The search for deposits and perceptions of profitable opportunities similarly encouraged the banks to diversify their business activities, as well as to modify the practices of orthodox British banking. As a result, the British banks in Australasia and South Africa, and to a lesser extent elsewhere, combined international banking with multinational retail banking.

This was the entrepreneurial age of British multinational banks. They acted in an almost Schumpeterian fashion, opening new markets and expanding their business as the frontier of settlement and of European influence moved onward. They pioneered a new form of industrial organization—the multinational enterprise—as they applied multi-branch banking and other Scottish banking practices to distant colonies and, later, foreign countries.

The strength of the British overseas banks, like the merchant banks, rested on British economic and political pre-eminence in the nineteenth century. It was hardly surprising that banks headquartered in the City of London which serviced the requirements of the world's leading capital and goods exporter flourished in a world where there were few restrictions on foreign branch banking. The overseas banks were also, however, remarkably successful in establishing sound governance structures. Socialization strategies were used to good effect, combined with lifetime employment and on-the-job training systems for management cadres. This was both fortunate and essential, for overseas banking in the nineteenth century was a risky business. In the early 1890s the British multinational banks faced a test of the strength of their corporate structures.

# CHAPTER 3

# Crisis and Expansion

## 3.1. The Crisis of 1890–1895

There were major financial crises in almost every region in which British multinational banks operated in the first half of the 1890s. In a world without central banks or lenders of last resort, such crises could all too easily threaten the survival of banks. In South Africa, a financial panic in 1889 was followed by the collapse of most of the local banks. In 1890 London's leading merchant bank, Barings, all but collapsed due to over-exposure to Latin American loans. Although Barings was rescued by the Bank of England, the result caused a major crisis of confidence in the City and in Latin America. There followed major financial crises in Argentina and Uruguay, and a civil war in Chile in 1891, followed by revolutionary uprisings in Brazil in 1892 and 1893. In Australia, there was a series of failures culminating in the great bank crash of April to May 1893, by which time 54 of the 64 banks operating two years previously had closed, 34 of them permanently. In the East, a sudden rapid and unexpected fall in silver prices after September 1890, which lasted until the turn of the century, caused considerable financial instability and exacerbated the problems of banks operating in the region.

An initial view of the impact of these external crises on the overseas banks can be ascertained from the sample of British banks whose financial performance has been examined in detail in this study. The shareholders in over half of the sample banks would have done better between 1890 and 1895 to have invested in Consols—British government stock—than in their banks. By this measure, the early 1890s rank with the 1930s as an exceptionally bad period for the banks. A particular problem was diminishing investor confidence which weakened the share prices of the overseas banks, but their aggregate published profits also moved down sharply, though there was a wide range in profitability between different banks.[1]

The sample banks all survived, but a number of other banks were not so fortunate. There was a swathe of casualties among banks with assets between £8 million and £11 million—not the largest of the overseas banks, but a second tier of important enterprises. In the South American region, the English Bank of the River Plate collapsed in August 1891, with attempts

---

[1] This paragraph is based on the performance data of the sample banks given in Tables A5.2–4.

to revive and reconstruct the institution finally being abandoned three years later. In the East, the reconstructed Oriental Bank—known as the New Oriental Bank Corporation—suspended payment in June 1892. Four months later the Chartered Mercantile Bank of India, London and China was obliged to undertake a reconstruction, reopening (minus its Royal Charter) as the Mercantile Bank of India. In Australia, the Bank of South Australia—one of the smaller overseas banks—was saved from collapse by its acquisition by the Union Bank.[2] But the London Chartered Bank of Australia and the English, Scottish & Australian Chartered Bank suspended payment in April 1893. Both were reconstructed and reborn a few months later. Such reconstructions imposed heavy burdens on shareholders, who were obliged to provide large amounts of new capital and forgo dividend payments for years.[3]

Several other banks had painful experiences. Two new entrants into overseas banking were badly shaken. The Bank of Tarapaca and London, operating in Chile, was unable to make a dividend payment in 1891, and failed to pay a half-year dividend in 1894.[4] The Imperial Bank of Persia had to write down its capital by one-third in 1894 and declared no dividend in that year.[5] Longer-established banks were also affected. The total shareholder funds of the Hongkong Bank fell by a quarter between June 1891 and June 1892, and, in order to pay a sufficient dividend, the bank had to deplete a fund originally intended to assist staff who were forced to retire early through ill-health, or their widows.[6] Another creation of the 1860s, Standard Bank of South Africa, experienced heavy bad debts.[7]

New Zealand did not suffer a banking collapse of the severity seen in Australia, but the National Bank of New Zealand was in difficulties from 1885, when its capital had been written down by nearly a third. During 1891 and 1892 an informal committee of the larger shareholders on the London register investigated the bank. Its capital had to be written down by a further 60 per cent, and the sum replaced by a call to shareholders,

[2] S. J. Butlin, *Australia and New Zealand Bank* (London: Longman, 1961), 290–3.

[3] David Merrett, *ANZ Bank* (Sydney: Allen and Unwin, 1985), 198–200; id., 'Australian Banking Practice and the Crisis of 1893', *Australian Economic History Review*, 29 (Mar. 1989), 81; id., 'The 1893 Bank Crashes: The Aftermath', unpublished paper. The shareholders of the Bank of South Australia had to pay a large sum to the Union Bank. See Butlin, *Australia and New Zealand Bank*, 292–5.

[4] David Joslin, *A Century of Banking in Latin America* (London: Oxford University Press, 1963), 181, 184.

[5] Geoffrey Jones, *Banking and Empire in Iran* (Cambridge: Cambridge University Press, 1986), 66–8.

[6] F. H. H. King, *The History of the Hongkong and Shanghai Banking Corporation*, i. (Cambridge: Cambridge University Press, 1987), 438–45, 594–5.

[7] GMO, 8 Aug. 1899, in Alan Mabin and Barbara Conradie (eds.), *The Confidence of the Whole Country* (Johannesburg: Standard Bank Investment Corporation, 1987), 466.

while substantial lines of credit had to be extended to the bank by its London bankers, Lloyds. The colony's local bank, the Bank of New Zealand, experienced an even worse crisis after very rapid growth in the 1870s and 1880s. Bad debts and diminishing confidence in the bank led to a temporary move of the head office to London in 1890, and to the colonial government acquiring a shareholding in 1895.[8]

The causes of the monetary and financial disorders which afflicted so many regions were almost entirely specific to those regions, although many of them have to be placed against the background of the accelerating flows of European, especially British, capital into the extractive and agricultural resources of areas of recent settlement.[9] This distinguished the crisis of the early 1890s from the 1866 crisis, which originated in the City of London with the failure of Overend Gurney. The problems in South Africa in 1890 stemmed from a temporary collapse of one of the periodic speculative booms which affected the country following the development of the gold-mines of the Witwatersrand. The Australian economy went into a recession with falling investment in the pastoral industry and building, to which sectors the financial institutions were highly exposed. In Latin America, domestic political conflicts, and problems of over-borrowing and incautious lending, were the causes of the difficulties of the early 1890s. In the East, although much remains unclear about the sharp fall in silver prices, the decline was certainly exacerbated by the failure of attempts by countries on a bimetallic standard and other interested parties to secure an international agreement to support silver. The downward spiral was given a serious push in 1893 by developments in the United States, when the Sherman Act of 1890—which had required the Federal government to purchase a fixed amount of silver at pre-depreciation prices—was repealed.

Despite the region-specific nature of the crises, banks active in one region were sometimes affected by developments elsewhere. While the Baring Crisis had little impact on overseas banks not active in Latin America, it may have led to the collapse of the London market for Australian government funds in 1891,[10] and the overseas banks had to contribute to the Baring Guarantee Fund established by the Bank of England to support the stricken bank, and so preserve the London financial system.

The Australian banking crisis caused greater problems to other banks. In South Africa, new suspicions were raised about the banking system,

---

[8] National Bank of New Zealand Reports and Accounts; Balance Books, LB; B. A. Moore and J. S. Barton, *Banking in New Zealand* (Wellington: Bank Officers' Guild, 1935), 67–71; P. Colgate, D. K. Sheppard, K. Guerin, and G. R. Hawke, 'A History of the Bank of New Zealand, 1862–1982. Part 1: 1862–1934', Victoria University of Wellington Money and Finance Association, Discussion Paper No. 7, 1990.

[9] Herbert Feis, *Europe: The World's Banker, 1870–1914* (New Haven, Conn.: Yale University Press, 1930), 19–20.     [10] Butlin, *Australia and New Zealand Bank*, 280.

although the large Standard Bank did not suffer as a result.[11] However, it was the substantial British deposits collected by the Australian banks which became an issue. Some contemporaries blamed them for being the cause of the panic. In fact, no Australian bank suffered substantial withdrawals prior to May 1893, but the deposits were held to be vulnerable to panic withdrawals and were one factor in the instability of the situation.[12] Lack of confidence in the safety of deposits in the Australian banks helped cause a sharp fall in the London deposits of Hongkong Bank, a serious blow to its strategy of keeping 'on an even keel' in sterling.[13] There were similar problems at other overseas banks.[14]

The British multinational banks, then, faced a range of specific crises in their regions plus a general crisis of confidence in the wake of the Australian collapse. However, what turned an uncomfortable experience into a liquidation was not the overwhelming force of adverse exogenous circumstances, but rather management failure and imprudent banking. Inadequacies within banks rather than environmental factors caused the demise of the banks which failed.

The English Bank of the River Plate was a prime illustration of this point. In an unusual reversal of the normal situation, the bank's London management, rather than its managers on the spot, engaged in incautious lending to various Argentinian interests, some of which was long-term even though the bank never secured an adequate local deposit base. The bank was eventually overwhelmed through its involvement with a speculative and fraudulent syndicate designed to establish a national bank in Uruguay.[15]

Imprudence rather than dishonesty lay at the heart of the Australian banking crisis, the root cause of which was a general deterioration in prudential standards among the Australian banks in the 1880s following intensified competition in a largely unregulated environment.[16] The British banks which failed all manifested such problems. The Bank of South Australia, after devoting few resources to building up reserves, made a series

[11] GMO, 7 Feb. 1894, in Mabin and Conradie (eds.), The Confidence of the Whole Country, 342.

[12] N. Cork, 'The Late Australian Banking Crisis', Journal of the Institute of Bankers, 15 (Apr. 1894), 180; Butlin, Australia and New Zealand Bank, 305–7; A. S. J. Baster, The Imperial Banks (London: King, 1929), 151–6.

[13] King, The History of the Hongkong and Shanghai Banking Corporation, i. 422, 449, 472.

[14] For the Mercantile Bank, see Chief Manager to W. Jackson, 19 May 1893, File MB509, Mercantile Bank Archives, HSBC; for the National Bank of New Zealand see, National Bank of New Zealand Balance Books, LB.

[15] Charles A. Jones, 'British Financial Institutions in Argentine, 1860–1914', Ph.D. thesis, Cambridge University, 1983, 45–60.

[16] Merrett, 'Australian Banking Practice', 82. For an excellent case-study of the growing recklessness in a locally registered bank, see Margaret and Alan Beever, 'Henry Gyles Turner', in R. T. Appleyard and C. B. Schedvin (eds.), Australian Financiers (Melbourne: Macmillan, 1988), 120–7.

of bad loans in the second half of the 1880s. This trend culminated in the Melbourne manager providing large advances to land speculators. The bank had dismissed its inspector in 1884, and the absence of a local inspectorate had not helped the Adelaide-based management in controlling Melbourne. The London Chartered Bank of Australia likewise engaged in imprudent lending, which led to heavy bad debts, while the English, Scottish & Australian Chartered Bank had grown on the basis of insufficient liquid assets, and had a very high concentration of lending risk.[17]

The same picture of inadequate or imprudent banking emerges from the two Eastern Exchange banks which succumbed. The depreciation of silver heightened the risks faced by British banks in the East, but well-managed concerns could contain the problem. The branches of the New Oriental, like its predecessor, were too widely spread for efficient management, and some extremely poor banking decisions were taken. Large loans were made to the bank's directors, in circumstances which suggested fraud. The London management also made a considerable number of dubious advances and loans to assorted individuals and companies, while large bad debts were incurred at Melbourne branch by a manager who went mad and was subsequently committed to an asylum.[18] Chartered Mercantile was afflicted by a series of bad debts several years before the suspension of the New Oriental caused a run on its own Eastern branches. Further bad debts left the bank with no published reserves, and confidence among its shareholders and customers vanished.[19]

The banks which experienced problems in the early 1890s, but avoided collapse, were also often not merely the victims of adverse circumstances. The Imperial Bank of Persia, for example, established a viable commercial banking business in Persia, but made heavy losses in an incompetent attempt to build roads, in poorly managed branches in Iraq and Bombay, and through speculative investment activities.[20] The Bank of Tarapaca and London's troubles were not simply Chilean politics and economic difficulties. The bank experienced considerable initial management problems, mostly related to its dependence on the 'nitrate king' Colonel North, and the Bank of Tarapaca seems to have been aided in its recovery by North's death in 1896.[21]

---

[17] Merrett, 'Australian Banking Practice'; id., *ANZ Bank*, 197–8; id., 'The 1893 Bank Crashes: A Reconsideration', unpublished paper given to Monash Economic History Seminar, 13 Nov. 1987; Butlin, *Australia and New Zealand Bank*, 290–5.

[18] 'The New Oriental Bank Corporation: A Lesson in Bad Banking', *Bankers' Magazine*, 57 (1894).

[19] Annual Directors' Reports, Chartered Mercantile Bank, 1890, 1891, 1892, and Report of Committee of Directors, 27 Oct. 1892; King, *The History of the Hongkong and Shanghai Banking Corporation*, i. 404; typescript history of Mercantile Bank, date and author unknown, File MB 2176, HSBC.     [20] Geoffrey Jones, *Banking and Empire in Iran*, ch. 2.

[21] Joslin, *A Century of Banking in Latin America*, 181–5.

The years of crisis in the early 1890s had a considerable influence on British multinational banking, but there was a marked divergence between regions. In Australia, there was a noticeable shift towards prudence among local and British banks. The crisis exercised a fundamental influence on Australian banking for decades. The reputations of banks were enormously tarnished, laying the foundations for the widespread antagonism towards them that was to become such a noteworthy feature of twentieth-century Australia. The banks themselves became far more conservative. Aggregate liquidity ratios within Australia rose sharply over the following two decades. As part of this new caution, the taking of British deposits was largely abandoned. The two leading British banks—Bank of Australasia and Union Bank—and the leading local bank—the Bank of New South Wales—together held nearly a third of all bank liabilities and assets within Australia, and they settled down to a long period of cautious banking.[22]

The situation and reaction of the British banks in South Africa and Latin America was different. In these regions, the early 1890s had revealed the fragility of the local banks, and had thus enhanced the standing of the British banks. The collapse of a number of local banks in South Africa left Standard Bank in a very strong position.[23] The picture was similar in Latin America. In Argentina there was a widespread collapse of both state and private banking in 1891 and 1892. In 1891 London and River Plate Bank acquired one of Argentina's oldest and largest private banks, the Banco Carabassa. This merger, and the London and River Plate's stability in general, placed it in such a strong position in Argentina that it felt able to develop more liberal banking strategies, especially in the type of lending undertaken.[24]

Overall, the strength of the governance structures of the British multinational banks had been demonstrated. The Baring Crisis, the Australian banking collapse and its impact on confidence elsewhere, the disruption of the Eastern Exchanges, and various regional financial panics had reduced the profits, increased the bad debts, and depressed the share prices of many British overseas banks, but the survival of most of them was never in doubt. In the settler economies of the Southern Hemisphere, the sounder British banks proved considerably safer than many of their local counterparts, demonstrating the continued strength of their competitive advantages. The British banks which failed, or needed to be reconstructed, were brought down by management failure. The elimination of a swathe of such banks

---

[22] Merrett, 'Australian Banking Practice', 83; id., 'The 1893 Bank Crashes: The Aftermath'; C. B. Schedvin, *Australia and the Great Depression* (Sydney: Sydney University Press, 1970), 80–1.

[23] GMO, 9 Aug. 1893, in Mabin and Conradie (eds.), *The Confidence of the Whole Country*, 342.

[24] Joslin, *A Century of Banking in Latin America*, 127–131; Charles A. Jones, 'British Financial Institutions in Argentine', ch. 2.

left a more prudent set of institutions in place, whose reputations had been enhanced by their stability in the midst of crisis.

## 3.2. Growth and Performance, 1896–1913

After the financial disturbances of the early 1890s, the world economy experienced sustained growth in the two decades before the First World War. As always, there were diplomatic and political crises which affected specific regions and dented the confidence of markets—the Boer War (1899–1902), the Russo-Japanese War (1905–6), the Boxer Uprising and 1911 Revolution in China, and growing tension in Europe between the Great Powers. But the predominant feature of these years was growth. World trade continued to grow fast, despite the revival of protectionism by many countries. The temperate regions of European settlement boomed, as falling transport costs provided a basis for expanding primary commodity exports. Capital flows grew as country after country joined the gold standard.

These conditions provided an ideal environment for the British multinational banks, and they flourished. Their total assets grew by over a half between 1890 and 1913. Latin America emerged as the most important location for British banks, its share of total assets surpassing Asia and Australasia, the other two main host regions. The British banks active in Latin America expanded rapidly. By 1913 the London and River Plate Bank had overtaken the two leading Anglo-Australian banks, Standard Bank, Chartered, and the Hongkong Bank to become Britain's largest overseas bank in terms of asset size, and second only to the Hongkong Bank in market capitalization. The Anglo-South American Bank, only recently founded as the Bank of Tarapaca and London in 1888, experienced a more remarkable growth. Its assets expanded sixteenfold between 1890 and 1913, and its market capitalization seven times.

The number of British bank branches abroad almost doubled in these years. Australia, whose individual states had joined in the federal Commonwealth of Australia in 1901, and New Zealand continued to claim the lion's share of these branches. However, the number in South Africa, which had also become a federation in 1910, rose sharply, and by the eve of the First World War almost one-fifth of British multinational bank branches were in Southern Africa. The size of branch networks in Asia, Latin America, and elsewhere remained modest.

Branch expansion continued to stem from a number of motives and determinants: the desire to strengthen existing positions, entrepreneurial instincts in conditions of expanding frontiers, and a more systematic process of internalization. In Australia branch expansion was driven by the growth of towns in many states, as well as the need to match competitor banks in branch openings.[25] There were also examples of banks trying to diversify their risks by expansion into other countries. In 1907, for example, Ionian Bank opened a branch in Egypt, with the aim of reducing its overexposure to the Greek currant industry, and aware that there was political pressure against its note-issuing privileges.[26] Egypt was under British administration, expatriate Greeks played a very large role in Egypt's business life, and there were considerable Greek exports of tobacco to Egypt, which offered the prospect of desirable trade finance opportunities.

The entrepreneurial search for new opportunities led British bankers into pastures new in Africa and parts of Asia. In this period, sub-Saharan Africa was opened to British banking. In Southern Africa, Standard Bank opened branches in the Rhodesias (now Zambia and Zimbabwe) and Nyasaland (now Malawi) as British political influence expanded.[27] British banks also entered East Africa in the 1890s, again in the wake of British expansionism. Zanzibar, which had close trading links with India, was placed under British 'protection' in 1890. Three years later the National Bank of India opened a branch there. Expansion on the mainland followed, and in 1904 the first interior branch was opened, at Nairobi.[28] The entry of Standard Bank into the region in 1911 led to a spate of competitive branch openings between the two banks.[29] In West Africa, a branch at Lagos was opened in 1891 by the African Banking Corporation, in a flurry of activity which also took it to Tangier as well as its South African base. This bank soon discovered it did not have the resources to manage such a far-flung operation, and its branch and pioneering role in West Africa was taken over by the Bank of British West Africa, which established branches in Nigeria, the Gold Coast (Ghana), Sierra Leone, and The Gambia. A rival British bank founded in 1899, the Bank of Nigeria, also opened branches in West Africa before being acquired by its larger rival.[30]

There was also further expansion of British banks into 'virgin' territories in Asia. Hongkong Bank opened the first modern bank in Thailand in 1888, followed by Chartered Bank in 1894.[31] In Malaya, where British

[25] Butlin, *Australia and New Zealand Bank*, 331–3.

[26] Chairman's Statement, Ionian Bank Ordinary General Meeting, 12 Apr. 1910.

[27] J. A. Henry, *The First Hundred Years of the Standard Bank* (London: Oxford University Press, 1963), 118–29; *Standard Bank, 1892–1967: Three Quarters of a Century of Banking in Rhodesia* (Salisbury: Standard Bank, 1967), 12–29.

[28] Geoffrey Tyson, *100 Years of Banking in Asia and Africa* (London: National and Grindlays, 1963), 110–21.

[29] Henry, *The First Hundred Years of the Standard Bank*, 193–200, 206–13; J. J. Swanson, 'History of the Bank in East Africa', Memoirs, unpublished MS, June 1954, SC.

[30] Richard Fry, *Bankers in West Africa* (London: Hutchinson Benham, 1976), 42, 61–2, 66–8; African Banking Corporation files, SC.

[31] P. Sithi-Amnuai, *Finance and Banking in Thailand* (Bangkok: Thai Watana Panich, 1964), 33–9; F. H. H. King, *The History of the Hongkong and Shanghai Banking Corporation*, ii (Cambridge: Cambridge University Press, 1988), 129–35; Compton Mackenzie, *Realms of Silver* (London: Routledge & Kegan Paul, 1954), 194–7; 'The Chartered Bank in Thailand', *Standard Chartered London Newsletter*, Oct. 1974, SC.

political control was spreading from the 1870s, Chartered Bank was the first bank to penetrate the interior of the country, opening at Kuala Lumpur and Taiping in 1888. The Mercantile Bank of India began the opening-up of the peninsula's east coast by establishing a branch at Kota Baharu in 1912.[32]

Quite frequently, the establishment of branches in these countries was preceded, sometimes for long periods, by the use of independent agents. These agents were replaced by branches either when the volume of business increased or when the relationship appeared to be working inefficiently. National Bank of India's investment in Zanzibar seems to have arisen from the first cause. A firm of merchants had acted as the National Bank's agents but, following the declaration of Zanzibar as a free port in 1892, business grew so fast that the bank decided to establish its own office.[33] In Thailand, both the Hongkong Bank and Chartered had been represented by firms of continental merchants. Given the competition between merchant houses, there would appear to have been a reluctance to use rival firms as bankers. Certainly Hongkong Bank's branch rapidly captured most merchant accounts, apparently because of a general desire to preserve confidentiality.[34]

The internalization process can also be seen in the establishment by many of the British multinational banks of wholly owned branches or agencies in New York and Hamburg. Table 3.1 lists the foundation dates of these outposts, and the banks involved.

The backdrop to the establishment of these offices was the growing importance of American and German foreign trade in the world economy. In the United States, apart from the pioneering example of the Bank of British North America with its early establishment of a New York agency, the British banks initially appointed independent agents, such as Brown Brothers and Company, who represented Colonial Bank. However, the increasing volume of business, and the need for information, pushed banks towards seeking more direct representation. This process was encouraged by the United States legislation which made it difficult for American banks to engage in foreign trade finance or exchange dealing on their own account, so that although in New York state law forbade foreign banks to take local deposits, there were lucrative international banking opportunities with no local competitors.[35] As business grew, independent agencies were replaced by wholly owned facilities, which were designated

[32] Mackenzie, *Realms of Silver*, 215–6; King, *The History of the Hongkong and Shanghai Banking Corporation*, ii. 35–6.

[33] Tyson, *100 Years of Banking in Asia and Africa of Silver*, 111.

[34] Sithi-Amnuai, *Finance and Banking in Thailand*, 34; Mackenzie, *Realms of Silver*, 195–6; King, *The History of the Hongkong and Shanghai Banking Corporation*, ii. 130.

[35] Mira Wilkins, *The History of Foreign Investment in the United States to 1914* (Cambridge, Mass.: Harvard University Press, 1989), 463.

TABLE 3.1. *New York and Hamburg agencies/branches of British multinational banks, 1850–1913*

| Bank | Year opened New York | Year opened Hamburg |
|------|------------------|------------------|
| Bank of British North America | 1850s | — |
| Hongkong Bank | 1880 | 1889 |
| London and Brazilian | 1886 | — |
| Colonial Bank | 1890 | — |
| London and River Plate | 1891 | — |
| African Banking Corporation | 1900s | — |
| Chartered Bank | 1902 | 1904 |
| Standard Bank of South Africa | 1905 | 1904 |
| Anglo-South American | 1907 | 1905 |
| Commercial Bank of Spanish America | 1912 | — |
| Bank of British West Africa | — | c.1909 |

*Source*: Bankers' Almanac; Mira Wilkins, *The History of Foreign Investment in the United States to 1914* (Cambridge, Mass.: Harvard University Press, 1989), 464–5.

'agencies' rather than branches because of the restrictions on deposit-taking.

The Hamburg branches appeared for the same reasons—a growing trade volume, the need for information about and direct contact with customers, and the desire for control over what was done in the bank's name. Hamburg was a leading trading and shipping centre prominent in Germany's extra-European trade. There was also the consideration that German domestic banks were active both in trade finance and in establishing foreign operations to assist that business. Hongkong Bank opened its Hamburg branch in 1889 as a direct response to the formation of the Deutsch-Asiatische Bank and its establishment of China branches. Other British banks followed this path in response to the expansion of German trade and German banking activity in their areas.[36]

New York and Hamburg were the major American and continental centres of interest to British multinational banks before 1914, but other cities attracted attention if special trading or other links existed with the bank's region of specialization. The Bank of British Columbia and the Bank of British North America established branches in San Francisco in 1864, followed by Hongkong Bank in 1875, the latter being attracted by the considerable bullion and exchange business between China and San

[36] King, *The History of the Hongkong and Shanghai Banking Corporation*, ii. 538; Joslin, *A Century of Banking in Latin America*, 199; Henry, *The First Hundred Years of the Standard Bank*, 155.

Francisco.[37] In Europe, the London and Brazilian Bank opened branches in Portugal in the 1860s, through which it developed a successful business recycling emigrant remittances, while in 1881 the Hongkong Bank opened a branch in Lyon to participate directly in the extensive trade in raw silk between the Far East and that French city. It had formerly been represented by the important local bank, the Crédit Lyonnais. Fourteen years later the London and River Plate Bank opened in Paris. This bank had formerly used Rothschilds as its agents, but by the mid-1890s felt the need for 'detailed observation'.[38]

This world of expanding trade and imperial frontiers made profits for the British overseas banks, and good returns for their shareholders. In only one instance among the sample banks would shareholders have done better to put their money in Consols in these years. There were large gains to be made by investors in the shares of fast-growing new entrants, notably the Bank of British West Africa and Anglo-South. However, in quite a number of cases, an investment in a domestic bank might have earned a better return, at least judging by the two such banks included in this study.

The published profits of almost all the sample overseas banks showed a marked improvement on the 1890-5 period, although profit ratios varied widely between institutions. The aggregate profit ratios of the overseas banks moved upwards along with British domestic banks in the second half of the 1890s, and exceeded the domestic banks for much of the 1900s. In the middle of that decade, even the 'worse' five overseas banks in the sample narrowed the gap in profitability between themselves and the domestic banks.[39]

It was the policy of the British banks not to reveal their 'true' or 'real' profits to shareholders, but to transfer a portion of them to inner and secret reserves before declaring their published profits. This practice was completely legal, and was used by domestic as well as overseas banks. The justification was the argument that confidence could be better maintained in the banks if their published profits and dividend payments were 'smoothed' rather than fluctuating sharply according to actual business conditions. Moreover, the banks used their published reserves and their inner reserves in different ways. The published reserves were regarded as effectively part of capital, and visible proof of strength and stability. Transfers from them were only made at times of dire need, such as the

---

[37] Wilkins, *The History of Foreign Investment in the United States*, 460; King, *The History of the Hongkong and Shanghai Banking Corporation*, i. 95-6, 152.

[38] Chairman's Statement, 23rd Ordinary General Meeting, Bank of London and the River Plate, 15 Dec. 1895.

[39] See Graphs A5.1-2 which compare for the period 1890 to 1939 the aggregate published profit ratios of English and Welsh joint stock banks with the aggregate of the sample overseas banks, and the profit ratios of the 'best' and 'worst' five overseas banks.

early 1890s. In contrast, inner reserves could be used without publicity, and thus without fear of damage to prestige or loss of credit. Inner reserves, therefore, fluctuated—sharply in some cases—in contrast to the usual upward trend of the published reserves. They were tools of crisis management, the means to prevent a temporary downturn in trade or an exchange crisis from becoming a serious threat to the stability of the bank.

The existence of real profits and inner reserves conveys an aura of mystery and a sense of the improper to the activities of the British multinational banks. In reality, their existence needs to be kept in perspective. For the sample banks for which information on real profits and inner reserves exists, it can be seen that in most years real profits were higher than published ones, and for every bank the real profit ratio between 1896 and 1913 was higher than the published one. Some banks had accumulated considerable sums in their inner reserves by the eve of the First World War, but these amounts were significant rather than enormous in the context of the overall size of their balance sheets. The published figures distorted the true picture, but they were not fabrications. Already by the late nineteenth century, for example, it was a convention that a rise (or fall) in real profits was reflected by an upward (or downward) movement in published profits, although the size of the movement would be less, and this convention was not always followed. In summary, the evidence lends no support for any crude view that the British banks were extracting vast sums from their host economies in ways which were hidden from public view.

However, there was arguably a conflict of interest between the banks' stakeholders in this matter. The diversion of a portion of profits into inner reserves meant that shareholders received lower dividends than they might otherwise have expected. Depositors, on the other hand, benefited from the ensuing stability, as did managements, who were better equipped to secure the long-term survival of their banks. As might be expected from institutions which offered lifetime employment and developed strong corporate cultures, survival was ranked at least equally with maximizing shareholder value as a corporate goal. 'The Bank's principle', the man designated to open a branch of the London and River Plate in Valparaiso, Chile, was advised in 1906, 'is to consider safety before profit.'[40]

Unlike later periods, no clear geographical pattern emerges from the profitability figures, real or published. In terms of published profits, the best five banks between 1896 and 1913 included two Australasian, two Eastern Exchange, and one Latin American bank. The best ten included three Australasian, three Eastern Exchange, two Latin American, plus banks specializing in West Africa and Egypt. This was a cross-section of the different types of British overseas banks, and suggested that good profits

[40] E. Ross Duffield to R. Williams, 19 Dec. 1906, D7/1, Bolsa Archives, UCL.

could be earned in most environments. Interestingly, the four institutions with the lowest profit ratios included the three non-Australian pioneers of the 1830s, the Bank of British North America, Colonial Bank, and Ionian Bank, together with the Imperial Bank of Persia, which faced the daunting task of introducing British-style commercial banking into a backward and unstable Iran.

The Hongkong Bank, ranked second in terms of its published profits ratio between 1896 and 1913, merits additional comment. It was the most consistently profitable bank by this measure throughout the whole period of analysis, being ranked among the top two institutions every period between 1890 and 1920, and as the most profitable bank thereafter until 1975, except during the Second World War. A number of factors explain the bank's good performance. The fast-growing international trade in the East provided a good business environment for all well-managed Exchange banks before 1914, but the location of its head office in Hong Kong seems to have enabled this bank to take particular advantage of regional opportunities. This was evident in exchange operations. The bank's dollar balance sheet combined with the strategy of 'keeping on an even keel' gave it a competitive edge over sterling-based banks, which were more exposed to the problems caused by the depreciation of silver. Arguably, too, the location of the head office away from the City of London allowed more flexible business strategies to be envisaged. Certainly the opening of branches in San Francisco and Lyon was adventurous for an Exchange bank, while the Hongkong Bank's prominent and profitable foreign loan business— to be discussed in the next chapter—was atypical. A low ratio of paid-up capital to deposits also suggested a long-term efficiency at attracting deposits, an indication of effective organizational capability and sound reputation.

After the crisis of the early 1890s, then, British multinational banks had grown and prospered. Many more branches had been opened. Still entrepreneurial, new territories in Africa and Asia had been penetrated, along with footholds in New York and continental Europe. Most banks in most regions had made good profits, which were used in part to reward shareholders and in part to build reserves against the unexpected.

## 3.3. Entrants and Exits

The rapid growth of overseas bank branches and of the assets of the British multinational banks was not primarily the result of creation of firms, although new overseas banks continued to be founded in this period. Eleven of the banks active in the bench-mark year of 1913 had not featured in the 1890 list, but these enterprises accounted for only around 9 per cent of the assets and 11 per cent of all overseas branches of the British banks in 1913.[41] As a group, the character of the new entrants was different in some respects from their predecessors, particularly in the matter of their shareholding structure. While still 'free-standing' in some respects, many of these banks had stronger and more durable equity links with existing firms than had previously been the case, and in many cases their share-holding remained in limited hands.

The change was not a sudden one, and several of the new entrants had similarities with their predecessors. This was the case with the African Banking Corporation, one of only three overseas banks founded in the crisis years between 1890 and 1895. This was established to operate in South Africa, taking over the staff and business of a failed local bank, and it appears to have been a typical 'free-standing' British overseas bank.

The two banks founded in 1894, however, were of a different ilk. The moving spirit in the creation of the Bank of British West Africa in 1894 was Alfred Jones, the principal owner and chairman of the Elder Dempster Steam-ship Line, and he took up nearly 60 per cent of the first share issue. Jones by this period had secured a virtual monopoly over the external communications of British West Africa. His large ocean-going fleet had eliminated British competition, while in 1895 a cartel agreement—the West African Shipping Conference—was reached with the competing German shipping firm. Jones was, as a result, able to prevent any serious competition to his West African shipping monopoly until his death in 1909. With the benefit of this secure power base, Jones diversified into related services, into boating companies, coastal services, and the promotion of a credit and banking structure that allowed trade to expand. As will be discussed in Chapter 4, the Bank of British West Africa was primarily concerned with the provision of the silver coinage of the British territories in the region, and it was given a monopoly as silver agent to the colonial government.

The Bank of British West Africa, therefore, formed part of a diversified business group, and was not a 'free-standing' entity in any real sense. The bank's head office remained at Liverpool, the centre of the shipping group, until shortly before the First World War. It did not have a quotation on the London Stock Exchange until 1901. Jones was chairman of the bank as well as of Elder Dempster, and he dominated the management of the bank until his death, when he still owned almost a third of the capital.[42]

The Bank of British West Africa was not alone in its close association

---

[41] Calculated from Appendix 1. The assets of two new entrants—Grindlays and the London, County and Westminster Bank (Paris)—are unknown in 1913, but could not have been large. This calculation excludes three banks which were reconstructions of banks active in 1890 and so, technically, new banks.

[42] Fry, *Bankers in West Africa*, 26, 51, 57; P. N. Davies, *The Trade Makers: Elder Dempster in West Africa, 1852–1972* (London: Allen and Unwin, 1973), ch. 4 and 5.

with existing merchant groups. Its West African rival, the Bank of Nigeria —whose life-span (1899–1912) means that it fails to enter either the 1890 or 1913 bench-mark lists in this book—was similarly founded by a small group of merchant houses operating in West Africa, resentful of Elder Dempster's control of the Bank of British West Africa.[43] Similarly the Bank of Mauritius, incorporated in 1894 and still active in 1913, was largely owned by a small group of British trading interests on the island, where the economy was dominated by sugar exports.[44]

Another modestly sized new entrant, the Commercial Bank of Spanish America, also had a restricted shareholding. This bank had originated as a commission house, receiving and selling Colombian coffee in London and sending textiles to Colombia. It had been founded in 1881 by two Colombians resident in London, and they remained prominent among its shareholders. In 1904 this venture merged with the London Bank of Central America, a bank which had been registered in London in 1893, but which had been founded in Nicaragua five years previously. Following the merger, the Cortés Commercial and Banking Company was established, still with a strong Latin American influence among its directorate. The bank operated branches in Colombia, Nicaragua, El Salvador, Ecuador, and Peru, far beyond the normal confines of British overseas banking in Latin America. In 1910 the Anglo-South American Bank purchased a minority shareholding in the firm, and in the following year the name was changed to the Commercial Bank of South America, but it continued to function as a separate concern.[45]

A more equivocal case was the Eastern Bank, established in London in 1909. This was envisaged as a new Exchange bank, of the kind founded in the 1850s and 1860s. A Stock Exchange quotation was granted soon after its establishment and it had a larger capital than, say, the Bank of British West Africa. Yet it also had a number of powerful institutional shareholders, of which the most important was the Eastern trading house of E. D. Sassoon. There was a Sassoon on the first board, and the bank's first offices in the City of London were in the premises of E. D. Sassoon.[46] Very unusually, there were also two representatives from continental banks on the Eastern's board. The two banks were Société Générale of Paris and Banque d'Outremer of Belgium, which had combined interests in China. It seems likely that both banks had stockholdings in Eastern Bank. Banque

[43] Fry, *Bankers in West Africa*, 42; Davies, *The Trade Makers*, 122.

[44] When the Mercantile Bank made an offer to purchase the bank in 1916, the decision to accept was taken by a handful (eleven) 'principal shareholders' meeting in London. Meeting of Some of the Principal Shareholders of the Bank of Mauritius, 29 Feb. 1916, MB 1191, HSBC.

[45] Joslin, *A Century of Banking in Latin America*, 202–5.

[46] *Bankers' Magazine*, 88 (1909), 751; Stanley Chapman, *The Rise of Merchant Banking* (London: Allen and Unwin, 1984), 131–2; Geoffrey Jones, *Banking and Empire in Iran*, 248.

d'Outremer's representation continued into the 1930s. Eastern Bank and Banque d'Outremer were subsequently allied in an Anglo-Belgian syndicate designed to negotiate China loans, and it seems probable that it was interest in China finance that brought the Sassoons and the Belgians together.[47]

The remaining six new entrants to the British multinational banks active in 1913 were unusual types of a kind not seen before the 1890s. Grindlay & Co. and Cox & Co. were both old-established enterprises, linked to the British Army, which evolved into overseas banks. Their shareholding was limited, and neither was publicly quoted. Grindlays originated in the 1830s as a London-based agency specializing in handling the business affairs of British civil servants and military coming and going from the East. Branches in Calcutta and Bombay had been maintained by an autonomous Indian-based partnership until 1908, when the London Grindlays purchased them.[48] Cox & Co. were a firm of Army agents which opened a branch in Bombay in 1905 to service its military customers' requirements while they were in India. Other Indian branches followed, and some non-military business was undertaken, largely discounting local bills plus the purchase of bills in India as a means of remitting funds from the branches to England.[49]

Two new entrants established just before the First World War were one-branch Paris subsidiaries of English domestic banks. Some of the domestic banks had, by the turn of the century, built up a considerable foreign trade business, using networks of foreign correspondents. The establishment of London branches by continental banks from the late nineteenth century provoked further innovations. In 1905 Midland Bank opened its own foreign exchange department, and it briefly flirted with the idea of establishing a branch in the United States.[50] Two other domestic banks did take the route of foreign direct investment. In 1911 Lloyds purchased Armstrong and Company of Paris, formerly the independent agent of various English banks, and formed it into a wholly owned subsidiary, Lloyds Bank (France). The bank, as one of its management later observed, 'was established mainly for the purpose of dealing with English-speaking people'. To emphasize the point the bank proudly proclaimed—in English—that it was 'A British Bank conducted on British lines'. In September 1913 the London, County

---

[47] King, *The History of the Hongkong and Shanghai Banking Corporation*, ii. 479; Mackenzie, *Realms of Silver*, 207; G. Kurgan-van Hentenryk, *Leopold II et les groupes financiers belge en Chine* (Brussels: Palais des Académies, 1972), 767 n. 1.

[48] Tyson, *100 Years of Banking in Asia and Africa*, 193–7.

[49] Undated Memorandum on Indian Business, A56b/101, LB; R. S. Sayers, *Lloyds Bank in the History of English Banking* (Oxford: Clarendon Press, 1957), 190–3, 202.

[50] A. R. Holmes and Edwin Green, *Midland: 150 Years of Banking Business* (London: Batsford, 1986), 132–4.

TABLE 3.2. *Fate by 1913 of British multinational banks active in 1890*

| No. in 1890 | Continued | Continued Reconstructed | Failed/ liquidated | Acquired by non-British bank | Acquired by British bank |
|---|---|---|---|---|---|
| 33 | 17 | 3 | 5 | 5 | 3 |

and Westminster Bank established a Paris subsidiary, also conceived as a British bank for British clients in France.[51]

The National Bank of Egypt and the National Bank of Turkey were also a new species of overseas bank. They were semi-political creations, designed to act as state banks in their respective countries and registered in them, albeit with influential London-based directors. Their foundation will be discussed in the following chapter, but in the present context it is noteworthy that the same individual had a very large shareholding in both banks.

Almost half of the 33 banks active in 1890 did not survive, at least in their existing form, until 1913. Table 3.2 summarizes their fates. Of the 16 banks which had disappeared by 1890, 3 were victims of the early 1890s, and existed in their reconstructed forms twenty-three years later.[52]

Five of the 1890 banks had failed or had been put into liquidation. The New Oriental and the English Bank of the River Plate collapsed in the early 1890s. The Union Bank of Spain and England led an undistinguished existence after its foundation in 1881 and was finally put into voluntary liquidation in 1896.[53] Agra Bank went into voluntary liquidation in 1900, apparently because of over-exposure to the Indian tea industry.[54] The Bank of Egypt suspended payment in October 1911, a victim of incautious mortgage-lending on property.[55]

Five of the British banks were acquired by local interests in the countries where they operated. In 1912 the Bank of Africa and its branches in South Africa were acquired by the National Bank of South Africa. It was in North America, however, that this process was the most visible. In 1900 the Bank of British Columbia was acquired by a Canadian bank, while

[51] Geoffrey Jones, 'Lombard Street on the Riviera: The British Clearing Banks and Europe, 1900–1960', *Business History*, 24 (1982), 187.

[52] These were the Mercantile Bank of India, the London Bank of Australia, and the English, Scottish & Australian Bank.

[53] A. S. J. Baster, *The International Banks* (London: King, 1935), 49.

[54] Mackenzie, *Realms of Silver*, 217, 225; King, *The History of the Hongkong and Shanghai Banking Corporation*, i. 456.

[55] Baster, *The International Banks*, 77–8; *National Bank of Egypt, 1898–1948* (Cairo: National Bank of Egypt, 1948), 33–4.

all three of the British banks centred on California were 'localized' in the 1900s.[56]

Three banks active in 1890 had been acquired by other British overseas banks. The Anglo-South American Bank acquired two of them, the Anglo-Argentine Bank and the London Bank of Mexico and South America, as part of a strategy of diversification away from Chile. The small Anglo-Argentine Bank had branches in Buenos Aires and Montevideo in Uruguay.[57] The London Bank of Mexico and South America functioned as a kind of investment company, holding shares in local banks in various countries, which gave their London business to the British bank.[58] Both these banks were fully absorbed into Anglo-South. The same fate befell the Bank of South Australia, acquired by the Union Bank during the Australian banking crisis.

The tiny number of mergers and acquisitions with other British overseas banks made a striking contrast to the domestic banking sector, which was transformed by widespread mergers in these years, to emerge as highly concentrated by the end of the First World War.[59] The multinational banks stayed out of this merger movement, although they were a little more active in acquiring small local banks overseas. In South Africa, the African Banking Corporation acquired some local banks soon after its foundation, while the London and River Plate was able to take advantage of the Argentinian banking crisis of the early 1890s to acquire a leading local bank (see above, Section 3.1). Later, in the 1900s, the Mercantile Bank of India strengthened its business by acquiring the Bank of Calcutta, owned by the Yule family, who were leading expatriate figures in the Calcutta business community. The Mercantile Bank thereby acquired the custom of an important business group, and the alliance was cemented by the appointment of the chairman of the Bank of Calcutta, David Yule, to the board of Mercantile.[60]

It was striking that the banks which failed or otherwise disappeared were mostly smaller institutions. Ten of the 13 1890 banks which disappeared completely were in the smallest 16 of the banks listed in that year. The two larger banks which failed—the New Oriental and the English Bank of the River Plate—succumbed in the early 1890s banking crisis. This pattern was related in part to the date of foundation, as only 2 of the 13 banks were founded before 1862, while 5 were creations of the late 1870s and 1880s. The other trend was the elimination of British branch

[56] Wilkins, The History of Foreign Investment in the United States, 459–61, 850 n. 43.

[57] Joslin, A Century of Banking in Latin America, 197–9.    [58] Ibid., 207–14.

[59] Michael Collins, Money and Banking in the UK: A History (London: Croom Helm, 1988), 78–81.

[60] Agreement of 21 Mar. 1906 between Bank of Calcutta, David Yule, and Mercantile Bank, Mercantile Bank Archives, 1946; Rajat K. Ray, Industrialization in India (Delhi: Oxford University Press, 1979), 266–7.

banking from the United States and Canada, apart from the Bank of British North America.

The 1890s and 1900s, therefore, saw a considerable turnover in institutions engaged in multinational banking. Thirteen of the 1890 banks did not reach 1913—and 3 more had to be reconstructed—while 11 of the 1913 banks were new entrants. The significance of this high turnover was less than might be seemed, however, as both the entries and the exits were mostly of modest-sized banks. The entrepreneurial age when individuals promoted 'free-standing' British banks to operate in distant countries was nearing its end.

## 3.4. Centralization and Management Control

The two decades before the First World War saw, for many banks, a further increase in the importance of 'London' in general, and bank boards in particular, in decision-making. There were a number of pressures working in this direction. The age of pioneering was, in many regions, over and attention could shift to consolidation and the formalization of management systems. Improvements in communications allowed London to exert a greater control over distant branches. The crisis of the early 1890s had revealed the dangers of imprudent banking and encouraged the directors, as 'principals', to monitor more closely the actions of their 'agents' overseas. The growing interest of a number of banks in loan issues also worked to enhance the importance of 'London' within banks, for it was in the City of London that such loan issues were made, and where contacts and information were the prerequisite for success.

The growth in the authority of London was most noteworthy in the case of the British banks in Australia, so badly shaken by the events in the early 1890s. Local boards were finally phased out during the 1890s. In both the Union Bank and the Bank of Australasia there was a very evident shift of power to London. Small subcommittees of directors were formed to enable much closer monitoring of banking business in Australia, and these were supported by London managers with enhanced powers. The Union Bank's Standing Committee was formed in 1895, and met twice a week right through until the merger with Bank of Australasia in 1951. By the years shortly before the outbreak of the war, the directors of both banks frequently gave their Melbourne-based CEOs detailed instructions, and regularly overruled Melbourne's advice. In the Union Bank, in particular, London's control extended to the smallest detail.[61]

[61] For the Union Bank's directors' views on a spring lock to be used on the door of a new branch in Brisbane, see Standing Committee to General Manager, 21 Nov. 1913, U/61/10, ANZ Archives; Butlin, *Australia and New Zealand Bank*, 318–22, 331, 336–7; Merrett, *ANZ Bank*, 47–9.

The power of London was a constant theme in the histories of many other banks in these years. The Imperial Bank of Persia's board retained a tight control over the bank's business, using two powerful subcommittees, which met at least once a week. In 1908 the board exercised its authority by forcing the resignation of the bank's first chief manager.[62] By the 1890s the board were firmly in control of the National Bank of India.[63] There was a similar pattern in the new entrants after 1890, such as the Bank of Mauritius and Eastern Bank. In the Bank of British West Africa, the board closely monitored everything from personnel matters to advances. It only met monthly until 1901, and thereafter weekly, but this gave little indication of the extent of directors' control because Alfred Jones dictated the policy of the bank, and frequently took personal actions without consulting fellow directors. The death of Jones ended this era of autocratic rule, but not the domination of policy from Britain.[64]

In the Hongkong Bank there was also a growth in the role of London, but in a form which did not threaten the ultimate authority of the chief manager and the board in Hong Kong. During the 1900s a division, or sphere of influence, developed within the bank. Hong Kong took responsibility for Eastern exchange banking. Meanwhile, London became the focus for the bank's merchant banking activities, which grew in importance as international consortiums were formed to negotiate loans for China and elsewhere. The bank's London Consultative Committee was transformed into an independent, but subsidiary, authority, especially after the appointment in 1903 as its permanent and salaried chairman of Sir Thomas Jackson, following his final retirement from Hong Kong. While the existence of two centres of authority might have been expected to cause internal tensions, conflict seems to have been avoided by careful and well-defined specialization of function.[65]

The attractions of the London capital market and communications improvements, then, worked to enhance the importance of London in the decision-making of many banks, but as always there were exceptions. There was no evidence of a great surge in London's influence in the Standard Bank of South Africa. Although the system of local directors was, as in Australia, phased out, the general manager in South Africa had considerable autonomy, which must have been enhanced by Standard's continued adherence to the practice of rotating its chairman every week. When Standard Bank decided to diversify into East Africa in 1911, the new branches were administered from South Africa until 1925, even though conditions were totally different in the two regions.[66]

---

[62] Geoffrey Jones, *Banking and Empire in Iran*, 76–7, 101–8.

[63] Tyson, *100 Years of Banking in Asia and Africa*, 128.

[64] Fry, *Bankers in West Africa*, 51–3, 59–60; Fry's Digests of the BBWA Board Minutes, Fry's History Files, BAC S/90, SC.

[65] King, *The History of the Hongkong and Shanghai Banking Corporation*, ii. 27–31, 556–8.          [66] Swanson, 'History of the Bank in East Africa', 24.

The banks which did take a large share of their business decisions in London faced potential problems. The City was an ideal base for a bank specializing in foreign trade finance and exchange. However, London-based boards were less obviously qualified to assess domestic banking risks in distant markets. Moreover, there was room for conflict over the priority to be afforded different types of banking—trade and exchange versus purely domestic or retail. These problems were to begin to become real, rather than potential, in the changed environment after the First World War.

## 3.5. Flexibility and Conservatism

Despite the great diversity between the activities of the British overseas banks in different regions, it can be said that trade finance and related exchange business remained the core activities in the twenty years before 1914. They were multinational trade banks which financed the movement of commodities and minerals around the globe. In West Africa the British banks financed the cocoa exports, providing the funds to cover the seasonal purchase, transport, and shipment of the beans.[67] In Thailand, they financed that country's growing exports of tin, rice, and rubber.[68] In Argentina the British banks financed the flows of Argentinian crops, meat, and wool, on to world markets. In Brazil they were at the centre of the country's foreign trade, financing the exports of coffee and rubber, and imports of manufactured goods as well. Their establishment of branches in various regional centres in Brazil made it possible for them to match imports in one port with exports at another, according to season.[69] The British banks in Australasia were similarly extremely involved with the pastoral industries of their countries.

The prudent finance of a crop or a mineral continued to require detailed knowledge of the commodity and its market. In Egypt, to give one example, the British banks before 1914 were closely involved with cotton, which had become the dominant part of the economy. The Egyptian cotton crop was harvested between mid-August and mid-November. The banks were engaged, in part, in financing the cultivators during the growing period from February to September. Funds were provided to large landowners through bills discounted, made against a satisfactory guarantor, and with an undertaking to sell the cotton through an agent nominated by the bank. The British banks were much less interested in making advances to the smaller cultivators, who generally obtained funds from merchants, local money-lenders, or a specialist agricultural bank established in the 1900s.

[67] Fry, Bankers in West Africa, 31.

[68] King, The History of the Hongkong and Shanghai Banking Corporation, ii. 131–2.

[69] Joslin, A Century of Banking in Latin America, 130–1, 162–5; Richard Graham, Britain and the Onset of Modernisation in Brazil, 1850–1914 (Cambridge: Cambridge University Press, 1968), 95–8.

The banks did lend to up-country cotton merchants, who on-lent to local cultivators against growing crops or cotton delivered to them for sale on certain conditions. Advances made to the native merchants were always on condition that a certain amount of cotton should be delivered to the bank for sale. The advances were made against cotton deposited in approved 'ginning' factories, in the name of the bank. The cotton was then ginned and sent down to Alexandria in the bank's name, where it was stored by the bank until it was sold on the Alexandria markets. Great skill was required in discounting bills to merchants and large landowners as it was essential to know both the creditworthiness of the borrowers and the quality of the cotton against which funds were being lent. Much depended on the quality of the agents employed by the bank, who were usually locally born Europeans who could speak Arabic.[70] Cotton sold on the Alexandrian market went into the hands of the export merchants, who also required financing from the banks until the cotton was shipped and the advance could be paid off by a bill drawn on a spinner or a bank in Britain or elsewhere.

The British banks in the Middle and Far East found, as the banks in Australia had previously, that they had to modify the terms on which they offered credit. In the decades before the First World War the Eastern Exchange banks offered credit facilities against a variety of different types of security, against goods in the bank's possession, against the deposit of share certificates, and against title deeds to mortgages. In South-east Asia merchants also offered 'trust receipts' as security for loans and advances. These offered banks security of unspecified goods or produce, and were designed for merchants handling a range of commodities which were constantly being processed. Often the banks employed staff whose sole duties were to monitor and supervise the goods or produce hypothecated to the bank and stored in warehouses, or godowns as they were known.[71]

In Vietnam (then part of French Indo-China) Hongkong Bank opened a branch in Saigon in 1870, and Chartered Bank in 1904. Saigon was the major rice-trading centre, and the Exchange banks became active in the finance of the rice trade. The problem was to find a safe system for making advances against paddy (that is, rice before it is milled) and rice. A system evolved which was designed to facilitate the banks' quest for security. The Exchange banks leased godowns from rice-millers, in which each bank had the sole use of either all or part of a godown. This gave them greater control over 'their' produce—the goods against which they were advancing money. Customarily, paddy was delivered to a godown, and a receipt obtained which was taken to the bank by the would-be borrower, either

[70] Chairman's Annual Report to Ionian Bank Shareholders, Mar. 1912; Memorandum on Egyptian Branches, 19 Feb. 1923, A56c/155, LB.

[71] e.g. Madras Advice, 26 Nov. 1908, in Branches/Agencies Special Advices File, 1907–9, Chartered History Files, SC.

the miller or a Chinese merchant. Against this receipt, the borrower would receive an advance of, usually, 80 per cent of the value of the paddy deposited. As the mills only received payment for the product of the paddy, it was necessary to release the paddy from the godown to be milled. Application to proceed with this had to be made to the bank, which granted a 'delivery order'. The paddy was then milled, and the resulting rice shipped, the documents being delivered to the purchasing bank, which was not necessarily the lending bank. The loan was then repaid. It was a complex process![72]

In South Africa it was trade in precious metals and foodstuffs that was of particular concern to the British banks. The finance of gold shipments from the newly discovered deposits of the Witwatersrand formed a considerable part of Standard Bank's activities. In the mid-1890s perhaps half the gold output of the Transvaal passed through the hands of the Standard Bank on its way to Britain. A great deal of the work of the bank's Johannesburg branch revolved around the handling of gold and its dispatch to London for sale. The bank had its own assay equipment and in 1892 a full assay office was opened, which smelted bars of gold, and tested samples. With its own assay office, the bank was in a position to buy gold outright as well as advancing against it, and it could make higher advances on smelted gold. During the 1890s Standard Bank also developed a close relationship with De Beers, who acquired a large share of the South African diamond industry in that decade. Standard did not, however, confine its interest to De Beers, but forged a link with one of that company's most powerful rivals in the 1900s, the Premier Mining Company.[73]

Boards and head offices in London considered the exchange business associated with foreign trade finance particularly desirable. Exchange profits were made by the rapid turnover of funds prized in banking orthodoxy and stood in contrast, in orthodox eyes, to the more dubious profits earned from interest on advances, which might never be repaid. In the 1890s and 1900s this viewpoint caused many clashes with managers 'in the field', who argued that advances to producers and merchants within the country formed part of the total process of foreign trade finance, even though they themselves did not involve exchange business.[74] It was the Eastern Exchange banks where, naturally enough, the emphasis on exchange was

[72] Saigon Advice, 21 Dec. 1912, in Branches/Agencies Special Advices File, 1909–28, Chartered History Files, SC; Mackenzie, *Realms of Silver*, 197–9.

[73] Henry, *The First Hundred Years of the Standard Bank*, 76–7, 102, 140–1; GMO, 10 Feb. 1890, GMO, 17 Feb. 1892; GMO, 4 Aug. 1897, GMO, 8 Feb. 1899, in Mabin and Conradie (eds.), *The Confidence of the Whole Country*, 264–5, 308, 429, 457; Standard Bank, South Africa to London, 1 Feb. 1905, 8 Feb. 1905; in South Africa Box, SC; James Henry, 'The Standard Bank's Early Days in Johannesburg, 1886–1900', in *Africana Notes and News*, Sept. 1956, SC; William H. Worger, *South Africa's City of Diamonds* (New Haven, Conn.: Yale University Press, 1987), 304–5.

[74] e.g. Geoffrey Jones, *Banking and Empire in Iran*, 97, 136–7; Chartered Bank, Hong Kong to London, 30 May 1898, Hong Kong Correspondence File 5 (i), SC.

particularly strong. Managers of such banks regularly found themselves admonished to pursue energetically this form of business.[75] Conversely, although boards in London liked exchange profits derived from movements of trade, they strongly disliked such profits if they were the product of pure speculation and arbitrage, activities which could go very badly wrong.[76]

In Brazil in the 1890s, London and Brazilian's business was largely centred on exchange, but there was considerable tension about the legitimacy of some business. London sought to prohibit dealing with speculators. Policies were laid down in London designed to make managers undertake only exchange business arising from genuine trade. Branch managers, however, often pleaded that this was too conservative and risk-averse. The upshot was often a compromise. 'We hesitate to prohibit purchases of Exchange from Speculators in view of your advice', the bank's London office wrote to its Rio manager in 1897, 'but we do not like the commodity. Your sellers may be wealthy but you have no legal redress against them if they see fit to repudiate their engagements, as we know full well to our cost!'[77]

Exchange banking in fact involved constant judgemental decisions and it was a moot point what could be considered speculative. Timing lay at the heart of its success. In the late 1890s, Chartered's London management ascribed the good profits earned by its branches in the Straits Settlement 'to the ability of the Branch Managers to purchase Sterling during the time when margins between bills for immediate delivery and ready purchase of silver in London ensured considerable profits'.[78] Timing was also a prerequisite for success in the large bullion and specie business undertaken by the Eastern Exchange banks in the late nineteenth and early twentieth centuries. Chartered Bank's London management monitored such bullion operations closely, to see that the branches in the East operated the possibilities of exchange and arbitrage as efficiently as possible, giving detailed instructions on how to cut in and out of bullion and exchange operations.[79]

Exchange business was no less prized by the British banks in the settler economies. The British banks in Australia remained prominent exchange-dealers and they had large exchange turnovers before the war.[80] In South

[75] e.g. Mercantile Bank, London to Mr Ormiston, 27 Mar. 1902, MB 512, HSBC.

[76] Geoffrey Jones, *Banking and Empire in Iran*, 69, provides one example.

[77] Extra 35/33, 13 Aug. 1897, G3/3, Bolsa Archives, UCL. See also Graham, *Britain and the Onset of Modernisation in Brazil*, 98–9, and Joslin, *A Century of Banking in Latin America*, 161.

[78] Chartered Bank, Hong Kong Branch to London, 30 May 1898 (comments on letter from J. H. Gwyther) in Hong Kong Correspondence File 5 (i), Chartered History Files, SC.

[79] e.g. Chartered Bank, Mr Hoggan to Inspector in Calcutta, 414a, 13 Aug. 1909, and Head Office to Hong Kong, 25a, 23 July 1909, Bullion File, Chartered History Files, SC.

[80] For the Bank of Australasia's exchange turnover pre-1914, see e.g. the Superintendent's Yearly Review, Oct. 1917, A/141/5, ANZ Archives.

Africa Standard Bank was an energetic pursuer of exchange business. In the 1890s it often lamented that because De Beers always received part-payment for its diamonds in sterling in London, the bank missed out on handling most of the exchange business of the diamond industry.[81] However, the Boer War (1899–1902) gave the bank the opportunity to earn high exchange profits, for its contract with the British Army Pay Department enabled it to 'practically control the exchange market, and to compel the other Banks, in the absence of mining and mercantile exchange, to purchase from us, on favourable terms'.[82]

Movements in the exchange rate remained a threat, as well as an opportunity. Banks frequently bemoaned the effect of such movements on their balance sheets, and more especially when the currency of the country they operated in depreciated against sterling, which had the effect of reducing the balance sheet value of assets in the foreign country. In the late 1890s, for example, Brazilian currency depreciated sharply against sterling. In Brazil, British banks were blamed for this fall, because of alleged speculative activities. The British banks, in their private correspondence, more often blamed political instability and 'reckless emissions of paper money' by the government,[83] but, whatever the cause, the result was a problem for sterling balance sheets. The London and Brazilian Bank had to suspend its normal annual bonus to shareholders in 1898 on this account. Again, Ionian Bank felt itself badly affected by fluctuations in the drachma/pound exchange rate around the turn of the century, and between 1901 and 1908 switched to converting its Greek assets into sterling for balance sheet purposes at a fixed rate of exchange.[84]

Many of the overseas banks, when they made internal calculations of their profit, made a distinction between interest, exchange, and—usually a much smaller sum—commission profits. Given the different ways of calculating profits, too much weight could be put on these calculations, but a few illustrations provide some insights at least of variations between banks. In the Imperial Bank of Persia, for which relevant data survives for a few years, interest profits were considerably more than those earned from exchange in the years 1905 to 1908 and then, following the appointment of a new chief manager and the adoption of a revised business strategy, this situation was reversed up to 1914.[85] There was a somewhat similar pattern in the Bank of Mauritius, where interest profits were two and a half times greater than its exchange profits between 1903 and 1909,

[81] GMO, 12 Aug. 1896, in Mabin and Conradie (eds.), *The Confidence of the Whole Country*, 403.

[82] GMO, 8 Aug. 1900, in ibid., 487. See also GMO, 13 Aug. 1902, 522 for an estimate of the turnover involved.

[83] Extra 35/51, London to Rio, 23 Dec. 1897, G3/3, Bolsa Archives, UCL. See also London to Rio, 22 Dec. 1899, G3/4.

[84] Annual Report to Ionian Bank Shareholders, May 1901.

[85] Geoffrey Jones, *Banking and Empire in Iran*, 106, 137.

but less than 10 per cent higher between 1910 and 1914.[86] In the London and River Plate Bank in 1911 and 1913 (the two pre-war dates for which the data survive), receipts from interest were over six times those from exchange operations.[87]

By the pre-war decades the British banks in the English-speaking settler economies were long established in domestic or retail banking through their extended branch networks, but there were divergent trends between the economies. In Australia, structural changes in the economy, reaction to the banking crisis of the early 1890s, and the creation of state-sponsored credit institutions to farmers led to a fall in domestic lending to the building trade and to farmers, with a shift towards trade finance in line with the growing importance of foreign trade in the Australian economy.[88] In South Africa, in contrast, while Standard Bank of South Africa had tried to avoid lending against mortgages up to the 1890s, after the Boer War the bank appears to have lent more to farmers, including advances against the security of landed property.[89] This was the main activity of Standard Bank's up-country inland branches, in contrast to the branches at ports which dealt chiefly with trade finance, and those offices which specialized in precious metals, notably Johannesburg (gold) and Kimberley (diamonds).

In Latin America also, from the 1890s an intentional and sustained process of product diversification is discernible following the period of high orthodoxy in the late 1870s and the 1880s. This development has been most closely studied in the case of Argentina, where two factors combined to encourage a liberalization of lending policies. On the one hand, the British banks faced growing competition from local banks and merchant houses. On the other hand, there was a substantial growth of Argentinian bank deposits as the economy and population grew. Total Argentinian bank deposits grew over three times between 1900 and 1914, and although the foreign bank share of these fell from 39 per cent to 23 per cent, the British banks still had an increase in resources to finance more local lending. The London and River Plate, with its reputation for stability, was for a time particularly successful in attracting small deposits from immigrants. With extra resources and the spur of competition, the British banks modified their lending policies. The London and River Plate

[86] Memorandum on Analysis of Mauritius Operations, MB1191, HSBC.

[87] Amalgamated Profit and Loss Account for the Head Office and Branches, 30 Sept. 1911 and 3 Sept. 1913, Bolsa, LB. London and Brazilian's Buenos Aires branch followed this pattern. Between 1897 and 1915 interest earnings always exceeded those from exchange, and between 1910 and 1914 they were nearly nine times as great. Profit and Loss Account, G39, Bolsa Archives, UCL.

[88] Butlin, *Australia and New Zealand Bank*, 322, 338–40; Merrett, 'The 1893 Bank Crashes: The Aftermath'.

[89] GMO, 4 Aug. 1897, in Mabin and Conradie (eds.), *The Confidence of the Whole Country*, 422; Henry, *First Hundred Years of the Standard Bank*, 151–2.

began offering overdrafts on current accounts (rather than only loans for fixed sums) and also began to lend against the security of shares and mortgages (rather than solely against 'genuine' bills of exchange). From the mid-1890s several smaller British banks entered the mortgage market, using funds from Belgium and later Scotland.[90]

In Brazil, the British banks also diversified beyond exchange and foreign trade, but at a slower pace than in Argentina. Nevertheless, by the early years of the twentieth century the British banks were lending to the textile industry and to a wide group of industries in the São Paulo region. There was some diversity between industries in this respect. The London and Brazilian Bank had a very strong position in the exchange market, while the two other British banks had a greater incentive to find new sources of business. The British Bank of South America, for instance, became active in lending to local entrepreneurs, especially in the 1900s, and in order to enhance its resources it led the way, in 1909, in attracting small fixed deposits from the general public.[91]

In the 1900s the fast-growing Anglo-South American Bank was prepared to lend without security in order to expand its role in Latin America. Such lending had its dangers, however, and by 1907 even this bank had become so distressed at the losses arising from the extensive facilities granted at many of the branches in the shape of unsecured overdrafts that the directors had to introduce more formal procedures. Recognizing that the bank needed to grant unsecured credit on occasion in order to 'maintain a position in the front rank in the countries where the Bank is established', the directors reminded their managers to examine carefully the business of firms before offering such facilities, and only to allow such credit up to the equivalent of 20 per cent of a firm's capital. The overall amount of lending a branch manager could authorize without reference to London was also limited.[92]

In Asia, the Eastern Exchange banks also became more involved in their local economies as time passed. The Exchange banks established 'up-country' branches beyond the ports where initial operations had been located. Chartered Bank's first branches in the interior of Malaya, at Taiping and Kuala Lumpur, began by granting loans to petty traders and small contractors, and these interior branches became heavily involved in domestic banking.[93] Nor did branches of the Exchange banks at ports confine themselves solely to foreign trade finance. The Treaty Ports on the

---

[90] Charles A. Jones, 'British Financial Institutions in Argentine', ch. 2.

[91] Graham, *Britain and the Onset of Modernisation in Brazil*, 136; Joslin, *A Century of Banking in Latin America*, 165–72. The private letters from Rio to the Brazilian branches of the London and River Plate, which opened in Brazil in 1892, suggest this bank had also become involved in local lending in the 1900s. See file D8/2, Bolsa Archives, UCL.

[92] Anglo-South American Bank Circular, No. 13/33, 6 Dec. 1907, C2/4, Bolsa Archives, UCL. [93] Mackenzie, *Realms of Silver*, 216.

China coast had many locally registered public companies, usually established by expatriate Europeans of various nationalities, and active in utilities, services, and consumer goods manufacture. The Hongkong Bank provided substantial overdraft facilities to a number of these companies, financing fixed capital investment in some instances.[94]

The Exchange banks' dealings with the indigenous sector in Asia were often conducted through intermediaries. There were, in fact, two streams of business activities within these banks: European managers lent to Western—and occasionally Asian—business, while local staff dealt with the indigenous sector. In China and other countries with a Chinese business community, such as the Dutch East Indies, Singapore, and the Philippines, the key figure was the comprador. The use of a comprador enabled the Exchange banks to conduct business with a community which had both a language and a business culture very different from their own. He was, crucially, the provider of information. Although there were minor differences between branches of the same bank, in general the comprador was responsible for the recruitment and conduct of all Chinese staff of the banks. He paid them and was financially responsible for any shortages caused by them. One result was that compradors recruited members of their family and clan, who could be relied upon. The comprador negotiated and secured the business of banks with Chinese customers. Although he received a monthly salary, his main source of income was a commission on the business he controlled. A comprador had to provide sufficient security to protect a bank against misuse of its funds, and a cash sum would be deposited with a bank in advance, supplemented by a lien against property. Compradors usually had guarantors from within the Chinese community.

The compradoric system had both advantages and disadvantages. Even if the British staff of the Exchange banks had been able to learn Chinese—a task few of them ever attempted—they would have lacked the contacts and the information on the Chinese business community to be able to lend safely to it. Compradors provided the means by which foreign banks could lend to Chinese traders or banks. For a bank, the main disadvantage of the system was the loss of control over a proportion of its funds. Banks depended on the reliability of the comprador. However, because compradors frequently engaged in business on their own account, there was always a risk that the bank's funds would be misused and when this happened a bank could suffer serious loss.[95]

In China, the Exchange banks had substantial dealings with the well-developed indigenous banking system. Major cities had their own banking

[94] King, *The History of the Hongkong and Shanghai Banking Corporation*, i. 507–9.
[95] Carl T. Smith, 'Compradores of the Hongkong Bank', in F. H. H. King (ed.), *Eastern Banking* (London: Athlone, 1983).

systems—Hong Kong in 1886 had some twenty Chinese banks—which were interconnected by specialized remittance banks operating throughout the country. Through loans to these banks the Exchange banks were able to lend further sums to the indigenous economy without the risks that would have been involved in direct lending.[96] The British banks and the native banks borrowed from, and lent to, each other on a daily basis, according to market conditions, and with the comprador as the intermediary. The native banker would normally never meet any British staff during the course of such business.[97]

The use of intermediaries by the Exchange banks in order to conduct business with the Chinese indigenous economy had parallels elsewhere in Asia. In Ceylon, for example, the 'guarantee shroff' performed a very similar function to that of the comprador. This person was responsible for arranging loans to the indigenous sector, which he guaranteed. There were further intermediaries for small and medium-sized borrowers. These were the Chettiars, a south Indian banking caste who, before the British banks opened branches, provided all the banking services in Ceylon, and in other parts of South-east Asia. The shroffs of the Exchange banks guaranteed loans to Chettiars in return for a commission. Lending to the Chettiars enabled the Western banks to capture some of the profits gained from the high interest rates prevailing in the rural credit market, with a much-reduced risk.[98] In other areas, the British banks employed intermediaries who did not guarantee loans, but performed a vital role in providing information on the local economy and creditworthiness of local borrowers. In Iran, each branch of the Imperial Bank of Persia had a mirza, or 'interpreter'. Mirzas did not formally guarantee customers and staff, but they advised on the recruitment of local staff and on the creditworthiness of potential customers. In line with the Imperial Bank's desire that its British staff should have direct contact with their local customers, the mirzas were also often required to give Persian lessons to European staff, a function which compradors seem rarely if ever to have undertaken. With the aid of the mirzas, the Imperial Bank before 1914 at times made substantial sums available to large merchants or indigenous bankers (sarrafs) which must have been on-lent to the local economy.[99]

These intermediaries were subsequently to be strongly criticized for

[96] King, The History of the Hongkong and Shanghai Banking Corporation, i. 503-4.
[97] The evidence in a legal case brought by five native banks in Hankow against Chartered Bank allows this business to be followed in detail. See Transcript of Privy Council Proceedings on the Tung Ta Bank and Others versus the Chartered Bank of India, Australia and China, 20 Mar. 1907, Posterity Files, SC.
[98] King, The History of the Hongkong and Shanghai Banking Corporation, i. 518; H. L. D. Selvaratnam, 'The Guarantee Shroffs, the Chettiars, and the Hong Kong Bank in Ceylon', in King (ed.), Eastern Banking.
[99] Geoffrey Jones, Banking and Empire in Iran, 105-6, 156.

preventing indigenous borrowers from dealing directly with the Western banks, and thus forcing up the cost of borrowing. The counter-argument of the banks was that they would never have lent money without the use of such intermediaries. Both arguments had validity.

In West and East Africa, the links between the British banks and indigenous merchants were fewer than in many parts of Asia, and bank lending remained more firmly restricted to expatriate firms. However, the British banks in East Africa, although they did little business with Africans, had much closer contacts with Asian merchants active there. Retail trade, and the distribution of imports into the interior arriving at Mombasa, was almost entirely in the hands of the Indian population. In order to conduct business with the Indian community, the British banks employed 'brokers' on the same principle as the intermediaries used in Asia. The brokers who were active at the East African branches in the 1900s were sometimes staff members, but sometimes independent agents working on a commission basis. They were naturally always Asians. While nominally employed to collect bazaar information, in fact they performed a wide range of functions.[100]

In West Africa, the local business of the British banks was largely concerned with lending to European trading companies, who on-lent to African traders and producers. The problem of obtaining adequate security for loans from Africans was a particular obstacle to direct lending.[101] As usual, challenger banks were more flexible than market leaders, and in the 1900s the Bank of Nigeria actively lent to Africans.[102] The Bank of British West Africa had a much more conservative attitude, being largely content to confine its business to the large British trading companies and its lucrative role as silver agent for the colonial governments. It was only in the immediate years before the First World War, and after the acquisition of the Bank of Nigeria, that BBWA began to show a marginal interest in lending small sums to Africans, usually against the security of property.[103]

The greater involvement in domestic banking in their host economies of British multinational banks must be kept in context, for trade finance and exchange remained core activities. The location of head offices in the City of London continued to yield competitive advantages for the overseas banks in international banking. It provided essential information and contacts. They knew of large loans, impending investments, and changing business conditions earlier than local competitors. Interlocking directorships with other overseas British business interests provided a flow of new business

---

[100] Swanson, 'History of the Bank in East Africa'.

[101] Fry, *Bankers in West Africa,* 110; 116–17.

[102] Draft letter from Sir Walter Egerton to Colonial Secretary, 26 Nov. 1907, No. 43456; Colonial Office Minute by H.A.B., 31 Dec. 1907, No. 43456. Colonial Office Files, Co520/50, PRO.

[103] BBWA Board Minutes, 26 Feb. 1913, 27 Aug. 1913, 17 Dec. 1913, in Fry's Digests of Minutes, BBWA Board Minutes, Fry's History Files, BAC s/90, SC.

and fresh information. London's bill market continued to be a key part of international trade finance. The credit provided by the London bankers of the overseas banks played an essential role in helping them balance the seasonal flows of funds, especially after the practice of taking British deposits declined following the crises of the early 1890s. The money market was a profitable home for the temporary surplus funds which accumulated in London when primary commodity exports to Britain were sold and the bills were met. It was not surprising that although the London offices of the banks were small in staff numbers, the business transacted by them was of considerable importance for the institutions. In Australia, the business undertaken by the Anglo-Australian and local banks was almost identical, but the Anglos were distinguished by the greater share of their assets involved in their London business, and by the disproportionate share of bills in their balance sheets.[104]

London provided an excellent location for the long-term investments of the banks, whose investment portfolios grew rapidly in the two decades before the war. In the 1890s the overseas banks invested largely in Consols, as did domestic British banks. Consols were highly prized for their liquidity as well as their earning ability. Subsequently, however, a fall in their price led banks to diversify their portfolios, and those that did not do so quickly enough faced losses. The Colonial Bank was particularly badly affected, as it had a high investment ratio, and had placed large amounts of its resources in gilt-edged securities. In 1904 it had to establish a special reserve to cover depreciation on investments, and after 1908 regular sums needed to be set aside from profits to cover depreciation.[105]

Most bank investment portfolios became more diversified in the 1900s, often with a bias towards stocks originating from the country or countries in which they specialized. The Imperial Bank of Persia's investment portfolio between 1892 and 1900 was dominated by the 1892 Persian Government Loan Stock. The bank had floated the loan, but the issue had not been a success, failing even to secure a quotation on the London Stock Exchange. After the loan was redeemed in 1900, the Imperial Bank diversified into British government, colonial, and municipal stocks, but it also had many small investments in Chinese, Japanese, United States, Mexican, South American, and Russian government, municipal, and railway stock. In 1911 the bank also purchased a substantial share of a new Persian government loan which it had issued.[106] The National Bank

---

[104] David Merrett, 'Paradise Lost? British Banks in Australia', in Jones (ed.), *Banks as Multinationals* (London: Routledge, 1990), 71.

[105] Standard Bank had similar problems in 1907. See Directors' Report, 88th Ordinary Meeting of SBSA, 15 Oct. 1907; *A Banking Centenary: Barclays Bank (Dominion, Colonial and Overseas), 1836–1936* (London: Barclays Bank, 1936), 58; Colonial Bank Balance Sheets.

[106] Geoffrey Jones, *Banking and Empire in Iran*, 73–4, 111.

of New Zealand, in 1910, had over 30 per cent of its portfolio in New Zealand government stock, almost 20 per cent each in British government and Bank of England securities and British railway, utility, and municipal stock, 15 per cent in Indian government and railway stock, and smaller sums in government and railway stock of diverse countries.[107]

A third bank for which detailed information on investments has survived, the African Banking Corporation, had nearly 40 per cent of its investments in 1913 in South Africa, mostly in the form of government stock, with less than 1 per cent held in British government securities. The largest percentages outside South Africa were around 10 per cent each in Indian government and railway stock and various American railways, 6 per cent in Canadian railways, and 5 per cent in Brazilian government loans, with smaller sums spread around diverse government, municipal, and railway stock, and even some money in Consolidated Gold Fields of South Africa, the New York Telephone Company, and a British brewery.[108]

Despite the diversity of the business undertaken by British multinational banks in different regions, some generalizations can be made. The banks remained specialists in trade finance and exchange banking, which used the competitive advantages of being headquartered in London to good effect, but the process of evolution into institutions offering a wider range of financial products continued on the lines established before 1890. The banks active in the Australasian and South African colonies had long been engaged in domestic banking of various kinds. The banks in Asia, Africa, and Latin America evolved more in this direction in the pre-war decades, albeit at different paces and to different degrees. British banks were conservative institutions. They were prudent lenders, and discouraged their staff from involvement in speculative activities. However, their strong corporate cultures and the socialization of managers permitted flexibility in their business strategies, within certain parameters. As a result, and over time, credit was extended on more liberal terms, to people who were not white Anglo-Saxons, to sectors other than foreign trade, and even—on occasion and with guilt—to speculators.

### 3.6. Competition and Collusion

In many regions in which they operated, the competitive advantages of the British multinational banks over both local and other foreign institutions remained considerable right up to the First World War. First-mover advantages, the benefits associated with having a strong presence in London, and the organizational capability of the banks all combined to

---

[107] National Bank of New Zealand Balance Books, LB.
[108] African Banking Corporation papers, SC.

make it difficult for competitors successfully to challenge the British banks. Nevertheless, in several regions British overseas banks experienced competitive challenges.

In the United States and Canada, the competitive pressures from local banks were clearly so great that by 1914 only one bank remained in British ownership. In the neighbouring West Indies, the Colonial Bank was also badly affected by competition. This bank had a long-established strong monopoly position in the islands, but showed little interest in the custom of anyone but its traditional constituents, the big planters and proprietors.[109] Falling prices in the sugar industry, the financing of which had been the bank's preserve, hit profits, but even worse were the consequences of the growing commercial links between the West Indies and Canada and the United States. In 1889 the Canadian-owned Bank of Nova Scotia opened a branch at Kingston, Jamaica, followed by other branches there and on other West Indian islands. In the absence (as yet) of American branch banking abroad, the Bank of Nova Scotia was able to capture the business of American firms in the Caribbean. After establishing a branch in Boston in 1899, the Canadian bank obtained the Jamaican business of the United Fruit Company, which all but controlled the export of Jamaica's most important crop by the 1890s, bananas. In 1906 the Bank of Nova Scotia captured the account of the Jamaican government from the British bank. Moreover, Colonial Bank felt itself handicapped by certain conditions in its Royal Charter, especially the obligation that its notes should be encashable, not only at the branches of issue, but at all its principal branches, which meant that the Colonial Bank had to keep large reserves of unremunerative specie at each branch.[110]

In fact Colonial's misfortunes were largely the result of management failure. It was trapped in the mentality of being a single-commodity bank. When the major business declined, the board could think of nothing better to do than invest in British government stock, and suffered from its depreciation as a consequence. It was only with a change in its controlling interest that there was any sign of a competitive response. In 1911 the Canadian financier William Maxwell Aitken (the first Lord Beaverbrook) purchased control of the Colonial Bank, a year after settling in England. He became a director three years later, and served as chairman between 1915 and 1917. Aitken had previously been actively engaged in the promotion of companies in the West Indies, as well as being a leading promoter

---

[109] Republic Bank Ltd., *From Colonial to Republic: One Hundred and Fifty Years of Business in Banking in Trinidad and Tobago, 1837–1987* (Trinidad: Republic Bank, n.d.), 68.

[110] Neil C. Quigley, 'The Bank of Nova Scotia in the Caribbean, 1889–1940: The Establishment and Organisation of an International Branch Banking Network', *Business History Review*, 63 (1989). For Colonial Bank's complaints about its note-issuing obligations, see Minute by G.G., 27 Mar. 1911, Paper 9429, CO 318/327, PRO.

of mergers in Canada which had made him a millionaire by the age of 30, and he was soon able to use his entrepreneurial skills to secure the account of the United Fruit Company for the Colonial Bank. However, his main strategy was diversification away from the West Indies, first to West Africa and ultimately into a merger with Barclays Bank.[111]

In Latin America, it was not Canadian but German multinational banks that challenged the British banks. The specialist German overseas banks founded from the 1880s were designed to take over from the British banks the finance of German trade with Latin America, and they had made considerable progress in this direction by the First World War.[112] They found a natural client base in countries with substantial numbers of German immigrants, such as Chile, but they were also able to break out of ethnic banking, in some places securing the accounts of British firms even when there was a British bank in the city.[113] The Latin American activities of German electricity utilities provided another good source of business for the banks. The British banks in Latin America were clearly affected by the activities of their German competitors.[114] The German banks were successful in securing market share, but nevertheless the British banks almost everywhere remained ahead of their German rivals by the time of the outbreak of the First World War.

German banking competition also became a matter of concern in Asia, especially after the formation of the Deutsch-Asiatische Bank in 1889, but the Eastern Exchange banks were powerful institutions whose grip on the trade and exchange of the East was not easily overcome. On the China coast, the Hongkong Bank retained the accounts of many German merchants because its Hong Kong base enabled it to offer a superior service. In addition, the major German firms active in Hong Kong continued to be represented on the board of the Hongkong Bank up to 1914. Hongkong Bank collaborated rather than competed with German interests in such matters as Chinese government loans, and a form of symbiotic relationship developed.[115]

Continental European multinational banks emerged as competitors elsewhere in Asia, but the position of the British banks remained strong.

---

[111] Quigley, 'The Bank of Nova Scotia in the Caribbean'; Katherine V. Bligh and Christine Shaw, 'William Maxwell Aitken', in David J. Jeremy (ed.), Dictionary of Business Biography (London: Butterworths, 1984), 23–4; Sir Julian Crossley and John Blandford, The DCO Story (London: Barclays Bank International, 1975), 2–3; A Banking Centenary, 58–9.

[112] Peter Hertner, 'German Banks Abroad before 1914', in Geoffrey Jones (ed.), Banks as Multinationals, 102–7; Manfred Pohl, Deutsche Bank Buenos Aires, 1887–1987 (Mainz: Hase & Koehler, 1987), ch. 3.

[113] This was apparently the case in Valparaiso, Chile, in the mid-1900s. R. Williams to R. A. Thurburn, 23 May 1906, D7/1, Bolsa Archives, UCL.

[114] Joslin, A Century of Banking in Latin America, 111, 194–7.

[115] King, The History of the Hongkong and Shanghai Banking Corporation, ii. 544–8; Hertner, 'German Banks Abroad', 107–11.

Deutsch-Asiatische Bank established branches in Calcutta and Singapore, but these were minor affairs. The Banque de l'Indochine acquired new clients from the failure of the New Oriental and Chartered Mercantile, and later opened branches in Hong Kong (1894) and Singapore (1905), the bastions of British commercial influence in the East. However, the French bank was largely confined to French-related business, although the Singapore branch over time acquired the accounts of some Chinese merchants.[116] In Iran, a Russian rival to the Imperial Bank of Persia was launched in the early 1890s, but was never very successful, and had been reduced to a moribund state in the decade before the First World War. A Russo-Chinese Bank, formed in 1895, was a more serious proposition, but it was never a serious challenger to the preponderance of the Hongkong Bank in China.[117] The British banks in Asia and the Middle East did not welcome the competition of other European multinational banks, but were rarely too threatened by it. The overall importance of British trade and investment, and diplomatic and colonial influence, would have made any other outcome surprising.

In most of the settler economies, with the partial exception of South Africa, local banks grew in importance. In Argentina, depositors and businessmen slowly regained confidence in local institutions after the disastrous collapses of 1891 and 1892. In part this was because of their imitation of British banking practices. A new generation of Argentinian banks, notably the Banco de la Nación, expanded their market share. This bank was much more modelled on British-style commercial banking than its official predecessors, although it combined prudence with a bold strategy of branch expansion. The foreign bank share of Argentinian deposits fell from 39 per cent to 23 per cent between 1900 and 1914, while over this period the share of the Banco de la Nación doubled to reach 51 per cent.[118]

Local banks grew in importance elsewhere in Latin America too. In Chile, the Banco de Chile, and in Brazil, the Banco do Brasil, mounted challenges to the British banks even in the exchange markets, although an extremely severe banking crisis in Brazil at the turn of the century overwhelmed many local banks, and even the Banco do Brasil had to be reconstructed, leaving the British banks to acquire the better customers of their erstwhile competitors.[119] In Uruguay, the Banco de la República opened in 1896, to the initial disdain of British bankers.[120] But the Uruguayan government gave the new bank the sole right of note issue, obliging the

[116] Marc Meuleau, *Des pionniers en Extrême-Orient* (Paris: Fayard, 1990), 171, 291–3.
[117] Geoffrey Jones, *Banking and Empire in Iran*, 54–6, 98–9, 116, 119; King, *The History of the Hongkong and Shanghai Banking Corporation*, ii. 41.
[118] Charles A. Jones, 'British Financial Institutions in Argentine,' 83–5.
[119] Managing Director (British Bank of South America) to Sao Paulo Manager, 7 Dec. 1900, E2/1, Bolsa Archives, UCL.
[120] Manager's letter of 30 Oct. 1896, Head Office Confidential Letters, Book 2, LB.

London and River Plate Bank to call in the notes which it had circulated in that country for nearly forty years, and by 1914 the Banco de la República had captured a large share of the market.[121]

In Australia, the rapid loss of market share to local institutions in the forty years prior to 1890 ceased, but the British banks entered a long period of stagnation. To some extent this was true of all the commercial (or trading, as they became known) banks. Between 1890 and 1930 state savings banks, often officially guaranteed, raised their share of total deposits from 6 per cent to 30 per cent. However, the two leading British-owned trading banks failed to capitalize on the high reputations they achieved through surviving the banking crisis, which had been at its most destructive in their base of Victoria. 'Our prestige after the 1893 crisis was very great', Union Bank's general manager recalled forty years later, 'and for some years thereafter we could get practically what business we desired.'[122] Unfortunately they desired to continue to focus on their well-established business of lending to wool-growers and farmers, and financing the associate export trade, and as a result missed growth opportunities elsewhere. The limits to flexibility of British overseas banks were, perhaps, particularly evident in Australia. Over this period, the Bank of New South Wales strengthened its position as market leader, while smaller local banks such as National Bank of Australasia grew in importance.[123] Meanwhile, in New Zealand, the Bank of New Zealand was by far the largest bank—accounting for almost a half of non-government deposits in 1913—but the National Bank of New Zealand, the Union Bank, and the Bank of Australasia between them held 37 per cent of deposits and 44 per cent of advances, the latter a considerable improvement on their market share in the late 1880s.[124]

By the time of the First World War, modern banks owned by nationals existed in several Asian countries, but only rarely did they pose a threat to the Eastern Exchange banks. In Thailand, the Siam Commercial Bank was formed in 1906, but it did not flourish under its German management, and during the First World War the Hongkong Bank had to second managers to the bank to salvage it.[125] In China, expatriate merchants sponsored the formation of the London-registered National Bank of China in 1891, which had many Chinese shareholders and Chinese on the board of directors, but it, and the Imperial Bank of China founded in 1898, made

[121] Joslin, A Century of Banking in Latin America, 110, 137–8, 145, 165.

[122] General Manager to Standing Committee, 23 June 1936, UBL 191, ANZ Archives.

[123] Merrett, ANZ Bank, 35–6; Butlin, Australia and New Zealand Bank, 338–40.

[124] G. R. Hawke and D. K. Sheppard, 'The Evolution of New Zealand Trading Banks mostly until 1934', Victoria University of Wellington Working Papers in Economic History, No. 84/2, Mar. 1984.

[125] King, The History of the Hongkong Shanghai Banking Corporation, ii. 129–30, 236–7.

only very modest progress in challenging the Exchange banks. The National Bank was eventually put into voluntary liquidation in 1911, by which date the Imperial Bank was also in difficulties.[126]

In British India the modern banking system had three components, which only partially overlapped with each other. The three Presidency banks had been privatized in 1876, but they retained the privilege of holding government balances. They remained subject to regulatory restrictions. They could only lend against certain types of security; they were not allowed to borrow in England; and they could not undertake exchange banking. There were also a number of Indian-registered joint stock banks, which focused on domestic business; while some of these were owned by expatriate Britons, others were Indian-owned. This sector was subject to periodic crises, with large numbers of banks failing in the mid-1860s and again in 1913–14. The Exchange banks did not face competition in the exchange markets from the Presidency banks or the joint stock banks, while their London offices gave them the advantage in attracting the accounts of expatriate firms in India. There was competition for deposits and advances. There is some evidence that the Exchange banks were taking a growing share of bank deposits from the mid-1870s to the mid-1890s, but that subsequently the Indian joint stock banks became more powerful competitors.[127]

After 1880 the officially sponsored Yokohama Specie Bank made rapid progress in trade finance and exchange operations, and even participated in Japanese government loan issues on the London market. By 1914 British banks were still significant in Japanese foreign trade finance and foreign borrowing, but their importance was visibly declining.[128]

Inevitably the reaction of individual British banks to competition from other British institutions, foreign banks, and local banks varied widely with time and region. If a generalization about strategies can be offered, however, it is that over time the British banks became increasingly attracted to co-operation with other banks (of any nationality) rather than to unrestrained competition. Such a preference for collusion is probably an inherent feature of capitalism, but it was certainly strong in the British banking

[126] Ibid. i. 261, 263, 404–6, 457; ii. 42–3, 278–9.
[127] A. K. Bagchi, *The Presidency Banks and the Indian Economy, 1876–1914* (Calcutta: Oxford University Press, 1989), ch. 3; Dwijendra Tripathi and Priti Misra, *Towards a New Frontier: History of the Bank of Baroda, 1908–1983* (New Delhi: Manohar, 1985), 15–16; A. G. Chandavarkar, 'Money and Credit, 1858–1947', in D. Kumar (ed.), *The Cambridge Economic History of India*, ii (Cambridge: Cambridge University Press, 1983), 776–84.
[128] Norio Tamaki, 'The Yokohama Specie Bank: A Multinational in the Japanese Interest, 1879–1931', in Geoffrey Jones (ed.), *Banks as Multinationals*; R. P. T. Davenport-Hines and Geoffrey Jones, 'British Business in Japan since 1868', in R. P. T. Davenport-Hines and Geoffrey Jones (eds.), *British Business in Asia since 1860* (Cambridge: Cambridge University Press, 1989), 222–4; King, *The History of the Hongkong and Shanghai Banking Corporation*, ii. 43; Hugh T. Patrick, 'Japan, 1868–1914', in Rondo Cameron *et al*, *Banking in the Early Stages of Industrialization* (New York: Oxford University Press, 1967).

culture from which the overseas banks emerged. At least from the 1860s, English domestic banks had operated formal and informal agreements to restrict price competition, and this collusion was encouraged by the British Treasury and the Bank of England which found it easier to enforce official interest rate policy when dealing with cartelized banks.[129] The fact that in many markets it was the British banks which held the established position which was faced by competition probably encouraged a view that the best way to deal with new entrants was to contain them in collusive agreements, especially in matters of price. On the other hand, new entrants into banking were appearing in many regions, and this worked against collusion. Moreover, the considerable autonomy which distance alone gave to branch managers tended before 1914 to give rise to many local agreements, which frequently broke down after a few months.

Among the Eastern Exchange banks, collusive tendencies were noticeable early on, although there was strong competition in the opening of branches and for the 'best' accounts. After the banking crisis in 1866, the Eastern Exchange banks signed an agreement to shorten the usance period on bills from six to four months, an agreement which the newly founded Hongkong Bank declined to join, and which broke down in 1867.[130] By the turn of the century the Exchange banks were jointly lobbying on policy matters, such as their successful campaign against a central bank in India.[131] Exchange banks associations were formed at local level—in Calcutta and Bombay in 1892—and these became mechanisms through which agreements on rates could be negotiated. However, these local inter-bank agreements in India, and elsewhere in the East, were regularly undermined by accusations of cheating and the problems of monitoring their implementation.[132] There were often tensions between head offices and local managers in this matter. While a manager might be infuriated by the cheating of another British bank in his city, head office might value the collaboration of the same bank elsewhere, and be reluctant to offend it.[133]

It would appear that at any one time in India the Exchange banks had in force on a local basis a considerable range of agreements on exchange rates and interest rates, and terms for particular types of business. In 1913,

[129] Collins, *Money and Banking in the UK*, 80; Brian Griffiths, 'The Development of Restrictive Practices in the UK Monetary System', *Manchester School*, 41 (1973); Geoffrey Jones, 'Competition and Competitiveness in British Banking, 1918–71', in Geoffrey Jones and Maurice Kirby (eds.), *Competitiveness and the State* (Manchester: Manchester University Press, 1991), 121.
[130] Mackenzie, *Realms of Silver*, 64–5; King, *The History of the Hongkong and Shanghai Banking Corporation*, i. 85–6, 185.
[131] Tyson, *100 Years of Banking in Asia and Africa*, 140–4; Bagchi, *The Presidency Banks and Indian Economy*, 157–61.
[132] e.g. Report by Mr J. B. Lee on Prospects of Business in Madras, 1900, Posterity File 97, SC.
[133] e.g. Mercantile Bank, London to Mr Nicholl, 14 July 1905, MB Hist. 512, HSBC.

to give an example of the latter type, the British banks operated similar agreements in Delhi, Cawnpore, and Amritsar on the terms for lending to the cotton piece goods business. These agreements were very detailed and comprehensive. Under the Amritsar agreement, three Exchange banks and the Allahabad Bank, an Indian joint stock bank under British management, fixed such matters as the rate of interest on piece goods loans, the minimum margins to be maintained on loans after goods had been loaded in the Amritsar warehouse or godown, the rate for godown rentals and insurance, the rate for insurance of goods in transit, the interest on clearing charges, and the rates for bill collections, rail receipt collections, and commissions.[134]

It was probably in Australasia that the most stable pattern of collusion developed. In Australia, an industry association, the Associated Banks of Victoria, had been formed in 1877, but rates agreements frequently broke down. After the crisis of the early 1890s, however, competitive instincts waned, and industry agreements on rates and charges were easier to enforce than previously. The Australian banking system began its evolution into a closely knit oligopoly, with only one new domestic entrant between 1888 and 1981. There was still extensive non-price competition, especially in the opening of branches, but diminishing price competition. Agreements between the banks on the exchange rates were usually firm, breaking down only occasionally—in 1897–8 and 1904–6—in the pre-war period. Australian deposit rates were, by this date, also uniform, but through price-matching rather than formal collusion.[135] Collusive agreements were at least as strong in New Zealand, where the Associated Banks of New Zealand was formed in 1891, and by the following decade a range of rates agreements was in force.[136]

The competitive advantages of British multinational banks remained substantial in the decades before 1914, and as a result most challenges were contained. In the Far East, Latin America, and the West Indies the British banks faced new competition from other European and Canadian multinational banks. In several Latin American countries more stable indigenous banks were able to compete more effectively for domestic business. The market share of the British overseas banks was more often eroded than sharply reduced by these new entrants to the industry, but a preference for collusive agreements suggested, perhaps, an ebbing of competitive vigour.

[134] Chartered Bank, Amritsar letter, 129, 23 Oct. 1913, in File on Branches/Agencies Special Advices 1909–28, Chartered History Files, SC.

[135] Butlin, *Australia and New Zealand Bank*, 234–5, 258–60, 339–40; Merrett, 'Paradise Lost?', 72; *idem*, 'The 1893 Bank Crashes: The Aftermath'; Baster, *The Imperial Banks*, 145–7; R. F. Holder, *Bank of New South Wales: A History*, ii (Sydney: Angus and Robertson, 1970), 519, 524–7.

[136] Hawke and Sheppard, 'The Evolution of New Zealand Trading Banks', 46–9.

### 3.7. *Conclusion*

The period covered by this chapter began with financial crises and ended with a world war. In between, the British multinational banks had expanded along with a booming world economy. The number of overseas branches operated by British banks had almost doubled, and stood well in excess of 1,000. Almost half of the banks active in 1890 had not survived until 1913, but there were only a handful of severe failures from which nothing was salvaged, and most of the exits were among the smaller banks. There had also been a number of new British entrants to multinational banking, whose character differed in some respects from the established model of 'free-standing' institutions.

The British overseas banks were conservative institutions with flexible business strategies. Aware of the risks of multinational banking, their managements accumulated inner reserves out of profits to ensure their ability to survive periodic crises. In most cases, their governance structures and corporate cultures were effective in controlling risks. The failures of the early 1890s demonstrated the consequences if these structures and cultures were sub-optimal. The strong organizational capability of most banks permitted even those operating beyond the English-speaking settler economies to undertake some domestic banking as well as trade finance and exchange banking. In Asia, the Exchange banks developed organizational forms to enable them to engage in a parallel stream of business activity with the indigenous economy alongside the business undertaken with expatriate firms. There was a question mark, however, over the advantages of a London headquarters for a multinational retail bank, as opposed to a trade bank.

The competitive position of British overseas banks had declined in some of the first territories to which they had gone in the 1830s. In Canada, a single British-owned bank remained in operation. In the West Indies, Canadian multinational banks had challenged the British position. In Australia, the rapid relative decline of the British banks which began at mid-century slowed, but they entered a period of stagnation, failing to capitalize on their survival during the great banking crisis of 1893. Elsewhere, in most of the East except Japan, in much of Latin America, in South Africa, and in the British colonial territories in West and East Africa, the British banks remained extremely influential and, apparently, well able to defend themselves from assaults by other multinational or local banks.

# CHAPTER 4

# Banks and Governments

## 4.1. Empire, Public Policy, and Competitive Advantage

The growth and strength of British multinational banking between 1890 and 1914 cannot be understood without reference to political and public policy factors, which were highly favourable to their operations. The size and power of the British Empire was perhaps the single most important country-specific source of competitive advantage for the banks. This was most obviously shown by the direction of British multinational banking investment, for while Britain had extensive trading and investment links with the rest of Europe and the United States, it was imperial ties which were the major influence on the overseas banks. In Australasia and South Africa they served British settlers. In the East they financed the movements of British trade to and from the centres of British power, the Indian Empire, Singapore, and Hong Kong. Latin America by the late nineteenth century was fully part of Britain's 'informal Empire'. In the two decades before 1914, as the Empire expanded in Southern, West, and East Africa, branches of the overseas banks followed.

In more general ways, the public policy environment was favourable to the British banks. There were few prudential regulations and no exchange controls in the world economy. Receptivity towards foreign banks was high in most areas of the world. Many functions which were later to be the preserve of governments or their central banks were still left to the private sector, providing profitable opportunities for commercial banks. The exchange rate and international reserves of a country such as Australia were still determined by the individual actions of banks, acting without government direction. It was a world where the well-managed British multinational banks were able to exploit their competitive advantages to the full.

## 4.2. Governments as Regulators

Compared with the situation after the Second World War, home and host country regulatory controls over multinational banks were very limited in the nineteenth century. The United Kingdom had a liberal regulatory regime. Britain was slow to develop formal regulatory controls over banks, a situation which continued for much of the twentieth century.[1] There were no formal banking ratios. By the late nineteenth century the Bank of England, which remained privately owned until 1946, was well advanced in its evolution as a non-commercial central bank, but its private shareholders expected a reasonable return on their investment, which provided a constraint on its ability to act in the 'public interest'. The bank never made a public pronouncement of its willingness to serve as a lender of last resort, and in the nineteenth century it did not always provide such support. In 1866 it refused to save Overend's discount house, whose insolvency was considered to have been recklessly incurred, while even the rescue of Barings depended on the assistance of the commercial banks in offering guarantees against loss.[2]

There was no hint in Britain of the United States legislation which made multinational banking by American banks virtually illegal. Nineteenth-century British governments had no interest if private individuals wanted to establish, or invest in, overseas banks. The world's most *laissez-faire* government believed the state must remain well clear of such business decisions. The protection of note-holders and government deposits was, however, another matter, and this had been the concern of the government regulators who drafted the Royal Charters under which the first generation of overseas banks had operated.

In the context of Victorian Britain, not even the regulators felt happy about the degree of government intervention in banking matters which the granting of Royal Charters necessitated. The system offended the principles of *laissez-faire* by containing a hint of special privileges granted to only a few favoured banks. The Treasury was eager to shed its responsibilities, which often included giving permission for increases in capital, for purchases of land, for opening branches in places not specified in charters and even for sanctioning the re-election of retired directors. As a result, the granting of new charters soon ceased after the Companies Act of 1862 allowed banks to obtain the privilege of limited liability with no special government controls. The problem remained of the banks which already had Royal Charters. The Treasury's solution by the early 1880s was a new 'model charter' which every chartered bank would be required to accept as its existing charter expired. This relieved the Treasury of many responsibilities, and shifted other regulatory controls to the colonial governments.[3]

---

[1] F. Capie, 'The Evolving Regulatory Framework in British Banking', in Martin Chick (ed.), *Governments, Industries and Markets* (Aldershot: Elgar, 1990); Geoffrey Jones, 'Competition and Competitiveness in British Banking, 1918–1971', in Geoffrey Jones and Maurice Kirby (eds.), *Competitiveness and the State* (Manchester: Manchester University Press, 1991).

[2] Michael Collins, *Money and Banking in the UK: A History* (London: Croom Helm, 1988), ch. 6.

[3] A. S. J. Baster, *The Imperial Banks* (London: King, 1929), 134–6; S. J. Butlin, *Australia and New Zealand Bank* (London: Longman, 1961), 269–74.

By enforcing prudence in the entrepreneurial age of British overseas banking, before effective company legislation was in place, the Royal Charter system had enhanced the competitive advantages of British multinational banking.

Over time a number of banks gave up their Royal Charters and incorporated under the Companies Acts. The Oriental Bank Corporation lost its charter following its failure in 1884. Three more banks lost their Royal Charters as a result of failure or reconstruction in the early 1890s.[4] However, in 1889 the Treasury was obliged to grant a new Royal Charter to meet the special circumstances of the Imperial Bank of Persia. The Imperial Bank's promoters had obtained a concession from the Iranian government to found a state bank with, among other privileges, the exclusive right of note issue, but the Companies Act excluded a bank with the right of note issue from the privileges of limited liability as regards its note issue. Iran was a sensitive region of Anglo-Russian diplomatic rivalry bordering on the Indian Empire, and the British Foreign Office made a special case to the Treasury that the British 'national interest' was at stake in having a British-controlled state bank. A Royal Charter was duly issued which, like previous charters, carried a number of restrictions. In particular, the bank was obliged to hold a certain amount of reserves against its note issue; its loans to the Iranian government were limited to one-third of paid-up capital; its banking business was confined to Iran; and it was precluded from engaging in non-banking activities, such as mining.[5]

In the remaining decades before the First World War, and thereafter, the banks which held Royal Charters settled down to a stable situation whereby if they wished to undertake something beyond the powers of their existing charter, they applied for, and generally received, a Supplementary Charter. Increases of capital, expansion into new geographical areas, and renewals or changes to note-issuing power were the usual causes of requests for such Supplementary Charters. Treasury permission for such changes was not automatic. When the Imperial Bank of Persia required a Supplementary Charter to write down its capital in 1894, for example, the Treasury insisted that the reserve liability of shareholders was retained for the full paid-up value of each share. Later, after the First World War, the bank's desire to open branches anywhere outside Iran was restricted by the Treasury to a few specified countries.[6] In the West Indies the Colonial Bank was unhappy about its charter obligation to encash notes at all its principal branches, but the Treasury and the Colonial Office refused to relieve the British bank of its obligations.[7]

---

[4] Baster, *The Imperial Banks*, 130-1.
[5] Geoffrey Jones, *Banking and Empire in Iran* (Cambridge: Cambridge University Press, 1986), 24-5.       [6] Ibid., 67-8, 245-6.
[7] Minute by GG, 27 Mar. 1911, Paper 9429, Co318/327, PRO. See above, Sect. 3.6.

Host country regulations were at their most extensive in sovereign countries beyond the British Empire. The low receptivity towards foreign banks in the United States has already been discussed as one reason for the low level of British multinational banking investment in that country. The demise of the Anglo-Californian banks was influenced by declining receptivity in that state. After the 1909 California Banking Act it was difficult for foreign banks to have 'branches' in the state, prompting local incorporation or at least the segregation of the Californian branches' business from that of the rest of the bank. After 1913, a newly established foreign bank was not permitted to receive deposits.[8]

Beyond the United States, British banks encountered a variety of host government restrictions or demands, but these could rarely be dignified with the term 'regulation' in the American sense of the word. The Ionian Bank was the British bank with the largest number of branches in continental Europe, and it faced a Greek government with strong views on the duties of foreign banks. Ionian had a Greek charter and was the only non-Greek bank among the three 'privileged' note-issuing banks in the late nineteenth century. For the Greek government, such 'privileges' implied corresponding obligations. The Ionian Bank was obliged to lend to agriculture, and also to assist the perennially chaotic state of Greece's finances. In 1885 the bank was obliged to make a loan to the government amounting to around £150,000, as a quid pro quo for making its note issue legal tender, and it also had little alternative to making additional loans.[9] By 1897, when the Greek government was formally declared bankrupt, the indebtedness of the state to the Ionian Bank amounted to nearly £170,000, a sum only partially recovered under the regime of the International Financial Commission established under the auspices of the Great Powers to regularize the liabilities of the Greek state.[10]

By the early 1900s the Ionian Bank lived under growing fear that its Greek charter would not be renewed in 1905. The rivalry of the National Bank of Greece, which had acquired the other Greek note-issuer in 1900, focused growing attention on the Ionian Bank's position. In early 1901 Ionian heard informally that its note-issuing privileges would not be renewed, and the National Bank offered to negotiate with it for the transfer to itself of the remaining portion of Ionian's business.[11] Within months the government was insisting on a variety of conditions, including that the

---

[8] Mira Wilkins, *The History of Foreign Investment in the United States to 1914* (Cambridge, Mass.: Harvard University Press, 1989), 461–2.

[9] Draft letter, F. Larkworthy to Sir Edward Grey, Apr. 1908, 1898 2½% Greek Government Gold Bonds File, Box 1, Ionian Archives, LSE.

[10] Ionian Bank to President, International Financial Commission, 1909 (draft) in 1898 2½% Greek Government Gold Bonds File, Box 1, Ionian Archives.

[11] F. Larkworthy's Annual Report, 6 May 1902; Petition of Bank to Prime Minister Theotokis, 28 Mar. 1901, Charter/Extensions: 1905 Renewal File, Box 3, Ionian Archives.

bank become a Greek-registered company with its headquarters and board resident in Athens, and shareholders' meetings held in Greece.[12]

This was the kind of host government pressure against a foreign bank which was to become widespread and irresistible as the twentieth century progressed, but at this stage Ionian Bank was still able to reach a compromise solution. It appealed to the British Foreign Office for assistance, and the British Minister in Athens made a series of informal representations to the Greek government on Ionian's behalf.[13] The bank also tried to demonstrate its commitment to Greece in a number of ways, such as opening new branches and reducing the rate of interest on certain loans.[14] Finally, in 1903, the government agreed to renew Ionian's right of issue for a further period of fifteen years from 1905, provided the bank would surrender any legal claim it had for renewal thereafter. The Ionian Bank was also permitted to sell its privileges to the National Bank of Greece if satisfactory terms could be reached.[15] Subsequently, the proposed sale of the note-issuing privileges of the Ionian was defeated at a shareholders' meeting—mainly by proxy votes from the bank's Greek shareholders, who, at this time, held a majority of shares in the bank.[16] Ionian thus remained a bank of issue in Greece for another fifteen years, before losing its privilege to the National Bank in 1920—without compensation.

The British banks in Latin America also on occasion came under pressure from those seeking to restrict the activities of foreign banks. In Argentina, this pressure was at its height between the mid-1880s and the mid-1890s, when there was a drive to develop the Banco Nacional as a quasi-state or development bank, and to subject the British banks to taxation. This strategy, however, was gravely weakened by the collapse of the Banco Nacional along with other local banks in 1890. Its successor, the Banco de la Nación, was a powerful rival to the British banks, but it operated as a normal commercial bank following British-style banking orthodoxy. After 1895 the British banks in Argentina had little trouble from economic nationalism.[17] Elsewhere in Latin America, resentment of British banks did not translate into regulatory action before the First World War, although the British bank in Uruguay was obliged to give up its note issue in 1904.

[12] Court Minute, 31 Oct. 1901, Vol. 13, Ionian Archives.
[13] F. Larkworthy to T. Sanderson, 30 Jan. 1902: T. Sanderson to Ionian Bank, 20 Feb. 1902; Charter/Extensions: 1905 Renewal File, Box 3, Ionian Archives; F. Larkworthy's Report to AGM, 15 May 1903.
[14] Special Court Minute, 18 July 1902, Vol. 13, Ionian Archives.
[15] F. Larkworthy's Report to AGM, 15 May 1903, Ionian Archives.
[16] Proceedings of Extraordinary General Meeting, 18 Dec. 1903, Ionian Archives. There were 131 shareholders on the London Register, with 544 votes, and 266 shareholders on the Corfu Register, with 7,179 votes. The vote on the sale was 2,853 for and 6,817 against (all of which were proxies).
[17] Charles Jones, 'British Financial Institutions in Argentine, 1860–1914', Ph.D. thesis, Cambridge University, 1983, chs. 6 and 7.

In the East, the British banks operated in several sovereign nations, but it was a qualified sovereignty which restricted any regulatory controls they may have wished to exercise over foreign banks. In China, foreign banks operated under the privilege of extraterritoriality, subject to the jurisdiction of consular courts, supported by a British supreme court for China located in the Shanghai International Settlement. In Thailand, the banks also operated under conditions of extraterritoriality. However, the government was anxious to maintain economic sovereignty, and in 1902 the British banks were obliged to surrender their note-issuing privileges in favour of an exclusive government issue.[18]

Within the British Empire, the Colonial Banking Regulations continued to provide the basic regulatory framework through to the First World War. There was little else in the way of regulation, and no central bank existed in the Empire except the Bank of England. In Australia, however, there was a first hint of later developments. In 1910 the Commonwealth government introduced a Treasury-controlled note issue, while private banknotes issued or reissued were to incur a tax of 10 per cent—more than enough to secure their withdrawal. By 1914 the note issues of all trading banks in Australia were almost extinct. Soon after the legislation of the note issue came the foundation of the state-owned Commonwealth Bank of Australia. Some of the supporters of the Commonwealth Bank proposal hoped it would act as a central bank and greatly curb the role of the commercial banks, but what emerged was a conventional commercial bank which took over the Federal government business from the private banks. It was only after the First World War, and then rather hesitantly, that the Commonwealth's role as a central bank and regulator expanded.[19] In neighbouring New Zealand, the banks continued to issue their own notes until the 1930s and, though the government had a shareholding in the Bank of New Zealand, there was no central bank or government banking regulation until 1934.[20] In South Africa, the commercial banks operated without regulatory supervision until 1920, when the South African Reserve Bank was created with the sole right of note issue, and commercial banks were made subject to reserve requirements.[21]

In the decades before the First World War, therefore, regulatory

[18] F. H. H. King, The History of the Hongkong and Shanghai Banking Corporation, ii, (Cambridge: Cambridge University Press, 1988), 129; T. Pramuanratkarn, 'The Hong Kong Bank in Thailand: A Case of a Pioneering Bank', in F. H. H. King (ed.), Eastern Banking (London: Athlone Press, 1983).

[19] J. S. G. Wilson, 'The Commonwealth Bank of Australia', in R. S. Sayers (ed.), Banking in the British Commonwealth (Oxford: Clarendon Press, 1952); Butlin, Australia and New Zealand Bank, 340–54.

[20] G. R. Hawke, Between Governments and Banks: A History of the Reserve Bank of New Zealand (Wellington: Shearer, 1973), ch. 2.

[21] A. Day, 'The South African Reserve Bank', in Sayers (ed.), Banking in the British Commonwealth.

restrictions on the British overseas banks were very limited. Within Britain, the banks which continued to operate with a Royal Charter had some kind of Treasury regulation, but much less than in the early nineteenth century. Abroad, the extensive regulation in the United States was one factor which discouraged British multinational banking in that country. Occasionally, as in Greece, the activities and privileges of foreign banks came under active attack, and in countries as diverse as Uruguay, Australia, and Thailand the note-issuing privileges of British banks were curtailed by local governments. For the most part, however, the banks remained extraordinarily unrestrained in their banking operations.

## 4.3. Banking for Governments

The absence of banking regulations and of central banks before 1914 not only left the British multinational banks free to pursue their chosen business strategies. It also meant that the banks themselves performed some of the functions later acquired by central banks, including the management of government funds, and various currency matters. There were substantial profits to be made in some of these activities, although they also brought responsibilities which were not always welcome.

It was in part to take advantage of such opportunities, and in part to serve wider goals of promoting British influence, that a new type of British overseas bank emerged in the two decades before the First World War. The two most important of these 'state banks' were the National Bank of Egypt and the National Bank of Turkey. They were both linked in a family of such enterprises promoted by the same figure—Sir Ernest Cassel, a German and Jewish banker who had emigrated to Britain in 1869 at the age of 17 and subsequently made a fortune as an international financier.

The National Bank of Egypt was founded in 1898 to serve as a government bank in Egypt with the sole right of note issue. Its creation was one of a series of measures adopted by the British administration in the 1890s to promote economic development in Egypt. Cassel had become involved with Egyptian affairs, especially the finance of the infrastructure investments desired by the British administration, and the proposal to establish the National Bank of Egypt was another such project, which appealed to British officials because it would both facilitate the finance of other developments and cement Egypt's economic relationship with Britain.[22]

The National Bank was formed as an Egyptian company, with half of its

---

[22] P. Thane, 'Sir Ernest Joseph Cassel', in D. J. Jeremy (ed.), *Dictionary of Business Biography*, i (London: Butterworths, 1984), 607–8; id., 'Financiers and the British State: The Case of Sir Ernest Cassel', in R. P. T. Davenport-Hines (ed.), *Speculators and Patriots: Essays in Business Biography* (London: Cass, 1986).

capital of £1 million subscribed by Cassel and the rest by two merchants resident in Egypt. The board resided in Cairo, as did the bank's governor —a Britisher—but there was an important London committee. The bank issued notes, served as the main banker to the government, and floated foreign loans for the government. It also developed a commercial banking business. By 1914 nearly twenty branches had been opened in Egypt, plus a London office, and the bank had also diversified into neighbouring Sudan (ruled jointly by Britain and Egypt), where it had opened a further five branches. The National Bank also developed a limited lender-of-last-resort status, taking responsibility, for example, for the liquidation of Bank of Egypt, when it suspended payment in 1911. None of this served to convince Egyptian nationalists that the National Bank was anything but a 'foreign' bank. By the eve of the First World War nationalist writers were dreaming of the establishment of an Egyptian-owned 'national bank', dreams which were to culminate in the foundation of Bank Misr in 1920.[23]

The National Bank of Egypt and Cassel were involved in the creation of two affiliates, both of which had substantial National Bank shareholdings and interlocking directorships. The Agricultural Bank of Egypt was formed in 1902 to lend to small cultivators. It boomed in the ten years following its foundation, but a change in the law in 1911 which made small landholdings immune from seizure for debts meant that the small landowners were unable to provide adequate security for loans. The bank's business evaporated and it went into liquidation in the inter-war years.[24] The National Bank of Egypt was also intimately connected with the Bank of Abyssinia, formed as an Egyptian company in 1905, with a fifty-year concession to act as a 'state bank' from the Emperor of the last independently ruled 'native' kingdom in Africa.[25] The venture was never successful. Local resentment was caused by the location of the bank's headquarters in Cairo even though the concession stated this should be in Addis Ababa, and it became involved in a prolonged but unproductive tussle between British and French diplomatic and financial interests seeking railway concessions in the country.[26] Commercial banking was also slow to get going, in a country where banking had been previously unknown; it was

---

[23] *National Bank of Egypt, 1898–1948* (Cairo: National Bank of Egypt, 1948), ch. 3: Eric Davis, *Challenging Colonialism: Bank Misr and Egyptian Industrialisation, 1920–1941* (Princeton, NJ: Princeton University Press, 1983), 69–76; Robert L. Tignor, *State, Private Enterprise, and Economic Change in Egypt, 1918–1952* (Princeton, NJ: Princeton University Press, 1984), 62–7.  [24] *National Bank of Egypt*, 24–7.
[25] Sir John Harrington to Lord Cromer, 29 Nov. 1906, Fo371/3; Memorandum by G. Clerk, 26 Apr. 1909, in Sir Edward Grey to Sir Eldon Gorst, 7 May 1909, Fo371/594, PRO.
[26] Memorandum re Abyssinian Railway, enclosed in Lord Chesterfield to Sir Edward Grey, 3 Aug. 1906, Fo371/3; Memo by Sir John Harrington on Abyssinian Railway, 19 July 1907, Fo371/191, PRO.

1909 before the Bank of Abyssinia was able to record a profit, and by 1914 the bank was again in a major crisis.[27]

The problems faced by the Bank of Abyssinia and the Agricultural Bank of Egypt did not deter various other attempts at creating 'state' banks, several of which involved Sir Ernest Cassel. In 1906, for instance, he financed the establishment of a State Bank of Morocco on the lines of the National Bank of Egypt, but the dominant influence of France seems to have worked against the success of this venture.[28]

Equally unsuccessful was Cassel's more ambitious scheme in Turkey, where he had had investment interests since the 1880s. The idea of the National Bank of Turkey, which was launched in 1909, originated with the Young Turk government, which had overthrown its corrupt and feeble predecessors in the previous year and which was anxious to modernize the country. Cassel had arranged a £1.5 million loan for the new government, and he was its choice to organize a national bank which—the Young Turks hoped—could help develop the country. The Young Turks were anxious also to have a British counterweight to the strong German and French economic and financial influence in their country. While Britain was in fact a shareholder in the Imperial Ottoman Bank, which served as the state bank of the Ottoman Empire, French influence predominated in that bank and the British Foreign Office was discreetly enthusiastic about a more exclusively British institution, provided it could operate without offending Britain's diplomatic ally France.

The new National Bank of Turkey was modelled on the National Bank of Egypt. It had a subscribed capital of £1 million, of which £250,000 was paid up. The head office was in Constantinople, but six of the directors were to sit in London as a Special Committee and the board was to take the advice of this committee on such issues as loans and advances over £100,000. There was also to be a Consultative Committee consisting entirely of Ottoman subjects, but the whole tone of the bank was British. Cassel's choice for governor was Sir Henry Babington-Smith, a leading civil servant in the British Post Office and an ex-administrator of the Ottoman Debt. As in the case of the National Bank of Egypt, Cassel did not join the board, but he was in almost daily touch with Babington-Smith.[29]

---

[27] BA (Bank of Abyssinia) Balance Sheet for 1908, enclosed in Gorst to Grey, 14 June 1909, F0371/597; BA Balance Sheet for 1909, enclosed in Gorst to Grey, 4 June 1910, F0371/823; BA Annual Report for 1910, enclosed in W. G. Thesiger to Grey, 10 Feb. 1911, F0371/1043, PRO; *National Bank of Egypt*, 27–9.

[28] Thane, 'Sir Ernest Joseph Cassel', 608.

[29] Ibid., 610; A. S. J. Baster, *The International Banks* (London: King, 1935), 78–112, Marion Kent; 'Agent of Empire? The National Bank of Turkey and British Foreign Policy', *Historical Journal*, 18 (1975). For the Imperial Ottoman Bank, see Christopher Clay, 'The Imperial Ottoman Bank in the Later Nineteenth Century: A Multinational "National" Bank?', in Geoffrey Jones (ed.), *Banks as Multinationals* (London: Routledge, 1990).

The National Bank of Turkey did not make great progress against the banking and diplomatic realities of pre-war Turkey. There was never any prospect of the bank developing a serious commercial banking business, especially as British business interests in Turkey were negligible. It never stood a chance of dislodging the Imperial Ottoman Bank as the government's banker with the sole right of note issue. Its prospects of securing a substantial share of the business of infrastructure investment thus rested on being enthusiastically supported by the Foreign Office, but such enthusiasm never materialized. The British government's support for the National Bank always took second place to the imperatives of good Anglo-French relations. As a result, it was not given the same level of overt assistance the French gave the Imperial Ottoman Bank, and the Germans gave the Deutsche Bank, in Turkey. This was particularly vividly shown when the National Bank became involved in a consortium to develop an oil concession in alliance with the Shell oil company and the Deutsche Bank, neither of which the Foreign Office liked.[30] In the middle of 1913, after numerous difficulties, being frozen out of various business initiatives, and after abortive attempts to merge with the Imperial Ottoman Bank and subsequently the French-owned Banque de Salonique, the National Bank of Turkey resolved to withdraw from Turkey.[31] The Foreign Office persuaded the National Bank to stay in business, but in the early months of 1914 negotiations were under way to extend the shareholding to France and Russia. The negotiations were almost complete when they were overwhelmed by the outbreak of the First World War.[32]

In some countries, British multinational banks—rather than these quasi-political creations—performed certain state or central banking functions before 1914. In Iran, the Imperial Bank of Persia was the state bank with the sole right of note issue and it served as the government's banker, revenue collector, and paymaster, and even reformed the coinage system.[33] In some senses, the Hongkong Bank, as the leading foreign bank in China, performed a similar role in China. It was predominant in issuing Chinese government loans on the European capital markets, but also performed certain central banking-type responsibilities. In 1909 in Hankow, and in 1910 in Shanghai, for example, there were serious crises in the local money markets, and the Hongkong Bank was involved in rescue operations.[34]

[30] The immensely complicated story of the Mesopotamian oil concessions is given in Kent, 'Agent of Empire?', and id., *Oil and Empire: British Policy and Mesopotamian Oil, 1900–1920* (London: Macmillan, 1976), 33–94. See also Fritz Seidenzahl, *100 Jahre Deutsche Bank, 1870–1970* (Frankfurt am Main: Deutsche Bank, 1970), 224–7. For the Deutsche Bank's oil interests, see Hans Pohl, 'The Steaua Romana and the Deutsche Bank 1903–1920', *Studies on Economic and Monetary Problems and on Banking History*, Deutsche Bank, No. 24, 1989.
[31] Sir Henry Babington-Smith to Sir Edward Grey, 11 June 1913, Fo371/1826, PRO.
[32] Sir Edward Grey to L. Mallet, 23 Feb. 1914, Fo371/2127, PRO.
[33] Geoffrey Jones, *Banking and Empire in Iran*, esp. 78–86, 114–27.
[34] King, *The History of the Hongkong and Shanghai Banking Corporation*, ii. 456–60.

British overseas banks undertook a range of government business in the Empire, though their roles varied considerably between countries. In British India, the Presidency banks served as government banker. In Canada and Australia, the British banks occupied no special position *vis à vis* local banks, and the colonial governments never restricted their business to British institutions. Government business was awarded on a competitive basis, with—in Australia—a marked preference by colonial governments for local institutions.[35] In New Zealand, the Bank of New Zealand served as government banker. The existence of a government shareholding and representation at board level after 1895 ended the hopes of other banks that they might secure government business. In contrast, Standard Bank of South Africa was firmly established by the 1890s as the sole banker to both the Imperial government and that of Cape Colony.[36]

British overseas banks usually held the government accounts in the non-settler colonies, apart from British India. In the case of Hong Kong, the colonial government's current account was transferred from the Oriental Bank to the Hongkong Bank in 1872, and relations between this bank and the colonial government grew very close in the following decades. In the late 1880s and early 1890s, however, there was a dispute between the Hong Kong government, the Colonial Office, and the British Treasury about the permissible level of government balances held by the bank, with the Treasury working first to limit the total and then to share the excess between the four British chartered banks, despite the colonial government's wish for no limit and to retain the Hongkong Bank as its sole banker. Soon after this decision was taken, one of the other banks—the New Oriental Bank Corporation—failed and another—the Chartered Mercantile—was reconstructed as a non-chartered bank. Thus government accounts were in effect split between the Hongkong Bank and Chartered Bank, with the former having the lion's share.[37]

In the Straits Settlements and Malaya, government business was spread between the banks, sometimes being used as an inducement to encourage the opening of new branches. Chartered was the first bank to open branches in the interior of Malaya, and its branches in Taiping and Kuala Lumpur held the government accounts.[38] When the government of the Federated Malay States wanted Hongkong Bank to open a branch in Kuala Lumpur before 1914, it offered to share government business between it and the

[35] Butlin, *Australia and New Zealand Bank*, 191, 205–6, 253–4.

[36] J. A. Henry, *The First Hundred Years of the Standard Bank* (London: Oxford University Press, 1963), 144; GMO, 7 Feb. 1894 and GMO, 13 Feb. 1895, in Alan Mabin and Barbara Conradie (eds.), *The Confidence of the Whole Country* (Johannesburg: Standard Bank Investment Corporation, 1987), 351 and 370.

[37] King, *The History of the Hongkong and Shanghai Banking Corporation*, i. 160–1, 445–6.

[38] Compton Mackenzie, *Realms of Silver* (London: Routledge & Kegan Paul, 1954), 215–16.

Chartered Bank.[39] In 1910 Hongkong Bank was also appointed sole banker to the Johore State Government after opening the first bank in that state.[40]

In West Africa, the Bank of British West Africa (BBWA) took over the account of the government of Lagos when it acquired the business of the African Banking Corporation in 1894. As BBWA's branch network spread through West Africa, it acquired the accounts of the respective colonial governments—of Gold Coast in 1896, Sierra Leone in 1898, and Old Calabar (Southern Nigeria) and Bathhurst (The Gambia) in 1902.[41]

A very important part of this bank's business was its role as currency agent for these colonial governments. The promotion of a stable currency, on which an efficient system of credit could be based, had been a major motive behind Alfred Jones's entry into West African banking. British silver coins had become the principal currency of the region during the nineteenth century. These were supplied on demand by the Royal Mint in London. There had to be a constant flow of new coins because Africans not only valued them more highly than worn ones but also tended to hoard them. When the African Banking Corporation opened in Lagos in 1891, agreement was reached whereby it was given the right to import silver coins from the Royal Mint free of charges for packing, freight, and insurance. The bank was allowed to make a maximum charge of 1 per cent commission on new silver coins paid out, and its duties included collecting and shipping back to Britain, at its own expense, redundant silver. BBWA took over this agreement, and signed similar agreements as its branches spread through West Africa.[42]

There seems little doubt that the silver-importing business was a profitable one for BBWA, and this perhaps explains why the bank's commercial banking strategy was noticeably conservative. BBWA had a monopoly, and it could impose banking charges as well as commission for paying out new silver. It also did not have to import every bag of coin, but could reissue a great deal of the silver returning from circulation.[43] By the early 1900s the amounts of specie being imported into West Africa were becoming substantial. In the four years 1901 to 1904, BBWA imported on average £200,250 worth of specie each year into Nigeria.[44] However, the physical work of distributing silver money in West Africa also expanded

[39] King, The History of the Hongkong and Shanghai Banking Corporation, ii. 35.

[40] Chee Peng Lim, Phang Siew Nooi, and Margaret Boh, 'The History and Development of the Hongkong and Shanghai Banking Corporation in Peninsular Malaysia', in King (ed.), Eastern Banking, 365.

[41] Richard Fry, Bankers in West Africa (London: Hutchinson Benham, 1976), 20, 23–8.

[42] Ibid., 7–10, 19–21, 23–6. For an insight into the process whereby the British silver coins replaced indigenous currency systems, see Walter I. Ofonagoro, 'From Traditional to British Currency in Southern Nigeria: Analysis of a Currency Revolution, 1880–1948', Journal of Economic History, 39 (1979).  [43] Fry, Bankers in West Africa, 28–9.

[44] Cited in Fry's Digests of Board Minutes, 1904–1909, BBWA Archives, SC.

exponentially. The trading firms in the region needed large amounts of cash to pay for produce, with demand fluctuating violently between seasons. Forecasting how much coin would be required at a particular place, and physically getting it to outlying towns, were considerable problems.

BBWA's role as currency agent and government banker was never without its tensions. The bank felt aggrieved when colonial administrators tried on occasion to lessen their dependence on it by using alternative means of funding themselves. Conversely, BBWA's commission charges were regularly criticized. Some traders complained about the fact that the bank's monopoly favoured the Elder Dempster group. A number of colonial governments also felt unhappy about the whole system. The Royal Mint, as well as BBWA, made considerable profits from the difference between the exchange value of the silver coins and their intrinsic value, and it was not long before colonial governors began to press for a share of these profits.[45]

Difficulties regarding BBWA's monopoly over the importing of silver were most apparent in Southern Nigeria, the only territory on the British West African coast where, after the establishment of the Bank of Nigeria in 1899, there was a competitive situation. The Bank of Nigeria sought an equal share of government business and by 1907, after a period of rapid branch expansion by that bank which extended its operations far beyond Lagos, the colonial governor had become convinced that BBWA's monopoly agreement should be ended, both for the government's banking business and for silver importation, and that both banks should be dealt with on a competitive basis.[46] Many merchants active in West Africa also criticized the BBWA monopoly, but discussions about alternative procedures were repeatedly delayed. It was not until 1909 that a conference at the Colonial Office in London decided to cancel BBWA's silver import monopoly. In future, it was resolved, the supply of silver coin to West Africa would be controlled by the Royal Mint, which would give equal treatment to all recognized banks. The government banking business in Southern Nigeria was also to be divided between the two banks. The Bank of Nigeria seemed, finally, to have won its case and secured its own future, but at the last moment the Colonial Secretary—for unexplained reasons—decided to maintain the status quo, leaving BBWA's silver monopoly intact.[47]

It was only in 1911, after the appointment of a new Colonial Secretary, that a final decision was taken to end the formal agreements with the

[45] Fry, *Bankers in West Africa*, 35–6, 38–9.

[46] Sir Walter Egerton to Lord Elgin, 26 Nov. 1907, CO520/50, PRO; Fry, *Bankers in West Africa*, 42–4.

[47] Fry, *Bankers in West Africa*, 45, 49–51; Memorandum on Conference at the Colonial Office, 20 May 1909, CO520/86; Sir W. Egerton to Lord Crewe, 7 Mar. 1910, and minutes by J.A., 12 May 1910, on this letter, CO520/92, PRO.

colonial governments on which BBWA's silver monopoly was based and, secondly, to appoint a committee, under Lord Emmott, to inquire into the whole question of the currency of the West African territories. The report of this committee led to the establishment in 1912 of a West African Currency Board, charged with issuing new currency notes and coins for the West African colonies, and redeeming the old British silver coins.

The idea of a currency board was adopted in British East Africa after the First World War, and in other British colonies subsequently. As a monetary system, it facilitated monetization of the economy and created a stable currency, which helped trade. On the other hand, it was far from being a central bank with an independent monetary policy or regulatory powers. The West African and other boards were based in London, and their members were chosen by the Colonial Office and the British Treasury. The main function of the boards was to arrange the exchange of local pounds into British ones, to which they were linked at par.[48]

Regardless of the economic merits of the currency board system, however, it did not spell the end of BBWA's role in currency matters. The bank's chief manager was one of the seven members of the Emmott Committee, and he was also appointed to the Currency Board. The finance of the minting of coin and other initial expenditure of the board was arranged by a London clearing bank, but the operation of the new currency system in West Africa was given to BBWA, which had acquired its sole competitor, the Bank of Nigeria, in 1912. The bank undertook the delivery of the new currency and the redemption of the old one. Payment was initially on the basis of a commission as a percentage of turnover.[49]

The note issues of the British overseas banks, whose nineteenth-century evolution was discussed earlier, can also be considered in the context of their quasi-state bank activities. Table 4.1 shows the size and geographical distribution of their note issues in 1913. (See Table 2.1 for the situation in 1890.)

Between 1890 and 1913 the East—in effect the British colonies of Hong Kong and Singapore—had increased its share of the total British-controlled note issue to 43 per cent, while the Imperial Bank of Persia had also built up a substantial note issue in Iran. Conversely, the British-controlled note issue in South America had all but vanished, while Australasia's share of the total issue had fallen sharply, with almost all of the residual in New Zealand.

The main influence on this changing geographical distribution of notes was the decision by certain governments to take over note issues themselves, or concentrate them in indigenous hands. It was striking that even

[48] J. K. Onoh, *Money and Banking in Africa* (London: Longman, 1982), 36–7.
[49] Fry, *Bankers in West Africa*, 75–8.

TABLE 4.1. *Note issues of British multinational banks by region, 1913*

| Region | Notes issued (£ sterling) | No. of banks |
|---|---|---|
| The East | 3,313,169 | 3 |
| Southern Africa | 1,359,431 | 2 |
| Canada | 1,001,981 | 1 |
| Iran | 962,419 | 1 |
| Australia and New Zealand | 659,841 | 5 |
| West Indies | 373,093 | 1 |
| Greece | 290,878 | 1 |
| South America | 10,126 | 1 |
| TOTAL | 7,970,938 | 15 |

the dependent colonies of the British Empire became dissatisfied with private note issues as the century progressed. Moves to replace such issues by government ones got under way in various colonies in the late nineteenth century, encouraged by the dispute over the Hongkong Bank's issue of small-denomination notes in Hong Kong, and the consequences of the Governor of Ceylon's guarantee of the Oriental Bank note issue in Ceylon in 1884.[50] By 1890 the idea of a state note issue for all Crown Colonies had become an agreed Imperial policy, but implementing the policy was a slow process. The Straits Settlement government was an enthusiastic supporter of a state note issue. In 1892 the failure of the Chartered Mercantile Bank left only two banks of issue in Singapore—Hongkong Bank and Chartered Bank—and during the Chinese New Year in 1893 the colony ran short of money. After further delay, and tension between the administration and the banks, the Straits Currency Note Act was passed in 1899, which established a government note issue. Over the next fifteen years the government note issue slowly superseded that of the two banks.[51]

The profitability to banks of note issues continued to depend upon particular circumstances, and thus the loss of note-issuing privileges did not always represent a great financial blow to the British banks. In Iran, the Imperial Bank regarded the note issue as a profitable as well as prestigious activity, even though it made the bank more vulnerable to runs organized by its opponents. However, any profitability disappeared when the size of

[50] See above, Sect. 2.2.

[51] W. Evan Nelson, 'The Hongkong and Shanghai Banking Corporation Factor in the Progress towards a Straits Settlements Government Note Issue, 1881–1889', in King (ed.), *Eastern Banking*; King, *The History of the Hongkong and Shanghai Banking Corporation*, i. 484–7; ii. 226–9; Mackenzie, *Realms of Silver*, 190–1; Y. C. Jao and F. H. H. King, *Money in Hong Kong* (Hong Kong: Centre of Asian Studies, University of Hong Kong, 1990), 16 ff.

the issue exceeded a certain level, for the Imperial Bank's Royal Charter specified it had to hold a 100 per cent cash reserve against such 'excess' issue. The bank was naturally unwilling to expand its issue beyond that point. When, in 1930, the Imperial Bank was obliged to surrender its note-issuing privileges to the Iranian government, it received £200,000 in compensation, a valuation which the bank considered a considerable underestimate.[52]

In Cape Colony, the British banks found the profitability of their note issue affected by the Cape Bank Act of 1891. Prior to that date, the note-issuing power of banks had been restricted by their charters to the amount of their capital, and they had also been obliged to pay an annual note duty of $1\frac{1}{2}$ per cent to the government. The new Act provided for the issue of notes to be covered by a deposit of Cape government securities to the full extent of the issue. This made the profitability of the note issue dependent in part on the prices at which the government stock could be bought, and on the rate of interest receivable on it. The Act also specified that banknotes would be legal tender throughout the colony, which meant that notes could be issued at Cape Town and accepted everywhere else, rather than at individual branches. Banknotes were to be supplied by the government, and the duty reduced to 1 per cent, levied on their average circulation.[53] Standard Bank decided to continue to issue notes under the new regime. The bank's internal correspondence makes it clear that the benefits of the issue were held to exist in wider terms than simple accounting profits, and included publicity gains, which gave it some competitive advantage over smaller banks. However, the profitability of the note issue appears to have been much reduced by the requirement to retain the considerable investment in government stock as cover against the notes.[54]

In Australia, colonial government legislation appears to have rendered the private note issue unprofitable by the 1890s, and this explains why there was so little opposition to the introduction of the Commonwealth note issue. The general manager of the Union Bank of Australia told a government commission in 1895 that he did not think that there was 'any' profit in the bank's issue once the 'initial cost of the notes', note tax, and the reserve kept in coins were taken into account, not to mention 'clerical labour in handling, signing, narrating, writing off register, and distribution books, etc., besides postage and sending the notes about the country'.[55]

British multinational banks in the two decades before the First World War had continued to perform a range of activities which in later periods

---

[52] Geoffrey Jones, *Banking and Empire in Iran*, 80, 126, 223–4.

[53] Henry, *The First Hundred Years of the Standard Bank*, 112–13.

[54] GMO, 2 Feb. 1893, in Mabin and Conradie (eds.), *The Confidence of the Whole Country*, 324–5; Henry, *The First Hundred Years of the Standard Bank*, 153–4.

[55] Butlin, *Australia and New Zealand Bank*, 324.

would be taken over by the public sector. In the Middle East region, the Imperial Bank of Persia served as state bank of Iran, while Ernest Cassel promoted a series of state banks for Egypt, Turkey, and even Abyssinia. Such schemes were closely tied to the diplomatic rivalries of the period, and British imperial power. Elsewhere, British banks held government accounts, issued notes, and sometimes—notably in West Africa—played seminal roles in the entire currency system. These functions were not always as profitable as they might have seemed, but they often enhanced the reputations of the banks. The moves against private note issues and the creation of colonial currency boards suggested, however, that the quasi-state activities of the British banks were likely to be of a finite duration.

### 4.4. Loan Issues

By the late nineteenth century London was the world's leading international financial centre and Britain was the world's largest capital-exporting economy. A considerable proportion of this foreign outflow took the form of loans to colonial and foreign governments, or to their state-owned railways. For the most part, however, the arranging and issuing of such loans was undertaken by institutions other than the overseas banks.

In the first half of the nineteenth century, the merchant banks dominated the issue of foreign government and railway loans. The market leaders were the Rothschilds, followed by Barings, who from the mid-nineteenth century became extremely active in railway issues, especially those of North America. The second half of the century saw the advent of serious competitors to these banks, such as Hambros and, especially, the Anglo-American house of Morgan, which became very active in European and South American stock in particular. Successful participation in this business required, not a large capital, but the more intangible assets of reputation and connection, and it was in these areas that the leading merchant banks held their crucial advantage.[56]

Over time the loan issue process grew in complexity. Initially a single house preferred to issue a loan, but by the 1870s and 1880s loans were increasingly handled by syndicates of banks, though the leading merchant banks preferred to undertake issues alone if possible, at least until the Baring Crisis. In the 1900s syndicates were given a further boost by the British Foreign Office policy towards loans of a political nature. Closely related to the growth of syndicates in loan issues was the spread in the practice of underwriting, which seems to have been used by most of the merchant banks by the 1900s, and was in use for several decades beforehand.

[56] Stanley Chapman, *The Rise of Merchant Banking* (London: Allen and Unwin, 1984), chs. 1–3, 6; Vincent P. Carosso, *The Morgans: Private International Bankers, 1854–1913* (Cambridge, Mass.: Harvard University Press, 1987), chs. 6, 11, 14, 16.

Underwriting was one of the roles of many syndicates, whose members agreed to take a certain proportion of a loan in return for a commission when the public did not fully subscribe to it. Syndicates and underwriting groups were to a certain extent fluctuating and fragile relationships, but it seems that, despite this, there were alliances of a more permanent nature between particular merchant banks, stockbrokers, other City institutions, and particular individuals.[57]

There is no reason to dispute the conventional view that the merchant banks were the leading institutions in foreign government and railway issues prior to the First World War, yet over time competitors appeared. During the 1830s Glyn, Mills became involved in loans for the Canadian provinces, and the bank maintained an interest in colonial and foreign loans over the next eighty years.[58] Glyn's was an unusual bank, and a pioneer, but it was not alone among domestic banks in its interest in foreign loans. By the late nineteenth century the London and Westminster Bank was very active in loan issues on behalf of the Australian and South African colonies. Parr's Bank, originally a small country institution which became a London clearing bank in 1891, also developed an extensive loan business, issuing or playing a major underwriting role in Canadian, Brazilian, Chinese, and Serbian loans over the following decade, and becoming closely involved with the spate of Japanese government loan issues in London between 1899 and 1913. By the eve of the First World War even the Midland Bank, which had doggedly stayed out of foreign loans, had revised its strategy, and in 1909 issued a Russian railway loan, guaranteed by the Russian government.[59]

The British overseas banks rarely participated in foreign loan issues. In the 1870s there were a number of small issues by the Oriental Bank (Chile and Japan in 1873, Chile in 1875), Ionian (Greece in 1879) and Hongkong Bank (China in 1875), and in 1884 the Standard Bank raised a small loan for the Orange Free State. From the 1890s United States and continental European borrowing in the London market slackened, to be replaced by Latin American, Far Eastern, and colonial issues. These were regions where the British multinational banks operated branch networks, and it could have been anticipated that they would have become involved in capital as well as trade flows. Yet this was not the case. None of the Australian, Canadian, or South African loans after 1890 were issued by British overseas

---

[57] Chapman, *The Rise of Merchant Banking*, 88–9, 155–61; Carosso, *The Morgans*, 205–6; D. C. M. Platt, *Britain's Investment Overseas on the Eve of the First World War* (London: Macmillan, 1986), 141–5.

[58] Roger Fulford, *Glyn's, 1753–1953* (London: Macmillan, 1953), ch. 8, 160–1.

[59] A. R. Holmes and Edwin Green, *Midland: 150 Years of Banking Business* (London: Batsford, 1986), 135–6.

banks. They had only a marginally larger role in South American loans. Between 1890 and 1914 only four Latin American government loan issues were handled by the British overseas banks. London and River Plate Bank issued a £1.4 million Argentinian loan in 1892 and a £2.8 million one in 1903. London Bank of Mexico and South America issued a £1 million El Salvador loan in 1908, and Anglo-South American a Nicaraguan loan for £500,000 in 1909. In addition, several British banks in Latin America undertook smaller-scale loan issues than central government ones, including Treasury bill issues and provincial and municipal government loan issues. In Brazil, for example, the London and Brazilian Bank undertook the Para government loan issue in 1904, and three years later raised a £1 million loan for the São Paulo government. In 1905 and 1910 the bank also issued loans for the Bahia provincial government.

There were two exceptions to this overall modest picture. The minor exception was Iran, whose two issues on the London market (an 1892 loan for £500,000 and a 1911 loan for £1,250,000) were floated by the Imperial Bank of Persia.[60] The major exception was the Far East, and especially China and Japan. Between 1874 and 1895 the Hongkong Bank was responsible for the public issue of China loans with a nominal value of £12 million. After 1895, and following China's defeat by Japan and need to pay a large indemnity, China's borrowing requirements increased. Hongkong Bank played the predominant role in arranging this finance, having reached an agreement with the Deutsch-Asiatische Bank in early 1895 that all government loans would be split between the two. Between 1895 and 1914 the bank was involved in Chinese government issues worth at least £60 million.[61] Between 1897 and 1912 the Hongkong Bank also participated in the London issue of twenty-one Japanese loans, and between 1897 and 1930 the Hongkong Bank was involved in the issue of Japanese government and municipal loans with a total face value of £250 million. For these loans the Hongkong Bank always acted as a member of a syndicate, usually including Parr's Bank and the Yokohama Specie Bank. In addition, Hongkong Bank floated Thailand's first public loan, for £1 million in 1905, together with the Banque de l'Indochine, and in 1907 the Hongkong Bank was the lead bank in a £3 million loan designed for railway development, though subsequently the Thais, ever anxious to avoid

---

[60] Geoffrey Jones, *Banking and Empire in Iran*, 48–54, 120–3.

[61] King, *The History of the Hongkong and Shanghai Banking Corporation*, i. 535–62; ii, chs. 5, 6, 7, 8. King provides tables summarizing the main China loans by period between 1874 and 1895 in vol. i, pp. 548–9, and between 1895 and 1914 in vol. ii, pp. 312, 377, 451, 512. There is an in-depth study of China's first public loan, in 1874, in David J. S. King, 'China's First Public Loan: The Hongkong Bank and the Chinese Imperial Government "Foochow" Loan of 1874', in King (ed.), *Eastern Banking*.

dependence on either a single country or a single institution, turned to the London clearing bank National Provincial.[62]

Hongkong Bank's great British rival in the Far East, the Chartered Bank, played a less active role in loan issues. The bank issued a Chinese government loan for £1 million in 1895, usually referred to as the 'Cassel Loan' because Sir Ernest Cassel signed the loan contract in London for the British side. Chartered also took part with other banks in an 1897 Japanese loan for £4.4 million and in a £10 million Japanese loan in 1899. The 1899 loan was issued jointly by Chartered Bank, Hongkong Bank, Parr's Bank, and the Yokohama Specie Bank. Chartered was subsequently involved in further Japanese loan issues, in 1904 and 1905, but it was not until shortly before the First World War that the bank made a determined effort to become a serious participant in loan-issuing.[63]

The question arises why the role of the overseas banks in loan-issuing was largely limited to the Far East, and why in particular the Hongkong Bank stood out as such an exception. Part of the answer lies in the related qualities needed to succeed in loan-issuing—connections and reputation. Connections were needed both in the borrowing country, if the loan contract was to be secured, and in the City of London, if the issue was to be placed. Obviously the British multinational banks lacked connections in continental Europe and the United States, where they had few if any branches. In the colonies and Latin America they were better placed, but others had often established superior connections before them. In the case of Brazil, for example, the London Rothschilds were appointed sole financial agent of the government in 1855, and they virtually monopolized Brazilian foreign loan issues, at least until 1908, when a French bank issued a loan in Paris. The London Rothschilds were able to use their links with their cousins in Paris to issue Brazilian loans simultaneously in London and Paris.[64]

Connections in the City were equally important, because loan-issuing was so much of a matter of confidence. A merchant bank's credit rating rested not on the capital size of the firm, but on its personal reputation.[65] For most of the nineteenth century, Rothschilds and Barings had by far the strongest reputations in the City, and could thus place issues with the

---

[62] King, *The History of the Hongkong and Shanghai Banking Corporation*, ii. 97–101. King provides a summary of Japanese public loans with a Hongkong Bank participation on pp. 143–6. Norio Tamaki, 'The Yokohama Specie Bank: A Multinational in the Japanese Interest, 1879–1931', in Geoffrey Jones (ed.), *Banks as Multinationals*, 200–2; King, *The History of the Hongkong and Shanghai Banking Corporation*, ii. 133–5.

[63] Mackenzie, *Realms of Silver*, 203–4, 206; Thane, 'Financiers and the British State', 93–5; King, *The History of the Hongkong and Shanghai Banking Corporation*, ii. 98, 269; File on Japanese Sterling Loan of 1899, Posterity Files, and Court Minutes of 9 Nov. 1904 and 29 Mar. 1905 in Banking Operations File 3 (ii), Chartered History File, SC.

[64] R. Graham, *Britain and the Onset of Modernisation in Brazil, 1850–1914* (Cambridge: Cambridge University Press, 1968), 101–2; Chapman, *The Rise of Merchant Banking*, 86–7.

[65] Chapman, *The Rise of Merchant Banking*, 70, 81.

greatest ease. In the 1870s and 1880s Morgans had to struggle to gain recognition as an equal to Rothschilds and Barings by, for example, accepting participation in syndicates headed by the more prestigious houses, and by co-operating with an established London merchant bank, Hambros, in Scandinavian government issues, a region in which Hambros were specialists.[66] Among the clearing banks which undertook loan issues, London and Westminster Bank had the highest reputation and best connections in the City.[67] The overseas banks were not City institutions of the highest ranking, and although their London-based boards nearly always had directors with connections with other City institutions, their reputations were not of the standing of the great merchant banks.

The question of connections and reputation helps to explain why the British banks in Australia played such an insignificant part in that country's loan issues. Australian borrowing was undertaken by state governments before the First World War, despite Federation and the formation of the Commonwealth government in 1901. In the 1870s and 1880s the trading banks, both local and British, had issued some loans for state governments. The Union Bank, for example, was active on behalf of the Queensland government. From the mid-1880s, however, the major borrowers transferred their issuing business to leading London banks. New South Wales and Queensland turned to the Bank of England, while Victoria, Western Australia, and Tasmania made use of the London and Westminster Bank. In 1905 New South Wales also transferred to the London and Westminster. By 1914 only South Australia still issued loans without a London bank, preferring instead the locally registered National Bank of Australasia.

Despite their London head offices and multinational branch networks, therefore, the Anglo-Australian banks did not participate in Australia's heavy overseas borrowing. The Australian state governments chose the London banks because their prestige helped guarantee the issue would be successful. As Australian issues grew in size in the late nineteenth century, so did the importance of using a bank whose standing could, apparently, guarantee a successful outcome. The London banks, however, had more advantages than prestige. They could offer lower fees because of the large volume of stocks and funds they dealt with. Australian stocks could be added on at marginal cost. Syndicates formed by the London banks had the capacity to make issues far out of reach of the Anglo-Australian banks. The annual value of new issues of Australian government stocks in the 1880s was already around a quarter of the combined Anglo-Australian banking assets in Australia. Another important factor was that all the Australian governments used the London broking firm of Nivison and

[66] Carosso, *The Morgans*, 204–5.
[67] C. A. E. Goodhart, *The Business of Banking, 1891–1914* (London: Weidenfeld and Nicolson, 1972), 137 n. 24.

Company. Nivison had been an employee of London and Westminster before leaving to establish his own firm in the 1880s. During the 1890s he rose to prominence in Australian issues by developing the new techniques of underwriting syndicates. Working in alliance with the London and Westminster, he developed a network of contacts in the City through which loan issues could be underwritten, helped by the Colonial Stock Act of 1900, which conferred trustee status on Dominion stocks. Trustees had to confine their investments to British government or government-guaranteed stocks. Nivisons developed close relations with trustees and thus had easy access to a large supply of funds, which could almost guarantee the success of an issue. These arrangements worked well, and left no room for the Anglo-Australian banks to enter the business, even if they had wanted to.[68]

In Latin America the first-mover advantages and reputations of the merchant banks provided equally formidable barriers to entry to government loan issues for the British overseas banks. Rothschilds had a close long-term relationship with Brazil and Barings with several states, and there was little room for the overseas banks. On occasion, when the banks tried to penetrate the loan issue business, they found their role confined to being used as bargaining weapons by governments wanting to improve the terms offered by merchant banks.[69]

It was only in exceptional circumstances that an overseas bank secured loan issue business. The usual criteria were that the reputation of the borrowing country was (initially at least) low, that the bank was a specialist in that country, and that the bank had a close connection with a more prestigious City institution which could enhance its reputation. The fact that the 1892 and 1911 Persian loans were issued by the Imperial Bank of Persia can be explained in part in these terms. The bank was the state bank of the country and thus had a unique connection with the government. Iran was obliged to make the loan issue in 1892—its first—because it had cancelled a concession held by a Western company following an outbreak of violent anti-foreign protests. The country, therefore, had a zero credit rating on the London market. Finally, the Imperial Bank collaborated in both 1892 and 1911 loans with Glyn's, which had been one of the founders of the bank and served as its London bankers. Even Glyn's reputation, however, was insufficient to prevent only 3 per cent of the 1892 loan being taken by the public when it was issued, such was the poor

[68] A. R. Hall, *The London Capital Market in Australia, 1870–1914* (Canberra: Australian National University, 1963), 103–5; R. S. Gilbert, 'London Financial Intermediaries and Australian Overseas Borrowing, 1900–29', *Australian Economic History Review*, 11 (1971); R. P. T. Davenport-Hines, 'Lord Glendyne', in R. T. Appleyard and C. B. Schedvin (eds.), *Australian Financiers* (Melbourne: Macmillan, 1988), 190–205.

[69] The Anglo-South American Bank had such an experience in Chile in 1907. London to Santiago, 8 Nov. 1907, C2/4, Bolsa Archives, UCL.

reputation in the City of both Iran and the Imperial Bank. In 1911 Iran's standing had risen sufficiently for two second-rank London merchant banks to express an interest in a loan issue, but—as will be explained below—the Imperial Bank of Persia was protected by its status as the preferred instrument of the British Foreign Office.[70]

The Hongkong Bank's exceptional role in China loans can also be explained partly in these terms. The bank was not, unlike the Imperial Bank of Persia, a state bank, but it was a specialist in China. In the 1870s and 1880s China did not want to raise large foreign loans, and was therefore not an outstandingly attractive proposition for the great merchant banks, although both Barings and Rothschilds expressed interest in China loans in the 1880s. Moreover, China wanted, at least initially, to float loans on its own terms, denominated in obscure Chinese units of account, with interest calculated on a lunar-month basis and payments at inconvenient intervals. The Hongkong Bank was willing to meet such requirements—and was able as a Hong Kong-based institution to advance the government silver funds against loans not yet issued—and so was able to establish itself in a strong position by the time, from the mid-1890s, that Chinese borrowing assumed a larger scale.[71] Hongkong Bank's ability to place the early China loans on the London market without the help of the merchant banks was a considerable achievement, and rested on the fact that, as in the case of the Imperial Bank and Glyn's, it had an influential City ally—the stockbroking house of Panmure Gordon and Company. This firm was very active in loan issues, co-operating closely (for example) with Rothschilds over Brazilian loans. Its founder had extensive personal experience of China, and this provided a basis for a close relationship with the Hongkong Bank. Panmure Gordon provided Hongkong Bank with the essential City connections successfully to float its early loans.[72] Subsequently the bank developed substantial London expertise, with the growth in importance of its London Committee and the appointment of Charles Addis to its London office in 1905 after long service in the East. In London, Addis acquired a growing reputation as an international financier and China expert.[73]

In effect, Hongkong Bank opted not to hand the loan business to an existing merchant bank, but to 'internalize' the merchant-banking functions within itself. As a result, the Hongkong Bank became, virtually, two banks—an Exchange bank in the East, and a merchant bank in London.[74]

---

[70] Geoffrey Jones, *Banking and Empire in Iran*, 28–9, 48–54, 121–3.

[71] King, *The History of the Hongkong and Shanghai Banking Corporation*, i. 536–9.

[72] Ibid., 545; ii. 269; Carosso, *The Morgans*, 589. See also B. H. D. MacDermot, *Panmure Gordon & Co., 1876–1976: A Century of Stockbroking* (London: privately published, 1976).

[73] Roberta Allbert Dayer, *Finance and Empire: Sir Charles Addis, 1861–1945* (London: Macmillan, 1988), esp. ch. 3.

[74] 'Hongkong and Shanghai Banking Corporation', *Bankers' Magazine*, 96 (1913), 735; see also King, *The History of the Hongkong and Shanghai Banking Corporation*, ii. 242.

The bank contrived to maintain a good relationship with Barings and, especially, Rothschilds, while preventing them gaining a dominant role. Relations with N. M. Rothschild were particularly close. The Rothschilds acted as intermediaries in the negotiations which led to the accord on China loans between Hongkong Bank and Deutsch-Asiatische Bank in 1895. As a reward, Hongkong Bank agreed that if it needed help in placing a China loan in London, it would offer the business first to Rothschilds.[75] Subsequently, in 1899, Carl Meyer—a very close associate of the Rothschilds—joined the London Committee of the Hongkong Bank.[76] The bank also co-operated with the merchant banks over loan issues outside China, especially Japan, while it undertook the 1905 Thai loan after Rothschilds (and Schroders) had declined the business.[77]

Most of the overseas banks were, therefore, disadvantaged in the matter of loan issues compared to the merchant banks in terms of their connections and reputations. The Hongkong Bank overcame this handicap by issuing China loans at a time when they were relatively unattractive to others, utilizing its specialist knowledge of Chinese conditions. It penetrated the City of London through an alliance with a London stockbroking house, and over time built up its own in-house merchant-banking expertise. This process was not automatic, but was the result of entrepreneurial decisions by the Hongkong Bank to follow this independent route.[78] The policy was successfully implemented by means of strategic alliances, with Panmure Gordon, to some extent with Rothschilds, and, on the international scene, with Deutsch-Asiatische Bank after 1895. Conversely, it would appear that the explanation why most other overseas banks did not become involved in loan issues was not merely the size of the obstacles facing them, but that they lacked the desire or the entrepreneurial vigour to overcome them. Perhaps because their boards, unlike those of Hongkong Bank, were London-based and thus more exposed to the orthodoxies and highly specialized ethos of the British banking system, many banks believed that loan-issuing was beyond their proper business. Chartered Bank, for example, was very wary of 'political' loans such as the China ones, and held to a view—as its court of directors minuted in 1899—that loans for such purposes as railway construction, river improvement, or similar developmental projects were 'outside the province of an exchange bank and should not be entertained'.[79] This view only changed shortly before the First World

---

[75] King, *The History of the Hongkong and Shanghai Banking Corporation*, ii. 264–75.
[76] Ibid., 298.  [77] Ibid., 97, 133.
[78] Within the Hongkong Bank, the decision to pursue an independent strategy on loans was probably due to David McLean, the bank's Shanghai manager who had moved to London in 1872. King, *The History of the Hongkong and Shanghai Banking Corporation*, ii. 269.
[79] Court Minute, 28 Dec. 1899. Similar decisions were in Court Minute, 15 May 1901 and Court Minute, 15 Jan. 1902, in File 3 (ii), Box 3, Chartered History Files, SC.

War. Similarly, in 1884 Standard Bank of South Africa issued the first Orange Free State loan ever to be placed in London, but subsequently state loans were undertaken by Rothschilds or London and Westminster Bank. Standard's management does not seem to have felt distressed by this, perhaps because the bank felt contented with the substantial income it derived from lending funds to the Cape and other governments within South Africa.[80]

A final, but important, part of the explanation why Hongkong Bank and the Imperial Bank of Persia were more prominent in loan-issuing than many other overseas banks is political. By the turn of the century, it had become very important in diplomatically 'sensitive' parts of the world such as China and Iran, for Britain, and thus British banks, to be in the forefront of providing external finance so that control over such important sources of collateral as customs revenues did not pass into the hands of rival powers. To some extent Hongkong Bank and the Imperial Bank of Persia became the preferred instruments of the Foreign Office, and their position as loan-issuers was 'protected'.

The value of this protection was seen in the case of the 1911 Persian loan. Loans had become the arena of Anglo-Russian rivalry in Iran for the previous two decades, and by that period there was also German interest in the country. In 1910, because of fear that a German loan might materialize, the Foreign Office gave the green light to two merchant banks which had expressed interest in a Persian loan to proceed with their loan offers. The Iranian government took up one of the proposals, offering as security a first lien on the southern customs of the country. As soon as the negotiations became serious, however, the Foreign Office moved to protect the position of the Imperial Bank, the traditional instrument of British policy in Iran. Both the Iranian government and the merchant bank were warned off in very explicit terms, and Foreign Office support given to a counter-offer from the Imperial Bank made at the Foreign Office's request.[81]

The complicated story of the China loans in the two decades before the First World War, and of Hongkong Bank's complex relationship with the Chinese and British governments, has been analysed in detail by F. H. H. King, who has stressed that the bank was not a mere agent of British imperialism but a commercial private sector institution trying to act in the best interests of both its shareholders and the Chinese government.[82] Nevertheless, it cannot be denied that during the 1900s the Hongkong Bank had

[80] Henry, *The First Hundred Years of the Standard Bank*; 89; for Standard Bank's large advances to the Cape government, see e.g. GMO, 8 Feb. 1899, in Mabin and Conradie (eds.), *The Confidence of the Whole Country*, 464.

[81] Geoffrey Jones, *Banking and Empire in Iran*, 121; David McLean, 'International Banking and its Political Implications: The Hongkong and Shanghai Banking Corporation and the Imperial Bank of Persia, 1889–1914', in King (ed.), *Eastern Banking*, 5–6.

[82] King, *The History of the Hongkong and Shanghai Banking Corporation*, i, 558–9.

very strong support from the Foreign Office regarding the China loans. In these years China loans became progressively more a concern of international diplomacy and were negotiated by 'banking groups' representing the Great Powers. The 1895 agreement between the Hongkong Bank and the Deutsch-Asiatische Bank was followed from the mid-1900s by alliances between French, Belgian, and later American, Russian, and Japanese banking groups. In these groups, the Hongkong Bank alone represented Britain. This situation had the support of the Foreign Office. As one of the officials put it in 1912, 'the hitherto most effective means' of achieving British diplomatic goals in China had 'been the exclusive utilization of the Hongkong and Shanghai Bank and its attendant foreign groups'.[83] However, exclusive support for a single bank was not a comfortable public position for the Foreign Office, and the Hongkong Bank never received the kind of full commitment from the British government that the French and German groups received from their governments. After 1910 there was some government pressure for the bank to widen the basis of the 'British group'.[84]

The issue came to a head during the negotiations for a major 'Reorganization Loan' after the 1911 Chinese Revolution. Two other British overseas banks decided to make a serious assault on the China loan business, and Hongkong Bank's monopoly of it. One was the recently formed Eastern Bank and the other was the Chartered Bank, which had finally overcome its scepticism about participating in loans.[85]

Both banks faced obstacles from the Foreign Office. The Eastern Bank participated in an Anglo-Belgian syndicate formed to compete with the Four Power Consortium of the Hongkong Bank and the French, German, and American groups. This syndicate concluded a loan agreement for £1 million in March 1912, but the Foreign Office refused to take official notice of the advance, rendering the security vulnerable.[86]

Chartered Bank also faced Foreign Office obstacles in its path. Chartered decided that its best strategy was to try to join Hongkong Bank as joint British representative in the Four Power Group (which was soon to be reformed as the Six Power Group, Russian and Japanese banks joining those of the original four nations). Chartered secured the initial support of the

[83] Minute by J. D. Gregory on Future Policy of HMG if Reorganisation Loan Negotiations Failed, 26 Aug. 1912, FO371/1321, PRO.

[84] King, *The History of the Hongkong and Shanghai Banking Corporation*, ii. 412-13.

[85] William Hoggan, Secretary, London, to Inspector, Peking, No, 554a, 15 Mar. 1912, China Loans File 5, Chartered History Files, SC. See also Mackenzie, *Realms of Silver*, 206.

[86] Mackenzie, *Realms of Silver*, 207; King, *The History of the Hongkong and Shanghai Banking Corporation*, ii. 479-81; Lord Balfour of Burleigh to Foreign Office, 24 Jan. 1912, FO371/1340; Minute by Max Müller, 16 Mar. 1912; Minute by W. Langley, 16 Mar. 1912; Telegram 65, Sir Edward Grey to Jordan, 18 Mar. 1912; W. Langley to Eastern Bank, 19 Mar. 1912; Eastern Bank to Foreign Office, 18 Mar. 1912, FO371/1315; Minute by M. Müller on Eastern Bank, 10 Apr. 1912, FO371/1316, PRO.

Foreign Office for its inclusion in the British group, but when it approached the Hongkong Bank brandishing this support, all it received was an offer to participate in the underwriting of any loan agreed.[87] The Foreign Office, determined to avoid competition among rival lending groups and to ensure that the proceeds of loans were used for 'desirable' purposes, was not prepared to force the Hongkong Bank to make concessions. It resolved that, for the duration of the Reorganization Loan negotiations only, Hongkong Bank would be supported as the sole British issuing bank.[88]

Frustrated in this strategy, Chartered joined with other British financial institutions in a rival loan syndicate put together by a well-known company promoter Birch Crisp, which included several prominent London banks. Meanwhile, the Chinese government were increasingly impatient at the stringency of the Six Power Group's terms. In July 1912 they had applied directly to Chartered Bank to arrange a loan, though the British Minister in Beijing had managed to discourage the application.[89] The Crisp syndicate organized a loan of £10 million in August, which went ahead despite Foreign Office statements that the Hongkong Bank was the only British bank it was willing to support, and despite considerable British diplomatic pressure on the Chinese government to cancel the agreement. Crisp succeeded in issuing the first instalment of the loan, despite strong opposition from Whitehall, apparently because he secured support from some of the less prominent City institutions pleased that he had stood up to the 'Establishment'.[90] The objections of the Consortium, the Foreign Office, and the Hongkong Bank led, however, to the ultimate frustration of Crisp. Chartered Bank proved unable to manage the exchange operations of the loan without Hongkong Bank assistance, and Crisp eventually withdrew from China.[91]

Nevertheless, the confusion and embarrassment caused by the Crisp loan finally breached Hongkong Bank's exclusive position. In December 1912 the bank agreed to widen the British group, which became Hongkong Bank (33 per cent), Barings (25 per cent), London, Country and Westminster Bank (14 per cent), Parr's Bank (14 per cent), and the merchant bank Schroders (14 per cent). Chartered was offered by the Hongkong Bank an equal participation in the British group, but rejected the offer on the

---

[87] Whitehead to Hongkong Bank, 22 Mar. 1912; London letter, 13 Apr. 1912, in China Loans File 5, Chartered History Files, SC; C. Addis to Langley, 27 Mar. 1912 and minute by M. Müller on this letter, FO371/1316, PRO.

[88] Foreign Office to Chartered Bank, 13 May 1912 and minute by W. Langley, FO371/1317, PRO.

[89] Telegram 156 from Sir John Jordan, 16 July 1912, Fo371/1320, PRO.

[90] Mackenzie, *Realms of Silver*, 207–8; King, *The History of the Hongkong and Shanghai Banking Corporation*, ii. 490–3; Conversation between Crisp and J. D. Gregory, 23 Aug. 1912, Fo371/1321, PRO.

[91] King, *The History of the Hongkong and Shanghai Banking Corporation*, ii. 496–8; Carosso, *The Morgans*, 571–2.

grounds that it was not to be allowed a share in the loan-servicing or the exchange, and did not finally join the British group until 1916.[92]

The exclusive support of the Foreign Office, therefore, does not entirely explain the unusually prominent position of the Hongkong Bank in loan issues compared to the other British overseas banks. First-mover advantages, specialist knowledge of China, skilful use of strategic alliances in the City and elsewhere, and sheer entrepreneurial ability must all have greater explanatory power. Nevertheless, in the 1900s the coincidence of the interests of the bank and the Foreign Office undoubtedly strengthened its position in China loans.

For the most part, therefore, the flexible business strategies of the British multinational banks had not been extended to include foreign loan issues. They lacked the reputation and the connections in the City of London to offer competition to the merchant and large London banks. As products of a specialist financial system, they also lacked the desire to diversify into such business. The Hongkong Bank was the main exception to this picture, and it was a strategy that brought rewards. When the bank suffered from fluctuations in exchange in the East, the loan business provided an alternative source of profits, and was thus one of the reasons for that bank's profitability in the pre-war decades.[93]

### 4.5. Bankers and Diplomats

The Foreign Office's involvement in Persian and China loans illustrates the growing links between banking, finance, and international diplomacy in the period between 1890 and 1914. In certain other countries the ties between banks and national foreign policy goals were tighter than in Britain. It was all but impossible for a foreign government to float a loan on the Paris market without the permission of the French government, while French and German overseas banks worked closely with their respective Foreign Ministries. The links between British banks and the Foreign Office were less intimate and formal than in these countries, but nevertheless they were substantial.

The nature of the relations between British banks and British diplomats was very region-specific. In pre-war Latin America, the British government took a decidedly non-interventionist approach, declining, for example, to become directly involved in the Argentinian and Chilean economic crisis of the early 1890s despite pleas from British banking and financial interests. The Foreign Office was equally resolved not to interfere in the flotation

---

[92] King, *The History of the Hongkong and Shanghai Banking Corporation*, ii. 494–6, 579–80.

[93] King, *The History of the Hongkong and Shanghai Banking Corporation*, iv (Cambridge: Cambridge University Press, 1991), 11.

of Latin American government loans in London.[94] British financiers and bankers in the United States could expect support from the Foreign Office, but any assistance was never pushed to the point of disrupting Anglo-American relations.[95]

In contrast, in the countries where there was substantial Great Power rivalry, bankers and diplomats were drawn closely together. The principal countries which saw this phenomenon were Egypt, Turkey, Iran, and China. British governments did not promote banks in this period, but they certainly welcomed and encouraged the National Bank of Egypt, the Bank of Abyssinia, the National Bank of Turkey, and the Imperial Bank of Persia. In these countries the establishment of a 'British' bank was seen as a useful factor in British foreign policy—a means whereby British influence could be strengthened, and a reputable vehicle created through which British investment could flow to a country where a British commercial presence was deemed to be necessary.

The loans these countries sought became a matter of concern for diplomats, not least because of the collateral offered as security. Iran provided a classic illustration. In the 1890s and 1900s the country was an area of rivalry between Britain and Russia, sandwiched as it was between the borders of the Tsar's empire and British India. Both governments understood the links between loans and political influence, and the bankers had no choice but to operate within this highly politicized context. In the late 1890s the British were somewhat less willing than the Russians to become directly involved in such matters, the Treasury, for example, refusing to offer guarantees as a means of tempting British investors into Iranian securities. However, after a large Russian loan had been made in 1900, British diplomats were stung into pursuing more forceful policies, with the Imperial Bank of Persia being recruited as a front-line force in the attempt to strengthen British influence. In 1907 Russia and Britain neatly divided Iran into agreed 'spheres of influences' but in the years before the First World War the spectre of German loans—and with it German political influence—appeared.[96]

The Foreign Office also used the banks to channel funds to desirable administrations, or individuals. In Iran after 1903, British government funds were lent to the government, through the Imperial Bank of Persia, the bank earning a 1 per cent commission on the business. Several hundred thousand pounds were lent to the Iranian government in this fashion.[97] The Imperial Bank's own lending to the government was subordinated

---

[94] Joslin, *A Century of Banking in Latin America* (London: Oxford University Press, 1963), 103–4.
[95] Wilkins, *The History of Foreign Investment in the United States*, 592–3, 605.
[96] Geoffrey Jones, *Banking and Empire in Iran*, 83–7, 120–2.
[97] Ibid., 88–91, 123–4.

to the wishes of the Foreign Office.[98] Loans were made to particular individuals at the request of British diplomats and guaranteed by the British government. In 1903 the British Legation guaranteed an Imperial Bank loan to a group of mullahs, the powerful Islamic clergy with whom the British government wanted the best possible relations.[99] In China in 1900, the British government used the Hongkong Bank for the first time to make a political loan to a provincial viceroy.[100]

The involvement of British banks in road and railway and other infrastructure schemes also led them into close ties with the Foreign Office, for transport and communications were matters of strategic concern. The Imperial Bank of Persia's promoters originally envisaged that the bank would make more profits on mines and transport than on banking. The mining venture was soon spun off into a separate company, but the bank remained involved with roads for years. Transport, like much else in Iran, was a highly political matter. Russia forbade Iran to construct any railways between 1890 and 1910 (an arrangement Britain was quite happy to go along with), and this made the control of roads even more vital. In the early 1900s the Foreign Office restrained the Imperial Bank from selling its road investment, encouraged the formation of a joint venture with another British company, and offered a subsidy to the bank to retain its road interests. Later, after 1910, the Foreign Office also supported the Imperial Bank's involvement in various schemes to build railways in Iran.[101]

In China the Hongkong Bank was an active participant in a scramble for railway concessions in the late 1890s. In 1898 it joined with the trading company Jardine, Matheson to form the British and Chinese Corporation (B & CC). Railway concessions were, as in Iran, a matter of vital strategic concern, and the corporation was supported by British diplomats in China. In 1903 the Foreign Office, anxious to secure a valuable railway concession and concerned about French competition, engineered the creation of a new company, the Chinese Central Railways, into which the B & CC and a rival British venture, the Pekin Syndicate, merged certain of their interests. In the negotiation of railway concessions and other matters, the Hongkong Bank needed the support of the Foreign Office 'to confirm the Bank's status with Chinese authorities pressed by other Powers to accord concessions'.[102]

There were other links between diplomats and bankers. On occasion, the British government offered subsidies to overseas banks to open branches in areas which offered unattractive commercial prospects but fulfilled a

[98] Ibid., 116–17.
[99] Ibid., 92, 128; McLean, 'International Banking and its Political Implications', 5.
[100] King, *The History of the Hongkong and Shanghai Banking Corporation*, ii. 319–21.
[101] Geoffrey Jones, *Banking and Empire in Iran*, 61–4, 93–4, 129–31.
[102] King, *The History of the Hongkong and Shanghai Banking Corporation*, ii. 338, and *passim*; McLean, 'International Banking and its Political Implications', 9–10.

diplomatic purpose. The Imperial Bank of Persia received a subsidy between 1903 and 1908 to establish and maintain a branch in Seistan near
the borders of the Indian Empire, and sometimes—but not always—
acceded to other Foreign Office requests to open branches.[103] The practice
of subsidizing bank branches extended beyond the diplomatically sensitive
regions. In Malaya, the British colonial government used direct or indirect
subsidies to encourage banks to open branches in particular places. When
Hongkong Bank opened a branch in Malacca in 1909 at the behest of the
government, it was provided not only with temporary offices, free of charge,
but free accommodation for its manager, and a site, free of charge, for its
permanent office.[104] Even in the West Indies, the Colonial Bank received
subsidies to keep certain branches open.[105]

The connections between the British overseas banks and the Foreign
Office were, therefore, both substantial and inevitable in the circumstances
existing before the First World War. It would be far from true, however,
to say that relations between bankers and diplomats were harmonious.
Civil servants harboured considerable doubts—or rather prejudices—about
the morality of bankers. 'We are looked upon as shylocks and men without bowels of compassion for the poor browbeaten Chinese,' the British
and Chinese Corporation's agent in Beijing complained in 1906.[106] The
Imperial Bank of Persia was dismissed as 'usurious and somewhat shady'
by the Foreign Office a few years earlier.[107]

The bankers, in turn, never felt they got the support they merited from
their Foreign Office, a complaint which was voiced by many other sections
of British business before and after 1914.[108] The National Bank of Turkey
felt aggrieved that it never received the full backing of the Foreign Office
it thought it deserved, and had been promised. In Turkey preservation of
good Anglo-French relations was rated a far higher diplomatic priority
than support for a 'British' bank. The Imperial Bank of Persia was frequently critical of Foreign Office policies, as well as considering diplomats
far too willing to ask it to sacrifice profits on the altar of the national interest. 'Political considerations', one of the bank's senior managers observed
in 1909, 'do not pay our dividends,' and similar sentiments were expressed
in the Hongkong Bank.[109]

---

[103] Geoffrey Jones, *Banking and Empire in Iran*, 91–2, 128.
[104] Chee Peng Lim *et al.*, 'The History and Development of the Hongkong and Shanghai
Banking Corporation in Peninsular Malaysia', 366, 368; Mackenzie, *Realms of Silver*, 215–
16.        [105] Minute by G. G., 15 Dec. 1911, paper 40056, CO318/327, PRO.
[106] Cited by McLean, 'International Banking and its Political Implications', 10–11.
[107] Geoffrey Jones, *Banking and Empire in Iran*, 88.
[108] R. P. T. Davenport-Hines and Geoffrey Jones, 'British Business in Asia since 1860', in
R. P. T. Davenport-Hines and Geoffrey Jones (eds.), *British Business in Asia since 1860*
(Cambridge: Cambridge University Press, 1989), 22–3.
[109] Geoffrey Jones, *Banking and Empire in Iran*, 127–8; McLean, 'International Banking
and its Political Implications', 12.

In truth, in regions of acute international diplomatic rivalry, the Foreign Office and the overseas banks needed one another, but their interests were never fully identical.[110] The diplomats came to realize that the British policy goals could be served by the banks, but their concerns were wider than those of the banks and they were rarely happy about giving 'exclusive' support to an individual British enterprise. Banks such as the Imperial Bank of Persia and the Hongkong Bank felt responsibilities to their host economies, let alone their shareholders, which meant that they could experience a conflict of interest when asked to act as agents of the British government. Yet in countries such as Iran and China the support of the Foreign Office was essential for survival. 'You see how we dance to the piping from Downing Street and get more kicks than ha'pence for our trouble,' the Imperial Bank's chief manager wrote in 1910, 'and yet we must maintain in *all* quarters these good relations which are a *sine qua non* to our best interests'.[111] Similarly, in China, the banks could not do business with the Chinese government without the consent of the British Legation, which 'only assisted and registered agreements which were consistent with British foreign policy'.[112] Co-operation between bankers and diplomats was a necessary evil for both parties.

### 4.6. Conclusion

The decades before 1914 were, by later standards, remarkably free of government intervention in banking in most countries. Regulatory controls were few. There were almost no restrictions on flows of funds across borders. Beyond the United States, foreign financial institutions faced few discriminatory laws. State-owned banks were established in a few countries, but as yet they posed only a marginal threat to the activities of the British multinational banks. Meanwhile, British public policy had encouraged prudent business strategies in the overseas banks, while otherwise allowing them to follow their entrepreneurial instincts as they wished.

Many activities later performed by governments remained in the private sector before the First World War and provided business opportunities for British overseas banks. They acted, both in the Empire and outside it, as 'state banks' and government bankers, and as currency agents. They issued the paper currency of a variety of countries. They helped governments float loans on the London capital market, although their role was modest compared to the merchant banks and a number of the London banks.

In regions of Great Power rivalry, the British overseas banks were drawn

---

[110] Clarence B. Davis, 'Financing Imperialism: British and American Bankers as Vectors of Imperial Expansion in China, 1908–1920', *Business History Review*, 56 (1982), 260.
[111] Geoffrey Jones, *Banking and Empire in Iran*, 127–8.
[112] King, *The History of the Hongkong and Shanghai Banking Corporation*, ii. 518.

into a kind of symbiotic relationship with the Foreign Office. Although neither party felt entirely comfortable with the other, British diplomats felt obliged to become interested in the banks' loan issues and other activities in countries such as China and Iran, where British strategic interests clashed with those of other Powers. The banks, in turn, needed Foreign Office support if they were to survive in these areas.

The British multinational banks before 1914 were private sector institutions, seeking to make profits for their shareholders, but governments were already a part of their lives, a source of restrictions, business opportunities, sustenance, and frustration.

# CHAPTER 5

# War and Depression

## 5.1. Structure and Performance, 1914–1946

The thirty years after the outbreak of the First World War saw a deterioration in the favourable environmental conditions which the British multinational banks had previously enjoyed. The banks had specialized in supplying financial services to the primary-commodity-producing settler economies of the Southern Hemisphere and to Asia. Their core business was trade finance and exchange operations. After 1914 the world economy was buffeted by two world wars, the Great Depression, and a world financial crisis in 1931. There was a sharp fall in the terms of trade for many primary products, resulting in severe downward pressure on the incomes of countries which had specialized in their production and export. In addition, by the 1930s governments almost everywhere were interfering with the flow of capital and trade between nations by exchange controls and tariffs. Yet the vast British multinational branch network remained intact. Survival and continuity in the face of deteriorating conditions provides perhaps the most pervasive theme in the history of British multinational banks between 1914 and 1946.

In the first half of this period the assets of British multinational banks had continued to grow, and by 1928 they stood at over twice their 1913 level, even though the number of banks had fallen marginally. In contrast, the following decade was one of stagnation, finally ending the continuous expansion of British multinational banking assets since the 1830s. There was a striking shift in the geographical distribution of these assets, as Latin America lost importance in British overseas banking. By 1938 a new 'Triad' of host regions was established, consisting of Australasia, Asia, and Southern Africa, in which almost three-quarters of the assets of British multinational banks were located.

No country could match the number of overseas branches operated by British banks, which grew rapidly between 1913 and 1928, reaching well over 2,000 in that year, before stagnating in the 1930s. There was a substantial further increase in the number of British-owned bank branches in Southern Africa. Overall around three-quarters of all British overseas bank branches in 1938 were in the settler economies of Southern Africa and Australasia.

The financial performance of the sample banks examined in this book indicates a number of surprising features of this thirty-year period. The two world wars emerge as more of an opportunity than a problem for the overseas banks. Except in a handful of cases, the shareholders in banks during both world wars earned higher returns than if they had invested in Consols, and many of them did better by this measure than if they had held shares in the two domestic banks in the sample.

The British banks fared less well in the economic problems of the inter-war years than in the periods of military conflict. In the 1920s the aggregate published profits of the sample overseas banks fell from their wartime peak, and remained below those of domestic banks. The shareholders in nearly half of them would have done better to invest their funds in Consols. Predictably, the performance of the overseas banks between 1930 and 1938 was very weak. As a group, their published profits fell further, while the shareholders in all but two of them would have done better to invest in Consols.

In terms of their published profit ratios, the Eastern Exchange banks appear to have performed best after 1914, except during the Second World War. This group of banks provided four out of the five best banks in 1914–20 and 1930–38, and three of the five in the 1920s. In contrast, the profitability of the Latin American banks was noticeably weak, as was that of the Australasian banks after 1930. Latin America saw the one major corporate disaster of the inter-war years. The Anglo-South American Bank, the largest overseas bank measured by total assets in 1929, almost failed in July 1931, and the shattered remains were finally absorbed by another British bank five years later.

It was during the 1930s that there was the greatest discrepancy between the published and the 'real' performance of the British banks. While the published profit ratios of the Eastern Exchange banks placed them in the top end of the sample, the surviving data on inner reserves and real profits indicates a weaker performance. There were off-balance sheet transfers to support published profits and, for the two sample Exchange banks for which the level of 'real' profits is known, the ratio of real profits to shareholder funds was less than the ratio of published profits to shareholder funds. The 'star' of the Exchange banks, the Hongkong Bank, was no exception to this general trend, and was forced during the mid-1930s to draw on inner reserves to pay its dividends.[1] In contrast, the 'real' performance in this period of Standard Bank and Barclays (DCO)—whose foundation in 1926 will be discussed in the following section—was considerably better than their published profitability. South Africa provided the core business of both banks, and it is evident that in the 1930s it was a highly desirable location for a British bank.

[1] F. H. H. King, *The History of the Hongkong and Shanghai Banking Corporation*, iii (Cambridge: Cambridge University Press, 1988), 188–94, 196–200 contains a detailed discussion of that bank's financial performance in the inter-war years.

In summary, the British multinational banks had good wars but a difficult 1930s, during which profits fell, and the expansion of assets and overseas branches ceased. There was a geographical reorientation of British overseas banking, with Latin America being replaced by South Africa as one of the three main host regions, alongside Australasia and Asia. In the 1930s the two British banks active in South Africa also achieved a noticeably good financial performance. However, it was the survival of British multinational banks amidst the political, economic, and financial turbulence of this period which remains striking. Profits and dividends fell, but the structure remained intact.

The explanation for the stability of British multinational banking will be an underlying concern of much of the following discussion. The remainder of this chapter will examine the major developments in corporate organization and management structure between 1914 and 1946, and assess the response of the banks to crisis. Chapter 6 will focus more on their banking strategies, and examine their success in responding to the political and economic changes of the period.

## 5.2. The Clearing Banks and Multinational Banking

The most radical organizational innovation after 1914 was the long-delayed entry of Britain's domestic commercial banks into multinational banking. This was one aspect of a wider trend towards modifying the structure of functional and geographical specialization in British overseas banking. This inherited structure, however, proved very durable.

A number of factors put pressure on the traditional specialized nature of British multinational banking, and help to explain the entry of the clearing banks into overseas banking. One was the example of German multinational banking, with its closer ties between domestic and foreign banking operations. During the First World War the merits of greater integration between domestic and overseas banking were much discussed in a semi-political debate about competing economically with Germany after the end of military hostilities. It was in this atmosphere that a special committee was appointed under Lord Faringdon, whose report and the subsequent establishment of the British Trade Corporation will be discussed in Chapter 7. Although most British commercial bankers criticized Faringdon, the idea that there were benefits to be gained from a closer integration of domestic and overseas banks gained widespread adherence.

A second factor working against functional and regional specialization was the greater political and economic instability seen in many countries after 1914. Banks which had specialized in the finance of a few commodities produced by a few countries felt a need to diversify their risks, including forming equity alliances with domestic British banks. The British banks in

Latin America and the West Indies clearly felt the need for such diversification, and actively sought mergers and alliances. In region after region
economic problems and growing political risks stimulated such diversification strategies in the inter-war years. In Australia, during the late 1920s,
the growth of government intervention and competition from the state-
owned Commonwealth Bank also provoked such thoughts, though concrete plans never materialized. By 1929, for example, one of the English,
Scottish & Australian Bank's chief general managers was advocating 'a
union' with a British domestic bank in these terms:

We have always in our vision a Commonwealth Bank nourished and bolstered up
by the Government of the day more and more encroaching upon our profit-earning
ability and all the time attempting to exert a control which may in time be most
irksome . . . The Bank that is first to move in the direction indicated by me will . . . be
enormously strengthened and will certainly have a distinct advantage over all its
Competitor Trading Banks and the Bank so strengthened would be a powerful
force against the Government-owned Institution.[2]

A third factor working against the specialized structure of British overseas banking was an increase in both the ability and the desire of the
domestic banks to engage in multinational banking. The merger waves
among British domestic banks created large units which, in contrast to
their small nineteenth-century ancestors, were able realistically to consider
owning branches outside Britain. From the late nineteenth century the
clearing banks had begun to become involved in international banking.
Shortly before the First World War, the traditional dependence on correspondent relationships was challenged when the first tentative steps were
taken into multinational banking, and when two of the leading English
clearing banks established small French subsidiaries. The growth in size
and prestige of the domestic banks enhanced the advantages to be gained
from shifting from reliance on correspondent relationships to finance foreign trade towards owning their own overseas branches, which would permit the internalization of intangible assets such as knowledge and reputation.
The political and economic uncertainties of the First World War and immediate post-war years raised the transactions cost of market relationships
and prompted the clearers to exercise greater management control over
foreign operations. The incentive to internalize through multinational
banking was enhanced by weak share prices after the end of the war,
which reinforced the financial attractiveness of acquiring equity stakes in
the overseas banks, and by the enthusiasm of those banks for alliances
with domestic banks.

Lloyds and Barclays were, of Britain's 'Big Five' domestic banks, the
most active foreign direct investors, and this remained the case until the

[2] E. O'Sullivan to A. Williamson, 28 Nov. 1929, E/49/1, ANZ Archives.

TABLE 5.1. *Foreign direct investment by Lloyds Bank, 1911–1946*

| Region | Year | Bank | Original investment (£ sterling) | Lloyds share of issued capital (%) |
|---|---|---|---|---|
| Europe | 1911 | Lloyds Bank (France) | 39,888 | 100 |
| | 1917 | Becomes joint venture with National Provincial | | 50 |
| | 1918 | Renamed Lloyds and National Provincial Foreign Bank | | |
| South America | 1918 | London and River Plate Bank | 5,961,534 | 99 |
| | 1923 | Merger with London and Brazilian Bank | | 56.9 |
| | 1936 | Anglo-South American acquired | | 49.6 |
| India/Egypt | 1923 | Cox & Co. | 54,000 | 100 |

1970s. Lloyds' strategy was idiosyncratic. It acquired shareholdings in a range of banks active outside Britain. However, there was little consistent policy behind these investments, and no policy at all concerning their subsequent exploitation.[3] Lloyds' multinational banking strategy remained almost incoherent until the end of the 1960s. The result was, arguably, one of the great 'missed opportunities' of British multinational banking.

There were two dimensions to the expansion of Lloyds' activities abroad. First, it established, through a number of acquisitions, a branch network spanning Latin America, continental Europe, and India, over which it exercised some kind of managerial control, although—as will be seen below—that control was not very strong. Second, Lloyds also took small equity stakes in a large number of other overseas banks (both British- and non-British-registered). These investments did not carry any managerial control. The two strategies are best dealt with separately.

Lloyds made its first foreign direct investment in 1911, when Lloyds Bank (France) was established by the purchase of Armstrong and Company. Subsequent investments stemmed from a combination of the desire by Lloyds to have more direct representation abroad; the desire of certain banks to seek shelter under the umbrella of Lloyds; and Bank of England pressure to rescue ailing banks. Table 5.1 presents a simplified picture of the development of Lloyds' direct investments.

[3] J. R. Winton, *Lloyds Bank, 1918–1969* (Oxford: Oxford University Press, 1982), 30.

The First World War presented profitable business opportunities for Lloyds Bank (France), and by 1915 the capital of the bank had a book value of £240,000. In 1917 Lloyds agreed to let another large English clearing bank, the National Provincial Bank, acquire a half-share in the bank, and in the following year the French operation was renamed Lloyds and National Provincial Foreign Bank. By 1919 the bank had some 11 branches in France, Belgium, Germany, and Switzerland, and ten years later 19 continental branches were operating.[4]

In 1918 Lloyds acquired 99 per cent of the shares of the London and River Plate Bank, at a total cost of over £5.9 million, which was greatly in excess of market price. Lloyds believed that it could offer its British customers active in the Latin American market a better service by owning its own branches than by operating through correspondent relationships.[5] But it is also evident that London and River Plate welcomed and probably sought the Lloyds take-over. The profitability of this bank had fallen during the war years, and the immediate future for the bank looked full of risks. Several Latin American countries had undergone recessions or commercial crises on the eve of the war, and a recurrence of such problems was not unlikely. Moreover, during the war American banks had become much more active in Latin America, threatening the traditional state of affairs in which American trade with South America had often been financed by the British banks.[6] While there was an exchange of directors, Lloyds retained the existing structure of the bank, although it did strengthen its capitalization.

In 1923 London and River Plate Bank amalgamated with the other major long-established British bank in South America, London and Brazilian, to form the Bank of London and South America (Bolsa). London and Brazilian's position had gravely weakened in the immediate post-war years. It had increased its capital in 1919, although by appealing to its shareholders rather than capitalizing profits, as had the London and River Plate. The strengthening of resources was badly needed, for by the early 1920s London and Brazilian was facing the difficulties obviously foreseen by the management of London and River Plate. Owing to a fall in the sterling value of the Brazilian and Argentinian currencies, in 1920 London and Brazilian suffered an accelerating net depreciation of its capital employed in South America which amounted to £540,557 by 1922.[7] It seems that by the time

[4] Geoffrey Jones, 'Lombard Street on the Riviera: The British Clearing Banks and Europe, 1900–1960', *Business History*, 24 (1982), 187–90, 192–3.
[5] Chairman's Statement to Extraordinary General Meeting of Lloyds' Shareholders, 7 Aug. 1918.
[6] Winton, *Lloyds Bank*, 28; David Joslin, *A Century of Banking in Latin America* (London: Oxford University Press, 1963), 236; A. S. J. Baster, *The International Banks* (London: King, 1935), 222–3.
[7] London and Brazilian Bank Annual Reports for 1921, 1922, and 1923.

of the amalgamation of the London and River Plate and the London and Brazilian in 1923, the inner reserves of both banks had disappeared through a combination of bad debts and exchange depreciation.[8] Under the terms of the amalgamation, each bank brought into the new bank, Bolsa, all its assets and took shares out of the common stock in proportion to what they brought in. The upshot was considerably to reduce (to 56.9 per cent) the Lloyds Bank share of the capital of the new bank.

In 1936 Bolsa acquired the remaining British bank in South America, the Anglo-South American Bank, which had been more or less bankrupt since 1931. This move was made at the behest of the Bank of England and will be discussed in detail in Chapter 7. The acquisition was financed by the issue of further shares by Bolsa, which had the effect of reducing the Lloyds share of its issued capital to 49.8 per cent.

In 1923 Lloyds added two further continents to its sphere of operation when it acquired the business of Cox & Co., which had ten branches in British India and two in Egypt. Like the Anglo-South American Bank, Cox & Co. had effectively failed and its acquisition by Lloyds was also at the behest of the Bank of England. Lloyds spent £54,000 in purchasing the Indian premises, but no other payment was made for the Indian business, the Bank of England providing a substantial sum to cover Cox's losses. In 1926 the Egyptian branches were sold, but the Indian business was retained until 1960.

Through a series of acquisitions, therefore, Lloyds acquired influence over the entire British overseas banking branch network in Latin America and a number of branches in British India, while a green-field investment strategy had created a branch network in continental Europe. Little thought was given, however, to how to exploit and organize this considerable empire. Throughout the inter-war years there was an absence of any strategic management over, or even co-ordination between, the operations in different regions, or between them and Lloyds' domestic business. Except for the former Cox & Co. branches, the other banks were run as independent units. Cox's branches were formally incorporated into Lloyds Bank, being placed under a new Eastern department of the bank's London head office, and supervised by an Eastern Committee of the main board. But Lloyds diluted its overall control of the continental subsidiary in 1917, and the Latin American operations in 1923, and subsequently exercised little control over their activities. Such loose control and co-ordination was typical of many sectors of British business before the 1930s, and often much later.[9]

---

[8] Note respecting the Investment of Lloyds Bank Limited in the Bank of London and South America Limited, 9 Sept. 1930, Winton Bolsa File, LB.

[9] A. D. Chandler, *Scale and Scope* (Cambridge, Mass.: Harvard University Press, 1990), 286–7.

In 1943 there was an internal report by Lloyds' two chief general managers, Wilson and Parkes, on their bank's relations with Lloyds and National Provincial Foreign Bank, Bolsa, and a Scottish domestic bank, the National Bank of Scotland, in which Lloyds had acquired almost all of the issued stock in 1918. 'Although we are carrying full responsibility for these Banks and must necessarily do so,' this report observed, 'we have little knowledge of what is going on except when the Balance Sheets are produced and even then very scanty figures are given and little attention paid to them.' The general managers could find no evidence over the previous twenty years of any great exchange of business between the different institutions or their parent, which appeared to 'reap very few known advantages from the connection'. This even extended to publicity, for Bolsa only referred to the Lloyds connection in very small print on their balance sheet. By 1943 Lloyds' overseas investments had come to resemble not so much an overseas banking group as a kind of 'lock-up' of funds. 'Let us remember', Wilson and Parkes noted, that 'block purchases of shares such as we have made cannot be bought and sold like those of an ordinary investor—once in, generally speaking, we have to stay and we are dependent on the good management of the institution in which we have little control.'[10]

The dependence on 'good management' was particularly unfortunate since neither the continental nor the Latin American operations were blessed with this attribute, which was all the more damaging because both operated in regions where political and economic conditions were especially difficult for British banks. As a result, a second outstanding feature of the overseas banking interests of Lloyds Bank was their unsatisfactory financial performance.

The performance of Lloyds and National Provincial Foreign Bank was very poor. It paid small dividends up to 1930, but nothing thereafter until after the Second World War. During the early 1930s the bank accumulated large bad debts, and the two British banks eventually provided £1.5 million in off-balance sheet 'gifts' to keep their subsidiary afloat in this decade. Unfavourable exogenous circumstances, such as the freezing of German debts under the 'standstill' agreements of 1931 and the crisis of the French franc in the mid-1930s, explain much of this dismal record. Lloyds and National Provincial Foreign Bank was in the wrong place at the wrong time. However, serious problems were also caused by a weak business strategy and poor management. The bank was unclear what kind of business it wanted. During the 1920s hopes were still high that there were sufficient British people on the Continent for the bank to justify itself

---

[10] Memorandum of 21 July 1943 by R. A. Wilson and Sydney Parkes, Winton Investment File, LB; Winton, *Lloyds Bank*, 30.

merely by serving them, and only towards the end of the decade did the bank realize there was not enough 'British' business on the Continent to justify its existence, and that it had to become seriously involved in local commerce. Very few of its British managers, however, had the ability to build a foothold in such local business. After 1928 an increasing number of unwise advances were made, which were turned into bad debts by the Depression, revealing serious weaknesses in the Paris-based management. In 1937 there was a further blow when it was discovered that one of the few profit-making parts of the bank, the branch in the City of London, had derived all its profits from speculation in exchange.[11]

Bolsa was not the financial disaster of the Lloyds and National Provincial Foreign Bank. However, by most measures, its profitability and performance was average to poor. In opportunity cost terms the Lloyds investment was hardly satisfactory. By 1936 the original investment of £5.6 million had been written down in Lloyds' books to £2.6 million, and by 1943 Wilson and Parkes estimated the worth of the Bolsa investment at £2.4 million. They also calculated that the flow of dividends had been very unsatisfactory. Lloyds had increased its capital by £1,886,564 when the London and River Plate Bank was acquired in 1918. The amount required to pay a 12 per cent dividend to these extra shareholders was £226,837 per annum. However, Lloyds had received from Bolsa an average dividend of only £161,000, leaving, Wilson and Parkes complained, 'a large deficiency to be found to provide the dividend on the shares issued to acquire the investment'.[12]

Like Lloyds and National Provincial Foreign Bank, Bolsa was an inadequately managed bank in the wrong place at the wrong time. The inter-war years were a period of trade depression, exchange controls, and many other problems throughout Latin America. Weak management meant that Bolsa was not well equipped to respond to these problems. The years immediately after the merger with London and Brazilian Bank seemed particularly unfortunate in this respect. Bolsa's real profits declined steadily over the 1920s. Between 1923 and 1927 the bank lost £2.5 million through capital depreciation and bad debts, of which Brazil contributed a £0.9 million loss in capital depreciation and £0.4 million in bad debts. A Lloyds director who conducted a detailed investigation of Bolsa in 1930 concluded that many of the losses 'especially in Brazil and to a lesser extent elsewhere' were 'due to a defective organisation'. Controls over lending decisions were very weak. The management structure was very thin, with head office control mainly enforced by periodic visits of directors to South

[11] Geoffrey Jones, 'Lombard Street on the Riviera', 193–8.
[12] Memorandum of 21 July 1943 by R. A. Wilson and Sydney Parkes, Winton Investment File, LB. See Appendix 5 for a comparison of Bolsa's profitability and performance with those of other banks in this period.

America. A strengthening of the management structure followed, which will be discussed below, but there was a further spate of bad debts early in the new decade.[13]

Only the performance of the former Cox & Co. banking business offered a more optimistic scenario. In the 1920s Lloyds had also experienced management problems in the East, and a severe loss at Rangoon branch at the end of the decade revealed, as in Latin America, poor controls over lending and inadequate senior management. When Lloyds took over the Indian branches in 1923 substantial losses were occurring, which rose to £80,000 in 1924. However, until 1928 Lloyds managed the business under the guarantee of the Bank of England, and by 1928 the business as a whole was in the black. Lloyds was able to overcome management problems with greater ease than in Latin America and the Continent, and it was hardly a coincidence that the Eastern operations were the one direct investment that was wholly owned and integrated into the domestic bank. Better management as well as better trading conditions (compared to Latin America and the Continent) made Lloyds' Eastern business profitable in the 1930s. Between 1928 and 1942 the Indian branches and the Eastern department in London made a net profit of over £1 million after meeting all expenses and making full provision for bad and doubtful debts. Nearly £620,000 of this profit was remitted to head office.[14]

In addition to these direct investments, Lloyds also took small shareholdings in at least fourteen other banks. Table 5.2 lists these 'strategic stakes', and their outcome by 1943.

Like the more substantial investments, these smaller shareholdings were acquired for a variety of reasons and with no overall strategy evident. The most consistent theme was the desire of Lloyds to strengthen correspondent links, and this was particularly evident in the series of stakes taken in banks operating in Australia, both British- and locally registered. The investment in the locally registered National Bank of Australia in 1924, for example, took the form of a mutual purchase of shares, designed to facilitate a 'closer relationship' and 'the mutual interchange of business as far as possible'.[15] British multinational banks such as the Bank of British West Africa and the National Bank of New Zealand welcomed the prospect of an equity link with a strong English clearing bank. Lloyds were, for example, the London bankers of the New Zealand bank and during the

---

[13] Note respecting the Investment of Lloyds Bank Limited in the Bank of London and South America Limited, by Alwyn Parker, 9 Sept. 1930, Winton Bolsa File, LB; Report by Murray and Beane, May 1933, LB.

[14] Memorandum of 21 July 1943 by R. A. Wilson and Sydney Parkes, Winton Investment File, LB; Winton, *Lloyds Bank*, 126–9.

[15] Lloyds Investment Committee, 29 Feb. 1924, File 500, LB.

TABLE 5.2. *Shareholdings by Lloyds Bank in other overseas banks, 1906–1943*

| Year | Bank | Shares (no.) | Cost (£ sterling) | Value, June 1943 (£ sterling) |
|---|---|---|---|---|
| 1906 | English, Scottish & Australian | 20,000 | 20,000 | Sold 1932 for £12,071 |
| 1910/1925 | Australian Bank of Commerce | 11,666 | 11,666 | Sold 1929 for £8,953 |
| 1911 | Anglo-Russian Bank | 1,800 | 8,200 | 0 |
| 1916 | British Italian Corporation | 4,704 | 101,080 | Sold 1930 for loss of £1.1 m. |
| 1917 | British Trade Corporation | 15,000 | 100,000 | 4,875 |
| 1918 | Queensland National Bank | 30,000 | 30,000 | 21,750 |
| 1919 | Bank of British West Africa | 37,500 | 255,000 | 180,469 |
| 1919 | National Bank of New Zealand | 48,150 | 243,431 | 78,244 |
| 1919 | National Bank of South Africa | 5,000 | 65,000 | Sold 1932 for £51,210 |
| 1920 | P & O Banking Corporation | 10,000 | 101,250 | Sold 1927 for £104,625 |
| 1923 | Niederosterreichische Escompte Gesellschaft | 50,000 | 52,265 | Sold 1935 for £28,755 |
| 1924 | International Bank of Amsterdam | 300 | 25,478 | Sold 1936 for £26,383 |
| 1924 | National Bank of Australasia | 3,265 | 49,118 | 24,487 |
| 1935 | Anglo-Palestine Bank | 25,000 | 26,111 | 26,111 |

First World War their relationship had become particularly close.[16] In some cases the Lloyds investments were explicitly solicited by the recipient banks. This was true of the P & O Banking Corporation, whose foundation in 1920 as an offshoot of Lord Inchcape's P & O Steam Navigation Company will be discussed below. The Lloyds shareholding was invited by Lord Inchcape, after another clearing bank (National Provincial) had asked for a shareholding.[17] The British Trade Corporation and the British Italian Corporation were wartime creations sponsored by the British government (see Chapter 7), and the Lloyds participation was—at least in part—due to official pleas to lend support.

The financial performance of these small strategic stakes was no more satisfactory than that of the larger investments. Half of the investments made between 1906 and 1935 were sold before 1936, in five instances at a lower price than that at which they had been originally purchased. Total losses on these sales were in excess of £1.2 million. In the disastrous case of the British Italian Corporation, Lloyds not only lost its original investment of over £100,000, but also had to contribute £1.1 million towards a rescue fund for the institution. Of the shareholdings retained, most had lost value. Lloyds had a peculiar ability to buy at the top of the market. The 1919 share price of the Bank of British West Africa was not reached again until 1946. The National Bank of New Zealand share price actually peaked in 1928, but collapsed dramatically in the 1930s. In 1943 Wilson and Parkes were distressed to find that Lloyds' investment in that bank had declined in value by nearly 70 per cent compared to the 1919 purchase price.

Overall, it is hard to be positive about Lloyds' entry into multinational banking in the inter-war years. In 1943 Wilson and Parkes calculated that the bank had invested £7.5 million in overseas banks between 1910 and 1935, of which £4.8 million had been completely lost. In addition, the income from these investments had been 'negligible', as had 'non-monetary advantages' such as the introduction of new business. This calculation is not definitive. It seems to have excluded, for example, the income Lloyds gained from its Indian investments, and to have included the loss stemming from a £50,000 participation in an £800,000 7 per cent sterling loan made in 1916 to the 'Holy Synod of the Empire of Russia' to buy wax for use in Russian churches.[18] Nevertheless, the Wilson and Parkes estimate undoubtedly provides the right order of magnitude for the overall financial performance of the Lloyds investments.

Barclays was the second British clearing bank to make large overseas investments in the inter-war years, and its experiences contrasted with

---

[16] See the correspondence in T160/278, PRO.

[17] Lord Inchcape to Henry Bell, 26 Jan. 1920, File 5227, LB.

[18] Ibid., Memorandum of 21 July 1943 by R. A. Wilson and Sydney Parkes, Winton Investment File, LB; Winton, *Lloyds Bank*, 30.

those of Lloyds. While Lloyds acquired banks operating in Latin America and the East, Barclays focused its activities on the West Indies and Africa, and more specifically South Africa, Egypt, and West Africa. Moreover, while Lloyds made little or no effort to co-ordinate its various overseas interests, Barclays created a new and distinct bank. In both the regions it chose to operate in, and in the creation of a unified and co-ordinated managerial structure, Barclays made wiser decisions than Lloyds.

As in the case of Lloyds, the overseas banks acquired by Barclays were enthusiastic supporters of this development. Nevertheless, it would appear also that Barclays had a sharper strategic vision than Lloyds. The senior management of Barclays, especially F. C. Goodenough, who was appointed chairman in 1916, shared some of the concerns of the wartime Faringdon Committee. In August 1917 Goodenough wrote of the 'coming struggle for the markets of the world'. Bankers, he argued, were to play a key role in this struggle, providing 'not only, or even principally, financial help, but rather the hearty co-operation of the Banker in discovering fresh outlets for the manufacturer's wares'. If this was to be achieved, Goodenough concluded, it was essential 'that the Bank should have not only what is usually termed a "Correspondent" in the principal centres, but rather a Branch or the nearest approach to a Branch that can be arranged'.[19]

Goodenough's vision, therefore, was of a more entrepreneurial bank than conventionally seen in British banking, which, in his opinion, involved the internalization of former market arrangements within a multinational banking structure. Goodenough was also convinced that this multinational bank should focus on, and serve the interests of, the British Empire, to whose promotion as an economic unit he was dedicated.[20]

Fortunately there was an overseas bank which represented an ideal instrument for Goodenough's hopes of creating a multinational 'empire' bank—the Colonial Bank. Under the dynamic leadership of Max Aitken, a strategy of diversification had been adopted in order to escape the problems of Canadian competition in the West Indies. The Colonial Bank Act of 1916 extended the powers of the bank to carry on the business of a banker in the United Kingdom or anywhere in the British Empire. This enabled the bank to carry out its plan to extend its overseas branch network to West Africa, which had traditional trading links with the West Indies. The first West African branches, at Lagos and Accra, were opened in early 1917. Branches were also opened in Manchester and Liverpool, enabling the bank to get into closer touch with those trading houses concerned with the West Indies and West Africa. Further legislation in 1917 extended the bank's powers to carry on business anywhere in the world where British

[19] Memorandum by F. C. Goodenough, 31 Aug. 1917, File Private Papers of F. C. Goodenough, 3/2356/1, BBA, quoted in Jones, 'Lombard Street on the Riviera', 189.
[20] A. S. J. Baster, *The Imperial Banks* (London: King, 1929), 235.

citizens were able to transact business, a move probably designed to allow Colonial to compete with the Bank of British West Africa in the French and German West African colonies.

There was an obvious synergy between the strategic aims of Barclays and Colonial Bank. In January 1918 a joint committee of directors was established, and in the following March Barclays purchased £40,000-worth of shares in Colonial. There was a further link in the same year when Barclays acquired another domestic English bank, the London Provincial and South Western Bank, which also had a shareholding in Colonial. London Provincial's former chairman became deputy chairman of Barclays and in 1919 he joined the board of Colonial.[21] At this stage Goodenough's concept of his ideal multinational empire bank was of a sort of consortium bank owned by a number of existing banks drawn from the developed countries of the Empire. In 1919 he persuaded the Bank of Montreal and the National Bank of South Africa (both banks locally registered in their own countries) to invest in Colonial, and they gained representation on its board.

In 1920 the range of Barclays' overseas interests was extended with the acquisition of over 90 per cent of the shares of the Anglo-Egyptian Bank. Colonial Bank had expressed interest in Egypt as a possible area for diversification, but the initiative for the Barclays take-over in fact came from Anglo-Egyptian. It seems likely that the bank perceived that Egypt's wartime prosperity could not continue indefinitely, based, as it was, almost entirely on high cotton prices and levels of military expenditure. The threat of Barclays-backed competition may have been the final straw.[22]

The next stage in the development of Goodenough's strategy for an empire bank involved the National Bank of South Africa. This bank had rapidly expanded its branch network after the end of the war, only to be caught by the early 1920s depression. In 1922 the National Bank had failed to pay a dividend. As early as 1921 the bank approached Barclays about its taking a shareholding, but nothing transpired and National Bank's decline continued, with a steady leakage of deposits as public confidence waned. During 1924 and 1925 negotiations with Barclays were resumed, with the National Bank's directors reportedly 'deaf to any appeal which conflicts with [their] overwhelming desire' to find a way out of their plight.[23] By spring 1925, after a thorough examination of the bank's affairs, Barclays was ready to rescue the South African bank.[24]

The Barclays scheme involved the use of the Colonial Bank as the central vehicle to create a unified multi-regional banking group including the

[21] Sir Julian Crossley and John Blandford, *The DCO Story* (London: Barclays Bank International, 1975), 3–4.  [22] Ibid., 5–9.
[23] South African Reserve Bank to M. Norman, 1 Apr. 1925, G1/9, B. of E.
[24] Crossley and Blandford, *The DCO Story*, 9–19.

National Bank of South Africa. In August 1925 Colonial Bank was reincorporated by a private Act of Parliament. A month later, its name was changed to Barclays (Dominion, Colonial and Overseas). During November and December 1925 the shareholders of the Anglo-Egyptian and the National Bank agreed to the participation of these banks in the scheme.

Barclays (DCO) was controlled by Barclays, but not wholly owned by it. The bank had an authorized capital of £10 million, of which £6,975,500 was to be issued and £4,975,500 paid up. The share structure was divided up into 1,793,000 8 per cent cumulative preference shares of £1 each; 2,682,500 'A' ordinary shares of £1 each; and 500,000 'B' ordinary shares of £5 each, which were £1 paid. Barclays subscribed to all the 'B' ordinary shares thereby gaining majority voting rights, but it only held a minority of the remaining shares through its previous shareholding in Anglo-Egyptian.[25] In February 1926 some 9 per cent of the preference shares and 16 per cent of the 'A' shares were on the South African register of the bank, although over time this number fell. By March 1931 the corresponding percentages were 5 and 9.[26]

Barclays (DCO) offered a striking contrast to the overseas banking interests of Lloyds in several respects. The most obvious difference was that it was a unified banking group with a common board, general management, and strategic direction. The management structure and, in many cases, the senior staff of Barclays (DCO) were borrowed from Barclays Bank. Barclays in Britain operated a highly decentralized system based on local boards of directors, who usually represented banks that had been absorbed into the Barclays empire. This organizational pattern was followed in the new creation. At the top of the structure was a central board in London. Goodenough became chairman. The three former chairmen of the amalgamating banks, plus some of their directors, were also made directors, as was the general manager, John Caulcutt, who had been a senior general manager in Barclays. He had two assistants, one from Barclays and one from the National Bank of South Africa. They managed a small head office staff, mainly drawn from Barclays.

In accordance with Barclays' domestic experience, there was a strong emphasis on decentralization, and each bank initially preserved a separate identity. The boards of the old banks remained in existence and continued to function, operating under the powers delegated to each of them by the central board. Although they were designated 'local boards', those of the former Colonial and Anglo-Egyptian banks sat in London. The former National Bank of South Africa local board continued to sit in

[25] Barclays Bank Board Minutes, 24 Mar. 1927, 38/503; Chairman and General Manager's Correspondence, 3/211, BBA.

[26] Ibid., J. R. Leisk to F. C. Goodenough, 22 July 1931, Chairman and General Manager's Correspondence, 3/212.

Johannesburg, but that bank's London Committee continued to meet in London. The local boards were given considerable powers of discretion over lending, but within limits decided by head office. At the end of 1926, for example, the local board in South Africa was permitted to sanction proposals for renewals of existing limits for direct facilities in excess of £50,000, but proposals for new business involving direct facilities in excess of £50,000 had to be referred to London except in cases of emergency.[27]

Over time the inherited separate organizations of the bank were slowly merged, though the decentralized structure was maintained. In 1929 the London Committee of the National Bank and the London-based boards of the two other banks were merged. This new weekly committee exercised overall control over lending policy, with powers delegated from the central board. In 1932 a standing Chairman's Committee was formed, modelled on a similar body in Barclays. This consisted of the chairman, his deputy, and the vice-chairman, who could discuss urgent matters before they went to the full board, and liaise with the equivalent committee in the domestic bank. New local management centres were established. In the late 1920s the old centralized structure of the National Bank was modified, with the creation first of a Cape local board to take responsibility for the bank's business in the Cape area, and then (in 1928) of a Rhodesian Committee. The East African operations were also taken away from the direct supervision of Pretoria by the establishment of a control organization in Kenya. The Rhodesian and Kenyan committees initially reported to the South African board in Pretoria, but the latter soon passed under London control to take advantage of better communications. A local head office was also established in Egypt and then in Palestine, and it was only the former Colonial Bank regions where, for a time, the regional management concept was not applied, and the basis of the organization remained the managers of the large branches, reporting directly to London, which was the centre of the sugar trade. Throughout DCO considerable power remained below the level of head office, with the South African management in particular retaining a large measure of independence throughout the inter-war period.[28]

If the unified nature of Barclays (DCO) provided a strong contrast to Lloyds, so did the relationship between the overseas and parent banks. There seems to have been almost no relationship between Lloyds and its overseas associates, apart from the shareholding link and some links at board level. In contrast, although DCO was autonomous, there were close connections between it and Barclays, in addition to the interlinking directorships. After the foundation of DCO, a number of senior staff were transferred from Barclays to the overseas bank, sometimes to overcome

[27] Ibid., Note, 5 Oct. 1926, Chairman and General Manager's Correspondence, 3/211.
[28] Crossley and Blandford, The DCO Story, 22–30, 38–46, 59, 70–4.

immediate staff requirements.[29] Staff were seconded from one bank to the other for training, and it became an established practice that staff joining DCO should spend their first eighteen months with their local branch of Barclays, learning the basics of banking. Although there appears to have been some competitive rivalry and tension between DCO and Barclays' own international operations, these problems seem on the whole to have been overcome, perhaps because many former Barclays staff joined DCO.[30] A perception of common interest pervaded at least the higher echelons of both banks. This common feeling was obviously reinforced by the fact that Goodenough was chairman of both banks before his death in 1934, and naturally perceived the benefits of co-operation. Moreover, unlike the enthusiasm of Lloyds for diluting its shareholdings in overseas banks, Barclays took the opposite line. In the late 1920s and early 1930s Barclays purchased 'A' shares and disposed of preference shares in DCO as a means of achieving 'a greater consolidation of interests between the two concerns'.[31]

The financial performance of Barclays (DCO) was also a noticeable improvement on that of the Lloyds affiliates. DCO emerged as Britain's largest overseas bank following the collapse of Anglo-South American Bank. Its real profit performance was considerably stronger than its published profits, and it accumulated large inner reserves. Barclays did not need to provide any financial assistance for DCO, and received dividends from it throughout the period. This experience provides some support for those who have stressed the advantages for banks in operating in several markets and not being exposed to a single one.

A closer look at the profits of Barclays (DCO) reveals, in fact, that the group was heavily dependent on a single market, and used the profits earned in it to 'cross-subsidize' the branch network elsewhere. Table 5.3 gives a regional breakdown of the net profits of Barclays (DCO) before provision for bad and doubtful debts and various other cumulative transfers between 1928 and 1939.

The most striking feature of Table 5.3 is the importance of the National Bank of South Africa's contribution to DCO's total net profits, which reached 53 per cent by 1937 to 1939. Moreover, a considerable portion of the head office 'profits' seems to have been administrative charges for the South African operations, while the main contributor to the 'other' profits shown in Table 5.3 was Circus Place branch, the former London office of the National Bank of South Africa, which continued to handle much of the London end of DCO's South African business.[32]

[29] Ibid., 41.      [30] Ibid., 31.

[31] F. C. Goodenough to J. R. Leisk, 12 Aug. 1931, Chairman and General Manager's Correspondence, 3/212, BBA.

[32] Ibid., Circus Place's contribution to 'other' profits was 75% 1928–30, 79% 1931–3, 65% 1934–6, and 76% 1937–9, 38/251.

TABLE 5.3. *Net profits (losses) of Barclays (DCO) by region,*
*1928–1939 (£000)*

| Region | 1928–30 | 1931–3 | 1934–6 | 1937–9 |
|---|---|---|---|---|
| National Bank of South Africa | 1,281 | 864 | 2,056 | 2,587 |
| East Africa | 25 | (11) | 1 | 3 |
| Colonial Bank | 418 | 150 | 207 | — |
| West Indies | — | — | — | 344 |
| West Africa | — | — | — | 15 |
| Anglo-Egyptian | 248 | 130 | 204 | — |
| Egypt etc. | — | — | — | 77 |
| Palestine | — | — | — | 127 |
| Head office | 1,046 | 1,378 | 987 | 854 |
| Other[a] | 506 | 659 | 850 | 884 |
| TOTAL | 3,524 | 3,170 | 4,305 | 4,891 |

[a] The most important elements of this category were DCO's London branches.
The bank's Manchester and Liverpool branches in the United Kingdom, the New York
agency, and Hamburg branch are also included.
*Source*: Papers submitted to DCO Accounts Boards, 38/251, BBA.

South African-related business overall contributed around three-quarters
of DCO's profits in the 1928 to 1939 period, while the branch network
in East Africa and (from the evidence of the late 1930s) West Africa was
barely profitable.

A number of reasons explain DCO's superior financial performance
compared to that of the Lloyds affiliates. First, DCO was a better-organized
and -managed bank, which drew on the accumulated knowledge and
staff of its domestic parent. Secondly, inter-war South Africa offered far
more banking opportunities than Latin America. It was not simply a matter of Barclays being particularly successful in South Africa, for its rival,
the Standard Bank, also found the country profitable in the inter-war
years. Thirdly, Barclays also chose the banks it acquired with more skill
than Lloyds. The Colonial Bank and the National Bank of South Africa
were fundamentally sound institutions for, despite its injudicious over-
expansion in the early 1920s, the National Bank's difficulties were of a
temporary nature. Anglo-Egyptian was perhaps the weakest of the three
banks acquired because of the problems of a cotton-based economy, competition from a newly founded local bank, and managerial deficiencies.[33]

[33] Crossley and Blandford, *The DCO Story*, 39–42; Report on Sudan and Egyptian
Branches, 18 May 1927, by W. N. Bickett, Chairman and General Manager's Correspondence, 3/211, BBA.

Barclays' overseas expansion was not confined to the DCO group, and some of these other ventures had a less satisfactory performance. The bank's attempts to penetrate continental Europe were more successful than the Lloyds and National Provincial joint venture, but still loss-making. Barclays' association with France came about, like that of Lloyds with India, through the activities of Cox & Co. Cox & Co. followed the British Expeditionary Force to France in 1914. In 1915 a separate company, Cox & Co. (France), was incorporated, to which the London and South Western Bank soon subscribed half the share capital. The merger of London and South Western with Barclays in 1918 brought this French interest into Barclays' orbit. By the time of the merger Cox had six French branches, and further branches followed. In 1922 the business was completely taken over by Barclays, which formed Barclays Bank (Overseas), renamed Barclays Bank (France) in 1926. It was not long before Barclays experienced some of the problems which damaged Lloyds and National Provincial Foreign Bank. Ignorance of local conditions and ill-advised lending led to a growing bad-debt problem, especially during the early 1930s, and Barclays was obliged to provide off-balance sheet support to the bank. Barclays Bank (France) had to be 'given' over £400,000 by its parent to keep it in existence in the 1930s.[34]

In 1925 Barclays also established a wholly owned and Italian-registered bank, Barclays Bank SAI. This unwise initiative stemmed from over-optimistic intelligence that the bank might become bankers to the Vatican. In 1925, a Holy Year, a branch was opened in central Rome, and in the following year a second branch was opened in Genoa. Unfortunately, no business materialized from the Vatican except a small deposit, and by the early 1930s large bad debts had accumulated. 'The Bank', Goodenough observed in 1934, 'had passed through two phases—the first was one of disaster, and the second, one of liquidation.' Thereafter, business activity was much reduced, and the Genoa branch closed in 1937.[35]

Outside Europe, Barclays established Barclays Bank (Canada) in 1929. This was a chartered bank under Canadian law, and was jointly owned by Barclays Bank and Barclays (DCO), and designed to finance trade between Canada, Britain, and the rest of the Empire.[36] Local legislation, requiring a certain amount of the capital and reserves of a bank to be kept within Canada, obliged Barclays to establish a separate bank, even though Goodenough considered that a better performance would have been obtainable if the Canadian venture had been part of Barclays Bank or DCO.[37] Barclays

[34] Jones, 'Lombard Street on the Riviera', 189, 199; Secretary, Barclays Bank (France) to F. G. Bacon, 2 July 1954, B02H, BBA.

[35] Jones, 'Lombard Street on the Riviera', 199–200.

[36] F. C. Goodenough to Rt. Hon. Viscount Willington (Ottawa), 14 Nov. 1927, Chairman and General Manager's Correspondence, 3/215, BBA.

[37] Ibid., F. C. Goodenough to J. R. Leisk, 5 Nov. 1931, 3/212.

Bank (Canada) developed a small foreign exchange business, but stagnated from the mid-1930s. It was managed with a distinct lack of entrepreneurial flair, and failed even to attract the accounts of British companies operating in Canada.[38]

Finally, in the 1930s Barclays (DCO) built up an interest in the Eastern Bank. The motivation for this investment appears to have been that Barclays wished to develop its business with Arab customers, but was handicapped because of its strong Jewish customer base in Palestine.[39] In 1939 DCO's chairman joined the board of Eastern Bank, and during the early 1940s DCO made regular share purchases when market conditions were right, regarding Eastern Bank's shares as a reasonable investment in this period.[40] In contrast, Barclays consistently declined to take an investment in the Bank of British West Africa (BBWA), in which Lloyds and several other clearers already had stakes. An initial approach in the mid-1930s, in the context of reducing 'needless and wasteful competition in West Africa' between DCO and BBWA, was rejected. BBWA raised the matter again in 1939, and in 1943 its chairman tried—again unsuccessfully—to persuade Barclays to take over the whole of his bank.[41]

Apart from Lloyds and Barclays, two of the other 'Big Five' English clearing banks entered overseas banking, although on nothing like the same scale. The Westminster Bank's experience had some similarities to that of Lloyds. In 1913 it established a greenfield Paris subsidiary, which—as Westminster Foreign Bank—had acquired branches in Spain and Belgium as well as France. The whole venture was ill planned, and by 1921 the Westminster Bank had lost about £1 million on its continental operation. Thereafter, a policy of extreme caution was followed, and the Spanish branches were sold in 1924 after further large losses. In 1916 Westminster Bank invested £100,000 in the British Italian Corporation, and thus suffered from its subsequent disastrous performance. In 1920 Westminster Bank, National Provincial, and Standard Bank joined Lloyds as shareholders in BBWA. Lloyds had 12.5 per cent of the issued capital, and the other three banks 11 per cent each. In the same year Westminster Bank also joined Lloyds as one of the shareholders in the P & O Banking Corporation, selling its investment in 1927 when Chartered Bank acquired most of the equity.[42]

The National Provincial Bank had a sudden enthusiasm for overseas

[38] Ibid., Sir Julian Crossley Diaries, 17 Dec. 1946 and 23 Mar. 1948, 38/209, BBA; Extract from Sir George Bolton's Memorandum, 14 Oct. 1953, C48/152, B. of E.

[39] Crossley and Blandford, *The DCO Story*, 94.

[40] Sir Julian Crossley Diaries, 31 July 1944, 38/209, BBA.

[41] Richard Fry, *Bankers in West Africa* (London: Hutchinson Benham, 1976), 143–4; Sir Julian Crossley Diaries, 10 Sept. 1943, 38/209, BBA.

[42] Jones, 'Lombard Street on the Riviera', 187, 189–90, 198–9; Fry, *Bankers in West Africa*, 96.

investment during the war. In 1916 it took a shareholding in the British Italian Corporation, though only a quarter the size of the Lloyds and Westminster investments, and in 1917 purchased half of Lloyds' continental subsidiary. National Provincial was subsequently not only burdened with the losses made by the unsuccessful Lloyds and National Provincial Foreign Bank, but felt aggrieved that everyone continued to regard the venture as belonging to Lloyds alone, with the resulting loss of any related business.[43] In 1920 National Provincial took 11 per cent of the capital of BBWA and secured a shareholding in the P & O Banking Corporation. Finally, in 1924 National Provincial made its one wholly owned foreign acquisition when it purchased the entire share capital of Grindlay and Company, which a few years previously had begun to diversify from personal banking for Army personnel into more general commercial banking in India.[44]

The effect on the ownership structure of British multinational banking of the advent of the clearing banks was substantial. In 1938 Barclays controlled four overseas banks, including DCO, the largest measured by total assets and branch numbers. Bolsa, Grindlays, and Westminster Foreign Bank were wholly or partly owned by other clearers. Lloyds and National Provincial Foreign Bank was jointly owned by two clearers. BBWA was owned by the Lloyds, National Provincial, and Westminster Banks together with the Standard Bank of South Africa, while Eastern Bank and National Bank of New Zealand had equity stakes held by Barclays and Lloyds respectively.

The functional and geographical specialization of British overseas banking had been partially ended during the inter-war years by the clearers' entry into multinational banking, therefore, but any potential internalization advantages were dissipated by management and organizational failings. Opportunities for the co-ordination of business activities were often missed. The Lloyds overseas banking group represented the largest example of this failing. Only Barclays, by creating a multi-regional overseas bank with real management links to the domestic parent, was able to reap some internalization advantages. The main consequence of the entry of British clearing banks into overseas banking was the retention in existence of the substantial and unprofitable British branch networks in regions such as Latin America, the West Indies, parts of colonial Africa, and continental Europe. The support of the domestic banks provides, therefore, one explanation for the ability of the overseas banks to survive the turbulence of the inter-war years.

Meanwhile, there was one member of the 'Big Five' domestic banks which

[43] Jones, 'Lombard Street on the Riviera', 202.
[44] Geoffrey Tyson, *100 Years of Banking in Asia and Africa* (London: National and Grindlays Bank, 1963), 189.

avoided multinational banking. This was the Midland Bank, which had been the most innovative in its attitude to international banking business in the 1900s, and had been on the verge of opening a branch in Russia when the Communist Revolution of 1917 resulted in a sudden change of circumstances. However, the Midland Bank subsequently settled on a strategy of acting as 'bankers' bank' in London rather than competing with foreign banks on their own territory. Given the disturbed conditions prevailing in many countries in the inter-war years, this proved a sensible strategy, and during the 1930s in particular the Midland made substantial profits from its correspondent banking business.[45] Contrary to the expectations of the other clearing banks, Midland demonstrated that a successful international banking business could be conducted without multinational branching in this period.

The 'free-standing' structure of British multinational banking was modified in the inter-war years by the advent of equity links between domestic and overseas banks. The consequences of this shift in the ownership of some of the banks, however, were less radical than might have been envisaged. Only Barclays sought to merge its overseas interests into a multiregional multinational bank, whose business was co-ordinated with the domestic parent. For the most part the inherited 'free-standing' tradition of regionally specialized banks with no domestic British business remained in place, although the financial support of domestic banks helped to ensure the survival of part of the British multinational branch network.

### 5.3. Mergers, Concentration, and the Fall of Anglo-South

The main changes to the structure of British overseas banking came from the advent of the clearing banks into multinational banking, but there were also other developments. In 1918 the last British overseas bank in Canada, the Bank of British North America, was acquired by the Bank of Montreal. The removal of the former's ninety-two branches from British control spelled the end of a significant British-controlled branch network in North America until the 1970s.[46]

There was some consolidation between British banks active in the same region. In the East, the Indian business of the Delhi and London Bank was acquired in 1916 by the Alliance Bank of Simla, an Indian-registered but British-managed bank. Delhi and London Bank's English business passed to Boulton Brothers of London, which had been associated with the Alliance Bank since 1914. Unfortunately, Boulton Brothers engaged in fraudulent financial transactions and in 1923 they and the Alliance Bank—which

---

[45] Jones, 'Lombard Street on the Riviera', 187, 190–1, 200–1; A. R. Holmes and Edwin Green, *Midland: 150 Years of Banking Business* (London: Batsford, 1986), 133–4, 137–41.
[46] Baster, *The Imperial Banks*, 224–5.

operated no fewer than forty-five branches in India—crashed.[47] Another First World War merger initiative was the Mercantile Bank of India's acquisition of the small Bank of Mauritius. Although Mauritius was geographically distant from Mercantile's Asian base, there were strong trading links between the island and India.

A later intra-regional merger in the East was Chartered Bank's absorption of the P & O Banking Corporation. The Corporation was the single new overseas bank established after 1914 which was neither owned by the clearers nor a 'semi-official' bank such as the Anglo-International Bank (see Chapter 7). The prime mover behind the founding of the P & O Banking Corporation in 1920 was the first Earl of Inchcape, the chairman of the P & O Steam Navigation Company, the largest shipping combine in the world at that time. The shipping company had developed a substantial private banking business, and Inchcape considered that this profitable activity could be further enhanced if it was hived off into a separate institution, which could raise money to fund expansion. The bank made large loans to the shipping company to help with the purchase of new ships, and on the basis of this inter-group business initially expanded rapidly.[48] By 1921 it had four branches in India and one in the West End of London as well as a head office in the City. P & O also, in a radical move, purchased a controlling interest in the Allahabad Bank, another Indian-registered but British-managed institution, making it the first Exchange bank to possess a strong domestic banking business in the interior of India. Further branches followed during the first half of the 1920s, in Colombo, Shanghai, Hong Kong, Singapore, and Canton.[49]

This new creation did not fare well, and it was never able to overtake its older rivals. In 1927 Chartered Bank—anxious to remove a competitor and interested in entering Indian domestic banking through the Allahabad Bank—made an offer to buy the shares, and by mid-July it had acquired three-quarters of P & O's equity. The P & O Banking Corporation was in considerable difficulties by that time. At the end of March 1928, the amount standing to the credit of P & O's profit and loss account was only £82,453, while the amount required to pay the usual 5 per cent dividend was £105,000. All but two branches (Shanghai and Singapore) had made losses during the previous year, and the main source of revenue was derived from money market operations in London. In the East, the exchange markets were extremely competitive, while the Inchcape group of companies proved

---

[47] Ibid., 222–3; Memorandum on Report of the Liquidators, 19 Nov. 1924, G30/13, B. of E.

[48] Stephanie Jones, *Trade and Shipping: Lord Inchcape, 1852–1932* (Manchester: Manchester University Press, 1989), 123–4, 131.

[49] P & O Annual Reports and Accounts in 1920s; Compton Mackenzie, *Realms of Silver* (London: Routledge & Kegan Paul, 1954), 262.

loyal to their old bankers, the Imperial Bank of India, and were slow to transfer their funds to the P & O Bank. The new entrant had resorted to inferior business to build market share, and bad debts had resulted.[50] The P & O Banking Corporation was retained as a distinct entity over the next decade, although four Chartered directors joined the board and there was some rationalization of duplicated branches. However, the bank's earnings never again surpassed the level of 1927. It was never able to find adequate local deposits and its profitability continued to rest mainly on money market operations.[51] In February 1939 Chartered purchased the remainder of the capital of the bank, which was then totally absorbed and ceased to exist, although the Allahabad Bank was retained as a distinct entity.

There were also mergers among the British banks beyond the East. In South Africa, the African Banking Corporation was purchased by Standard Bank in 1921.[52] In the same year the London Bank of Australia was acquired by the English, Scottish & Australian Bank. By the 1930s there was considerable discussion among the British-owned trading banks in Australia about more extensive mergers, but—for reasons discussed below—nothing materialized until 1951, when the two largest banks merged to form ANZ.

It was in Latin America that the most extensive concentration occurred. London and River Plate and London and Brazilian Banks had come together in the Lloyds group during and immediately after the First World War. The aggressive growth of the Anglo-South American Bank resulted in further concentration of British banks. As the eventual collapse of this bank was one of the most serious episodes in the history of British multinational banking in the inter-war years, it is worth examining its performance in some detail.

Anglo-South had embarked on the path of growth through acquisition before the First World War. The driving force behind the bank's growth was R. J. Hose, who had joined it as secretary in 1896 (the day before the founder, Colonel North, died), and became managing director in 1911 and chairman in 1918. In 1920 Hose achieved his ambition to be represented in Brazil by purchasing the British Bank of South America, the rival of the London and Brazilian Bank. In that year, too, he acquired 60 per cent of the shares of Banco A. Edwardes y Cía, an old established banking house in Chile, which had run its business on orthodox British principles.[53]

[50] Memorandum re P & O Bank's Results at 31 Mar. 1928, Mr Keenan's File, BAC 63, SC.

[51] Ibid., Chartered's Memorandum on the P & O Banking Corporation, and Comment of 17 Oct. 1938, P & O Files, BAC 63.

[52] J. A. Henry, The First Hundred Years of the Standard Bank (London: Oxford University Press, 1963), 232–3.

[53] Charles A. Jones, 'Commercial Banks and Mortgage Companies', in D. C. M. Platt (ed.), Business Imperialism 1840–1930 (Oxford: Clarendon Press, 1977), 49.

The rapid growth of the bank continued in the following years. In 1921 a shareholding was taken in a Belgian private bank, the Banque Générale Belge. Two years later Anglo-South's Paris branch was converted into the locally registered Banque Anglo-Sud-Américaine, and its New York agency was converted into the Anglo-South American Trust Company. The acquisition and establishment of affiliates was accompanied by a rapid expansion of the branch network, and penetration into new territories. The Commercial Bank of Spanish America, which had been acquired before 1914, was used as a vehicle to diversify into a number of Central American and Caribbean countries, such as Guatemala.[54]

The pace of growth was not matched by enhanced profitability. While the size of the bank grew, a weakening share price sharply reduced the market value of its capital during the 1920s. By 1928 Anglo-South was the largest British multinational bank measured by total assets, but only around twelfth in terms of market capitalization. Although the bank's real profits are unknown, its published profits ratio in this decade was very low compared to most of the sample banks, while its shareholders would have done better to invest in Consols than hold its equity.

Several things went wrong for the Anglo-South American Bank in the 1920s. The entrepreneurial spirit of the bank was not matched by organizational capability. The central direction of the group and its highly diversified interests was over-concentrated in the hands of Hose.[55] Anglo-South, the British Bank, and the Commercial Bank operated three different head offices in London. In Latin America, the group was slow to rationalize the branch network, and acquired banks continued to function as independent units. In Uruguay in 1924 the British Bank took over the business of Anglo-South, but four years later the decision was reversed and Anglo-South reopened. Only in the mid-1920s were steps taken to rationalize the activities of the Commercial Bank, which became involved in trading activities as well as banking. In 1926 the Commercial Bank's branches in Central America, Colombia, Venezuela, and Ecuador were incorporated into Anglo-South, and a more conventional banking business was subsequently followed.[56]

Managerial and organizational defects were accompanied by insufficient care for prudent finance. Dividend payments were more generous than the bank's underlying profitability would have indicated. In 1927 £800,000 was taken from the published reserves to provide for capital depreciation in Latin America, and less than a fifth of this sum had been restored by 1930. By 1929 and 1930 the dividends of the British Bank of South America exceeded the profits it earned. Anglo-South raised cash for itself by selling

[54] Joslin, *A Century of Banking in Latin America*, 257–62.
[55] Ibid., 260.    [56] Ibid., 261–2.

TABLE 5.4. *Production and prices of Chilean nitrates, 1918–1934*

| Year | Production (000 tons) | % total world production | Price ($US per ton) |
|------|------------------------|--------------------------|----------------------|
| 1918 | 487.5 | 42 | 58 |
| 1922 | 182.6 | 21 | 52 |
| 1926 | 346.1 | 23 | 43 |
| 1930 | 419.7 | 19 | 34 |
| 1934 | 144.8 | 7 | 19 |

*Source*: Based on Thomas F. O'Brien, 'Rich beyond the Dreams of Avarice: The Guggenheims in Chile', *Business History Review*, 63 (1989), tables 1 and 2.

some of its real estate to its own property company, which then issued mortgage debentures, the principal and interest of which were guaranteed by the parent bank. There was evidence, too, that the bank was responding to pressure on its profitability by shifting assets into higher-earning, but illiquid, business.[57]

These weaknesses in management and finance were, perhaps, a consequence of fast entrepreneurial growth, which could have been rectified if the business climate had continued to offer profitable opportunities. Unfortunately the impact of falling commodity prices on the Latin American economies created anything but ideal conditions for a bank, especially as Anglo-South remained over-exposed to one particular commodity, nitrates.

Anglo-South had its origins as the 'nitrate bank'. In the late nineteenth century Chilean nitrates were an excellent business for a bank to link its fortunes to. In 1894 Chile supplied over 70 per cent of the entire world nitrate market, and prices were generally maintained and supported by cartel agreements. Such price-fixing, however, encouraged the development of substitute products. Already by 1914 nitrogen, usually derived from coal distillation, was a serious competitor to Chilean nitrates. The First World War stimulated the production of synthetic nitrogen.[58] The consequences for the prices and relative importance of Chilean nitrates can be seen in Table 5.4.

By the mid-1920s the competitive threat posed by synthetic nitrates to natural nitrates was well known,[59] but Anglo-South's exposure to Chile

[57] Ibid., 263–4; Report by Deloitte, Plender, Griffiths on Anglo-South American Bank, 17 May 1932, C48/89, B. of E.

[58] Thomas F. O'Brien, ' "Rich beyond the Dreams of Avarice": The Guggenheims in Chile', *Business History Review*, 63 (1989), 132–9.

[59] See e.g. General Manager to W. E. Stokes, 19 May 1925, enclosing cutting entitled 'Nitrate Sales' from *Financial Times*, 19 May 1925, B2/3, Bolsa Archives, UCL.

and the nitrate industry was so great that substantial diversification away from them was difficult. Moreover, there was a considerable vote of confidence in the industry's future by the Guggenheims, the diversified American mining group. In 1924 the Guggenheims made their first investment in Chilean nitrates, confident in the belief that a new production process would enable them to reduce costs, and in 1929 they acquired the most important nitrate-producer in Chile. Anglo-South, with one-third of all its advances tied up in nitrates, eagerly welcomed the arrival of the Guggenheims, and their plans to reorganize the industry, and 'secretly assisted' them in the 1929 takeover bid.[60] Unfortunately a continuing fall in prices undermined the ambitions of the Guggenheims. Early in 1930 Anglo-South finally began to limit further lending to nitrate interests, but the bank was so committed to the industry that it had little alternative but to continue to support it in the hope that the situation could be saved by some reorganization.

In March 1931 the Chilean government and private producers finally agreed a reorganization plan. The Compâniá de Salitre de Chile (Cosach) was formed to undertake the production and sales of natural nitrate, with the Guggenheims controlling the management, and with special fiscal concessions from the government. Anglo-South gave advances to Cosach to get it started, on the understanding that Cosach would issue bonds in New York and London in order to pay off the creditors. The financial structure of Cosach, however, was weak, and external circumstances were less than propitious. The situation of the financial markets in 1931 meant that it was impossible for the loan for Cosach to be floated, while in July of that year the Chilean government that had helped form Cosach was overthrown. Anglo-South extended short-term credit to Cosach in the form of acceptances, but from July there was a run on deposits and on 10 September the bank's managing director had to go to the Bank of England for help.[61] Anglo-South's subsequent fate is explored in Section 7.3.

The inter-war years saw some concentration among the overseas banks not involved with the clearing banks. In the East, Australia and South Africa smaller banks had been absorbed by their larger brethren, although not to the extent that the structure of British overseas banking had been fundamentally changed. The process had gone furthest in Latin America, where all British multinational banking had been reduced to a single bank by the end of the 1930s, in part because of the failure of the entrepreneurial Anglo-South American Bank. This institution had created a branch network spread all over Central and South America, and begun building a presence in the United States and Europe. If the vision had worked,

---

[60] O'Brien, 'The Guggenheims in Chile', 139–47.
[61] Ibid., 149–53; Joslin, *A Century of Banking in Latin America*, 266–8.

Anglo-South might have developed as an organization broadly similar to Barclays (DCO)—a multi-regional bank, but without a domestic bank shareholder. Unfortunately the combination of the inter-war primary-product price difficulties and organizational deficiencies proved fatal.

## 5.4. Management Structures

A striking feature of the inter-war years was the extent to which the management structures already in place before 1914 remained in existence. There were strong similarities in the composition of boards, and of their relationship with CEOs and branch managers. The unstable conditions of the inter-war years probably discouraged organizational innovation, but there was also an aura of stagnation about many banks, which had only just begun to change in the prelude to the Second World War.

The recruitment of the boards of directors of the overseas banks remained very similar to the pre-First World War years. The same family dynasties often presided. This was true of the directors of the Bank of Australasia and the Union Bank of Australia, many of whom were elderly and long-serving figures until, towards the end of the 1930s, deaths and resignations cleared a path for a new generation.[62] The board of the Imperial Bank of Persia had a similar static quality. The seven members of the board had an average age of 71 in 1936, and they were led by an 83-year-old chairman who had become a director in 1913.[63] Chartered Bank had the same chairman between 1904 and 1932—he had been born in the same year as the foundation of the bank, and was 79 on his retirement.[64]

Regardless of the age of their members, the boards of many overseas banks continued to exercise executive functions. They continued to recruit junior executive staff; to make decisions on lending above the limits allowed to their CEOs and managers; and to take the final decisions on overall strategies. In the Union Bank of Australia, the Standing Committee of the board met twice a week during the inter-war years, playing a major role in policy formation. The Imperial Bank of Persia's board obliged two successive chief managers to retire, in 1935 and 1939.[65] In the Bank of British West Africa there was some shift of power away from the board to the general management, especially during the tenure of Leslie Couper as general manager between 1918 and his death in 1929. Couper had a strong independent standing in Whitehall and the City which reinforced his authority. However, even during the 1920s there were many *ad hoc* board committees to discuss policy matters, and after Couper's death the power of the directorate seems to have reasserted itself, especially for the

[62] D. T. Merrett, *ANZ Bank* (Sydney: Allen and Unwin, 1985), 29, 54.
[63] Geoffrey Jones, *Banking and Empire in Iran* (Cambridge: Cambridge University Press, 1986), 186, 211–12.    [64] Mackenzie, *Realms of Silver*, 270–1.
[65] Geoffrey Jones, *Banking and Empire in Iran*, 210–33.

ten years after 1937 when there were two men serving as joint managing directors.[66]

There were exceptions to this pattern, as there had been before the First World War. In the Standard Bank, whose chairmanship continued to alternate on a weekly basis, the general management in South Africa had considerable authority all through the inter-war years. The Hongkong Bank's board, too, remained non-executive. Although the board had to be respected and consulted, the chief manager continued to run the bank.[67]

Boards remained important for the commercial intelligence and business links they provided a bank. Members of the Hongkong Bank's board continued to be elected largely because of their business affiliations. They were drawn from the most important agency houses in Hong Kong and the China coast, and these firms in turn had connections throughout the Far East, in other regions such as the Persian Gulf, and in London.[68] Before its troubles, the Anglo-South American Bank's board boasted an array of men with powerful Latin American and international business connections, notably the Bolivian magnate Don Antenor Patiño, who was in the process of consolidating much of the world tin industry under his control.[69] In Latin America, the East, Australia, and elsewhere, business flowed between banks and other enterprises linked at director level, creating networks of long-term relationships.

As before 1914, the CEOs of some banks, notably those active in Australia and South Africa, were located in these countries, while the Eastern and Latin American banks had their executives in London. Long-serving chief executives were often found. The English, Scottish & Australian Bank had the same general manager between 1909 and 1933, when he retired aged 76. The Bank of Australasia's superintendent was in the post for eighteen years before his retirement in 1944, aged 71. Chartered Bank had the same man as chief manager between 1920 and 1933, but then three incumbents in the post in the subsequent seven years.

The power of 'London' in decision-making which had grown in many banks before 1914 was not reversed in the inter-war years, although there remained considerable variations even among British banks within the same region, and within the same bank over time. In inter-war Australia, there was a spectrum in the degree of London control. At the one extreme, the board of the Union Bank exercised exceptionally close control over its Melbourne-based executive, and this only began to be modified during the Second World War.[70] In the Bank of Australasia the voice of London was also strong,

[66] Fry, *Bankers in West Africa*, 40–1, 141. Fry's Digests of BBWA Board Minutes, BAC S/90, SC.

[67] King, *The History of the Hongkong and Shanghai Banking Corporation*, iii. 38, 290–9.

[68] Ibid., 40–6.      [69] Joslin, *A Century of Banking in Latin America*, 260–1.

[70] Merrett, *ANZ Bank*, 48–50, 58–9.

though perhaps less so than in the Union Bank. In contrast, after the First World War the Australian executive of the English, Scottish & Australian Bank appears to have had more power. The implications of these variations for the business strategies of the three banks will be discussed below.

In many other banks London-based boards and managements remained highly influential. The views of London featured prominently in the Imperial Bank of Persia. The advice of that bank's Tehran-based chief manager in the 1930s that facilities should be granted to assist the government's industrialization programme was overruled in London, on the grounds that such lending was 'contrary to the tenets of British banking'.[71] Among the Eastern Exchange banks, London remained the dominant voice in the Chartered Bank, Eastern Bank and the P & O Banking Corporation. In the Ionian Bank, the general management moved from Athens to London in 1921, leaving behind a regional management for Greece.

During the 1900s the Hongkong Bank's London Committee had secured a special place in that bank's affairs as the focus for its merchant-banking activities. In 1919 the Committee was reorganized, with the bank's senior London manager, Sir Charles Addis, appointed the ex-officio chairman. Addis was joined by representatives from Hongkong Bank's London clearer, and leading merchant banks, indicating a continuing strong interest in international finance. When Addis retired from the bank's staff in 1922, he became permanent chairman of the committee. However, changing circumstances in China (which will be more fully examined in Chapter 6) placed a question mark over the usefulness of the London Committee. None of the investment and loan projects in which the bank was interested came to fruition in the 1920s. Over time Hong Kong also became uneasy about the London Committee. The need for such a high-powered group of financial experts which had become progressively divorced from the bank's London management, with whom it had little contact by the late 1920s, was questioned. In 1933 these tensions culminated in the decision of the bank's chief manager to retire Addis from the chairmanship of the committee, and, for the remainder of the decade, the authority of 'London' within the Hongkong Bank was weak, with Hong Kong exercising a decisive influence on policy matters.[72]

The outbreak of the war in the Pacific resulted in a dramatic and unprecedented transformation in this situation. In December 1941 Hong Kong was overrun by the Japanese Army, and the bank's erstwhile headquarters taken over as the result of the new Japanese administration. In August 1943 its chief manager died in a Japanese prison camp. The bank's senior London manager, Arthur Morse, who had transferred from Hong

[71] Jones, *Banking and Empire in Iran*, 229.
[72] King, *The History of the Hongkong and Shanghai Banking Corporation*, iii. 46–50, 94–8, 217–30, 371–5, 465–8.

Kong to London in 1939, became the acting chief manager of the bank. The members of the London Committee became the *de facto* board, and in 1943 Morse was elected chairman of the board. It was not until June 1946 that the head office of the bank was re-established in Hong Kong.[73]

The growth in size of many banks was not matched by the development of appropriate managerial hierarchies, with the result that the organizational capabilities of a range of institutions came under strain. The apex of the management structures was often insufficient given the growth in scale and scope of many institutions. This was evident in the case of Anglo-South American Bank, where R. J. Hose combined the posts of chairman and managing director between 1918 and 1928, when a CEO was belatedly appointed. With only a small support staff at the group's three London head offices, the managerial task facing Hose was formidable. The Australian banks manifested similar, if less damaging, problems. In the 1930s the Bank of Australasia's superintendent, supported by a staff of twenty-four in Melbourne, handled a vast range of administrative tasks, signing every letter to London, making all large loans, and making all senior staff appointments. It was not surprising that the superintendent, and his equivalent in the Union Bank where a similar system prevailed, found themselves overwhelmed by detail, with little time for strategic planning even if their London-based boards had permitted such autonomy.[74] In the inter-war English, Scottish & Australian Bank, the general management in Melbourne combined their overall supervision of the bank with the management of its business in the state of Victoria.[75] There was a similar situation in the Hongkong Bank, where the chief manager in Hong Kong ran both the local business in the colony and the international branch network. There was little sign of a distinct head office, although the establishment of an inspectors' department in Hong Kong in 1936 marked its embryonic development.[76]

Some banks evolved a more elaborate general management structure. Standard Bank had several layers of senior management in South Africa, though the exact structure shifted with personality changes within the bank. By 1921 there was a senior general manager in South Africa, supported by three joint general managers and two assistant general managers. In 1927 this was replaced by two joint general managers and two deputy general managers. In 1930 there were three joint general managers, two deputies, and one assistant, and by 1934 the bank had reverted to a sole general manager with supporting executive staff.

[73] Ibid., chs. 12 and 13; ibid., chs. 1 and 2.
[74] Merrett, *ANZ Bank*, 16, 17, 45–7.
[75] J. Ewing's Memorandum of 3 July 1936, E/49/2, ANZ; Merrett, *ANZ Bank*, 206.
[76] King, *The History of the Hongkong and Shanghai Banking Corporation*, iii. 447.

The creation of management organizations at regional level offered one solution to the problems of managing a geographically diffuse banking business. Most progress in this area in the inter-war years was made by the overseas banks with a clearing bank connection. Barclays (DCO)'s system of local boards and local management centres was particularly effective. However, there was always the problem with regional levels of authority that they would complicate rather than facilitate decision-making within a bank, and develop as rival centres of power to boards or CEOs. It was for this reason that some banks had phased out local boards of directors from the late nineteenth century. Regional *managements* rather than directors was one solution, for as salaried servants of the board their officers might be expected to show less independence. This reasoning was no doubt an important factor in Standard Bank's decision after the First World War not to appoint a local board in South Africa, but instead to widen the powers of its general managers.[77]

The Bank of London and South America also developed a regional management system in response to the bad-debt and other difficulties it faced in the years immediately following the merger in 1923. The first step came in 1927, when the start of a regional management system was put in place. Bolsa's general manager sat in London. Under him there had been a chief manager in Buenos Aires, but—as in the case of the Hongkong Bank—he had both supervised the bank's branches in Argentina and managed the large Buenos Aires branch. Under the 1927 reforms, the chief manager was ordered to delegate his local branch management functions, but was given stronger powers over all the Argentinian branches and the branch in Paraguay. However, regional management remained partial in Bolsa at this stage. In Uruguay, the manager at Montevideo controlled all the branches in that country and reported to London, and was requested only to 'seek the counsel and co-operation of the Chief Manager at Buenos Aires'. In Chile, on the other hand, each branch reported directly to London. This was also true for Brazil, where each branch was directly controlled from London, 'the duties of the Chief Manager at Rio de Janeiro Branch being solely consultative'. It was a similar situation in Colombia. There were obvious problems of co-ordination with such a structure, to overcome which it was hoped that managers would 'make a point of meeting more frequently'.[78]

In 1931, as Bolsa's financial performance deteriorated yet further, this organizational system was modified. The chief manager at Buenos Aires took control over the branches in Uruguay and Chile as well as those in Argentina and Paraguay. At the same time the powers of his equivalent in

[77] Henry, *The First Hundred Years of the Standard Bank*, 176.
[78] Report of the Special Committee, 15 Nov. 1927, Bolsa Board Minutes, LB.

Brazil were also much enhanced. The chief manager in Rio de Janeiro henceforth controlled the Brazilian branches in the same way as his colleague in Buenos Aires controlled his branches, except in the matter of lending limits. These continued to be fixed by London 'owing to the great variations in local conditions, and mentality of clients over such a vast area'. A chief manager was also appointed to control the bank's branches in Colombia.[79] This basic system seems to have remained in place for the rest of the decade, although it had to be modified when the acquisition of Anglo-South American Bank's business in 1936 resulted in the absorption of a network of Central American branches into the Bolsa fold.

A regional management structure was found in a number of other banks. The Bank of British West Africa had a number of district managers for each area, such as Gold Coast, Nigeria, Sierre Leone, Morocco, and Egypt. When the bank appointed joint managing directors in 1937, their responsibilities were split on geographical lines, one taking care of West Africa and Morocco, the other everywhere else plus the management of investments and exchange.[80] Between the wars, Ionian Bank also had a regional management system in operation in Greece (which had the most autonomy and importance) and Egypt, together with a weaker local organization in Cyprus. Some banks had no formal regional management, but certain branches were more significant than others and exercised a quasi-regional function. This was true, for example, of Chartered Bank's Singapore and Hong Kong branches.

The control and motivation of managers at branch level remained an important issue for banks. By the inter-war years a range of formal procedures and rules were in operation. This included discretionary limits on the amount of facilities a manager could grant without reference to higher authority; standing orders and regulations; requirements to produce regular reports on branch business; and periodic visits by inspectors. However, individual managers needed sufficient autonomy to be able to make a profit in the local markets that they knew better than did people in London. Each branch manager was thus akin to an entrepreneur, forever seeking new business opportunities.

In these circumstances there were many potential pitfalls. Senior management had to recognize the realities of information asymmetry, and that market and cultural traditions varied widely. 'When in Rome', Bolsa's deputy chairman observed in 1931, 'one must do as Rome does.'[81] When a new manager took over the Mercantile's Shanghai branch in 1929, he received the following letter from London, from the man who became chief manager a few years later:

---

[79] Ibid., Board Minute, 10 Feb. 1931.
[80] BBWA Directors' Private Minute Book, 15 June 1937, SC.
[81] Richard Foster to G. F. Thorburn, 20 July 1931, B34, Bolsa Archives, UCL.

One thing you are not likely to get from Head Office is instructions how to run your Branch . . . if we could run Shanghai, we wouldn't have sent you out there on a large salary to do it for us. Our knowledge of the day to day conditions in your market is practically nil. If we see you going obviously wrong or too deep, we shall call attention to it, but a Branch like yours must be left very much to the Manager to make what he can of it.[82]

However, no British overseas bank applied such a doctrine too literally, both because London-based boards expected some approximation to British banking orthodoxy in their institutions, and because the habits of 'Rome' could lead all too easily to bad debts.

There was thus a tension between allowing managers to act entrepreneurially and the requirements of banking prudence. Too much entrepreneurship at branch level was potentially dangerous, but over-rigid controls and all-pervading conservatism could leave managers lacking motivation and competitive vigour. This seems to have been the case with the Bank of Australasia and the Union Bank, especially from the late 1920s. Reinforced by the bad-debt problems associated with the Depression, the advances of each branch were closely watched by the inspectors. Managers became risk-averse, concerned to avoid mistakes rather than generate new business.[83]

Corporate culture and socialization remained the most important means of ensuring co-ordination between branch managers, and preventing behaviour that was not too aberrant. The multinational banks which operated in countries not settled by Europeans continued to recruit their future executives from Britain, and from a particular social and educational background within Britain. These staff followed a similar career path, working their way up from junior to manager and occasionally beyond. They remained a small group. Hongkong Bank's Eastern staff peaked in the inter-war years at 274. The Imperial Bank of Persia's British overseas executive staff was a mere 68 in 1930, and had fallen to 43 by 1940. The P & O Banking Corporation had a British overseas staff of 50 in 1927 and 45 in 1939. The smallness of numbers and the similar background encouraged a group identity, corporate loyalty, and willingness to abide—in general—in the tradition and practices of the institution.

The recruitment policies of the overseas banks were exemplified by Mercantile Bank of India's response to an enquiry from the Institute of Bankers in 1942. Four general observations were made by the bank's chief manager. First, 'we do not recruit from universities'. Secondly, 'of recent years about half our total recruitment has been from Headmaster's Conference Schools' (i.e. the better fee-paying independent or 'public' schools).

[82] J. B. Crichton to J. B. Ross, 17 Oct. 1929, MB Hist. 1002.8, HSBC.
[83] Merrett, ANZ Bank, 43.

Thirdly, 'very occasionally in special circumstances we have taken boys from other secondary schools in England'. Fourth, 'none from other schools'. Public schools, and occasionally grammar schools, were the only sources of recruitment for the British overseas banks. Mercantile Bank still had some preference for prior banking training, but this was no longer as strong as it had once been, and 'character' had assumed an even greater importance than before 1914. 'We are very largely influenced', the chief manager wrote, 'by a personal interview when appearance, manners, general intelligence and personality count for much. We have frequently found that boys with the best examination records have no personality at all.'[84]

Entry arrangements naturally varied between banks. Hongkong Bank insisted on one or two years' experience in another firm before it would entertain an application, and potential recruits also had to pass a written examination. Emphasis was placed on participation in sports, for 'sports in the East were seen as essential to health, mental and physical, for making contacts inter-house and for learning more of one's own colleagues'. Above all, the bank sought men who would, in the classic British phrase, 'fit in'—who could represent the bank and attract business with confidence.[85] Similar sentiments echoed through other banks. 'We regard personality as one of our greatest assets,' the board of the Imperial Bank of Persia noted in 1929. 'We must look to our representatives in the East, of whatever grade of service, to conduct themselves in and out of office with unremitting regard to the obligations of their position.'[86] In inter-war Australia and South Africa (as well as, for the most part, Ionian's operations in the Mediterranean), the executive staff were overwhelmingly locally recruited rather than being the scions of British public schools, but the ethos and corporate cultures of these local recruits had many similarities to those of the British public school boys.[87]

Common backgrounds, social and sporting links, and lifelong employment bound together the executive staff of the British overseas banks. Formal training was conspicuous by its absence. In some banks, such as the Hongkong Bank, juniors in London were expected to pass a part of the Institute of Bankers' exam before being sent overseas, but overwhelmingly the emphasis remained on learning on the job. Staff continued to learn their jobs by watching others, and by being watched by others.

Nevertheless, some of the larger banks began to consider more formal training for their British staff. Bolsa appointed a staff manager, and had a staff development programme of sorts in operation. In 1927 the bank's

[84] J. B. Crichton to C. Lidbury (President, Institute of Bankers), 10 Apr. 1942, MB Hist. 1002.9, HSBC.
[85] King, *The History of the Hongkong and Shanghai Banking Corporation*, iii. 317–24.
[86] Quoted in Geoffrey Jones, *Banking and Empire in Iran*, 273.
[87] Merrett, *ANZ Bank*, 19–20.

Rules and Instructions to all managers included the obligation to 'periodically transfer members of the staff from one department to another so as
to make each member of the staff thoroughly conversant with the various
duties appertaining to each department'. From 1931 inspectors had to
provide written reports on all executive staff, together with a numerical
assessment of other British staff. Bolsa also had an elementary system of
talent-spotting:

The names of clerks who are particularly well reported upon are extracted at Head
Office on the 'List of Promising Clerks' under the respective countries . . . care is
taken to ensure that promising men are moved to different Branches as often as
possible (with due regard to economy) in order to give them a wide experience
while young.[88]

There is no evidence, however, that most banks achieved even this level of
organization in staff development matters in the inter-war years.

In the circumstances, it is not surprising that the recruitment of university graduates was not a high priority for banks which prized 'personality'
over intellectual ability or academic training. However, there were a few
tentative and unsuccessful experiments. Before the First World War Charles
Addis, who had graduated in economics at Edinburgh University, attempted
to encourage the recruitment of graduates into the Hongkong Bank, arguing that the 'old rule-of-thumb' methods of training were outdated, that
more formal training was needed, and that men who had been trained how
to think were the best candidates in such circumstances. However, his
plans never progressed because of the absence of any accelerated promotion scheme, which meant that graduates had to start at the same level and
salary as the school leaver despite being three or four years older. The
prospect was not a particularly attractive one, especially as there were
many managers in the Hongkong Bank—as in all the others—who dismissed the value of an academic education. The numbers of graduates in
the Hongkong Bank, therefore, remained tiny in the inter-war years.[89] In
the mid-1930s the general management of the Union Bank, concerned
about declining market share in Australia and anxious 'to improve the
calibre of our staff', discussed the need

to push on those men who by the study of Accountancy or a course of Commerce
at the Universities and subsequent successful examinations show that they have
ambitions and capacity. These officers should be fit for Managerial and Executive
positions at an earlier age than is the common experience and they should therefore
be of greater service to the Bank.

[88] Memorandum on Staff Training attached to Staff Manager (Bolsa) to F. A. Beane, 19
May 1933, File 2384, LB.
[89] King, *The History of the Hongkong and Shanghai Banking Corporation*, iii. 264–5; ii
(Cambridge: Cambridge University Press, 1988), 185–8.

Similar sentiments were being voiced in the local Bank of New South Wales at the time, but in practice the concern for formal educational qualifications seems to have remained limited, in both institutions.[90]

The managers recruited because of their character and trained on the job steered the British banks through the many hazards of the inter-war years with skill and some success. They did what they always had done well. The real question was their ability to adjust to changing circumstances, and here there were doubts. The British banks tended to experience problems when they attempted geographical and product diversification, a point which will be explored later in this book. Their human-resources policy resulted in a bias towards stability rather than innovation, which was unfortunate because in the inter-war years political and economic realities started to change.

There was already a contrast with some of the larger American banks. When National City Bank (later Citibank) began to establish foreign branches during the First World War, a shortage of skilled personnel was identified, and the management turned immediately to the higher-education system. In 1915 the bank developed a special programme with several American universities which included some practical training in international banking, with the tacit understanding that the successful participants in the programme would later join the bank. In the same year a College Training Program was initiated, which took selected university graduates through a one-year course 'working in various departments of the bank, studying foreign languages, and attending lectures by bank officers'.[91] In the inter-war years formal in-house training programmes were developed. National City Bank was part of the wider 'professionalization of management' which was spreading throughout American business at this time.[92] For the most part, this trend passed British business by, and the overseas banks simply shared the general British view that formal education and training had little to offer practical men of business.

The nineteenth-century corporate governance structures of the British multinational banks stayed in place in the inter-war years. An unkind observer might describe these structures as being largely composed of a cadre of untrained public schoolboys presided over by very elderly directors. In fact, the socialization of the executive staff and the strong corporate cultures remained powerful tools to reduce agent–principal conflicts. Indeed, the sound governance structures of the banks provide a further

[90] General Manager to Standing Committee, 23 June 1936, UBL 191, ANZ Archives; C. B. Schedvin, 'Sir Alfred Davidson', in R. T. Appleyard and C. B. Schedvin (eds.), *Australian Financiers* (Melbourne: Macmillan, 1988), 339–40.

[91] Harold van B. Cleveland and Thomas F. Huertas, *Citibank, 1812–1970* (Cambridge, Mass.: Harvard University Press, 1985), 79–80.

[92] Alfred D. Chandler, *The Visible Hand* (Cambridge, Mass.: Harvard University Press, 1977), 464–8.

explanation for their ability to survive the turbulent inter-war years, although their ability to respond dynamically to change was more questionable.

### 5.5. Crisis Management

The strength of the governance structures of the British multinational banks was put to its greatest test in this period during the two world wars and the economic and financial crisis associated with the Great Depression. Such events heightened the risks of multinational banking, but the British banks proved themselves masters of crisis management.

Graphs 5.1 and 5.2 allow a closer look at the impact of the wars on bank profits. They chart the movements in aggregate published and real profits for all the overseas banks for which real profit data exists in each period. In both periods the banks included are reasonably well distributed by size and region, although no Australasian bank is included. The result is one measure, albeit an imperfect one, of the impact of the wartime shocks.

There was a similar pattern in both conflicts. An initial period of dislocation was followed by rising profits. The Second World War emerges as having had a more disturbing influence on the real profits of the sample banks, which fluctuated sharply at the beginning of the conflict, before settling on an upward trend.[93]

This common pattern can be readily explained. Both wars interrupted the flows of trade in whose finance the British multinational banks were so committed. Both also led to a much higher level of government intervention in their affairs, with exchange controls and other measures transforming their normal business practices.[94] The initial outbreak of war was often accompanied by financial dislocation: for example, there was a wave of panic and moratoria in Latin America, Egypt, and elsewhere in 1914. Branches in enemy-occupied territories were lost. This meant, in the First World War, the loss of the Hamburg branches of the banks and closures in the Middle East.[95] The Turks closed Eastern Bank's branch in Baghdad (then part of the Ottoman Empire), while in 1915 and 1916 the Imperial Bank of Persia lost control over a number of its branches in Iran to Ottoman and German forces.[96] Enemy action took a much greater toll in the Second World War, especially for the Exchange banks. By 1943 the Hongkong Bank had 33 of its 37 Eastern branches overrun by the

[93] For other measures of profitability and performance in the two world wars, see Appendix 5.

[94] See e.g. S. J. Butlin, *Australia and New Zealand Bank* (London: Longman, 1961), 355, 413: Crossley and Blandford, *The DCO Story*, 102.

[95] David J. S. King, 'The Hamburg Branch: The German Period, 1889–1920', in F. H. H. King (ed.), *Eastern Banking* (London: Athlone, 1983), 529–41.

[96] Geoffrey Jones, *Banking and Empire in Iran*, 170–1.

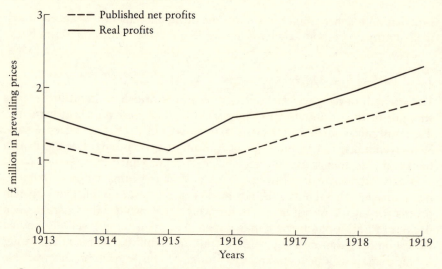

GRAPH 5.1. Aggregate published and real profits of six British multinational banks, 1913–19 (Chartered, Standard, Colonial, Ionian, Imperial Bank of Persia, London and River Plate)

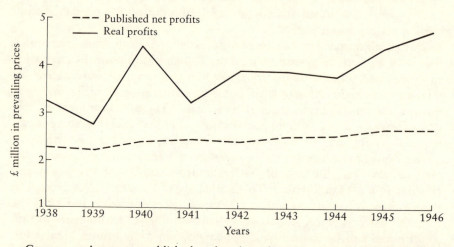

GRAPH 5.2. Aggregate published and real profits of ten British multinational banks, 1938–46 (Chartered, Standard, Barclays (DCO), Ionian, Imperial Bank of Iran, Bolsa, Mercantile, Eastern, Bank of British West Africa, Lloyds and National Provincial Foreign Bank)

Japanese, while the Mercantile Bank of India lost half of its 24 branches, and Chartered 30 of its 43 overseas branches. Conversely, the surge in real profits observable in 1940 was largely the result of the operations of those banks whose branches were located in regions (as yet) untouched by the war, notably Bolsa, Barclays (DCO), and Chartered Bank.

The banks responded well to wartime difficulties, a reflection of the strength of their administrative structures and of their corporate cultures. The most striking instance was the Hongkong Bank in the Second World War, which survived the loss of most of its branches and its head office, the latter being successfully reconstructed in London. The bank's survival was considerably helped by the fact that by the 1930s it had transferred most of its reserves into British securities in London, a move initially undertaken to overcome exchange risks and subsequently maintained because of lack of opportunities for the profitable use of funds in the East.[97]

On a smaller scale, the banks proved adept at maintaining confidence in local markets in the face of adversity, and at responding to unexpected opportunities. British phlegm and being on the winning side proved a successful combination in surviving wartime difficulties. The outbreak of the First World War, for example, caused a serious crisis of confidence in Greece, and a run on the banks. The government declared a moratorium, but the Ionian Bank's administration in Athens publicly refused to take advantage of it and continued to honour all demands made on the bank. Within days Athens was having to draw on head office funds in London. This was unfortunate because much of the bank's liquid resources there which had—in the tradition of the bank—been placed on the London money market had been frozen by a British government moratorium. The Ionian Bank secured temporary assistance from the Bank of England and the Treasury, which enabled it to remit funds to Greece, and the bank emerged with its reputation in Greece enhanced.[98] British bankers excelled at the kind of sang-froid which calmed over-excitable 'locals'. In late June and early July 1942 there was an (understandable) run on the banks in Egypt when it appeared that the German Army was about to overrun the country. Barclays (DCO), however, remained calm and open—paying out £7 million in cash in a week. Branch managers were informed by their local head office that they had a 'unique opportunity . . . to set, by our attitude of forbearance, fortitude and calm, an example to the populace at large'.[99]

---

[97] King, *The History of the Hongkong and Shanghai Banking Corporation*, iii. 178–9, 188, 633.
[98] Chairman's Statement to Shareholders, Ionian Bank, 13 Apr. 1915; *Ionian Bank Ltd.: A History* (London: Ionian Bank, 1953), 37.
[99] Crossley and Blandford, *The DCO Story*, 128–9.

In South Africa, the Standard Bank was directly affected by the First World War when, in October 1914, a rebellion broke out, supported by both anti-war and pro-German elements. Communications were interrupted, and some of Standard's branches in disturbed areas had to be closed. However, the bank was skilled at remaining on good relations with all sides, to such an extent that it was later able to grant loans to the rebels to enable them to meet the fines imposed on them without having to sell stock or land.[100] Further to the north, in East Africa, Standard was ever alert to new opportunities. The defeat of the Germans in German East Africa in 1916 was immediately followed by the despatch of the bank's Kampala manager (in neighbouring British Uganda) to Dar-es-Salaam to open a new branch.[101]

In most countries war quickened the pace of economic activity, and in the process provided new business opportunities for the banks. During the First World War many of the economies in which the overseas banks operated were boosted by rising commodity prices. South Africa profited from high wool prices. Egypt prospered because of high cotton prices. The Bank of British West Africa benefited from the expanding exports and high prices of the West African staples, cocoa and edible nuts and seeds. Anglo-South American's Chilean branches boomed alongside the wartime surge in demand for nitrates. Wartime inflation did more than boost the nominal size of assets. It also created profitable opportunities for exchange operations and arbitrage. Naturally the extent to which an individual bank benefited from such conditions depended upon its own skills. During the First World War, for example, the conservative local managements of the Bank of Australasia and the Union Bank of Australia declined, despite the urgings of their London offices, to adopt policies which would have enabled them to take full advantage of Australia's booming export economy.[102]

In both wars, too, several banks obtained lucrative business servicing the requirements of the British government and its Armed Forces. In Iran in the First World War, the Imperial Bank devoted the bulk of its resources to meeting the requirements of the British government. In the Second World War, after the Allied occupation of Iran in August 1941, the Imperial Bank was again active in servicing British military requirements, and it also benefited from the relaxation of many previous Iranian government restrictions to its operations.[103] In Egypt during the First World War, the Anglo-Egyptian Bank flourished as the official banker for the Army: its chairman described the Army of Occupation as a boon to Egypt which was 'as good as a second cotton crop'.[104] In Iraq, although the Eastern Bank

[100] Henry, *The First Hundred Years of the Standard Bank*, 167.
[101] Ibid., 214–17.   [102] Butlin, *Australia and New Zealand Bank*, 361–3.
[103] Geoffrey Jones, *Banking and Empire in Iran*, 176–82, 298–311.
[104] *A Banking Centenary* (London: Barclays Bank (DCO), 1936), 97.

had had its Baghdad branch seized by the Turks in 1914, as the fortunes of war changed the bank profited from the official support of the British authorities. It opened new branches in the region on the basis of handling the government of India's banking business.[105] There were similar stories in the Second World War. Barclays (DCO)'s Egyptian business, for example, boomed as the bank inherited the Anglo-Egyptian's role as Army banker. Turnover at the Cairo branch of the bank, which in 1939 was less than £6 million, rose to nearly £300 million during the four subsequent years.[106]

The financial crisis of 1931 presented another, but equally grave, challenge to the British multinational banks. 1931 was, as the chairman of Eastern Bank ruefully told his shareholders, 'the most difficult and eventful year in the history of banking, industry and commerce, in living memory'.[107] Britain's enforced departure from the gold standard in September of that year followed several months of diminishing confidence in sterling, and the collapse of the Austrian and German banking systems between May and July. This financial crisis came two years after a major recession had begun in the United States which reduced that country's real gross national product by 30 per cent between 1929 and 1933. The American banking system experienced a series of crises, with almost 9,000 banks closing their doors between the late 1920s and 1933. Meanwhile, the economic problems of the United States spread rapidly, causing a sharp jump in unemployment, price deflation, and falling incomes in most of the industrialized world. The Great Depression had also accelerated a decline in the prices of foodstuffs and raw materials, with devastating consequences for producer countries.

Not surprisingly, these events had an adverse effect on the British overseas banks. The general context of 1931 was clearly the final straw for the gravely weakened Anglo-South American Bank, but the profitability of many institutions was much reduced. Graph 5.3, compiled on the same basis as the equivalent graphs for the two world wars, is suggestive of the severity of the impact on the banks. The aggregate real profits of the seven banks for which data exists fell sharply in 1930 and became briefly negative in 1931, before staging a recovery. Even the 'smoothed' published profits were a third lower for the seven banks in 1931 than two years previously. The aggregate figures contained wide discrepancies between institutions. Both Chartered—the one Eastern Exchange bank in the sample—and Bolsa made large real losses in 1931, in excess of £700,000 each, while most other banks merely had their real profits reduced over the previous year.

[105] Eastern Bank, London to Basra Branch, 6 Sept. 1915, Precedents' Book, Eastern Bank Archives, SC.
[106] Crossley and Blandford, *The DCO Story*, 127–8; for DCO's general wartime role, see *A Bank in Battledress* (London: Barclays Bank (DCO), 1948), 49–50.
[107] Eastern Bank Chairman's Report, Mar. 1932.

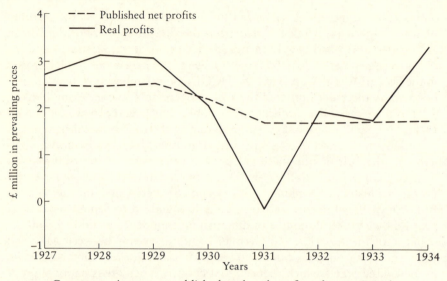

GRAPH 5.3. Aggregate published and real profits of seven British multinational banks, 1927–34 (Chartered, Standard, Barclays (DCO), Ionian, Imperial Bank of Iran, Bolsa, Lloyds and National Provincial Foreign Bank)

The financial and related crises of 1931 hit the British banks in several ways. Falling commodity prices and incomes in producer countries reduced trade flows, which in turn hurt exchange profits, which were dependent on turnover. The difficulties of customers translated into growing bad debts. Those banks which had conducted business with Germany and Central Europe found their funds abruptly frozen in 1931 by exchange controls and 'standstill agreements'.[108]

The collapse of the gold standard caused severe disruption. Chartered blamed its wretched performance in 1931, and the subsequent need to transfer £1 million from published reserves to support profits in that year, directly on exchange losses due to Britain going off the gold standard.[109] All the Exchange banks were affected by uncertainties about silver, to which the Chinese currency remained linked, and which began a new period of depreciation in the late 1920s, reaching a low point against sterling in March 1931, before moving upwards once more.[110] Standard Bank and Barclays (DCO) were placed in exceptional difficulties when South Africa declined to follow Britain off the gold standard. The Union

[108] See e.g. Geoffrey Jones, 'Lombard Street on the Riviera', 198–9; Eastern Bank Profit and Loss Files, R/21, SC. Eastern Bank had £273,403 frozen under the 'standstill' agreements, virtually all of which had been written off by 1939.

[109] Mackenzie, *Realms of Silver*, 240.

[110] King, *The History of the Hongkong and Shanghai Banking Corporation*, iii. 172.

was not finally forced to abandon the gold standard until December 1932. In the intervening period the country's economy was subjected to severe deflationary pressures, while the British banks had a major foreign exchange crisis to face. Standard's overall losses on exchange between 1931 and 1933 were estimated at almost £700,000.[111]

The collapse of the gold standard was perhaps the greatest shock to the British trading banks in Australia. During the 1920s the trading banks had continued to control the Australian exchange rate and hold the country's international reserves using the mechanisms developed in the nineteenth century. Even between 1915 and 1925, when both Australia and Britain were off the gold standard, the exchange rates between the two currencies did not diverge very greatly.[112] In the late 1920s this world disintegrated when the Australian economy encountered a major external liquidity crisis. During the 1920s Australia had borrowed heavily in London and New York.[113] There was growing criticism in London of the size and prudence of Australian borrowing and, by early 1929, in conditions of rising interest rates, it had become impossible to issue Australian debt on the London market.[114] Debt-servicing became dependent on exports of Australia's main primary commodities, wool and wheat, whose prices were falling. As a result, the London funds held by the trading banks—Australia's reserves—fell dramatically during the second half of 1929, raising the possibility of default and national disgrace.

The traditional adjustment mechanisms operated by the trading banks to maintain exchange parity were overwhelmed by this sudden crisis. Their control over the exchange rate and reserves passed to the government through a prolonged and painful process, during which the Bank of New South Wales took a series of initiatives which the British banks in Australia found themselves obliged to follow. At the beginning of 1930 the Commonwealth Bank acquired compulsorily all the available gold reserves of the trading banks, in readiness for a forced sale abroad, and the country effectively left the gold standard. Six months later, as the impact of the Great Depression of Australia intensified, the Bank of New South Wales's general manager, Sir Alfred Davidson, persuaded the other trading banks to give the government priority claim over their holdings of foreign exchange under a voluntary 'Mobilization Agreement'. Pressure on the exchange

---

[111] Henry, *The First Hundred Years of the Standard Bank*, 235–48. Notes on Working of the Bank for the Four Years Ended 31 Mar. 1935, in Ledger in Miscellaneous South Africa Box, SC. Crossley and Blandford, *The DCO Story*, 52–5, 59–62.

[112] *Report of the Royal Commission Appointed to Inquire into the Monetary and Banking Systems at Present in Operation in Australia* (Melbourne, 1936), 43.

[113] R. S. Gilbert, *The Australian Loan Council in Federal Fiscal Adjustments, 1890–1965* (Canberra: Australian National University Press, 1973), 79.

[114] C. B. Schedvin, *Australia and the Great Depression* (Sydney: Sydney University Press, 1970), 96–107.

TABLE 5.5. *Profits (losses) of English, Scottish & Australian Bank, 1927–1933 (£ sterling)*

| Source | 1927 | 1928 | 1929 | 1930 | 1931 | 1932 | 1933 |
|---|---|---|---|---|---|---|---|
| Australia[a] | 475,892 | 418,119 | 406,000 | 448,984 | 318,115 | (418,592) | 275,272 |
| London | 71,956 | 81,795 | 192,133 | 20,559 | (23,393) | 453,824 | 7,400 |
| TOTAL[b] | 547,848 | 499,914 | 598,499 | 469,543 | 294,721 | 35,232 | 282,672 |
| Published profits | 550,988 | 598,769 | 601,262 | 542,736 | 266,658 | 147,719 | 219,327 |

[a] These figures include bad debt recoveries.
[b] These profits are net but are before British income tax. They are not, therefore, equivalent to the 'real' profits of other banks given elsewhere.

*Source*: Melbourne to London, 5 July 1930, E/3/15; Melbourne to London, 8 July 1932, E/3/18; Melbourne to London, 6 July 1933, E/3/19, ANZ Archives.

rate continued, however, as the banks attempted to hold parity with sterling. In January 1931 Davidson broke the trading banks' agreement on exchange rates and led a devaluation of the Australian pound, which by the end of the month had fallen 30 per cent against sterling.[115] Twelve months later the Commonwealth Bank took responsibility for setting the exchange rate and the control of exchange policy passed from the trading banks to the central bank.

These events were a shock to all the trading banks in Australia. Not only was the normal course of business subjected to a deep trauma, but the rules under which the banks had operated for decades were changed fundamentally. The British banks in Australia, unlike their British counterparts in the East and Latin America, had extremely limited experience of major exchange fluctuations, and of the losses that could follow from them. They had their business and their profits buffeted and, given their particular focus on exchange and trade finance, they were probably more exposed to the disruption than many of the local banks.

Although the real profits for the Anglo-Australian banks are not available, the data which does survive gives some idea of the shock experienced by them in these years. The Bank of Australasia's London exchange turnover, for example, fell sharply. Having averaged around £42 million in the five years 1924 to 1929, it entered a sharp decline to £38 million in 1929, £27 million in 1930, and a mere £17 million in 1931, before recovering in subsequent years. Turnover was £25 million in 1932, £27 million in the following year, and £35 million in 1934.[116] The profits of the English, Scottish & Australian Bank were severely affected, as Table 5.5 shows.

[115] Schedvin, 'Sir Alfred Davidson', 346.
[116] Superintendent's Yearly Reports, 1931 and 1939, A/145/13 and A/141/13, ANZ Archives. These figures include Australian and New Zealand exchange transactions.

Moreover, the 'abnormal' exchange situation (as it was often described in internal bank correspondence) had the effect of causing wide fluctuations in the bank's sources of profits as between London and Australia. This was particularly evident in the years 1929 to 1933, when London's profit figures varied dramatically. For a time, the British trading banks in Australia had clearly ridden a whirlwind.

They were not alone. Multinational banks of every country found their business very badly affected by the events of the early 1930s. Although comparative financial data is unavailable, anecdotal evidence makes clear the risks of multinational banking in these years. National City Bank, the American bank with the largest multinational business in the inter-war years, recorded negative earnings for its foreign branches for each of the five years 1930 to 1934.[117] The Banque de l'Indochine's profits fell sharply in the early 1930s as French Indo-China was badly affected by the Great Depression.[118] The leading German overseas bank in Latin America, the Deutsche Ueberseeische Bank, was unable to pay its dividend in 1931, and also passed its dividend in several subsequent years.[119] Given the extent of the British multinational banking interests and the severity of the crisis of the early 1930s, the fact that it was only the Anglo-South which seriously floundered is remarkable.

There are a number of plausible explanations. The concern of the Bank of England to prevent a banking collapse was important, and will be discussed in Chapter 7. Again, the wisdom of certain overseas banks in seeking shelter under the umbrella of large clearing banks also seemed justified by the 1931 crisis. If the British banks active in Brazil, Egypt, or the West Indies had still been the independent institutions of the pre-1914 era, their prospects of survival might have been in doubt. For example, the aggregated geographical breakdown of Barclays (DCO)'s profits given in Table 5.3 disguises the severity of the fall in profits faced by the former Colonial and Anglo-Egyptian Bank operations in the early 1930s.[120] In a wider sense, the overseas banks benefited from their adherence to British banking orthodoxies. The banking crises of these years were at their worst in those countries where commercial and investment banking had been combined, for such banks with long-term loans to industries found their

---

[117] Cleveland and Huertas, *Citibank*, 207.

[118] Y. Gonjo, 'La Banque coloniale et l'État: la Banque de l'Indochine devant l'interventionnisme, 1917–1931', *Le Mouvement social*, 142 (1988), 74; Marc Meuleau, *Des pionniers en Extrême-Orient* (Paris: Fayard, 1990), 360–401.

[119] Manfred Pohl, *Deutsche Bank Buenos Aires, 1887–1987* (Mainz: Hase and Koehler, 1987), 76.

[120] The Egyptian profits declined from £101,089 in the year ending Sept. 1929 to £77,803 in 1930 and £34,288 in 1931. Profits from the former Colonial Bank branches in the West Indies and West Africa declined from £151,104 to £109,865 and £38,877. Papers submitted to DCO Accounts Boards, 38/251, BBA.

solvency affected by the declining value of their assets, while banks with substantial share portfolios were vulnerable to declining security prices.[121]

The survival of the banks also rested, as in the world wars, on effective crisis management. In the short term this consisted of a skilful combination of policies designed to preserve public confidence while achieving private prudence. The published and inner reserves built up by earlier generations of managers were now used for the purpose for which they had been intended—to preserve confidence during crisis conditions. Bolsa, Chartered, Bank of Australasia, and English, Scottish & Australian Bank were among the institutions which reduced their published reserves by at least £1 million in 1931. Other banks drew on their inner reserves to pay dividends and strengthen their public appearance. Dividends were cut in most banks, although not too drastically, and a variety of economy measures were implemented, often involving a reduction in directors' fees, sometimes the reduction of staff salaries, some redundancies, and the closure of marginal branches.[122] Corporate cultures were sufficiently strong that bank staff were prepared to tolerate falling incomes and declining promotion prospects in order to ensure the survival of the whole institution. In some instances the branch closures were substantial. The Imperial Bank of Persia's branch network shrank from 29 to 14 in the ten years after 1929, while the Bank of British West Africa's numbers fell from 58 in 1929 to 40 over the same period. It all amounted to an effective cost control programme in the face of declining revenues and growing bad debts.

The longer-term response of the banks to the new circumstances caused by the Great Depression and the collapse of the gold standard was a shift in business strategy. The 1930s saw large increases in the investments held by the banks. Exactly the same phenomenon can be seen in the balance sheets of British domestic banks, and the reasons were very similar. While safe commercial lending opportunities were in decline, the attraction of holding British government securities rose. The low interest rate policies adopted in Britain from 1932 raised the capital value of gilts, while a shift in the composition of government debt from short- to long-term borrowing had the effect of lengthening the average life of securities held by the banks.[123] The ratio of investments to deposits rose sharply for almost all of the British multinational banks between 1929 and 1938, regardless of

---

[121] Harold James, Introduction, in Harold James, Hakan Lindgren, and Alice Teichova (eds.), *The Role of Banks in the Interwar Economy* (Cambridge: Cambridge University Press, 1991), 7.

[122] See e.g. King, *The History of the Hongkong and Shanghai Banking Corporation*, iii. 191–2; Merrett, *ANZ Bank*, 203; Fry, *Bankers in West Africa*, 135–6; Joslin, *A Century of Banking in Latin America*, 253.

[123] Michael Collins, *Money and Banking in the UK: A History* (London: Croom Helm, 1988), 247–51.

their area of operation.[124] These investments played a major role in securing the continued existence of several banks. An extreme case was the
Imperial Bank of Persia, whose main source of profit after 1931 was the
income from investments managed by the London office.[125] However,
investment income was important for many other banks. By the mid-1930s
the Hongkong Bank had 'a high proportion' of its funds in sterling securities, and in 1935 the bank's chief manager wrote to one branch manager
that it would be more profitable to close his branch 'and invest the expenses
saved in a Post Office savings account'.[126]

In Australia, all the trading banks in the 1930s placed considerable
funds in Commonwealth Treasury Bills. Although such bills had been
issued in small numbers in the 1920s, the banks had generally looked
askance at them. The situation was transformed in June 1931 when the
Commonwealth Bank, in search of bank credit in order to finance government deficits, undertook to rediscount bills held by the banks virtually
at par. In a period of high liquidity and low profitability, Treasury Bills
provided an ideal outlet for the banks' funds. The trading banks' holdings
of Treasury Bills expanded from £1.5 million in the fourth quarter of
1929, to £20.7 million in the same period in 1931, and £38 million twelve
months later. The British banks became eager converts to Treasury Bills
but, as so often, it was the Bank of New South Wales which first perceived
their usefulness.[127]

The stability of the British multinational banks during the world wars
and the crisis of the early 1930s demonstrated their strength as business
institutions. They were able to overcome short-term dislocations, and also
make appropriate adjustments to medium-term strategies.

## 5.6. Conclusion

Given the severity of the political and economic crisis in the world economy
between 1914 and 1946, the most striking characteristic of the history
of the British multinational banks in this period was that they and their
branch networks largely survived intact. Only one major institution, Anglo-
South American, failed, and even that did not crash but was liquidated in

---

[124] Between 1929 and 1938 Standard's investment/deposit ratio rose from 11 per cent to
25 per cent; Chartered's from 20 per cent to 49 per cent; Barclays (DCO)'s from 15 per cent
to 33 per cent; the Bank of Australasia's from 11 per cent to 22 per cent; Eastern Bank's from
45 per cent to 79 per cent; and the Imperial Bank of Persia's from 56 per cent to 94 per cent.
[125] Geoffrey Jones, *Banking and Empire in Iran*, 215–17.
[126] King, *The History of the Hongkong and Shanghai Banking Corporation*, iii. 179.
[127] *Report of the Royal Commission Appointed to Inquire into the Monetary and Banking
Systems . . . in Australia*, 82–91; H. W. Arndt, *The Australian Trading Banks* (Melbourne:
Cheshire, 1957), 76–7; R. F. Holder, *Bank of New South Wales: A History*, ii (Sydney: Angus
and Robertson, 1970), 791.

good order. The other banks active in the primary producing countries of the Southern Hemisphere and Asia had, not surprisingly, experienced difficulties and a poor financial performance in the 1930s, but their existence was not threatened. Likewise, the Hongkong Bank survived the loss of its headquarters and most of its branches in the Pacific war. The British banks were well equipped to survive in crisis situations. Their strong corporate cultures enabled them to respond effectively to extreme adversity. They were well managed. Their reserves, built up over the years, stood them in good stead when the Great Depression and the financial crisis of 1931 struck. The use of off-balance sheet transfers enabled the banks to maintain confidence in the face of severe business fluctuations.

In a longer-term perspective, the changes in the world economy between 1914 and 1946 had helped bring into question the continued viability of the nineteenth-century structure of British multinational banking. The functional and geographical specialization of the sector was modified by clearing bank investments in overseas banks, and by mergers between overseas banks. By the end of the 1920s three groups existed which were breaks with the specialized past. Barclays (DCO) was controlled by a domestic bank, and had an extensive branch network spanning Africa and the West Indies. Another domestic bank, Lloyds, had full or part ownership of banks active in Latin America, continental Europe, and India, and smaller equity stakes in a range of institutions active elsewhere. Finally, the Anglo-South American Bank operated branches in much of Central and South America, and was reaching out to other regions.

Ten years later it was evident that the specialist structure of British overseas banking was not to be so rapidly overturned. Anglo-South had disappeared. Its remnants had been absorbed into Lloyds' Latin American interests, but it was clear that Lloyds was unwilling or unable to forge its diverse overseas banking empire into a unified multinational banking group. Only Barclays (DCO) had developed as a more integrated organization. The external environment was clearly unfavourable to a reorientation of corporate stuctures. Anglo-South might have survived but for the traumatic fall in nitrate prices. Nevertheless, organizational shortcomings emerge as persistent themes, despite the strong corporate cultures which enabled banks to survive crises. Anglo-South's management structures in the 1920s failed to match the bank's entrepreneurial ambition and scope of operations. Lloyds allowed itself to continue for decades in a position of ownership without control. The next chapter will explore in greater detail how the management structures of the banks affected their ability to respond to the changing environments of their host economies.

# CHAPTER 6

# Banking Strategies in the Inter-war Years

## 6.1. Market Shares and Competitive Advantages

Multinational banking can be regarded as a mature industry in the inter-war years. Products and technologies changed little, and growth prospects declined. There were opportunities for new entrants in retail banking in some economies, and as a result the British banks faced competitive challenges from new local banks in various markets. However, the economic and political environment offered limited prospects in international banking. The British banks faced few new multinational banks owned by other countries. German overseas banking was decimated by the First World War and its aftermath, and the main new entrants into multinational banking came from the United States. During the First World War National City Bank began to construct a multinational branch network, and by 1930 the bank had almost 100 foreign branches, two-thirds of them in Latin America. Other American banks established a smaller number of foreign branches. American multinational banking activity was a novel development, but it remained relatively small-scale in the inter-war years.[1]

In the nineteenth century the British overseas banks had developed and flourished by using the strategy of multinational branch banking to exploit the competitive advantages of being based in the United Kingdom. After 1914, some elements of the 'diamond' of national competitive advantage became less favourable to the British banks.

Factor conditions remained favourable for British multinational banks, but perhaps less so than previously. The London market remained an excellent place to raise equity, but in fact very few banks raised capital after the immediate post-First World War period. The depressed economic conditions from the late 1920s explain this in part. However, it also appears that many banks may have been reluctant to raise capital because they were not generating additional profits sufficiently rapidly to allow the continuation of high dividend rates on a larger capital.[2] The British

---

[1] Thomas F. Huertas, 'US Multinational Banking: History and Prospects', in Geoffrey Jones (ed.), *Banks as Multinationals* (London: Routledge, 1990), 249–53; Harold van B. Cleveland and Thomas F. Huertas, *Citibank, 1812–1970* (Cambridge, Mass.: Harvard University Press, 1985), 76–9, 121–7, 205–8; John Donald Wilson, *The Chase* (Boston, Mass.: Harvard Business School Press, 1986), 12–14, 23–4. Canadian banks also developed multinational operations in Latin America in the 1920s.

[2] See e.g. D. T. Merrett, *ANZ Bank* (Sydney: Allen and Unwin, 1985), 43; id., 'Paradise Lost? British Banks in Australia', in Geoffrey Jones (ed.), *Banks as Multinationals*, 78.

overseas banks continued to have access to the large pool of skilled labour which existed in a country with such a well-developed domestic banking system. However, a number of factors may have diminished this advantage. Casualties in the First World War led to staff shortages in the immediate post-war period, and banks seem to have experienced problems finding and retaining staff of adequate quality.[3] There were similar problems after the Second World War.[4] Conversely, in the depressed early 1930s most banks sought to reduce their staff, rather than recruit. Easier staff transfer from domestic to overseas banks was one potential internalization advantage which could have arisen from the clearing bank investments in overseas banks, but in practice any such transfers seem only to have taken place within the Barclays group. The general quality of British banking staff in the inter-war years may also not have been uniformly high. The rapid amalgamation process among the domestic banks gave the new large banking groups a miscellaneous staff from the various merged banks who may not have been particularly appropriate for the bigger group into which the smaller banks were absorbed.[5] The fact that formal staff training was largely eschewed exacerbated this problem.

The inter-war years saw some deterioration in the demand conditions which had favoured British multinational banks. Their core market—servicing the requirements of British business—had entered a period of long-term relative contraction. Britain's exports stagnated in the inter-war years, resulting in a fall in its share of total world exports from 14 per cent in 1913 to 10 per cent in 1937. However, the effect of this trend on the overseas banks was mitigated by the growing importance of the Empire in Britain's foreign trade, the result of a number of factors, including the declining competitiveness of British manufactured goods in developed country markets, and the imperial preference schemes in operation in the inter-war years. Between 1930 and 1938 the Empire proportion of total British exports and imports increased from 43 per cent to 50 per cent, and 29 per cent to 40 per cent, respectively. Nevertheless, British exports, especially textiles, experienced considerable losses through import substitution in various markets where the banks had financed British trade, including India and Latin America.[6]

The weakening after 1918 of British 'free-standing' companies active in the extractive and other sectors of many developing countries posed a

[3] Geoffrey Jones, *Banking and Empire in Iran* (Cambridge: Cambridge University Press, 1986), 267–8.

[4] Richard Fry, *Bankers in West Africa* (London: Hutchinson Benham, 1976), 173–9; Geoffrey Tyson, *100 Years of Banking in Asia and Africa* (London: National and Grindlays, 1963), 207; J. A. Henry, *The First Hundred Years of the Standard Bank* (London: Oxford University Press, 1963), 315.

[5] Geoffrey Jones, 'Lombard Street on the Riviera: The British Clearing Banks and Europe, 1900–1960', *Business History*, 24 (1982), 205.

[6] Derek H. Aldcroft, *The British Economy* (Brighton: Wheatsheaf, 1983), 34–6, 81–2.

greater problem for banks, with whom they often had close business connections. The significance of British expatriate business within India waned as, for example, a large portion of the previously British-owned jute industry passed into Indian hands.[7] There was a similar story in much of Latin America, where trade ties with Britain weakened alongside a collapse in British capital exports. American multinationals made considerable investments in Argentina, Brazil, and elsewhere, sometimes buying out former British enterprises. For the most part, their business went to American banks.[8] However, the demise of British expatriate business was a slow process, and it still provided an important customer base for the banks. In Latin America, for example, Bolsa in the 1930s continued to provide large facilities for British traders and others such as Gibbs and the many British-owned utilities. A particularly valuable customer was the Union Cold Storage Company, managed by the Vestey family. By the 1920s this firm had become the largest meat-retailer in the world, accounting for one-third of the refrigerated storage capacity in Britain and 20 per cent of all meat imported into Britain, and with a network of suppliers in Latin America.[9] Bolsa supplied the credit requirements of the Union Cold Storage through overdrafts, acceptance credits, and other instruments. The level of credit obviously fluctuated continuously. However, at one bench-mark date, December 1936, Bolsa was providing total facilities of over £1.6 million to the Vestey group of companies through branches in Argentina, Uruguay, Brazil, Portugal, Spain, and London. Half of this sum was in sterling and the remainder in local currencies.[10]

In other markets the managers of British banks discovered that there was insufficient 'British' business to run a profitable branch. The continental subsidiaries of the British clearing banks in the inter-war years were badly affected by this problem, and they were not alone. The larger customers of Lloyds' Indian branches in the inter-war years were the British importers and agency houses, but competition among the banks for such desirable business was acute and thoughts turned to other possible sources of income. 'With the very keen competition for the limited amount of business of the European firms and larger Indian Firms,' one of Lloyds' senior managers reported on the Rangoon branch in 1930, 'it would be necessary for us to strike out a new line and the proposal is that we should

[7] B. R. Tomlinson, 'British Business in India, 1860–1970', in R. P. T. Davenport-Hines and Geoffrey Jones (eds.), British Business in Asia since 1860 (Cambridge: Cambridge University Press, 1989), 96–100.

[8] David Joslin, A Century of Banking in Latin America (London: Oxford University Press, 1963), 231–3. The expansion of American multinationals in inter-war Latin America is discussed in Mira Wilkins, The Maturing of Multinational Enterprise (Cambridge, Mass.: Harvard University Press, 1974), sects. 2 and 3, and in Colin M. Lewis, 'Immigrant Entrepreneurs, Manufacturing and Industrial Policy in the Argentine, 1922–28', The Journal of Imperial and Commonwealth History, 16(1) (1987), 89–90.

[9] Alfred D. Chandler, Scale and Scope (Cambridge, Mass.: Harvard University Press, 1990), 376–8.   [10] Bolsa Board Minutes, Dec. 1936, LB.

open a sub-office in the Sooratee Bazaar,' all of whose streets were occupied 'by Mahamedon [*sic*] and Chinese Merchants, both exporters and importers'.[11]

The decline of the relative importance of British business was matched by wider structural changes in the world economy which adversely affected the demand for the trade finance and foreign exchange services in which the British banks had specialized. The most striking change was the sharp decline in international trade, whose finance had so concerned the overseas banks. Worse still for the banks was the shift in the commodity terms of trade against primary producers.[12] The banks which had originated as the 'nitrate bank' and the 'cocoa bank' and the 'currant bank' found the prices of the commodities they had financed falling, and with falling prices came less business and more bad debts.

In West Africa, for example, the three main export crops of cocoa, palm-oil, and ground-nuts experienced sharp price falls with the Depression. Barclays and the Bank of British West Africa (BBWA) did not finance the African producers, but they did finance the trading houses, whose business fell away dramatically. The African cocoa producers in the Gold Coast reacted to declining prices by organizing a series of output restrictions, culminating in a total refusal to sell their produce in 1937. Moreover, as this dispute came to a head cocoa production was hit by an outbreak of 'swollen shoot' disease, which further undermined what had been one of the major areas of trade finance for the banks.[13] The profits of the British banks active in the region plummeted.[14]

In inter-war East Africa, the three British-based banks (Standard, Barclays (DCO), and National Bank of India) largely financed European settlers and plantation-owners, who were very badly affected by the falling commodity prices of the inter-war years. In Kenya, the principal crops were coffee, sisal, and maize. From 1930 the prices of these settler crops collapsed. The total value of coffee, sisal, and maize exports fell from £2.5 million in 1930 to less than £1 million in 1934. In contrast the low-cost African cereal producers with whom the banks had almost nothing to do fared much better in the 1930s.[15] In Kenya, Standard Bank began to

[11] Mr Knox's Reports on Indian Branches, Mar.–Apr. 1930, File 2321, LB.
[12] James Foreman-Peck, *A History of the World Economy* (Brighton: Wheatsheaf, 1983), ch. 7.
[13] Fry, *Bankers in West Africa*, 138–41.
[14] BBWA Profit and Loss (Branches) File, West Africa Box, SC. BBWA's branch profits for Nigeria and the Gold Coast fell from £93,802 and £72,261 respectively for the year to Mar. 1929 (out of total branch profits for all areas of £180,138) to £15,478 and £7,916 respectively (out of a total of £48,195) for the year to Mar. 1939.
[15] David Anderson and David Throup, 'The Agrarian Economy of Central Province, Kenya, 1918 to 1939', in I. Brown (ed.), *The Economies of Africa and Asia in the Inter-war Depression* (London: Routledge, 1989); Henry, *The First Hundred Years of the Standard Bank*, ch. 23.

foreclose on a large number of farms from 1930 onwards, often having itself to hold and maintain such foreclosed property. One former Standard manager, recalling the early 1930s, remembered Standard as 'probably for the time being the largest landowner in Kenya'.[16] This chronic situation was only relieved when the colonial administration founded a Land Bank, raising money in London to on-lend to farmers at lower interest rates than current market rates, thus enabling many farmers to discharge their existing mortgages to banks.

There were similar stories for many primary producers in Latin America, Australia, and New Zealand in the 1930s. New Zealand's export prices in 1931 were only 58 per cent of those in 1928.[17] The prices of Brazilian coffee, Argentinian wool, and Chilean nitrates tumbled. One of the few commodities to do well was gold, whose good fortune helped to make South Africa 'both commercially and industrially one of the more prosperous countries in the world' by the mid-1930s, and which also helped banks in West and East Africa to weather the crisis.[18]

Despite the problems of commodity prices there was economic growth in many of the economies in which the overseas banks operated. The collapse in primary product trade and prices used to be seen as a major disaster for the Third World, but in fact there were some positive outcomes. Many primary producing communities were able to use devices such as a partial return to subsistence production to mitigate the effect of falling incomes, while incomes were also sustained by falls in prices of manufactured imports and foodstuffs.[19] Trade barriers and the rise of indigenous entrepreneurial groups led in a number of countries to a substantial growth in manufacturing through import substitution. Indian manufacturing output grew at a rate well above the world average in the inter-war years, and faster than that of Britain, the United States, or Germany.[20] In Latin America there was a rapid recovery from the crisis years of 1929 to 1932, as the manufacturing sector expanded. Argentinian manufacturing output, for example, grew at 3 per cent per annum between 1929 and 1939. There was particular progress in many Latin American economies in textiles, tyres,

---

[16] J. J. Swanson, 'History of the Bank in East Africa', Memoirs, June 1954, p. 68, East Africa Box, SC.

[17] S. J. Butlin, *Australia and New Zealand Bank* (London: Longman, 1961), 390.

[18] Henry, *The First Hundred Years of the Standard Bank*, 254; Fry, *Bankers in West Africa*, 146–7; in East Africa, Standard Bank profited from the discovery of gold at Kakamega, near Kisumu, in the early 1930s. Ralph Gibson's Report on his Visit to East Africa Branches, Mombasa, 29 Feb. 1936, SBSA East Africa Box, SC. Barclays (DCO) Report and Accounts, 9 Dec. 1937, 38/351, BBA.

[19] I. Brown, Introduction, in Brown (ed.), *The Economies of Africa and Asia in the Inter-war Depression*, 1–2.

[20] Morris D. Morris, 'The Growth of Large-Scale Industry to 1947', in D. Kumar (ed.), *The Cambridge Economic History of India*, ii (Cambridge: Cambridge University Press, 1983), 609; Rajat K. Ray, *Industrialization in India* (Delhi: Oxford University Press, 1979).

pharmaceuticals, and food-processing for the home market. The fact that they could service the requirements of these new industries has been given as one reason why almost no Latin American banks collapsed in the Great Depression.[21]

The problem for the British multinational banks was that their past focus on trade, exchange, and the finance of primary commodities did not place them in a good position to benefit from such growth as occurred through import substitution or through peasant agriculture. Their products and policies were attuned to different requirements. They had weak ties with the indigenous entrepreneurs and peasants who seem to have been behind much of the economic growth in the developing world in the inter-war years. Modern Indian business, for example, came to be dominated by Marwari business groups, who both had their own credit arrangements and shared general Indian nationalistic sentiments.[22] The Exchange banks in India had limited connections with the Marwaris. In Iran, the Imperial Bank had financed the requirements of British business and local merchants since its foundation, but it was not accustomed to meeting the requirements of the government factories and private entrepreneurs who were responsible for that country's industrialization in the 1930s.[23] Often the branches of the British banks were simply located in the wrong places—ports and entrepôts—to take advantage of the new sources of growth.

A further problem for the British overseas banks was that in many regions local banks appeared which offered real, or at least potential, competition for domestic-oriented business, such as the finance of local industry. In New Zealand the Bank of New Zealand had dominated the market since its foundation, while, in Australia, local banks, especially the Bank of New South Wales, were market leaders. However, by this period sound modern banking institutions were also no longer a rarity in Latin America and Asia, and their customer appeal was on occasion reinforced by nationalism and anti-imperialism.

In Egypt and Iran, for example, such nationalistic feeling led to the establishment of local banks, Bank Misr and Bank Melli, which competed vigorously for deposits and business, often appealing to nationalist sentiments.[24] In British India, the Exchange banks began to be criticized for not

---

[21] Carlos F. Diaz Alejandro, 'Latin America in the 1930s', in Rosemary Thorp (ed.), *Latin America in the 1930s* (London: Macmillan, 1984). See also E. V. K. FitzGerald, 'Restructuring through the Depression: The State and Capital Accumulation in Mexico, 1925–40', in id., 268. [22] Ray, *Industrialization in India*, 71–2.

[23] Geoffrey Jones, *Banking and Empire in Iran*, 228; W. Floor, *Industrialisation in Iran, 1900–1941*, Centre for Middle Eastern and Islamic Studies, University of Durham, Occasional Paper No. 23, 1984.

[24] For Bank Misr, see Eric Davis, *Challenging Colonialism* (Princeton, NJ: Princeton University Press, 1983). For Bank Melli, Geoffrey Jones, *Banking and Empire in Iran*, 206–8, 217–27, and Frances Bostock and Geoffrey Jones, *Planning and Power in Iran* (London: Cass, 1989), 32–49.

lending sufficiently to Indians, and for not employing Indians at a senior level. British banks were attacked and boycotted alongside British political institutions, with these sentiments peaking in the early 1930s. When representatives of the Exchange banks in India gave evidence to the Central Banking Enquiry Committee in 1930, they were accused of exercising 'discrimination against Indian firms and Indian business from racial bias'.[25] The Ceylon Banking Commission of 1934 heard similar complaints about the British banks, and there were particular complaints that Ceylonese were unable to borrow directly from the banks, but instead had to go through shroffs, a procedure which raised the cost of borrowing.[26]

In China there was less of an explicit attack on British banks, but their roles were changed as a modern and unified nation state emerged. In 1927 the Kuomintang achieved the apparent political unification of the Republic of China, though in the 1930s Japanese military intervention was to destroy this stability almost as soon as it had been achieved. Chinese nationalism limited the role of the foreign banks. Up to the end of the 1920s the Hongkong Bank, and to a lesser degree the other foreign banks, had fulfilled quasi-central banking roles. The Hongkong Bank held the reserves of the Chinese Maritime Customs and Salt Administration; its banknotes circulated freely; the exchange rates quoted by it were accepted as the official rates by the market in Shanghai. Between 1928 and 1936, however, monetary reforms resulted in significant changes in the banking system. A new Central Bank of China took over government revenues. The institution of a managed currency in 1936, and the nationalization of the silver stocks held by the banks, took the quotation of exchange rates out of the hands of the foreign banks. After 1936 the issues of government banks were the sole legal tender. Government and other Chinese modern banks competed with the British banks, and the competition was not solely in terms of price or quality of service. Chartered Bank's Beijing manager complained in 1935 about the 'large measure of political influence which the larger Chinese banks now appear to enjoy'.[27] There were fears by the 1930s that the government would prohibit the foreign banks from accepting Chinese deposits, thereby eliminating a flow of 'cheap funds'. A move to achieve this was under way in 1937, but was abandoned following the Japanese invasion of China in August of that year.[28]

Nationalistic sentiments and local banks, therefore, helped reduce some of the competitive advantages of British multinational banks. Nevertheless,

[25] C. Knox to F. A. Beane, 3 Sept. 1930, File 2321, LB. See also memorandum by A. Murray, File 2381, LB.
[26] F. H. H. King, *The History of the Hongkong and Shanghai Banking Corporation*, iii (Cambridge: Cambridge University Press, 1988), 527–9.
[27] Chartered Peking Branch Letter, 15 Mar. 1935, Eastern Banking between the Wars File, Chartered History Files, SC.
[28] King, *The History of the Hongkong and Shanghai Banking Corporation*, iii. 360–1, and ch. 7 and 8 generally for the Hongkong Bank in China between 1927 and 1941.

British banks were still regarded as stable institutions which, compared with the disastrous banking failures in continental Europe and the United States in the early 1930s, they were. Many of the new local banks in the Third World in the inter-war years were fragile creations or prone to injudicious policies. In Egypt, for example, Bank Misr succumbed to a major liquidity crisis in 1939 following a period of rapid expansion and diversification.[29] When local banks got into difficulties, British banks usually benefited and sometimes assisted. In the disturbed conditions of the inter-war years, a reputation for stability remained a strong competitive advantage.

There was also some decline in the third element of Porter's 'diamond'— the presence of related or supplier industries. The changed position of the City of London, and of sterling, compared to 1914 was important here. There was a shift into dollars for trade finance in Latin America in the years immediately following 1918, which was only partially arrested by Britain's return to the gold standard in 1925. The City of London's role as the world's leading capital market declined as the Bank of England imposed informal restrictions on portfolio capital exports in the 1920s, with more powerful controls after 1932. In 1926–9 Nivison's, the Australian government's financial advisers in London, advised their clients to turn to New York for loans in response to the Bank of England's controls.[30] Latin American governments began serious loan issues on the New York market in the 1920s, and there was a huge speculative boom in Latin American issues in New York between 1925 and 1928, most of which later defaulted.[31] London was not about to be eclipsed by New York, or sterling by the US dollar, but by the inter-war years some of the competitive advantages of being a sterling bank with a head office in London were waning.

At the same time the advantages which British banks could derive from switching funds between countries were diminished by the problems of the gold standard and, more generally, the increase in government intervention in the banking sector. The inter-war years saw the emergence of widespread central banking. In the early 1920s the creation of central banks was the chosen instrument in the international attempt to restore exchange stability. During this period many Latin American countries established central banks. There was a similar trend in the Commonwealth, encouraged and guided by the Bank of England. The South African Reserve Bank was formed in 1920, and by the 1930s the state-owned Commonwealth

---

[29] Davis, *Challenging Colonialism*, 166–7; Robert L. Tignor, *State, Private Enterprise, and Economic Change in Egypt, 1918–1952* (Princeton, NJ: Princeton University Press, 1984), 162–74.

[30] R. S. Gilbert, 'London Financial Intermediaries and Australian Overseas Borrowing, 1900–29', *Australian Economic History Review*, 11 (1971), 39.

[31] Carlos Marichal, *A Century of Debt Crises in Latin America from Independence to the Great Depression, 1820–1930* (Princeton, NJ: Princeton University Press, 1989), ch. 7.

Bank was developing as an Australian central bank. In 1934 the Reserve Bank of New Zealand opened, followed by the Reserve Bank of India in 1935.[32] In the British colonies in East and Central Africa and the West Indies, currency boards were established on the lines of the West African Currency Board, which had been set up in 1912.

For the British banks, the imposition of exchange controls and other restrictions on the free movement of funds was one of the most unwelcome aspects of increased government intervention in banking. The competitive advantages of the British banks in being able to move funds between countries, and their regular and often large exchange profits, were disrupted almost everywhere, and eliminated in some places. From 1929 restrictions on movements of capital grew, and after 1931 were widespread all over the world. Exchange controls caused havoc with the traditional exchange and trade finance business of the British banks. 'In the past history of the Bank', a Bolsa report noted in 1933, 'exchange and the profits therefrom have always contributed the most important feature of its business.' This was particularly true in the case of Brazil, where most branches were located in ports. Tight exchange controls helped to reduce the 1931 profits of the bank's Rio de Janeiro branch to only 30 per cent of their 1930 total.[33] In Iran, fixed exchange rates and exchange controls left the Imperial Bank throughout the 1930s short of its previous exchange profits, constantly threatened with the withdrawal of its right to deal in foreign exchange, and often unable to remit profits.[34] In Australia, as noted in the previous chapter, the trading banks lost their long-established role in setting the exchange rate. From 1932 the Commonwealth Bank set the exchange rate and the first comprehensive foreign exchange controls were introduced in August 1939. They were to last until 1983.

British banks were fully aware of the consequences of this growing government intervention in their affairs. In 1938 one of the directors of P & O Bank, which was about to be fully absorbed into Chartered Bank, noted how, in the inter-war years,

Banking, as a business, has been profoundly affected and to its disadvantage by the control and regulation which is being exercised almost universally by Governments, directly and indirectly, over money and interest rates, discount rates and exchanges . . . there are symptoms almost everywhere suggesting that the State is seeking to enlarge its activities and operations in the direction of harnessing

[32] Joslin, *A Century of Banking in Latin America*, 229–30; R. S. Sayers (ed.), *Banking in the British Commonwealth* (London: Clarendon Press, 1952), ch. 2, 6, 9, 11; id., *The Bank of England, 1891–1944*, i. (Cambridge: Cambridge University Press, 1976), 201–10; Rajul Mathur, 'The Delay in the Formation of the Reserve Bank of India: The India Office Perspective', *Indian Economic and Social History Review*, 2 (1988).
[33] Bank of London and South America. Some Notes and Suggestions Arising out of the Visit of Sir Alexander Murray and Mr F. A. Beane to South America, Jan.–May 1933, 69–72, LB.    [34] Geoffrey Jones, *Banking and Empire in Iran*, 222–5.

existing Banking Institutions to its own needs, and of excluding Banks from exercising the functions which they have in the past discharged in the financing of trade and commerce.[35]

The increased role of governments was distressing, and even perplexing, for many British bankers. Their own country also saw the growth of government intervention in economic affairs, including the introduction of widespread trade protectionism after 1931, but the prevailing culture remained one of liberal *laissez-faire*. For most inter-war British businessmen, state intervention in economic affairs was not simply inefficient, it was immoral.

Central banks themselves were not always looked upon as unmitigated disasters by the British banks, although the latter usually opposed their foundation. Standard Bank's management, for example, could find no 'special need in South Africa for a Central Reserve Bank' in 1920, and feared that it might 'be developed in such a way as to materially interfere with the operations of the private Banks'.[36] However, what the British banks were most concerned to prevent was the development of the Reserve Bank as a direct competitor to the commercial banks and, once this fear had subsided, relations were calmer, except in the gold standard crisis of 1931 and 1932.[37] In inter-war British India, the Exchange banks lobbied for as little regulation as possible, and certainly objected to the compulsory deposits they were obliged to make with the Reserve Bank,[38] but once the system was established their relations with the Reserve Bank were satisfactory.

Relations between British overseas banks and the authorities were more problematic when the banks feared that a central bank would become a competitor. This lay at the heart of the many tensions between the trading banks and the Commonwealth Bank in inter-war Australia, tensions made worse by the distrust felt by the banks for the authorities, and the bitter criticism of the banks widely expressed in Australia. In 1934 the Labour Party in Australia adopted nationalization of banking as a major plank in its federal election campaign. Labour lost, but the tensions did not subside and the nationalization question reappeared after the Second World War.[39] The trading banks felt under siege from government for reasons they did not fully understand. 'I hate to see [the Union Bank] have to face created difficulties by Governments after its long pioneering history,' the acting general manager wrote to his chairman in London in 1938. 'Certainly we have not got nationalisation, but we are called on to deal with governmental

[35] Comment by P & O Board Member on Mr Cockburn's Report on P & O Bank, 21 Oct. 1938, BAC 63, SC.
[36] Notes on the Working of the Bank, 1920 and 1921, SBSA Misc. Box, SC.
[37] Henry, *The First Hundred Years of the Standard Bank*, 178–92, 235–48.
[38] Note of a Meeting at the National Bank of India . . . to consider the provisions of the new proposed Reserve Bank Bill, 4 Oct. 1933, MB Hist. 427. HSBC.
[39] Butlin, *Australia and New Zealand Bank*, 398–9, 402–3, 406–8; Merrett, *ANZ Bank*, 107–8.

influences which affect us, to some extent, as if we had.'[40] The banks felt similar feelings of victimization in New Zealand. Union's general manager observed to London in 1936,

the Government has now taken our gold, the right of Note issue, the financing of dairy products, and we are compelled by law to keep with the Reserve Bank 7% of our demand and 3% of our time liabilities in New Zealand. On the latter we pay interest and receive no return from the Reserve Bank. We cannot use this compulsory balance and we pay income tax thereon.[41]

In terms of firm strategy and structure—the fourth determinant of national competitive advantage—the previous chapter has already outlined much of the story. The British overseas banks were well-managed institutions able to survive the serious crises seen in the thirty years after 1914. However, it is less clear that these structures were changing sufficiently fast to enable them to adjust their strategies to respond to the changing environment of the inter-war years. Financing foreign trade, especially British trade, with the Southern Hemisphere and the East was no longer the goldmine it had once been. The new growth opportunities were to be found in industries growing through import substitution and other sectors of domestic economies. Product and geographical diversification strategies were in order. However, as Chandler has discussed in relation to the growth of the modern industrial enterprise, expansion in foreign markets and, still more, product diversification and product improvement and innovation require considerable organizational capability.[42] The corporate cultures of the overseas banks, which had worked so well in the nineteenth century, based on the recruitment of public school boys, lifelong employment, and on-the-job training, generated skills that were region- and product-specific, and were not well equipped to sustain diversification.

A particular facet of the organizational structure of the British overseas banks acted as a constraint on product diversification. This was the role of the London-based boards and headquarters in decision-making. A London board was ideal for a nineteenth-century bank financing international trade. However, it was less ideal as banks became more involved in local economies. Directors and staff in London found it harder to assess domestic banking risks than indigenous banks, and were thus prone to be conservative. They were also prone to give a higher priority to the London-based foreign exchange and treasury operations of their banks. As a result, some of the British banks developed into virtually two banks within the same institution, with retail operations managed overseas and other activities from London.

[40] Acting General Manager to Sir John Davidson, 4 Oct. 1938, UBL 309, ANZ Archives.
[41] A. W. McNicol to Standing Committee, 11 Aug. 1936, UBL 191, ANZ Archives.
[42] Chandler, Scale and Scope, 374–5, 603–5.

This organizational constraint on diversification was clearly seen in the cases of the two leading British banks in Australia, the Union Bank and the Bank of Australasia. Their London directors—most of whom were involved in other capacities in Anglo-Australian trade—were not interested in developing retail or domestic banking *per se*, and in acquiring larger deposits to finance such business. They considered that the business of their banks in Australia was to finance trade, especially exporters, which would lead to an accumulation of funds in London, which could in turn be used in short-term money market operations.[43] This mechanism was at work in the Bank of Australasia all through the 1920s, as lending in Australia was restricted and rationed in order to meet the needs of trade and of London. 'Our present severe restrictive policy', the bank's superintendent reported to his directors in 1923, 'is largely due to the necessity for conserving funds for the purchase of wool and produce bills.'[44] Four years later he reported that there was 'keen demand for accommodation at all points, and no difficulty should be experienced in increasing our figures if our resources permit. However . . . we are still adopting a restrictive policy owing to the necessity of conserving funds for the purchase of wool bills, etc.'[45]

The role of their London-based boards further restricted the growth of the Union Bank and the Bank of Australasia in the domestic Australian banking market because they stood aside from the merger wave which transformed Australian banking between 1917 and 1931. There was a rush of banking amalgamations in this period. Banks which were still confined to a single or a few states in 1914 had become truly 'national' banks by 1931. However, the British directors of the Union Bank and the Bank of Australasia feared that a merger with a local bank would mean their loss of control over the institution, which would shift domicile to Australia. The problem was that market share was largely determined by the number and location of its branches. Other Australian banks were rapidly able to expand their branch networks through mergers. Moreover, both the British banks were over-dependent on the state of Victoria and on rural and provincial towns. Australian economic growth after 1900, however, was located in the larger towns and, especially, the state of New South Wales and its capital, Sydney. Only a merger could have enabled the two British banks to reverse their under-representation in these areas.[46]

It was not until 1927, ten years after the merger wave had begun, that the first stirrings of concern became noticeable within the two banks, and especially the Union. The bank's Standing Committee noted how it had 'fallen behind other banks' in market share of deposits, and it readily

[43] Merrett, *ANZ Bank*, 50–1.
[44] Superintendent's Yearly Review, Oct. 1923, A/141/5, ANZ Archives.
[45] Superintendent's Yearly Review, Oct. 1927, A/141/6, ANZ Archives.
[46] Merrett, *ANZ Bank*, 41–3.

became apparent that the bank was badly under-represented in the new suburbs of the big cities of Sydney and Melbourne.[47] Perception of the problem, however, came well before the implementation of effective corrective measures. Negotiations for the acquisition of a local bank (the Ballarat Banking Company) were entered into, but went adrift because of the deteriorating economic conditions in 1930.[48] In 1928 and 1929 nine new branches were opened in the suburbs of Melbourne and Sydney, but this initiative was also overwhelmed by the Depression, and seven years later the bank's under-representation in the great population centres was still felt acutely.[49] Further attempts to reverse the Union Bank's decline came with a wartime shift of control over lending policy from London to Melbourne, but the problems stemming from the organizational structure of the Anglo-Australian banks were not to be quickly solved.

The third British-owned bank in Australia—the English, Scottish & Australian Bank (E, S & A)—provided some contrasts with the Union and the Bank of Australasia. By the beginning of the 1920s the Melbourne management of the bank held considerably more authority *vis-à-vis* their board than did their counterparts in the other two banks. The general manager between 1909 and 1927, and joint general manager from 1928 to 1933, was later said to have had 'a strong prejudice against any "interference from London"'.[50] Perhaps because of this greater Australian influence, the bank was a very active participant in the merger movement of the 1920s. In February 1920 the British bank tried to buy the Bank of Victoria, a local bank, and when this offer was rejected, it bid for the British-based London Bank of Australia. The London Bank had been planning a fusion with a local bank, the Commercial Bank of Tasmania, mainly because one of their clients, the British chocolate firm of Cadbury, was planning to erect a factory in Tasmania, and both the London Bank and the Commercial Bank were duly acquired by E, S & A.[51] In 1927 another local institution, the Royal Bank of Australia, was acquired.

These mergers allowed a rapid expansion of market share in the 1920s. The E, S & A penetrated Western Australia and Tasmania for the first time. In New South Wales and Victoria its deposits in 1920 had been well

---

[47] Standing Committee to General Manager, 17 Feb. 1927, U/61/11; General Manager to Standing Committee, 14 Apr. 1927, UBL 182, ANZ Archives.

[48] General Manager to Standing Committee, 9 July 1930, UBL 185, ANZ Archives. The Bank of Australasia had attempted to purchase another local bank, the Bank of Adelaide, in 1928, but had been rebuffed, while the British bank's directors had declined to make an offer to the Queensland National Bank in 1930 despite their local management's recommendation. See Merrett, *ANZ Bank*, 42.

[49] Standing Committee to General Manager, 14 May 1936, U/61/13, ANZ Archives.

[50] S. M. Ward to J. Ewing, 6 Sept. 1937, E/49/1, ANZ Archives.

[51] London Bank of Australia, Directors' Minute Book No. 8, Minute of 22 Sept. 1920, LBA/25.B, ANZ Archives; Melbourne to London, 19 Aug. 1920, E/3/1, ANZ Archives; Geoffrey Jones (ed.), *British Multinationals: Origins, Management and Performance* (Aldershot: Gower, 1986), 98–9, 103–5.

behind those of the Bank of Australasia and the Union Bank, but by 1930 they exceeded them.[52] E, S & A was also notably profitable in the 1920s. Unfortunately, fast expansion was not matched by improved administration. A fragile managerial structure had, by the early 1930s, resulted in large bad debts, especially in a few large accounts in which the bank's lending was particularly concentrated. Particularly large losses were made following the bankruptcy in 1936 of a trader on the Sydney Stock Exchange to whom the bank had provided large facilities, apparently used for speculative purposes.[53]

The Bank of New South Wales, which gained market share through the inter-war years, provided a sharper contrast to all the British-owned trading banks in Australia. This bank, under its dynamic general manager, Sir Alfred Davidson, took the major initiatives during the exchange crises of the early 1930s, and in general followed an innovative and aggressive business strategy which avoided the misfortunes of the E, S & A. Even at the height of the Depression, this bank opened new branches and sought to expand lending, and it was among the first to see the potential usefulness as liquid assets of Commonwealth government Treasury Bills.[54]

In respect of their management structures and other matters, therefore, it can be argued that the original competitive advantages held by the British multinational banks in the nineteenth century weakened after 1914. Yet this weakening only rarely translated into serious losses in market share, in so far as these can be estimated in the inter-war years. Table 6.1 provides a crude assessment of the changes in the market shares of British banks by region between 1914 and 1946.

In a few countries the inter-war years saw a substantial decline, or even disappearance, of British banking activity. The sale of the Bank of British North America after the First World War eliminated British institutions from Canadian domestic banking, and Barclays Bank (Canada), established at the end of the 1920s, remained a very small institution. In Iran, the establishment of the state-owned Bank Melli in 1928 combined with restrictive government legislation led to a drastic decline in the market share of the Imperial Bank of Persia, which had formerly held almost all modern bank deposits and advances in that country. By 1939 the Imperial Bank claimed a mere 9 per cent of bank deposits, and 6 per cent of advances.[55]

[52] Merrett, *ANZ Bank*, 200–1; Deposit Figures by State 1920 to 1935, attached in General Manager to Standing Committee, 23 June 1936, UBL 191, ANZ Archives.

[53] Merrett, *ANZ Bank*, 200–4; London to Joint General Managers, 10 Dec. 1932, E/3/17, ANZ Archives. See above, Sects. 5.4 and 5.5. The Sydney trader in question was Keith Brougham Docker. See S. Salisbury and K. Sweeney, *The Bull, the Bear and the Kangaroo* (Sydney: Allen and Unwin, 1988), 262–3.

[54] C. B. Schedvin, 'Sir Alfred Davidson', in R. P. T. Appleyard and C. B. Schedvin (eds.), *Australian Financiers* (Melbourne: Macmillan, 1988), 339 ff.; R. F. Holder, *Bank of New South Wales: A History* (Sydney: Angus and Robertson, 1970), ii, ch. 36 and *passim*.

[55] Geoffrey Jones, *Banking and Empire in Iran*, 235–6.

TABLE 6.1. *Market share performance of British banks by region or country, c.1914–c.1946*

| Changes in market share | Region/country |
| --- | --- |
| Elimination/severe decline | Canada, Iran |
| Stagnation/slight decline | Australia, New Zealand, Latin America |
| Stable | The East, West Indies, colonial Africa |
| Growth | South Africa |

A more usual pattern was the stagnation or slow loss of market share seen in inter-war Latin America, Australia, and New Zealand. In Latin America, Bolsa and, until its demise, Anglo-South American remained important in many countries, but there was competition from local institutions, and also from American and Canadian banks. The shift into dollars for trade financing in this region placed the British banks at a disadvantage *vis-à-vis* the Americans, especially as other British business and trade links with the sub-continent were weakening.[56]

In inter-war Australia, the British banks maintained around 30 per cent of the Australian-domiciled assets of private trading banks, although the trading banks' share of all financial assets continued to decline in favour of other financial intermediaries, such as savings banks and life assurance companies, which grew in importance. For reasons explained above, the market share of the two leading British banks stagnated or even fell against that of the local Australian banks. The Union Bank and the Bank of Australasia were outdistanced by the two Sydney-based local banks, the Bank of New South Wales and the Commercial Banking Company of Sydney, but the acquisition strategy of the English, Scottish & Australian Bank improved its market share.[57] Market shares in inter-war New Zealand were also stable. While the three British banks accounted for 37 per

[56] Cleveland and Huertas, *Citibank*, 123–5; Joslin, *A Century of Banking in Latin America*, 215–33. In Brazil, the overall importance of all foreign banks declined in this period. The sight deposits in the six leading foreign banks declined as a percentage of total deposits from 41 per cent in 1914, to 11 per cent in 1938, and 8 per cent in 1945. Data contained in Maria Barbara Levy to the author, 7 Dec. 1990. In Argentina, Charles Jones gives data suggesting that the British share of deposits had fallen to 11 per cent in 1927. They held 20 per cent of gold deposits, and a much smaller 9 per cent of local currency deposits. Charles Jones, draft chapter for Colin M. Lewis and Rory Miller (eds.), *British Business in Latin America* (Cambridge: Cambridge University Press, forthcoming).

[57] Between 1914 and 1939 the Union Bank's share of deposits fell from 11.2 per cent to 8.2 per cent, and its share of advances from 9.4 per cent to 9 per cent. The Bank of Australasia held 10.6 per cent of deposits and 9.3 per cent of advances in 1914, and 10.4 per cent of deposits and 10.7 per cent of advances in 1939. Merrett, 'Paradise Lost?', 74–6; id., *ANZ Bank*, 35–42; Butlin, *Australia and New Zealand Bank*, 377, 409; R. C. White, *Australian Banking and Monetary Statistics, 1945–1970*, Reserve Bank of Australia, Occasional Paper No. 4B, Sydney, 1973, table 41.

cent of non-government deposits in 1913 and 44 per cent of advances, the corresponding figures in 1939 were 39 per cent and 39 per cent.[58]

In the developing countries of the British Empire, British banks remained strong and their market share stable. This was true, for example, in British colonial Africa. An African-owned bank, the National Bank of Nigeria, was founded in 1933, but by 1939 it only had £10,000-worth of deposits, although they rose during the Second World War.[59] In the British West Indies, Barclays (DCO) and the Bank of Nova Scotia had a virtual duopoly in the banking market. In British India, the Exchange banks (which were mostly British) saw their share of deposits of the modern banking sector decline gently from 34 per cent to 29 per cent between 1919 and 1937, and following the creation of the Reserve Bank in 1935 they were also faced with a new competitor in the exchange markets in the shape of the Imperial Bank of India, which was finally freed from the prohibition from dealing in foreign exchange.[60] However, there appears to have been no precipitate decline in their exchange business because of this competition.

South Africa was the one country where British banks very sharply *increased* their market share in the inter-war years. Following the acquisition of the National Bank by Barclays (DCO) in 1926, virtually the entire domestic banking sector of South Africa was British-controlled, although the banking sector as a whole was—as in Australia—losing ground to non-bank financial intermediaries such as building societies and insurance companies. Among the banks, the only competition to the two British giants were the Dutch-owned Netherlands Bank, and two small local institutions. In 1939 Barclays (DCO) and Standard had 96 per cent of commercial bank deposits in South Africa (57 per cent and 39 per cent respectively). In stark contrast to Australia, locally owned banking virtually disappeared from South Africa in the inter-war years, and the country emerged as the very pinnacle of British multinational banking influence.[61] The duopoly of the British banks in South Africa, the absence of strong locally owned competitor banks, and the prosperity of the economy underpinned by the flourishing gold industry provides a convincing explanation for the good profitability of Barclays (DCO) and Standard Bank in the 1930s.

For the most part, therefore, the British multinational banks in the inter-war years held on to the market shares they had captured in earlier

[58] G. R. Hawke and D. K. Sheppard, 'The Evolution of New Zealand Trading Banks mostly until 1934', Victoria University of Wellington Working Papers in Economic History, No. 84/2, Mar. 1984, tables 1 and 2.　　[59] Fry, *Bankers in West Africa*, 216–17.
[60] A. G. Chandavarkar, 'Money and Credit, 1858–1947', in Kumar (ed.), *The Cambridge Economic History of India*, ii. 775–84.
[61] Stuart Jones, 'The Apogee of the Imperial Banks in South Africa: Standard and Barclays, 1919–1939', *English Historical Review*, 103 (1988). National City Bank opened a Cape Town branch in 1920, but closed it within two years. Richard W. Hull, *American Enterprise in South Africa* (New York: New York University Press, 1990), 130–3.

years, despite any weakening in their competitive advantages. A number of factors explain this. They had established excellent franchises in many regions in which they operated, which were not easily overturned, except by aggressive host government action. As most of their operations remained in the British Empire, they were largely immune from hostile policies against them as British banks. The Australian government, for example, blocked new entry by 'foreign' banks from the early 1920s, but the existing British-owned banks were excluded from this category. In most countries the British banks possessed extensive physical assets in their branch networks. Some of these branches were imposing buildings in their local contexts. Their reputations for honesty and stability were also considerable assets in the disturbed conditions of the period. The participation in their shareholding of British clearing banks enhanced their reputation for stability.

Two other factors deserve longer consideration. The first is the nature of competition in many inter-war markets, which will be discussed in the following section. Secondly, the British banks showed sufficient flexibility in their business strategies to make adjustments to changed conditions. This will be the concern of subsequent sections of this chapter.

## 6.2. Competition and Cartelization

The British overseas banks faced competition from other institutions in the inter-war years, but this competition was rarely sufficient to overwhelm their market shares. Multinational banking by other countries remained limited. Competition for retail business by local banks was often restricted by collusive agreements. As a result, franchises were sometimes eroded, but rarely overturned.

This would not be the impression gained from a rapid reading of the internal correspondence of the banks in the inter-war years. The declining business opportunities of the period often made managers feel they were under competitive pressure, especially compared with the golden age before the First World War. At branch level managers often felt themselves facing intense competition for *desirable* foreign exchange and trade-related business. This was very evident in the Eastern Exchange banks in this period. The banks in India, for example, competed fiercely for exchange business, and the entry into exchange banking of the Imperial Bank of India in 1935 added another factor to the struggle. In regard to exchange generally, Chartered Bank's chief manager noted in 1938, that

the competition nowadays at every point is so keen, that it is doubtful whether the Banks as a rule make more than $1/32$ per cent on ready transactions, while it is pretty evident at the end of each half year, that the cloud of inter-bank transactions result in little or no profit whatsoever, and seem to be designed to benefit the brokers' pockets entirely.[62]

Mercantile Bank's manager in Hong Kong in 1936 found

Competition . . . very keen. European business is tightly held. Chinese tend to gravitate towards Chinese banks to avoid Compradore charges . . . Genuine trade turnover alone cannot possibly support the 23 Banks engaged in exchange business here.[63]

Even the mighty Hongkong Bank found itself under competitive pressure in China, Ceylon, and elsewhere.[64] Local banks sometimes made inroads on deposit bases. Eastern Bank in Bombay, for example, experienced such unwelcome competition for savings deposits:

Newly established Indian Banks are keen to obtain deposits from the public, and are willing to pay a high rate. This type of constituent in India is not so well-informed as the average current account holder, and, consequently less inclined to query the standing of the Bank in which he deposits his savings.[65]

Such competition with local banks, and rivalries between British banks for premium business, was conducted in most countries in the context of widespread collusive agreements covering both price and non-price competition. The economic conditions of the period were precisely those most likely to prompt collusive behaviour. Demand for the banks' product was inelastic, innovations were few, while political and financial risks were high. Almost everywhere collusive agreements were unstable, but they were persistent.

The main focus of collusive activity was in controlling price competition. By the inter-war years there was general agreement among all the banks in Australia not to indulge in price competition, leaving non-price competition (especially opening new branches) as the main strategy if a bank wanted to expand market share. There was even a 'gentlemen's agreement' against managers in one bank trying to persuade a customer to transfer his account.[66] In inter-war South Africa the duopoly of Barclays (DCO) and Standard Bank operated a wide-ranging banking cartel.[67] Such agreements were easy to enforce in South Africa and Australia because there were so few entrants to the banking industry. The established banks' control of the clearing house for inter-bank settlements of cheques served

---

[62] Memorandum on the P & O Banking Corporation (undoubtedly by W. R. Cockburn of Chartered Bank), 17 Oct. 1938, BAC 63, SC.
[63] R. Kennedy to Chief Manager, 7 July 1936, MB Hist. 1002.4, HSBC.
[64] King, *The History of the Hongkong and Shanghai Banking Corporation*, iii. 366–71, 501–3.          [65] Eastern Bank Inspector's Report on Bombay, July/Aug. 1939, SC.
[66] Merrett, *ANZ Bank*, 40; id., 'Two Hundred Years of Banking' (unpublished paper); Butlin, *Australia and New Zealand Bank*, 400.
[67] Stuart Jones, 'The Apogee of the Imperial Banks in South Africa', 894.

as a powerful entry barrier. The cartel agreements on borrowing and lending rates, and the gentlemen's agreements on poaching customers, represented further entry barriers.[68]

Nevertheless, even price competition was not entirely eliminated in inter-war Australia. As observed already, the Bank of New South Wales was prone to break cartel agreements, or take assertive steps to change rate levels, and the British banks found themselves regularly discomfited by his actions. To give one example of a regular scenario in the 1930s, in August 1932 the Melbourne management of the English, Scottish & Australian Bank reported to their London office that the Bank of New South Wales's general manager, Davidson, had 'again become restless on the subject of Interest payable on Fixed Deposits of all currencies'. He had written to the chairman of the Associated Banks of Victoria,

suggesting a further reduction, and, on being advised that the Victorian Banks thought the time inopportune, he intimated that his deposits were keeping up in such volume that he would be forced again to reduce deposit rates, but that he did not wish to have to act alone . . . We were hoping that we had resisted him when he wrote announcing that he would, irrespective of what other Banks might do, make a reduction in his rates.[69]

Even Australia in the 1930s did not see the complete elimination of competition among the trading banks.

In parts of the non-settler Empire, Latin America, and in the East, collusive agreements were widespread, but still subject to frequent disruption. Barriers to entry were lower, and some of the new entrants were indigenous institutions anxious to secure market share and, sometimes, unwilling to collude with British banks. Nevertheless, in most regions rates and other agreements were made, and there was some tendency for such agreements to become more comprehensive over time. In West Africa, for example, from the late 1920s the two British banks were reaching agreements not to open or reopen branches in certain places without giving an agreed period of notice to the other bank.[70] There were also sporadic rates agreements which were eventually codified in a formal agreement headed 'Cooperation between Banks in West Africa' signed in January 1945. Some forty-four 'matters' were agreed between the banks, and 'no deviation or exception was permitted' without the 'mutual consent of the head offices in London'. The agreement remained in force until 1957.[71]

Collusion was often more difficult when non-British banks were active

---

[68] For Australia, see Merrett, 'Paradise Lost?', 72; id., 'Two Hundred Years of Banking'.

[69] Melbourne to London, 18 Aug. 1932, E/3/18, ANZ Archives.

[70] BBWA Board Minutes of 12 Sept. 1929, 8 June 1932, 10 Aug. 1932, Fry's Digests of BBWA Board Minutes, BAC S/90, SC.

[71] BBWA Board Minutes, 22 Nov. 1944, Fry's Digests of BBWA Board Minutes, BAC S/90, SC; Fry, *Bankers in West Africa*, 146.

in the market. In the East there had been many local rates agreements since the nineteenth century, and these became much more comprehensive in the inter-war years. The British Exchange banks achieved a considerable amount of co-operation with each other and other foreign exchange banks. The codified resolutions of the Eastern Exchange banks, agreed to at various times by their managers in London, which applied not only to eight British banks but also to French, American, Belgian, Chinese, and Japanese banks, represented a comprehensive collusive pattern which covered the range of business transacted by the banks, from the fixing of rates and charges to the specification of the formulas to be followed in the negotiation of bill contracts and advances.[72] However, Indian banks were less enthusiastic about such agreements, and even British banks broke agreements when it suited them. In 1928 Mercantile Bank's Calcutta manager bemoaned the policies of Lloyds, 'a thorn in the flesh' who were 'still endeavouring to attract business by granting facilities on terms that we are not prepared to give'.[73] Rates agreements rarely covered all the products offered by the banks, leaving room for price competition in some areas.[74]

Tacit as well as explicit collusion was in evidence among the Exchange banks in the inter-war years. It was not unusual for the better-established banks in a particular market to attempt to use their influence or market power to eliminate price competition, though the success of this strategy depended very much on the characteristics of individual markets. Eastern Bank's Calcutta branch was able to resist pressure from Lloyds in 1936 to reduce the interest it offered on savings deposits,[75] but another small British bank, the Mercantile Bank, had no such leeway in Hong Kong, where the Hongkong Bank was able to exercise effective price leadership. Mercantile's manager reported to London on the situation as it appeared to him in 1932:

You would hardly credit the hold that the Hongkong Bank has on the Colony. They seem to be prepared to carry business that no home Bank would look at. Most Companies, firms and individuals are indebted to them in one way or another. They watch all cheques drawn on them payable to other Banks and, should it be found that the cheque is in connection with exchange business, the merchant and broker concerned have the pleasure of an interview with Grayburn [the chief manager of Hongkong Bank].

[72] Summary of Resolutions agreed to at various times by the Managers of Eastern Exchange banks in London, 8 Nov. 1929. Banking Enquiry File, Eastern Bank, Box 371. See also Terms of Agreement between the Imperial Bank of India and the Exchange Banks at Colombo, 10 Dec. 1936, Eastern Bank Inspection Report on Eastern Bank Colombo, Oct.–Dec. 1939, SC.

[73] Manager, Calcutta to J. B. Crichton, 15 Mar. 1928, MB Hist. 1002.1, HSBC.

[74] e.g. Inspection Report on Eastern Bank, Madras, Oct. 1939, SC. The Exchange banks had no agreement on rates for advances in that city in the late 1930s.

[75] Inspection Report on Eastern Bank Calcutta, Jan. 1936, SC.

Brokerage is $\frac{1}{8}$ on merchant business, $\frac{1}{16}$ on interbank. Too high! The National City Bank tried to get Ferguson of the Chartered to call a meeting to consider a reduction. Ferguson promised but has gone to London without doing anything. Grayburn gives out that, as long as he is here, the brokerage will not be reduced.[76]

In the ports of Asia, in the dependent British colonies, and in South Africa, the British banks were sufficiently strong to keep collusive agreements in place, despite inevitable jockeying for position between individual banks. In Australia and New Zealand they were firmly placed within banking cartels to which outside entry was all but impossible. The stability of the market shares of British banks was not surprising.

The consequences for overall economic welfare are less clear-cut. Economic theory would predict a negative impact on consumer welfare, to which the anecdotal evidence offered by the Mercantile's manager's remark about the level of brokerage charged in Hong Kong in the 1930s would lend support. However, and not only in the East, there were continual enforcement problems, which make it doubtful if excessive monopoly profits could have been secured for long. There was in part a trade-off between innovation and stability. A South African banking historian has argued that that country was saved the horrors of the American banking collapses after 1929 by the duopoly exercised by Standard Bank and Barclays (DCO).[77] Conversely, specialists on Australian banking history—which also had no major banking collapse—stress the conservatism and lack of innovation which was part of the cost of the cartelized structure.[78] In the economic and financial conditions of the period, there were considerable benefits for welfare in avoiding American or Central European-type banking collapses. The problems, perhaps, came later, for the collusive caution of the inter-war years was often carried over into the new conditions pertaining after the Second World War.

## 6.3. Geographical Diversification

In the nineteenth century the British overseas banks—or at least those that survived—were conservative institutions which nevertheless pursued flexible strategies within the parameters of what was considered prudent banking. In the inter-war years this tradition continued, and the banks responded to changes in their competitive advantages with further modifications of their strategies.

The problems of commodity prices, and sometimes of political risk, encouraged geographical diversification. The mergers and amalgamations

[76] Manager, Hong Kong to J. B. Crichton, 13 Dec. 1932, MB Hist. 1002.1, HSBC.
[77] Stuart Jones, 'The Apogee of the Imperial Banks in South Africa', 915.
[78] Merrett, 'Two Hundred Years of Banking'.

discussed in Chapter 5 must be seen in this context. The overseas banks which sought links with the clearers were, among other things, attempting to lessen their dependence on single countries or regions.

Some banks also pursued geographical diversification strategies through greenfield investments in new countries. Apart from risk-spreading, there were usually other motives behind such moves, including securing profitable opportunities and wishing to forestall competitors. This latter consideration, for example, helped encourage the Mercantile Bank of India to open branches on the east coast of Malaya in the inter-war years. 'A principal point which you must keep in view is the protection of our existing interests in Kota Bahru,' Mercantile's chief manager wrote to his manager in Singapore in October 1927 in the context of opening a new branch in the small town of Kuala Krai; 'it is of paramount importance that we should not be forestalled in opening an agency by another Bank which may damage the business we have already built up in Kota Bahru.'[79]

In the Mediterranean, Ionian Bank's diversification to Egypt before 1914 had proved a relative success.[80] Encouraged by the Egyptian experience, Ionian attempted to extend further its area of operation during the inter-war years. When the bank surrendered its note-issuing rights in Greece after the First World War, its relations with the Greek authorities became less tempestuous, but nevertheless inter-war Greece had an unstable economy, with high inflation and a depreciating currency, and there was a considerable incentive to spread assets beyond its shores. Ionian followed a policy of establishing branches where there were Greek communities it could serve. In 1922 the bank opened in Istanbul (Constantinople) by taking over the branch of an American bank. However, the branch lost money almost continuously, in part because of continuing tensions between Greece and Turkey, and in 1928 the branch was taken over by Deutsche Bank.[81] A branch was opened in Nicosia in Cyprus in 1926, followed by a number of other agencies in the following year. Cyprus, with its large Greek population, offered fertile ground, and despite the long-established position of the Imperial Ottoman Bank, and the presence of a local bank

---

[79] Chief Manager to R. D. Cromartie, 6 Oct. 1927, MB Hist. 1190, HSBC. Mercantile opened an agency in Kuala Krai in 1929, at a time of optimism about the results of the extension of the railway to north-east Malaya, but closed it two years later. See S. W. Muirhead, 'The Mercantile Bank of India on the East Coast of Malaya', in F. H. H. King (ed.), *Eastern Banking* (London: Athlone, 1983), 656.

[80] During the First World War high cotton prices helped to make the Ionian's Egyptian business a profitable one. In the seven years 1914 to 1920, Ionian's Greek branches earned profits of £318,623, nearly one-third of which were made in a single peak year of 1918. In contrast, the recently established Egyptian business made profits of £262,380, which were much more evenly spread on an annual basis. Annual Account Ledgers 1914–20, Ionian Bank Archives, LSE.

[81] *Ionian Bank Ltd.: A History* (London: Ionian Bank, 1953), 37–8; Annual Account Ledgers, 1925–8, Ionian Bank Archives, LSE.

and the Bank of Athens, Ionian had captured nearly one-quarter of all commercial bank deposits by 1930. It was less easy to make profits. The Cyprus operations lost money every year except one between 1926 and 1935, but, as market share fell (to 11 per cent by 1946), profits improved.[82]

Two British banks diversified into the Arab side of the Gulf, which lacked any modern financial institutions until after the First World War, and was under British 'protection'. The pioneer was the Eastern Bank, which opened a branch in Bahrain in 1920. Eastern Bank's late foundation had meant that it faced a hard struggle to compete for business in British India against the longer-established Exchange banks, and had an incentive to search for opportunities elsewhere.[83] Eastern Bank was strong in Bombay, which had close trading links with Bahrain, which, although not a colony, was under British 'protection', administered by a political agent responsible to the government of India. There were many Indian merchants in Bahrain, and almost all of Bahrain's imports came from India. The bank's establishment of a branch on the island was welcomed by the British authorities, and they protected its monopoly there until 1944.

One of the problems faced by banks seeking geographical diversification in the inter-war years was that the weakness of commodity prices which handicapped their traditional business was a world-wide phenomenon. Diversification could mean, therefore, that banks simply faced more of the same problem. Bahrain's economy in the 1920s was heavily based on the pearling industry. Bahrain's pearls were despatched to Bombay, where sorting, stringing, and polishing was carried out before world-wide distribution. The Great Depression, however, caused a collapse in the demand for pearls, which was exacerbated by the export of cultured pearls from Japan. Eastern Bank's diversification strategy, like the entire Bahrain economy, appeared doomed, but both were unexpectedly saved in the early 1930s when an American oil company discovered oil. The Middle Eastern oil industry had hitherto been confined to Iran and Iraq, where oil had been discovered in 1908 and 1927 respectively. In 1934 Bahrain began to export oil, and in the following year a refinery was built. By the late 1930s Eastern Bank was making substantial and growing profits in Bahrain, almost entirely from meeting the finance and exchange operations of the oil industry.[84] Good luck, therefore, was perhaps the major reason for the positive outcome of Eastern's diversification strategy in Bahrain.

By far the most extensive geographical diversification strategy of any

[82] Kate Phylaktis, 'Banking in a British Colony: Cyprus 1878–1959', Business History, 30 (1988), 422–5. The Cyprus branches lost a total of almost £14,000 between 1926 and 1935, while they earned profits of £25,000 between 1936 and 1945; Annual Account Ledgers 1927–46, Ionian Bank Archives, LSE.

[83] Rodney Wilson, 'Financial Development of the Arab Gulf: The Eastern Bank Experience, 1917–1950', Business History, 29 (1987), 180–1.

[84] Eastern Bank Inspection Report on Bahrain, Feb. 1938, SC.

of the British overseas banks was that of the Imperial Bank of Iran into the Arab side of the Gulf. This was a classic example of an escape from a market whose growth prospects were poor, or even non-existent. The regulatory and political conditions faced by the Imperial Bank in Iran deteriorated rapidly from the 1920s. The bank lost its note-issuing rights. The government established the Bank Melli, which competed vigorously for business. Exchange controls and industrialization through import substitution cut into the bank's traditional business. For much of the 1930s the Imperial Bank made little or no profit from its large branch network in Iran, and its main source of profits was income from sterling investments in London.[85] The bank opted to diversify, initially in the most difficult circumstances of the Second World War. New branches were opened in Kuwait in 1942, Bahrain in 1944, and Dubai in 1946. The circumstances which led to this decision, and its consequences, will be discussed in Section 9.3.

The Eastern Bank and the Imperial Bank had diversified into neighbouring territories under British political influence which had commercial links with their main host economy. Those banks which attempted diversification into banking markets where their skills were not transferable tended to experience considerable difficulties in becoming established and, more often than not, found themselves climbing up an expensive learning curve of bad debts and other unpleasant traps which face unwary bankers. The Imperial Bank of Iran, for example, found it an uphill struggle to maintain a branch in Bombay between 1919 and 1934, and experienced a series of bad debts.[86] The Bank of British West Africa fared no better when, in a surge of post-war optimism, it established branches in Egypt, Morocco, and elsewhere. In Egypt, branches were opened in Alexandria and Cairo in 1918 and 1920, but large losses followed and in 1925 the business was sold to Lloyds. The bank opened a branch in Tangier in Morocco in 1915, and further branch expansion followed in this French territory, but bad debts and irregularities soon ensued. Branches began to be closed after 1929.[87] British bankers who ventured into continental Europe in the inter-war years experienced similar difficulties in understanding local banking conditions, while, in Australia, the two leading British banks found it difficult to diversify even into other states.

Geographical diversification was one possible strategic response for British multinational banks faced with declining competitive advantages in the inter-war years. It spread risks and could even offer a transformation in corporate prospects, but growth opportunities were limited. Moreover, the successful implementation of geographical diversification was constrained

---

[85] Geoffrey Jones, *Banking and Empire in Iran*, ch. 8.    [86] Ibid., 259–65.
[87] Fry, *Bankers in West Africa*, 96–7, 136, 156–7.

by the region-specific skills of the banks. Their corporate cultures and on-the-job training produced executives who 'knew' particular regions well, but whose skills were not easily transferable. Given the importance of knowing your customers in banking, this served the banks well, unless they attempted to penetrate areas whose business cultures were radically different.

## 6.4. Product Diversification

A second possible strategic response to declining competitive advantages was product diversification. Although the inter-war years were not an ideal environment for a bank as compared to the periods of fast economic growth seen in the nineteenth century, or again in the 1950s and 1960s, there was at least some potential if the banks were able to shift their product focus to meet new circumstances, such as growth of domestic industries through import substitution.

The British banks had a conservative image in the inter-war years, and in some cases the reality was very much in line with the image. In Australia, the British banks were conservative within a conservative context. The few product innovations seen in inter-war Australia were marginal, such as the introduction of ladies' banking chambers, travel services, and small personal loans. All the banks continued to look towards foreign trade finance for much of their lending business, and were slow to grasp the opportunities to supply the fixed and working capital requirements of the growing numbers of large industrial firms, many of them subsidiaries of foreign multinationals. The Union Bank and the Bank of Australasia were particularly conservative, clinging to their traditional rural and pastoral lending for too long, and under-represented in the industrial growth areas of New South Wales. In 1938, 41 per cent of the Bank of Australasia's lending (by amount) was to farmers, a further 4 per cent to primary-product-related industries, 16 per cent to private individuals, and 9 each to merchants and wholesalers, and to 'manufacturing and productive industries'.[88] By the same year the Union Bank was convinced of 'the necessity for taking all possible steps to reduce the percentage of advances relating to Primary Producers and increasing that relative to Mercantile and Industrial Accounts'.[89]

It would, however, be a caricature to argue that the British banks entirely avoided the new sources of Australian growth in the inter-war years. The Bank of Australasia had been the bankers of the Broken Hill Proprietary Company 1886 (BHP) since a year after BHP's foundation. Although

[88] Superintendent's Yearly Report, 1938, A/141/15, ANZ Archives.
[89] Standing Committee to General Manager, 15 Nov. 1938, U/61/14, ANZ Archives.

originally an import and export business, by the inter-war years BHP had become a major Australian heavy industrial group. The Bank of Australasia also held the accounts of some of the American, Swiss, and British multinationals which built factories in inter-war Australia, such as AT & T, Nestlé, and Unilever.[90]

An extreme lack of product innovation was manifested in the inter-war years by the Imperial Bank of Iran, especially its board in London, which declined to support the Iranian government's industrialization programme. It did provide, from the mid-1930s, some of the short-term facilities required by foreign contractors employed on government projects, especially railway construction, but the bank refused to become involved in longer-term investment projects as 'contrary to the tenets of British Banking'. It is hard to avoid the conclusion that both business opportunities in Iran and the opportunity to re-establish a working relationship with the Iranian government were lost by such policies.[91]

Banks which did attempt substantial product innovation ran into difficulties. Although the Anglo-South American Bank was finally overcome by Chilean nitrates, it is clear that its vigorous pursuit of market share had led it to be far more 'flexible' than its British competitor, Bolsa, but that weaknesses in the bank's managerial structure had meant that such flexibility had not been matched by sufficient banking prudence. Arguably the English, Scottish & Australian Bank was afflicted by the same problem in the early 1930s. It would seem that British overseas banks found it hard to match entrepreneurial ambition with requisite managerial structures, and that deviations from orthodoxy led all too easily to serious difficulties.

A further example of unsuccessful product—and geographical—diversification was Cox & Co., which failed in 1923 and had to be acquired by Lloyds at the behest of the Bank of England (see Chapter 7). By the end of the First World War the bulk of Cox's deposits and profits in India derived from fully commercial business rather than its former Assay business.[92] In 1919 Cox opened a branch in Alexandria in Egypt, and in the following year in Cairo. It enthusiastically entered the cotton finance business, and in 1920 purchased two cotton-spinning factories. However, by 1923 the Egyptian business had lost almost £95,000, although the factories themselves were profitable.[93] Cox also established, in collaboration with several local financiers, the Eastern Company registered in Egypt

[90] The bankers of individual customers can be found in *The 'Digest' Yearbook of Public Companies of Australia and New Zealand*, published annually. An estimate of the share of banks in public company business by industry is given in the first edition of H. W. Arndt, *The Australian Trading Banks* (Melbourne: Cheshire, 1957), 21–2. Later editions did not carry this table. [91] Geoffrey Jones, *Banking and Empire in Iran*, 229. [92] Undated Memorandum on Indian Business, File 3042, LB. [93] Memorandum on Egyptian Branches, 19 Feb. 1923; W. G. Johns to H. Bell, 11 Apr. 1923. File 2476, LB.

in 1920 to finance 'propositions . . . outside [Cox's] scope as bankers'. This venture, in turn, promoted a company to transport the produce of one of Cox's spinning factories and 'with a view to a subsequent amalgamation of all the Nile Transport Companies'.[94] There was also a small investment in a shipping company on the Danube, and Cox & Co. was linked through interlocking directorships with Cox's Shipping Agency, which formally ran a shipping and insurance business, but also undertook merchanting on occasion.[95] Cox appears to have been engaged in considerable product diversification after the First World War, therefore, but its management structures were not strong enough to hold the venture together. Diversification, once again, was at the expense of necessary banking prudence.

It would be wrong, however, to suggest that product innovation or diversification was either always absent, or always fatal. Barclays (DCO), the overseas bank with perhaps the most effective managerial hierarchy, pioneered lending to the indigenous agricultural sector in the 1930s. In 1935, and building on the expertise of the Anglo-Egyptian Bank, it took a 'leading part' in the formation of the Agricultural Mortgage Corporation of Palestine 'in order to provide a type of finance not readily forthcoming from the banks'. The bank also lent to agricultural co-operatives in Cyprus, where it had opened a branch in 1937. The island had had co-operative credit societies for decades, but their financing had been on an insecure basis until 1938 when the Co-operative Central Bank was established, which accepted surplus funds for deposit of various co-operative societies, and lent to other societies in need of funds. Barclays (DCO) lent funds on overdraft to the new institution, providing, during 1938, some 45 per cent of the Co-operative Bank's working capital.[96]

In many regions, the British banks responded to the condition of the inter-war years by edging closer to purely domestic business, and modifying their conditions for making loans. This was, of course, a continuation of a long-term trend. With limited opportunities for exchange profits and (often) increased competition, banks often found their best hope of obtaining exchange business was to extend credit 'down the line'. There were many examples of this in both Asia and Africa. During the 1920s the British banks at Harbin in Manchuria, to give one example, participated in the boom in soya bean production and exports. They provided finance for both middlemen and shippers, and this was seen as the best way to obtain the exchange business related to the trade.[97] In Uganda, the British banks

[94] Memorandum on the Eastern Company, File 1251, LB.
[95] O. V. G. Hoare to W. Goodenough, 3 May 1921, File 3035, LB.
[96] Phylaktis, 'Banking in a British Colony', 425; Sir Julian Crossley and John Blandford, *The DCO Story* (London: Barclays Bank International, 1975), 78, 90–1.
[97] Inspection Letter 412a, Harbin to London, 1 Mar. 1929, Special Advices from Agencies and Branches No. 3, Chartered Box, SC; Felix Patrikeeff, 'Prosperity and Collapse: Banking and the Manchurian Economy in the 1920s and 1930s', in King (ed.), *Eastern Banking*.

gave credit to the Asian cotton-ginners who purchased the crops of the African producers. The banks then expected to get the exchange business attendant on the sale and shipment of ginned cotton.[98]

The purchase of local banks with a domestic business represented a more radical strategy to get closer to local markets, but there was only a handful of such examples in the inter-war years. Anglo-South American's purchase in 1920 of a controlling interest in the Chilean private bank of Banco A. Edwards y Cia was the first of these. Banco A. Edwards appears to have been well run and profitable, and survived the fall of Anglo-South, continuing as a subsidiary of Bolsa. In 1921 the P & O Banking Corporation purchased the Indian-registered Allahabad Bank, which in time passed into the hands of Chartered Bank. Finally, in what retrospectively can be seen as a piece of poor timing, in January 1939 Ionian Bank purchased a majority of the shares of the Banque Populaire SA of Athens, which was one of the 'Big Five' banks in Greece and a serious competitor of Ionian Bank. In an even more dramatic innovation, Ionian formed an Athens-registered fire insurance company in March 1939. Within a year, however, Greece had been engulfed by the Second World War, and these two ventures disappeared into enemy hands until Greece's liberation in 1944.[99]

In Asia, the Middle East, and Africa, British banks displayed a greater willingness to lend on security, which would have been considered most undesirable before the First World War. For the banks in the Middle East, more local lending often meant more unsecured lending. Islamic law made property a very dubious security against which to lend, and in any case customers often considered it an insult to be asked for any security beyond their good name. It is quite clear, therefore, that in a country such as Iraq the British banks by the 1930s were lending largely on an unsecured basis.[100] This was more an instance of enforced innovation than anything else, and the practice was not liked by London managements.[101] Nevertheless, by the 1930s British banks almost everywhere were modifying their rules on collateral, often against their better judgement.

In Asia, the Exchange banks became further involved in local lending. Local lending had always been undertaken through intermediaries, and this continued. In China, the British banks continued to use compradors, who introduced local business and assessed its creditworthiness. There remained, therefore, a kind of 'bank within a bank'. In the Hongkong Bank's Shanghai branch in the inter-war years, there was even a separate Chinese banking hall. The British banks also continued their close connections with the

---

[98] Ralph Gibson's Report on his Visit to Standard's East African Branches, Mombasa, 29 Feb. 1936, SBSA East Africa Box, SC.   [99] *Ionian Bank Ltd.*, 38–9.
[100] Geoffrey Jones, *Banking and Empire in Iran*, 252.
[101] See e.g. Private and Confidential Letter to Basra Manager, 8 Mar. 1939; see also General Manager to Amarah Manager, 21 Apr. 1939; Eastern Bank Inspection Reports, SC.

TABLE 6.2 *Security for overdrafts on current account at four Eastern Bank branches, 1936 (% of total overdrafts)*

| Branch | Property | Commodities | Shares | Government security | Clean |
|---|---|---|---|---|---|
| Calcutta | 15 | 40 | 24 | 19 | 2 |
| Bombay[a] | 0.1 | — | 82 | 15 | — |
| Madras | 4 | 1 | 37 | — | 58 |
| Singapore | 7 | 65 | 4 | — | 24 |

[a] Eastern Bank in Bombay also had 2.9 per cent of its overdrafts lent against other security such as fixed deposits. Minor items for other securities at the other branches have been ignored.

*Source*: Eastern Bank Inspection Reports, 1936, SC.

Chinese native banks, although in the early 1930s the role of these banks in the Treaty Port banking system dramatically declined. In the 1920s, however, such native banks provided a low-risk avenue of lending to the local economy. Chartered Bank's Shanghai branch, for instance, made loans to native banks against the security of godown warrants for silk, cocoons, and other produce. The actual goods were pledged in the first place to the native banks by Chinese merchants, and, when these banks were pressed for funds, they applied to the foreign banks for accommodation. When pledging their cargo, the Chinese merchants signed a document authorizing the native bank to repledge it if necessary to foreign banks. Thus the native bank would, on obtaining a loan from Chartered Bank, for example, give Chartered an open-date 'pro note' for the amount of the loan, and also sign the ordinary loan bonds. In addition the loan would be guaranteed by Chartered's comprador.[102]

In some areas, when the banks made local loans directly they made unsecured—or 'clean'—advances, but they also took commodities, government securities, property, and shares as security. The lack of surviving data makes it hard to discern how practices changed over time, but Table 6.2 which shows the security taken on overdrafts on current account at four of Eastern Bank's branches in 1936 demonstrates, at least, the considerable diversity between regions.

The Exchange banks considered lending against commodities or government securities to be by far the most satisfactory procedure. However, the need to maintain or increase local lending in the inter-war years led them

[102] King, *The History of the Hongkong and Shanghai Banking Corporation*, iii. 347–54, 365; Shanghai to London, 948a, 20 Oct. 1922, Special Advices from Agencies and Branches No. 2, Chartered Box, SC.

to lend increasingly against property and shares. Both were considered risky and there was often uncertainty about the legal status of such securities. In Ceylon, for example, the law made it impossible to realize pledged security for loans. This should have ruled out loans against mortgages, but in fact even such banks as the Hongkong Bank undertook this business in the inter-war years, and accumulated bad debts.[103] In Singapore all the Exchange banks lent against the security of property, but tried to confine such lending within certain rules, such as that any advances should be only temporary and that they offered the prospects of other, sounder, business.[104] The problems which could follow from such lending against property were illustrated at Eastern Bank's Calcutta branch in the 1930s. The bank had to foreclose on many mortgages and became the owner of 'extensive properties' in the city. On the other hand, the paucity of other types of business meant that these repossessed properties became a useful source of income. In 1936 the working profits of Calcutta branch were found to 'depend largely upon the yield obtained from their properties'.[105] The British banks also lent against shares—as Table 6.2 makes evident. The growth of local stock exchanges and companies meant this kind of security was both more regularly offered and accepted, but a major problem remained of the marketability of shares quoted only on minor stock exchanges.[106]

One constraint on how far the banks modified their traditional lending policies was their continuing desire to be seen as stable orthodox British banks. This image had provided one of their competitive advantages over local institutions and, with their boards located in London and their shareholding drawn mainly from the United Kingdom, there was a limit on the extent banks wanted to be seen to be following unorthodox banking practices. It was on these grounds that the chairman of Barclays (DCO) opposed suggestions that the bank should enter the mortgage market in South Africa in 1926:

I do not like the plan, especially for such a bank as ours, whose reputation will be enormously increased if we preserve a strict banking attitude . . . It is considered in this country that the class of business . . . is strictly that of a Mortgage Company or a Building Society, and if we should undertake it, I think it would be prejudicial to us in the long-run.[107]

Concern to maintain the standards of banking orthodoxy did not rule out product innovation, but it often constrained it. For banks whose staff had

[103] King, *The History of the Hongkong and Shanghai Banking Corporation*, iii. 503–4.
[104] For Eastern Bank's rules, see Private and Confidential Letter to Singapore Manager, 15 Apr. 1940, Eastern Bank Inspection Reports, SC.
[105] Inspector's Report on Calcutta Branch, 23 Jan. 1936, SC.
[106] Acting Inspector's Report on Madras Branch, 1936, SC.
[107] F. C. Goodenough to J. R. Leisk, 11 Nov. 1926, 3/211, BBA.

TABLE 6.3 *Note issues of British multinational banks by region, 1938*

| Region | Notes issued (£ sterling) | No. of banks |
|---|---|---|
| Hong Kong | 14,907,869 | 3 |
| West Indies | 1,230,955 | 1 |
| Rhodesia | 942,088 | 1 |
| Australia and New Zealand | 3,756 | 2 |
| TOTAL | 17,084,668 | 7 |

skills that were product-specific as well as geographically specific, some caution on undertaking very new types of business was prudent.

The British banks sometimes had no alternative but to modify their business strategies, in view of changes beyond their control. In Asia, collapse of the Chettiar bankers during the Great Depression, through whom the British banks active in Ceylon, Burma, and elsewhere in South-east Asia had on-lent considerable sums to indigenous economies, left the Eastern Exchange banks with large bad debts.[108] It also stimulated more direct lending to local merchants.

The increased role of governments in banking and finance also resulted in some 'enforced product innovation'. Table 6.3 indicates that the banks continued to lose their note-issuing rights. Although the nominal sterling value of banknotes issued by British banks was higher in 1938 than twenty-five years previously (see Table 4.1), the numbers of countries in which there was a private note issue had fallen sharply.

Standard Bank lost its note issue in South Africa after the establishment of the Reserve Bank, and though it retained an issue in the British colony of Rhodesia. In 1920 the Ionian Bank's note-issuing privilege was transferred to the National Bank of Greece. Ten years later the Imperial Bank of Iran surrendered its right of note issue under official pressure. In the mid-1930s the trading banks in New Zealand had to surrender their note issues, leaving only a tiny residual by 1938. A major exception to this trend was Hong Kong, where the note issues of the three British Exchange banks were made legal tender in 1935. This was one consequence of China's departure from the silver standard in that year (see above, Section 6.1), which the British colony had followed. Hong Kong established a monetary system known as the sterling exchange standard, a variant of the

---

[108] King, *The History of the Hongkong and Shanghai Banking Corporation*, iii. 512–16; H. L. D. Selvaratnan, 'The Guarantee Shroffs, the Chettiars and the Hongkong Bank in Ceylon', in King (ed.), *Eastern Banking*, 416–17. Lloyds Bank in Burma was owed 27 lacs in defaulted Chetty loans in July 1933. See Lloyds (Calcutta) to Eastern Department, 19 Sept. 1934, Box 1557, LB.

colonial Currency Board system. Working in the context of a government-operated Exchange Fund, to which the note-issuing banks surrendered their silver held against notes, the banks agreed to issue notes on demand. Although the sterling exchange standard was ended in 1972, the private note issue of the banks continued into the 1990s.[109]

British banks handed over many of their quasi-central banking roles to governments and their newly founded central banks, although occasionally new roles were found. One of the more extraordinary reversals was again in the East. By the mid-1930s the Hongkong Bank had lost virtually all of its quasi-central bank functions in China, but subsequently, as the country suffered from both Japanese aggression and the problems of the new managed currency, the Hongkong Bank, with the help of the Chartered Bank, attempted to stabilize the Chinese currency, partly through secret exchange operations on the Shanghai market.[110]

It is hard to give more than an impressionistic picture of how far the British overseas banks adjusted their product strategies in the inter-war years. It is evident that there was an adjustment, but product innovation was usually incremental rather than revolutionary. One imperfect measure of the extent to which the business of the banks changed was the balance of exchange and interest earnings within institutions. By the 1930s interest earnings within a range of banks seem to have become more important than those from exchange, which suggests a refocusing on local business, although the surviving data is scattered and is suggestive rather than conclusive.

An Exchange bank like the P & O Banking Corporation, for example, found its earnings from exchange falling from the late 1920s.[111] In 1938 a director of this bank reflected how the P & O's 'large and profitable exchange business' in Calcutta had 'necessarily changed in character, and like older Eastern Exchange Banks, the bank in India [was] being directed more towards local banking and investment in India Government securities'. The Exchange banks had, he argued,

in the past, looked for their profits to the financing of the Exchange of the raw materials of the East for the manufactures of the West—business which was carried through by Bills of Exchange earning an interest profit as well as yielding an exchange profit. A very considerable amount of trade which formerly flourished

---

[109] Y. C. Jao and F. H. H. King, *Money in Hong Kong* (Hong Kong: Centre of Asian Studies, University of Hong Kong, 1990), 27–9, 51 ff. The note-issuing banks were (are) the Hongkong Bank, Chartered Bank (later Standard Chartered), and the Mercantile Bank of India (between 1911 and 1978).

[110] King, *The History of the Hongkong and Shanghai Banking Corporation*, iii. ch. 8; id., 'Defending the Chinese Currency', in King (ed.), *Eastern Banking*.

[111] In the year 1936 net earnings from interest of £207,000 surpassed those from exchange of £61,000. Memorandum on P & O Bank (undoubtedly by W. R. Cockburn, of Chartered Bank), 17 Oct. 1938, BAC 63, SC.

between the East and Europe, particularly Central Europe, is now being conducted on the barter basis. British Exchange Banks do not now participate in the financing of this trade, save to a very limited extent, and then only subject to state regulations and attendant risks.[112]

Evidence from the British banks in Latin America and South Africa also suggests the declining importance of exchange earnings over time. Bolsa in the 1920s made the majority of their profits in Argentina and Brazil from exchange operations, but this was no longer true by the end of the 1930s, especially in Brazil, where exchange controls were by then in place.[113] In South Africa in the 1930s, Standard Bank's exchange earnings became progressively less important as the bank's overall profitability grew.[114]

The British multinational banks adapted some of their banking strategies to the new circumstances of the inter-war years. The changes were, however, incremental rather than revolutionary, more evident in some regions than in others, and sometimes dictated by external events. A modification in lending policies occurred in most regions, and the problems of the international economy prompted the British banks to undertake more business not directly related to foreign trade and exchange. These changes took place within a number of constraints. These included the product-specific skills of staff, the need to safeguard a conservative and safe image, and the evident fate of banks such as Cox and Anglo-South American which appeared to favour entrepreneurship over prudence. The conservatism of the Anglo-Australian banks also indicated that, at least beyond a certain stage, control from London constrained the extent to which banks could engage in domestic or retail banking, at least compared to locally based competitors.

## 6.5. Local Staff in Africa and Asia

The changing circumstances of the inter-war years prompted a revision of the employment policies of some of the overseas banks. The executive staff

---

[112] Memorandum by P & O Director on Mr Cockburn's Report, 21 Oct. 1938, BAC 63, SC.

[113] Between 1923 and 1932 Bolsa's Argentine group of branches earned 66 per cent of their total working profits from exchange, and the Brazil group some 69 per cent. Comparable figures for the late 1930s are not available, but there is data for gross *receipts* (not profits). In the four years 1936 to 1939, in the Argentine group of branches receipts from exchange were £735,048, or 28 per cent of those coming from interest, which amounted to £2,637,131. In Brazil, where exchange controls were now in place, receipts from exchange of £110,928 were only 7 per cent of those from interest, which totalled £1,546,089. Bank of London and South America. Some Notes and Suggestions Arising out of the visit of Sir Alexander Murray and Mr. F. A. Beane to South America, Jan.–May 1933; Bolsa Consolidated Profit and Loss Accounts, LB.

[114] Standard Bank's working profits in South Africa were £369,870 in 1933, £883,911 in 1935, £1,220,936 in 1937, and £1,042,496 in 1939. The percentage derived from exchange profits was 94 per cent, 29 per cent, 20 per cent, and 21 per cent. SBSA Profits, BAC P/25, SC.

of the banks which operated outside the regions of Anglo-Saxon colonial settlement and the Mediterranean had always been British nationals recruited in the United Kingdom. The British staff were living proof to customers that these were *British* banks, safe and honest institutions, while the common cultural background and lifetime employment of the management cadre provided important means of ensuring co-ordination between branch managers and preventing opportunistic behaviour. The Eastern Exchange banks had employed intermediaries such as compradors when they wanted to undertake indigenous business.

These policies looked less satisfactory during the inter-war years as even the banks in Africa and Asia moved away from exchange banking and trade finance towards greater involvement in local economies, which suggested the need for a much greater level of information about those economies. Such detailed information was most readily found among nationals rather than British expatriates. Growing nationalism pointed in the same direction, for the employment of expatriate managers was visible evidence of the foreignness of British banks. Equally, the weaker financial performance of the banks in the inter-war years, and especially the 1930s, suggested that costs could be contained if expensive expatriates were replaced by cheaper nationals. Yet such a cost reduction strategy ran counter to the banks' competitive advantage in being *British* banks. As a result there were constant worries about how far the benefits of the British image—and the apparent reality of British probity—would be dissipated should nationals be appointed to the executive staff. Progress on the promotion of local staff was, on the whole, painfully slow, with considerable differences between regions.

The Bank of British West Africa was a pioneer in the employment of nationals in senior positions. This may well have been due to the fact that the West African coast was a singularly unhealthy environment for Europeans, and in consequence the bank found it difficult to recruit and keep suitable British staff. Already, in 1916, BBWA offered small prizes and assistance with fees 'in connection with shorthand and typewriting' through the directors of education in Freetown and Lagos 'with a view to encouraging commercial education amongst natives'.[115] In 1917 the board resolved that an attempt should be made to get the African staff interested in the bank as shareholders by offering them shares which could be paid for gradually.[116] A year later, two Africans were appointed as managers of small sub-branches.[117] Further such appointments followed in the inter-war years. In 1931 the board agreed to a suggestion from their Lagos

---

[115] BBWA Board Minutes, 15 Mar. 1916, in Fry's Digests of BBWA Board Minutes, BAC S/90, SC.  [116] BBWA Board Minutes, 30 Mar. 1917, SC.
[117] BBWA Board Minutes, 6 Dec. 1918, SC.

management that an African clerk should be placed in charge of a sub-branch 'subject to the District Manager being satisfied that the African clerk selected provided acceptable security for his fidelity'. In addition, safeguards were to be taken for the general supervision of the sub-branch.[118]

There were no such employment prospects for Africans in East Africa until the 1950s. In so far as 'locals' were allowed to undertake responsible work, they were Asians. In the case of Standard Bank, it was decided in 1936 that, in the interests of economy, some of the work formerly done by European officers should in future be done by Asian clerks.[119]

The British banks in Asia also seem to have found the employment of nationals in executive positions a difficult process, and there were no significant developments until the 1930s, when the Depression focused minds on salaries and costs. In 1932 the management of Lloyds' Indian branches began to consider granting additional responsibilities to certain Indian staff, almost entirely for reasons of economy. The proposals do not seem to have made much progress, out of concern for the need to keep 'the scope for irregularities . . . to a minimum compatible with the working of a reasonable system' and promotion of Indian staff to executive staff in Lloyds did not take place until the early 1950s.[120]

The Mercantile Bank of India made more progress in this direction than most of the Exchange banks in this period. Consideration of employing Indians at a more senior level seems to have begun in 1936 when Lord Catto, the former head of the great Anglo-Indian mercantile house of Andrew Yule and Company and a supporter of Dominion status for India, wrote to Mercantile's chief manager suggesting that a young Indian might be employed in the bank in a more than clerical capacity.[121] The 26-year-old man was a physics graduate from Madras University whose father had worked for the Mercantile Bank in Madras and finished up as a partner of Andrew Yule, and whose father-in-law was a director of the Madras board of the Reserve Bank of India. The bank took up Catto's suggestion, in part in the hope that this well-connected man could 'influence a certain amount of new business' in the direction of the bank.[122]

The experiment was a success and in 1938 the bank created a new grade of Indian Assistant, 'solely with a view to economy in administration'. The bank sought '*well educated* young men, preferably graduates, of good family

---

[118] BBWA Board Minutes, 26 Mar. 1931, SC.

[119] Report by Ralph Gibson, 29 Feb. 1936, SBSA East Africa Box, SC.

[120] Memorandum by District Manager, Calcutta to the Chief General Manager, 14 Feb. 1933, File 2407, LB; J. R. Winton, *Lloyds Bank, 1918–1969* (Oxford: Oxford University Press, 1982), 129.

[121] Lord Catto to J. B. Crichton, 6 Mar. 1936, MB Hist. 978, HSBC; R. P. T. Davenport-Hines, 'Thomas Sivewright Catto', in D. J. Jeremy (ed.), *Dictionary of Business Biography* (London: Butterworths, 1984), i.

[122] Mercantile Bank to Mr Graves, 23 Apr. 1936, MB Hist. 978, HSBC.

and of steady and reliable character', who would be taken on for a probationary period and, after having passed the first examination of the Indian Institute of Bankers, appointed to the new grade. Initially they were to be given only very restricted 'signing powers' for the bank, but the British officers in the bank were expected to treat them with respect. 'We suggest', the chief manager wrote to his Bombay manager, 'that from the outset the Indian Assistants should be addressed by all officers as "Mr".'[123]

By 1943 the Mercantile Bank had twelve Indian Assistants in post. During the war they began replacing assistant accountants and the bank decided that Indians could now become eligible for formal promotion to this grade, formerly the preserve of British officers. By this time the matter was one of high policy, and was the subject of a long memorandum by the Bank's chairman which was entered into the board minutes. He feared that his Indian Assistants would be poached by other banks if their further promotion was blocked, but by now—if not sooner—the real argument for liberalizing employment practices had become 'political':

One of the most bitter complaints made against the Eastern Exchange Banks operating in India is that the higher ranks in the Bank's services are closed preserves for Europeans, and that Indians are relegated to purely subordinate positions. After the War the Exchange Banks may in any event have a difficult position, and we ought to take steps, as far as we reasonably can to remove all legitimate causes for complaint.

Yet the constraints on the appointment of Indian executive staff were still felt by the chairman to be considerable. He identified two of them. 'We have to remember', he minuted, 'that the Mercantile Bank of India is a British Bank . . . it might be dangerous and it might affect our business if the impression got abroad that we were Indianizing the Bank.' Secondly, there was the problem of executive staff mobility in a small bank. The chairman could not envisage that locally recruited staff could, or should, be internationally mobile. Both these factors were to be much discussed within the British overseas banks over the next three decades. For Mercantile's chairman, they meant that the scheme had to be kept relatively small. On the other hand, he was prepared to make a firm declaration of principle which would have shaken his predecessors: 'The essential principle is that there should be no discrimination on racial grounds. There will be differences, of course, but the differences will arise from the fact that the Indians are serving in their own country, whereas Europeans are serving abroad.'[124]

Such a commitment to end racial discrimination was a major breakthrough. Events in contemporary Iran clearly demonstrated the need for

---

[123] Chief Manager to Manager, Bombay, 10 Feb. 1938, MB Hist. 978, HSBC.
[124] Memorandum by the Chairman, 12 Oct. 1943, Board Minute Book No. 11, MB Hist. 2308:13, HSBC.

the change of attitude. The Imperial Bank's most prominent local employee, Abol Hassan Ebtehaj, had been recruited in 1920, but during the early 1930s had become increasingly unhappy about the denial of status afforded to him, merely because he was an Iranian. In 1936 he resigned from the bank, joined government service, and by 1942 had re-emerged as governor of the Bank Melli. As governor over the following eight years, he made the existence of the Imperial Bank extremely uncomfortable. Although he always denied that he was pursuing a vendetta against the British bank, there is little doubt that his policies were a major factor in the decision of the Imperial Bank to disinvest from the country.[125]

By 1945, therefore, at least some of the British banks active in parts of Africa and Asia had taken their first steps to promote nationals to more senior positions, and so avoid the 'Ebtehaj syndrome'. A recognition of changing political realities was one reason, but banks were also eager to reduce staff costs, while the more their lending moved towards the domestic economy, the greater was their need for staff with knowledge of local cultural and business conditions.

## 6.6. Conclusion

In the inter-war years the British multinational banks were faced by declining competitive advantages in a mature industry. Life became harder for them. The banks, however, retained substantial first-mover advantages, and they were successful in surviving the major crises of this period. They had excellent franchises. Competitive challenges were limited in most markets. In Australasia and South Africa—two of the three major regions of operation—strong banking cartels were in operation which blocked new entrants, and severely restricted if not totally eliminated competition between existing banks. In the light of such factors, it was unsurprising that they retained market share in many countries and remained profitable, albeit at a reduced level in the 1930s.

The British banks showed some flexibility in their banking strategies, and this was another reason why market share had been maintained. They had always adjusted to host economy conditions, and continued this tradition in the inter-war years. Nevertheless, the overall policy of the banks can be characterized as 'sticking to the knitting',[126] and product and geographical diversification was modest. The changes in ownership discussed in the previous chapter—notably the advent of domestic banks into

[125] Geoffrey Jones, *Banking and Empire in Iran*, 283–6, 305–9, 317–32; Bostock and Jones, *Planning and Power in Iran*, 19–24, 70–84.
[126] For the concept of 'sticking to the knitting', see Thomas J. Peters and Robert H. Waterman, *In Search of Excellence: Lessons from America's Best-Run Companies* (New York: Harper and Row, 1982), ch. 10.

multinational banking—did not result in any great change to business strategies. 'Sticking to the knitting' is a sensible business strategy, and perhaps especially so given the uncertainties of the inter-war years. In conditions of a mature industry, incremental changes can be less costly (in a number of ways) than attempting to win new customers through entirely new products.[127] However, growth opportunities were missed in some markets, perhaps in Australia especially, and it would seem that the banks were constrained by a number of factors which meant that departures from 'knitting' were painful and hazardous. A fundamental problem was limited organizational capability. Within banks, management structures and cultures were designed to control risks in an emerging industry, not to generate new business in a maturing one. Skills were product- and region-specific, and the system of recruitment and training reinforced this situation. Organizational structures designed for multinational trade banks were less satisfactory for institutions which were evolving into multinational retail banks. Structure had lagged behind strategy, and limited the degree to which strategy could be modified.

Meanwhile, it remains to consider the home government environment faced by the British multinational banks. In the nineteenth century the British Treasury had played a large role in shaping the structure of the banks, especially its specialized nature. As the competitive advantages of the overseas banks declined in the inter-war years, an appropriate response from the British government and the Bank of England might have been expected. The next chapter turns to British official policy towards multinational banking.

[127] Michael Porter, *Competitive Strategy* (New York: Free Press), 243–4.

# CHAPTER 7

# The British Government, the Bank of England, and Multinational Banking

## 7.1. State-Sponsored Multinational Banking

During the First World War, and in the unstable inter-war years, the British government and the Bank of England came to play a much more direct role in multinational banking. The government promoted banking institutions. The Bank of England tried to influence the business strategy of the clearing banks towards multinational banking. Finally, the rescue of various banks was organized, and arrangements made so that their troubles did not damage the health of the rest of the financial community. The latter was one factor in the survival of British multinational banking in this era, but the other official policies did little to enhance the competitive advantages of British banks.

The most extraordinary departure from previous British traditions was the British government's promotion, in 1917, of a new bank designed in some respects to perform the functions hitherto performed by overseas and domestic banks. This was by no means the sole break with liberal *laissez-faire* tradition induced by the war. The government had been forced to introduce extensive controls over much of industry, had imposed limited import tariffs, and had even promoted and taken half the equity of a dyestuffs company designed to overcome Britain's dependence on imported dyes from Germany. Nevertheless, direct intervention in the sacrosanct world of the City of London was in many ways the most shocking of this spate of state intervention.

The idea of creating a British Trade Bank originated with concern felt in some quarters that British exporters were not being provided with adequate financial facilities compared to their German counterparts. German banking, with its apparent willingness to lend long-term to German industry, was much admired by many British observers anxious to explain Germany's successful competition in certain industries, especially in 'new' ones such as chemicals where British business appeared woefully deficient. In July 1916 an expert committee was appointed by the government, chaired by Lord Faringdon, a businessman and close friend and colleague of Sir Ernest Cassel. Faringdon had been one of the three promoters of the National Bank of Turkey. His committee included two men from the

Treasury and the Board of Trade, together with representatives of Barings and various other London banks.[1]

The handful of witnesses called before the committee expressed a number of reservations about the specialized British financial system, which was felt not to be assisting British exporters and manufacturers as well as its German counterpart. The closer integration of German domestic and overseas banking and industrial interests was more effective in winning overseas contracts in South America and elsewhere, and in promoting exports.[2] Witnesses pointed to the more professional nature of the German banks, and especially their employment of technical experts. A former employee of the Deutsche Bank gave a description of that bank's intelligence department, which provided sufficiently good commercial data on foreign markets to enable German bank managers 'to teach the merchant how to extend his business abroad'.[3]

The evidence presented at the Faringdon Committee was far from comprehensive and obviously self-selected. Yet the message seemed clear. The British financial system worked well enough in its individual parts, but more integration was required if Britain was to compete successfully with Germany after the war. British finance and British industry needed to work more closely together. Financial institutions needed more technical knowledge and commercial intelligence. What was required was an institution prepared to initiate projects and explore markets, and perhaps even provide venture capital for new enterprises.

These sentiments were reflected in the report of the Faringdon Committee which, unlike the evidence submitted to it, was published. The report praised the work of both the overseas and domestic banks, but complained that there was no co-ordination between them. Faringdon argued that what was needed was 'a new bank to fill the gap between the home banks and the Colonial and British-Foreign banks and banking houses, and to develop facilities not provided by the present systems'. A wide variety of potential tasks were identified for the proposed new institution. Great weight was given to its value in collecting and providing information, and the whole thrust of the new institution was to be more proactive than reactive in its strategy. 'It is essential that British products should be pushed, and manufacturers, merchants and bankers must combine to push them.' All of this required extensive contacts abroad, but Faringdon envisaged a sort of correspondent relationship with existing overseas banks. The

---

[1] A. S. J. Baster, *The International Banks* (London: King, 1935), 193–4; R. P. T. Davenport-Hines, *Dudley Docker* (Cambridge: Cambridge University Press, 1984), 137–9. The banks on the Committee were National Provincial Bank, Westminster Bank, Glyn, Mills, Liverpool and Martins Bank, the Midland Bank, and the Bank of England.

[2] Evidence of Vincent Caillard to Faringdon Committee, 7 July 1916, BT 55/32, PRO.

[3] Evidence of Edward F. Davies, 12 July 1916, BT 55/32, PRO.

Institution, the report believed, 'would largely use, under agreement, the existing banks and the facilities which they could afford', though some staff secondment was also envisaged. Integration, the provision of information, the identification of entrepreneurial opportunities, and a close relationship with existing institutions were the most important features of the Faringdon Report.

The committee ended its report with a specific proposal to create a 'British Trade Bank', constituted under a Royal Charter. The bank was to have a privately subscribed capital of £10 million. It was to have a foreign exchange department and 'a credit department for the issue of credits to parties at home and abroad'. However, as the bank was intended not to unduly interfere with existing banks, banking houses or financial institutions', the 'British Trade Bank' was not to accept deposits at call or short notice, and only open current accounts 'for parties who are proposing to make use of the overseas facilities which it would afford'.[4]

The Faringdon Report was unpopular in the City. The representative of Barings refused to sign it; and there was considerable adverse comment in various journals. *Bankers' Magazine* considered the report 'a too hastily prepared document', with insufficient support from the banking community.[5] Charles Addis, who was emerging as a prominent defender of free trade principles, published a strong attack on the proposed new bank in 1916. He predicted that, since competition with existing institutions was ruled out, the bank would inevitably 'be confined to a class of business which existing banks have discarded as unprofitable or unsafe', and he objected in principle to state interference in the working of the market.[6]

The unpopularity of the Faringdon proposal dampened the enthusiasm of the government for supporting the new institution. In November 1916 Faringdon raised the question of financial assistance for his new bank. It was proposed that it should receive a subsidy of £50,000 in its first year, followed by £40,000, £30,000, and £20,000 in the following three years. Faringdon explicitly did not want a 'government bank', but felt that the task of creating a viable, well-staffed institution needed some subsidy. By mid-April 1917, however, the idea of such a subsidy had been ruled out, the Treasury offering only to pay for any services rendered to the government 'on the basis of fair market value'. The idea of having a government director on the board was also briefly discussed, and as briefly rejected, because too close an association with the government was not considered

---

[4] Report to the Board of Trade by the Committee Appointed to Investigate the Question of Financial Facilities for Trade, Cd. 8346, 1916.
[5] 'The Proposals for a British Trade Bank', *Bankers' Magazine*, 102 (Nov. 1916), 545.
[6] 'A British Trade Bank', *Economic Journal* (Dec. 1916); Roberta Allbert Dayer, *Finance and Empire* (London: Macmillan, 1988), 87–8.

desirable.[7] Despite such caution and the fact that the government had responded to City criticism and dropped the name 'bank' from the title, substituting 'corporation', when the bill to create the proposed new institution came before the House of Commons in May 1917, it was widely attacked. The government had to promise Parliament that the corporation would receive no special state aid, no exclusive access to government information, and no monopoly as regards the representation of British trade abroad.[8]

The new British Trade Corporation (BTC) received its Royal Charter in April 1917. Faringdon was appointed its governor. The six other directors included three bankers (the senior partner of the merchant bank Huth Jackson, the chairman of National Provincial, and a director of Liverpool and Martins Bank), and three prominent armaments and steel industrialists, including Dudley Docker, who was very much a moving spirit behind the whole proposal. There was little interest in the City in acquiring shares. On 24 April 1917 the President of the Board of Trade summoned a meeting of leading joint stock bankers, and asked them to subscribe to the initial £1 million share issue. Lloyds' chairman offered £100,000 provided it was clear that the corporation would not be a direct competitor, but enthusiasm cooled following the issue of the prospectus. The list of the initial fifty applicants for the capital included Barclays, Glyn, Mills, five other domestic banks, two British overseas banks (London and River Plate and Standard Bank of South Africa), a recently established foreign trade bank (the British Bank of Northern Commerce), and the National Bank of South Africa. However, the sums committed were not large, and the majority of the share issue was taken up by the public. Nevertheless, the capital was raised, and BTC was able to appoint as its manager an experienced man whose working background included the Imperial Ottoman Bank, the Ionian Bank, the Anglo-Egyptian Bank, and the National Bank of Egypt.[9]

The BTC proved a forlorn experiment. It paid a 2.5 per cent dividend in 1918, and 4 per cent in 1919 and 1920, but nothing thereafter. In 1922 half the capital had to be written off. The corporation faced three interrelated problems. First, its business strategy was to penetrate former spheres of German trading influence where the German, Austrian, Turkish, and Russian empires had collapsed. Yet a British-based bank had few, if any, competitive

---

[7] President of the Board of Trade to Chancellor of the Exchequer, 6 Nov. 1916; Memorandum on Interdepartmental Conference, 22 Nov. 1916, BT 13/72; B. Law to A. Stanley, 14 Mar. 1917; Treasury to R. W. Matthew, 16 Apr. 1917, BT 13/83, PRO.

[8] Baster, *The International Banks*, 194–5; Davenport-Hines, *Dudley Docker*, 141–2.

[9] Baster, *The International Banks*, 195; Davenport-Hines, *Dudley Docker*, 142; id., 'Alexander Henderson, First Lord Faringdon', in D. J. Jeremy (ed.), *Dictionary of Business Biography*, iii (London: Butterworths, 1985), 155; Bankers' Meeting, 24 Apr. 1917, Deputation from the Clearing House Bankers, 1 May 1917, List of Applicants for £1 million capital, BT 13/83, PRO.

advantages in such regions. Secondly, this problem was compounded by its commitment only to operate in areas not already served by a British bank. Given the extensive British overseas bank branch network, this was virtually equivalent to condemning the BTC to operate in places no one had ever considered financially viable. Its initial branches were, therefore, located in such unlikely places (for a British bank) as Batoum (in southern Russia), Belgrade, and Danzig (on the Baltic). Finally, both these problems were compounded by the fact that the British government, as it had already demonstrated before 1914 in the case of the National Bank of Turkey, was not prepared to commit its whole-hearted support even to institutions which it had encouraged or sponsored.[10]

During the war BTC could do little except set up an information bureau, but by early 1919 it had purchased 96 per cent of the stock of the National Bank of Turkey, which had become completely moribund during the war. At the same time BTC purchased the newly founded Levant Company, a trading venture designed to replace German influence in the Near East, of which Lord Faringdon was on the board. Another purchase was the mercantile firm of Whittall, which had branches at Salonika and Constantinople. BTC's activities were not, however, limited to the eastern Mediterranean. It invested £100,000 in the Portuguese Trade Corporation, designed to compete with German interests active in pre-war Portugal. In 1918 BTC also founded, jointly with the London and Brazilian Bank, the Anglo-Brazilian Commercial and Agency Company, intended to replace German merchants by British ones in Brazil. These and other minor ventures were all failures. By 1922 the Brazilian and Levant Company investments had both had to be written off, while the National Bank of Turkey was never wholly revived.[11] BTC's most positive achievement was the formation of a subsidiary to insure foreign trade credits, the Trade Indemnity Company, which appeared—if only briefly—to find a demand for its services. It also built up a reasonably successful acceptance business, and by the mid-1920s it had become more of an acceptance house than anything else.

BTC's investments designed to assist British foreign policy ended in fiasco and failure. The corporation became involved with British intervention in the Russian civil war after the Bolshevik Revolution. The branch at Batoum was opened in response to a request from the British Army active in that area, and soon afterwards in 1919 BTC formed the South Russian Banking Agency (together with three clearing banks, Lloyds Bank, Westminster, and National Provincial) designed to facilitate British interests in south Russia.

[10] Davenport-Hines, *Dudley Docker*, 143.
[11] David Joslin, *A Century of Banking in Latin America* (London: Oxford University Press, 1963), 244: M. Kent, 'Agent of Empire? The National Bank of Turkey and British Foreign Policy', *Historical Journal*, 18 (1975), 388; Paper 44421, FO368/2204, PRO.

This venture collapsed following the Bolshevik victory in the civil war. Equally unproductive was an excursion into China loans. In 1919 the British Foreign Secretary insisted that the corporation (as well as Rothschilds) should be admitted to the British group of banks in the 'Four Power Consortium' which had been formed before the war. But no loans were negotiated in this period. By 1926 the corporation was no more than a name.[12] During 1925 an American syndicate attempted to purchase a 25 per cent stockholding in what was left of the corporation, a development strongly disliked by the government given that it had 'a Royal Charter and is in a special position to assist British Trade'. In the following year the Bank of England saved the corporation from such American 'scorpions' by arranging a merger with the Anglo-Austrian Bank, a venture which was not only government-inspired but also had a large Bank of England shareholding.[13]

Anglo-Austrian Bank had been founded in the middle of the nineteenth century by British interests, but by 1875 shareholding and control had shifted to Austria.[14] Before the war the bank, which belonged to the exclusive circle of Viennese *crédit mobilier* banks, had an office in London, and was indebted to various British and other concerns for over £2 million. The sterling assets of the bank were insufficient to meet the sterling liabilities, and the collapse of the Austrian currency at the end of the war meant that funds could not be remitted from Vienna. The Bank of England, under instructions from the Treasury, had financed many of the acceptances signed by the bank after the outbreak of war, in order to save a panic. As a result, it was the largest creditor for over £1.6 million. In order to try to recover the debts, and as an aspect of the ambitious plans of the Governor of the Bank of England, Montagu Norman, for the postwar monetary reconstruction of Central Europe and Germany, a debt to equity scheme was devised under which the Anglo-Austrian Bank was reconstructed as a British-registered institution, largely controlled by the Bank of England. Anglo-Austrian had, as a result of the break-up of the Austro-Hungarian Empire, a substantial branch network spread over six independent countries: in 1920 it operated 33 branches in Austria, 29 in Czechoslovakia, 3 each in Hungary and Romania, 2 in Italy, and 1 in Yugoslavia. The Bank of England's resolve to become a majority shareholder in such a venture represented an even more startling innovation than the

[12] Davenport-Hines, *Dudley Docker*, 143–7; Baster, *The International Banks*, 196–7. On the failure of the 'New Consortium' see F. H. H. King, *The History of the Hongkong and Shanghai Banking Corporation*, iii (Cambridge: Cambridge University Press, 1988), 87–98.

[13] Summary of the Bank of England's schemes for the Reconstruction of the Anglo-Oesterreichische Bank, 1927, C40/119; M. Norman to General Sir Herbert Lawrence, 17 Aug. 1926, C40/120, B. of E.

[14] P. L. Cottrell, 'London Financiers and Austria, 1863–1875: The Anglo-Austrian Bank', *Business History*, 11 (1969), repr. in R. P. T. Davenport-Hines (ed.), *Capital, Entrepreneurs and Profits* (London: Cass, 1990).

creation of the BTC, especially as the Bank expressed an interest to take 'an active part' in Anglo-Austrian's affairs.[15]

Anglo-Austrian Bank was registered as a British company in March 1922, with a substantial capital of £1,406,370. The Bank of England held just over a quarter of the equity, and a further £700,000 in certificates of indebtedness which could be converted at any time into shares. The Articles of Association gave the Bank of England majority voting power so long as it held a minimum of £200,000 shares. The Czechoslovakian branches were, for political reasons, turned over to a new Anglo-Czechoslovakian Bank, which was locally incorporated, and in which the Anglo-Austrian Bank held around 70 per cent of the shares and the Czech government most of the remainder.

Like the BTC, the reconstruction of the Anglo-Austrian represented a good idea which was not turned into a viable commercial scheme. In the immediate post-1922 period the bank did play some positive role in Central European reconstruction. The Anglo-Austrian and Anglo-Czechslovakian Banks, for example, took an active part in the flotation in London of reconstruction loans for Austria, Hungary and Czechoslovakia.[16] However, commercial success proved elusive. The management of the new anglicized Anglo-Austrian Bank initially hoped that control could be firmly centred on London, and that British banking principles could be followed. This strategy was never likely to be easy to implement given that Anglo-Austrian was a classic example of the continental 'mixed banking' tradition, its main business consisting of giving credits to various industrial concerns which it controlled. These Central European banking practices proved puzzling to the bank's British staff, many of whom knew little about the business culture or even the German language.[17] Financial disorder, heavy taxation, and violent exchange fluctuations added to the problems of managing the bank.

[15] Baster, *The International Banks*, 199–200; M. Norman to Sir Basil Blackett, 13 Apr. 1921, C40/115, B of E. For the wider context of the Bank of England's involvement in the Anglo-Austrian Bank, see R. S. Sayers, *The Bank of England, 1891–1944*, i (Cambridge: Cambridge University Press, 1976), 163–83; P. L. Cottrell, 'Aspects of Western Equity Investment in the Banking Systems of East Central Europe', in Alice Teichova and P. L. Cottrell (eds.), *International Business and Central Europe 1918–1939* (Leicester: Leicester University Press, 1983), esp. 316–21; Robert Boyce, *British Capitalism at the Crossroads, 1919–1932* (Cambridge: Cambridge University Press, 1987), 39. For a detailed discussion of the Bank of England and the Anglo-Austrian Bank, see Alice Teichova, 'Versailles and the Expansion of the Bank of England into Central Europe', in N. Horn and J. Kocka (eds.), *Law and the Formation of the Big Enterprises in the Nineteenth and Early Twentieth Centuries* (Göttingen: Vandenhoeck and Ruprecht, 1979), 368–80. See also Eduard März, *Austrian Banking and Financial Policy* (London: Weidenfeld and Nicolson, 1984), 457–62.

[16] Baster, *The International Banks*, 201.

[17] Cottrell, 'Aspects of Western Equity Investment in the Banking Systems of East Central Europe', 331–3; see also P. Bark to M. Norman, 28 Dec. 1921; Memorandum of 27 Dec. 1921; C40/116, B. of E.

In November 1922 the Bank of England purchased a further £300,000 shares because Anglo-Austrian was short of capital, and during 1924 the Bank of England had to offer a credit of £1 million in conjunction with Glyn's, a member of which—General Sir Herbert Lawrence—was Anglo-Austrian's chairman. The Austrian branches ran a large annual loss, said, by 1926, to have reached £1 million.[18] As the bank approached liquidation there was no alternative but to abandon multinational aspirations. The bank's Italian branches were sold to the Banca Italo-Britannica—an institution whose dismal career will be discussed below—and its Yugoslavian and Hungarian branches were sold to local banks. In July 1926, in the largest deal of all, the Austrian branches were sold to Credit Anstalt of Vienna. In every case there was an exchange of shares and directors. In September 1926 the remainder of Anglo-Austrian fused with the British Trade Corporation to form the Anglo-International Bank, with a paid-up capital of £1,960,000. As Anglo-Austrian was virtually bankrupt, the Bank of England, acting for the Treasury, purchased £600,000 shares which were issued for £1 million so as to recapitalize the new institution.[19] Lawrence became the new chairman, with the Bank of England owning around 55 per cent of the equity.

The career of the Anglo-International Bank was as ill-fated as that of its predecessors. The general manager was Peter Bark, the last Minister of Finance in Tsarist Russia, who had drifted into the orbit of Montagu Norman. He maintained Anglo-Austrian's policy of abandoning the multinational branches and relying on a correspondent strategy. By 1929 only two Romanian branches remained in the bank's possession, and these were finally disposed of in 1932. Anglo-International concentrated on acting as a bankers' bank, replacing direct commitments to commercial firms abroad by credits granted to foreign banks, and refocusing the business on Germany rather than Central Europe.[20] It also undertook business on behalf of the Bank of England. For some time, for example, the Bank of England sold dollars in London using the Anglo-International Bank. After September 1931 Anglo-International operated on the foreign exchange market for account of the Bank of England, and it also assumed a number of obligations at the request of the Bank of England, including taking up a German government bond issue.[21] These things helped to make Montagu Norman very protective of Anglo-International: in June 1928, for instance,

---

[18] M. Norman to O. Niemeyer, 14 June 1926, C40/120, B. of E.
[19] Memorandum on Anglo-International Bank, Chief Cashier's Office, 2 Mar. 1932, C40/119; Memorandum of 20 Oct. 1930, C40/120, B. of E.
[20] Memorandum by P. Bark, 16 Nov. 1933, C48/90, B. of E.
[21] Bank of England Memorandum, 17 Oct. 1932, C40/119; Memo on Anglo-International Bank Ltd., 7 Oct. 1932, C48/90, B. of E.; R. J. Truptil, *British Banks and the London Money Market* (London: Jonathan Cape, 1936), 175; Sayers, *The Bank of England*, ii, 426 n. l.

he declined an offer from Deutsche Bank to buy the Bank of England's holding in the bank.[22]

Such services on behalf of the Bank of England could not save Anglo-International from the ravages of the Great Depression and, especially, the Central European financial crisis in 1931. The collapse of Credit Anstalt in May 1931 was a devastating blow, for much of Anglo-International's business derived from its old Austrian connection. The bank's German business was likewise ruined. The shareholdings in Credit Anstalt and the other associated Central European banks were rendered worthless. By October 1932, 83 per cent of Anglo-International's assets were 'more or less frozen', but the Bank of England resolved to soldier on because a formal bankruptcy would 'reflect adversely on British Banking prestige—and, in particular, on that of the Bank of England and Glyns who have acted as sponsors'.[23] The Bank of England purchased Anglo-International's shares on the market to prevent a total collapse of the share price. However, by 1933 Anglo-International had an excess of current liabilities over liquid assets of over £1.1 million. The Bank of England had to grant a credit of £1 million to the distressed bank, and in November 1933 a policy of 'private orderly liquidation' was decided upon.[24] Lawrence was replaced as chairman by Sir Bertram Hornsby, who had been Governor of the National Bank of Egypt between 1921 and 1931. He had been installed to run Anglo-South American Bank after its collapse in 1931, and now found himself managing two 'dead dogs' on behalf of the Bank of England.[25]

Anglo-International Bank lingered on during the remainder of the 1930s, unable to develop any new sources of income and, as Hornsby at one stage reflected, was not 'a good advertisement for British Finance'.[26] In 1943 the Bank of England calculated that it had lost some £1.6 million since 1927 through its support for Anglo-International, including share purchases.[27] In 1944 the 'goodwill' of the business was given to Glyn, Mills, who took over the few remaining liabilities to the public, but it was not until 1962 that the Anglo-International Bank was finally liquidated.

A further costly official intervention in overseas banking was the British Italian Corporation. The idea of establishing a British bank to operate in Italy originated with the London, County and Westminster Bank, which sent a man from its Paris branch to Italy in early 1915 to explore the possibilities. It soon became apparent that the best option might be to take a shareholding in an Italian bank. By August the British Foreign Office had

---

[22] Memorandum, 13 June 1928, G14/84, B. of E.
[23] Bank of England Memorandum, 17 Oct. 1932, C40/119, B. of E.
[24] Memorandum to Governor, 25 Sept. 1936, C40/119; K. O. Peppiatt to H. Read, 20 Nov. 1933, C48/90, B. of E.    [25] Memorandum of 3 Dec. 1934, C48/90, B. of E.
[26] Memorandum by B. Hornsby, 17 Nov. 1939, C48/91, B. of E.
[27] Memorandum 24 February 1943, C48/92, B. of E.

become interested in the scheme, though the Treasury as usual was hostile to any government financial commitment to any project. Over time the project became broader, and the eventual outcome in 1916 was the creation of two institutions, the British Italian Corporation in Britain and the Compagnia Italo-Britannica in Italy.

Probably because the initiative for the project had come from the banks rather than a government committee, the Italian venture attracted far more City support than the British Trade Corporation. A considerable number of domestic and overseas banks took shareholdings. An analysis of the shareholding in 1929 showed that some 51 per cent of the issued capital of £1 million was in the hands of British joint stock banks, with a further 20 per cent held by British insurance companies (notably the Prudential), and the rest by trust companies, shipping companies (the Ellerman company), commercial firms, and private individuals. Three of the 'Big Five' English clearing banks were major shareholders: Lloyds and Westminster Banks for £100,000, and National Provincial £25,000.[28] Half of the capital of the Compagnia Italo-Britannica was taken by the corporation, and half by an Italian group of banks.

The aims of the British Italian Corporation were similar to those of the British Trade Corporation. The object was 'the development of the economic relations between the British Empire and Italy, and the promotion of undertakings in the commercial and industrial field in Italy'. It was hoped that competing British manufacturers could be brought into contact with one another through the corporation, and 'wasteful competition' avoided. Considerable emphasis was placed on challenging the former German strength in many Italian industries before the war, such as electricity. These wider aims probably help to explain the most extraordinary feature of the scheme. Despite the reluctance of the Treasury, and in contrast to the British Trade Corporation, the British government offered financial support to the venture. An agreement of 8 June 1916 provided for an annual subsidy of £50,000 for ten years, while a supplementary agreement on 18 October 1917 provided for an additional government payment of an amount equal to the income tax or excess profits duty to which the corporation might become liable in consequence of the payment to them of the annual subsidy.[29]

The British Italian Corporation soon experienced problems. It became involved in shipping finance, and was caught in the post-war shipping

[28] Annual Report of British Italian Corporation, 1918; Analysis of shareholding of British Italian Corporation, 1929, OV36/35, B. of E.

[29] Luciano Segreto, 'La City e la "Dolce Vita" romano: la storia della Banca Italo Britannica, 1916–1930', *Passato e Presente*, 13 (1987), 69–73; Baster, *The International Banks*, 197–8; Annual Report of the British Italian Corporation, 1917; Board of Trade to Treasury, 26 Oct. 1920, T161/498, PRO.

slump with a substantial shareholding in a shipping company. There was a lack of co-ordination with the efforts of the British Trade Corporation. The plans to penetrate the Italian electricity industry failed, as did hopes of establishing exclusive relations with major British companies active in Italy, notably the armaments firm Vickers. The joint venture with the Italian banks was abandoned, and in 1922 the whole Italian operation passed into a wholly owned subsidiary, the Banca Italo-Britannica. The government subsidy was terminated at the same time, the corporation receiving the £283,418 paid up to then as a present, free of tax. The corporation's dividend payments—which totalled £210,000 between 1917 and 1921—had rested entirely on this subsidy.[30]

For a time the Banca Italo-Britannica appeared to flourish. It developed a substantial branch network, managed from its head office in Milan, and in 1926 it acquired the Italian branches of Anglo-Austrian Bank. The Banca became the fourth or fifth largest among the Italian commercial banks. Unfortunately the corporation in London lost control of what was being done in Italy, and by 1926 'irregularities' occurred in the Banca Italo-Britannica. In 1929 rumours about the bank's standing led to crisis. In January 1929 the Bank of England was advised that, if the Banca Italo-Britannica did not find £2.6 million within a week, it and the British Italian Corporation would have to go into liquidation. The Bank of England obliged the 'Big Three' clearing banks to put up the sum, even though they formed only a minority of the eighty or so shareholders. The Bank itself offered a minor contribution of £250,000, and agreed to accept any sterling acceptances that were placed on the London market. The assistance of Mussolini and the Italian central bank was also secured in the rescue operation.[31]

A subsequent Bank of England investigation revealed some of the full horror of the incompetence and corruption at the Banca Italo-Britannica. By mid-February the Bank's investigator had established that the Italian institution was 'absolutely insolvent'.[32] Investigations of the branch network revealed an institution devoid of management controls. Turin branch was reportedly managed 'by methods which it is charitable to term merely incompetent'.[33] The worst problems were at Rome, where large sums of money had been borrowed on short term from foreign banks in sterling and dollars, and had either been utilized for the purchase of securities or been lent without authority to various debtors. The transactions had been

[30] Segreto, 'La City e la "Dolce Vita" romano', 74–7; Baster, *The International Banks*, 198.

[31] Minutes of the Committee of Treasury, 23 Jan. 1929 and 6 Mar. 1929, G14/250, B of E; Sayers, *The Bank of England*, i, 260–1.

[32] Francis Rodd to Deputy Governor, 16 Feb. 1929, OV36/35, B. of E.

[33] Memorandum on Mr Palmer's Reports on Venice, Trieste, and Turin Branches, 21 Sept. 1929, OV36/38, B. of E.

kept secret in separate books and the balance between the totals of the debits and credits carried into the authorized books of the bank under false names. The Banca's most senior staff had been involved in the bribery of politicians and in prostitution. Its managing director, a naturalized British subject of Italian extraction, was inculpated in the scandal, resigned, and fled to France, later being sentenced to nine years in prison in his absence.[34]

The underlying problem was the tension between British and Italian banking practices, which had led to misunderstanding and, ultimately, management failure. 'The Italian conception of Banking is different from the British,' one of the British investigators gloomily observed in June 1929, in a direct echo of the difficulties of Anglo-Austrian.[35] In 1930 the business was sold to the Bank of America. Lloyds and Westminster Banks lost between £1.1 million and £1,877,522 each, and National Provincial as much as £1,690,871, in their support of the Banca Italo-Britannica, making a maximum total loss for the three clearers of £5,445,964. The Bank of England also wrote off its £250,000 contribution.[36]

The British Trade Corporation, the British Italian Corporation, and the Anglo-Austrian Bank represented remarkable departures from pre-1914 orthodoxies. In the first two instances, the government had sponsored and even in one case subsidized banks to operate in geographical areas previously barely touched by British multinational banking. Moreover, both banks were intended to break down the specialized nature of British banking by mixing finance with other types of business and linking domestic and overseas banking. The Bank of England's reconstruction of the Anglo-Austrian Bank in 1922 stemmed from less evangelistic motives, being essentially an imaginative solution to the problem of debt in the context of Montagu Norman's efforts to influence the financial stabilization of Central Europe. The result was just as unorthodox, however, with the British central bank owning and controlling a 'mixed' commercial bank with a multinational branch network.

The results of all this unorthodoxy were dismal. The government and the Bank of England, and all the other parties involved, made large financial losses with little but a bizarre record of failure to show for them. A number

[34] Segreto, 'La City e la "Dolce Vita" romano', 80–92; Memorandum concerning the Financial Position of the British Italian Banking Corporation and the Banco Italo-Britannica, 1929; Memorandum, Apr. 1931, File 7692, LB.

[35] C. H. Evans to F. Ashley Cooper, 4 June 1929, File 7692, LB.

[36] The higher figures are from Lloyds Advances and General Purposes Committee, 1 Oct. 1930, File 2209, LB. At the time Lloyds hoped that the banks might recover up to £1,200,000 of the £5,445,964. A Lloyds Bank report in 1943 put the bank's loss at £1,079,757, Memorandum of 21 July 1943 by R. A. Wilson and Sydney Parkes, Winton Investment File, LB. See also Sayers, The Bank of England, i, 261–3 and J. R. Winton, Lloyds Bank, 1918–1969 (Oxford: Oxford University Press, 1982), 57–9.

of reasons lay behind this poor performance. The inter-war years were not an ideal time for new banking ventures in Germany, Italy, and Central Europe. British bankers also had few skills and little experience in the new geographical regions or new types of business being sought. Poor management often resulted. Excessive dependence on 'locals' on the spot led to bad debts. As other British commercial interests in these new regions were not substantial, the new banks had no ready-made customer base among its own nationals.

In retrospect, it can be seen that the economic logic for these banks was weak. The decline of international trade, and of the British share of world trade, provided an inhospitable environment for new British multinational trade banks. Arguably, too, the great era of mixed banking was already over by the First World War. In the unstable economic conditions of the inter-war years, the mixed banking systems of several continental countries collapsed or were replaced. Faringdon and others like him were to some extent attempting to emulate a model whose time had passed. More active government support might have enabled the banks to survive or carve out a market niche. However, although the official sponsors of these new institutions sometimes welcomed their assistance, positive support to make them commercial successes was never forthcoming, nor was any attempt made to co-ordinate their activities. Moreover, from the Faringdon Report onwards, there was a consensus that the new banks were not to compete with existing institutions. This constraint fatally curbed any entrepreneurial initiative, and amounted to a virtual sentence of commercial death.

## 7.2. The Bank of England and the Clearers

Curiously, while the British government was sponsoring banks designed in part to overcome the specialized nature of British multinational banking, the Bank of England was actively attempting to thwart the private sector's attempt to achieve the same goal. For over two decades the Bank of England opposed the entry of the clearing banks into multinational banking, although its opposition proved singularly ineffective.

The Bank of England's policy evolved in the context of mounting concern about the structure of British banking as a whole. By 1918 the banking system of England and Wales had become concentrated in the hands of the 'Big Five'. This raised monopoly fears in some quarters, while the Bank of England was concerned about the implications for banking stability. Concern at the pace of bank amalgamations led to the Colwyn Committee, which in its report in 1918 recommended legislation requiring prior official approval of any further amalgamations. No legislation ever materialized, but it became established policy that the 'Big Five' in England and Wales would refer any amalgamations among themselves to the Treasury for approval, and a set of rules to this effect was codified in 1924.[37]

A sub-theme of this debate was the implications of the clearers' new involvement in overseas banking. This matter had first become an issue in 1918, following the spate of overseas investments by Lloyds Bank. The Indian authorities had raised objections to Lloyds' negotiations about taking an equity stake in the National Bank of India. As a result, the Colwyn Committee had refused Lloyds permission to proceed.[38] In 1919 Lloyds' proposals to take shareholdings in the National Bank of New Zealand and the Bank of British West Africa also ran into difficulties. The Colwyn Committee declined both proposals in March 1919, on the grounds that Lloyds had agreed not to make further acquisitions in the previous year. Although the agreement essentially applied to domestic banks, the committee considered that 'large purchases such as those now proposed, coupled with seats on the Board, came under the head of amalgamations'.[39] In this case, however, the government was lobbied hard by both of the banks involved to allow them to forge a link with Lloyds. The Colonial Office also supported both the West African and New Zealand purchases. As a result, in June 1919 the Colwyn Committee allowed the schemes to proceed.[40]

In these early discussions, the authorities had treated Lloyds' policies in the context of the overall government policy on bank mergers. By the early 1920s, however, the focus had shifted and become more specific. The concern became the potential threat to banking stability should one of the clearers' overseas ventures go badly awry. One of the first people to articulate such worries was Gaspard Farrer, a director of Barings who had given evidence to the Colwyn Committee opposing further bank mergers, and who subsequently became a member of a small committee to advise the Chancellor of the Exchequer on policy in this area. He had also been the one member of the Faringdon Committee who had declined to sign the report calling for the establishment of a British Trade Bank.[41] In February 1923 he wrote to Lord Colwyn saying that a warning should be given against British domestic banks taking over banks active abroad, because the British government would be forced to help them if their foreign adventures went awry, which was more than likely. 'There can be no excuse

---

[37] Sayers, *The Bank of England*, i, 235–43.

[38] Winton, *Lloyds Bank*, 23; G. Tyson, *100 Years of Banking in Asia and Africa* (London: National and Grindlays Bank, 1963), 152–3.

[39] Report of Bank Amalgamation Committee, 13 Mar. 1919; Note by C. P. Stocks, 13 Mar. 1919, T160/278, PRO.

[40] National Bank of New Zealand to Austen Chamberlain, 20 Mar. 1919; Foreign Office to Board of Trade, 19 June 1919; Lord Selbourne to A. Chamberlain, 5 Apr. 1919; Shorthand Notes on Deputation to Lord Inchcape *re* LB and BBWA, NBNZ, and West Yorkshire Bank, 11 June 1919; Advisory Committee Meeting, 11 June 1919. T160/278, PRO.

[41] Sayers, *The Bank of England*, i, 237–8. For Farrer, see Philip Ziegler, *The Sixth Great Power: Barings, 1762–1929* (London: Collins, 1988), 272–3.

for these extensions abroad,' he noted, 'nothing but greed and megalomania.' Farrer was particularly exercised about the dangers faced by Lloyds in Latin America, obviously remembering Barings' near-fatal problems in the late nineteenth century. 'Experience tells one how easily trouble can arise among these excitable Latin races.'[42]

Farrer's views were readily espoused by Norman. By early March he expressed his hope of 'leaving India again free from the Clearing Banks', and it was very soon the governor's established policy that the clearing banks should not extend their interests abroad.[43] 'If there is a crisis in any part of Africa or in the West Indies,' Norman wrote to the governor of the South African Reserve Bank objecting to the formation of Barclays (DCO) in 1925, 'are we in London to risk the credit of a Clearing Bank being affected?' For Norman, the whole idea threatened the specialized nature of British financial institutions, which he held to bring stability. 'The Clearing Banks exist mainly to care for trade and industry in this country; for those domestic and foreign financial transactions as are conducted here; and for the private individuals needs.'[44]

Norman maintained this line over the next twenty years, to no result. He faced two problems in making his policy effective. First, while the Treasury supported the policy that there should be no amalgamations among the 'Big Five', he found no strong support within the government for his views on divesting the clearers of their foreign interests. The two issues were seen as quite distinct, and the Treasury was much less concerned about the second one.[45] Secondly, Norman found himself encouraging the *further* expansion of these interests in several instances when the imminent collapse of banks threatened the financial system. Lloyds was, as will be seen below (Section 7.3), prompted in 1923 to rescue Cox's (with their Indian and Egyptian branches) and, more spectacularly, to add the Anglo-South American Bank to their Latin American empire in 1936. Such inconsistencies did not prevent Norman, usually, from persisting in his opposition to multinational investments.

After watching helplessly the amalgamation in 1923 of London and Brazilian Bank with the London and River Plate Bank owned by Lloyds, the first big clash came two years later over the formation of Barclays (DCO). The Bank of England regarded this proposal as 'against the public interest'.[46] Representations were made to Barclays, which steadfastly ignored

[42] Gaspard Farrer to Lord Colwyn, 15 Feb. 1923, G1/9, B of E; Sayers, *The Bank of England*, i, 243–4.
[43] M. Norman to Sir Basil Blackett, 9 Mar. 1923, G1/9, B of E; Sayers, *The Bank of England*, i, 242–3.
[44] M. Norman to Governor of South African Reserve Bank, 11 Mar. 1925, G1/9, B. of E.
[45] Memorandum on Barclays Bank, Canada, 27 Dec. 1929, T160/278, PRO.
[46] Committee of Treasury, 1 Apr. 1925, G14/73, B of E; Sir Julian Crossley and John Blandford, *The DCO Story* (London: Barclays Bank International, 1975), 24.

them. In June 1925 the Bank of England decided on principle to close down the accounts and discriminate against the acceptances of overseas banks controlled by clearers. When Barclays (DCO) began operations, the Bank of England refused to open an account for it or discount their bills. By May 1929 this treatment was being applied also to Barclays' French and Canadian subsidiaries, Bolsa, the Bank of British West Africa, Lloyds and National Provincial Foreign Bank, the National Bank of New Zealand, Westminster Foreign Bank, and the British Overseas Bank. Only the acceptances of the British Italian Corporation were taken by the Bank of England, its dire condition confirming Norman in his worst fears about the dangers of foreign entanglements. All through the 1930s the bills of these overseas banks carried slightly higher rates of discount due to the discriminatory policy of the Bank of England.[47]

The Bank tried a variety of schemes to rid the clearers of their overseas subsidiaries. In November 1936 Norman got the committee of the Treasury of the Bank of England to agree that 'if an opportunity presented itself, the Governor might make a definite offer to the Chairman of Barclays Bank to take over for cash their interest in Barclays Bank (DCO) at a price to be mutually agreed upon'.[48] However, nothing concrete emerged from this extraordinary proposal, which would have made the Bank of England the owner of Britain's largest overseas bank, and all Norman could do was to throw occasional obstacles in that bank's path. In 1936, for example, he attempted to get the Colonial Office to block Barclays' plans to open a branch in Cyprus, but again with no success.[49]

Norman was equally active—and ineffective—in trying to persuade Lloyds to divest itself of its overseas subsidiaries. He had a particular dislike of Lloyds' operations in India, which he described in 1925 as 'less justifiable than any other venture'.[50] In 1934 the Bank of England attempted to persuade Lloyds to sell their Indian branches to the Imperial Bank of India, but after an examination of their profitability the British bank declined to sell.[51] In 1936 Lloyds asked for the discrimination against Bolsa to be dropped as, following the Anglo-South American merger, the clearer now held less than 50 per cent of the shares. The Bank of England, however, 'could not agree that this fact in any way altered the position'.[52]

The Bank of England maintained its struggle into the Second World War. As late as 1943 the Bank was discussing methods of divesting the clearers of control of their overseas interests. In April of that year the idea

[47] Committee of Treasury, 3 June 1925, 1 May 1929, G14/73, B. of E; Sayers, *The Bank of England*, i, 244–8.   [48] Committee of Treasury, 25 Nov. 1936, G14/73, B. of E.
[49] M. Norman to A. H. Reid, 16 Dec. 1936; R. V. N. Hopkins to M. Norman, 24 Feb. 1937, G1/367, B. of E.   [50] Secret Memorandum, 17 June 1925, G14/73, B. of E.
[51] Committee of Treasury, 24 Oct. 1934 and 5 Dec. 1934, G14/73, B. of E; Lloyds Advances and General Purposes Committee, 28 Nov. 1934, File 2210, LB.
[52] Committee of Treasury, 28 Oct. 1936, G14/73, B. of E.

was floated of creating a 'trust company', which could take over the shares of Bolsa, Barclays (DCO), and Lloyds' Indian branches, but this was abandoned as 'unworkable'. Less ambitious schemes proposed to deal with each bank separately and on an incremental basis. It was thought, for example, that if Lloyds' chairman would cease acting as chairman of Bolsa, it might be 'a significant and important starting point'.[53] It was not until after Montagu Norman's departure as governor that the Bank of England's policy began to soften.

Montagu Norman's attack on the overseas interests of the clearers was quite impotent. However, it provided an unhelpful context for attempts to renew the competitive advantages of British multinational banking, by ending the geographical and functional specialization of the multinational banking sector. It may help to explain part of the reason why Lloyds failed to merge its disparate overseas interests into a more coherent structure. Certainly the hostility of the central bank to the integration of domestic and overseas banking provided no incentive to Lloyds' management to integrate the various aspects of their business.

## 7.3. Bank Rescues

The Bank of England's aversion to the risks of multinational banking may be related in part to the support it had to give to a number of troubled banks in the inter-war years, both in the domestic and overseas banking sectors. At the end of the 1920s it had to rescue the Lancashire-based clearing bank Williams Deacon's, which had accumulated large bad debts in the cotton industry. The Bank of England spent over £3 million in supporting the bank and arranging its acquisition by the Royal Bank of Scotland.[54] Similar rescue operations were needed for a number of overseas banks, in addition to the cases of the Anglo-Austrian Bank and the British Italian Corporation which have already been mentioned. The Bank of England was remarkably successful in preserving British banking stability, but, ironically, only at the cost of enlisting the support of one of the clearing banks Norman most wished to keep out of overseas banking.

The first crisis came in 1923 with the problems of Cox & Co. This bank's ambitious growth has been surveyed earlier (see above, Section 6.4). Already by 1918 rumours about the bank's stability were being heard. The Governor of the Bank of England gave a partner 'a friendly hint' that the firm had 'better be extremely careful in future to confine their operations to the most strictly purist Bankers' business'.[55] The 'hint' was not taken,

[53] Memorandum, 7 Apr. 1943, G14/73, B. of E.; Memorandum, 14 Apr. 1943 on Barclays (DCO) and Bolsa, C48/152, B. of E.    [54] Sayers, *The Bank of England*, i, 253–9.
[55] Governor's Memorandum, 1 June 1918, C40/125, B. of E.

and on 29 January 1923 Cox's auditor called on Montagu Norman with the distressing news that the bank's accounts showed a loss of £1 million against capital and reserves of between £1.2 million and £1.4 million, and that a run against the bank was expected. It emerged that Cox's had approached Lloyds about six weeks previously with an amalgamation proposal, but Lloyds had been unenthusiastic. Norman saw the chairman of Lloyds on the same day and told him that 'in the interest of the community it appeared essential that the proposed amalgamation be carried through with the least possible delay'.[56]

The 'interest of the community' meant financial support to Lloyds to undertake this operation. Lloyds received guarantees from the Bank of England amounting to £900,000, of which the Treasury originally covered £400,000. The Bank of England also provided that Lloyds would run Cox & Co., including the Indian and Egyptian branches, as a separate business over a management period ending in December 1927, when the assets would be valued and any liabilities of the Bank of England under its guarantees assessed. The Treasury agreed to approve the merger without reference to the Amalgamation Committee.

The acquisition of Cox & Co. by Lloyds averted any crisis of confidence stemming from the failure of a bank, albeit a small one. Norman, however, was distressed that one outcome was the ownership by Lloyds of a branch network in India and Egypt. In 1926 he was able to arrange the sale of the Egyptian branches to the National Bank of Egypt, by offering the latter bank a payment of £50,000.[57] However, the Bank of England never succeeded in persuading Lloyds to divest the Indian business. Meanwhile, the total cost to the Bank of England of the rescue of Cox's (including the £50,000 paid to rid Lloyds of its Egyptian branches) amounted to £267,000.[58]

A more prolonged and expensive rescue operation was needed with the collapse of the Anglo-South American Bank. When this bank's managing director went to the Bank of England on 10 September 1931 (see above, Section 5.3), he reported that his bank was having problems placing its acceptances on the market, and that it had lost £5 million in deposits over the last ten weeks. This was not an ideal moment for the Bank of England, as Britain was in the last days of the financial crisis which was to force it off the gold standard. The initial advice to Anglo-South was to seek assistance from its London bankers. But the depth of the crisis soon became apparent. On 22 September the Bank of England agreed to advance up to £1.5 million to the stricken bank, and by the following day up to

---

[56] M. Norman to Sir Warren Fisher, 2 Feb. 1923, c40/125, B. of E.
[57] M. Norman to B. Hornsby, 9 Dec. 1926, G1/9, B. of E.
[58] Sayers, The Bank of England, i. 242; Winton, Lloyds Bank, 22–5.

£3 million.[59] For the Bank of England, the real horror of Anglo-South American Bank's plight was not the potential failure of the institution itself, but the crippling effect the failure would have on the London discount market, which in the circumstances of September 1931 could have been utterly disastrous. Moreover, it was feared that—again in the circumstances—there would be an inevitable spill-over effect on overseas confidence in other British banks.[60]

As in the Cox's crisis, the Bank of England's thoughts soon turned to Lloyds Bank, part-owner of the other London-based South American bank, Bolsa. On 23 September Lloyds' chairman was approached about a takeover of Anglo-South, but on the following day came the reply that Lloyds 'would prefer only to look after the Bank of London'.[61] This was hardly surprising in view of Bolsa's large 'real' losses in 1930 and 1931, and the general problems of the South American economies. The Bank of England consequently called upon all clearers to come to the rescue. Lloyds resolutely refused to become involved, but the other four members of the 'Big Five' agreed to provide £500,000 each for a rescue operation, and the Bank of England a further £3 million. A condition of the support was the resignation of Anglo-South's directors, and by mid-October the Bank of England had installed Sir Bertram Hornsby as chairman.[62] At the end of the month Anglo-South's managing director was still expressing his 'great faith in the ability of the Guggenheims . . . Nitrate had had its ups and downs but always came right in the end,'[63] but by November the situation was so critical that Montagu Norman was obliged to ask the Chancellor of the Exchequer for a formal guarantee that its losses would be met by the government. By the end of January 1932 the 'Pool' of supporting banks had made £8.5 million of advances to the stricken bank. In May there was another crisis, when the Press finally published details of the depth of the problem, and at the end of the month Anglo-South's largest customer, the Bolivian tin magnate Patîno, threatened to withdraw his total deposits of £750,000. At the Treasury there was a discussion as to whether it would be 'better to take the ruthless but orthodox view . . . and cut our loss'. Anglo-South's acceptances had been reduced and so the 'Discount Market could probably stand the shock of a collapse now', but the problem remained that 'if the ASAB were to go, there is grave risk other institutions might fail also'.[64]

[59] Memorandum by K. O. Peppiatt, 10 Sept. 1931, Credit Committee Meeting, 22 and 23 Sept. 1931, C48/68, B of E; Sayers, *Bank of England*, i, 263–4.

[60] Memorandum by K. O. Peppiatt, 10 Oct. 1931, C48/68, B. of E.

[61] Memorandum of 23 Sept. 1931; Credit Committee 24 Sept. 1931. C48/68, B. of E.

[62] Credit Committee, 30 Sept. 1931, 2 Oct. 1931; Memorandum of 2 Oct. 1931. C48/68, B. of E.    [63] Note of an Interview with Mr Wells, 30 Oct. 1931, C48/69, B. of E.

[64] *Daily Herald*, 18 May 1932; *The Times*, 20 May 1932; Treasury Memorandum to Sir Richard Hopkins, 30 May 1932, T160/633, PRO.

In these crisis conditions, the support of the 'Pool' was formalized by the creation of a new company, Chilnit, with a nominal capital of £1,000. The Pool's advances of £8.5 million were taken over by Chilnit. In turn, Chilnit took as assets £7.5 million doubtful nitrate accounts and £1 million new preference shares in the Anglo-South American Bank, which gave it voting control over the bank. This procedure transferred a sight liability into a deferred contingent guarantee, and was a device to revive confidence in Anglo-South. In June 1932 Montagu Norman also decided to lend a further £2 million, and perhaps £1 million more, of Bank of England funding to Anglo-South.[65]

For a time it seemed that Anglo-South might have been saved. In October 1933 a leading financial journal reflected that 'the bank has been enabled to retreat from the valley of the shadow of death'.[66] Anglo-South was, however, burdened by debt, and had no opportunity to recover given the economic circumstances of South America in the 1930s.[67] A more permanent solution was necessary. In 1935 Norman approached the Royal Bank of Canada through the governor of the Canadian central bank to ascertain if it was interested, but it was not.[68] By September 1935 Anglo-South's position was so dire that Norman concluded that, 'owing to lack of practicable alternatives', the only way forward was a merger with Bolsa, even though it 'involved the condoning of Lloyds' "sin" in South America'.[69] It took a year of negotiations before, in July 1936, agreement was reached, and Bolsa took over the business and assumed the liabilities of Anglo-South. In return, Chilnit was given £100,000 Bolsa shares (at £5 each) and Bolsa and Lloyds agreed to pay staff compensation up to £350,000. Anglo-South's shareholders received nothing. After the sale of the Bolsa shares and other realizations, the total cost to the Pool of the Anglo-South American rescue amounted to £4,568,000, of which the Bank of England contributed £2,351,000.[70] Potentially the most serious crisis faced by the British banking community in the inter-war years had been averted.

There were other rescues also. One involved the British Overseas Bank, a quasi-multinational institution. The idea of establishing a specialist foreign bank owned by medium-sized domestic banks had been discussed by the Union Bank of Scotland and Glyn, Mills before the First World War. During the war, and in the context of the Faringdon Report, the project

---

[65] Sayers, *The Bank of England*, i, 266; Memorandum, 20 June 1932, C48/74, B. of E.
[66] *Financial News*, 16 Oct. 1933.
[67] Secret Memorandum by B. Hornsby, 21 Feb. 1934, C48/79, B. of E.
[68] M. Norman to G. F. Towers, 5 June 1935; G. F. Towers to M. Norman, 4 July 1935, C48/80, B. of E.    [69] Meeting in Governor's Room, 12 Sept. 1935, C48/81, B. of E.
[70] Memorandum of Agreement between Bolsa and Anglo-South, 6 July 1936, and Supplementary Agreement, C48/83; Memorandum, 24 Sept. 1948, C48/84, B. of E.; Sayers, *The Bank of England*, i, 266–7.

proceeded, with a larger number of banks becoming involved. In 1919 the British Overseas Bank was formed. Eight banks subscribed £1 million in 'B' shares, while a further £1 million was raised from the public in 'A' shares, of which the Prudential insurance company took £100,000.[71] The British Overseas Bank, like the BTC, represented an attempt to integrate domestic and overseas banking more closely. Like the BTC, it also looked eastwards. It founded the Anglo-Polish Bank in 1920 after taking over a Warsaw private bank; acquired control over an Estonian bank and a stake in a Latvian bank; and in 1924 absorbed the London and Liverpool Bank of Commerce, which had a large continental acceptance business. It made no attempt, unlike the BTC, to establish greenfield branches.

The ownership structure caused initial problems. Two bank shareholders, the Imperial Ottoman Bank and Anglo-South American Bank, found a conflict between their own business activities and those of the British Overseas Bank. In 1924, as a result, six banks agreed to sell their shares at par, and Williams Deacon's, the Union Bank of Scotland, and the Prudential became holders of one-third each of the 'B' capital.[72] Subsequently, the British Overseas Bank appeared to flourish, developing a large trade finance business with Eastern Europe and Spain (due to the inheritance of the London and Liverpool Bank). Although Montagu Norman objected to its clearing bank ownership, in 1931 the Bank of England began using the institution to operate in the foreign exchange markets, alongside the Anglo-International Bank. In 1936 the Bank of England persuaded the British Overseas Bank to take over Frederick Huth and Company, a merchant bank which had been in difficulties since the early 1920s and in which the Bank of England had lost £1 million in supporting operations.[73] Overall the British Overseas Bank appeared, in the mid-1930s, to have avoided the disasters which had afflicted the 'official' banks.[74]

In fact, the British Overseas Bank could no more avoid the consequences of events in Central Europe than any other British institution. By December 1937 it was apparent that no proper provision had been made against 'Standstill' debts or frozen assets in other countries, and that the bank was

---

[71] Baster, *The International Banks*, 202–3; Memorandum by Mr Gairdner on the origins of the British Overseas Bank, 30 Nov. 1938, C48/129; N. Hird to B. G. Catterns, 19 Oct. 1938, C48/128, B. of E. The initial eight bank shareholders were Glyn's, the Union Bank of Scotland, Williams Deacon's, Anglo-South American Bank, the Dominion Bank of Toronto, Hoare & Co, Northern Banking Company (of Belfast) and the Imperial Ottoman Bank. A Board Minute of Williams Deacon's (5 June 1919) states that the British Overseas Bank was to be 'a protective alliance, firstly for the promotion of mutual interests, and secondly for the development of business in fresh fields'. Memorandum on the British Overseas Bank, contained in P. Winterbottom to author, 12 August 1991.
[72] Memorandum by Mr. Gairdner, 30 Nov. 1938, C48/129; Prudential to M. Norman, 25 Apr. 1924, C48/128, B. of E.
[73] Sayers, *The Bank of England*, ii, 426 n. 1, 268–71; N. Hird to B. G. Catterns, 19 Oct. 1938, C48/128, B. of E.         [74] Baster, *The International Banks*, 204.

'insolvent'.[75] By November of the following year the Bank of England had agreed to deposit £1 million with the bank, Williams Deacon's deposited a further £750,000, and Union Bank £250,000, and a new chairman was appointed.[76] Nevertheless, the bank was slowly run down, and in 1944 the residual business was sold to Glyn, Mills for £7,000. It is unclear how much money was lost in the rescue, but it seems that at least £300,000 of the special deposit was written off.[77]

In addition to these rescue attempts, the Bank of England became involved on occasion in advising on the appointment of directors to certain banks, and in making small share purchases to assist policy. In the mid-1930s, for example, the Bank of England advised on the appointment of a director to the Ionian Bank, which had heavy bad debts. Norman agreed to fund his director's share qualification if necessary.[78] In another example of Bank of England intervention, the Bank made small purchases of Ottoman Bank shares after 1926, and persuaded a number of British merchant banks to do likewise. This was designed to counter the French influence in the bank, and increase the influence of its London Committee.[79]

The Bank of England's success in preventing a major overseas banking collapse in the inter-war years was a considerable achievement, given the problems of the world financial and economic system, especially in the 1930s. Bank rescues were handled effectively and efficiently. There was, however, a price to be paid. The rescues of Cox's and Anglo-South American cost the Bank over £2.6 million; that of British Overseas Bank maybe a further £150,000. Nearly £2 million more was spent on the rescue of the British Italian Corporation and the support for the Anglo-International Bank. On the other hand, £5 million was perhaps not an excessively large sum for the preservation of financial stability. To put it in perspective, it was the equivalent of the Bank of England's profits for the two years 1935 and 1936.[80]

## 7.4. Conclusion

The overall assessment of the public policy impact on British multinational banking in the inter-war years must be equivocal. The Bank of England deserves credit for helping to prevent any major crisis in the sector. The collapse of the Anglo-South American Bank in 1931, in particular, might

[75] Memorandums, 23 Dec. 1937 and 14 Jan. 1938, C48/128, B. of E.
[76] M. Norman to Gairdner, 16 Nov. 1938, C48/129, B. of E.
[77] Financial Times, 26 June 1944.
[78] Notes by M. Norman, 23 Dec. 1935 and 5 Feb. 1936, G1/367, B. of E.
[79] Confidential Memorandum, Ottoman Bank, 16 June 1926; M. Norman to General Sir Herbert Lawrence, 27 Oct. 1926; letters from Chief Cashier to various institutions, 8 Nov. 1926; C40/130, B. of E.
[80] Sayers, The Bank of England, apps., 343, gives Bank of England profits, 1890–1939.

have had serious repercussions for the smaller overseas banks. Like the banks themselves, the Bank of England was effective at crisis management.

The more proactive public policy initiatives were less productive. The Bank of England and British government departments were involved in a series of loss-making ventures, and all too often found themselves the hapless victims of fraudulent or incomprehensible Italians and Central Europeans. The half-hearted promotion of new multinational trade banks, and the attempt to run a Viennese *crédit mobilier* bank, were not good advertisements for what happens when governments or their agents become involved in commercial banking.

The Bank of England's opposition to the clearing banks' entry into multinational banking, unsuccessful as it was, had the most negative adverse consequences of all the official policies. Fears of the consequences of exposure to 'excitable Latin races' and other non-British cultures were understandable in the inter-war years. The competitive advantages held by British multinational banks were in decline and the political and economic environment was unstable. The Bank of England had no way of predicting the remarkable growth of the world economy seen in the 1950s and 1960s: its officials were more likely to have had forebodings of another world war.

There was, however, a misapprehension that the preservation of the specialized financial system, designed to reduce risk in the nineteenth century, would have a similar effect in the twentieth century. In fact the advent of the clearers into multinational banking was, in part, a response to the new risks faced by overseas banks which had specialized in commodities or regions whose prices or politics had become unpredictable after 1914. There might have been more Anglo-South-type failures among British banks, or at least those active in South America, the West Indies, and parts of Africa, if the domestic banks had not taken shareholdings. Not only did the Bank of England not recognize this, but it also contributed to the situation whereby the changed ownership was not translated into a more effective relationship between overseas and domestic banking. Indeed, an unfortunate by-product of the Bank's successful crisis management was that it added to the heterogeneous nature of the Lloyds overseas banking empire, and further diluted Lloyds' ownership of the Latin American part of it.

# CHAPTER 8

# Grand Designs

## 8.1. Competitive Challenges in the Post-war World

The world economy grew very fast between the 1950s and 1973, banishing—for a time—the spectre of economic misfortune seen in the inter-war years. This was the era of 'economic miracles', which saw sustained fast economic growth in most of Western Europe as well as of Japan. British multinational banks were relieved from the problems of world war and financial crisis, but in several respects the 'diamond' of national competitive advantage which they had exploited continued to deteriorate. Changes in business strategy became more urgent, as did the need for structural and organizational change. This chapter focuses on structure, while Chapter 9 examines the strategies of the British banks in their host economies.

The relative economic and political decline of the United Kingdom was the root cause of much of the deterioration in the competitive advantages of the banks. Britain emerged from the Second World War as the master of an enormous colonial empire spanning Africa and Asia. Twenty years later this had all been swept away. Britain had become, in reality if not in its own estimation, a modest European power. During the 1950s and 1960s it missed the 'economic miracle', with an economic growth rate persistently slower than its European neighbours.[1]

The demand component of the 'diamond' was particularly adversely affected by these developments. The banks which had helped finance Britain's foreign trade found their core market was shrinking. In 1929 the United Kingdom had accounted for 23 per cent of world exports of manufactured goods. In 1953 the figure was 16 per cent, and by 1970 the figure was down to 8 per cent.[2] More seriously, import substitution and other factors cut further into traditional British markets in many countries in which the banks had specialized. Britain's share of Latin American imports, for example, declined from 13 per cent to 5 per cent between 1938 and 1955.[3]

In a long-term perspective, the structure of British exports changed, with

---

[1] B. W. E. Alford, *British Economic Performance, 1945–1975* (London: Macmillan, 1988), 11–19.

[2] B. R. Mitchell, *British Historical Statistics* (Cambridge: Cambridge University Press, 1988), 524.

[3] D. J. Joslin, *A Century of Banking in Latin America* (London: Oxford University Press, 1963), 286.

a shift away from low-technology products, such as textiles, to more sophisticated products, such as chemicals and electrical goods. In turn this involved a shift in markets, away from the Empire and the developing world
and towards developed economies. By 1971, 45 per cent of Britain's exports went to Europe. There was also a parallel shift in the sources of
British imports. Once dominated by raw materials and foodstuffs, from
the 1950s the share of manufactured goods began to rise, from 20 per cent
in 1951 to over 60 per cent thirty years later. Such manufactured goods
came, for the most part, from Europe and the United States.[4] In the
nineteenth century the British overseas banks had left the finance of Britain's
trade with the United States and Europe to others, and as a result they had
minimal representation in those regions. By the 1960s such specialization
seemed destined to confine the banks to an ever-dwindling market.

Even in the settler economies of the Commonwealth, there was a shift
in trade patterns away from the United Kingdom towards other countries.
After the Second World War Britain purchased a smaller share of Australian
and New Zealand exports and supplied less of their imports. These countries
found new markets for their wool and meat in the United States and Japan
and purchased their imports from a wider range of developed economies.
By the mid-1960s Japan was Australia's largest export market and North
America the most important source of imports.[5] An internal memorandum
of the Standard Bank of South Africa in 1967 commented on the consequences for the British multinational banks of the advent of American,
Japanese, and continental European competition in these markets:

Their trade with the Commonwealth is growing rapidly and in the case of many
countries, has long since, in aggregate, surpassed that of the U.K. Banking opportunities are less and less related to U.K. oriented trade. It would appear that
more and more trade is being carried on in other than sterling or sterling related
currencies with all of the implications that has for the traditional Overseas bank
approach.[6]

In other words, the competitive advantage of being a British bank was, in
region after region, in danger of becoming a competitive disadvantage.

The decline in the use of sterling noted by the Standard Bank presented
particular problems for the British banks. Britain's declining competitiveness put sterling's role as a reserve currency on par with the dollar under
growing pressure after 1945, which a devaluation in 1949 did nothing to
halt. It was only after a further devaluation in November 1967 that British
governments came to recognize that sterling's days as a reserve currency

[4] C. H. Lee, *The British Economy since 1700: A Macroeconomic Perspective* (Cambridge: Cambridge University Press, 1986), 218–33.
[5] D. T. Merrett, *ANZ Bank* (Sydney: Allen and Unwin, 1985), 173–4.
[6] Secret Memorandum, 18 Jan. 1967, enclosed with C. E. Fiero to W. G. Pullen, 24 Jan. 1967, Standard 'Grand Design' File, South Africa Box, SC.

were over. Meanwhile, in the 1950s and 1960s the British multinational banks active in countries with large sterling balances, such as Kuwait and Hong Kong, found themselves under pressure from the British government to help support the currency. Instead of the banks gaining competitive advantage from being sterling institutions, they were expected to contribute to keep the weakened currency alive. When devaluation finally came in 1967, the Hongkong Bank and the British Bank of the Middle East (BBME) were among banks which made substantial losses.[7]

The problems of sterling handicapped the British banks in their traditional business of international trade finance. The overseas banks found themselves based in a currency which fewer people wanted to use, and short of a currency—the dollar—which was replacing it. The American dollar became dominant in Latin America after the Second World War, while even the Eastern Exchange banks and the British banks in East, Central, and West Africa and the West Indies had to face the consequences of the disintegration of the Sterling Area. Until the 1950s the local currencies of these regions had a fixed parity with sterling. This had not only meant that their trade was financed in sterling, it had also been the fundamental factor which had enabled the banks to operate their business in unified fashion, with funds flowing between London and the host economies. During the second half of the 1950s the old Currency Boards which had operated the colonial monetary system began to give way to central banks, which undertook discretionary monetary management. In many cases, and over time, monetary reserves were shifted out of sterling.[8] The monetary system which had given British banks active in the Empire such an advantage slowly disappeared.

The British banks had not only serviced the requirements of British foreign trade, they had also been closely involved with the multifarious British overseas business interests active in the world economy. This had been a fortunate position for, as late as 1938, Britain may have remained the world's largest foreign direct investor. It lost this role to the United States after the Second World War, but in 1971 Britain was—with 14 per cent of total foreign direct investment—the world's second largest multinational investor.[9] Yet the direction of this British direct investment moved

[7] Geoffrey Jones, *Banking and Oil* (Cambridge: Cambridge University Press, 1987), 65–8, 146–8; F. H. H. King, *The History of the Hongkong and Shanghai Banking Corporation*, iv (Cambridge: Cambridge University Press, 1991), 738.

[8] 'Currency and Banking Developments in Certain Commonwealth Countries during the Past Ten Years', *Bank of England Quarterly Bulletin*, 2 (Mar. 1962), 25–35; G. O. Nwanko, 'British Overseas Banks in the Developing Countries. 2: The Break-up of the Empire', *Journal of the Institute of Bankers*, 93 (Aug. 1972), 254–9.

[9] John H. Dunning, 'Changes in the Level and Structure of International Production: The Last One Hundred Years', in Mark Casson (ed.), *The Growth of International Business* (London: Allen and Unwin, 1983), 87.

sharply to the disadvantage of the overseas banks. In 1929 only around 14 per cent of British direct investment had been located in Europe and the United States, while three-quarters was in the developing world, especially Latin America and Asia, and largely involved in natural resources and public utilities. From the Second World War many such British-owned resource and utility investments disappeared, often through nationalization. By 1962 the developing world accounted for only 36 per cent of British outward direct investment. In the 1950s British direct investors had focused on Canada, Australasia, and South Africa—in the latter two regions the British multinational banks were of course extremely well positioned—but from the early 1960s there was a sharp reorientation towards Western Europe and the United States.[10]

As in the case of British foreign trade, therefore, British direct investment was shifting away from the regions in which the overseas banks had their branches. The British-owned utilities, plantations, mines, and trading companies, which had provided deposits and exchange business, were a dwindling customer base. British multinationals still offered good business opportunities for British banks, but not ones which the overseas banks were well positioned to exploit. Apart from the serious problem of geographical location, the banks often had closer links, especially at director level, with the 'older' forms of British business, such as the trading companies and agency houses of Asia, than with the large British industrial firms which became the driving force of British multinational investment, and which looked to their clearing banks for credit facilities. Moreover, the British multinationals of the post-war world often both needed large credit facilities and had financing requirements in a number of countries. On both counts the comparatively small and geographically specialized British overseas banks were not well placed to respond. They needed access to larger resources. They needed to offer facilities in a wider range of countries, and they required access to the new generation of potential British corporate customers.[11] These needs reinforced the pressures working against the specialized structure of British overseas banking.

More generally, the capital structure of the overseas banks became a growing disadvantage in the post-war world. The paid-up capitals of most banks stayed at their 1920s levels until the mid-1950s, with substantial increases only coming in the following decade. A number of factors explain this phenomenon. The existence of large inner reserves made managements less concerned about published capital ratios. The Anglo-Australian banks, and probably many others, remained concerned to maintain share prices and dividend rates, and sceptical that fresh capital

[10] David Shepherd, Aubrey Silberston, and Roger Strange, *British Manufacturing Investment Overseas* (London: Methuen, 1985), 9–12.
[11] Richard Fry, *Bankers in West Africa* (London: Hutchinson Benham, 1976), 250.

would generate additional profits sufficiently rapidly to maintain dividend payments.[12] The Hongkong Bank, whose dollar paid-up capital was stationary between 1921 and 1955, developed a strong reluctance to entertain a rights issue, apparently fearing a loss of confidence by Chinese constituents.[13] In fact, small capitals made the British banks look vulnerable to big business and other big customers, despite their fabled—but secret—inner reserves. There was an increasing recognition that the banks needed size if they were to be taken seriously.[14] The issue of 'undercapitalization' became a major preoccupation as many host governments initiated specific capital ratios for banks in their countries.

The incentives to expand the scale and scope of the British multinational banks were reinforced by the advent of stronger competition. Local banks grew in importance in many developing countries, while there were new entrants into international and multinational banking, especially from the late 1950s. During the 1950s the British clearing banks took advantage of their larger size, their domestic customer base, and their networks of foreign correspondents to encroach on business the overseas banks had once regarded as their own. The overseas banks felt that the clearers were gaining market share in export finance.[15] Moreover, the British overseas banks in Asian and other developing countries found themselves outflanked by the British clearing banks, who forged links with new local banks, which they sometimes helped to grow.[16] The Midland Bank, which had no foreign branches but a vast overseas correspondent network, was particularly active in this regard. It seconded men to a series of newly founded local banks in the 1950s (such as the National Bank of Kuwait, the Jordan National Bank, and the Sudan Commercial Bank) with one eye on the long-term benefits which could flow from a good correspondent relationship.[17]

A still greater competitive threat came from American multinational banks. The advent of the Eurodollar market at the end of the 1950s, which will be discussed in Chapter 10, heralded a transformation of the multinational banking industry. One consequence was an enormous expansion in multinational activity by American banks. These banks serviced the requirements of American corporations which had engaged in unprecedented levels of foreign direct investment in the 1950s. A few banks such

---

[12] Merrett, *ANZ Bank*, 172.

[13] King, *The History of the Hongkong and Shanghai Banking Corporation*, iv, 5 n. c, 244.

[14] e.g. Geoffrey Jones, *Banking and Oil*, 73.

[15] Note for Mr Pullen from H. E. Faulkner, *re* Memorandum for the Radcliffe Committee, 1 Oct. 1957, Radcliffe Committee Papers, 'Miscellaneous' File, Chartered Box, SC.

[16] W. G. Pullen to John Mellor Stevens, 6 Apr. 1961, C48/158, B of E; C. R. Wardle to I. M. W. Ward, 27 May 1960, Mercantile Bank Archives, HSBC.

[17] Chief Foreign Manager to F. I. Ashton, 26 Sept. 1952; Memorandum by H.M.O., 22 Dec. 1952, Midland Bank Archives; Geoffrey Jones, *Banking and Oil*, 71, 143.

as Citibank and Chase established global branch networks. Many others opened branches in leading financial centres and selected countries.[18] The large American banks had the scale and scope which the British overseas banks lacked. Their client base was drawn from the world's largest multinational investor, and they had dollar-denominated capitals and deposit bases. Finally, they were hungry to grow fast internationally. They marketed aggressively, with a particular focus on international banking services and term loans. The American banks were not simply strong competitors of the British overseas banks: they were potential predators. The first wave of overseas bank amalgamations in the late 1950s was carried out against the background of real or imagined American takeover threats.

In much of the developing world, the British overseas banks faced competition for retail and domestic business from local banks. Such banks had the advantage of being local institutions, close to their home market, and so well equipped to meet its particular requirements. In many countries the directors of the local banks were directors of other local businesses, whose custom they would divert to their bank. In the 1950s many British banks were still able to compete with local banks and there was a rapid expansion of branch networks to meet this challenge, but in the following decade controls were often introduced to restrict foreign bank activity, especially the opening of new branches. This increased the vulnerability of banks dependent on a particular region and acted as a major incentive for diversification. Their decline in importance made the British banks feel more insecure. 'As the Overseas banks become less vital to the countries within which they operate,' Standard Bank's management observed in 1967, 'their ability to influence their regulatory environment and to influence opinion in their favour is substantially weakened, accelerating their relative decline.'[19]

The location of most British multinational banking investment was a further problem. The Southern Hemisphere settler economies never recovered the dynamism seen in the nineteenth century, and after 1945 their relative decline continued. In Australia, New Zealand, and South Africa—where three-quarters of all British-owned overseas bank branches were to be found—economic growth rates were below those of Western Europe and Japan. Australia's and New Zealand's dependence on primary commodity exports and their small populations constrained their growth. Both countries found it extremely hard to diversify their economies. Pastoral products were responsible for around 50 per cent of total Australian exports

[18] Thomas F. Huertas, 'US Multinational Banking: History and Prospects', in Geoffrey Jones (ed.), *Banks as Multinationals* (London: Routledge 1990), 253–4. Derek F. Channon, *Global Banking Strategy* (Chichester: Wiley, 1988), 11–20.
[19] Secret Memorandum, 18 Jan. 1967, enclosed with C. E. Fiero to W. G. Pullen, 24 Jan. 1967, Standard's 'Grand Design' File, South Africa Box, SC.

until the late 1950s.[20] South Africa experienced considerable industrialization in the 1950s and 1960s, but in the context of the apartheid regime introduced by the Nationalist Party in 1948, which included a plethora of state invervention measures including tight exchange controls, as well as a strong hostility to the English-speaking business community.[21] Moreover, the massacre of sixty-nine Africans by the South African police at Sharpeville in March 1960 confirmed that country as one with serious political risk.

Much of Asia, Africa, and Latin America offered even fewer growth opportunities for their British banks. Sub-Saharan African and South Asian countries had relatively poor economic growth rates in the 1950s and 1960s, and many adopted import substitution and anti-foreign economic strategies which confined the roles of British banks even within a slow-growth context. Among the Latin American economies, Brazil achieved considerable economic progress but growth rates in other major economies like Argentina (where British banking activity was strongest) were poor in the 1950s and 1960s, and everywhere import substitution policies, state interventionism, inflation, and political instability made life unpredictable for foreign banks.[22]

The British multinational banks, therefore, were specialized in a range of countries which, for a number of reasons, were the growth laggards of the post-1945 world. There were two main exceptions. First, in Asia in the 1950s and 1960s Singapore and Hong Kong diverged from much of the Third World and pursued export-led growth strategies. Their reward (and that of South Korea and Taiwan a little later) was a surge of economic growth which transformed them into NICs (newly industrialized countries).[23] Two of the Eastern Exchange banks, Chartered and Hongkong Bank, held long-established strong positions in both Singapore and Hong Kong, and were well placed to take advantage of the growth of their host economies, which continued to welcome 'foreign' banks. A second region where British overseas banks found a hospitable environment was the oil-rich Gulf states. As open economies which (at least until the 1970s) allowed British banks to operate freely, they offered havens of prosperity and a rich source of deposits.[24]

There was, therefore, a range of pressures after 1945 working against

[20] A. G. Kenwood and A. L. Lougheed, *The Growth of the International Economy, 1820–1980* (London: Unwin Hyman, 1983), 309–10; C. B. Schedvin, 'Staples and Regions of Pax Britannica', *Economic History Review*, 43(4) (1990).

[21] Stuart Jones, introduction, in Stuart Jones (ed.), *Banking and Business in South Africa* (London: Macmillan, 1988), 16–22.

[22] Lloyd G. Reynolds, *Economic Growth in the Third World: An Introduction* (New Haven, Conn.: Yale University Press, 1986), 78, gives economic growth rates for a large number of developing economies between 1950 and 1980.

[23] James Riedel, 'Economic Development in East Asia: Doing What Comes Naturally?', in Helen Hughes (ed.), *Achieving Industrialization in East Asia* (Cambridge: Cambridge University Press, 1990).  [24] Geoffrey Jones, *Banking and Oil*, ch. 2.

the inherited structure of British multinational banking with its pattern of small, geographically specialized banks. The circumstances of this period might have seemed to dictate further movements in the directions seen in the inter-war years, particularly in a greater integration between domestic and overseas banking, and the formation of multi-regional groups, if only as a form of risk diversification. In practice, the corporate reorganization of British multinational banking proceeded at a remarkably slow pace. The list of the British multinational banks active in 1955 was shorter than in 1928, but similar in every other respect. It was not until the end of the 1960s that a major reorganization occurred. The geographical distribution of British multinational bank assets and branches in 1970 also showed a strong continuity with earlier periods.

The struggle to achieve structural change in British multinational banking forms the subject of the next two sections. However, in order to put the complex merger negotiations in context, some general reasons for the slow pace of corporate reorganization can be identified here.

First, developments in the multinational banking sector have to be put in the context of the British financial system as a whole, in which organizational change was very slow to occur in the two decades after the end of the war. The highly specialized nature of British financial institutions remained firmly in place until the late 1950s. The Bank of England and the British government strongly discouraged deviations from traditional practices. The situation began to change around 1958, when lending controls on clearing banks were temporarily relaxed, and when they were allowed to form links with hire purchase finance companies. The growth of the Euromarkets, and a government decision in 1967 to permit further clearing bank mergers, represented further milestones on the path leading to the end of the specialized system, but it was not until the 1970s that major diversification occurred and 'financial conglomerates' began to form.[25]

Secondly, the overseas banks after 1945 faced little of the domestic rivalry stressed by Michael Porter as a stimulus to change. They had carved out the world between them. Regional specialists did not compete in other regions. Collusive agreements were widespread in many countries. Official lending controls, exchange controls, and barriers to entry were pervasive. Managements continued to disguise the true performance of their banks. The British Companies Act of 1948 had excluded banks from the general requirement to disclose true profits. The overseas banks maintained the view all through the 1950s and 1960s that non-disclosure was in the best

---

[25] James Maycock, *Financial Conglomerates: The New Phenomenon* (Aldershot: Gower, 1986), ch. 2 and 3; Geoffrey Jones, 'Competition and Competitiveness in British Banking, 1918–71', in Geoffrey Jones and Maurice Kirby (eds.), *Competitiveness and the State* (Manchester: Manchester University Press, 1991), 127–30.

interests of depositors.[26] The policy was only changed after 1969 when the British clearing banks announced their intention to publish their true profits and reserves. Two overseas banks, Barclays (DCO) and National and Grindlays, resolved to follow the same route in their 1970 accounts, prompting all the banks except the Hongkong Bank to follow.[27]

A third reason for the slow pace of structural change was that, whatever the long-term decline in their competitive advantages, the world economy in the 1950s and 1960s was sufficiently vigorous to allow the British banks to pay enough dividends to please their shareholders. Investors earned better returns from investing in the shares of the sample multinational banks than from either Consols or—in many cases—the shares of the two sample domestic banks. Published profit ratios were a considerable improvement over the 1930s and the war years. The 'real' profitability of all the sample banks was higher than their published figures, and in a number of cases considerably so. Although shareholders benefited from this profitability, managements also took the opportunity to strengthen inner reserves. The upshot was that the banks faced no immediate profits crisis which could have focused their minds on reorganization.

The attitude of one large shareholder in British overseas banking deserves special mention as an obstacle to faster corporate reorganization. The multinational banking strategy of Lloyds Bank remained erratic in these years, with no sign of any willingness to bring order into the disparate group of banks in which it had invested. For most of the 1960s Lloyds left it to Bolsa, its affiliate, to develop an international strategy, and it was only from 1969 that more coherent policies began to emerge. It was a misfortune that the bank lacked both the vision and the competence to take any initiative to reorganize British-owned multinational banking.

Finally, one legacy of the specialist structure of British overseas banking was that it had created highly institution-specific corporate cultures which were hard to merge. Managements were often reluctant to lose their identities and suspicious of banks which operated in regions other than their own. Early talks about a possible merger between Chartered and Standard, for example, were handicapped because neither institution wanted 'to sacrifice his separate identity'.[28] In several cases the managements of banks had an extreme attachment to their institutions and resisted the amalgamation schemes of their boards. This problem emerged as a substantial issue when the boards of the Bank of Australasia and the Union Bank agreed to merge immediately after the Second World War. While their

---

[26] Evidence of the Eastern Exchange Banks' Association to the Company Law Committee (probably Mar. 1960), General Manager's Letters File, Chartered Bank Records, SC.

[27] Note to Chairman from Deputy Chairman, Standard Bank, 6 July 1970, SBSA Box; Standard Chartered Annual Report, 1972, SC.

[28] Governor's Note, 3 Dec. 1959, C48/158, B. of E.

London directors thought that this was an excellent idea, their Australian managements—who had not been consulted—were very far from pleased. Union Bank's senior management opposed the merger and the bank's inspector resigned, helping to delay the amalgamation negotiations until mid-1947, when the Australian government's announcement of bank nationalization legislation brought them to a complete halt.[29] A few years later, in 1954, the general manager of the BBME managed to wreck his chairman's scheme to merge with the Chartered Bank, an institution which he disliked.[30] The corporate cultures which helped make the banks such durable institutions could also provide formidable barriers to organizational change.

Although powerful incentives to structural change in British multinational banking existed, therefore, the banks' profitability in the era of fast economic growth, their protection from external takeover and shareholder criticism, the indecisiveness of Lloyds Bank, and institutional factors combined to temper the urgency of the matter. Moreover, the British financial system as a whole only slowly evolved from its specialist heritage, with few changes until the late 1950s.

## 8.2. The First Mergers 1945–1960

The pace of corporate reorganization was slow in the first fifteen years after the end of the Second World War. A number of mergers were effected, and more discussed, but the structure of regional and functional specialization remained firmly in place in 1960. Table 8.1 summarizes the main mergers and acquisitions of this period. Table 8.2 gives a list of abortive merger proposals, including only those schemes where serious negotiations were entered into.

A number of themes stand out from the mergers and attempted mergers of this period. The first was that the inter-war attempt to integrate domestic and overseas banking was partly put into reverse. One of the 'Big Five' domestic banks, the National Provincial Bank, had a clear strategy to withdraw from overseas banking. In 1948 it sold its 100 per cent shareholding in Grindlays Bank to the National Bank of India, for whom it had long served as London banker, and seven years later it withdrew from the unsuccessful continental joint venture with Lloyds, which as Lloyds Bank (Foreign) became a wholly owned subsidiary of Lloyds.[31] Barclays' enthusiasm for multinational banking also cooled. In 1957 Barclays, which together with Sassoon interests had held 65 per cent of the shares of the

[29] Merrett, ANZ Bank, 78–89.    [30] Geoffrey Jones, Banking and Oil, 75–7.
[31] Geoffrey Tyson, 100 Years of Banking in Asia and Africa (London: National and Grindlays, 1963), 189–90. Geoffrey Jones, 'Lombard Street on the Riviera: The British Clearing Banks and Europe, 1900–1960', Business History, 24 (1982), 202.

TABLE 8.1. *British overseas bank mergers and consolidations,*
*1945–1960*

| Year | Banks | Regional | Multi-regional |
|------|-------|----------|----------------|
| 1948 | National Bank of India/Grindlays Bank | X | |
| 1951 | Union Bank/Bank of Australasia | X | |
| 1954 | Lloyds acquire 100% Lloyds and National Provincial Foreign Bank | X | |
| 1957 | Chartered/Eastern Bank[a] | | X |
| 1957 | Chartered acquire Ionian's Cyprus branches | | X |
| 1959 | Hongkong Bank/Mercantile Bank of India | X | |
| 1960 | Hongkong Bank/BBME | | X |
| 1960 | National and Grindlays acquire Lloyds Indian branches | X | |

[a] Eastern Bank's activities spanned the Middle East and the East.

TABLE 8.2. *Abortive British overseas bank mergers, 1945–1960*

| Year | Banks | Regional | Multi-regional |
|------|-------|----------|----------------|
| 1953–6 | BBME and Ionian | | X |
| 1954 | E, S & A and National Bank of New Zealand | X | |
| 1954–5 | BBME and Chartered | | X |
| 1955 | E, S & A and ANZ | X | |
| 1956 | Chartered and Ionian | | X |
| 1958–9 | BBME and National and Grindlays | | X |

Eastern Bank, reached an agreement with Chartered Bank which enabled Chartered to acquire Eastern. In return there was an exchange of shares between Barclays and Chartered.[32] Barclays had also sold its small Italian and Canadian subsidiaries in 1950 and 1955 respectively.

Although Lloyds acquired full control of the continental subsidiary, the general direction of its policy suggested some disengagement from multi-national banking. During 1943 it had been decided to reduce its shareholding in Bolsa still further in view of the poor performance of the bank, and by the end of 1954 Lloyds owned only 29.7 per cent of the shares. In 1960 Lloyds also sold its wholly owned Indian and Pakistan branch network to National and Grindlays, in consideration for shares in the latter bank

[32] Memorandum, 2 May 1957, C45/158, B. of E.

which gave Lloyds around 25 per cent of National and Grindlays.[33] Lloyds ended the decade of the 1950s with an even less integrated and coherent group of overseas banking activities than it started out with.

The main result of the mergers in the fifteen years after 1945 was further to concentrate British banking within regions. British banking in Latin America was already the preserve of Bolsa. After 1945 British banks in Australia also consolidated. In 1951 the Union Bank and the Bank of Australasia finally merged to form the Australian and New Zealand Bank, and the next few years saw a number of abortive attempts to achieve a further consolidation within the region. In 1954 ANZ approached the other remaining British bank in Australia, the English, Scottish & Australian, about a merger, but negotiations were unsuccessful. ANZ's main motive was defensive, as had been the earlier merger between its two constituent banks. The British banks were continuing to lose market share to local banks and saw amalgamation as a way to reverse the trend. Equally abortive were the English, Scottish & Australian Bank's attempts to interest the National Bank of New Zealand in a merger.[34] The British trading banks in Australasia remained isolated from British overseas banks elsewhere and from the British domestic banks, although there was a link of sorts with Barclays. Sir Geoffrey Gibbs, a director of the Bank of Australasia who was elected chairman in 1947 and subsequently served as chairman of ANZ from 1951 to 1967, was also a director of Barclays (DCO) between 1945 and 1971, becoming vice-chairman in 1949 and deputy chairman in 1955. In 1948 he seems to have been interested in achieving the integration of the Bank of Australasia and the Union Bank into the Barclays group, but the scheme did not proceed, and Barclays confined itself to holding a small equity stake in ANZ after the merger.[35]

There was also concentration among the Eastern Exchange banks, with three main groups emerging, each reaching out to other regions. The acquisition of Grindlays' twelve overseas branches in the Indian sub-continent strengthened the National Bank of India's South Asian business. The subsequent purchase of Lloyds' Indian branches in 1960 gave the group the largest foreign-owned branch network in South Asia. In the 1950s National Bank's African interests were also enhanced by Grindlays' opening of a series of branches in the Rhodesias, then a British settler economy undergoing a substantial boom. The first branch, at Salisbury, opened in 1953.[36] By 1960 National and Grindlays (as the bank became

[33] J. R. Winton, *Lloyds Bank, 1918–1969* (Oxford: Oxford University Press, 1982), 134–7. [34] Merrett, *ANZ Bank*, 233–4, 211–12.
[35] Sir Julian Crossley Diaries, 16 Mar. 1948, 38/209; Memorandum for DCO Accounts Board, 23 Nov. 1959, 38/251, BBA. In 1959 Barclays Bank and Barclays (DCO) together held 7.5 per cent of ANZ's capital.
[36] Tyson, *100 Years of Banking in Asia and Africa*, 191, 224.

known in 1958) had a branch network spanning South Asia and East and Southern Africa, and was 25 per cent owned by Lloyds.

The Chartered Bank was another nucleus of activity. By the mid-1950s Chartered was faced with a number of frustrations in its traditional region of operations. After the Communist Revolution in 1949, it retained only one branch in China—in Shanghai—while its branches in India, Burma and Ceylon were located in countries increasingly dedicated to import-substitution (and high tax) economic policies. Chartered resolved to diversify where growth opportunities were greater. The BBME, sitting on a rich deposit base and exclusive banking concessions in the Gulf, was an obvious target, but (as noted above) the merger scheme was effectively sabotaged by BBME's general manager. Chartered, therefore, turned its attention towards the other major independent British institution in the area, Eastern Bank, which also had branches in South and South East Asia that overlapped with those of Chartered. This bank had been gravely weakened by bad debts in excess of £1.2 million in Bombay and Calcutta, contributing to a real profit performance only marginally better than the published figures. Probably as a consequence, Barclays actively supported Chartered's acquisition of Eastern. This acquisition gave Chartered branches in the Arab Gulf, and in 1959 it added to these Middle Eastern interests by establishing a joint venture operation in Iran.[37]

In 1957 Chartered also extended its geographical sphere of operations yet further by acquiring the Cyprus branches of the Ionian Bank. The Ionian Bank's region of specialization looked increasingly unwise after the Second World War, provoking merger thoughts both within and outside the bank. 'The bank is in a difficult position, Greece and Egypt, currants and cotton,' a Bank of England official observed in 1948, 'and would do well to explore means of broadening the base of operations by amalgamation.'[38] As a small bank with substantial inner reserves, it was of interest to financial speculators, and its shareholding became unstable as a result.[39] During the war a substantial number of the bank's shares (probably over 18 per cent by 1953) were acquired by a Middle East Jewish family (the Zilkhas) whose long-term intentions were suspect.[40] After the failure of negotiations with the British Bank of the Middle East,[41] in September 1956 Ionian began to negotiate a merger with the Chartered Bank, and an agreement between the two banks which would have preserved the identity of Ionian was soon reached in principle. The deal was vetoed in November,

[37] Meeting at Barclays (DCO) between Eastern, Chartered, and DCO representatives, 6 June 1957, Eastern/Chartered Merger File, Box 22, SC; Standard Chartered Bank, *A Story Brought up to Date* (London: Standard Chartered Bank, 1980), 7.
[38] Memorandum, 24 Mar. 1948, C48/154, B. of E.
[39] F. C. Hawker to Sir Herbert Brittain, 7 June 1957, C48/154, B. of E.
[40] Memorandum 3 July 1952, C48/154, B. of E.
[41] Geoffrey Jones, *Banking and Oil*, 50.

however, by a new group of shareholders who had purchased the equity formerly held by the Zilkhas. The moving force in this syndicate was the stockbroking firm of Behrens Trusted, which specialized in takeover bids, and which demanded the break-up value of the bank, which Chartered was not prepared to pay.[42] Thereafter the focus of attention shifted to breaking up the bank. In January 1957 the bank's Egyptian branches were sequestrated in the wake of the Suez Crisis. In August of the same year Ionian's Greek business was sold to the Commercial Bank of Greece. Two months later Chartered purchased the Cyprus business. The Ionian Bank effectively ceased to operate as an overseas bank, though it continued in existence as a form of merchant bank.

By 1960, therefore, Chartered Bank had, like National and Grindlays, both consolidated its position within its own region and also diversified into other regions. The acquisition of Eastern Bank had resulted in a cross-shareholding with Barclays,[43] but there were no operational consequences and DCO's proposals to increase the shareholding further were strongly opposed by Chartered.[44]

The third grouping of Eastern Exchange banks was centred on the Hongkong Bank. This bank's good financial performance over the long term has been remarked upon on several occasions. The 1930s and the Second World War had been difficult periods, but in the post-war decades the Hongkong Bank's profitability ratios, both published and real, were again well in excess of those of the other sample banks, including Chartered Bank. This performance rested on the economic vitality of its main host economies, especially Hong Kong, whose export-led growth and status as an 'open market' within the Sterling Area provided excellent opportunities for an Exchange bank, and which remained as a British colony. After the war the colony also emerged as a low-tax area compared to Britain, and the Hongkong Bank also benefited—as an overseas company—from tax concessions on investments held inside the United Kingdom. The Hongkong Bank exploited these opportunities in an entrepreneurial fashion. Hong Kong alone provided 46 per cent of Hongkong Bank's gross profits between 1947 and 1961.[45]

---

[42] Note for Record, 22 May 1956, C48/154, B. of E. Draft Letter from Ionian's Board to Permanent Secretary, HM Treasury, Oct.–Nov. 1956; draft Court Minute, 30 Oct. 1956; J. M. Trusted to A. H. Reid, 30 Oct. 1956; H. M. Morford to A. H. Reid, 6 Nov. 1956, Box 1: Old Historical Records, Ionian Bank Archives, LSE.

[43] In May 1958 Chartered had some 1.5 per cent (or £200,000) of Barclays (DCO) stock, while Barclays (DCO) and Barclays held nearly 14 per cent (or over £600,000) of Chartered's shares.

[44] Note from Sir John Tait, 5 May 1958; Sir John Tait to V. A. Grantham, 7 May 1958; V. A. Grantham to Sir John Tait, 12 May 1958; Eastern/Chartered Merger File, Box 22, SC.

[45] King, The History of the Hongkong and Shanghai Banking Corporation, iv, 327. For the Colony's status as an open exchange market, see ibid., 345–7. The bank's role in Hong Kong's industrialization is discussed in Sect. 9.3, below.

Despite, or rather because of, its good performance, the Hongkong Bank was slow to diversify outside its traditional region. It was aware that American banks were becoming more active in the East, but felt under no threat itself, particularly as the bank had a statutory limitation on the beneficial holding of its shares which made the prospect of a take-over attempt on it remote. In 1955 its San Francisco agency, established in 1875, was converted into a separate subsidiary, the Hongkong and Shanghai Banking Corporation of California (see Chapter 10), but the first really substantial move was the acquisition of the Mercantile Bank. The activities of a Hong Kong-based share speculator, George Marden, were the initial reason for the acquisition of Mercantile Bank. Marden began buying Mercantile shares in 1953, with the hope of selling them at a profit to Hongkong Bank. When Hongkong Bank declined the offer, he offered the shares to the Bank of America, which was also not interested. A plan to break up the bank and sell it off in bits was frustrated by the Bank of England. Finally in the summer of 1957 Hongkong Bank agreed to buy the 14 per cent of Mercantile's stock held by Marden 'if only to prevent Mercantile being sold elsewhere'.[46] Mercantile's board declined the cash offer made by the Hongkong Bank for the remainder of the shares and stalemate ensued until Chase Manhattan emerged as a potential bidder for Mercantile in 1958. A further offer was made for Mercantile shares and in 1959 it became a fully owned subsidiary of the Hongkong Bank.[47]

In the following year the Hongkong Bank acquired the British Bank of the Middle East (BBME). This bank's diversification in the 1940s out of Iran into the Arab world paid handsome dividends as oil discoveries brought unprecedented wealth to Kuwait and other Gulf states, in several of which it held, for a time, monopoly banking agreements. Like the Hongkong Bank, it held a large deposit base in a booming region, which was under British political influence but exempted from Sterling Area exchange controls.[48] However, as a small bank with substantial inner reserves and a valuable franchise it was also an obvious take-over target, which its board attempted to pre-empt by merging with another bank. The directors' initial proposals to merge with Chartered had faltered, as had negotiations with the Ionian Bank. During the summer of 1958 merger negotiations had begun with National and Grindlays, and at the beginning of 1959 both banks approached the Hongkong Bank about taking them over to achieve a fundamental realignment of Eastern banking.[49]

The inclusion of National and Grindlays in such a realignment found

---

[46] King, *The History of the Hongkong and Shanghai Banking Corporation*, 499.

[47] Ibid., 507–14.

[48] BBME's development will be examined more closely in ch. 9.

[49] King, *The History of the Hongkong and Shanghai Banking Corporation*, iv, 533; Geoffrey Jones, *Banking and Oil*, 78.

little favour with the Hongkong Bank. While the Mercantile Bank of India had profitable branches in South-east Asia, National and Grindlays was heavily dependent on India, which, with its high taxes and restrictive attitude to foreign business, was not a tempting market. BBME was a much more attractive proposition, especially when Hongkong Bank learned the size of its inner reserves and the level of its real profits. Moreover, the American threat remained a factor.[50] In November 1959 the Hongkong Bank made a cash or share exchange offer for the smaller bank, and by spring 1960 it held virtually all the shares.[51]

The results from the mergers achieved between 1945 and 1960 were sometimes less than might have appeared, because the integration of different banks often proved a slow process. In this characteristic, the British banks followed a well-established tradition in British business whereby mergers between independent firms were often not followed by integration of the formerly independent firms, which continued to operate as separate units in many respects.[52] This was not the case in Australia, where the Union Bank and the Bank of Australasia were rigorously forged into a new, and more dynamic, entity after 1951,[53] but the Eastern Exchange banks were slower to take this route. It was written into the board minutes of the National Bank of India following the acquisition of Grindlays in 1948 that it was 'a major object in achieving the capital of Grindlays Bank Ltd. . . . to develop its business as a separate entity'.[54] Grindlays thus continued to function as a separate entity apart from National Bank representation at board level, until 1958 when, after a series of problems at Grindlays including heavy bad debts in Calcutta,[55] the two banks were merged into a single organization. Similarly, Eastern Bank retained its own management and balance sheet until 1971, and the Hongkong Bank also allowed the Mercantile Bank of India and the BBME to retain their separate identities, boards, managements, and balance sheets. In 1966 Mercantile's head office was transferred to Hong Kong, and the bank was increasingly integrated into the Hongkong Bank.[56] In contrast, BBME—operating in the Middle and not the Far East—was allowed to continue to function as a separate bank for a long period, and until the mid-1970s it

---

[50] Geoffrey Jones, *Banking and Oil*, 79.

[51] Ibid., 81–6; King, *The History of the Hongkong and Shanghai Banking Corporation*, iv, 535–9.

[52] A. D. Chandler, *Scale and Scope* (Cambridge, Mass: Harvard University Press, 1990), 287.

[53] Merrett, *ANZ Bank*, 97–103.

[54] Board Minute, 16 Dec. 1948, Grindlay and Company Minute Books, 1941–9, Grindlay Archives, ANZ Archives.

[55] Board Minutes 23 Dec. 1953, Grindlay Bank Board Minutes, 1950–4, Grindlay Archives, ANZ Archives.

[56] King, *The History of the Hongkong and Shanghai Banking Corporation*, iv, 514–17, 607–8.

even maintained a separate recruitment from the rest of the Hongkong Bank. It was not until 1980 that the bank's autonomy was ended, with the transfer of the head office to Hong Kong and the integration of senior management functions, though the bank continued to exist as a separate legal entity.[57]

Between 1945 and 1960, therefore, mergers reduced the number of British banks in Australia to two, while Eastern Exchange banking had been concentrated in three groups, all of which had branches outside Asia. Lloyds had a shareholding in one of the Exchange banks, and Barclays in another plus ANZ, but there was little progress being made in achieving a real integration of domestic and overseas banking.

## 8.3. Grand Designs, 1960–1971

The long struggle to modify the functional and geographical specialization of British multinational banks continued through the 1960s. By this decade their positions had declined further in the face of the competitive threats facing them. They resembled 'a lot of weak structures propping each other up'.[58] The result was a series of 'grand designs' or ambitious plans to forge multi-regional banking groups. Tables 8.3 and 8.4 summarize the real and abortive merger proposals of these years.

The theme of regional consolidation continued into the 1960s. In Africa, Standard Bank acquired the Bank of West Africa in 1965. As early as 1955 the Bank of West Africa's general manager (freshly arrived from the Midland Bank) had suggested that the bank might merge with another British overseas bank operating in a different area. However, his board disliked the idea of the bank 'losing its identity'. Ten years later the bank was approached by Standard Bank, which had branches in many areas of Africa but not West Africa, and which had a shareholding in the bank alongside three clearing banks. In an arrangement which will be looked at in greater detail below, Standard took over the West African bank, paying by the issue of new stock, which was taken up by British clearing banks and Chase Bank of the United States. The West African bank was renamed the Standard Bank of West Africa in 1966, but as usual the process of integration was a slow one.[59]

The 1960s also saw the final consolidation of all the British multi-national banking interests in Australia. ANZ's market share performance had improved from the late 1950s, but the smaller English, Scottish & Australian Bank (E, S & A) was constrained by capital inadequacy and the caution of its board. In the early 1960s it rejected merger offers from two

[57] Ibid., 544–9; Geoffrey Jones, *Banking and Oil*, 86–8, 274–5.
[58] Pencil Note on Memorandum by Sir George Bolton, 8 Dec. 1965, C48/156, B. of E.
[59] Fry, *Bankers in West Africa*, 250–7.

TABLE 8.3. *British overseas bank mergers and consolidations, 1960–1971*

| Year | Banks | Regional | Multi-regional | Domestic |
|------|-------|----------|----------------|----------|
| 1965 | Standard/Bank of West Africa | X | | |
| 1965 | Lloyds acquire National Bank of New Zealand | | | X |
| 1969 | National and Grindlays acquire Ottoman Bank's London Group business | | X | |
| 1970 | ANZ and E, S & A | X | | |
| 1970 | Standard/Chartered | | X | |
| 1970 | Bolsa/Lloyds Bank Europe | | X | X |
| 1971 | Barclays acquire Barclays (DCO) | | | X |

TABLE 8.4. *Abortive British overseas bank mergers, 1960–1971*

| Year | Banks | Regional | Multi-regional | Domestic |
|------|-------|----------|----------------|----------|
| 1962–7 | E, S & A and Chartered | | X | |
| 1964–8 | Standard/Chartered/ANZ/ National and Grindlays | | X | |
| 1965–8 | Lloyds/Barclays/Bolsa/ National and Grindlays | | X | X |

Australian-owned banks, but it accepted an offer from Chartered in December 1962. Two months later the arrangement was blocked by the Australian government, on the grounds that it might precipitate a flood of applications from foreign banks, but it was not until 1967 that both banks abandoned all hope of a merger.[60] There remained one obvious partner for E, S & A—their larger twin, ANZ. ANZ's management feared that, sooner or later, foreign banks would be allowed entry into Australia, and they would attack ANZ's areas of strength, especially international business. The acquisition of E, S & A was, therefore, a defensive move designed to strengthen ANZ's domestic business ahead of any such liberalization of entry terms, and, especially, to prevent any American bank from acquiring the smaller British bank and using it as a host for entry into the Australian market. In December 1968 the two banks announced that they were to merge, and in 1970 the new Australia and New Zealand Banking Group opened.[61]

[60] Merrett, *ANZ Bank*, 245–9.     [61] Ibid., ch. 11.

Much more grandiose amalgamation schemes were also afoot in the 1960s. The negotiations of these years were complex and overlapping, but at the risk of oversimplification it can be argued that two banks took the lead in trying to reorganize British overseas banking. These were Bolsa and Standard Bank, under the chairmanships of George Bolton and Cyril Hawker respectively. Their schemes both overlapped and clashed with one another, but for the sake of analysis they can be dealt with one by one.

It was not surprising that Bolsa should have assumed a lead role in attempting to reorganize British overseas banking, for its Latin American base made the bank particularly vulnerable after 1945. British trade and investment in the sub-continent fell away dramatically after 1945. American banks were very active and the dollar supreme. Latin American governments were prominent in pursuing import substitution and economic nationalism policies. Finally, Bolsa was part of the disorganized Lloyds overseas banking empire. Yet Bolsa had stood aside from the first phase of the reorganization of British overseas banking. It needed an entrepreneurial figure who could take a strategic view of what was happening and perceive opportunities to do something about it.

In 1957 such a figure arrived at the bank, George Bolton. Bolton's first job had been as an exchange dealer with the London branch of Société Générale de Paris, and during the 1920s he had worked for a merchant bank. In the early 1930s he was recruited by Montagu Norman to join the Bank of England's embryonic foreign exchange department, and he played a leading role in planning the exchange control system implemented during the Second World War. In 1948 he was appointed an executive director of the Bank of England. During the 1950s he actively supported the liberalization of financial markets, culminating in 1958, when sterling and a number of other currencies were made internationally convertible. A year previously, he accepted the offer to become chairman of Bolsa.[62]

Bolton's career had given him an overall strategic view which few if any other chairmen or CEOs of British overseas banks matched. By the time he joined Bolsa he had two firm ideas. The first was that sterling's role as a reserve currency was doomed. The second was that, if controls were relaxed, the City of London could be reborn as the world's leading financial centre, because its agglomeration of financial services gave it a unique advantage. On the basis of these insights, Bolton devised a plan for the strategic renewal of Bolsa. As one contemporary described the bank at the time, it was 'a wonderful old vehicle in a state of disuse'. Bolton decided that the 'vehicle' still had *potential* use which could be unlocked if the

---

[62] Richard Fry (ed.), *A Banker's World* (London: Hutchinson, 1970), 18–38. For a summary of his career, see R. P. T. Davenport-Hines, 'Sir George Lewis French Bolton', in David Jeremy (ed.), *Dictionary of Business Biography*, i (London: Butterworths, 1984), 364–9.

bank could reposition itself away from being a sterling bank engaged in trade finance and Latin American retail banking, and towards business that could take advantage of its base in a potentially resurgent City of London. In an interview in 1970, Bolton described the 'major steps' he resolved to take to reposition Bolsa:

a deliberate withdrawal from sterling activities in the belief that the international use of sterling would virtually cease; the organisation of an active exchange department; a decision that our responsibility lay in assisting the growth of the host countries more than the bank being regarded as a vehicle for the finance of British trade; and a decision to buy deposits at the going rate rather than solicit industrial customers to become customers.[63]

An early move by Bolton was the purchase of the old-established British merchant banking firm of Balfour Williamson and Company. This private company had an extremely diversified business involving trade finance, especially confirming, shipbroking, and timber, and with operating companies spread over much of North and South America as well as the United Kingdom.[64] This acquisition enabled Bolsa to diversify out of retail banking and short-term trade facilities into wider financial and trading operations, and the Balfour Williamson subsidiary was also used as a means to diversify beyond the Americas. In 1963, for example, it acquired the Allied National Company, a British company with financial interests in Africa, Australia, and Asia.

The key element of Bolton's strategy, however, was the resolution to withdraw from 'sterling activities'. Bolsa became one of the first-movers in the new Eurodollar market (see Section 10.2), but Eurodollars were not an ideal base for Bolton to undertake the kind of medium- and long-term lending that would form a part of his 'assisting the growth of . . . host countries', and he also sought a more secure access to dollar resources which could come from a dollar capital base. Soon after becoming chairman of Bolsa, Bolton began discussing the potential for a partnership with the Bank of Montreal. The upshot was the formation of a Bahamas-registered joint venture, the Bank of London and Montreal (Bolam), to which Bolsa contributed its branch network in Central America and the Bank of Montreal provided Canadian dollars. By 1963 Bolton was searching for an American banking partner, and was in negotiations with a US bank holding company, Western Bancorporation. These negotiations were not productive, but in 1965 Bolton had more success with another American institution, Mellon National Bank. The Bank of England would not allow a foreign bank to acquire more than 15 per cent of the issued capital of a British bank, and in August 1965 Mellon acquired such a stake in

[63] Interview in *The Banker*, Feb. 1970, cited in Fry (ed.), *A Banker's World*, 180.
[64] H. A. Holley, 'Bolsa under Sir George Bolton', in Fry (ed.), *A Banker's World*, 216.

Bolsa, at a cost of over £5 million.[65] One result of this arrangement was that Lloyds' share of Bolsa equity fell further, to 24 per cent by the end of 1965.

Bolton's plans to reshape the face of British overseas banking reached their apogee in the mid-1960s. The plan was no less than to unite the overseas banking interests of Lloyds and Barclays with those of Mellon to create an Anglo-American multinational bank. Bolton, like many contemporary Britishers, remained cool to the idea of British integration with the other Western European economies. Instead he looked to the United States, arguing that Britain's historic political and military alliance with that country should 'be cemented by the closest possible relations between the American and British banking and financial systems'.[66]

The group of banks in which Lloyds had shareholdings looked particularly attractive as a basis for a global Anglo-American bank. These included Bolsa, the 25 per cent share of National and Grindlays acquired in 1960, and the wholly owned Lloyds Bank Europe. In 1965 Lloyds sold its shares in the Bank of West Africa as part of the Standard takeover, but in the following year acquired 100 per cent of the shares of the National Bank of New Zealand. If Barclays (DCO) was added, Bolton argued, a multinational bank could be created with branches spanning Latin America, continental Europe, Africa, Asia, and New Zealand, with a headquarters in London, and access to dollars through an American shareholder.

The problem was to find a formula to fuse this mosaic into a unified state. In 1964 Bolton entered negotiations with National and Grindlays about a possible merger, but these were unsuccessful after an accountant's report on the two banks showed that National and Grindlay's reserves were much stronger than those of Bolsa.[67] He was initially more successful with Barclays (DCO), which in 1964 acquired a one-third share in Bolam,[68] and by 1965 Bolton was suggesting a merger of all the Lloyds and Barclays interests.[69] The proposal, however, did not find favour with the Bank of England, which considered all the overseas banks in question 'grossly undercapitalised', and 'to bring them together would make a vast organisation without substance'.[70]

During 1966 and 1967 Bolton persisted with the idea of a merger of Barclays' and Lloyds' overseas banking interests, but neither bank was willing to lose control over 'their' subsidiaries by merging them into a wide

[65] Memorandum to the Deputy Governor, 5 Aug. 1965, C48/156, B. of E.
[66] A speech by Sir George Bolton at the Bank's centenary dinner, 25 Oct. 1962, *Bolsa Quarterly Review*, 3(1) (1963).                    [67] Winton Files, LB.
[68] Sir Julian Crossley and John Blandford, *The DCO Story* (London: Barclays Bank International, 1975), 217.
[69] Memorandum by Sir George Bolton, 8 Dec. 1965, C48/156, B. of E.
[70] Memorandum, 15 Dec. 1965, C48/165, B. of E.

new bank, and it only proved possible to achieve a much looser arrangement. In 1967 Barclays, Barclays (DCO), Bolsa, and the National Bank of New Zealand—plus Chartered Bank and ANZ, in which Barclays held small shareholdings—formed Intercontinental Banking Services (IBS), a new organization with big ambitions to provide finance on 'an almost world-wide basis in most currencies'. Barclays had been galvanized into action by the plans of Standard Bank, which will be discussed below, to merge with Chartered and ANZ. The initial proposal was that Barclays and/or Lloyds would purchase (if they did not already hold) a large interest (around 20 per cent) in each of Bolsa, Chartered, ANZ, and the National Bank of New Zealand. National and Grindlays declined to get involved in the scheme at all. Chartered vetoed the equity exchange idea, so that a much looser consortium structure than originally envisaged emerged.[71] However, IBS was eventually launched just before a major sterling crisis and the devaluation of sterling in November 1967. British government lending restrictions crippled its growth and by 1970 it had ceased to take on new business.[72]

There was another false dawn for Bolton's schemes in 1968 when Lloyds and Barclays (together with a smaller English clearing bank, Martins) announced they were to merge. The idea had nothing to do with overseas banking *per se* but was a hasty reaction to the merger plan announced by two of the 'Big Five' English clearing banks, Westminster and National Provincial. However, Lloyds and Barclays placed considerable emphasis on the international benefits of this proposed alliance when their merger was referred by the British government to its antitrust agency, the Monopolies Commission. Three of their six stated reasons for the merger concerned international banking, and in particular the benefits to be gained from integrating domestic and overseas banking in a way that could counter the competitive challenge posed by American banks, by providing British customers with the chance to deal with the same bank at home and overseas. The Monopolies Commission was not convinced. It rejected the merger between Barclays and Lloyds, although the formation of National Westminster was allowed to proceed. Fears of a duopoly in domestic banking were foremost in this decision, but the Commission also failed to perceive any benefits in international banking from the merger. The Commission stressed the virtues of efficiency and cost rather than scale in competing with American banks, and saw little competitive merit in bringing together two sets of similar branch networks in the developing world.[73] The

---

[71] Charles Fiero to George Champion, 21 Sept. 1967, 'Grand Design' File, South Africa Box, SC.    [72] Winton, *Lloyds Bank*, 183–4.
[73] Monopolies Commission, *Report on the Proposed Merger of Barclays Bank Ltd., Lloyds Bank Ltd., and Martins Bank Ltd.* (London, 1968) 18–19, 44–60; Winton, *Lloyds Bank*, 183–4. See also Sect. 10.1, below.

Monopolies Commission verdict meant that the various Lloyds and Barclays affiliates went their separate ways.

Both Bolsa and National and Grindlays looked for salvation across the Atlantic. In July 1968 the Bank of England allowed Bolsa to increase the Mellon shareholding to 25 per cent. Meanwhile Lord Aldington, National and Grindlays' chairman, travelled to New York intending to persuade Chase Manhattan to invest in his bank. Eventually it was Citibank which invested.[74] In a complex arrangement designed to maintain British control over the bank, Citibank took 40 per cent of the equity, with Lloyds retaining another 25 per cent. In 1969 National and Grindlays also purchased a significant part of the banking business of the Ottoman Bank, including its London business and branches in Cyprus, the Middle East, and East Africa. In addition a new joint venture bank, Banque Ottomane (France) SA, was formed to take over the greater part of Ottoman's business in Paris, Marseilles, and Geneva.

In the aftermath of the failed merger scheme, Lloyds and Barclays moved to take firmer control over their overseas affiliates. In February 1969 Lloyds Bank began a belated examination of its overseas strategy. In 1970 Bolsa bought out the shares of Mellon and Barclays (DCO) in Bolam, making it a wholly owned subsidiary. The next stage was a merger of Bolsa and Lloyds Bank Europe, and in May 1971 both banks became subsidiaries of a new bank, Lloyds and Bolsa International Bank. Lloyds Bank acquired 55 per cent of the capital, and Mellon Bank nearly 13 per cent, with the remainder in public and institutional hands. Meanwhile, Bolton had retired as chairman of Bolsa in 1970. His vision of an integrated Anglo-American multinational bank spanning the globe remained unfulfilled.

Barclays followed a similar route to Lloyds. In 1971 it bought out the minority shareholders in Barclays (DCO), which was merged into Barclays' interests in continental Europe to form a new international bank, Barclays Bank International.

If Bolton had been one of the moving forces behind a reorganization of British overseas banking, the other main figure was Cyril Hawker of the Standard Bank. Hawker had served as deputy to Bolton when the latter became head of the Bank of England's foreign department in 1934,[75] but ironically they were to be more rivals than collaborators in the 1960s, following Hawker's appointment as chairman of Standard Bank in 1962.

Standard Bank had begun a search for a partner some years before Hawker's arrival. The bank had become increasingly concerned about the political and economic prospects of Africa during the late 1950s. Its South African base had obvious political risks, while the South African connection

---

[74] Harold Van B. Cleveland and Thomas F. Huertas, *Citibank, 1812–1970* (Cambridge, Mass.: Harvard University Press, 1985), 435.     [75] Fry (ed.), *A Banker's World*, 20.

was a stigma in the newly emerging countries of Africa. In 1959 the idea was floated of attracting a minority American shareholding in Standard, with the name of Bank of America being mentioned, but the Bank of England advised that the idea 'would not be welcome'.[76] Ideas of mergers with Lloyds, an Australian bank, or Chartered were discussed, but to little effect in the face of the problems of reconciling strong corporate cultures. In 1961 Standard held talks with National and Grindlays, which collapsed after the latter bank offered merely to take over Standard's East African operations.[77]

It was not surprising that while Bolton, from his Latin American base, initially focused on the need for his bank to obtain non-sterling resources, Hawker sought a merger to achieve geographical diversification out of the troubled waters of Africa. Within a few months of his appointment as chairman, he was advocating the formation of a giant 'British Overseas Bank' as part of a 'grand design' to reorganize the sector. Like all the merger schemes of the 1960s, the resultant negotiations were complex and fluctuating, but there were three main and related dimensions: a link with a UK domestic bank; a link with a US bank; and a merger between a group of overseas banks.

At the end of 1962 Hawker floated the idea that Midland Bank should participate in the 'British Overseas Bank'. A few years previously such a suggestion would have been ludicrous, because of Midland's traditional policy of reliance on correspondent banking. However, the problems of sterling and the formation of the European Community, among other factors, had led to an internal reassessment of that bank's international strategy, and by 1962 a new strategy of deeper international involvement through collaborative alliances had been devised. An initial idea was the formation of a banking group, led by Midland, and including Standard, Chartered, and English, Scottish & Australian, but Chartered had deep reservations about becoming involved with Africa, and declined to get involved. By May 1963 Midland too had come to prefer a looser association of 'Commonwealth banks'. The upshot was the formation in 1964 of London's first consortium bank, Midland and International Banks, or MAIBL. MAIBL was jointly owned by Midland (which held 45 per cent of the capital), Standard Bank, Commercial Bank of Australia, and Toronto-Dominion Bank, and its purpose was the finance of large-scale development projects using wholesale deposits.[78] In 1965 Standard further strengthened its link with Midland when, as a result of the merger with the

[76] Memorandum by Deputy Governor, 9 Feb. 1959; H. C. B. Mynors to E. Hall-Patch, 17 Feb. 1959, C48/157, B. of E.

[77] Note of a Conversation with Sir Edmund Hall-Patch, 4 Oct. 1961, C48/157, B. of E.

[78] A. R. Holmes and Edwin Green, Midland: 150 Years of Banking Business (London: Batsford, 1986), 249–54; Notes on Discussions with CBA, Toronto-Dominion, and Standard Bank in New York, Oct. 1963, in Maibl File, Management Committee Box 289, Midland Bank Archives; Memorandum 14 May 1963, C48/157, B. of E.

Bank of West Africa, Midland took over Lloyds' share in that bank and as a result acquired a 5 per cent shareholding in Standard Bank.[79] Neither this equity stake nor MAIBL, however, amounted to the strong integration with a domestic bank which Hawker originally envisaged.

By 1963 Hawker had also reached the view that Standard needed a link with an American bank, and, while negotiations with Midland were proceeding, talks also began with Chase Manhattan. This bank had established a small branch network in South Africa, and also a branch in Nigeria, and it posed a potential competitive threat in both areas unless some co-operative arrangement was arrived at. Hawker's first idea was to hive off Standard's East African operations into a new bank with Chase participation, possibly also involving continental banks, as a further way of defusing nationalist criticisms. This scheme did not progress. Instead, under the Bank of West Africa merger arrangements, Chase acquired 15 per cent of Standard, which effectively defused the competitive threat. An amalgamation of the Standard and Chase operations in South Africa was arranged, while in West Africa Chase's Nigerian branch was sold to the British bank. Subsequently Chase also seconded managers to Standard who helped introduce 'some new banking techniques and a spirit of aggressive competition'.[80] This arrangement left Standard with Midland Bank, National Provincial, and Westminster Banks owning 4.9 per cent each of its equity, and Chase with 14.5 per cent.

The final element of the Hawker 'grand design' was the amalgamation of a group of the British overseas banks. The acquisition of the Bank of West Africa in 1965 was a first part of this strategy, but Hawker found it hard to make further progress. Chartered, National and Grindlays, and ANZ were the desired partners, but problems arose with each one. A proposal in 1964 to create an 'African Banking Corporation' including the Bank of West Africa and the Central and East African branches of Standard and National and Grindlays collapsed because National and Grindlays wanted its Indian branches included in any amalgamation, while Standard argued that the growing unpopularity of Asians in East Africa made this undesirable. Chartered continued to be unhappy about a merger with Standard, and this reluctance grew following Chase's involvement, because it was felt that Chartered's business with the People's Republic of China might be threatened if it became known that it had an American association. As for ANZ, Chase had been declined permission to open a branch in Australia, and it was feared by ANZ that any scheme involving the American bank would be seen by the Australian government as Chase trying to enter the country through a back door.[81] It was in this situation

[79] Fry (ed.), *A Banker's World*, 252–4.    [80] Ibid., 252.
[81] Charles Fiero to John A. Hooper, 20 June 1967, 'Grand Design' File, South Africa Box, SC.

of conflicting and competing interests that Barclays launched its rival amalgamation scheme in 1967, which led, ultimately, to the formation of Intercontinental Banking Services.

The events of 1968 finally cleared away some of the confusion in the negotiations. While the threat of the Lloyds–Barclays merger focused minds, the Citibank acquisition of 40 per cent of National and Grindlays removed that bank from the range of merger possibilities. Similarly, the decision of the two British trading banks in Australia to merge, combined with the continued Australian government opposition to foreign banks, removed them from the merger debates.

During March and April 1969 two of Standard's shareholders attempted to gain virtual control. The newly created National Westminster and Chase proposed to raise their shareholding to 20 per cent each, as part of a new rights issue. Chase had always wanted a larger shareholding, while National Westminster was anxious to expand internationally, an arena in which both of its constituent banks were weak. National Westminster promised to direct business towards Standard, and provide the bank with greater resources to meet competitive challenges, but Hawker was less than pleased by the proposals. His 'grand design' had always stressed the need for links with a range of clearing banks and an American bank, and he had no wish for an exclusive relationship with just two banks. In May the scheme was dropped.[82]

This left Standard with Chartered. Merger negotiations began in the first half of 1969, and on 1 October it was announced they had agreed to amalgamate. On 1 January 1970 a new holding company came into existence, the Standard Chartered Banking Group, which controlled all the issued stock of both Standard and Chartered. Each bank came into the merger with its major institutional alliances intact. Chase held 14.5 per cent, National Westminster held around 8 per cent, and Midland around 5 per cent of Standard, while Barclays held 15 per cent of Chartered, although Barclays divested its shareholding almost immediately.

During the 1960s, therefore, two outsiders to British overseas banking—Bolton and Hawker—had struggled to reorganize their sector. The results of their efforts can be seen in Figure 8.1.

By 1971 British multinational banking had become concentrated in six main groups. Five of these were multi-regional, with only ANZ confined to Australasia plus its London business. However, there had been only limited progress in integrating the 'free-standing' overseas banks with British—or American—domestic banking. Only Barclays Bank International was wholly owned by its domestic parent. Lloyds was on its way to full

---

[82] Cyril Hawker to Sir George Harvie-Watt, 24 Apr. 1969, 'Grand Design' File, South Africa Box, SC.

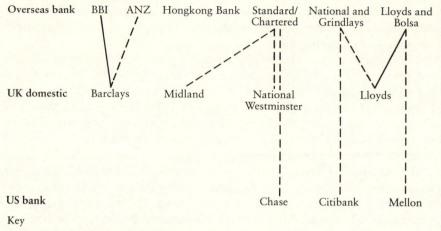

FIG. 8.1 The main British multinational banking groups, 1971

ownership of Lloyds and Bolsa, but in 1971 there was still also a Mellon shareholding. Three of the other banks had British clearing and American banks as minority shareholders, while the Hongkong Bank remained without any large institutional shareholder.

This corporate reorganization had taken a long time to achieve, and opportunities were missed as a result. Bolton's perception was surely correct that there were excellent prospects for British banks which combined the historic branch networks in the developing world with an active role in the City of London, reborn as the leading international banking centre, though his plans to create an Anglo-American bank were arguably more nostalgic than realistic. In the 1960s, as Chapter 10 will discuss in more detail, the world multinational banking industry changed very fast, and it was unfortunate that British bankers chose to spend most of the period simply talking about how best to respond to these changes.

## 8.4. The Regulators and the Grand Designs

The public policy environment deserves special mention as an obstacle to corporate reorganization in British overseas banking. The banks operated in a context defined by their home and host country regulators, who for the most part had other priorities than the creation of competitive British multinational banks.

Some of the regulatory constraints on the banks have already been identified in the preceding two sections. The Australian government effectively blocked all the attempts to merge the British-owned trading banks with banks active elsewhere. Any hope of creating a powerful British multinational bank with a firm base in the politically stable, if small, Australian market was dashed as a result. The British Monopolies Commission had blocked the Lloyds–Barclays merger in 1968. The regulators with the largest influence on the overseas banks, however, were those at the Bank of England.

By the mid-1950s the Bank of England had come to the conclusion that the structure of small, geographically specialized overseas banks had had its day. The Bank was particularly worried about the Eastern Exchange banks, which it believed might become a target for asset-strippers or, even worse, American banks. It looked favourably on mergers between them, and saw the continuation of competition between the banks as dangerous, in that it might open the door to unwelcome visitors from across the Atlantic.[83] The Bank of England, however, continued to govern the City of London not by regulations but by 'nods and winks'.[84] It did not coerce, or make any suggestion that would involve it in taking responsibility for the consequences of a decision. As a result, the Bank would not act directly to overcome negotiations deadlocked by vested interests and distinctive corporate cultures.

In a characteristically British fashion, the Bank of England attempted to influence the strategy of British overseas banking not by regulation but by suggestion, placing its officials on the boards of the banks. An early example was Sir Geoffrey Eley, a member of the Court of the Bank of England between 1949 and 1966, who was appointed a director of BBME in 1950 and served as its deputy chairman from 1952 to 1977. During the merger negotiations of the 1950s Eley kept the Bank of England informed of progress, and acted as a liaison figure.[85] In the mid-1950s the governor had talks 'about the future of Bolsa' which culminated in the appointment of Bolton as chairman.[86] When Bolton retired as Bolsa's chairman he was replaced by Sir Maurice Parsons, another Bank of England official who had worked for a long period with Bolton on international matters.[87] In 1962 Cyril Hawker followed in Bolton's footsteps, moving from the Bank of England to the chairmanship of an overseas bank, Standard.

The view that if the 'right man' was put in charge appropriate policies would be pursued was sensible, but only to a point. Bolton and Hawker arrived at their banks with clear-headed strategies for corporate renewal. However, the Bank of England thereafter left them to their own devices to overcome the structural obstacles to their plans. Neither Bolton nor Hawker

---

[83] See, e.g. Geoffrey Jones, *Banking and Oil*, 75–6.
[84] Geoffrey Jones, 'Competition and Competitiveness in British Banking, 1918–1971'.
[85] Geoffrey Jones, *Banking and Oil*, 75–8.
[86] Governor's Note, 5 July 1955, C48/156, B. of E.
[87] Fry (ed.), *A Banker's World*, 20.

could call on the special assistance of their old colleagues at the central bank.

As an institution, the Bank of England in the 1950s and 1960s assisted the various merger schemes when it could. At the end of the 1950s, for example, it helped the Hongkong Bank secure tax concessions from the British Inland Revenue which eased the acquisitions of the Mercantile Bank and BBME. It would, on occasion, urge banks to 'get on with amalgamation negotiations'.[88] However, if people turned a blind eye to the Bank's nods and winks, its policy was revealed as quite impotent. In the 1950s, for example, it watched passively as the Ionian Bank was dismembered (see above, Section 8.2). From 1953 the Bank of England was informally helping Ionian search for an appropriate partner among British overseas banks, but it would not coerce Ionian to do anything.[89] The Bank of England's passive attitude continued as Behrens, Trusted secured a majority of shares, and then proceeded to break up Ionian. The Bank deeply distrusted Behrens, Trusted—whom it regarded as speculators in Treasury bonds—and disliked even more the break-up of a British overseas bank. However, it would not interfere directly, and the limit of its sanction was to make subsequent life in the City uncomfortable for them. 'They had no interest in banking as such, but only in a quick profit', a Bank of England official minuted later. 'They were not interested in considering our ideas of strengthening British banking in the Middle East and in consequence their actions incurred our displeasure.'[90]

While the Bank of England would do little to coerce the individual banks into merging, it was rather more active in preventing their integration with either British domestic or American banks. After 1945 the Bank of England's overt hostility to multinational activity by the clearing banks weakened, but the policy remained in place.[91] Barclays was encouraged to dilute its shareholding in DCO, and loosen links between the domestic and the overseas bank.[92] When BBME mentioned the idea of a possible merger with Lloyds or another clearer in 1955, this was firmly ruled out by the Bank of England on the grounds that 'they and the rest of the Clearers have more than enough with which to occupy themselves at home'.[93] In the following year a tentative mention of a possible link with the Royal Bank of Scotland was rapidly squashed by the governor.[94] When in 1959 and 1960 Standard Bank floated the idea of a link with Lloyds, the Bank

[88] Geoffrey Jones, *Banking and Oil*, 80–5.

[89] Note for the Record, 27 Nov. 1953; Note, 21 Oct. 1954, Note, 15 Dec. 1955, C48/154, B. of E.

[90] Memorandum, 14 Jan. 1958; Memorandum by H. S. Clarke to Chief Cashier, 16 Jan. 1961. C48/155, B. of E.    [91] Memorandum, 21 May 1951, C48/152, B. of E.

[92] Governor's Note, 25 Sept. 1951 and 27 Apr. 1955, C48/152, B. of E.

[93] Secret Memorandum to Governor, 2 November 1955, C48/392, B. of E.

[94] Governor's Note, 5 July 1956, C48/392, B. of E.

of England strongly discouraged any idea of a full take-over, though it was prepared to countenance the clearer taking a small equity stake.[95] It was not until after C. F. Cobbold's retirement as the Bank's governor in 1961 that a policy change can be detected. When Standard approached the Bank of England in 1963 about a possible link with Midland, the response was more welcoming, one official observing that 'times have changed'.[96] Nevertheless, the Bank of England preferred the looser association of MAIBL, and it was perhaps only in the late 1960s that it became fully reconciled to domestic banks undertaking multinational banking.

One reason why the Bank of England modified its policies towards the clearers in the 1960s was its growing alarm about American penetration of the British banking system and its determination to prevent Americans from acquiring any of the overseas banks. The Bank of England had supported the amalgamation movements among the Eastern Exchange banks in the 1950s against the background of a fear of American intervention. In the 1960s the Bank of England bowed to the view that an American shareholding was inevitable and even desirable, but worked to keep the shareholding as a minority one. In the early 1960s the acceptable figure was 15 per cent. Mellon's investment in Bolsa and Chase's stake in Standard Bank in 1965 were kept to this level at the Bank of England's request. In 1968 Citibank was allowed to take a 40 per cent stake in National and Grindlays, but only on the conditions that British control was retained and that the American bank did not purchase further shares without the agreement of the governor of the Bank of England.[97]

The regulators, then, made a distinct contribution to the reorganization of British overseas banking. The Bank of England facilitated the multi-regional mergers, but allowed them to take place at a leisurely pace, while it blocked schemes to achieve greater integration between British domestic and overseas banking, or to achieve greater integration with American banks. In retrospect, as the remaining British overseas banks were to spend the twenty years after 1970 searching for a domestic partner, it has to be concluded that the Bank of England's contribution was to turn a difficult historical legacy into a near-fatal institutional handicap.

## 8.5. Management Structures

The British banks remained slow to change the management structures inherited from the nineteenth century. These structures had stood the test of war and financial crisis, but their value by the 1960s was less evident.

[95] Governor's Note, 20 Sept. 1960, C48/157, B. of E.
[96] Memorandum to the Governor, 26 Mar. 1963, C48/157, B. of E.
[97] Geoffrey Jones, 'The British Government and Foreign Multinationals before 1970', in Martin Chick (ed.), Governments, Industries and Markets (Aldershot: Elgar, 1990), 205.

The composition of bank boards offered testimony to the theme of continuity. Banks in the 1950s and 1960s often recruited directors from the same firms as had their nineteenth-century predecessors. The Eastern Exchange banks, for instance, still found most directors from among the old Eastern commercial and mercantile firms. The Hongkong Bank's board continued to consist of representatives of the traditional 'hongs', with only one new firm represented after 1945—Britain's largest chemicals company, ICI.[98] Probably the most important new source of recruitment was the appointment of former Bank of England officials to boards, notably Bolton and Hawker.

However, there were some innovations. Transport improvements enabled directors to visit more often the countries in which their banks operated. The advent of transcontinental air travel enabled the directors of the Anglo-Australian banks, for example, to visit the Southern Hemisphere much more frequently.[99] There were similar developments in other banks. In 1946 Lord Kennet became the first chairman of the Imperial Bank of Iran to visit the Middle East during his period of office, and he subsequently made other visits.[100]

A second discernible trend was a professionalization of decision-making by boards. Standard Bank of South Africa, for example, finally appointed a permanent, and full-time, chairman in 1952.[101] In most banks directors withdrew from taking executive decisions on matters of detail, though the pace of this development varied considerably between institutions, and over time banks began to appoint executive directors. By the mid-1950s the directors of the Bank of British West Africa 'were content to confine themselves to overall policy leaving the general manager and the management committee to run the Bank'.[102] In a number of banks it was evident by the 1950s that CEOs carefully controlled the information given to directors so as to ensure that they made the 'correct' decisions.[103]

Unsurprisingly, Sir George Bolton strove to achieve a greater professionalization of board decision-making following his appointment as chairman of Bolsa. During the 1950s the bank had a Daily Committee of Directors, which took many executive decisions on loans and other aspects of business. There was also an Establishments Committee and a Policy Committee active by the middle of the decade. Furthermore, directors were still actively involved in executive matters. Bolton became a full-time chairman of Bolsa, and moved very rapidly to improve the board's administrative procedures.

---

[98] Geoffrey Jones, *Banking and Oil*, 39–40; Merrett, *ANZ Bank*, 194; King, *The History of the Hongkong and Shanghai Banking Corporation*, iv, 252–7.
[99] Merrett, *ANZ Bank*, 230.   [100] Geoffrey Jones, *Banking and Oil*, 5.
[101] Henry, *The First Hundred Years of the Standard Bank* (London: Oxford University Press, 1963), 318.   [102] Fry (ed.), *A Banker's World*, 189.
[103] Ibid., 230; Geoffrey Jones, *Banking and Oil*, 40.

Head office functions were divided into two—banking and administration—with two full-time directors 'charged with policy direction and supervision of these two main functions'.[104] In 1959 all the board committees were abolished and replaced by a single Chairman's Committee, consisting of the chairman, his deputy and a small group of directors. The committee met 'weekly or whenever necessary' and was attended by the general managers of the bank. Its functions were to authorize credit, and to approve expenditure on premises and equipment up to a certain level.[105]

Managerial hierarchies deepened in the 1950s and, especially, the 1960s. During the 1950s specialist departments began to appear at head offices. At Melbourne, ANZ developed an economics and statistics department, which evolved into a *de facto* strategic planning unit. Methods and data-processing departments followed within the general manager's office, although well into the 1960s there was a considerable confusion between line and staff functions, and specialists were distrusted.[106]

Head office structures were even less developed in most other banks. The Hongkong Bank's head office, for example, was a very small one, with an executive staff of only seven in 1961. The chief manager was advised by a small group of inspectors who examined the monthly returns coming in from each branch. He read the correspondence of all the bank's branch managers, who were, however, largely left to function as independent profit centres. This organization had its merits, including flexibility, but it was not well equipped to manage a bank growing rapidly in size and diversity, and it created serious problems when other banks began to be acquired.[107] During the 1960s there were more vigorous attempts to modify organizational structures in the light of new complexities and product diversity. In the Hongkong Bank the number of executive staff at head office increased to twenty-six in 1971. Line functions were identified. Legal and tax specialists were appointed. In 1967 the bank's chief manager also became chairman, and in 1969 there was a major restructuring resulting in the creation of an executive board.[108]

Between 1967 and 1970 many of the British banks employed the services of management consultants. They were not alone in this decision. In the United States Citibank had McKinsey and Company investigate its organization in 1967. Dozens of British firms hired management consultants, usually either McKinsey or Urwick Orr and Partners. The usual advice was to adopt the multidivisional structure (M form) developed in

[104] Bolsa Board Minutes, 18 June 1957, LB.
[105] Bolsa Board Minutes, 25 Aug. 1959, LB.
[106] Merrett, *ANZ Bank*, 138–9, 155–6, 192–3.
[107] King, *The History of the Hongkong and Shanghai Banking Corporation*, iv, 581; S. G. Redding, 'Organisational and Structural Change in the Hongkong and Shanghai Banking Corporation, 1950–1980', in F. H. H. King (ed.), *Eastern Banking* (London: Athlone, 1983), 612, 618. [108] Redding, 'Organisational and Structural Change', 618–19.

the United States before the Second World War. British domestic banks such as Midland and National Westminster were among those seeking enlightenment from across the Atlantic.[109]

In 1967 and 1968 an Urwick Orr investigation of Barclays (DCO) led to a new management system being introduced based on the then fashionable concept of 'management by objectives'. Each layer of management was given an 'objective', with targets and results compared on a regular basis.[110] National and Grindlays called in McKinsey at the end of the decade and received a similar lesson in the virtues of planning and of divisional structures based on products and markets. As a result of the McKinsey report, the board's executive functions were largely given to a powerful Office of the Chairman. This supervised four profit-earning centres. The overseas division controlled the overseas branches, conducting traditional banking. International division controlled merchant banking overseas and was responsible for new ventures. A merchant banking division was responsible for merchant-banking activities in London. Finally there was a finance division in charge of money market operations.[111]

Managerial structures based on product or regional divisions had generally been adopted by British overseas banks by the early 1970s. These managerial hierarchies enabled the banks to pursue product and geographical diversification with more confidence, although the events of the 1970s and 1980s were to demonstrate that they offered no protection from the consequences of poor strategic decision-making.

For much of the immediate post-war period, the British multinational banks retained their structure as, with the important exception of Hongkong Bank, London-headquartered banks operating branches overseas. In most banks London remained important in decision-making, despite the development of regional management structures in the inter-war years. This continued to be a potential constraint on banks as they sought to develop more domestic business in their host economies, a point which will be explored more fully in the following chapter.

Over time this structure also began to come under external pressure. There began to be pressure in a number of host economies for 'localization', or the abandonment of branch banking in favour of the establishment of locally registered banks, sometimes with local equity participation. In some cases regulatory changes made this obligatory, while elsewhere the growth of nationalist feelings simply made a greater local identity desirable. The British banks disliked such localization, stressing the economies

[109] L. Hannah, *The Rise of the Corporate Economy* (London: Methuen, 1983), 152; Derek F. Channon, *The Strategy and Structure of British Enterprise* (London: Macmillan, 1973), 132; Holmes and Green, *Midland*, 282–8; Cleveland and Huertas, *Citibank*, 279.
[110] Crossley and Blandford, *The DCO Story*, 237–9.
[111] National and Grindlays Board Minutes, 22 Sept. 1970, ANZ Archives.

of scale and scope gained by their horizontally integrated corporations,[112] but were often powerless to resist it.

The British banks in Africa were among the first to have to face the issue of localization. From the 1940s, the two British banks in South Africa had begun to feel pressure to move closer to their host economy. Wartime banking legislation limited a bank's operations to the proportion of its capital and published reserves within South Africa, while the British banks were not popular with the Nationalist governments in power after 1948. In 1961 South Africa left the British Commonwealth. Meanwhile, beyond South Africa, the South African links of the British banks became an increasing liability as the Black African colonies approached political independence, and as resentment at apartheid grew.

In 1948 Barclays (DCO)'s chairman had already reached the (private) conclusion that the creation of a separate South African bank would 'prove to be a right move'.[113] This idea was not pursued, but in 1953 DCO added two new local boards (for Natal and the Orange Free State) to its already existing structure of a Cape local board and an overall South African board of directors based in Pretoria.[114] Standard Bank began serious consideration of the separation of the South African business into a subsidiary company in 1951.[115] However, the initial response of Standard, like Barclays, was to appoint local directors rather than break up the unity of the bank. In 1953 a South African Board was created with general supervisory responsibilities in South Africa, and in addition a Cape Board was established with special responsibilities for Cape Province and South African-occupied South West Africa (Namibia). A year earlier, the administrative headquarters of the bank were moved from Cape Town to Pretoria, the seat of government located in the Afrikaans province of Transvaal.[116]

The creation of local subsidiaries, however, raised more fundamental problems for the British banks. The South African operations of DCO and Standard Bank remained at the very heart of their profitability. In the early 1950s South Africa was contributing between 40 and 50 per cent of DCO's profits (before tax and provision for bad debts), though this proportion had dropped to around one-third by the end of the decade.[117] There were technical problems concerning, for example, whether a South African subsidiary should also control operations in neighbouring countries outside the borders of the Union. And there was the familiar problem of control,

[112] Chairman's Statement to Shareholders at 41st Ordinary General Meeting of Barclays (DCO), 4 Jan. 1967, 38/401, BBA; Geoffrey Jones, *Banking and Oil*, 90–1.
[113] Sir Julian Crossley Diaries, 10 May 1948, 38/209, BBA.
[114] Crossley and Blandford, *The DCO Story*, 279–80.
[115] R. E. Williams to W. G. Hall, 9 Apr. 1954 *re* Gibson's Report of 1951 and correspondence, Subsidiary Company File, SBSA Historical Archives Box, SC.
[116] Henry, *The First Hundred Years of the Standard Bank*, 318–20.
[117] Papers submitted to DCO Accounts Board, 38/251, BBA.

and possible duplication of, or competition with, London headquarters. Standard Bank's senior management were clearly unhappy about the implications of hiving off the South African business, and the various merger schemes discussed by the bank at the end of the 1950s (see above Section 8.4) can be regarded in part as alternative strategies to accepting the unpalatable one of localization.

The pace of independence in Black Africa, and the consequent need to increase the distance between Standard and the apartheid regime, finally pushed that bank towards localization in South Africa. The imperative of independence in the East African colony of Tanganyika (subsequently Tanzania) to a large extent determined the timing of the exercise when it finally came about.[118] In 1962 the parent bank was renamed the Standard Bank and a new South African registered subsidiary was created, the Standard Bank of South Africa, which took over the 700 branches (out of a total of 900 in Southern Africa) of Standard which were located in the country. The new bank was wholly owned by its British parent, and had four Standard Bank directors on its board. Eight years later a holding-company structure was formed in South Africa. Standard Bank Investment Corporation (SBIC) was established, which controlled Standard Bank of South Africa and other subsidiaries active in financial services, fund management, property, and credit cards.

External pressures continued to push Standard towards yet further 'localization'. During the 1960s Afrikaans business interests continued to grow in importance, and the local management of the bank felt the pressure acutely. The tension was felt in a growing distance between the London and South African managements of the bank. 'In some quarters in South Africa', the London management complained in 1967, 'little more than lip service is paid to the value of the links with us in London, and . . . the fact that we are at present sole shareholders . . . is accepted with some reluctance as a fact of history to which they must resign themselves.'[119] In 1968, when Standard Bank of South Africa's capital was increased, a local shareholding was issued with some 11 per cent of the capital becoming publicly owned, and by 1970 SBIC had a public participation of around 14 per cent.

By this time government pressure had become more direct. In 1970 a government commission—the Franszen Commission—recommended that all banks and insurance companies should be controlled by South African shareholders. The pressure was now so great that DCO abandoned its opposition to localization and in 1971 incorporated a local subsidiary, Barclays National Bank.[120] During the early 1970s the British banks came

---

[118] E. Hall-Patch to Cavendish-Bentinck, 14 Sept. 1961, Chairmen's Letter Book, East Africa Box, SC.

[119] Note for Chairman, 19 May 1967, SBSA Future Capital Requirements File, South Africa Box, SC.     [120] Crossley and Blandford, *The DCO Story*, 284.

under pressure to allow at least a 50 per cent local shareholding in their subsidiaries, and by 1973 the government was even suggesting that the British banks cut their shareholding to a mere 10 per cent.[121] In practice, the government permitted a slower reduction in British shareholding, recognizing that the limited size of the South African capital market restricted the opportunities for raising the local equity stake. By 1975 Standard's interest in SBIC had been reduced to 73 per cent, and by 1980 it was down to 58 per cent.

During the late 1960s the British banks in Black Africa experienced similar pressures to create locally registered subsidiaries, often with a local shareholding. In Nigeria, a government decree in 1968 declared that all foreign companies would be 'deemed' to be incorporated in Nigeria. Barclays Bank DCO (Nigeria) and Standard Bank Nigeria were formally incorporated in 1969. In 1970 a similar local incorporation took place in Ghana. There were similar developments in East and Central Africa, except Tanzania, which nationalized foreign banks in 1967. In 1969 government legislation in Uganda specified that banks had to be locally incorporated with immediate effect. A year later the government announced that 60 per cent of the shares in most companies were to be acquired by the government but, after the military coup in 1971 by the infamous General Amin, the British banks were permitted to retain a 51 per cent majority shareholding in their subsidiaries.[122]

By 1970 the local incorporation of subsidiaries had had a dramatic impact on the structure of a bank like Standard. It had virtually ceased to be a multinational branch bank and had become a holding company for a series of subsidiary and affiliate companies locally incorporated in various African countries and in which Standard held various percentages of equity. As it was in Africa that the pressure for local incorporation was greatest in the 1960s, it was the British banks active in that continent which were obliged to make the most radical changes in their structures. By the time of the merger with Standard, for example, Chartered Bank remained largely a multinational branch bank. However, over time, political and regulatory pressures obliged other British banks active in many parts of the developing world and elsewhere to incorporate local subsidiaries.[123]

The human resources policies of the banks changed only slowly. Recruitment and training remained stuck in traditional modes for a considerable period. The British banks continued to prefer to recruit as future

[121] A. Davies to C. Hawker, 12 Oct. 1970; Memorandum to Board by C. Hawker, 9 June 1973, Papers on Franszen Commission and Foreign Control of Banks, 1970–3, South Africa Box, SC.
[122] Crossley and Blandford, *The DCO Story*, 247, 262–3, 272–9; *A Story Brought up to Date*, 14–17.
[123] R. G. Dyson, 'New Patterns in British Banking Overseas', *Journal of the Institute of Bankers*, 94 (June 1973), 141–2.

executives middle-class and privately educated men with a few years experience with a domestic bank, who were then employed for life. Social and sporting skills—encapsulated in the concept of 'character'—were weighed far more highly than academic qualifications, which if too high were a positive bar to recruitment.[124] University graduates were recruited with reluctance. They were, BBME's general manager advised his board in 1955, 'of little use and that is the common experience of all the British overseas banks. University life fits them for a more sheltered existence than we can offer.'[125] Only towards the end of the 1960s, with an increasing number of British school-leavers going on to a higher education, did a belated reconsideration of recruitment policies take place.

Leaving aside the suspicion of university graduates—which was a distinctively cultural phenomenon shared by most sectors of British business—the human resources policies of the British banks were similar in most respects to the stereotyped image of Japanese corporations after 1945.[126] However, there was a marked difference in attitudes towards training, which in the British banks remained of the most basic on-the-job variety. This began to become a serious handicap as multinational and international banking was transformed during the 1960s. While the techniques involved in bills of exchange or lending on overdrafts could be passed from one generation to another by the traditional methods, more formal training was needed for bankers to understand the more complex and changing world of global capital and money markets. Moreover, the system of making junior expatriate officers perform routine clerical tasks for years forced up the costs of expatriate officers, especially as increasingly such jobs could be performed by well-qualified local staff.[127]

In Barclays (DCO), staff training schemes began in the 1950s, largely as an outgrowth of similar developments in the parent bank.[128] By the late 1950s ANZ had staff training schemes and a number of training schools in operation in Australia and New Zealand.[129] Standard Bank also had training schools in South Africa in this period. By the following decade training schools were in operation also in several African countries as well as in London, and in 1965 Standard opened a 'flagship' training college in Johannesburg, popularly known as 'the University of Banking'.[130]

Although progress in modifying the learning-on-the-job system was made, it must be said that the training courses offered by the British banks seem

[124] King, *The History of the Hongkong and Shanghai Banking Corporation*, iv, 275.
[125] Cited in Geoffrey Jones, *Banking and Oil*, 104
[126] James C. Abegglen and George Stalk, *Kaisha: The Japanese Corporation* (New York: Basic Books, 1985), 198 ff.
[127] King, *The History of the Hongkong and Shanghai Banking Corporation*, iv, 320.
[128] Crossley and Blandford, *The DCO Story*, 172–4.
[129] Merrett, *ANZ Bank*, 152–3.
[130] Standard Bank Report and Accounts, Mar. 1956, Chairman's Statement; Standard Bank London Newsletter, 5 Oct. 1969, SC.

to have been largely confined to rather elementary skills, and were not the equivalent of the management development programmes being introduced in American banks like Citibank.[131] Standard's 'university', as well as many training schools, continued to place a lot of emphasis on social skills, and extensive sports facilities were often provided. The Eastern Exchange banks seemed particularly loath to adopt formal training. Hongkong Bank's managers could remain ignorant of 'Eurodollars' for some years after the term had been introduced into the daily vocabulary of international bankers.[132] BBME's general manager in the 1970s still gave junior executives in London awaiting their first post in the Middle East 'odd jobs to do', like buying his cuff-links in Harrods.[133] This was no longer quaint British eccentricity, but a wilful amateurism and ignorance of changing market conditions.

There was, therefore, a strong element of continuity in the management structures of British multinational banks after the Second World War, but over time changes occurred. Managerial hierarchies deepened, management consultants were utilized, training policies were upgraded. The pace of change was slow until the late 1960s. Possibly this was because so much senior-management time was preoccupied with 'grand designs'. The inherited strong corporate cultures may have also provided obstacles to change. External pressures often had a faster impact. By 1970 host country pressure for localization had resulted in significant organizational change in certain cases, as multinational branch banking gave way to banking groups.

## 8.6. Conclusion

British multinational banking fared well in the twenty-five years after the end of the Second World War, despite any deterioration in competitive advantages stemming from the relative political and economic decline of Britain. The number of overseas branches had grown to almost 4,000 by 1970, excluding major localized subsidiaries in South Africa and elsewhere. Profitability had been good by comparison with earlier periods, while the 'real' profits of most banks were much better than their published figures. An evident adjustment to changing competitive advantages was visible in the growth of concentration. By 1971 six large multinational banking groups had emerged, five of which were multi-regional. After sixty years, Lloyds had finally decided to bring some coherence to the overseas banking interests it had acquired.

On a less optimistic note, the limitations of these changes were also self-evident. The clustering of British banking assets in the slow-growing Southern Hemisphere economies remained. The grand designs of Bolton

---

131 Cleveland and Huertas, *Citibank*, 284–6.
132 King, *The History of the Hongkong and Shanghai Banking Corporation*, iv, 672.
133 Geoffrey Jones, *Banking and Oil*, 107–8.

and Hawker had not been fulfilled. The integration of British domestic and overseas banking had only been partially achieved, and the legacy of free-standing banking remained. In 1970, Hongkong Bank, ANZ, Standard Chartered, and National and Grindlays remained without a domestic British banking base. All but the first of these had equity links with British clearing banks, but these did not result in integration, and proved transient. Even this degree of integration had taken twenty-five years to achieve, and meanwhile the industry had been revolutionized by the advent of global banking. Managerial hierarchies and training did not match the levels of the American money centre banks and looked arcane in comparison with them.

The British banks often preferred looser or informal links to full internalization. For decades Lloyds held equity stakes in a range of overseas banks, but declined to take full control of them. Barclays did create the integrated DCO organization, but subsequently its small shareholdings and overlapping directorships in ANZ and Chartered remained short of integration. Grand designs had a tendency to end up in the creation of new and ultimately rather marginal organizations, such as MAIBL and IBS. Mergers rarely led quickly to the integration of operations between the formerly independent units.

The internal momentum to achieve structural change within the banks was limited. Their distinctive corporate cultures worked against it. The profitability of the banks reduced any sense of urgency. The use of inner reserves helped protect them from any shareholder pressure, while the Bank of England protected them from American take-over bids, if not always those of British speculators. The highly specialized structure of the entire British financial system was only slowly modified. Change usually came from external influences. Bolton and Hawker, the two really dynamic strategic thinkers of this period, were imported into the British overseas banks from the Bank of England. Fear of American competition, if not take-overs, pushed the banks towards mergers. The creation of locally registered subsidiaries was forced on the banks by much resented political and regulatory pressure in host countries.

Bolton and Hawker had attempted to achieve faster structural change, and a more radical departure from the specialized tradition of British overseas banking. They had perceived long-term opportunities if existing assets could have been reorganized to achieve greater co-ordination between British domestic and overseas banking, and between both and the new world of international banking being created in the City of London. If three or four British banks had been created on such lines in the first half of the 1960s, competing vigorously with one another across regions, the competitiveness of British-owned multinational banking would surely have been enhanced. However, such a scenario was almost the last thing the Bank of England of the period would have wanted.

# CHAPTER 9

# Banking Strategies in the Post-war World

## 9.1. *Market Shares, Competition, and Receptivity*

Although the grand designs for the structural reorganization of British multinational banking were at best only partially achieved, the British banks continued to sustain their positions in many of the domestic banking markets in which they were established. They remained profitable and successful examples of multinational service and retail banking, despite many changes in their political and economic environment in the post-war decades.

Table 9.1 provides crude estimates of the changes in the market shares held by British banks in the twenty-five years after the end of the Second World War, while Table 9.2 estimates the share of deposits held by British-owned banks at the beginning of the 1970s. For many countries, market share data on an institutional level remain elusive, and this table merely suggests an order of magnitude. No attempt is made to include every country in which British banks were active.

The British multinational banks retained their prominent positions in the domestic banking systems of the English-speaking settler economies of the Southern Hemisphere. By 1970 the two British banks between them still held 73 per cent of commercial bank deposits in South Africa.[1] In Australia the British-owned banks continued, very slowly, to lose market share to local banks, but when the combined ANZ Group was formed in 1970 it held only a marginally smaller market share (24 per cent of deposits) than the largest bank in Australia, the Bank of New South Wales.[2] In New Zealand, in 1970, ANZ and the National Bank of New Zealand held between them 40 per cent of non-government deposits, or almost the same share as 1939.[3]

The other areas of British multinational banking strength were overwhelmingly in countries where British political influence was, or had been,

---

[1] Katherine Munro, 'Monetary Policy, Commercial Banking and the Political Imperative, 1965–85', in Stuart Jones (ed.), *Banking and Business in South Africa* (London: Macmillan, 1988), 114.

[2] D. T. Merrett, *ANZ Bank* (Sydney: Allen & Unwin, 1985), 273. R. C. White, *Australian Banking and Monetary Statistics, 1945–1970*, Reserve Bank of Australia, Occasional Paper No. 4B, Sydney, 1973, table 41.

[3] G. R. Hawke and D. K. Sheppard, 'The Evolution of New Zealand Trading Banks mostly until 1934', Victoria University of Wellington, Working Papers in Economic History, No. 84/2, Mar. 1984, table 1.

TABLE 9.1. *Market share performance of British banks by region or country, c.1946–c.1971*

| Changes in market share | Region/country |
|---|---|
| Elimination | China (1949), Egypt (1957), Greece (1957), Syria (1961), Burma (1963), Iraq (1964), Tanzania (1967), Kuwait (1970) |
| Sharp decline | Latin America, South Asia |
| Stagnation/moderate decline | Australia, South Africa, Singapore, Malaysia, Hong Kong |
| Stable | West, Central, and East Africa,[a] New Zealand |
| Growth | Lebanon |

[a] English-speaking Commonwealth countries, excluding Tanzania.

TABLE 9.2. *British bank share of commercial bank deposits in selected markets, c.1971*

| Market share (%) | Region/country |
|---|---|
| > 50 | South Africa, West, Central, and East Africa,[a] Oman |
| > 30 | Hong Kong, New Zealand, Bahrain, Dubai |
| > 20 | Australia, Malaysia, Singapore |
| > 5 | Lebanon, India |
| 1–5 | Argentina |
| Negligible | Europe, United States, Canada, Japan. |

[a] English-speaking Commonwealth countries, excluding Tanzania.

strong. British banks remained influential at the beginning of the 1970s in most of the new countries which had emerged from former British colonial territories in West, Central, and East Africa, and where challenges from local banks and foreign banks were just beginning. In Hong Kong and in the former colonial territories of Malaysia and Singapore there was much more competition and the relative positions held by the Exchange banks declined from their former peaks. But the British banks remained powerful. In 1970 Chartered alone held 11 per cent of Hong Kong's deposits, 13 per cent of Singapore's, and 19 per cent of Malaysia's. Its great Eastern rival, Hongkong Bank, also held significant market shares in all three countries, and it dominated banking in its Hong Kong base, where it and its subsidiaries accounted for around 36 per cent of total bank loans and advances in 1969.[4] British banks also held strong positions in the British-protected Gulf sheikhdoms. The former French protectorate of Lebanon was perhaps the only new, and non-Empire, country where British banks were able to build a substantial market share after the Second World War. The British Bank of the Middle East (BBME), the larger of the two British banks active in Lebanon, had opened a branch in Beirut in 1946. In 1965 it held 6 per cent of total deposits. The figure was almost certainly higher five years later, and it was probably the second largest bank in Lebanon in terms of deposits in these years.[5]

In some regions the British banks rapidly lost influence. The Exchange banks steadily lost ground in India. In December 1949, two years after Independence, the Exchange banks held 19 per cent of the deposits of the new state of India, nine-tenths of which were held by the six British overseas banks. Twenty years later, the foreign bank share of total deposits in India had fallen to 9 per cent. Five British banks held 68 per cent of this, or around 7 per cent of total Indian commercial bank deposits. In Latin America, Bolsa retained branches in twelve Central and South American countries, but Argentina was the only one where its overall importance in the banking system was significant, and even there its market share of total deposits had shrunk to less than 5 per cent by the 1960s.

British banks lost entire markets through nationalization. British banking was effectively eliminated in China after the 1949 Communist Revolution, although both the Hongkong Bank and Chartered retained branches in Shanghai through the 1950s and 1960s. The growth of Arab nationalism decimated British banking in some areas of the Middle East, beginning with Egypt, where foreign banks were nationalized in 1957. Syria, Iraq, and Libya followed this strategy in subsequent years. BBME had been the first bank in Kuwait, and was the only foreign bank ever allowed to operate in that country, but in 1971 its concession was not renewed, and the bank was obliged to divest from the country.[6] There were other nationalizations involving British banks in Burma and Tanzania, while in India in 1969 the Allahabad Bank, in which Chartered had held a 92 per cent interest for thirty-one years, was nationalized alongside other large domestic Indian banks.[7]

Throughout the period to 1970, British overseas banks had a near-zero market share in Europe (including the United Kingdom), North America, and Japan. The main British foothold in domestic banking in continental

---

[4] Y. C. Jao, 'Financing Hong Kong's Early Postwar Industrialization', in F. H. H. King (ed.), *Eastern Banking* (London: Athlone, 1983), 560.
[5] Geoffrey Jones, *Banking and Oil* (Cambridge: Cambridge University Press, 1987), 191, 204.     [6] Ibid., 147-9.
[7] Standard Chartered Bank, *A Story Brought up to Date* (London: Standard Chartered Bank, 1980), 4.

Europe, Ionian Bank's business in Greece, was eliminated in 1957 by the sale of that bank's Greek assets. Ionian and its wholly owned subsidiary the Banque Populaire had held between them around 10 per cent of the deposits of all the commercial banks in Greece.[8]

Each market had its individual characteristics, but two variables in particular exercised a fundamental influence on the performance of the British banks in their host economies. These were competition and receptivity. The British banks retained their market shares in economies where competitive forces were constrained. This was true of Australia, New Zealand, and South Africa before 1970. The banks there were highly regulated as part of macro-economic policies which aimed to control aggregate demand. Non-price competition was sometimes vigorous, but it was only pursued within well-defined parameters. One result was that in all three economies non-bank financial intermediaries grew in importance. In Australia, for example, the trading bank share of total financial assets declined from 32 per cent in 1948 to 22 per cent in 1970.[9] Within such regulated and oligopolistic market conditions, the British banks were at most only exposed to a slow loss of market share to local institutions. Moreover, in Australia and New Zealand the government prohibited new foreign bank entry, although American banks did open offices in South Africa at the end of the 1950s, and were able to develop a business servicing the subsidiaries of American corporations.[10]

Similarly, it was for the most part only in the late 1960s that the British banks in Black Africa and the Arab Gulf began to come under strong competitive threat. Table 9.3 gives the date of the first local and first American bank in selected African and Arab Gulf economies.

American banking activity in East, Central, and West Africa was minimal before the 1970s. Bank of America opened a branch in Nigeria in 1960 followed by Chase in 1961, but the Chase operation was sold to the Bank of West Africa in 1965. The Bank of America also had an interest in the locally registered Commercial Bank of Africa founded in Tanganyika in 1962. In the Gulf, American banks were never permitted to open in Kuwait and only secured a foothold in Oman in 1972, when the first local bank—the National Bank of Oman—opened, with the Bank of America having the management contact.[11] The first American bank branches opened in Dubai in 1964, and Bahrain seven years later, but it

---

[8] H. M. Morford to B. A. Sweet-Escott, 24 Sept. 1956, File on Various Takeover Negotiations, Box 1, Old Historical Records, Ionian Bank Archives, LSE. The Commercial Bank of Greece, however, had close connections with the British merchant bank, Hambros, and so to an extent a British 'influence' in Greek banking persisted.

[9] David Merrett, 'Two Hundred Years of Banking' (unpublished paper).

[10] Richard W. Hull, *American Enterprise in South Africa* (New York: New York University Press, 1990), 221.   [11] Geoffrey Jones, *Banking and Oil*, 169.

TABLE 9.3. *Dates of first local and American commercial banks in selected African and Arab Gulf countries, 1946–1970*

| Country | Date of first local bank | Date of first American bank |
|---------|--------------------------|------------------------------|
| Nigeria | 1924 | 1960 |
| Ghana | 1953 | — |
| Kenya | — | — |
| Uganda | 1965 | — |
| Kuwait | 1952 | — |
| Bahrain | 1957 | — |
| Dubai | 1963 | 1964 |
| Oman | — | — |

was not until the oil price rises in 1973 that American multinational banks arrived in the region in force.

Indigenous banks were largely a post-1950 phenomenon in both the Arab Gulf and Black Africa. In the Gulf sheikhdoms, the most successful local bank was the National Bank of Kuwait, which opened in 1952. By 1959 it had passed the BBME in size of deposits. However, the two banks worked closely together, and it was only with the arrival of three new Kuwaiti-owned banks after 1961 that a more competitive climate appeared, in which BBME faced a decline in its market share of deposits from 27 per cent to 10 per cent in eight years.[12] In West Africa, an indigenously owned bank in Nigeria had opened as early as 1924, but this institution went bankrupt six years later, and this set an unfortunate pattern of banking instability in the country. Over 100 indigenous banks were established in the 1940s and 1950s, practically all of which failed, leaving just a few medium-sized local banks. In neighbouring Ghana, the Ghana Commercial Bank originated in 1952, but it also suffered from severe management problems.[13] In Kenya and Uganda, indigenous banking was extremely limited before the end of the 1960s, when the British banks began to register their operations locally and take minority or majority local equity stakes. The most vigorous local bank in East Africa was the Uganda Commercial Bank, set up in 1965, on the basis of a credit institution founded in the previous decade, which began to make inroads into the business of British banks in the second half of the 1960s.

The market share of the British banks usually declined where local banking competition was very strong, or American banks were active.

[12] Ibid., 145.
[13] J. K. Onoh, *Money and Banking in Africa* (London: Longman, 1982), 95–7; Sir Julian Crossley and John Blandford, *The DCO Story* (London: Barclays Bank International, 1975), 246.

Both elements were at work in Latin America. A number of American banks operated extensive networks of branches and subsidiaries on the sub-continent by this period. In the 1960s Chase acquired interests in banks active in many Latin American countries. The Brazilian subsidiary Banco Lar proved particularly dynamic.[14] Bolsa faced intense competition almost everywhere it was established. Managers' reports even in the 1950s bemoaned the situation and, often, the unscrupulous tactics of some competitors. For example, Bolsa's manager in Montevideo, Uruguay, complained that 'in a city of a million inhabitants already saturated with 120 banking offices . . . the methods resorted to, to glean business, even if appearing to keep to the letter of inter-Bank agreements, often do not bear close scrutiny when the spirit of the agreement is involved'.[15] Bolsa in Venezuela found itself in an economy booming because of oil, but also one with many banks in operation, and little chance of reaching comfortable inter-bank agreements. Bolsa's situation in Venezuela was particularly weak because it had almost no oil company accounts in the 1950s, even though the economy was dominated by oil. All the American oil companies gave their business to Citibank, and—worse still—even some important British concerns chose the American bank instead of Bolsa.[16]

In South-east Asia, the British banks came under such competitive pressure only from the 1960s. In Malaysia two local banks were established in 1960, and by 1966 the branches of domestic banks outnumbered those of foreign banks. British bankers found the success of the new local banks 'astonishing', and complained that they 'employed . . . every dirty trick in the book'.[17] Singapore developed a locally owned banking sector in the inter-war years, and the powerful Overseas Chinese Banking Corporation dated from 1932. An American bank, the International Banking Corporation, had established a branch in Singapore in 1902, which duly passed to Citibank in 1915.[18] However, competition remained less than cut-throat before the mid-1960s. The British banks had long-standing ties with expatriate business houses and there were 'gentlemen's agreements' not to poach the customers of other banks. This calm atmosphere gave way to a more hectic one in the late 1960s, as Singapore's economy began to grow rapidly, and after the establishment of the Asian Dollar Market in 1968.

[14] John Donald Wilson, *The Chase* (Boston, Mass.: Harvard Business School Press, 1986), 163–6. [15] Bolsa Half-Yearly Results, June 1956, LB.
[16] Bolsa Half-Yearly Results, Dec. 1956, LB.
[17] C. Wardle to M. Turner, 29 Dec. 1961, MB 1325. Mercantile Bank Archives, HSBC; Chee Peng Lim, Phang Siew Nooi, and Margaret Boh, 'The History and Development of the Hongkong and Shanghai Banking Corporation in Peninsular Malaysia', in King (ed.), *Eastern Banking*, 375–6.
[18] Raj Brown, 'Chinese Business and Banking in Southeast Asia since 1870', in Geoffrey Jones (ed.), *Banks as Multinationals* (London: Routledge, 1990), 180; Harold van B. Cleveland and Thomas F. Huertas, *Citibank, 1812–1970* (Cambridge, Mass.: Harvard University Press, 1985), 81, 125.

By 1970 there were 37 commercial banks with branches in Singapore, of which 26 were foreign.[19] The British banks found their privileged position eroded as new competitors entered the market offering the same, or improved, banking products.

Hong Kong and the Lebanon were two markets where British banks sustained their positions against really strong competitive onslaughts, but in both markets special conditions applied. By 1955 there were 91 licensed banks with 94 branches in Hong Kong, and by 1970 there were 73 banks with 399 branches. However, the Hongkong Bank, as the 'local bank', was in an immensely strong position, functioning as the British colony's *de facto* central bank, and issuing 90 per cent of the banknotes.[20] In Lebanon, BBME faced nearly 90 foreign and local banks by 1965, but the British bank was again favoured by special circumstances. Local banks had a reputation for instability, which was fully justified when the largest bank—Intra Bank—collapsed in 1966, while the American banks initially made poor lending decisions as they travelled up the learning-curve of Middle Eastern banking.[21]

The degree of receptivity towards British banks was a second key determinant of their performance in different markets. There were wide variations between countries in their degree of receptivity, but the general trend in the 1950s and 1960s was for the introduction of restrictions on foreign banks. Table 9.4 gives a rough estimate of the extent of receptivity in selected countries towards British banks around 1970, excluding countries which had nationalized foreign banks.

There was a close correlation between high market share and high receptivity towards British banks. In Australia and New Zealand the long-established British trading banks were excluded from the general prohibition of foreign banks. They were effectively regarded as national institutions. Lebanon and Hong Kong were both free market entrepôts where there were no restrictions on foreign institutions. The Arab Gulf states, only emerging into full independence in the early 1970s, did not introduce restrictions on foreign banks until later in that decade.

Such havens, where British banks could compete on equal terms with local banks, became progressively rarer in the post-war world, and especially in the 1960s. During this era governments tightened controls over their banking systems, introducing new liquidity ratios and sometimes more direct controls over lending. Many of these controls applied to all banks, regardless of their nationality, but even these sometimes had a specially adverse effect on the British banks. After the Second World War,

[19] Hafiz Mirza, *Multinationals and the Growth of the Singapore Economy* (London: Croom Helm, 1986), 127.
[20] F. H. H. King, *A History of the Hongkong and Shanghai Banking Corporation*, iv (Cambridge: Cambridge University Press, 1991), 334–69, 621–5.
[21] Geoffrey Jones, *Banking and Oil*, 196–8, 199–204.

TABLE 9.4. *Receptivity towards British multinational banks in selected countries, c.1971*

| High[a] | Medium[b] | Low[c] |
|---|---|---|
| Australia | India | Uganda |
| New Zealand | Pakistan | Nigeria |
| South Africa | Sri Lanka | Ghana |
| Hong Kong | Malaysia | Iran |
| Dubai | Singapore | |
| Bahrain | Thailand | |
| Oman | Japan | |
| Lebanon | Saudi Arabia | |
| | Argentina | |

[a] High = No discriminatory legislation against existing British banks.
[b] Medium = Discriminatory legislation against British banks, such as a limit on branch expansion.
[c] Low = British banks only permitted to operate in joint ventures with local interests, or with local equity participation.

for example, governments began to introduce regulatory requirements which related the deposits and loans of banks to some ratio of the capital held by the bank within the country. The British banks had traditionally been reluctant to lock up their capital in such a fashion, preferring to keep it available in London, so this legislation had a painful impact on their business. By the end of the 1940s such regulations were widespread in Latin America. In Uruguay deposits could not exceed eight times the level of capital and reserves. Capital and reserves had to total a minimum of 15 per cent of deposits in Colombia, while in Venezuela deposits were limited to six times the level of capital and reserves, unless the excess was covered by a 40 per cent cash reserve.[22]

During the 1950s and 1960s such regulations spread from Latin America to Asia and Africa. There were also a growing number of attempts to force banks to assist economic development. In India, for example, the government introduced a policy of 'social control' over all banks. They were expected to devote a certain percentage of their resources to lending to priority sectors, such as agriculture and small-scale industry. 'The Banks are now being told just where and how they should place their surplus funds,' a branch manager of Chartered Bank reported to London in 1969, 'and to all intents and purposes we might consider ourselves to be nationalised.'[23]

[22] Bolsa Memorandum on Capital Resources on Branches Books: Restrictions on Deposits and Loans, June 1949, C48/156, B. of E.
[23] Chartered (Calcutta) to Head Office, 8 June 1969, File India: Merchant Banking, SC.

Some regulations were specifically targeted on foreign banks. Over time governments began to limit the opening of new branches. By the mid-1950s, for example, the Exchange banks in the old Indian Empire were being discouraged or prevented from opening further branches.[24] Initially the restrictions were often informal rather than formal. In 1956 Mercantile Bank was informed during a meeting between the governor of the Reserve Bank in Pakistan and one of its managers that the government intended 'to confine the operations of the Exchange Banks to the ports unless they were already established in the interior of West or East Pakistan'.[25] Such branching restrictions were an important factor in the decision of Lloyds to sell its South Asian branches in 1960.[26] By the late 1960s it was all but impossible for a foreign bank to open a new branch in India. After the nationalization of locally owned banks in India in 1969, there was a huge expansion of bank branches into the Indian countryside, but foreign banks were not permitted to participate in this development.

Branching restrictions on foreign banks spread like an epidemic. From 1962 foreign banks in Thailand were only permitted to establish themselves in Bangkok, and then only with a single office. After 1965 foreign banks were not allowed to open further branches in Malaysia.[27] By 1968 the Singapore authorities were preventing the opening of new branches by foreign banks, although such banks were permitted to open branches to operate in the new offshore market which began in that year. By the end of the decade countries as diverse as Saudi Arabia and Argentina had greatly restricted or even prohibited further branch expansion by foreign banks.[28] In 1967 even *laissez-faire* Hong Kong introduced restrictions on branching, as the result of a severe banking crisis two years previously. Prior approval from the colony's Banking Commissioner had to be obtained for opening branches, and an annual licence fee paid for each branch. This legislation, however, favoured the two large British banks in the colony, and its main impact was to check the branching of small banks. Some governments not only restricted new branches, but even limited the deposit-raising capacities of existing ones. In 1961 the government of Sri Lanka (Ceylon) introduced legislation under which foreign banks could not accept new deposits or an increase in present deposits from Sri Lankan

---

[24] For the case of India, R. N. Drake to Sir Cyril Jones, 26 Jan. 1954, MB Hist. 1000:12, HSBC.     [25] C. F. Pow to Mercantile Bank Karachi, 1956, MB Hist. 1794, HSBC.
[26] J. R. Winton, *Lloyds Bank, 1918–1969* (Oxford: Oxford University Press, 1982), 134–6.
[27] Thiravet Pramuanratkarn, 'The Hongkong Bank in Thailand: A Case of a Pioneering Bank', 430, and Chee Peng Lim et al., 'The History and Development of the Hongkong and Shanghai Banking Corporation in Peninsular Malaysia', 375, both in King (ed.), *Eastern Banking*.
[28] Geoffrey Jones, *Banking and Oil*, 179–80; Report of the Directors to AGM of Bolsa, 31 Dec. 1969.

nationals or companies, the latter defined as those with at least one Sri Lankan director. As a result between 1963 and 1968 the percentage of deposits held by British banks in that country declined from 32 per cent to 23 per cent.[29]

Anti-foreign bank restrictions were sometimes accompanied by positive discrimination in favour of local institutions. Government accounts were often placed with local banks. Within five years of Ghana's independence in 1957, for example, the accounts of government and other public corporations had been moved from the British banks to the state-owned Ghana Commercial Bank.[30] It was a similar story in Malaysia in the 1960s, when the fast growth of local banks was underpinned by a shift of many public accounts to them away from the British banks. Even the British banks in Australia suffered, to some extent, from this phenomenon. Public bodies, like the Wheat Marketing Board, gave their business to the state-owned Commonwealth Bank in the 1950s and 1960s, rather than to the commercial trading banks, either British- or Australian-owned.[31]

Some governments took their opposition to foreign banks further by insisting they could only operate in their countries if they took local partners. By the late 1960s several African countries had insisted on such 'localization' (see Chapter 8) and legislation of this kind was also in place in various other countries, such as Iran.[32]

By 1970 British banks, therefore, had retained substantial market shares in a range of economies where they had long been established, but Lebanon provided the only example of British banks achieving substantial penetration of a new market. British banks held their market shares best when competitive forces were constrained, and where there was no discrimination against foreign banks. This was unsurprising, but it also cast doubt over the long-term viability of the kind of multinational retail banking being performed by the British banks for, in country after country, receptivity towards foreign institutions appeared to be on the wane, and competition on the increase.

## 9.2. Banking in the Southern Hemisphere

The economic environment in the Southern Hemisphere settler economies was a considerable improvement on the inter-war years, but their comparatively slow growth and small size, and the extensive range of regulatory controls, limited profitable opportunities and constrained product

---

[29] King, *The History of the Hongkong and Shanghai Banking Corporation*, iv, 461–2.
[30] Richard Fry, *Bankers in West Africa* (London: Hutchinson Benham, 1976), 245.
[31] Information from David Merrett.
[32] Geoffrey Jones, *Banking and Oil*, 51, 249–50; Standard Chartered Bank, *A Story Brought up to Date*, 7.

innovation. Price competition was rare, and struggles for market share mainly took place by the opening of new branches, advertising, and similar strategies.

In Australia, the trading banks operated under the handicap of central bank controls over interest rates and lending levels, which depressed rates of return and dampened any desire to innovate. Controls over asset ratios made banks deploy a considerable proportion of their funds in low-yielding assets. Tight controls were in operation over exchange rates and capital movements. Through the 1950s the trading banks also had to face active competition from the central bank's trading arm, which until 1953 was not subject to all the restrictions that were imposed upon them. This anomalous situation was not fully resolved until 1960, when the central-banking functions of the Commonwealth Bank were transferred to a new institution, the Reserve Bank of Australia.[33] In New Zealand, there were also tight controls over interest rates and lending, and a system of variable reserve ratios, in operation between 1952 and 1969, was at the centre of monetary policy.[34]

Within this restrictive context, the British banks continued to be further handicapped by the division of decision-making between boards in London and general management in Australia and New Zealand. The board of ANZ, for example, continued to give considerable weight to the London business of the bank, even at the cost of constraining domestic business in Australia and New Zealand. The British directors sought to retain a large share of the bank's resources in London, and in general were far more concerned about immediate profits than considerations of market share. This caused considerable difficulties when, from 1952, the Commonwealth government imposed liquidity requirements on banks active in Australia, which in effect stipulated that only liquid assets and government securities held within the country would be counted. ANZ had more than half of its liquid assets and government securities held outside Australia when the new convention began, and did not fully meet the liquidity requirements until 1958. Ultimately the requirement was met in part by reducing the bank's domestic lending, which set ANZ back in its attempt to regain market share after the merger, and in the process caused tensions between the board and the Melbourne-based executive.[35]

The appointment of a particularly strong general manager at ANZ in 1961 was followed by a shift in authority from London to Melbourne, and a more expansionist policy began to be pursued by the bank. In his six years as general manager 127 new branches were opened, many in urban centres of New South Wales where the constituent banks of ANZ had

---

[33] Merrett, *ANZ Bank*, 130–3.
[34] G. R. Hawke, *Between Governments and Banks* (Wellington: Shearer, 1973), chs. 8 and 9.
[35] Merrett, *ANZ Bank*, 110–28.

always been under-represented. There was also a new emphasis on advertising, with a drive to create a marketing image of ANZ as 'Australia's Most Progressive Bank'.[36]

Differences of opinion, and of priority, between London and Melbourne also had their impact on the business strategy of ANZ's smaller British competitor, the E, S & A. In the first decade after the war, the bank's general manager—in the tradition of the E, S & A—had considerable power *vis-à-vis* the board in internal decision-making. He pursued an aggressive lending policy and was responsible in 1953 for a bold diversification into hire purchase, but he disliked government regulation of banking and ignored the liquidity requirements of the central bank, plunging E, S & A into a highly illiquid condition by the time of his retirement in 1955. Subsequently, the board assumed greater control over decisions and, as at ANZ, generally opted for improving profits rather than market share. An imaginative scheme in 1960 to provide resources for expansion by introducing some form of gearing in E, S & A's balance sheet was ultimately rejected by the board, uncertain of, and suspicious about, the Australian government's fiscal and monetary policies.[37]

Despite both the regulatory environment and organizational problems, there was product innovation by the British banks in Australia in the 1950s and 1960s, although they were more usually cast in the role of followers than leaders. The most striking entrepreneurial move was E, S & A's diversification into selling hire purchase in the early 1950s, after the general manager had observed the involvement of large American banks in this activity during a visit to the United States. There was an Australian precedent because the Commonwealth Bank had started writing hire purchase business in 1945, but this was a pioneering move for a trading bank. The enterprise proved successful, and in 1955 it was passed to a new wholly owned subsidiary, Esanda. By the 1960s, Esanda was making a substantial contribution to profits, and was in many ways the jewel in the crown of the business. ANZ was much slower into this area. In 1954 an invitation to take an equity stake in one of Australia's largest hire purchase companies was turned down. There were, again, differences of opinion between Melbourne and London over the appropriate mode of entry into the business. Eventually, it was only an announcement in 1957 by the Bank of New South Wales that it was taking a substantial shareholding in a hire purchase company that ended ANZ's indecision, and it acquired 14 per cent of the shares of the Industrial Acceptance Holdings, which were retained until the merger with E, S & A in 1970.[38]

[36] Ibid., 136–8, 166–71, 186.

[37] Ibid., 215–45; R. C. White, *Australian Banking and Monetary Statistics, 1945–1970*, Reserve Bank of Australia, Occasional Paper No. 4B, Sydney, 1973, table 41.

[38] Merrett, *ANZ Bank*, 143–7, 220–2, 231–2, 239, 271.

The 1950s also saw ANZ diversify into savings bank business. From the 1890s deposits in savings banks had risen faster than those in trading banks, partly because deposits were guaranteed by states. Establishing a savings bank was one means whereby the trading banks could, indirectly, secure deposits, but there appeared to be serious regulatory obstacles to such a course after the Second World War. In 1955, however, the Bank of New South Wales launched itself in this direction by forming a wholly owned savings bank subsidiary, whose deposits were guaranteed by itself so as to place it on a more equal footing with existing savings banks. ANZ responded soon after by forming a wholly owned (and London-registered) subsidiary, the Australia and New Zealand Savings Bank, which began business in January 1956 and soon attracted substantial deposits. Such savings bank subsidiaries were particularly useful to their parents because they operated through the trading banks' own branches. E, S & A did not emulate this successful strategy until 1961.[39] Nevertheless, by the time of the 1970 merger between ANZ and E, S & A, the two banks were more deeply involved in the domestic Australian economy than ever.

The regulatory environment in South Africa gave that country's banking market considerable resemblance to Australia in the 1950s and 1960s. The two British banks dominated the market, and they pursued the familiar mix of retail and commercial business within the parameters permitted by official monetary policy, which included banking ratios and exchange controls. The commercial banks in general steadily lost market share to non-bank financial intermediaries, and, as in Australasia, blamed regulatory controls for their lack of competitiveness. More critical observers, however, suggested that the merchant banks and building societies which took their business displayed more energy and entrepreneurship as they responded to changing circumstances.[40]

Yet the South African market was less static than that of Australia and New Zealand. Standard Bank, for example, saw its proportion of total advances in South Africa fall from 45 per cent in 1949 to 38 per cent ten years later. The main gainer was Volkskas, an Afrikaner-owned and pro-government bank, to which accounts of many state agencies and of Afrikaner businesses were transferred. In the mid-1960s Standard's management even toyed with the idea of an exchange of shares with Volkskas to gain access to Afrikaner business, but the scheme was never pursued.[41] Barclays' business was less vulnerable to competition because it had the accounts

---

[39] Ibid., 139–43, 241–2.

[40] Chairman's Statement, SBIC Ltd., Annual Report, 1973, SC; Munro, 'Monetary Policy, Commercial Banking and the Political Imperative', 122.

[41] Report on Business in the Union, 21 Oct. 1959, Business in the Union File; Alwyn Davies to Cyril Hawker, 5 Aug. 1965, South Africa Box, SC; Stuart Jones, Introduction, in Stuart Jones (ed.), *Banking and Business in South Africa*, 22.

of much of South Africa's mining business, especially the Anglo-American Corporation, and also of the principal public utility companies. As a result it retained its market share—at around 41 per cent of advances—through the 1950s. All the banks, however, had to compete more vigorously for deposits and, as in many other countries from the 1950s, there was a strong increase in the proportion of deposits bearing interest, the ratio of time to demand deposits in the Union rising from 30 per cent in 1954 to 73 per cent by 1962.

Government policy was less hostile to product innovation in South Africa than in Australia, and in some instances prompted it. Standard Bank, for example, had established a savings bank department as early as 1917.[42] After the Second World War the authorities exercised pressure on the banks to move away from orthodox British-style commercial banking. In 1949 the Reserve Bank obliged the banks and other financial institutions to contribute to the capital of a new institution, the National Finance Corporation of South Africa, which was designed to establish a short-term money market in the country.[43] Eleven years later the Reserve Bank expressed a preference for American-style term loans over the traditional overdraft system, which stimulated the banks to consider a move in the direction, although failure to agree among themselves led to a delay in the introduction of such lending.[44]

As the diversification of the South African economy proceeded in the 1960s—by 1963 manufacturing contributed as much to the national income as mining and agriculture together—the British banks diversified their product range. Competition from other financial institutions, and the sharp reduction in non-interest-bearing deposits, acted as spurs.[45] In the early 1960s Standard began to give consideration to providing facilities for medium- and long-term finance in South Africa.[46] During the late 1950s aggressive discount houses, especially Union Acceptances, which had been promoted by the Anglo-American Corporation and thus had a close association with Barclays, had begun taking deposits directly from the public and lending to the customers of the banks. This prompted Standard Bank to enter merchant banking in South Africa. In 1963 it became one of the principal sponsors alongside various insurance and mining groups of a new merchant bank, City Merchant Bank. There were problems with the mixed ownership of this bank, and in 1969 it was merged into a larger

[42] J. A. Henry, *The First Hundred Years of the Standard Bank* (London: Oxford University Press, 1963), 172.

[43] Ibid., 288; Crossley and Blandford, *The DCO Story*, 167; Sir Julian Crossley Diaries, 26 and 31 Oct. 1949, 38/209, BBA.

[44] General Manager's Conference, 1960 and 1962, in General Managers' Conferences, SC.

[45] Munro, 'Monetary Policy, Commercial Banking and the Political Imperative', 121–4.

[46] General Manager's Conference, 1962, in General Managers' Conferences, SC.

group, called Central Acceptances or Sentak, whose shareholders included government agencies as well as Volkskas.

Another route into merchant banking was the wholly owned Standard Bank Development Corporation of South Africa (or Devco) launched as a source of medium-term finance in 1964. Barclays reacted very strongly to Devco's formation, regarding it as a means of bypassing the provisions of the various banking arrangements in existence in order to gain market share of deposits, and for a time at least abandoned the rates agreements so far as these concerned deposits. In 1972 Devco became Standard Merchant Bank, and in the same year Standard withdrew from Sentak. Barclays, meanwhile, had entered merchant banking through a medium-term finance subsidiary launched in 1967.

In the second half of the 1960s product diversification intensified. In 1966 Standard acquired a controlling interest in the South African subsidiary of Diners Club, and so became the first bank to enter the charge card business. Three years later Barclays introduced its credit card—Barclaycard—into South Africa. In 1968 Standard acquired entire control of a large hire purchase company, the National Industrial Credit Corporation, in which it had had a part-ownership since 1963.

By the early 1970s both Standard and. Barclays in South Africa were diversified financial services operations, including commercial and merchant banking, hire purchase, factoring, and leasing. They had an uncomfortable relationship with the government and with the Afrikaner business community, but they remained the most important banks in the country. They still held the largest share of commercial bank deposits, and conducted much of South Africa's international banking business, not only with Britain—which remained the country's largest trading partner and foreign investor—but also with the United States, whose trade with and investment in South Africa grew rapidly in the 1960s and early 1970s. An analysis of the banking relationships of 300 American companies listed as doing business with South Africa in 1973 revealed that Standard had a connection with 61.5 per cent of them, Barclays with 37.2 per cent, and Citibank only 19.3 per cent.[47]

While South Africa shared many of the characteristics of the other Southern Hemisphere settler economies, there was one enormous social difference—the descendants of the European settlers formed only a minority of the total population. Until the 1950s the commercial banking sector had very little contact with the indigenous Africans, the majority of South Africa's population. However, the benefits of the economic growth of that decade, although distributed very unfairly, did spread to sufficient Africans to bring them to the attention of the banks as potential customers.

[47] Hull, *American Enterprise in South Africa*, ch. 6; Memorandum on the Banking Business of American Companies in South Africa, Oct. 1973, South Africa Box, SC.

While Africans came to be regarded as a useful source of savings deposits, it was considered that such deposit business had to be constrained. 'The African as a current account customer in possession of a cheque book', Standard Bank's management noted in 1958, 'is still, with comparatively few exceptions, prone to abuse the privilege,' and Africans were not considered seriously as potential borrowers.[48]

These attitudes changed rapidly soon after. At Standard Bank, the volume of African savings bank business increased from 27,805 accounts with resources of £1.2 million to 48,968 accounts with resources of £1.8 million in the space of the two years after March 1958. Standard reported a greater awareness by its managers 'of the importance attached to African business', though the political structure of the apartheid system hindered the bank in pursuing this business. Official restrictions on the ownership by Africans of fixed property in urban areas particularly handicapped their access to banking accommodation.[49] By 1962 Standard Bank's senior management was convinced that in the long term economic realities would doom apartheid and lead to 'a gradual integration of the two races'. The bank welcomed this prospect, and the potential African business that it could provide, but was content to watch the flow of history take its inevitable course, rather than assume the role of pioneer, or perhaps martyr:

Friction and loss of business would be experienced if we were to attempt to pioneer the path towards greater social and political rights for the Bantu. If, however, we are prepared to learn our lessons from the North and to move forward in step with contemporary public thinking there is no reason why the Bank's business should do otherwise than benefit from the growth of African nationalism.[50]

Unfortunately for South Africa's Black population, the path towards greater social and political rights was to prove longer and more tortuous than Standard's management thought in 1962.

In Argentina, the decade after the end of the Second World War was a particularly difficult one for Bolsa. Heavy state intervention in the economy and the banking sector created a hostile environment. In 1946 the Perón dictatorship nationalized the Banco Central, which came under the direct control of the government, and introduced an onerous form of control over bank credit known as the 'nationalization of deposits', which was in effect a 100 per cent cash reserve ratio applied to the entire banking system. The Banco Central assumed detailed control over the quantity and nature of bank credit, while the external sector of the economy was isolated by means of rigid trade and exchange controls. This regime remained in place until 1958.

[48] General Manager's Conference, 1958, in General Managers' Conferences, SC.
[49] General Manager's Conference, 1960, in General Managers' Conferences, SC.
[50] General Manager's Conference, 1962, in General Managers' Conferences, SC.

TABLE 9.5. *Percentage share of branches, deposits, and lending in Argentina, 1945, 1957, 1965 (%)*

| Institution | Offices | | | Deposits | | | Loans | | |
|---|---|---|---|---|---|---|---|---|---|
| | 1945 | 1957 | 1965 | 1945 | 1957 | 1965 | 1945 | 1957 | 1965 |
| Official Banks | 72 | 75 | 65 | 57 | 69 | 55 | 55 | 82 | 68 |
| Private Banks | 28 | 25 | 35 | 43 | 31 | 45 | 45 | 18 | 32 |
| Foreign | 5 | 4 | 5 | 17 | 10 | 15 | 13 | 6 | 9 |
| Argentine | 23 | 21 | 30 | 26 | 21 | 30 | 32 | 12 | 23 |

*Source*: Julio Gonzalez del Solar, 'The Argentine Banking System', *Bolsa Quarterly Review*, 6(4) (Nov. 1966).

Bolsa's management in Argentina had virtually no freedom of man-œuvre within such a context, and watched events as almost hapless victims. The nationalization of the British-owned railway system in 1948 removed an important source of deposits. Although Britain remained a major pur-chaser of Argentinian beef, dwindling British exports to the country dimin-ished the opportunities for trade finance and exchange operations. Profits could only be remitted to an extent determined as a percentage of capital and resources employed in the country, which trapped much of Bolsa's profit within Argentina.[51]

Table 9.5 shows the impact of the regulatory regime established in 1946. The Argentine banking system was divided into official banks, in-cluding national, provincial, and municipal banks, and private banks, which comprised foreign and locally owned institutions. Between 1945 and 1957 there was a shift of market share of deposits and loans to the official banks, with the foreign-owned private banks experiencing a particular decline. The fall of Perón was followed in 1957 by reforms which aban-doned most aspects of the regime put in place in 1945, including the 'nationalization of deposits'. As a result, the foreign banks were able to recover some market share, though more in deposits than loans. Bolsa remained, in the mid-1960s, the leading foreign bank out of a total of 14. In December 1965 it accounted for 27 per cent of total foreign bank deposits, 9 per cent of total private bank deposits, and 4 per cent of total Argentine bank deposits. However, the bank's freedom to innovate remained strictly circumscribed by the Banco Central, which closely dictated the lending policies which it expected all banks to follow.[52]

[51] Bolsa Board Minutes, 29 July 1952, 3 Mar. 1953, 17 July 1956, LB.
[52] Julio Gonzalez del Solar, 'The Argentine Banking System', *Bolsa Quarterly Review*, 6(4) (Nov. 1966).

Within these official confines, during the 1960s Bolsa's business developed in quite similar ways to those seen in Australia and South Africa. There was a drive to attract deposits, through renewing and expanding the branch network, which grew from 22 in 1955 to 31 in 1971. During the first half of the decade a new central office was built in Buenos Aires, branches were opened in suburbs likely to yield deposits, and in 1967 there was a new innovation when a branch was opened inside a new department store in Buenos Aires.[53] Bolsa diversified the financial services it offered in Argentina. In 1961 a new locally registered finance company was launched. This offered investment management and advisory services, the placing of shares on the local stock exchange, and medium-term finance. It also entered the field of hire purchase. In 1965, Bolsa established a wholly owned insurance company, and four years later the bank launched a credit card in Argentina.

The diversification away from commercial banking into other financial services was perhaps the most noteworthy theme in the history of the British banks in the Southern Hemisphere settler economies after the Second World War, especially in the 1960s when the pace of financial innovation intensified. Hire purchase, insurance, and merchant banking were the main areas of diversification. At the same time, the 1960s saw a new concern to raise deposits, as competition for funds from non-bank financial intermediaries and from local banks intensified. Everywhere regulatory and exchange controls set the parameters of bank strategies. In addition, the British banks experienced mild official discrimination in South Africa, and overt discrimination in Perónist Argentina. Meanwhile, Australia offered the clearest evidence of the continuing problems faced by banks with London head offices which were extensively involved in domestic banking.

## 9.3. *Continuity and Change in the Developing World*

Criticism of the business strategies of the British multinational banks in Asia and Africa pre-dated the Second World War but the criticisms intensified in the 1950s and 1960s. The British banks were variously accused of being excessively preoccupied with providing short-term credit for trade finance and exchange operations; of lending to expatriates in preference to locals; of making borrowing expensive and difficult in some countries by the use of intermediaries; of collecting deposits in capital-short economies and investing them in London; and of pursuing racist employment practices.

There was validity in each of these criticisms, although none could be accepted entirely even before the Second World War. Moreover, there was

[53] Bolsa Chairman's Annual Report to Shareholders, 31 Dec. 1967.

often a clear banking rationality behind policies which looked objectionable to outsiders. For example, while even wartime British Colonial Office advisers grew restive at the sight of British banks collecting deposits in poor countries and investing them in London,[54] bankers could claim that this strategy was necessary because there were insufficient safe outlets for lending. Such a claim could still be criticized on the grounds that the definition of 'safe' was too restrictive, however. In British West Africa, it was striking that a trading company like the United Africa Company extended more credit than the British-owned banks in the immediate post-war period, yet such conservatism had an explanation, if not a fully convincing one. West Africa, like most of the developing world, lacked money market assets and securities markets in which the banks could invest part of their funds in order to preserve their liquidity.[55]

The critique of British banks in the developing world drew strength from the fact that their business strategies appeared slow to adapt to new political and economic realities in the 1950s and 1960s. The kind of business undertaken and the banking techniques used in these decades showed strong continuities with earlier periods. Financing the movement of commodities remained the core business of the British banks in Africa and Asia, although the details of the finance were sometimes altered by new institutional arrangements. In West Africa, for example, the financing of produce remained the major concern of the British banks in the 1950s and 1960s. However, the institutional structure of this business was changed by the creation of produce marketing boards in the late 1940s, which developed as sole produce-buyers, and by the consequent withdrawal of the large trading companies such as the United Africa Company from their former role as quasi-banks in much of the West African interior.[56] The British banks provided substantial credit facilities for the West African marketing boards in the 1950s.[57]

Lists of the most important customers of the British banks in West Africa in the 1950s continued to read like a roll-call of British and American multinational enterprise active in the region. Most of the largest facilities were granted to British and American oil companies, such as the local subsidiaries of Esso, Mobil, and Shell; the British chocolate companies such as Cadbury which secured most of their cocoa from the region; British contractors such as Costain and Taylor Woodrow; and other large multinationals, such as Singer Sewing Machines. Yet, as ever, the British

[54] Minutes by W. A. Lewis, 1 June and 16 Aug. 1944, and G. P. Lamb, 5 June 1944, C0852/554/1, PRO.

[55] W. T. Newlyn, *Money in an African Context* (Nairobi: Oxford University Press, 1967), 42–6. [56] Fry, *Bankers in West Africa*, 184–6.

[57] Fry's Digest of BBWA Board Minutes, 18 Dec. 1952, 19 Nov. 1953, 21 Mar. 1957, 18 Dec. 1958, 10 Nov. 1960, BAC S/90, SC.

banks were sufficiently flexible to take advantage of more entrepreneurial activities. In 1949 the British Bank of West Africa (BBWA) opened an up-country branch at Bo, in Sierre Leone. The timing was fortuitous for in 1952 Bo became the centre of a new diamond-producing area, initially developed illegally by Africans digging in areas nominally reserved to an international mining company. By the 1960s diamonds had become Sierra Leone's most important export commodity. BBWA's branch at Bo prospered as a result of the diamond boom. At first the bank bought diamonds from the illicit African diggers, but over time focused on financing the dealers. In 1956, when the government legalized both the digging and exporting of diamonds, both BBWA and Barclays got export licences, although three years later diamond-exporting was concentrated in an official agency, managed by the South African mining company de Beers.[58]

In East Africa in the 1950s and early 1960s the British banks were heavily focused on the finance of trade in the region's agricultural and pastoral products. In 1962 around 25 per cent of Standard Bank's advances in East Africa were to agricultural interests, produce-brokers, and agricultural exporters. No finance was offered to the African smallholders, who, for example, largely cultivated the East African cotton crop. Instead the banks financed the subsequent processing and export stages, usually in the hands of Asians. Another quarter of Standard's advances was directed to industries and manufacturers, but much of this was to grain-millers, sugar-refiners, meat- and fruit-carriers, and other businessmen with close links to the agricultural sector. Another large category of loans, to wholesalers and retailers, also had agricultural connections.[59]

The emphasis on providing trade finance was naturally accompanied by a continued preference for short-term lending on the part of the British overseas banks. The short-term, self-liquidating credit remained the ideal; a long-term 'lock-up' of funds remained the dread. Of Standard Bank's total advances of £179 million at 31 March 1960, only 5.3 per cent was in the form of commitments for periods in excess of three years, and it is reasonable to assume that this figure is a fair proxy for the average British overseas bank in the developing world around that date.[60] For example, a list of Mercantile Bank's medium-term obligations in India and Pakistan in 1961 showed only 7 enterprises (including industrial firms, steamship companies, cotton mills, and a tea-planter) with modest-sized loans of durations from three to eight and a half years, while another 37 enterprises had overdrafts which were renewed annually, but were formally repayable on demand.[61]

[58] Fry, *Bankers in West Africa*, 208–12.
[59] Notes on Talk for the Training School, East Africa and Agencies Department, Nov. 1962, SC.
[60] General Manager's Conference, 1960, in General Managers' Conferences, SC.
[61] C. Wardle to M. Turner, 20 Apr. 1961, MB Hist. 1325, HSBC.

In some regions the desire for short-term lending, and caution about the kind of security taken, was increased by worries about political risk. After the Second World War most Eastern Exchange banks, for example, instituted tight limits over lending in South-east Asia in particular, fearing that the region might fall to the communists. The communist-led insurgency in Malaya in the 1950s reinforced such a fear. London head offices particularly disliked taking property as a prime security in countries considered under threat, and instead facilities were often made available on the basis of a letter of hypothecation over stocks as the prime security and property as collateral. When advances were made against property, an individual manager's discretion was normally limited to the amount he could advance on a clean basis. Such policies remained the norm among the Eastern Exchange banks at least until the 1970s.

The ethnic bias in the lending of the British banks continued into the 1950s. In East Africa, during the 1950s, Standard and other banks did attempt to make some loans to Africans, although somewhat reluctantly, and against an underlying assumption 'that the African has not yet achieved a full sense of monetary and commercial responsibility'.[62] The British banks made their lending decisions on commercial criteria, but their assessments of risk and creditworthiness were based on assumptions about ethnicity. Loans were often made to African farmers on the basis of a recommendation by the colonial District Commissioner, or, later, on the advice of retired expatriate farmers, and the numbers of such loans were few.[63]

In Asia, too, the British overseas banks, at least initially, retained pre-war attitudes on lending to 'locals'. In post-Independence Sri Lanka, the British banks at first clung to the guarantee shroff system, despite its unpopularity. The Exchange banks had to be subjected to forcible official pressure to effect a policy change. For example, at a meeting with representatives of all the Exchange banks in 1954, the governor of the Central Bank of Ceylon was forced to request explicitly that 'Ceylonese business must be encouraged,' and that the use of shroffs 'should cease'.[64] Even after such a request, the system lingered for a year or so.[65]

Traditional ideas on race and ethnic matters persisted within the British banks. This was not surprising in banks whose management systems rested on socialization strategies which were built around the British public school ideal. Every aspect of bank policy, from lending to personnel, was influenced

[62] General Manager's Conference, 1958, in General Managers' Conferences, SC.
[63] R. E. Williams to D. J. M. Frazer, 18 Jan. 1965, Development Finance File, Kenya Cabinet, SC.
[64] Meeting at Chartered Bank between Representatives of the British Banks with Branches in Ceylon and N. U. Jayawardena, Governor, Central Bank of Ceylon, 24 Mar. 1954, MB Hist. 610, HSBC; H. L. D. Selvaratnam, 'The Guarantee Shroffs, the Chettiars, and the Hongkong Bank in Ceylon', in King (ed.), *Eastern Banking*, 409–20.
[65] Inward letter to R. N. Drake, Sept. 1955, MB Hist. 1000:7, HSBC.

by racial considerations. There remained, for example, strong opposition in all banks well into the 1960s to marriages between their British staff and women of Asian or African origins. In 1961 Mercantile's chief manager, for example, was informed of yet another case of an officer getting 'himself involved with a Chinese girl clerk in his office', and his reaction was indicative of prevailing opinion:

I am getting utterly sick and tired of these incidents as they are now occurring far too frequently. We have recently had to get rid of a man in Ceylon, someone else is a nuisance in Hong Kong... I suppose the reason is that under modern conditions our men come more easily into contact with these attractive young Asian women... It seems to me that these associations cannot possibly be avoided. What must be prevented at all costs is them becoming too serious. I feel that the only possible thing we can do is for all Managers, including myself, to take every opportunity to explain in forceful language the effect which a mixed marriage can have on the folks at home, a man's career in the Bank, and above all, his social conditions. Perhaps more important still is that individuals should be warned, before they get into trouble, that if they do get mixed up with women of other races they may have to find other employment.[66]

In 1962 Mercantile's Management received a 'policy indication' from their parent to prevent mixed marriages, but the Hongkong Bank was not prepared 'to put this into print as exceptional cases may arise where... it might be extremely embarrassing to the Bank'.[67]

Yet for all the continuities in attitudes and policies, the business strategies of the British multinational banks in Africa and Asia continued to evolve, as they had done before the Second World War. The banks may have sought to stick to their 'knitting', but fundamental political and economic changes were altering the whole pattern of their host economies, and they had to respond. Host government pressure to assist economic development, competition from indigenous and American banks, and rivalry among the British banks themselves sometimes provided powerful incentives to change or modify traditional policies.

The complex rates agreements which British banks had erected in each region had never entirely stifled all price or non-price competition. From the 1950s the advent of new competitors from local and American banks made collusive agreements even harder to enforce, exposing the British banks to more open competition from sources which often did not respect the canons of orthodox British banking.

Colonial Africa remained a haven for British banks in this respect until the 1960s, and in each geographical area there was a complex system of rates agreements in force. Such agreements were the subject of considerable

[66] C. R. Wardle to T. J. McWilkie, 31 May 1961, MB Hist. 2132, HSBC.
[67] C. R. Wardle to J. M. Gregoire, 16 Mar. 1962, MB Hist. 2137, HSBC.

criticism in an official report on the East African monetary system by Erwin Blumenthal, commissioned by the British colonial government of Tanganyika in 1963. Blumenthal drew attention to the fifty-page Summary of Banking Arrangements which had set the charges and conditions operated by all the expatriate banks in East Africa since 1929. 'Agreements as far reaching as those contained in the Arrangements', Blumenthal noted, 'could hardly be approved under normal conditions.'[68] In their private response to the report, the British banks acknowledged that it could not 'be denied that the agreement is in fact a price maintenance arrangement', although they did consider the prices to be fair and to reflect economic realities in East Africa.[69] Competition was, in practice, never wholly eliminated. As the East African banking agreement only laid down minimum rates, banks often attempted to improve their market share of deposits by offering more favourable rates. In 1962, to give one of many examples, Barclays' management complained of the 'farcical' behaviour of one of its British competitors in this respect, which made 'a mockery of the agreed rates stucture'.[70]

The need for change was well articulated by a member of Standard's senior management in 1965. British banks had been at their most 'traditional' in colonial Africa, and the sudden advent of independence in the 1960s called for particularly sharp reorientation:

Successful banking requires a stake in the country, involvement in its fortunes, identification with its interests. In Africa especially, with the sensitivities and suspicions of new governments, we cannot expect to stand apart, to take out profits over the years and to put nothing back. If we are not prepared to take a risk . . . we shall lose the confidence of governments and businessmen . . . If we are too cautious, too fearful, we shall bring about what we fear. If we consistently turn away from profitable and sound lending because of lack of funds the business will go to Barclays DCO.[71]

Self-interest thus blended with a genuine recognition that banks needed to help developing countries to develop.

In fact, over the 1950s and 1960s, at different speeds in different regions and between different institutions, the British banks in the developing world became more flexible about whom they lent to and on their lending

[68] Erwin Blumenthal, *The Present Monetary System and its Future*, Report to the Government of Tanganyika, 1963, paras. 50 and 51.

[69] Memorandum on The Summary of Banking Arrangements: East Africa, *re* Blumenthal Report and 'Criticisms Implied', 21 Feb. 1963, attached to Note for Mr Roberts, 8 June 1964, Blumenthal Report File, Tanzania Box, SC.

[70] Barclays (DCO) Local Head Office, Nairobi to General Managers, 11 Aug. 1962, enclosed in Julian Crossley to Cyril Hawker, 16 Aug. 1962, Miscellaneous, SC.

[71] Standard Bank Board Paper, 6 Sept. 1965, *re* Employing the Bank's Resources in East, Central, and West Africa, Standard Box, SC. See also F. Seebohm, 'The Role of the British Overseas Banks', *Journal of the Institute of Bankers*, 88 (June 1967), 171.

terms. In West Africa, their finance of produce marketing boards and Sierre Leonean diamonds was only part of a new willingness to deviate from the orthodoxies of British banking. As early as 1947 BBWA had begun to provide long-term development loans, to begin with to the colonial administration, but later to the private sector. At least from the late 1950s, a growing number of loans were made to Africans, and the scale of lending to African firms was substantial.[72]

In East and Central Africa, as already indicated, British banks functioned on more 'traditional' lines for longer, but some change was discernible. Barclays (DCO) built on its earlier experience of lending to co-operatives in Palestine and Cyprus and became a substantial lender after the war to East African co-operative societies, especially in Tanganyika, where this form of marketing organization particularly flourished. For the British banks, this was a 'safe' way to lend to Africans. A Standard Bank training document in 1962 explained the advantages of lending to East African co-operatives: 'Lending by banks to individual Africans for crop finance would be almost impracticable and the co-operative system which is subject to special laws and close control, provides the banks with the opportunity to make bulk finance available to Africans.'[73] Standard Bank followed Barclays' lead and also became an active lender to co-operatives. In the early 1960s about 10 per cent of the bank's lending in Tanganyika was made direct to co-operatives. In addition, Standard and the other two British banks provided indirect facilities to the co-operatives through participation in consortium loans to agricultural marketing boards which on-lent the funds to co-operative societies. After 1962, when the Cooperative Bank of Tanganyika was formed and all co-operative accounts with the commercial banks were transferred to it, the British banks financed the co-operative movement by lending to the Cooperative Bank. However, the nationalization of banks in Tanzania in 1967 eliminated the business entirely.

In neighbouring Kenya, the British banks had traditionally financed the White settlers who had dominated the country's farming sector. After Independence in 1963, many of these European farmers had their land redistributed to Africans. The British banks were active in providing finance for the few large-scale African farmers who replaced the Europeans, although facilities to smallholders were confined to lending to co-operatives.[74]

A new interest in medium-term lending and in the opportunities of

---

[72] Fry, *Bankers in West Africa*, 168–9, 234–5. Several large loans to Africans were approved at one board meeting in Dec. 1962 although their purpose was unspecified. Three of these, at Sokoto in Nigeria, totalled no less than £270,000. Fry's Digests of BBWA Board Minutes, 20 Dec. 1962, and *passim*, BAC S/90, SC.

[73] Notes on Talk for the Training School, East Africa and Agencies Department, Nov. 1962, Miscellaneous, SC.

[74] 'Banking and Agriculture in Africa: Kenya', *Standard Bank London Newsletter*, 6 Feb. 1970.

lending to the indigenous economies of Asia and Africa led four British banks to establish wholly owned subsidiaries, known as development corporations, which offered medium- or long-term loans. These originated in a new concern for colonial development which emerged during the Second World War and which culminated in the formation of a specialist government agency, the Colonial Development Corporation, launched in 1948. Barclays was the pioneer among the British overseas banks. Its subsidiary, Barclays Overseas Development Corporation, was founded in 1946 and remained the most important.

The development corporations were indicative of the changed atmosphere among the British overseas banks, but their limitations were evident. They were all required to make commercial profits by their parents, which limited the kind of project which could be financed. There was a trend for loans to go to large companies rather than small ones and the resources committed to the development corporations were limited. Moreover, perhaps only Barclays was really enthusiastic about the idea until the 1960s. The bank corporations are best seen as transitory phenomena. With the advent of independence in Africa and elsewhere, and the assumption of development roles by governments, their original role largely disappeared, and they evolved into merchant banks. However, their performance, in the 1950s at least, bears comparison with the Colonial Development Corporation, which funded a series of ill-advised projects, indicating severe management failure.[75]

Apart from its status as a British colony, Hong Kong stood in sharp contrast to the African and West Indian countries which were the primary concern of the bank development corporations, for by the 1960s it had embarked on fast, export-led industrialization. The British banks in the colony again showed their flexibility in this context, notably so in the case of the Hongkong Bank. The Hongkong Bank lent on flexible terms to Chinese industrialists to finance their working capital, and also to finance fixed capital, especially for factory construction. Loans for this latter purpose were nominally repayable on demand, but in practice extended over up to four years. One estimate is that the Hongkong Bank provided as much as 48 per cent of total bank finance to the colony's manufacturing sector at a bench-mark date of June 1966, with a higher percentage in certain industries, including the textile industry, which played a leading role in the export-led growth. Unusually—and here the fact that the bank's head office was in the colony rather than London must have been important—the

[75] Frances Bostock, 'The British Overseas Banks and Development Finance in Africa after 1945', *Business History*, 33 (1991), provides a full account of these development corporations; see also Crossley and Blandford, *The DCO Story*, 144–5. Standard, National Bank of India, and Chartered established development corporations in 1947, 1948, and 1955 respectively.

Hongkong Bank acquired equity stakes in Hong Kong-based shipping interests, and in Cathay Pacific, the colony's airline. This was a radical departure from British banking orthodoxy, which allowed the bank to capture a higher share of the benefits of Hong Kong's rapid development.[76]

As the British banks in Africa and Asia moved away—at very different speeds in different environments—from trade finance and exchange banking towards longer-term commitments, they began to experience constraints on the funding side of their balance sheets. By the late 1950s, strains were showing in the traditional system whereby the banks financed their lending from locally raised deposits, a proportion of which was often transferred overseas and invested in the London money market. The problems of the Sterling Area and creation of national financial systems were one source of difficulty. Equally severe a problem was the growing search for resources to support expanded lending.

Such pressure, and its impact on the business strategies of the British banks, became evident in East Africa in the early 1960s when the imminence of political independence for the East African colonies produced a severe capital flight, which in turn reduced deposits. The British banks' ability to provide seasonal finance, especially for Uganda cotton, was put in doubt, and eventually at the end of 1961 the East African Currency Board put into operation a limited scheme for refinancing advances by the banks in respect of the marketing of a number of vital crops. This arrangement solved the immediate crisis, but over the next few years the strategies of the banks had to change. The British banks moved from a situation whereby a considerable portion of their locally raised deposits were invested in London to one where—by the mid-1960s—their East African branches were overdrawn on their London head offices.[77]

There was an identical trend in Asia. In India and Pakistan, by the early 1960s, the Exchange banks were having to finance their operations by drawing on London funds.[78] This raised the problem which had concerned the British overseas banks since their inception—the problem of risk: 'the risk being', as Mercantile's chief manager observed in 1960, 'that at some future date the Indian Government may refuse to permit the repatriation of such funds'.[79]

The changed circumstances stimulated a new interest in deposits. In most of Asia and Africa, even by the 1960s, there was no way to fund lending except by either natural deposits or resources transferred from

[76] King, *The History of the Hongkong and Shanghai Banking Corporation*, iv, 349–63, 561, 620–9, 693, 720–1.

[77] C. Hawker to A. Lawrie, 28 Apr. 1965, Chairman's Letter Book, East Africa Box, SC. See also Newlyn, *Money in an African Context*, 42–9.

[78] C. R. Wardle to M. Turner, 1 Mar. 1961, MB Hist. 1325, HSBC.

[79] C. R. Wardle to Lydall, 2 Nov. 1960, MB Hist. 1321, HSBC. See also King, *The History of the Hongkong and Shanghai Banking Corporation*, iv, 430–2.

Britain, for inter-bank money markets were virtually non-existent. 'A successful bank must have cheap money,' Mercantile's chief manager remarked in 1960. 'In other words—deposits.'[80] The search for deposits assumed a new priority.

The historical legacy of the British overseas banks put them at a disadvantage in this respect, for their branches were overwhelmingly clustered in commercial centres and entrepôts, where they could conduct exchange banking and finance trade. The Eastern Exchange banks, for example, had their branches located in the business centres of the ports and entrepôts of Asia. They had not actively sought deposits which did not bring exchange business within them. The intermediaries such as compradors who introduced indigenous business to the British banks had rarely been given incentives to attract simply deposit accounts. Moreover, in some British colonies, such as Malaya, local governments had held their accounts with British banks, thereby providing a reliable source of funds. By the early 1960s, competition was undermining this system because it simultaneously forced the Exchange banks—and their equivalents elsewhere in the developing world—to lend more while limiting their ability to find the money locally to finance the increased lending.

The British banks followed a number of strategies to expand their deposit bases. There was a considerable branch expansion in many countries, and the search for deposits was a major incentive for this trend. 'Our prime object in East Africa', noted National and Grindlays' chairman in 1967 in support of his policy of continued branch expansion, 'was the collection of further deposits.'[81]

In Hong Kong—to give one illustration—the Exchange banks had never seen the attraction of small deposits as their concern, and the grand banking halls of their few offices were not places where small Chinese depositors could feel comfortable. After the Second World War worries about Hong Kong's political future and, initially, constraints imposed by the assumption that a branch needed an expatriate manager, further diminished interest in branching. In 1961 the Hongkong Bank only had 16 branches in the colony. Subsequently, the search for funds and the threat of competition caused a policy reversal. Between 1962 and 1971 the number of Hongkong Bank branches in Hong Kong rose to 48, most of which were in new residential areas, and were managed by Hong Kong Chinese. Over the same period Chartered's branches in Hong Kong rose from 6 to 18, and the total number of bank branches in the colony from 190 to 438.[82]

[80] C. R. Wardle to S. W. P. Perry-Aldworth, 1 Apr. 1960, MB Hist 3140.4, HSBC.
[81] Regional Committee 'B' Meetings, 1965–9, Grindlays Archives, ANZ Archives.
[82] King, The History of the Hongkong and Shanghai Banking Corporation, iv, 367–72; Victor F. S. Sit, 'Branching of the Hongkong and Shanghai Banking Corporation in Hong Kong: A Spatial Analysis', in King (ed.), Eastern Banking, 629–54.

In 1965 the Hongkong Bank was able to strengthen its deposit base further by acquiring 51 per cent of the shares of Hang Seng Bank. This bank, owned by Hong Kong Chinese, grew rapidly in the 1950s and early 1960s, with an aggressive but prudent lending strategy. By 1965 it had become one of the largest private Chinese banks in Hong Kong in terms of deposits. However, it suffered a major run on deposits in that year following a banking crisis in the colony, and the bank's directors eventually had to offer a controlling interest in their institution to the Hongkong Bank or face closure.[83] The opportunities for similar purchases were minimal. In 1970 National and Grindlays secured 49 per cent of another Hong Kong Chinese bank, Dao Heng Bank, but this venture proved ill-fated, and in 1982 Dao Heng (by then wholly owned by the British bank) was sold to Hong Kong interests.

The Exchange banks, and Hongkong Bank in particular, were able to expand—in absolute if not relative terms—their deposits in Hong Kong by branching. Much of the Hongkong Bank's post-war success can be attributed to this strong deposit base, which was exploited in an entrepreneurial fashion. However, such a strategy became progressively more difficult elsewhere, as restrictions on the opening of new branches by foreign banks spread in the 1950s and 1960s (see above, Section 9.1).

The British banks also had to pay more to attract deposits. In country after country, British banks found the proportion of interest-free to total deposits falling. The days had passed when the security and stability of British banks alone would attract depositors. In colonial Africa the British banks actively pursued African savings accounts through 'mobile units' and other devices designed to attract previously hoarded funds into the banks.[84] The banks needed a stable deposit base to engage in longer-term lending, and they often employed ratios which explicitly linked the two. Standard Bank in the 1960s, for example, attempted to confine its term lending (two years and over) to a level which represented 90 per cent of savings bank deposits.

The British banks elsewhere also faced the end of the era of cheap funds. Chartered Bank, for example, experienced a remarkable shift in the structure of its deposit base. Table 9.6 illustrates the sharp increase in the proportion of interest-bearing fixed deposits over a twenty-year period. This trend was even discernible in the Gulf, despite the Islamic principles of many customers in the region, which meant that they would not accept interest. In the early 1950s the majority of BBME's deposits were interest-free, but by 1964 BBME was paying interest on approximately 70 per cent of its deposits.[85]

[83] King, *The History of the Hongkong and Shanghai Banking Corporation*, iv, 701–6; Y. P. Ngan, 'Hang Seng Bank Limited: A Brief History', in King (ed.), *Eastern Banking*, 709–16.    [84] Newlyn, *Money in an African Context*, 54.
[85] Geoffrey Jones, *Banking and Oil*, 60–1.

TABLE 9.6. *Structure of Chartered Bank deposits, 1946–1965* (£m.)

| Year | Current | % of total deposits | Fixed | % of total deposits | Total |
|------|---------|---------------------|-------|---------------------|-------|
| 1946 | 96  | 92 | 8   | 8  | 104 |
| 1955 | 172 | 85 | 31  | 15 | 203 |
| 1965 | 323 | 56 | 253 | 44 | 576 |

*Source*: SC, various files.

One possible strategy for banks in search of deposits or faced with unwelcome political risks was geographical diversification. However, in the 1950s and 1960s examples of this—other than by merging with another British bank—remained few. The single substantial example was the transformation of the Imperial Bank of Iran into the British Bank of the Middle East, which had begun during the Second World War (see Section 6.3). In 1945 Iran still provided over half of the bank's profits. Seven years later the bank could withdraw from that country, and the Iranian contribution was entirely matched, and far surpassed, by the new branches in the Arab world, which extended to almost every Arabic-speaking country by the end of the decade.[86] Other examples of greenfield diversification were rare. In Africa, Grindlays opened branches in the Rhodesias in the 1950s, but at least two other Exchange banks—Hongkong Bank and the Mercantile Bank—considered and declined the idea of opening branches in Africa.[87]

The lack of geographical diversification has a number of explanations including a recognition by the banks of the region-specific skills of their staff, the declining receptivity towards foreign banks in many regions after 1945, and the unattractive political and economic prospects of much of Africa and Asia. However, differences in entrepreneurship and in organizational structures between banks were also important variables on occasion.

This can be seen by contrasting the strategies of BBME and Eastern Bank in the Middle East, and Mercantile Bank and Hongkong Bank in Asia. Eastern Bank had been the first British bank on the Arabian side of the Gulf, with its Bahrain branch opening in 1920, but its enterprise faltered during the Second World War, leaving the BBME to take the initiative and secure monopoly banking agreements in Kuwait, Dubai, and other sheikhdoms.[88] In Asia, the Hongkong Bank after 1945 not only had

[86] Ibid., chs. 1–3.
[87] King, *The History of the Hongkong and Shanghai Banking Corporation*, iv, 480, 500, 528; the Thomas Report on East Africa, c.1950, and comments thereon, MB Hist. 808, HSBC.
[88] Geoffrey Jones, *Banking and Oil*, 9–15.

valuable franchises in growth economies such as Hong Kong, but it had the enterprise to exploit them. In contrast, the cautious board and senior management of Mercantile Bank chose to focus their attention on India, and rejected proposals from their own managers, for example, to expand their branch network in Hong Kong. The colony, the bank's CEO later observed, was 'a place where we missed the bus badly in 1948 by not opening offices in Kowloon'.[89] The bank was equally cautious in Thailand, Singapore, and elsewhere in the 1950s.

Organizational structures were an influence also on different strategies. The power of London in decision-making in both Eastern and Mercantile Banks was strong, and this power was used in a conservative way.[90] In contrast, the Hongkong's senior management were arguably better placed to judge risk because of their base in the colony. Again, BBME's diversification was the initiative, not of London, but much further down the managerial hierarchy. The pressure to open in Kuwait came from one of the bank's managers on the Iranian side of the Gulf, who had been depressed by the closing of Iranian branches in the 1930s, and had had news of the prosperity which oil had brought to neighbouring Bahrain. He was encouraged by a senior British diplomat in the region who wanted a British bank in Kuwait, and had tried and failed to persuade Eastern Bank to open there. This partnership also prompted BBME to open in Bahrain and Dubai. BBME's board responded positively to these suggestions, but its role was reactive rather than proactive. In the 1950s a series of new branches were opened as the result of initiatives by branch managers or other staff, who reported on banking opportunities in neighbouring countries.[91]

There appears to be no single reason why BBME allowed such individual initiatives. Before the 1940s its board had been more noteworthy for forcing its staff to follow policies designed in London. One important factor was almost certainly that senior management attention was focused on Iran, which paradoxically enabled flexibility on the margins. Between 1941 and 1945 Iran was occupied by British and Soviet armies, which relieved the then Imperial Bank from the host government's attacks on it, provided a valuable source of profits, and kept management's mind on the wartime emergency. After 1946 the bank's management was preoccupied with the complex difficulties it faced in its relations with the Iranian government. The fact that the concession under which the bank operated in Iran expired in 1949 helped defuse resistance to those looking beyond

---

[89] Mr Pow's Tour of Eastern Branches, 1963, MB 1045; see also Hong Kong to E. W. Paton, 21 May 1948, MB 1003:11, HSBC. Kowloon is the part of the colony located on the Chinese mainland.

[90] After the Hongkong Bank merger, the malign influence of London was frequently cited by Mercantile managers to explain performance in various markets; e.g. C. R. Wardle to J. H. Wickers, 13 Oct. 1959, MB 2128, HSBC.

[91] Geoffrey Jones, *Banking and Oil*, 47–8.

Iran, as did the long and painful tensions the bank had experienced in that country during the 1930s. BBME faced an explicit choice between diversification and liquidation.[92] Once the first diversifications had been successful, an entrepreneurial ethos developed within the bank, which was intensified by the proven presence of oil in the region, which meant that the potential opportunities were unusually clear.

The 1960s also saw the first attempts of the British overseas banks to follow the shifting geographical pattern of British foreign trade and investment by expanding in the United States and Europe. These efforts, the forerunner of more ambitious plans in the following decade, are best reserved for the next chapter.

The business strategies of the British multinational banks in the developing world in the twenty-five years after the Second World War showed both continuity and change. They retained their preference for short-term lending and liquidity. Traditional views on ethnicity lingered. Yet competition and the changing nature of their environment led to considerable product innovation in some respects. There was a rise in medium- and long-term lending, combined with a new willingness to lend to indigenous customers. The availability of deposits constrained these developments, and the branches of British banks searched for customers among populations previously little affected by British banking. These changes were evolutionary rather than radical but, given the limited organizational capabilities of the banks, it is perhaps surprising that they went as far as they did, and were as successful. However, by the 1960s external constraints, especially regulatory ones, had gravely limited the ability of the British banks to innovate, even if they wished to do so, while few opportunities remained for greenfield diversification within the developing world.

## 9.4. Local Staff in Africa and Asia

The first moves to raise the status of the Asian and African local staff of the British banks during the inter-war years have been discussed earlier (see Section 6.5). Developments after the Second World War further enhanced the case for giving more responsibility to local staff. As the British banks edged towards greater exposure to indigenous customers, and adapted their lending policies to their requirements, they needed more information and local contacts. Nationalist criticism of foreign banks and competition from local banks suggested that the British banks needed to assume stronger local identities. The branch expansion strategy enhanced the cost argument in favour of employing nationals rather than expatriates. While a 30-branch

[92] Geoffrey Jones, *Banking and Empire in Iran* (Cambridge: Cambridge University Press, 1986), ch. 12.

bank in the East could afford to employ expatriates as managers for every branch, the cost of such a strategy for a 300-branch bank would have been enormous.

Yet the employment of nationals at executive levels continued to be contentious. The socialization strategies employed by the banks worked most efficiently in a culturally homogeneous society, for they rested on judgements about character and 'type' rather than formal educational qualifications. Theoretically they could be applied more widely, with Asians and Africans being socialized into the corporate cultures of the banks. However, such a route was a costly and difficult one, for it required the banks to assess 'characters' of people from cultures very different from that of Britain. A further problem was one of differentiation. The customers of the banks had chosen to deal with *British* banks, and many expected to see a British face when they walked into a branch. It was frequently claimed that many local customers—and not just expatriate businesses—preferred to deal with British managers, who could be relied upon to maintain confidentiality and were not involved in local rivalries.[93]

There remained also the problem of mobility. The British banks had international officers who were rotated between branches in different countries. Staff were expected to be available for service everywhere within the bank's domain. It was far from clear that such a system could be maintained with non-British international officers. They might not want to move. More seriously, while most governments were likely to grant a work permit for a British officer to function as a branch manager in a British bank, would an African government grant such a permit for an Indian to be manager of a British bank, or vice versa? One possibility was for the banks to abandon the concept of an internationally mobile cadre of officers in favour of each country having its own nationals occupying all levels within that bank. However, the banks were convinced, probably rightly, that such a radical step would have fragmented their organizations beyond repair.

These considerations explain the hesitant moves of the British banks in their employment of local nationals. But the longer they hesitated, the more a further problem emerged. By the 1960s employment in a British bank was no longer the ideal for the younger generation in many developing countries. Often public service offered higher salaries or more prestige. Employment in a local bank or business offered more prospects for advancement, for it was never suggested that British banks would open their top management positions in London to non-British citizens. The upshot was that many British banks found it hard to recruit appropriate nationals to managerial positions, when eventually these positions were opened up

[93] Geoffrey Jones, *Banking and Oil*, 125–6.

to them. This problem was very evident in the Arabian Gulf by the 1960s. British banks such as BBME found it immensely difficult to recruit nationals and had to resort to hiring Indians and Pakistanis in the sub-continent for employment in the Gulf branches.[94]

Among the Eastern Exchange banks, there were some marked differences between institutions in the speed they moved on changing the status of local staff. The Mercantile Bank of India had begun to recruit Asians to executive positions in the mid-1930s. The National Bank of India appointed its first Indian at executive officer level in 1946.[95] However, it was not until 1954 that Chartered's court decided to follow this step. In the following year nine such appointments were made.[96]

In the mid-1950s Mercantile Bank, the pioneer among the Exchange banks, reviewed its position and considered further radical steps. Commenting on the pressure from various South Asian governments for the Asianization of executive posts in foreign-owned businesses, Mercantile's chairman argued that the bank needed a 'comprehensive policy' on the matter. He suggested that Mercantile continue to appoint only British nationals as managers and sub-managers at all branches, but that a proportion of the remainder of the officer staff should be Asian. He envisaged that this Asian cadre would be internationally mobile, with 'a large part of their service' in countries other than their own, and that they would be 'socialized' into the corporate culture by attending the bank's residential training centre in Britain and working in London office for a period of up to three years. Finally, he proposed that promotion beyond the bank's category of assistant accountant to the rank of accountant, and even beyond, be opened up to Asians.[97]

The chairman's initiative provoked considerable hostility from inside the bank. As various other chairmen discovered when they had attempted to merge their banks with others after 1945, their organizations had strong but inward-looking corporate cultures which resisted external threats to their existence. An agreed statement of Mercantile's management stressed that

the future success of the Bank is bound up in the maintenance of its British character ... The integrity and impartiality of [the] European Officers largely holds and extends the business of the Bank in the face of strong local propaganda for the utilisation of the service of indigenous Banks ... This is, and will remain, our strongest card in competition with local banks.[98]

[94] King, *The History of the Hongkong and Shanghai Banking Corporation*, iv, 304; Geoffrey Jones, *Banking and Oil*, 122-3.
[95] Geoffrey Tyson, *100 Years of Banking in Asia and Africa* (London: National and Grindlays, 1963), 208.
[96] Chartered Bank Annual Report and Balance Sheet, year ended Dec. 1955, Chairman's Report.      [97] Chairman's Memorandum, 7 Mar. 1955, MB Hist. 836, HSBC.
[98] Agreed Views of Management at a Meeting on 11 Mar. 1955 on the Chairman's Memorandum on Asianization, MB Hist. 836, HSBC.

These protestations seem to have had their desired effect, and the chairman's radical proposals were shelved.

Perhaps in part for similar reasons, no British bank in Asia—or elsewhere—went down the route of trying to recruit any significant number of non-British nationals to its international staff. However, over time, the status and prospects of local staff rose, and by the 1960s in several countries nationals were appointed as managers of smaller branches. In turn the various indigenous intermediaries whom the banks had used to deal with the local business slowly faded away or were transformed. The Hongkong Bank appointed its last Hong Kong comprador in 1953. In 1960 his title of comprador was changed to that of Chinese Manager. He continued to guarantee his staff and receive commissions on business introduced, but both these practices ceased when he retired in 1965, marking the final end of the compradoric system.[99]

In general, 'localization' of staff proceeded faster in Asia than in Africa. Within Africa, however, West Africa continued to lead the way. The Bank of British West Africa had already begun to employ Africans as clerks and senior clerks during the inter-war period. After the war they began to be appointed to more senior posts. Africans were appointed to branch management positions from the early 1950s, and promising nationals were also sent to London for training or, more precisely, socialization. By 1958 BBWA had thirteen African branch managers, and this number doubled in the space of the following two years. Barclays (DCO) seems to have had an equal commitment to Africanization.[100]

In East Africa, for the first two decades after 1945, localization essentially meant the promotion of locally employed Asians rather than Africans. Standard Bank, for example, recruited large numbers of Asians in the years after 1945 as a result of branch expansion and the growth of business. However, they were confined to filling junior positions as tellers and clerks, a policy which in turn meant that the bank had severe problems attracting high-quality recruits.[101] In 1958 Standard had a mere fifty-two African clerks in East Africa, 'of whom only one has proved of marked ability'.[102] The arrival of independence led to a more sustained drive to attract Africans as staff, but Standard and other British banks in East Africa found that it was far from easy to recruit suitable people. The civil services of the new states offered better prospects, while tribal differences often limited the mobility of African staff even within a single country.[103]

[99] King, *The History of the Hongkong and Shanghai Banking Corporation*, iv, 310.

[100] BBWA Chairman's Statements, Annual Meetings, 1958 and 1960; Fry, *Bankers in West Africa*, 232; Crossley and Blandford, *The DCO Story*, 246.

[101] Report by R. D. Roberts on Tour of East Africa, 6 May–4 July 1958, East Africa Box, SC.

[102] Standard Bank Manager's Conference, 1958, Standard Bank Managers' Conferences, SC.

[103] Ibid., 1962; Report on Visit to Kenya/Uganda by A. A. Lawrie, Jan.–Feb. 1968, East Africa Box, SC; National and Grindlays Report and Accounts, year ended Dec. 1967, Chairman's Statement.

In the twenty-five years after 1945, therefore, the prospects and status of the local staff employed by the British banks improved. In this area as in others, the banks were aware of changes in their environment and attempted to respond to them. However, as so often, the administrative heritage of the banks constrained the speed of change, as did the external environment. By the 1960s, in a range of countries, many British banks were more anxious to appoint nationals to executive posts than there were well-qualified nationals willing to work for them.

### 9.5. Conclusion

The performance of the British multinational banks in their host economies in this period supports the evidence presented in the previous chapter that this was a successful period for the banks. They held market share in many places where regulatory conditions permitted, although they fared best where competitive forces were not strong. First-mover advantages explain their continuing role, but they also had sufficient flexibility to upgrade their competitive advantage as their environment changed. In Australia, South Africa, and Argentina they diversified into non-banking financial services. In the developing world traditional policies towards lending and deposits were further modified, as were policies towards local staff. The willingness to innovate, and to change, accelerated during the 1960s.

The limitations imposed by their structures on the strategies pursued by British multinational banks remained evident, as they had in the inter-war years. London head offices were a handicap in competing with local banks in retail markets. Skills remained product- and region-specific. The corporate cultures and socialization strategies of the banks hindered their ability to acquire greater local identities. However, the problem for the British multinational banks lay less in retaining and adapting their old multinational retail banking business, which they did well, than in taking full advantage of the new opportunities which were dawning in the era of global banking after 1960. The next chapter turns to this new world.

# CHAPTER 10

# The Rise and Fall of Globalization

## 10.1. The Transformation of Multinational Banking

British multinational banks after 1945 had demonstrated sufficient flexibility in responding to changing conditions that they were often able to maintain their established positions in multinational trade and retail banking, even if some loss of market share was evident. This was a real achievement, yet the kind of banking they were doing, even in the 1960s, was fundamentally similar to that seen in the nineteenth century. Regulatory controls on capital flows and currency convertibility had reduced the importance of international banking, and minimized the scope for innovation. In contrast, manufacturing industry over this period had been revolutionized by new production methods and processes.

From the 1960s international banking underwent its own transformation, which was so dramatic that later writers could find few similarities with the industry which had existed previously. The catalyst was the emergence of the Eurodollar market. This new international money market was largely unregulated, and rapidly captured a rising share of financial intermediation from sheltered and conservative domestic banking markets. The birth of Eurobonds in 1963 resulted in a similarly unregulated capital market.[1] The nature of international banking was transformed. Formerly, it had been closely tied to international trade flows and related exchange operations. But, over time, the Eurocurrency, Eurobond, and foreign exchange markets became largely uncoupled from international trade. Multinational banks became the dominant players in these new financial markets, while lending to multinational corporations and to governments was undertaken on a dramatically enhanced scale. The globalization of financial markets prompted many governments to deregulate their financial markets, and to open them to foreign banks. The nature of international banking, and the opportunities for multinational banks, were transformed as a result of these developments.[2]

---

[1] There are numerous studies of the origins and development of the global money and capital markets, with perspectives changing over time as the markets themselves changed. There are valuable insights in Fritz Maschlup, 'Euro-Dollar Creation: A Mystery Story', *Banca Nazionale del Lavoro Quarterly Review*, 94 (Sept. 1974); Brian Scott-Quinn, *The New Euromarkets* (London: Macmillan, 1975); John Grady and Martin Weale, *British Banking, 1960–85* (London: Macmillan, 1986), 130–5.

[2] Michael R. Darby, 'The Internationalization of American Banking and Finance: Structure, Risk, and World Interest Rates', *Journal of International Money and Finance*, 5 (1986), 404; Derek F. Channon, *Global Banking Strategy* (Chichester: Wiley, 1988), ch. 1.

British banks lost rapidly their pre-eminence in this revitalized industry. The two previous chapters have already drawn attention to the rise of American multinational banking. American banks took the lead in the new era of international banking; in the process the banking system of the United States was transformed from being essentially local in character to being highly integrated with the world financial and banking system. In 1960, 8 American banks operated a total of 124 foreign branches. Ten years later 79 American banks possessed a total of 532 foreign branches. By 1980, 159 American banks had 799 foreign branches. During the 1970s Japanese and continental European banks expanded their multinational activities on a large scale also.[3]

The complexity of the post-1960 multinational banking industry makes an assessment of market share and of competitiveness a complex matter. A full analysis would involve an examination of a number of individual product markets, as well as an assessment of the overall competitive position of institutions.[4] Nevertheless, a crude proxy for the importance of British banks was their share of the international assets of all banks. By 1984 they held 7.5 per cent of total international bank assets, in fourth place behind the United States (26.4 per cent), Japan (23 per cent), and France (8.9 per cent), but more important than German banks (6.4 per cent). Six years later, at the end of 1990, British-owned banks owned 4.6 per cent of total assets, behind Japan (35.5 per cent), the United States (11.9 per cent), Germany (10.1 per cent), and France (9.3 per cent). They had been pushed into sixth place, behind Italian banks, which held 5.5 per cent of international bank assets in 1990.[5] British banks had pioneered and dominated the first era of multinational banking, but they had become modest players in the second one.

The modest international position of British banks by the 1980s can be readily, and with much justification, correlated with the equally modest role of the entire United Kingdom economy by this period. However, this chapter argues that managerial factors further handicapped the competitiveness of British banks, reinforcing their relative decline. The

---

[3] Darby, 'The Internationalization of American Banking and Finance', 405–7; Lawrence G. Goldberg and Denise Johnson, 'The Determinants of US Banking Activity Abroad', *Journal of International Money and Finance*, 9 (1990), 126–7; Thomas F. Huertas, 'US Multinational Banking: History and Prospects', in Geoffrey Jones (ed), *Banks as Multinationals* (London: Routledge, 1990), 254; Henry S. Terrell, Robert S. Dohner, and Barbara R. Lowrey, 'The US and UK Activities of Japanese Banks: 1980–1988', *International Finance Discussion Papers, Federal Reserve System*, 361 Sept. 1989; Channon, *Global Banking Strategy*, 11–34.

[4] For an analysis on these lines, primarily concerned with American banks, see Beverly Hirtle, 'Factors Affecting the Competitiveness of Internationally Active Financial Institutions', *Federal Reserve Bank of New York Quarterly Review*, 16(1) (Spring 1991), 38–51.

[5] *Annual Reports of Bank for International Settlements, 1985–1991.* Comparable data was not published before 1984.

administrative heritage of the banks constrained their response to the new opportunities of multinational banking, while a number of major errors in business strategy depleted their capital and exhausted their managements.

The following three sections discuss the problems faced by the British banks in their administrative heritage, and their attempts to build new corporate structures more appropriate to the era of global banking. Subsequently, two aspects of their new strategies in the 1970s and 1980s will be examined in greater detail: cross-border lending, and multinational banking in the United States.

## 10.2. The Administrative Heritage and the Competitive Diamond

During the 1970s and 1980s British economic decline continued to undermine many of the original competitive advantages held by British multinational banks. Britain's share of world exports continued to fall. An exceptionally severe recession in 1979–81 resulted in the bankruptcy of around a fifth of British manufacturing industry, and in 1983 Britain had its first trade deficit in manufactured goods for 200 years. A considerable share of manufacturing in Britain, from colour televisions to motor cars and around 20 per cent of industrial output in total, was controlled by the subsidiaries of foreign multinationals. Britain, as Michael Porter observed in his 1990 study, continued to 'slide'.[6]

Nevertheless, other aspects of the 'diamond' were more favourable to British-based banks and offered the prospect of renewed competitive advantages in multinational banking industry. London became the main home of the new Euromarkets. It offered an existing agglomeration of financial services, a reputation for stability and honesty, and freedom from tight regulation—an essential requirement, for the new markets were above all driven by the desire to escape from regulatory controls. Foreign banks were welcome to establish London branches, which did not require separate capitalization, and the Bank of England followed a flexible approach to foreign currency operations with non-residents. There were no reserve requirements or maturity constraints. There was no Glass-Steagall Act, as in the United States, to separate commercial and investment banking.[7] As a result, throughout the 1970s and 1980s London held a pre-eminent role

[6] Michael Porter, *The Competitive Advantage of Nations* (Macmillan: London, 1990), 482–507.
[7] The importance of London as an international financial centre in the 1970s and 1980s, and some reasons for this importance, are discussed in 'London as an International Financial Centre', *Bank of England Quarterly Bulletin*, 24(9) (1989), and E. P. Davis, *International Financial Centres: An Industrial Analysis*, Bank of England Discussion Papers, No. 51, Sept. 1990.

in international banking, foreign exchange dealing, and most other financial markets.[8]

In addition to being headquartered in the world's leading international financial centre, British banks had a uniquely rich experience of international activity. Collectively they had several thousand branches worldwide. Although most of these were located in the developing world or the Southern Hemisphere, British banks also had long-established positions in many of what became the leading financial centres of Asia and the Middle East—Hong Kong, Singapore, Bahrain, though not Tokyo. British banks had also decades of experience in foreign exchange operations and in moving funds around the world. The challenge for British banks was to create an appropriate firm structure, and to devise effective business strategies, in order to take full advantage of the new opportunities offered by the transformation of their industry.

The ability of British banks to achieve these goals was circumscribed by their administrative legacy.[9] They entered the era of global banking with a long organizational history, a long-established pattern of asset distribution, and strong corporate cultures. Even in the pre-1960s period of multinational banking, these structures and cultures had not been ideal. The separation of overseas and domestic banking had been under criticism since the First World War, while the organizational structure of the overseas banks had in some cases restrained their ability to function as multinational retail banks. In the post-1960s banking industry, the administrative legacy of British banks was an even greater handicap, which had to be overcome.

British banking, for example, had been characterized by a high degree of market segmentation. The clearing banks were primarily concerned with the domestic British market, while the overseas banks had specialized in different foreign markets. The advent of the global capital and money markets, a simultaneous sharp fall in the cost of transmitting electronic information, and the institutionalization of household savings, which created a pool of professionally managed capital, broke down such segmentation of national markets, and replaced it—to some extent—with a

---

[8] In 1990 Britain accounted for around 18 per cent of total international bank lending. Japan, which had become the largest centre, accounted for 19 per cent, and the United States 8 per cent. 'Developments in International Banking and Capital Markets in 1990', *Bank of England Quarterly Bulletin*, 31(2) (1991). One estimate of market shares in the foreign exchange markets at the end of the 1980s placed London first, followed by New York, Singapore, Hong Kong, Zurich, and Tokyo. 'The Asian Surprise in the Forex Markets', *Financial Times*, 2 Sept. 1991.

[9] This section draws heavily on Christopher A. Bartlett, 'Building and Managing the Transnational: The New Organisational Challenge', in Michael E. Porter (ed.), *Competition in Global Industries* (Boston, Mass.: Harvard Business School Press, 1986), 372–5.

single, global market-place. Bankers needed to have operations across the world—or at least in the leading international financial centres—to take full advantage of such new opportunities, and to tap the new international money markets.[10]

The large corporate customers of banks increasingly expected to be serviced on a world-wide basis, but this was not a service which the traditional structure of British banking was well placed to provide. The clearing banks, with the partial exceptions of Barclays and Lloyds, had largely relied on correspondent relationships abroad to provide the trade finance and exchange operations required by their corporate clients, but the speed and complexity of the new financial markets shifted the weight of advantage towards internationalization rather than the use of market mechanisms. The overseas banks had a different problem. They had almost no clients among the large British corporations, or, rather, they often served as bankers to individual subsidiaries of British multinationals in particular markets but had weak links with their head offices in the United Kingdom.

The client base of British banks was, in any case, a problem. A fundamental factor behind the rapid growth in the importance of the American multinational banks was the growing use of the Eurodollar market by American corporations. The United States government imposed restrictions on the export of investment dollars, forcing American multinationals to seek overseas sources of capital for expansion, while interest rate restrictions led American corporations to place surplus offshore funds in the Eurodollar market. American banks established branches in London to tap into the Eurodollar market, often using these funds to lend to their head offices.[11] There was a lag before most British companies began to co-ordinate their overseas subsidiaries in ways similar to American corporations, and to demand services on a world-wide scale. The Monopolies Commission report which rejected the Barclays and Lloyds merger in 1968 explicitly rejected the contention that British business wanted a global service from their banks, on the grounds that

as a general rule companies operating overseas go to the bank which provides the cheapest and most efficient local service, including often a local branch network. In many countries these banks are indigenous banks, but even where they are British banks the companies are influenced by local conditions and not by their relationships with the parent banks in this country.[12]

---

[10] Huertas, 'US Multinational Banking', 263–4.

[11] 'The Euro-Currency Business of Banks in London', *Bank of England Quarterly Bulletin*, 10 (March 1970).

[12] Monopolies Commission, *Report on the Proposed Merger of Barclays Bank Ltd., Lloyds Bank Ltd., and Martins Bank Ltd* (London, 1968), 49. See also Sect. 8.3, above.

Yet if such a situation was still true in 1968, it did not survive the collapse of the fixed exchange rate system in the early 1970s. Thereafter any multinational corporation had to regard the global foreign exchange and money markets as critical to their businesses.

The specialist skills of the British banking system were also a handicap in the age of global banking. During the 1960s American banks led the development of the Euromarkets through rapid product innovation, developing new lending investments such as floating-rate loans and syndicated loans. As most transactions were in dollars or dollar-denominated instruments, they had a natural advantage, but British banks also lagged in their willingness to innovate. The clearing banks were retail bankers, who left complex corporate financing to merchant banks, and who existed in a highly cartelized and regulated domestic market. They were not well equipped to develop innovative lending products and, indeed, rapidly lost market share in commercial lending even in Britain after 1960.[13] The British clearers did not make a determined entry into the Eurocurrency markets until the 1970s.

Likewise, the traditional skills of the overseas banks in exchange and retail banking needed upgrading if they were to participate fully in an industry whose complexity and scale was transformed. There was more of a perception of new opportunities among some of the overseas banks than among the clearers. In particular, Bolsa, under George Bolton, was among the pioneers of the Eurodollar market. One of his first acts on appointment as chairman in 1957 was to set up a foreign exchange department, with the dealers instructed to look for deposits in foreign currencies. At the end of 1962 Bolsa estimated that it was 'amongst the three of four largest operators in the London market'.[14] However, Bolsa did not long sustain a prominent position in the Euromarkets, and few other British overseas banks followed their lead. Chartered Bank's chief manager only seems to have become fully alerted to the potential of the new markets in 1968, at the same time noting the constraints within the bank on expansion into that area:

Bolsa are perhaps four-fifths orientated towards London and the Continent and they make very large profits in the Eurodollar and Eurobond market and other projects ... we may have a better and more profitable overseas branch network, but it is impossible to escape the feeling that ... we [may] be missing out in London ... At the moment, and this is said without casting any aspersions on the

---

[13] Geoffrey Jones, 'Competition and Competitiveness in British Banking, 1918–71', in Geoffrey Jones and M. W. Kirby (eds.), *Competitiveness and the State* (Manchester: Manchester University Press, 1991), 124–5.

[14] Richard Fry (ed.), *A Banker's World* (London: Hutchinson, 1970), 32; Head Office Memorandum by R.V.L., 22 Nov. 1962, Eurodollar File, LB. For Bolton's motivation, see above, Sect. 8.3.

ability of our general managers, they are brought home from branches where their background and experience is not altogether the best training for them to be plunged into the differing aspects of business in London, and often they have to learn in the job instead of bringing expertise to it.[15]

Somewhat belatedly, Chartered established an international banking division in 1969 headed by a retiree from Bolsa's international division.

The socialization strategies which had sustained the overseas banks through war and depression were of less value in post-1960s multinational banking. There was a belated recognition of this fact and over time the banks started to recruit staff with more formal education, in recognition that 'character' was no longer a sufficient qualification. National and Grindlays began regular graduate recruitment in 1969, in recognition that banking had become more complex and that 'competition is greater and the speed of decision from a Bank like ours is much greater'.[16] In 1977 the Hongkong Bank undertook a major review of its personnel policy and, thereafter, the recruitment of university graduates became the norm.[17] Corporate cultures based on lifetime employment were also modified as mid-career specialists were recruited, especially in merchant and investment banking. When the Hongkong Bank established its own merchant bank in the 1970s it recruited staff from outside the bank.[18] Some banks bought entire merchant banks to enhance their skills.

The inheritors of the 'free-standing' overseas banking tradition faced particular problems. In the nineteenth century, London-based boards had provided considerable advantages for multinational trade banks. In post-1960s multinational banking, a London branch became a prerequisite for any bank in the world which conducted international business, but a London-based board provided no advantages in the global money and capital markets. Moreover, the overseas banks—like the British merchant banks which were also prominent in the initial stages of the Eurodollar market—were constrained in their ability to accept foreign currency deposits by the relatively small sizes of their capitals. And, like other non-dollar-based banks, they were faced with possible dangers in regard to their dollar exposures. They were particularly handicapped in this regard because sterling was a weak and depreciating currency. As a result, British banks had to restrict the percentage of deposits in dollars against the

[15] Memorandum by W. G. Pullen, 27 Mar. 1968, File on International Division, Chartered Archives, SC.
[16] Draft of Chairman's Statement for 1970, Office of the Chairman, 1970–72, Grindlays Archives, ANZ Archives.
[17] F. H. H. King, *The History of the Hongkong and Shanghai Banking Corporation*, iv (Cambridge: Cambridge University Press, 1991), 665–6, 917–18.
[18] Ibid., 672. There was a similar process in the clearing banks. See London Clearing Banks, *Evidence by the Committee of London Clearing Bankers to the Committee to Review the Functioning of Financial Institutions* (London, Nov. 1977), 160.

possibilities of a crisis leading to difficulty in renewing foreign currency deposits, and they also had to limit the expansion of their total deposits to an acceptable ratio of capital and reserves.

British banks, therefore, entered the new era of multinational banking with a number of advantages. However, they also entered it with an administrative heritage which offered constraints on their ability to take full advantage of new opportunities in the industry.

## 10.3. Multinational Banking and the Clearers

During the 1970s and 1980s British commercial banks attempted to modify radically their inherited organizational structures and asset configurations. Many of the strategies adopted, such as diversification into related financial services, were common to both the clearing banks and the overseas banks, and to banks elsewhere in the English-speaking world. In the context of the history of British multinational banking, however, the most striking phenomenon was the continued struggle to overcome the institutional separation of overseas and domestic banking. This section considers the attempts of the British clearing banks to become multinational in their own right, and to become 'global banks'.

Barclays was the largest of the British clearing banks in the early 1970s, and the one with the most successful history of multinational banking. The concentration of its overseas banking interests in the wholly owned Barclays Bank International (BBI) marked a further stage in Barclays' evolution as a multinational bank. Over the 1970s BBI evolved a holding-company structure, as investments in associate and affiliate banks replaced wholly owned branches in many regions. In Africa and most of the developing world, BBI had shareholdings in many locally registered banks, the localized successors to the former DCO branch network. By 1976 the BBI shareholding in Barclays National Bank, the largest commercial bank in South Africa, had fallen to around 60 per cent, while it held 40 per cent of Barclays Bank (Nigeria), the next largest group operation in Africa after South Africa. In contrast, BBI had full ownership in a number of banks established to operate in developed market economies, including Barclays Bank of California, Barclays Bank of New York, and Barclays Canada.[19]

During the 1970s BBI expanded into wholesale banking, and into related financial services including leasing, merchant banking, and corporate finance. In 1984 it was merged into the parent domestic bank to form a unified bank able to offer its customers services on a global basis. After the deregulation of the London market in 1986—'Big Bang'—Barclays also

[19] Derek F. Channon, *British Banking Strategy and the International Challenge* (London: Macmillan, 1977), 128.

invested heavily to build up a presence in investment banking with the creation of a subsidiary, Barclays de Zoete Wedd (BZW), which became a multinational bank in its own right, establishing offices in other international financial centres.

Barclays remained a multinational bank in the traditional sense of owning branches or affiliates abroad, owning—in 1990—1,100 offices in 73 countries. However, the structure of the business had changed sharply over twenty years. Most of the retail business in the developing world was sold, as was the residual shareholding in the South African bank in 1986. The United States and Europe became the location for most of Barclays' assets outside the United Kingdom, while participation in multinational retail banking was largely confined to various European countries, including France, Spain, and Greece.[20]

This change in corporate structure and asset distribution was not achieved without costs. The initial years of involvement in investment banking yielded financially poor returns, as was the general experience of most commercial banks. The attempt to develop a large retail and consumer finance business in the United States had to be abandoned. (See below, Section 10.6.) Yet Barclays did manage to avoid the worst of the misfortunes which befell British banks in these years. At the beginning of the 1990s it had the strongest claim of any British bank to be regarded as a global bank. The main organizational challenge appeared to be to find a means whereby commercial and investment banking could coexist within one bank.[21]

The administrative heritage of Lloyds in multinational banking was an unhappy one, but the formation of Lloyds and Bolsa International Bank in 1971 appeared as a positive development. Within two years Mellons and the other minority shareholders had been bought out, giving Lloyds Bank International (LBI), as the bank was renamed, full ownership of an extensive multinational branch network spanning Latin America and Western Europe.

Lloyds, however, continued to experience difficulties in the management of its multinational banking interests. Some of its overseas interests remained outside the control of LBI, including Grindlays Bank and the National Bank of Zealand, both of which were under the administrative umbrella of the domestic parent, as were several new overseas subsidiaries. The most important example was Lloyds Bank California, created in 1974. LBI and its parent operated their own correspondent banking businesses, foreign exchange dealing departments, corporate banking divisions, and export finance divisions. Foreign currency lending was also divided between

[20] See Table A.4.2, and the list of principal overseas subsidiary and associated companies given in Barclays PLC Report and Accounts (1990).

[21] 'Divergence of Structure for the Convergence of Markets', *Financial Times*, 1 Nov. 1990.

the two banks. Investment management was split between the investment department and the trust division of the domestic bank, with LBI also performing a limited amount of portfolio management.

There were also problems with LBI itself. During the 1970s the bank adopted an aggressive growth strategy. There was a particular emphasis on expansion to the Far East, with branches and representative offices being opened in all the leading regional financial centres. Executives who had come from the Bolsa side of the business had a very different corporate culture from that prevailing in the domestic bank, with whom they had never had any real contact. They were excited by the opportunities for world-wide growth, a welcome chance to escape from the constraints of Latin America, and were determined to take full advantage of such opportunities. An entrepreneurial culture flourished, encouraged by a substantial staff recruitment, at middle and senior levels, of bankers from other institutions, as well as professionals such as lawyers, industrialists, and accountants. The upshot was that although LBI was wholly owned by Lloyds Bank Limited, the two banks were virtually entirely separate operations, with highly distinctive corporate cultures.[22] Within LBI itself there were also culture clashes between a senior management committed to entrepreneurial growth in international banking and a staff with a different tradition. 'This bank has its roots in Latin America,' one LBI executive observed in 1983. 'Its corporate culture is steeped in more than a century of dealing in that continent. While your directors may want change, the bulk of your staff were brought up one way and that's going to take time to change.'[23]

In the early 1980s LBI's rapid growth strategy experienced serious problems. There were bad debts in the Far East and elsewhere. The traditional branch network in Argentina was under threat of sequestration for a time during the Falklands War. Far more serious, however, was LBI's pursuit of asset growth by extensive cross-border lending (see below, Section 10.5). The outbreak of the world debt crisis in 1982 all but doomed LBI, which was ultimately merged into the domestic bank four years later. As part of the reorganization Lloyds established, in 1985, its own merchant bank, which took over LBI's merchant-banking and corporate finance divisions, together with the export finance activities of both the international and domestic banks. In 1984 Lloyds also disposed of its shareholding in Grindlays Bank.

The tradition of strategic incoherence continued, however. At the beginning of 1986 Lloyds sold its Californian subsidiary. This might have been taken as a signal that the bank intended to withdraw from

---

[22] 'The Last Days of Lloyds Bank International', *Euromoney* (Dec. 1984).
[23] 'LBI Gets Caught in the Cross Fire', *Euromoney* (Feb. 1983).

world-wide ambitions, but in the following April it launched a take-over bid for Standard Chartered. Lloyds claimed that the merged bank would represent 'a global financial institution strong in capital, in management, in its substantial share of its home market, and in the breadth and depth of its overseas network'.[24] This was the first hostile banking take-over bid ever seen in Britain: it was also Lloyds' bid to be a global bank.

Both bids failed. By July Standard Chartered had defeated Lloyds (see below, Section 10.4). Lloyds resumed its erratic course—it purchased a Canadian bank in 1986, renamed it Lloyds Bank Canada, but sold it again in 1990—but the overall trend became one of withdrawal from multinational banking, except in niche products and activities. The bank withdrew from commercial banking in the United States, and in the Far Eastern financial centres except Tokyo. Its attempt to develop Lloyds Merchant Bank as an equivalent to BZW was abandoned when the bank withdrew from most securities market activities. Instead, Lloyds focused on the domestic British market. It diversified into estate agency business, following a pattern seen in the United States, innovated in retail banking products, and in 1988 merged with a leading British life assurance company. By 1990 the multinational activities of Lloyds were much reduced. It still had 360 offices in 20 countries, but the proportion of its assets in the United Kingdom had risen from 43 per cent in 1985 to 82 per cent in 1990.

Midland and National Westminster, the two remaining 'Big Four' English clearing banks after 1968, faced a more difficult task than Lloyds and Barclays if they wished to become global banks, for they had few pre-existing interests in multinational banking. This virgin status meant they were unburdened by unprofitable or embarrassing branch networks in the developing world or South Africa, but it also meant that their managements had little international experience.

Both banks explored strategies designed to capture a share of the new opportunities of international banking without recourse to large-scale multinational banking. The Midland Bank was the principal exponent of a strategy of forming alliances and joint ventures with foreign banks. This policy had originated in the 1960s, when Midland had reconsidered its former exclusive reliance on correspondent banking. In 1963 it had joined with three continental banks to form the European Advisory Committee (EAC) to develop areas of co-operation on the basis of not directly competing with one another in the territory of the other three. This 'club' led to the establishment of joint venture banks or consortia, a form of bank already pioneered by Midland when it helped establish MAIBL in 1964 (see Chapter 8, Section 8.3). In 1967 the four EAC banks formed the Banque Européenne de Credit à Moyen Terme, a Brussels-based bank

---

[24] Lloyds Bank PLC offer for Standard Chartered PLC, Apr. 1986.

set up to develop facilities in Europe for medium-term loans of substantial amounts for major industrial projects, and other ventures followed.[25]

National Westminster did not join a 'club', but it was also active in the foundation of consortium banks, based both in Britain and abroad, such as the Orion Bank, which by the mid-1970s had become the largest consortium bank in Britain. The member banks of the consortium sought to develop new areas of business and expertise while sharing the risk with others, and they were particularly attractive to European banks without substantial international business which were searching for an appropriate competitive response to the large American money centre banks.[26]

The British clearing banks, especially Midland and National Westminster, were prominent in the London consortium banks. Table 10.1 lists their investments in them in 1977.

Within a decade this network of consortium banks and clubs had been dismantled. Many partners in the consortium banks decided to establish their own multinational branches, causing conflicts of interest. The unwritten rules about not competing with fellow members of the club were slowly discarded. The consortium banks also suffered from management problems, especially as much of their senior management was seconded from parent banks. Many consortium banks also lent heavily to developing countries, and were, as a result, badly affected by the debt crisis. For some Japanese and continental European banks, the consortium banks may have formed a useful intermediate step on the way to multinational banking, but it is more likely that for the British banks they consumed large amounts of management time with only modest results.[27] They may even have provided a handicap for some of the clearers, especially the Midland, in developing their own skills in the Eurocurrency markets. MAIBL's principal activity, for example, was Eurocurrency lending, which meant that Midland and its other shareholder banks either had to stay out of the market or compete with their own creation.

There was an equally unsatisfactory outcome from the Midland and National Westminster shareholdings in Standard Chartered. In the 1960s Cyril Hawker had placed great hopes on the benefits of such equity links, but in practice they did little to enhance the competitiveness of any of the banks concerned. In 1976 National Westminster sold its shares, followed by the Midland Bank three years later.[28]

---

[25] A. R. Holmes and Edwin Green, *Midland: 150 Years of Banking Business* (London: Batsford, 1986), 253–5. Two other British banks were active in 'clubs', Williams & Glyns and Barclays. The membership of these three 'clubs' in 1977 is given in London Clearing Banks, *Evidence by the Committee of London Clearing Banks to the Committee to Review the Functioning of Financial Institutions*, table 28.
[26] Alberto A. Weissmüller, 'London Consortium Banks', *Journal of the Institute of Bankers*, 95 (August 1974), 203–16; Channon, *Global Banking Strategy*, 20–1.
[27] Channon, *Global Banking Strategy*, 22–3; Holmes and Green, *Midland*, 257.
[28] Channon, *British Banking Strategy*, 131; Holmes and Green, *Midland*, 296.

TABLE 10.1. *Clearing banks' investments in consortium banks, c.1977*

| Clearing bank | Consortium bank | Location | Percentage shareholding | Specialization (if any) |
|---|---|---|---|---|
| Midland | Banque Européenne de Crédit | London | 14 | Latin America |
| | Banque Européenne pour l'Amérique Latine | Brussels | 16 | United States |
| | European-American Bancorp | New York | 20 | Middle East |
| | European Arab Holding and its subsidiaries: | Luxemburg | 5 | Middle East |
| | European Arab Bank | London | | Middle East |
| | European Arab Bank (Brussels) | Brussels | | Middle East |
| | Europäisch-Arabische Bank | Frankfurt | | Middle East |
| | European Asian Bank (branches in Asian centres) | Hamburg | 14 | Asia |
| | European Asian Finance (HK) | Hong Kong | 10 | |
| | European Banking Company | London | 14 | International merchant banking |
| | Euro-Pacific Finance Corporation | Melbourne | 15 | Australia |
| | Iran Overseas Investment Bank | London | 6 | Iran |
| | Midland and International Banks | London | 45 | |
| | Ship Mortgage International Bank | Amsterdam | 25 | Shipping |
| | UBAF Bank | London | 25 | Middle East |
| National Westminster | Libra Bank | London | 5 | Latin America |
| | Orion Bank and its subsidiaries including: | London | 20 | Far East |
| | Orion Pacific (75%) | Hong Kong | | International merchant banking |
| | Roy West Banking Corporation | Nassau | 40 | Iran |
| | Saudi International Bank | London | 5 | |
| Williams & Glyn's | Development and Investment Bank of Iran | Tehran | 4 | Far East |
| | Inter-Alpha Asia | Hong Kong | 14 | |
| Barclays | United International Bank | London | 10 | East Europe |
| | Anglo-Romanian Bank | London | 30 | |
| | Banque de la Société Financière Européenne | Paris | 12 | West Europe |
| | Euro-Latinamerican Bank | London | 5 | Latin America |
| | International Energy Bank | London | 15 | Energy |
| | Iran Overseas Investment Bank | London | 6 | Iran |

*Source:* The London Clearing Banks, *Evidence by the Committee of London Clearing Banks to the Committee to Review the Functioning of Financial Institutions,* (London, Nov. 1977), table 48.

The comparative failure of alternative strategies led National Westminster and Midland into multinational banking on their own account. National Westminster had inherited the modest Westminster Foreign Bank, which operated a small number of branches in France and Belgium, and this was transformed into a new subsidiary, International Westminster Bank, which developed a large presence in wholesale and Eurocurrency markets. During the 1970s branches were established in New York, Chicago, and San Francisco, in leading continental centres such as Frankfurt, and in Bahrain, Singapore, and Tokyo.

The Midland Bank had been reassessing its whole business strategy since the late 1960s, when the decision by all the clearing banks to disclose their inner reserves had revealed that it, rather than Lloyds, was the most undercapitalized of the clearing banks, and that its profitability was much weaker than its competitors.[29] In 1974 a review of the banks' international strategy demonstrated Midland's inordinate dependence on Britain for its profits compared to the other clearing banks. The result was a historic decision that Midland Bank needed to establish its own representation in major overseas centres and to aim to raise the contribution of international business to its profits.[30] Over the next five years Midland established a number of branches, representative offices, and affiliates in foreign countries.

Between 1979 and 1982 Midland embarked on a series of foreign acquisitions, culminating in early 1980 in a preliminary agreement to acquire 51 per cent of Crocker National, one of California's largest banks. The acquisition made Midland Bank the tenth largest banking organization in the world.[31] A few months previously, National Westminster Bank also purchased a large American bank on the East Coast.

At the time, large-scale acquisitions appeared the most effective means to achieve a rapid shift in assets, but it soon became apparent that these clearing banks lacked the management skills necessary to control rapid diversification into multinational banking, investment banking, and other areas greatly removed from their traditional concerns.

Initially National Westminster made progress. It passed Barclays in the early 1980s to become Britain's largest bank by asset size. It had less exposure to Third World debts than the other British clearers, and in 1987 it became the first British bank in history to report profits of over £1 billion.[32] Subsequently, however, diversification into investment banking resulted not only in heavy losses but also in involvement in a major financial scandal which led in 1989 to the resignation of National Westminster's

---

[29] Holmes and Green, *Midland*, 244–5.
[30] Ibid., 257–60, 287. Chairman's Statement, 1979 Report of the Directors and Accounts, Midland Bank.
[31] 'How Midland was Struck by a Californian Earthquake', *Financial Times*, 25 Jan. 1988.
[32] 'Nat West's Profit Soars Past £1bn.', *Financial Times*, 25 Feb. 1987.

chairman and three other directors. Multinational banking in the United States also resulted in substantial financial losses (see below, Section 10.6). In 1990 National Westminster had reverted to the status of being Britain's second largest bank by asset size, behind Barclays. The bank still had over a quarter of its assets outside the United Kingdom, yet global ambitions had been replaced by a desire to be a large European bank, with a core commercial banking business in the British market.[33]

The 1980s proved to be the worst decade in the Midland Bank's history. Heavy losses eventually forced the sale of Crocker National in 1986, minus most of its bad debts and all its Latin American loans, which Midland was obliged to retain. The bank's total losses in California were estimated at around £1 billion. The disastrous Crocker episode was only a severe manifestation of more general failings in the bank's organization and senior management. Its export finance division, for example, made losses approaching £100 million over the same period, largely because of a defence affiliate with links to Britain's security services, whose activities were unknown to senior management.[34] The purchase of a leading London stockbroker, Greenwells, during 'Big Bang' also resulted in losses in excess of £30 million within fifteen months.

In 1987 a former deputy governor of the Bank of England, Sir Kit McMahon, was appointed chairman and chief executive officer. The bank sold its profitable regional subsidiaries in Scotland and Ireland to bolster its capital, and withdrew from equity trading on the London market. However, this restructuring was interrupted by a resurgence, in a different guise, of global ambitions. In December 1987 Hongkong Bank acquired 14.9 per cent of Midland's shares. Hongkong Bank agreed not to increase its shareholding further for three years, but the conventional wisdom was that a full merger would follow in due course. Meanwhile, there was an exchange of directors between the two banks.[35] A merged bank offered the prospects of a global bank strong in Europe, Asia-Pacific, and North America. Subsequently, there was some rationalization of branches between the two groups, but the problems of merging an overseas bank and a British clearing bank had been underestimated, especially when the latter was burdened by a large Third World debt provision and heavy commercial bad-debt provisions because of a severe recession in Britain at the end of the 1980s. In December 1990 both banks decided not to proceed with a merger in view of mounting losses and weak share prices.

Midland Bank was left with a business very similar to the one which it had operated twenty years previously. It was essentially a British domestic

---

[33] 'A Cautious Repair Strategy for the Mistakes of the Past', *Financial Times*, 19 Apr. 1991.
[34] 'Tinker, Tailor, Soldier, Banker', *Financial Times*, 15 July 1991.
[35] 'A Special Relationship—If not exactly a Marriage', *Financial Times*, 11 Dec. 1987; 'The Road to Britain', *Far Eastern Economic Review*, 26 Nov. 1987.

bank which conducted international banking through a large network of correspondents and had a substantial foreign exchange business. However, its viability as an independent institution remained in doubt. In 1990 it became the first British clearing bank to cut its dividend for fifty years. A new chairman and a new CEO were appointed, the latter imported from Barclays Bank.[36] During 1991 Lloyds Bank began to explore the opportunities for a merger with Midland, whose profitability had begun to recover, and by March of the following year a merger agreement between the two banks was almost in place. It was against this background that the Hongkong Bank renewed its interest in Midland with an agreed take-over bid.[37]

During the 1970s and 1980s, therefore, all four British clearing banks sought to become global banks. Three of the banks had their ambitions cruelly curbed by Latin American debt, Californian banking, and investment banking. Barclays, the fourth, avoided a major catastrophe in these years, and was able as a result to aspire to be counted as a global bank in the new decade. The experiences of the British banks must be set in the context of a general malaise in the world banking industry. Many American, Japanese, and continental European banks were also weakened by unsuccessful strategies of international expansion and diversification into new markets, particularly in investment banking. Arguably, the aggregate performance of the British clearing banks could be compared favourably with that of the American money centre banks. Nevertheless, the inadequacies of the strategies and structures of the British banks are evident. These failings were not simply the result of a particularly flawed generation of senior bank executives, but need to be understood in the context of the institutional legacy which the banks had inherited, and the problems of overcoming it.

## 10.4. Globalization and the Overseas Banks

While the British clearing banks sought to become multinational banks, the descendants of the overseas banks were confronted with the difficult inheritance of their free-standing structures, which also appeared a handicap if they were to become global banks.

ANZ felt itself under a particular competitive disadvantage in the early 1970s. Apart from a board of directors and substantial international banking business located in London, ANZ's business was almost entirely confined to Australia and New Zealand. It had Barclays as a minority shareholder,

---

[36] 'McMahon to Quit Midland', *Financial Times*, 6 Mar. 1991; 'A Look Back at Years of Living Dangerously', *Financial Times*, 12 Mar. 1991.
[37] 'Lloyds and Midland Merger was Blocked by Threat to Quit', *Financial Times*, 25 Mar. 1992.

with around 8 per cent of the equity, but the Australian regulatory authorities had made it explicit that a merger with a British clearing or other overseas bank was out of the question. ANZ was a substantial bank, but its past history and current regulatory conditions appeared set to confine its ambitions to the small Australasian markets.

As the Bretton Woods fixed exchange rate system broke down, both the Australian and British governments sought to influence capital flows, and ANZ's legal status emerged as a major problem for capital-raising. The British authorities were determined to defend a, by now, fragile sterling. In 1974 the Bank of England only approved an ANZ rights issue on condition that the funds were not remitted outside the Overseas Sterling Area. ANZ's management had wanted to extend the group's operations to Asia and the United States. A further blow came in 1975, when the bank was informed that it would not be allowed to remit out of the United Kingdom any of the proceeds of another planned rights issue.

The result was the extraordinary decision in 1976 to transfer the group's domicile to Australia, even though over 95 per cent of ANZ's shareholders were residents of the United Kingdom. The old board in London was dissolved, and a new one based in Melbourne was formed. By the end of 1977 just over 50 per cent of ANZ's shares were listed on the Australian registers, and by 1981 the proportion had risen to 70 per cent.[38] British multinational banking had begun in Australia in the 1830s, and the emigration of ANZ was truly the end of an era.

ANZ's emigration was the neatest solution to the problems caused by the free-standing structure of British overseas banking. It followed, belatedly, the fate of many of Britain's nineteenth-century free-standing companies in other sectors, management control of which seems often to have transferred to the host country before the First World War once the British headquarters became superfluous.[39] The three other surviving overseas banks were not able to take the ANZ route. The host economies of Standard Chartered and Grindlays in Africa and Asia did not offer hospitable locations to transfer domicile, while even the Hongkong Bank's base in Hong Kong was subject to political uncertainties.

During the 1970s and 1980s all three banks attempted to overcome their peculiar administrative heritage by seeking to develop banking and financial activities in the United Kingdom. They appeared to have obvious advantages. Their boards and senior management were almost exclusively British, as was their shareholding, with the partial exception of the

[38] David Merrett, *ANZ Bank* (Sydney: Allen and Unwin, 1985), 295–301.
[39] Mira Wilkins, *The History of Foreign Investment in the United States to 1914* (Cambridge, Mass.: Harvard University Press, 1989), 161–2.

Hongkong Bank.[40] Yet none of the banks succeeded in their British ambitions, while two out of three of them experienced acute problems in their overall strategies and organization.

At the beginning of the 1970s Grindlays appeared to possess reasonable prospects. In 1965 it had acquired two-thirds of the shares of the family-dominated British merchant bank of Brandt, which had been gravely weakened by bad debts. The Bank of England had prevented Grindlays from securing full control,[41] but nevertheless it provided a mechanism to participate in the developing global money markets. By the beginning of the new decade Grindlays had more than 50 per cent of its profits coming from its London operations, which suggested that it had built up a successful Eurocurrency business.[42]

The problem was to devise an appropriate organizational structure to take full advantage of this potential. This proved exceptionally difficult. At the apex of Grindlays was a complex shareholding structure. Lloyds held 41 per cent of Grindlays Holdings, a holding company, which in turn controlled 60 per cent of the shares of Grindlays Bank. Citibank held 40 per cent of the shares of Grindlays Bank directly. This structure satisfied the Bank of England's desire to prevent Grindlays from falling under American domination, but worked to prevent either large shareholder from intervening in the management of Grindlays.

This management was less than optimal. There was confusion and overlapping between the international division of Grindlays, which oversaw commercial banking activities, and the merchant-banking functions performed by Brandts. The bank had diversified with little thought to overall strategic intent. It was only in 1970 that the first 'one-year plan' was devised within the bank, and in the following year the bank's chairman, Lord Aldington, whose family (the Lows) had worked for Grindlays Bank almost continuously since 1856, produced the first attempt at an overall strategic plan, which was called the Strategic Concept. This set a number of overall financial objectives, including an annual return on capital employed after taxes of 11 per cent, and 'a rate of growth of activity and profit of around 10 per cent', without any substantial increase of capital from shareholders. Pessimism about the growth prospects in South Asia and Africa led the planners to look instead to Europe and the Pacific Basin, and particular emphasis was given to the need to build up fee-based

[40] The Hongkong Bank closed its London share register in 1974, at which time 70 per cent of shares were held there. By mid-1982, 73 per cent of shares were held by shareholders with registered addresses in Hong Kong. See King, *The History of the Hongkong and Shanghai Banking Corporation*, iv. 569.

[41] Channon, *British Banking Strategy*, 137; Geoffrey Jones, 'Competitive Advantages in British Multinational Banking since 1890', in id., *Banks as Multinationals*, 50.

[42] G. O. Nwanko, 'British Overseas Banks in the Developing Countries. 3: The Future of the Overseas Banks', *Journal of the Institute of Bankers*, 93 (Oct. 1972), 334.

activities of the kind undertaken by merchant banks, building on the expertise of Brandts.[43]

However, the involvement with Brandts and British merchant banking rapidly undermined rather than sustained the Strategic Concept. Grindlays had finally secured full control of Brandts in 1972, but it did not seek to exercise any management control over the merchant bank's lending policies. At the end of 1974 Brandts had outstanding property loans of £90 million. A sudden collapse in property prices associated with the British secondary banking crisis rendered many of these bad, and in the following year Brandts was obliged to make large debt provisions. A large loss was declared in 1975, and Grindlays paid no dividends.[44]

Lloyds and Citibank were obliged to mount a support operation for the bank's endangered capital position. In 1975 Citibank put more equity capital into Grindlays Bank, thus taking its stake up to 49 per cent, while Lloyds Bank provided two five-year subordinated loans, retaining, thereby, 40 per cent of Grindlays Holdings, but the latter now only controlled 51 per cent of Grindlays Bank. In return for its assistance, Citibank seconded staff in an attempt to improve Grindlays' management performance. A senior Citibank banker was installed in the new post of chief executive, and soon afterwards Lord Aldington retired as chairman. Seconded Citibank personnel attempted to improve the management systems at Grindlays, but the ownership position seems to have handicapped their efforts in this direction.

Grindlays never fully recovered from the crisis of 1974 and 1975. In 1980 Lloyds and Citibank made a new subordinated loan of $US75 million. The world recession in the early 1980s caused bad debts to rise, and Grindlays began to dispose of parts of its business. In 1983 additional large bad-debt provisions stimulated a further realignment of the shareholding, with Citibank increasing its commitment yet again. Under these arrangements Grindlays Bank became a wholly owned subsidiary of Grindlays Holdings, in which Citibank took a dominant 48.6 per cent share, and another former Citibank banker was hired as chief executive. The Lloyds shareholding fell to 21.3 per cent, and Lloyds ceased to have representation at director level.

It came as a relief to almost everyone when, in 1984, ANZ made an offer for Grindlays. The offer, valued at £182 million, was worth considerably more than the bank's current market value, and was readily accepted by Citibank and Lloyds. ANZ, having emigrated to Australia in 1976, had decided to pursue a strategy of multinational expansion beyond

---

[43] Memorandum from the Chairman to Board of Directors, 20 Dec. 1971, Office of the Chairman, 1970–72, Grindlays Archives, ANZ Archives.

[44] Grindlays Bank Ltd, Statement by the Chairman; Channon, *British Banking Strategy*, 136. See also Appendix 5.

its new home economy, and was attracted by Grindlays' branch network in Africa, Asia, and the Middle East. 'At last', Grindlays' chairman reflected, 'we shall have a shareholder who really wants us.'[45] The bank remained incorporated in the United Kingdom, but its operations were increasingly integrated with those of ANZ, and ultimate control passed from London to Melbourne. By a peculiarly circular route, ANZ's acquisition of Grindlays finally achieved the integration of the Anglo-Australian banks with British overseas banks active elsewhere.

Like Grindlays, Standard Chartered discovered during the 1970s that the ownership of its equity by large British and American banks created more uncertainty than profits. The eventual disposals of their holdings by National Westminster and Midland have already been noted. In addition, United States regulations meant that the Chase Manhattan shareholding was under question from the very beginning. Under law Chase could not own stock in another American bank, which meant that the new group would have to sell the Chartered Bank of London, Chartered's San Francisco subsidiary. When Standard Chartered's management declined to follow this course, Chase had to sell its shares in 1975.[46]

Standard Chartered also faced organizational problems. It was not surprising that the task of integrating the two banks did not prove an easy one. They had distinctive corporate cultures, developed over the previous century and influenced by the nature of their host economies. The Chartered staff were skilled in trade finance and exchange banking, while Standard's past focus had been in retail banking. Moreover, at the time of the merger the two banks had quite different organizational structures. Standard Bank was essentially a holding company for a series of subsidiary companies locally incorporated in African countries, while Chartered had remained a branch-based bank with its commercial banking operations not normally conducted through subsidiary companies. The upshot was that there was duplication of functions within the group for some years after the merger, and the full integration of the two head offices was not achieved until 1975.

Notwithstanding such difficulties, the bank embarked on a large-scale diversification strategy in the 1970s, in pursuit of global ambitions. This was a central part of the group's first exercise in corporate planning, the five-year Corporate Plan launched in 1975.[47] The man who became Standard Chartered's CEO in 1977 later recalled the new 'grand design'

[45] 'ANZ Launches £182 million Offer for Grindlays', *Financial Times*, 14 June 1984; Merrett, *ANZ Bank*, 318.

[46] John Donald Wilson, *The Chase* (Boston, Mass.: Harvard Business School Press, 1986), 170–1.

[47] Standard Chartered Bank, *A Story Brought up to Date* (London: Standard Chartered Bank, 1980), 24, 28.

TABLE 10.2. *Major acquisitions of Standard Chartered, 1970–1980*

| Year | Company | Equity participation (%) | Activity |
|------|---------|--------------------------|----------|
| 1973 | Hodge Group | 100 | UK finance |
| 1973 | Mocatta and Goldsmid | 55 | UK bullion |
| 1973 | Mocatta Metals Corporation | 30 | US bullion |
| 1974 | Liberty National Bank | 100 | California commercial banking |
| 1976 | Wallace Brothers | 94.7 | UK merchant bank |
| 1977 | Tozer Standard and Chartered | 100 | UK merchant bank |
| 1978 | Mutual Acceptance Ltd. | 51.98 | Australian finance |
| 1978 | Commercial and Farmers National Bank | 100 | California commercial banking |
| 1979 | Union Bank | 100 | California commercial banking |

*Source*: Standard Chartered Annual Reports, 1973–80.

enunciated in 1975: 'There were two corner stones to that strategy: we wanted to become big in the U.S., through the acquisition of a major banking unit, and we wanted to establish a strong domestic base in the U.K.'[48]

Acquisitions provided the means by which Standard Chartered sought to achieve these goals. Table 10.2 reviews the most important of these in the 1970s. In the United States, a series of acquisitions of small Californian banks culminated in the acquisition of Union Bank (see below, Section 10.6). In Australia, the British bank acquired majority control over a hire purchase and leasing company, in which Chartered had held a shareholding since the 1960s. A joint venture merchant bank was begun in 1973 and brought under full control in 1977, when it was renamed Standard Chartered Merchant Bank. Other merchant banking interests came into the group through Standard Chartered's rescue—at the Bank of England's request—of Wallace Brothers, another victim of the mid-1970s collapse in the British property market. Standard Chartered also acquired a large shareholding in the Mocatta Group, leading bullion-dealers.[49]

There remained the goal of 'a strong domestic base' in Britain. In the age

[48] 'A Banking Mastermind', *Financial Times*, 21 Mar. 1981.
[49] Margaret Reid, *The Secondary Banking Crisis, 1973–75* (London: Macmillan, 1982), 145. There is a study of the history of Wallace Brothers before 1973 by A. C. Pointon, *Wallace Brothers* (Oxford: Oxford University Press, 1974). See also Appendix 2, entry on Sassoon Banking Company; Standard Chartered Bank, *A Story Brought Up to Date*, 37.

of global banking, Standard Chartered was handicapped by its lack of contacts with the headquarters of large British multinationals. It had no British deposit base, which meant that it had to buy all of its deposits on the money markets. This meant, in turn, that the cost of funds, and hence the profit margins of foreign trade financing, fluctuated with interest rate movements outside the bank's control. Standard Chartered was also short of British earnings, which placed it in a disadvantaged fiscal position. It derived most of its profits from outside the United Kingdom, while British corporation tax effectively discriminated against foreign income. The bank lacked sufficient British profits to provide it with taxable allowances to offset overseas earnings and reduce its liability to corporation tax.

Standard Chartered attempted a number of strategies to enter the British market. In 1973 it acquired the entire capital of the Hodge Group, in which Chartered Bank had acquired a minority interest in 1968. The group was predominantly a British retail operation extending mainly small-scale credit to, and attracting deposits from, individuals through a large United Kingdom branch network. In addition, it had around 100 operating companies with a wide range of activities, including cinemas and caravan parks. The acquisition proved ill-fated, for it was a difficult period for British finance houses, with low levels of consumer demand, volatile interest rates, rising costs, and bad debts. The diversified Hodge Group, which Standard Chartered left its founder Sir Julian Hodge to run as chairman, suffered a particularly high incidence of bad debts, and a considerable management effort was required to divest the group of many of its non-core businesses. In 1978 Standard Chartered suffered a humiliation when a British government agency threatened to refuse the bank a licence to conduct consumer credit business after receiving complaints about the conduct of the bank's business. The consumer finance operation was renamed Chartered Trust in 1979, but further extensive bad debts were made during the 1979–82 recession.[50]

Standard Chartered also attempted greenfield branch expansion in Britain, where a dozen new branches were opened over the 1970s. However, neither the new branches nor the Hodge Group were satisfactory responses to the shortage of sterling deposits. While the latter had the potential to become a provider of 'cheap' funds to Standard Chartered, in practice during the 1970s the finance group worsened the funding problem

[50] Standard Chartered Bank, *A Story Brought Up to Date*, 29, and Timothy O'Sullivan, *Julian Hodge: A Biography* (London: Routledge & Kegan Paul, 1981), 89–96. For contemporary discussion of the affair of the consumer credit licence see *Daily Express*, 18 Dec. 1978; *Financial Times* and *Guardian*, 21 Dec. 1978; Office of Fair Trading Press Release, 20 Dec. 1978, 'Consumer Credit Act Licensing: Hodge Group Companies', transcript of interview of Sir Julian Hodge on BBC2 TV 'Money Programme', 11 Oct. 1978.

TABLE 10.3. *Geographical distribution of Standard Chartered's assets and pre-tax profits at 31 December 1980*

| Region | Assets | | Pre-Tax Profits | |
|---|---|---|---|---|
| | £m. | % | £m. | % |
| United Kingdom | 4,240 | 27.5 | 7,376 | 3.2 |
| North America | 3,027 | 19.6 | 33,583 | 14.4 |
| South Africa | 3,510 | 22.8 | 54,489 | 23.4 |
| Africa (except South Africa) | 1,097 | 7.1 | 45,956 | 19.8 |
| Far East | 2,608 | 16.9 | 79,042 | 34.0 |
| Other | 935 | 6.1 | 12,034 | 5.2 |
| TOTAL | 15,417 | 100.0 | 232,480 | 100.0 |

*Source*: Monopolies and Mergers Commission, *A Report on the Proposed Mergers of the Hongkong and Shanghai Banking Corporation, Standard Chartered Bank Limited and the Royal Bank of Scotland Group Limited* (London, Jan. 1982), 35.

as it itself required assistance from wholesale funds obtained from the market by Standard Chartered. The branch expansion programme also offered little relief, for it would have taken a considerable number of branches for Standard Chartered to be able to compete in retail banking with the clearers, and in practice the new branches led to an increased need to fund operations through the money markets.

Despite the unresolved problems in Britain, Table 10.3 shows that in the ten years following its formation Standard Chartered had significantly modified its inherited structure. The bank had shifted its business away from the traditional areas of Africa and the East—although four-fifths of profits were still derived from these regions—and held one-fifth of its assets in North America by 1980. Over a quarter of the bank's assets were in the United Kingdom, but in headquarters or other activities which yielded few returns.

During 1980 Standard Chartered's management concluded that the only way to improve radically its banking presence in Britain was by acquisition. The four largest clearing banks were beyond Standard Chartered's grasp, but a number of smaller clearing banks were potential candidates. The most appealing was the Royal Bank of Scotland Group, in which Lloyds Bank was the largest shareholder with around 16 per cent of the ordinary share capital. The group owned the Royal Bank of Scotland, one of the 'Big Three' Scottish clearing banks, and a small English clearing bank, Williams & Glyn's. There appeared a near-perfect synergy between the Royal Bank, whose business was largely domestic banking, and Standard Chartered. The two banks had had inconclusive merger discussions in 1976, but the Royal Bank became more interested in the proposal in 1979 when Lloyds made unwelcome amalgamation proposals. During 1980 the Royal Bank and Standard Chartered began negotiations. The Bank of England was informed and, unlike in earlier years, supported the proposed integration of domestic and overseas banking, believing that it might enhance the competitiveness of British international banking as well as create a desirable 'fifth force' in domestic banking. Agreement to merge was reached, and on 17 March 1981 Standard Chartered announced a £334 million agreed bid for the Royal Bank of Scotland Group.[51]

Three weeks later the Hongkong Bank made a higher counter-bid for the Royal Bank, and battle was joined between the two main surviving Eastern Exchange banks, both seeking to come 'home'. Hongkong Bank's situation in the early 1970s had some similarities to that of Standard Chartered. It had also only limited representation in the United States or Europe, but its unique position in Hong Kong continued to provide a low-tax environment and an accommodating regulatory system. Hongkong Bank did not follow the British clearing banks in the 1970s when they made public their inner reserves; local regulation permitted it to retain the practice of non-disclosure of 'true profits' and of the amount of inner reserves.[52]

During the 1970s the Hongkong Bank continued its diversification into other financial services.[53] Most of the diversification from commercial banking was achieved by the foundation of new companies. For example, a greenfield merchant bank, Wardley, was founded in 1972.[54] One of the few acquisitions, the purchase in 1973 of 30 per cent of the equity of Anthony Gibbs, the London merchant bank, also provided one of the few problem areas in this decade; in 1980 full ownership was acquired and it was merged into Wardley.[55] The overall performance of the Hongkong Bank Group was impressive. Net published profits doubled between 1971 and 1975, 1975 and 1978, and 1978 and 1980, while true earnings were considerably higher. Moreover, the growth had been internally financed. The bank had no long-term debt, and there had still been no rights issue since 1921.[56]

Nevertheless, the Hongkong Bank remained heavily dependent on Hong

---

[51] Monopolies and Mergers Commission, *A Report on the Proposed Mergers of the Hongkong and Shanghai Banking Corporation, Standard Chartered Bank Limited and the Royal Bank of Scotland Group Limited* (London, Jan. 1982), 4, 62,
[52] King, *The History of the Hongkong and Shanghai Banking Corporation*, iv. 572-3.
[53] Ibid., 717-19, 747-61.  [54] Ibid., 712-13.
[55] Ibid., 714-16, 869-70.  [56] Ibid., 875.

Kong in particular, and the Far East more generally, and, in the age of global banking, this appeared to be a disadvantage. In 1980 the Hongkong Bank acquired 51 per cent of Marine Midland Bank of New York State, and it also turned its attention to Britain, where it was evident that the bank could only radically improve its position by means of an acquisition. The Royal Bank of Scotland presented an obvious target, but any move was delayed by the final arrangements for the purchase of Marine Midland. Standard Chartered's agreed bid for the Royal Bank focused the Hongkong Bank's mind, and on 7 April it made a counterbid, valued at £498 million, or £164 million more than Standard Chartered's offer.[57]

An intense battle followed. Standard Chartered made an increased offer, valued at £481 million. The matter was referred to the British government's regulatory agency, the Monopolies and Mergers Commission, which reported against both bids, largely on the grounds of the need to retain an autonomous Scottish banking system, with ultimate decisions taken in Scotland.[58]

A number of factors lay behind this decision. Important elements in Scotland argued vocally for the retention of Scottish banking autonomy. The Hongkong Bank's offer ran into the particular obstacle of the opposition of the Bank of England, which had agreed to the Standard Chartered bid and, when Hongkong Bank's chairman advised of his intentions, had asked him not to proceed. When the Hongkong Bank ignored this advice the Bank of England did everything possible to block its bid. The evidence of the Bank of England to the Monopolies and Mergers Commission objected to its 'overseas' ownership and control and suggested that Hong Kong's banking regulations were inadequate. However, the fundamental objection was that the governor's authority in the City of London would be fatally weakened if his authority were flouted.[59] Although it supported the Standard Chartered offer, the extreme ferocity of the Bank's opposition to the Hongkong Bank contributed significantly to an atmosphere in which the preservation of the Royal Bank's Scottish identity became the crucial matter.

The Royal Bank of Scotland affair was full of irony. Generations of Scots had provided much of the management of the Exchange banks, yet their attempt to buy a Scottish bank had been defeated by Scottish nationalism. The Bank of England, which had for sixty years worked to prevent the integration of overseas and domestic banking, had been finally

[57] Ibid., 891–3.
[58] Monopolies and Mergers Commission, *Report on the Proposed Mergers of the Hongkong and Shanghai Banking Corporation*, 84–7.
[59] *Ibid*, 61–5; King, *The History of the Hongkong and Shanghai Banking Corporation*, iv. 893–6; R. Fay, *Portrait of an Old Lady* (London: Viking, 1987), 122–6.

reconciled to the idea in the case of Standard Chartered and the Royal Bank, only finally to contribute yet again to its rejection. The Hongkong Bank, the traditional symbol of British financial power in the East, found itself regarded as a 'foreign' bank.

The performance of both Standard Chartered and the Hongkong Bank weakened after the Royal Bank affair, but it was the former that suffered the most. Initially Standard Chartered appeared to recover from the defeat of its British strategy. In 1984 it acquired clearing bank status in Britain, while in the following year agreement was reached to purchase United Bank of Arizona, which represented a further geographical diversification within the United States. Meanwhile, the historic reliance on Africa continued to decline as subsidiaries were localized and, partly for political reasons, the bank reduced its involvement in South Africa. In 1985 Standard Chartered did not participate in a rights issue by the South African holding company Standard Bank Investment Corporation Ltd (SBIC), and as a result the British parent's shareholding fell to 39 per cent.

Yet there was evidence of a loss of strategic direction in this period, and managerial weaknesses were suggested by a threefold growth in commercial bad debt provisions between 1981 and 1983. It was in a weakened state that, in April 1986, Lloyds made a hostile take-over bid (see above, Section 10.3). Standard Chartered's management were determined to maintain the independence of their bank, and this was achieved three months later when a number of prominent Far Eastern and Australian business groups, which were customers of the bank, assumed the role of 'white knights', taking a large shareholding amounting to 40 per cent of the equity, sufficient to defeat Lloyds.[60] Although preserved as an independent bank, however, Standard Chartered's problems became acute. The unusual shareholding structure created constant uncertainty about its future, and its shares became a speculative stock.[61] In 1987 Third World debt provisions resulted in a large loss, and the bank was further burdened by substantial commercial bad debts and poor performing subsidiaries in Canada and elsewhere.

Asset sales and a management purge followed. In 1987 the group's residual investment in SBIC was sold, and in the following year Union Bank and United Bank of Arizona were sold, ending the bank's American strategy. Meanwhile, in March 1988, shortly before the 1987 results were declared, the head of the Bank of England's banking supervision was appointed executive chairman. The existing group managing director

---

[60] The three key 'white knights' were Sir Yue-Kong Pao, a leading Hong Kong magnate and shipowner, who acquired 14.9 per cent of the equity, a Malaysian businessman Tan Sri Khoo Teck Puat, who purchased 5 per cent, and the Bell Group of Australia led by Robert Holmes à Court, which acquired 7.4 per cent.

[61] Lex Column, *Financial Times*, 7 Apr. 1987.

resigned and, in the following October, the former chairman retired. A rights issue was made to boost further the group's capital strength, and the bank sold its head office in London and its Singapore headquarters. Over time the bank's unusual shareholding structure was resolved, with most of the equity held by the 'white knights' being sold.[62]

A recovery plan—or 'Break out' as it was known—made a virtue of what had become a necessary *fait accompli*. Standard Chartered resolved to confine itself to traditional 'core' businesses. The Far East–Pacific and Africa were the main areas of operation, with a focus on traditional business such as trade finance. Commercial and retail banking was to be confined to countries where Standard Chartered had an established position, such as Hong Kong and Zimbabwe.[63]

In 1990 Standard Chartered remained a major multinational bank, with 743 offices in 56 countries (of which 121 were in the United Kingdom). It had 38 per cent of its assets in Europe including Britain, 47 per cent in Asia–Pacific, and 5 per cent in Africa, but it was the latter two regions which provided almost all the profits.[64] The bank had reverted to what it had been in 1970: an institution which combined London-based international banking activity with an extensive commercial bank branch network inherited from Chartered Bank in the Asia–Pacific region, and a profitable banking business in parts of English-speaking Black Africa.

The Hongkong Bank avoided the traumas of Standard Chartered. Like Standard Chartered, its response to the failure of the Royal Bank bid was to seek diversification elsewhere. It joined in the rush of commercial banks to buy London stockbroking firms, in anticipation of major changes in the City's securities market. In 1984 it purchased 29.9 per cent, the maximum permitted by Stock Exchange rules, of James Capel, a leading London brokerage house, with an outstanding reputation as investment analysts. Two years later Hongkong Bank acquired 100 per cent ownership of the firm.[65] In commercial banking, it entered Canada and Australia as these countries deregulated their banking systems. It was permitted to establish commercial banks in both countries. In Canada, a substantial branch network was built up by means of the acquisition of a troubled domestic bank (in 1986), and the subsequent purchase of the Canadian operations

---

[62] 'Bond Sells £165m Bank Stake', *Financial Times*, 5 Nov. 1988; 'Y. K. Pao Sells 10% Stake in Standard', *Financial Times*, 20 June 1989. By 1990 only Tan Sri Khoo remained a significant shareholder, with around 8 per cent of the equity.

[63] 'Breaking out of a Turbulent Era', *Financial Times*, 17 Aug. 1989.

[64] See Table A.4.2 for Standard Chartered's asset distribution in 1990. Total trading profits in that year were £183m. Asia Pacific contributed £153 million, Africa £33m. and Europe £19m. In addition, the Middle East and South Asia made profits of £24m. while North America and Australia lost £11m. and £35m. respectively.

[65] 'James Capel Tops Analysts' League Table', *Financial Times*, 21 Oct. 1986. 'Going Solo after Big Bang', *Financial Times*, 22 Oct. 1986.

of both Lloyds and Midland banks. The Hongkong Bank of Canada was the largest foreign bank in Canada by the end of 1990.[66]

As the 1980s progressed, it became evident that the Hongkong Bank faced two serious problems. The first was its home base. Hong Kong's future was clouded by the fact that much of its land—the New Territories—had been only leased to Britain for 99 years by the Chinese government in 1898. The remainder of the colony, including Hong Kong island, was not a viable entity without the leased territory. At first the Hongkong Bank pretended that 1997 did not exist. Symbolically, in 1982 it restated its faith in the future by offering twenty-year home mortgages.[67] Two years later the British government negotiated an agreement under which the entire colony was to be returned to China in 1997, but with a guarantee of continuity in the territory's economic life-style for a further fifty years beyond 1997. The agreement inspired little confidence and, by the time of the Tiananmen Square massacre in China in June 1989, a mass emigration of business and professional people was already under way.

The second problem for the Hongkong Bank was its diversification strategy. During the 1980s the bank had continued its federated managerial approach to many of its subsidiaries. Hang Seng Bank, Marine Midland (which was not wholly owned until 1987), and James Capel were run as autonomous units. In the mid-1980s this policy appeared a source of strength, overcoming problems of the corporate culture clashes which occurred in many mergers and acquisitions. In fact, the policy was more a sign of managerial weakness than of strength. The Hongkong Bank had introduced formal training for its staff, but its executives' skills remained specific to certain regions and products. As a result there was little alternative to leaving existing managements in place, as a retrospective assessment by the bank's deputy chairman made clear:

We have managed our strategy of expanding overseas with difficulty and we have not always been successful. . . . In neither the US nor Australia did we try to import our own culture, which was a weakness and a strength. In James Capel, there were also culture problems because Capel had a strong, established culture of the securities industry . . . I don't think we had the skills to be more hands on, especially in the US, where it would have been very difficult, and with James Capel.[68]

Table 10.4, which gives the published profits of the Hongkong Bank's new subsidiaries between 1985 and 1990, including the American securities

[66] King, The History of the Hongkong and Shanghai Banking Corporation, iv, 862; 'HK Bank may Buy Lloyds Canada', Financial Times, 2 Feb. 1990. Hongkong Bank Annual Report, 1989.
[67] King, The History of the Hongkong and Shanghai Banking Corporation, iv, 911 n. 1.
[68] 'Culture Shock Delays the Wedding Bells', Financial Times, 16 Oct. 1990.

TABLE 10.4. *Published profits (or losses) of selected Hongkong Bank subsidiaries, 1985–1990*

| Year | James Capel (£000) | CM & M ($US000) | Marine Midland ($US000) | HSBC Canada ($C000) | HSBC Australia ($A000) |
|------|------|------|------|------|------|
| 1985 | n.a. | n.a. | 125,119 | 408 | — |
| 1986 | 16,675 | 3,236 | 144,944 | 1,133 | 350 |
| 1987 | (13,985) | 17,576 | (408,765) | 6,009 | 6,667 |
| 1988 | (32,381) | (30,946) | 160,531 | 20,837 | 10,753 |
| 1989 | 358 | (4,743) | 13,886 | 34,818 | (81,564) |
| 1990 | (30,350) | 407 | (295,631) | 48,688 | (273,198) |

*Note*: n.a. = not available.

*Source*: Hongkong Bank Annual Reports, 1985–1990.

business CM & M acquired in 1983, provides a crude indication of the problems in this period. Hongkong Bank largely avoided Third World debt, but during the second half of the 1980s it more than made up for this by bad debts in the developed Anglo-Saxon economies. Market conditions became extremely difficult in UK and US securities after the October 1987 Stock Market crash, but the losses at CM & M, and especially James Capel, were compounded by management problems. Capel's chief executive resigned in 1990 after failing to persuade Hongkong Bank to sell the firm, and subsequently the firm's high degree of autonomy was ended.[69] There were similar problems elsewhere. Only Canada, where the bank had a core business based on expatriate Chinese immigrants, provided a more optimistic picture at the turn of the decade.

The Hongkong Bank's difficulties were relative rather than absolute. Its published profits declined in 1990, a year of great difficulty for banks throughout the world, but even then it had no need to resort to its still-secret inner reserves. Indeed, the bank's underlying strength became evident in 1992 when the historic decision was made to reveal its inner reserves and real profits. The bank's published net profits of £376 million in 1989, £272 million in 1990, and £465 million in 1991 were translated into real profits of £610 million, £380 million, and £707 million respectively once transfers to inner reserves were disclosed. Hongkong Bank's overall level of inner reserves, which had been the subject of considerable speculation, were shown to have stood at £859 million in 1989, £923 million in 1990, and £1,141 million in 1991. The main problem for the Hongkong Bank was the source of its profitability. Although the diversification strategy had given it over 1,300 offices in around 50 countries and

[69] 'Exodus Tests James Capel's Leading Role', *Financial Times*, 30 Apr. 1990; 'HK Bank Tightens Grip on J. Capel', *Financial Times*, 15 Jan. 1991.

about one-quarter of its assets in the United States and Canada, Hong Kong remained the jewel in the crown. The British colony accounted for 87 per cent of the bank's profits before tax in 1991.[70]

The urgent need to reduce dependence on Hong Kong, and to acquire a more politically secure base, led first to the decision to invest in the Midland Bank in 1987, and subsequently to a complex corporate restructuring. A new group holding company called HSBC Holdings was created, based in London. The structure appeared to give the Hongkong Bank the safety of British citizenship without a British tax burden. At the end of March 1991 the Hongkong Bank's shares disappeared off the Hong Kong and London markets, reappearing in early April as those of HSBC Holdings.[71]

Twelve months later the Hongkong Bank made a take-over offer for the Midland Bank, with the agreement of the latter's board. A rival approach from Lloyds Bank was finally defeated after the Hongkong Bank raised its offer to £3.9 billion, and in June 1992 Midland was finally acquired. The result was the creation of a banking group which combined the provision of international banking services with extensive retail banking franchises in Britain, North America and Asia. It was envisaged that HSBC Holdings would become the London-based corporate headquarters of the new merged group, though with operating units retaining considerable independence.[72] It was the start of a new episode in the long struggle to create a global bank by merging a domestic and an overseas bank.

During the 1970s and 1980s the descendants of the overseas banks had, like the clearing banks, attempted to adjust radically their inherited structures. They had diversified, to new countries and new products. However, such diversification, especially when achieved by acquisition, had revealed managerial weaknesses. Britain had caused constant problems for the banks. Grindlays' investment in merchant banking there had exposed it to the vagaries of the British property market. Standard Chartered had become involved in a consumer finance business it did not understand; had lost strategic direction when it failed to acquire a Scottish bank; and had had its shareholding structure destabilized by an abortive take-over bid from Lloyds. The Hongkong Bank had also been accident-prone in Britain. The acquisition of Anthony Gibbs and James Capel proved unsatisfactory, while the acquisition of the Royal Bank was abortive. The free-standing legacy proved an enduring one.

[70] 'The Beginning of an Era of Change for Hong Kong Investors', *Financial Times*, 15 Apr. 1992.

[71] 'The Bank Does a Bunk', *Far Eastern Economic Review*, 27 Dec. 1990; 'Bank Seeks to Retain its Privileges', *Financial Times*, 18 Jan. 1991.

[72] HSBC Holdings PLC offer for Midland Bank PLC, May 1992.

## 10.5. Global Debt

If British banks were handicapped by their history, they also pursued strategies which compounded their problems. Their participation in extensive cross-border lending was one of the more costly new strategies. British bankers, both in the clearing and the overseas banks, had been notorious for confining their business to short-term lending, yet by 1982 the direct descendants of this tradition were entangled in the world debt crisis—the largest 'lock-up' in history.

International lending by commercial banks grew enormously in the 1970s. Net international bank lending stood at around $40 billion in 1975. It reached $90 billion in 1978 and $160 billion in 1980.[73] This was a largely new phenomenon, which was made possible by the emergence of the Euromarkets. Multinational banks initially used the new global markets largely to service the requirements of their multinational clients. This situation was transformed by the 1973–4 oil crisis, which gave oil-producing countries massive surpluses and non oil-producing countries equally massive deficits. The commercial banks assumed an intermediary role. Oil-producing countries placed their surplus funds with the banks, who 'recycled' them to finance the balance of payments deficits of less fortunate countries. The nature of the banks' customers was substantially altered as a result, as governments and public agencies emerged as the prime customers.[74] The fast international growth of American banks in this decade was very largely driven by this cross-border lending, as most of their executives subcribed to the view that the primary goal of bank management was to increase the size of a bank's assets, and that international lending to anyone who would borrow was the fastest means to achieve this goal.

While there was a range of international borrowers from banks in this period, developing countries and, especially, Latin American countries were particularly prominent. Their indebtedness grew rapidly after 1973, and a growing percentage of this debt was held by commercial banks. One estimate is that their share of Latin American debt rose from 60 per cent in 1973 to 78 per cent seven years later.[75] There appeared to be a synergy between the interests of borrowers and lenders. Developing countries had never received sufficient assistance from official or governmental agencies, and were faced by large balance of payments deficits following the oil price rises. The credits offered by the banks were particularly attractive because

---

[73] P. Campagne, 'The Impact of Multinational Banks on the International Location of Banking Activity and the Global Hierarchy of Financial Centres', Ph.D. 1990 thesis, Reading University, 27.

[74] Channon, *Global Banking Strategy*, ch. 5.

[75] Robert Devlin, *Debt and Crisis in Latin America* (Princeton, NJ: Princeton University Press, 1989), 44.

they did not carry the conditions which often accompanied loans from official institutions. Western commercial banks, in turn, were extraordinarily liquid, and encouraged to lend to many developing countries because there was a boom in the export prices of many of the primary products which they produced. The banks believed not only that sovereign debt was risk-free, but that any dangers of international lending had been minimized by the introduction of variable interest rates on loans and the use of syndicated loans. Syndicated loans were organized by a lead manager, who would assemble a small group of major banks willing to underwrite the loan, and then a larger group of smaller banks willing to take a share in it. The organizers earned fees and commission income, while the smaller banks could participate in international lending at apparently low risk and at little administrative cost.[76]

American banks were the leaders in syndicated lending to the developing world in the 1970s, but British banks were prominent too. During 1976–7 American banks mobilized over one-half of the value of international syndicated loans, but British banks also played an important role, accounting for 16 per cent of such loans. German (16 per cent) and consortium banks (6 per cent) were also significant. In the years 1978 to 1982 there was a rapid growth in non-American bank organization of syndicated credits, especially Canadian (13 per cent), Japanese (9 per cent) and French (5 per cent), but American and British banks continued to dominate as lead managers.[77]

The outbreak of the world debt crisis in August 1982, following the Mexican announcement of a ninety–day moratorium on repayments to banks of all the principal of its debt, was followed by a flurry of recriminations about the lending strategies of the banks. They were variously accused of excessive lending with insufficient regard for loan quality (perhaps in order to get loan fees up front), of 'pushing' loans on borrowers, and of being incompetent at risk assessment, perhaps because of little recent evidence of country default.[78] It was also evident that banks

[76] United Nations Centre on Transnational Corporations (UNCTC), *Transnational Bank Behaviour and the International Debt Crisis* (Sept. 1989), 19–22; Carlos Marichal, *A Century of Debt Crises in Latin America* (Princeton, NJ: Princeton University Press, 1989), 233–6.

[77] UNCTC, *Transnational Bank Behaviour and the International Debt Crisis*, 46. This report gives a ranking of the principal twenty-five banks organizing syndicated credits, by volume of capital mobilized, between 1976 and 1982. National Westminster ($22.5bn.) and Lloyds ($21.3bn.) were ranked sixth and seventh respectively, behind Citicorp ($57.4bn.), Chase Manhattan ($52.7bn.), Bank America Corp ($35.1bn.), J. P. Morgan ($32.8bn.), and Manufacturers Hanover ($25.7bn.). Two other British banks figured in the list: Barclays ($13.4bn.) and Midland ($13.2bn.), sixteenth and seventeenth respectively.

[78] William Darity, 'Did the Commercial Banks Push Loans on the LDCs?', in Michael P. Claudon (ed.), *World Debt Crisis* (Cambridge, Mass.: Ballinger, 1986); Devlin, *Debt and Crisis in Latin America*, 79–83.

demonstrated a tendency to 'herd behaviour', with the result that lending was only loosely related to the underlying strengths of economies.[79]

On closer analysis, at least three different strategies can be discerned among the various multinational bank lenders to the developing world in the 1970s.[80] The 'leaders' were five large American banks, which dominated the process of syndicated sovereign loans, as they sought to achieve an accelerated growth of their assets. They pursued lending strategies that emphasized wide margins and large volumes of loans. Secondly, there was a group of ten relatively smaller banks which were 'challengers' to the 'leaders'. Lloyds Bank was the only British institution in this group, which included the Bank of Tokyo, Chemical Bank, and the Bank of Montreal. These banks aimed to increase their market share by way of ever larger transactions and were prone to assume excessive exposure to insolvency due to 'disaster myopia', or a naïve belief that all debt would be repaid. Thirdly, there was a group of more passive 'follower' banks, which included the other three British clearing banks, which were active in organizing syndicated credits, but less active than the other banks.

There was nothing uniquely British about the world debt crisis. The strategies of the British banks are best seen as pale imitations of their larger American cousins. However, they were more active in developing-country lending than other European banks, and as a result were more exposed to problem-country debt. By end-1985, American banks had 61 per cent of their total loans with developing countries and British banks 45 per cent, while Swiss banks had a mere 18 per cent.[81] Table 10.5 highlights the considerable British exposure to Latin American debt, which was almost that of French and German banks combined.

Perhaps the main criticism of the British banks was that, given Britain's unique history of international banking, they should have been so willing to disregard past experience and to follow the American lead. 'There were plenty of historical precedents on Latin American lending', a chairman of one British bank later observed, 'which should have put the red light up for everybody.'[82] The 'red light' should have been particularly prominent at Lloyds Bank International, the inheritor of over a hundred years of British branch banking in Latin America, yet this bank was prominent as a 'challenger' bank, anxious to expand its balance sheet at almost any cost.

[79] Graham Bird, *Commercial Bank Lending and Third World Debt* (London: Macmillan, 1989), 21; ch. 2 gives a detailed critical analysis of banks' assessment of developing country creditworthiness.

[80] This analysis is based on UNCTC, *Transnational Bank Behaviour and the International Debt Crisis*, 9–10. The five American 'leader' banks are identical with the principal organizers of syndicated credits, given in n. 79, above.

[81] UNCTC, *Transnational Bank Behaviour and the International Debt Crisis*, 46.

[82] Interview with the Chairman of National Westminster Bank. 'Outsider with a Fresh Eye', *Financial Times*, 24 June 1991.

TABLE 10.5. *Exposure of principal creditor banks
(by nationality) to Latin American Debt as of end-1985 ($US m.)*

| Creditor banks | Debtor countries | | | |
|---|---|---|---|---|
| | Brazil | Mexico | Argentina | Total Latin America |
| US | 25,600 | 24,100 | 8,900 | 90,500 |
| UK | 9,140 | 8,669 | 3,677 | 30,046 |
| Japan | 8,200 | 10,000 | 4,300 | 29,730 |
| France | 6,802 | 4,500 | 1,500 | 17,047 |
| Canada | 5,559 | 5,481 | 1,438 | 16,619 |
| Germany | 4,680 | 3,570 | 2,540 | 14,790 |

*Source*: United Nations Centre on Transnational Corporations, *Transnational Bank Behaviour
and the International Debt Crisis* (New York, Sept. 1989), 63.

'The ethos was to expand,' a former manager later explained. 'We wanted
to keep large chunks of syndicated loans because we were so small compared with Lloyds Bank, and compared with the other clearers.'[83] Lloyds
Bank International was one of the most prominent lead managers of credits
to Argentina, and to a lesser extent to Brazil and Mexico. Lloyds was left
with the highest exposure of any British bank to Latin American sovereign
debt. At the end of 1983 the group had a total cross-border exposure to
Latin American loans of around £3.5 billion, compared to total shareholder funds of £2.3 billion. It also had the highest exposure of any bank
to Poland when that country rescheduled its debt in 1981.

The other British banks had been more cautious. Both Barclays and
National Westminster had much less exposure to Latin American debt,
although by the mid-1980s Barclays had had South Africa and Nigeria—
two of its traditional areas of operation—join the list of countries which
could not repay their debts. However, Midland Bank was active in Latin
American loans, and when the debt crisis developed in 1982 it had total
loans outstanding to developing countries of $3.2 billion, or £2 billion.
The direct descendants of the overseas banks, Hongkong Bank and Standard Chartered, were far more conservative. They largely avoided cross-
border sovereign lending, especially in Latin America, although Standard
Chartered was exposed to African indebtedness in the mid-1980s.

Subsequently, both Hongkong Bank and Midland acquired sovereign
debt as an unwanted by-product of their multinational bank strategies in
the United States. Both Crocker National and Marine Midland had made

[83] 'The Last Days of Lloyds Bank International', *Euromoney* (Dec. 1984), 60.

large LDC loans. In 1988, the year after Hongkong Bank acquired full control of Marine Midland, the American bank had total loans outstanding to less developed countries of $1.5 million, or over £800 million. The worst instance of buying LDC debt was by Midland. Crocker National had a high LDC debt exposure, which Midland was obliged to keep when Crocker was sold. As a result, Midland acquired a further $2.6 billion in outstanding developing-country loans, giving the group a total exposure of $5.8 billion, or £3.2 billion.[84]

The financial history of the last two hundred years included many defaults by governments, but for the most part long-term finance for capital projects had been provided by bond issues to private investors, and it was they who suffered when a default occurred. It was the fact that it was some of the world's leading commercial banks which were the principal creditors that gave the debt crisis a different, potentially more serious character. The leading American multinational banks found themselves in particularly exposed positions. As income levels fell in indebted Latin American and other countries, various unsuccessful attempts were made to resolve the problem, although actual defaults were always prevented. In May 1987 Citibank made a public recognition that many sovereign risks were unlikely ever to be repaid when it established a $3 billion reserve provision, amounting to 26 per cent, against its outstanding LDC debt. As a result Citibank made the largest single quoted loss in world banking history.[85]

British banks were obliged to follow Citibank. In August 1987 the Bank of England wrote to all British-incorporated banks with problem debts to encourage them to reconsider the adequacy of their provisions.[86] The resulting debt provisions meant that Lloyds, Midland, and Standard Chartered reported losses in that year. They were the three banks whose multinational strategy had been the least successful over the previous decade, and the debt crisis served to compound already difficult situations, especially for Midland and Standard Chartered. Over the following years British banks made extensive provisions against Third World debt. In 1989 the Bank for International Settlements also introduced new capital standards for banks, requiring them to maintain capital equivalent to 8 per cent of assets, designed to force them to strengthen their balance sheets and, in the process, prevent the kind of over-lending seen in the 1970s.

British banks had never engaged in cross-border sovereign lending, but in the 1970s they indulged themselves in the new and unregulated Euromarkets. They were neither alone nor original in their strategies. Their

[84] Midland Bank PLC, Annual Report and Accounts, 1989.
[85] Channon, Global Banking Strategy, 174–8.
[86] Bird, Commercial Bank Lending and the Third World Debt, 88–90; Stephany Griffith-Jones, 'The New Bank of England Rules for Provisioning', IDS Bulletin (Apr. 1990), 61.

emulation of American banks led the British banks to ignore the past history of regions which they knew so well, particularly so in the case of Lloyds, and to put asset growth before prudence.

## 10.6. Multinational Banking in the United States and Europe

During the 1970s and 1980s British banks attempted to build a second multinational banking empire. They turned their attention from the Southern Hemisphere and Asia towards Europe and, especially, the United States. The globalization of financial markets made it essential to establish branches in leading European and American financial centres to undertake wholesale and corporate banking, but the British banks also pursued the more ambitious strategy of multinational retail banking.

Apart from the flurry of Anglo-Californian banks founded in the mid-nineteenth century, British bankers had generally avoided large-scale direct investment in United States banking. The larger overseas banks maintained wholly owned 'agencies' in New York, which financed trade and acted as sources of information but were prohibited by law from collecting local deposits, while the clearing banks conducted their American business on a correspondent basis and in the inter-war years sometimes appointed individual 'representatives' in the United States.[87] In the mid-1950s a modification in this strategy became discernible, while after 1974 British banks engaged in large acquisitions of American banks.

Between 1955 and 1973 British banks engaged in modest greenfield direct investment in the United States. This period began with the decision of the Hongkong Bank to convert its long-standing San Francisco agency into a separate subsidiary, but this remained a modest operation with only nine branches by 1970.[88] During the 1960s, Chartered and Barclays (DCO) also incorporated Californian subsidiaries. Chartered launched a new subsidiary, the Chartered Bank of London, in 1964. Barclays Bank of California was incorporated in 1965, building on the basis of DCO's representative office in San Francisco. Barclays Bank Limited, the British parent bank, took 25 per cent of the capital, and Barclays (DCO) the remaining 75 per cent.[89]

British banks also enhanced their representation in New York. In 1962 a change in New York law permitted foreign banks to convert their agencies in New York City into branches which could transact domestic business. Barclays (DCO) did this in 1963, and opened a second New York branch

---

[87] For the work of the Lloyds Bank representative in the inter-war years, see Memorandum by Mr Fea, 27 June 1928, File 2330, LB.

[88] King, *The History of the Hongkong and Shanghai Banking Corporation*, iv, 489–93; Annual Report of Hongkong Bank, 1970.

[89] Crossley and Blandford, *The DCO Story*, 242–3, 324.

in 1964, although no more until 1970.[90] In 1971 Barclays created a new subsidiary, Barclays Bank of New York, and began to develop retail banking services. The other overseas banks also upgraded their New York agencies in the 1960s, and they were joined in the city by new British entrants to multinational banking, such as National Westminster, which opened a New York branch in 1969.

The background to the renewed interest in the United States beginning in the 1950s has been sketched in earlier chapters. The shift of British trade and foreign direct investment towards the United States and Europe put into question the traditional correspondent arrangements used by British banks to service the requirements of British business. However, there was no explicit link between British banking activity in the United States and the overall pattern of British direct investment,[91] and host country factors exercised a more immediate influence. While changing regulatory conditions were the most important factor in the opening of New York branches, in California entrepreneurial perceptions of profitable opportunities were significant. It was the fastest-growing state in the United States, with a liberal regulatory position on branch banking.

Also important was the growth of American multinational banking, which disrupted traditional banking relationships. Chartered's chief manager explained the decision to launch the California subsidiary in these terms:

One of the reasons is the much more aggressive action now being taken by the Californian banks in our territories, or what they are now describing as their territories. Some years ago it was customary for them to use our branches and pass their business through us: now they all want a large foreign department for prestige reasons and their men travel round the East exchanging business with small local banks and by-passing us. Perhaps in this war of attrition it is a good thing to counter-attack.[92]

Later in the 1960s, the British clearing banks experienced American competition in their home market. While American banks initially settled in London to participate in the Euromarkets, they also rapidly gained market share in corporate lending, their aggressive marketing and use of term loans attracting British corporate customers as well as the subsidiaries of American corporations.[93] The United Kingdom had the largest amount

---

[90] Ibid., 214–15.

[91] It was also difficult to relate the growth of Japanese bank assets in the United States in the 1980s to Japanese direct investment. See Rama Seth and Alicia Quijano, 'Japanese Bank Customers in the United States', *Federal Reserve Bank of New York Quarterly Review*, 6(1) (Spring 1991).

[92] W. G. Pullen to W. H. Quasha, 19 July 1963, File on USA, Chartered Archives, SC.

[93] Janet Kelly, *Bankers and Borders: The Case of American Banks in Britain* (Cambridge, Mass.: Ballinger, 1977).

of American banking activity, measured in terms of total assets of any country.[94]

The first stages of the British 'counter-attack' in California were not very successful. Although the market was large, it was also complex and competitive, and success within it called for considerable management expertise. The Hongkong Bank managers sent to supervise the Californian subsidiary had learnt their banking in the East, and were ill-equipped to run an American bank, while experienced American bankers were difficult to recruit to a bank in which they could not progress to senior management. Locating an appropriate position in the market was another problem. While the subsidiary should have focused on international trade finance, it exhibited a long-term tendency to become involved in general banking, yet its branch network was too small to be a successful retail bank.[95]

The Chartered Bank of London proved equally problematic for its British parent. It also became involved in domestic banking in an effort to develop a profitable business. The subsidiary opened during an economic boom with rising land prices, and it made a large number of real estate loans. When interest rates rose, defaults followed. Further real estate loans were made before lending procedures were tightened as the dangers of financing real estate speculation became apparent. By the end of 1969 the subsidiary had lost $3 million on bad debts, or the entire amount of its original capital in 1964. These losses also meant that the subsidiary had to be provided with Eurodollar deposits at concessionary rates. In 1968 and 1969 the bank estimated the total cost of such operations at US $2.3 million.[96] The losses were curbed subsequently, but it continued to yield a very low return on capital; the Chartered Bank of London developed as a small retail bank offering a wide range of services largely to individuals. The result was a high-cost, low-return operation with little synergy with the rest of Standard Chartered's business.

The unpromising performance of these Californian operations did nothing to diminish the enthusiasm of British banks for the United States market. In 1974 the period of greenfield expansion gave way to that of acquisition. Table 10.6 gives the major British acquisitions of American banks and financial service companies between 1974 and 1990.

The wave of British acquisitions of American commercial banks began in a modest fashion, in accordance with the general pattern of foreign bank acquisitions of American banks. Prior to 1970 there had been only

---

[94] Goldberg and Johnson, 'The Determinants of US Banking Activity Abroad', 128–9.
[95] King, *The History of the Hongkong and Shanghai Banking Corporation*, iv. 495–8; 776–7.
[96] Ian G. Thompson to Chief General Manager, 18 Mar. 1968; Memorandum to the Chairman, 2 Nov. 1970, Chartered Bank of London File, SC.

TABLE 10.6. *Principal British acquisitions of American commercial banks and financial services companies 1974–1990*

| Date | British bank | US bank | Cost ($US m.) | Fate[a] | California | New York, New Jersey[b] | Other |
|---|---|---|---|---|---|---|---|
| 1974 | Lloyds | First Western | 118 | 1986s | X | | |
| 1974 | Barclays | First Westchester | n.a. | c | | X | |
| 1974 | Standard Chartered | Liberty National | 16 | 1988s | X | | |
| 1978 | Standard Chartered | Commercial and National Farmers | 7 | 1988s | X | | |
| 1979 | Standard Chartered | Union Bank | 400 | 1988s | | X | |
| 1979 | National Westminster | National Bank of North America | 429 | c | | X | |
| 1979 | Barclays | American Credit Corporation | 210 | 1990s | | | X[c] |
| 1979 | Barclays | Beneficial Corporation | 145 | 1990s | | | X[c] |
| 1980 | Barclays | Aetna Business Credit Corporation | 165 | 1990s | | | X[c] |
| 1980 | Lloyds | Talcott Factors (60%) | 118 | 1986s | | | X[d] |

| Year | Bank | Subsidiary | Amount ($m) | Status | | | |
|---|---|---|---|---|---|---|---|
| 1980 | Hongkong Bank | Marine Midland (51%) | 314 | | | | X |
| 1987 | Hongkong Bank | Marine Midland (49%) | 770 | c | | | |
| 1981 | Midland Bank | Crocker National (57%)[e] | 822 | | | X | |
| 1985 | Midland Bank | Crocker National (43%) | 224 | 1986s | | | |
| 1987 | Standard Chartered | United Bank of Arizona | 335 | 1988s | X | | X |
| 1987 | National Westminster | First Jersey National | 820 | c | | | X |
| 1988 | Royal Bank of Scotland | Citizens Financial | 440 | c | | | |
| 1988 | National Westminster | Ultra Bancorporation | 282 | c | X | | X |

*Note*: n.a. = not available.

[a]  s = sold, c = continued in 1990.

[b]  This category is of banks whose main business was in the states of New York or New Jersey. They were not necessarily incorporated there.

[c]  Consumer finance companies which operated in various states.

[d]  James Talcott Factors Inc. had credit factoring and commercial finance services in New York, Atlanta, Dallas, and Los Angeles. 100 per cent control in 1984.

[e]  The Midland Bank paid $597 for 51 per cent of Crocker National in Oct. 1981. It paid $112 m. in Jan. 1982 to increase the shareholding to 54 per cent, and $113 m. in Jan. 1983 to increase it to 57 per cent.

*Source*: Annual Reports of banks and *Financial Times*, various issues.

five foreign acquisitions of small American banks.[97] Standard Chartered acquired a small Californian bank in 1974. In New York, Barclays attempted to expand by acquiring a medium-sized bank, but this was blocked by regulators who, however, allowed the purchase in 1974 of the smaller First Westchester National Bank.[98] The most ambitious and expensive acquisition was by Lloyds Bank, when it acquired First Western Bank (renamed Lloyds Bank California). This and similar purchases raised the share of foreign banks in total banking assets in California from 5 per cent in 1970 to 13 per cent five years later.[99] The Lloyds acquisition made it the largest foreign-owned bank in California, ahead of the other British and Japanese banks in the state, and the eighth largest bank in the state in terms of deposits.[100]

After the initial spate of acquisitions, there was little activity until 1979–81, when a cluster of major acquisitions occurred. These took two forms. First, Barclays, in particular, and Lloyds acquired a number of consumer finance businesses. In 1979 Barclays bought the American Credit Corporation, a consumer finance, leasing and factoring, and mortgage loan company active in twenty-three states, which was renamed Barclays American Corporation, and other acquisitions followed.[101]

On a larger scale, Standard Chartered, Hongkong Bank, National Westminster, and Midland Bank paid between them $1,965 million for two commercial banks and majority shares in two others. After 1974 Standard Chartered continued to look for suitable acquisition prospects in California, particularly in the Los Angeles area. Another small California bank was bought, and this was followed by the acquisition of Union Bank, the sixth largest Californian bank in terms of deposits and the twenty-fourth largest bank in the United States. The Chartered Bank of London was merged into the Union Bank to create an institution which was ranked among the largest twenty-five commercial banks (by size of deposits) in the United States.[102]

Also in 1979, National Westminster Bank purchased the National Bank of North America, the thirty-seventh largest bank in the United States in

[97] King, The History of the Hongkong and Shanghai Banking Corporation, iv. 769–70.

[98] Derek Channon, Cases in Bank Strategic Management and Marketing (Chichester: Wiley, 1986), 286.

[99] Adrian E. Tschoegl, 'Foreign Bank Entry into Japan and California', in Alan M. Rugman (ed.), New Theories of the Multinational Enterprise (London: Croom Helm, 1982), 198.

[100] 'Competing in California', The Economist, 14 Dec. 1974, 79. The other large foreign banks in California at this time were Bank of Tokyo (ranked tenth in terms of deposits), Sumitomo (ranked eleventh), and Barclays (ranked fifteenth). Chartered were twenty-fifth and Hongkong Bank thirty-seventh.

[101] Channon, Cases in Bank Strategic Management and Marketing, 286.

[102] Standard Chartered Bank, A Story Brought up to Date, 34; King, The History of the Hongkong and Shanghai Banking Corporation, iv. 770–1; Standard Chartered Bank Limited News Release, 'Standard Chartered Bank Limited Merger of Californian Subsidiaries', 2 Jan. 1980.

terms of deposits. The National Bank had its headquarters in New York City and 140 branches in the Greater New York area, and was the thirteenth largest bank in New York state. A few years later the operation was renamed NatWest USA.

In the following year the Hongkong Bank acquired 51 per cent of another large New York state bank, Marine Midland. This was the largest foreign bank acquisition yet seen in the history of the United States. Discussions between the two banks began in early 1978, and a definitive agreement was approved by their shareholders in October. However, obtaining the appropriate regulatory permission from Federal and state regulators proved immensely complicated, and it was not until October 1980 that the acquisition of 51 per cent of the stock was accomplished.[103] In consideration of Federal regulatory requirements on interstate banking, the Hongkong Bank of California was sold to an American bank.

The Hongkong Bank acquisition of Marine Midland did not long remain the largest foreign bank acquisition in the United States. In 1981 the Midland Bank acquired 51 per cent of Crocker National, the eleventh largest bank in the United States. Midland Bank had searched for an American acquisition for some years, and it had attempted to buy a Chicago-based finance house, but withdrew when an investigation revealed bad debts. Under the terms of the Crocker acquisition, Midland initially acquired a 51 per cent holding, and it also agreed to raise this stake to 57 per cent over the following three years by paying $90 a share, or a total of $225 million. The acquisition was agreed in July 1980, but it was not until October of the following year that regulatory approval was obtained.[104]

In the early 1980s the British banks were the second largest owners of American banking assets, surpassed by the Japanese, but not dramatically so. (See Table 10.7.)

After a period of inactivity, British banks paid another $2,871 million between 1985 and 1988 for four new banks and for the minority shareholdings of the two banks partially acquired in 1979–81. Midland Bank purchased the remaining stock in Crocker National in 1985, and Hongkong Bank acquired the minority shareholding in Marine Midland two years later. In 1987 Standard Chartered diversified its business by the purchase (via the Union Bank) of the United Bank of Arizona. National Westminster made two large acquisitions of banks in New Jersey, which, from January 1988, permitted New York banks to operate in its state. Finally, the Royal Bank of Scotland—previously the owner of only a small number of foreign branches and offices—acquired Citizens Financial, the largest state chartered bank in Rhode Island, and subsequent small

[103] King, *The History of the Hongkong and Shanghai Banking Corporation*, iv. 776–848.
[104] 'How Midland was Struck by a Californian Earthquake', *Financial Times*, 25 Jan. 1988.

TABLE 10.7. *Total assets of United States banking institutions owned by foreign banks by country, 1980, 1985, 1990 ($US b.)*

| Country | 1980 | | 1985 | | 1990 | |
|---|---|---|---|---|---|---|
| | Assets | Rank | Assets | Rank | Assets | Rank |
| Japan | 72.5 | 1 | 178.6 | 1 | 435.5 | 1 |
| UK | 25.1 | 2 | 57.0 | 2 | 44.1 | 3 |
| Canada | 15.7 | 3 | 39.5 | 3 | 40.2 | 4 |
| France | 12.9 | 4 | 20.6 | 6 | 37.5 | 5 |
| Hong Kong | 11.9 | 5 | 23.3 | 5 | 22.4 | 7 |
| Switzerland | 11.3 | 6 | 18.3 | 7 | 25.6 | 6 |
| Italy | 9.2 | 7 | 29.1 | 4 | 48.0 | 2 |
| Germany | 7.2 | 8 | 8.8 | 8 | 16.2 | 8 |

*Source*: Faramarz Damanpour, *The Evolution of Foreign Banking Institutions in the United States* (New York: Quorum Books, 1990), 151–2. The 1990 figures were given in the *Wall Street Journal*, 23 Aug. 1991, and sent to the author by Mira Wilkins. The Hongkong Bank is included under 'Hong Kong' in this data.

acquisitions over the next two years gave it over 50 branches in the state.[105]

The British banks involved in the intensive acquisition waves were motivated by a desire to diversify their asset bases and to acquire a deposit base in a region where their funds could be profitably used. British banks which had developed corporate or wholesale business in the United States through a small number of branches or representative offices sought a cheaper source of deposits than the Eurodollar market. The banking acquisitions were also both part of, and a response to, a wave of British acquisitions of American companies. Between 1976 and 1986 British companies made 1,572 separate direct investments in the United States, with the number of investments reaching an annual peak of 188 in 1980.[106] The British banks can be regarded as following their clients, but it is more exact to say that they were emulating them. They also shared the contemporary belief held throughout British business that an American operation was a *sine qua non* of being a significant force in the world economy, and that it offered an escape from their own declining market. The United States, a director of the Midland Bank in the late 1970s later recalled,

[105] The most important acquisition was in 1990, when Citizens purchased the Rhode Island subsidiary of the Bank of New England Corporation. Linda S. Tissiere, 'Citizens Financial Group, Inc.: From the Past to the Present', *The Royal Bank of Scotland Review*, 171 (Sept. 1991).

[106] Jim Hamill, 'British Acquisitions in the United States', *National Westminster Bank Quarterly Review* (Aug. 1988), 12.

'was the golden place where all the excitement was ... You were considered a laggard if you weren't there.'[107] Given the bunching of the investments, there was also an element of oligopolistic reaction. The acquisitions of 1979–81 were made in an atmosphere where competitors were buying American banks, and the number of appropriate candidates was limited.[108]

Regulatory considerations were also important. Through the 1970s there was discussion at state and Federal level about restricting the activities of foreign banks, which could perform certain functions not permitted to American banks, and which were also not subject to Federal Reserve requirements.[109] These privileges were regarded as unfair, and as foreign bank activity increased, so did calls for controls over them. The acquisitions of British banks were made against fears that the 'door' might be shut against them. National and Grindlays, for example, took the decision to open a New York branch in 1973, arguing that such a step had to 'be taken quickly as U.S. Government might alter the rules regarding the influx of foreign banks'.[110] In the following year Standard Chartered decided to open branches in Chicago and Seattle partly as 'a pre-emptive act in relation to proposed Federal legislation aimed at restricting the activities of foreign banks'.[111]

The International Banking Act in 1978 put foreign banking organizations on a par with their American counterparts, and the ending of uncertainty in this respect may have made the American market more attractive to foreign banks. Nevertheless, there was an evident suspicion that the subsequent wave of foreign acquisitions would lead to further regulatory controls.[112] 'There is the possibility', Standard Chartered's chief manager in New York reported in January 1979, 'that further legislation might be introduced to restrict the activities of foreign banks in America and the door might then be completely shut.'[113] Such a view was public knowledge,[114] and it helps to explain the sometimes hasty decisions taken by British banks.

A final consideration was exchange movements. Both 1974 and 1979

[107] 'How Midland was Struck by a Californian Earthquake', *Financial Times*, 25 Jan. 1988.

[108] King, *The History of the Hongkong and Shanghai Banking Corporation*, iv. 771.

[109] Faramarz Damanpour, *The Evolution of Foreign Banking Institutions in the United States* (New York: Quorum Books, 1990), 45–67.

[110] National and Grindlays Overseas and International Banking Committee, 18 Dec. 1973, ANZ Archives. In fact, the bank never opened a branch.

[111] The Chartered Bank: Proposed Branch Expansion in the USA, Joint Managing Director, 2 July 1974, USA Box, SC.

[112] King, *The History of the Hongkong and Shanghai Banking Corporation*, iv. 771; 'How Midland was Struck by a Californian Earthquake', *Financial Times*, 25 Jan. 1988; L. G. Goldberg and A. Saunders, 'The Determinants of Foreign Banking Activity in the United States', *Journal of Banking and Finance*, 5 (1981), 29–30.

[113] Chief Manager, USA to Managing Director, 24 Jan. 1979, USA Box, SC.

[114] See e.g. 'Why British Banks are Storming US', *American Banker*, 29 Mar. 1979.

TABLE 10.8. *Principal divestments of American assets by British banks, 1986–1990*

| Date | UK banks | American subsidiary | Purchaser | Price ($ million) |
|------|----------|---------------------|-----------|-------------------|
| 1986 | Midland | Crocker National | Wells Fargo | 1,080 |
| 1986 | Lloyds | Lloyds Bank California | Sanwa Bank | 263 |
| 1986 | Lloyds | Talcott Factors | Congress Financial | n.a. |
| 1988 | Standard Chartered | United Bank of Arizona | Citicorp | 210 |
| 1988 | Standard Chartered | Union Bank | Bank of Tokyo | 750 |
| 1988 | Barclays | Barclays Bank of California | Wells Fargo | 125 |
| 1989 | Barclays | Barclays American Financial | Primerica | 150 |
| 1990 | Lloyds | US commercial banking | Daiwa | 200 |

*Note*: n.a. = not available.

*Source*: Annual Reports of banks and *Financial Times*, various issues.

were years when the US dollar was weak on the foreign exchange markets, and this was widely believed to have been a factor in foreign bank acquisitions of American banks.[115] However, it is more plausible that exchange rate fluctuations had an impact on the timing and size of the investment, rather than on the entire strategy.

The surge of British acquisitions of American banks appeared to signal a radical renewal of British multinational banking. In practice, the period of extensive British multinational bank investment in the United States proved short-lived. By 1990 British banking assets in the United States had fallen in absolute size since 1985, were less than those of Italy, and greatly exceeded by those of Japan. The principal cause of this decline was the flurry of divestments shown in Table 10.8.

Between 1986 and 1990 British multinational retail banking was completely eliminated from California, with the sale of two of the British-owned banks to Japanese banks, and of the remaining two to Wells Fargo, a local Californian bank. The terms of several of the sales indicated the poor conditions of the British banks. Midland sold Crocker at book value, but only after taking over $3.5 billion (£2,502.5 million) of Crocker's less desirable assets—including Latin American debt, and non-performing Californian property loans.[116] Lloyds sold its Californian subsidiary for a multiple of book value of 1.5, but only after taking on $250 million (£176.6 million) of cross-border lending, including $160 million to Latin America.[117] Barclays and Standard Chartered sales did not include having

[115] Damanpour, *The Evolution of Foreign Banking Institutions in the United States*, 120–1; 'Why British Banks are Storming US', *American Banker*, 29 Mar. 1979; Goldberg and Saunders, 'The Determinants of Foreign Banking Activity in the United States', 28–9.

[116] 'Midland Bank Sells Crocker for £715m. to Wells Fargo', *Financial Times*, 8 Feb. 1986.

[117] 'California Bank Sold by Lloyds', *Independent*, 15 Feb. 1986.

to take on dubious debt, but the latter had to sell its recently acquired Arizona bank for $80 million less than it had paid for it.[118]

By 1990 Standard Chartered, Lloyds, and Midland had abandoned branch banking in the United States. They were left with corporate banking and treasury business largely managed by New York offices, which was effectively the position with which they had started the 1970s. Barclays retained a larger presence in American corporate banking, but withdrew from Californian retail banking and also from its large consumer finance business. In 1992 it withdrew completely from American retail banking when it sold its 65 branches in New York to the Bank of New York.

In most cases, these divestments came after sustained periods of poor financial performance and, often, capital injections by the British parents. This was particularly true of the Californian subsidiaries.[119] The full cost of these poor-performing operations included the large amount of senior management time in the British parents which they occupied. Standard Chartered's Union Bank was the most successful British acquisition in California. Its net profit after taxation rose from $32 million to $56 million between 1980 and 1987, and it made a significant contribution to Standard Chartered's profits, peaking to 25 per cent of the entire group's pre-tax profit in 1986.[120] It was a considerable irony that the one British bank to achieve significant success in Californian banking had to withdraw because of the problems elsewhere of its parent.

In contrast to Union Bank, Midland's purchase of Crocker National was disastrous. In November 1983 American bank regulators examined Crocker's loan book and identified a large number of non-performing loans. Crocker had to allocate over $100 million dollars to its reserves, resulting in a small loss in that year. New American management was introduced; control from London tightened; and further debt provisions made. However, a year later regulators ordered further substantial bad-loan provisions, and demanded that the British parent prevent Crocker from failing. The American bank recorded an annual loss of $324 million in 1984. In January 1985 Midland invested a further $250 million in Crocker, and arranged a standby loan of $125 million, while five months later it purchased the Crocker minority shareholding. Finally, in May 1986, Crocker was sold to Wells Fargo, and the bank's name was rapidly abolished.[121]

[118] 'Standard Chartered £110m. US Bank Sale', *Financial Times*, 30 Jan. 1988. Barclays Bank of California was sold on a multiple of 1.7 and Union Bank of 1.3.

[119] 'Over there and Overdrawn', *Sunday Times*, 4 Mar. 1984; 'California Proves a Tough Testing Ground', *Financial Times*, 8 Feb. 1986.

[120] Standard Chartered Circular to Shareholders, 'Proposed Sale of Union Bank', 26 Apr. 1988.

[121] 'How Midland was Struck by a Californian Earthquake'; 'Midland Storm-troopers Fight to Stem Soaring Losses'; 'The £1bn. Cost of an Ill-Starred Excursion', *Financial Times*, 25, 27, 29 Jan. 1988.

The divestments of the second half of the 1980s left the Hongkong Bank and National Westminster as the main British banks still active in multinational retail banking in the United States, alongside the smaller Rhode Island operations of the Royal Bank of Scotland. These banks were more 'successful' than the other investments in the sense that they survived, but their financial performance was patchy. NatWest USA started the decade with losses or marginal profits, but after receiving $150m of new capital in the first three years, it appeared to recover slowly. A review of US bank performances gave Marine's average annual return on equity for 1980–6 as 10.4 per cent, compared with 13.8 per cent for the US money centre banks and 12.7 per cent for the US regionals.[122] Nevertheless, in the mid-1980s Hongkong Bank and National Westminster were regarded—at least in comparison with other British banks—as banks which had 'managed to master the fickle US market place'.[123]

At the end of the 1980s, however, the American banking market-place became exceptionally 'fickle'. Both the Hongkong Bank and National Westminster were severely affected by an economic recession which particularly affected the north-east of the United States and the property market. In 1990 both banks were required to provide new equity capital of $300 million to support their American subsidiaries. NatWest USA lost $140 million in 1989 and $352 million in 1990: the 1990 loss (equivalent to £167 million) was larger even than Crocker National's record loss in 1984, and brought unfavourable comparisons with Midland Bank's experiences.[124]

A variety of explanations can be offered for the demise of British multinational banking in California, and its problems elsewhere. There were powerful adverse exogenous circumstances. Californian banking became highly competitive in the 1970s and 1980s. Financial deregulation removed bank interest rate cartels, while permitting other institutions to enter commercial banking. Savings and loans institutions entered other areas of personal finance. Brokerage houses competed for deposits, as did large retailers.[125] Similarly, the problems of Marine Midland and NatWest USA on the north-east coast were in the context of a severe recession in which most competitor banks also fared poorly. The complex American regulatory procedures, which caused long delays between offers and approval of acquisitions, can be regarded as another adverse exogenous circumstance. This was particularly evident in the case of Crocker National, where the delay in receiving regulatory approval had serious consequences. Crocker's

---

[122] 'Marine Midland Sees Light at the End of the Tunnel', *Far Eastern Economic Review*, 22 Dec. 1988.
[123] 'California Proves a Tough Testing Ground', *Financial Times*, 8 Feb. 1986.
[124] Lex Column, *Financial Times*, 5 Apr. 1991.
[125] Channon, *Cases in Bank Strategic Management and Marketing*, 380–1.

management had wanted extra capital to expand. During the fourteen-month interval the bank increased its lending by $1.5 billion, much of which was on speculative real estate and to Latin America.[126]

There were, however, also failures in the strategy and management of the British banks. There were problems, for example, with the banks chosen for acquisition, and the terms. As a contested foreign take-over of an American bank was impossible, the banks acquired by the British had to be willing sellers. The management of a successful bank was unlikely to offer itself for sale to a British bank, and there was thus some justice in one observation (with regard to Marine Midland) that the lesson seemed to be 'to misquote Groucho Marx: never buy a bank that would have you as its owner'.[127] As a result, British banks had a tendency to pay a lot of money for banks which no one else wanted, or which had management problems. Lloyds began this tradition with the acquisition of First Western, a bank which 'had been passed from pillar to post and milked for profits by its sundry owners'.[128] Its latest owner, World Airways, had been obliged to divest from banking because of regulatory requirements. The purchase price—equivalent to £50 million for a bank with post-tax profits of £2 million—was widely regarded as excessive, but defended by Lloyds management as 'a rare opportunity' to buy a Californian bank.[129]

In other instances, American banks were anxious for funds to expand, and were able to force the British bank to provide these with minimal controls. Crocker National was only the most serious instance of this phenomenon. Marine Midland, for example, had passed through a severe crisis in the mid-1970s which had depleted its capital. Taking a foreign bank as a shareholder was the most realistic means of finding funds to finance a recovery, and Marine Midland was in a strong enough position to oblige Hongkong Bank to acquire only 51 per cent of the equity.[130]

A further failing was the absence in many cases of a focused business strategy. British banks, in their initial stages at least, attempted to penetrate a whole range of markets—retail, investment banking, and wholesale corporate—in which they lacked both the size and managerial expertise to be successful. The Union Bank was noteworthy for a more defined focus—serving the upper end of the medium-sized corporate market in California—a strategy which it had long pursued and which Standard Chartered allowed to continue. Ironically, the British bank felt under

---

[126] 'How Midland was Struck by a Californian Earthquake', *Financial Times*, 25 Jan. 1988.
[127] Shroff, *Far Eastern Economic Review*, 21 March 1991. See Darby, 'The Internationalization of American Banking and Finance', 409.
[128] 'Competing in California', *The Economist*, 14 Dec. 1974, 74.
[129] Interview with Jeremy Morse, *The Economist*, 9 Apr. 1975.
[130] King, *The History of the Hongkong and Shanghai Banking Corporation*, iv. 786–90, 793–4. See also Damanpour, *The Evolution of Foreign Banking Institutions in the United States*, 162.

pressure from Federal regulators and the Community Reinvestment Act of 1978 to shift Union Bank from its wholesale policy to a more consumer- and retail-orientated business, and a desire for a US dollar deposit base also encouraged interest in this area, but Union Bank eventually remained in its niche.[131] Multinational retail banking has proved difficult in every market, and Standard Chartered's product niche strategy was later recognized as the most effective competitive strategy for foreign banks.[132]

In many cases the relationship between the British parent and the American subsidiary was also troublesome. The usual pattern was that the British bank allowed its new acquisition a large degree of local autonomy. After a period, management difficulties arose, forcing the parent to assert much tougher control. Crocker National provides an extreme example. Midland had no control at all over the excessive lending undertaken during the period when regulatory approval was being sought. Even after October 1981 Midland was able to exert little influence over the bank it nominally controlled, and no co-ordination over their business activities. It was not until the end of 1983 that Midland sent British officials out to investigate Crocker's affairs, and not until the following year that Crocker's senior management was replaced and a senior Californian banker recruited to reconstruct the bank.[133] Hongkong Bank's relationship with Marine Midland developed in a similar fashion. After initially functioning as an autonomous entity, management problems led the Hongkong Bank to buy out the minority shareholding in 1987. It was not until 1988 that Hongkong Bank's director in New York secured offices in Marine Midland's building in the city. At the end of the decade the autonomy policy was abandoned, and senior staff were despatched from the parent bank to undertake 'radical restructuring'.[134]

An additional 'cost' of their American adventures may have been a neglect of continental Europe, to which the United Kingdom was joined by ever closer economic and political links, especially after Britain's accession to the European Community in 1973. During the 1960s the continental subsidiaries of the clearing banks, dating from the First World War, were revitalized, using the Euromarkets to expand their deposit base despite their small branch networks.[135] Some of the overseas banks, too, turned some attention to the Continent. Both Standard and Chartered, for

---

[131] 'California Proves a Tough Testing Ground', *Financial Times*, 8 Feb. 1986; Standard Chartered Bank, California Conference, 27 Nov.–1 Dec. 1978, Union Bank Files, SC.

[132] Hirtle, 'Factors Affecting the Competitiveness of Internationally Active Financial Institutions', 42.

[133] 'Midland Storm-Troopers', *Financial Times*, 27 Jan. 1988.

[134] 'Culture Shock Delays the Wedding Bells', *Financial Times*, 16 Oct. 1990; 'Marine Midland Losses Rise to $111.5 million', *Financial Times*, 1 Nov. 1990.

[135] Geoffrey Jones, 'Lombard Street on the Riviera: The British Clearing Banks and Europe, 1900–1960', *Business History*, 24 (1982), 202–4.

example, acquired shareholdings in small financial services and investment companies in Switzerland, Germany, Spain, Malta, and elsewhere, but there was no parallel in continental Europe with the subsequent dramatic expansion of British banks in the United States. Given the regulatory and other difficulties of acquiring domestic banks in most European countries, and the prohibitive cost of greenfield branch expansion, British banks largely confined themselves to shareholdings in merchant and private banks, and financial services.

The imminence of a post-1992 Single Market within the European Community caused speculation about an increase of multinational retail banking within Europe,[136] but the response of British banks was muted. Standard Chartered and Hongkong Bank effectively withdrew from the market. In 1989 the former sold all its continental European banking operations to Westdeutsche Landesbank, Germany's fourth biggest bank, together with half its merchant bank, which became the basis of a new joint venture, Chartered West LB.[137] The Hongkong Bank transferred substantial parts of its continental European business to the Midland Bank in the late 1980s.

There was more interest in continental Europe among some of the clearing banks. During the 1980s Barclays developed multinational retail and other subsidiaries in several European markets. National Westminster had a strategy of penetrating continental European banking through alliances and joint ventures with local partners, but the only concrete result was the purchase of a small number of branches in France, and by the turn of the decade any desire for extensive direct representation on the Continent had disappeared.[138] The Midland Bank also flirted with Europe in the late 1980s, acquiring nearly half of a Milan merchant bank and entering mortgage-lending in France, but several operations—such as French mortgage-lending—were rapidly abandoned.[139] Lloyds effectively withdrew from the Continent, apart from specialized niche areas, and even the historical Bolsa presence in Portugal was sold in 1990.

Direct investment by British banks in continental Europe remained small. In some southern European countries, notably Spain and Greece, they had a multinational retail presence. The local banks of these countries had been protected by restrictions on foreign bank entry, and—in the case of Greece—had been state-owned. They were often inefficient, and British

[136] Edward P. M. Gardener and Philip Molyneux, *Changes in Western European Banking* (London: Unwin Hyman, 1990), 139.

[137] 'Standard-bearing West LB Grabs the Political Initiative', *Financial Times*, 10 Oct. 1989; 'An Anglo-German Link-up', *Financial Times*, 14 Feb. 1991.

[138] 'Developing a European Branch Network', *Financial Times*, 17 Oct. 1988; 'Nat West to Withdraw from Belgian Market', *Financial Times*, 2 Feb. 1991.

[139] 'Midland to Sell Swiss Subsidiary', *Financial Times*, 28 June 1990; 'Woolwich to Buy French Group', *Financial Times*, 5 Mar. 1991.

and other foreign banks were able to offer a more efficient service, transferring techniques learned in more progressive markets. In Germany, Italy, and elsewhere, British banks operated a number of successful merchant- or investment-banking businesses.[140] Several medium-sized British banks also formed strategic alliances, cross-shareholdings, and joint ventures with continental banks.[141] These relationships were reminiscent of the era of 'clubs' in the 1960s, and their ability to provide more enduring benefits than their predecessors was far from certain.

In the era of global banking from the 1960s, therefore, British banks had attempted to construct a multinational banking business in the United States with considerable similarities to that which their predecessors had founded in the nineteenth-century settler economies. They had sought to combine international banking with a multinational retail business. In most cases this strategy was unsuccessful. The strategy of opening branches in New York and other major business centres in the United States had been correct, because the service and wholesale banking business of the British banks required such facilities. However, the British banks underestimated the problems of multinational retail banking in a developed market economy. They held no real advantage in the United States beyond an ability to finance acquisitions, and inadequate management had rapidly led to difficulties in a competitive and complex market. In contrast, British banks were restrained in their business strategies towards continental Europe. Such caution was perhaps understandable in view of the travails of the previous two decades.

### 10.7. Conclusion

The multinational banking industry was transformed from the 1960s. The advent of global financial markets changed the industry almost beyond recognition. Britain, or rather the City of London, retained a position of great international importance, for many of the new markets were physically located in the resurgent City, but British-owned banks rapidly lost significance.

The growth of American and, later, Japanese multinational banking reflected the size of their economies, their relative importance in the world

---

[140] In Germany, for example, Midland Bank owned 80 per cent of Trinkaus & Burckhardt, which established an innovative investment banking business. 'Institution is Banking on High Technology Products', *Financial Times*, 13 July 1991.

[141] In 1988 the Royal Bank of Scotland made an equity exchange agreement with Banco Santander of Spain. Two years later these banks initiated a European electronic banking network (IBOS), which Credit Commercial de France joined in 1991. In 1990 the Bank of Scotland purchased a third of the equity of a new Greek bank, and established a joint venture credit card operation in Germany. A third medium-sized British bank, TSB, formed a strategic alliance with Cariplo of Italy in 1991.

economy, and the strength of their currencies. The competitive advantages of British multinational banks in the nineteenth century had similarly rested on the importance of their home economy. The shrinking of British-owned multinational banking was, in this sense, 'inevitable'. However, British banks were also weakened by problems in their strategies and structures.

British bankers entered the era of global banking from the 1960s with an administrative heritage formed in quite different circumstances. It was based on segmented markets, specialist institutions, and strong corporate cultures. The British banks sought to modify this heritage, but it was a difficult task which was often undertaken too slowly and imperfectly. Matters were made worse by the unfortunate consequences of radical shifts in traditional business strategies. In the nineteenth century British overseas banks had pioneered multinational banking. In the process, they had secured franchises which were still yielding profits in the 1980s. But in the post-1960s multinational banking industry, British banks were more often followers than leaders. It proved neither a glamorous nor a rewarding role.

CHAPTER 11

# Conclusion

## 11.1. *British Multinational Banking: A Profile*

Beginning in the 1830s, British banks established extensive overseas branch networks during the course of the nineteenth century. They went first to British colonial settlements in Australia and Canada, and to the colonies in the West Indies. In the 1840s and 1850s new banks were established to exploit profitable opportunities in Asia, following the end of the East India Company's monopoly and the easing of regulatory barriers. In the 1860s and 1870s yet more British banks were founded to operate in the flourishing settler economies of the Southern Hemisphere—Argentina, Brazil, the South African colonies, and New Zealand. By the end of the nineteenth century the structure of British multinational banking was in place. A group of around thirty British banks owned and operated branches throughout the Southern Hemisphere and in all the leading ports of Asia.

In terms of numbers of branches, the Australian and New Zealand colonies were the heart of nineteenth-century British multinational banking. In terms of asset distribution, British overseas banks focused their attention on a 'Triad' consisting of Australasia, Latin America, and Asia in the fifty years before the First World War. In Australia and New Zealand, British banks, like their locally owned counterparts, owned large branch networks engaged in retail banking. In Asia, the British banks were mainly located at ports and trading centres. The British banks in Latin America were initially closer to the Eastern Exchange banks, but had a tendency towards developing more on the Australasian lines.

This geographical base offered the British banks superb opportunities in the nineteenth century. The booming production of and trade in primary goods, in which these areas specialized, provided excellent business, as did their import of manufactures from Europe, and especially Britain. The regions of recent settlement attracted large inflows of European labour and capital, which expanded markets and furthered economic development. The peasant economies of Asia benefited much less from trade in primary products, but nevertheless their exports of rice, cotton, opium, and other commodities expanded very rapidly alongside their imports of cotton textiles and other European goods. This favourable economic environment was greatly enhanced because British political control extended over the Australasian colonies and over most of the Asian trading centres. The risks of undertaking multinational banking were, as a result, much reduced. The

British overseas banks' business rested fundamentally on Britain's position as the world's largest capital-exporter, major world trader, and strongest imperial power.

The early British multinational banks competed with each other, and with other institutions, but the competitive structure of their industry was favourable to them. The rapid growth of American manufacturing and the international expansion of American multinationals was not matched by any significant United States multinational banking activity until the First World War. Multinational banks owned by other European countries did compete with British banks by the turn of the century, but were rarely able easily to overcome the first-mover advantages possessed by the British. In Australia and New Zealand, the British banks did face effective competition from banks established in the colonies, but in Latin America and Asia such local banks were either unstable or non-existent. The British banks were rarely active in those nineteenth-century countries outside the British Empire with well-developed domestic financial systems: the United States, Western Europe, and Japan after the Meiji Restoration.

The well-developed and extremely specialized British financial system also gave the early British multinational banks considerable room for expansion. Britain's domestic or clearing banks avoided most forms of international banking until the late nineteenth century, and did not even contemplate multinational banking until the early twentieth. Apart from conservatism, Britain's domestic bankers were discouraged from multinational banking by their relative smallness before the completion of the amalgamation movement, as well as by their underdeveloped skills outside retail banking. The merchant banks were international bankers *par excellence*. However, their family-based structures and small capitals would have been handicaps if they had sought to become multinational banks. In fact, their reputations and connections gave them immense advantages which rendered such strategies unnecessary. They and the overseas banks effectively specialized in different financial services and/or different regions. Competitive rivalries occurred, but, as in the case of the issue of Latin American loans, there often seems to have been a recognition that a certain activity belonged to one set of institutions rather than another.

The corporate structures of nineteenth-century British multinational banks were distinctive. They were free-standing entities which did no domestic banking business in the United Kingdom, apart from arranging trade finance and occasionally collecting deposits, particularly from Scotland. However, there were sometimes interlocking directorships between domestic and overseas banks, and occasionally domestic banks promoted new overseas banks. The British-based boards and small head offices exercised a close control over the lending and other parts of the business of their overseas branches. A variant of this pattern came when a British-owned and -managed bank was registered in a British colony, as in the case of the Hongkong Bank. Each bank specialized on a country, or at most a region.

This corporate form was most unusual in the history of multinational banking, but it was a typical form of nineteenth-century British foreign direct investment, seen in practically all economic sectors, which reflected both the abundance of capital available in the City of London and the limited growth of managerial hierarchies compared to the United States. Unlike most other free-standing firms, this organizational form persisted in British multinational banking through the inter-war years and beyond, although sometimes modified by clearing banks taking part of the equity.

The reasons for the survival of the free-standing form in multinational banking are clear. While a small head office and an elementary managerial hierarchy were a considerable handicap in industries which involved complicated processes or research and development, they remained much more viable in banking. The British banks made very effective use of socialization strategies to control their overseas branches, which reduced the need for a large head office to monitor staff. The British multinational banks were effective business institutions in the nineteenth century despite what appeared, by Chandlerian standards, underdeveloped management structures.

The British banks demonstrated considerable flexibility in their business strategies. They were initially multinational service banks concerned with international banking, especially trade finance and exchange. However, in almost all cases this led them into greater involvement with their host economies, and into multinational retail banking. In Australia this happened early in their corporate histories, but everywhere the finance of international trade drew banks into the domestic economy as they financed the distribution, and sometimes the growing, of crops. The issue of banknotes and the search for local deposits were also important influences leading to greater involvement with host economies.

The banks benefited greatly from their public images as bastions of financial orthodoxy. In practice, they had no choice but to adapt banking policies to the realities of the countries in which they operated, although this process regularly caused conflicts between London head offices and managers in the field. In particular, British banks modified the terms on which they would lend. Short-term lending gave way to the provision of longer-term credit. Mortgages were taken as security. In some cases, no security beyond a man's name came to be accepted.

These trends happened first when the banks operated in British colonies settled by British emigrants. The greater the political, legal, and cultural differences between Britain and the host economy, the less was the willingness to modify the rules of British banking orthodoxy. British banks in the nineteenth—and indeed the first half of the twentieth—century considered the risks of lending to Asians (let alone Africans) to be high, but the Eastern Exchange banks dealt with the indigenous sector in Asia using intermediaries such as compradors. Until the 1950s there were two streams of business activities within these banks. British managers lent to Western business, while locally recruited staff dealt with the indigenous sector. The latter's cost of borrowing increased as a result, but these links between the Western and indigenous business sector had benefits as well as costs.

The most striking theme in the history of British multinational banking in the sixty years after the outbreak of the First World War in 1914 was continuity. The geographical location, the organizational structure, and the business strategies of the British banks changed only slowly. In terms of geographical location, Australia and New Zealand continued to provide homes for the largest number of British-owned foreign branches from 1914 through to the 1960s, and its share of total British multinational banking assets stabilized at around 20 per cent. There continued to be relatively few branches in Asia, but that region accounted for around one-quarter of assets. The most significant change was the replacement of Latin America by Southern Africa as the third major area of British overseas banking. By 1955 there were almost as many British-owned bank branches in Southern Africa as in Australasia, while the region probably accounted for the largest share of assets.

The other locational changes were more modest. British banks pioneered modern banking in various parts of British colonial Africa and in the Middle East. They virtually withdrew from Canada and the United States after the end of the First World War, retaining only their modest representation in New York. The 1920s saw a rapid expansion—from almost zero base—of British bank branches in parts of Western Europe, but this was not sustained.

The theme of continuity also applied to the organizational structure of British multinational banking. The sector continued to consist largely of free-standing banks specializing in particular regions and not engaged in domestic banking, although there was a noticeable reduction in the numbers of banks over time, mostly achieved by mergers of banks specializing in the same region. After 1936 British banking was represented in Latin America by a single bank, while from 1951 there were just two British banks active in Australia.

The most radical organizational innovation was the entry of domestic banks into multinational banking. There was a surge of interest in multinational banking by the clearing banks between 1913 and the mid-1920s, but then few new initiatives until around 1970. The most important institutional result was the creation of Barclays (DCO), a large multi-regional bank largely controlled and partially owned by Barclays Bank. Lloyds Bank took a large, but fluctuating, equity interest in British banking in Latin America and acquired a branch network in South Asia, together with smaller holdings in other overseas banks. The clearing banks also established subsidiaries to undertake branch banking in continental Europe. These developments occurred despite the expressed wishes of the Bank of England, which sought to exclude the clearing banks from multinational banking.

There was also a strong continuity in the business strategies of British multinational banks. They largely stuck to their knitting, but modified their lending and other policies as circumstances changed. When international trade declined in the inter-war years, British banks became more involved in local lending, and more willing to relax rules on types of collateral. The 1930s saw Eastern Exchange banks begin to experiment with the recruitment of Asians into staff positions. After the Second World War some banks became involved in medium-term lending in Africa and Asia, and in other financial services such as hire purchase, savings banks, and unit trusts in the developed Southern Hemisphere economies. British banks were not radical innovators, but financial innovation was in any case closely controlled by official regulations in most countries after the Second World War.

From the 1960s the multinational banking industry was transformed by the advent of the global currency and capital markets. The large-scale multinational expansion of American banks, followed by other European and later Japanese institutions, dramatically changed the corporate players. Technological changes and deregulation in much of the developed world resulted in a blurring of distinctions between different types of banking and financial services.

The organizational structure of British multinational banking changed significantly in these years. Around 1970 there was a process of consolidation which featured the union of two of the remaining free-standing banks to form Standard Chartered; the formation of ANZ as a single Anglo-Australasian bank; and the merger of most of Lloyds' and Barclays' overseas interests into wholly owned international subsidiaries of the parent banks. These subsidiaries were later fully integrated into their parents. During the 1970s the two remaining large English clearing banks, Midland and National Westminster, made large-scale multinational investments for the first time.

The results of these developments were a considerable integration between overseas and domestic banking and the virtual ending of the traditional regional specialization of the banks. However, the old free-standing structure had left a legacy which was not easily overcome, and a number of multinational banks remained without a significant domestic British banking business. During the 1970s and 1980s there was a series of unsuccessful attempts to resolve this problem in the cases of Standard Chartered and Hongkong Bank, including rival take-over offers for the

Royal Bank of Scotland in 1981 and the Lloyds Bank take-over bid for Standard Chartered in 1986. ANZ resolved the problem by shifting domicile to Australia in 1976.

Corporate reorganization was accompanied by radical changes to business strategies and geographical location. The traditional focus on providing trade finance and international banking services, combined with retail banking, in the Southern Hemisphere economies and Asia was greatly qualified. British banks engaged in extensive cross-border sovereign lending for the first time. They diversified into other financial services on a large scale. There was also a dramatic geographical reorientation. British multinational banking virtually disappeared from the old bastions of Australia and South Africa, and became relatively insignificant in Latin America, although substantial investments remained in various Asian and African countries. There was a surge of major bank acquisitions in the United States, designed to build a second British multinational banking empire.

Unlike their nineteenth-century predecessors, however, the 1980s generation of British multinational banks found it hard to sustain their position. Most of them divested from retail banking in the United States, often after heavy losses. Sovereign lending resulted in a burden of Third World debt second only to that of the American banks. Diversification into related financial services, too, often resulted in losses and excessive burdens on management time. By 1990 British banks had rediscovered the merits of sticking to their knitting, but the wrong turnings and mistaken strategies of the previous two decades had taken their toll. They were chastened, and considerably less important in world banking than thirty years previously. Nevertheless, the British misfortunes of this period were by no means unique. American and other banks suffered from similar flawed strategies in international banking, and at least one British bank steered a sufficiently safe course through the perils of these years to remain a 'global' bank of the early 1990s. Hongkong Bank's acquisition of Midland Bank in 1992 created another large British-based international bank with a 'global' retail deposit base.

## 11.2. Origins and Competitive Advantages

Within the general history of British multinational banks, this book has explored specific themes related to their origins and competitiveness over time. The evidence from the foundation of the British multinational banks in the nineteenth century lends support to the existing models of the origins of multinational banking. Although the banks did not so much follow their corporate clients over national borders as were established by those clients to service their needs, the general point is valid that the British multinational banks came into being to service flows of British and imperial trade and capital. Theories of multinational banking which stress that foreign banks need an 'advantage' over local competitors find support in the empirical evidence presented here. British banks were either the first modern banks or else they introduced new methods—such as branch banking—which gave them advantages over local competitors. The decision to establish multinational branches rather than use market arrangements can also be interpreted within an internalization framework. There would have been high transaction costs in the use of the market in many of the countries in which British banks were interested in the nineteenth century, as trusted correspondents were lacking.

Two further factors deserve emphasis in the origins of British multinational banking. The first is the importance of entrepreneurial decisions. The first banks were founded by men who took the view that a type of banking organization devised to allow an English bank to do business in Ireland could be applied to colonies thousands of miles away. British industrial and imperial hegemony created the opportunities for such banking, but it was entrepreneurial judgement that perceived the opportunities and acted upon them. Later generations perceived opportunities beyond the British Empire, in Latin America, the Middle East, and Asia. Subsequently, entrepreneurial judgement took the banks from their origins as trade banks into retail banking in their host economies.

The second factor of importance was the influence of the institutional and regulatory environment in shaping the corporate forms in which entrepreneurial ambitions were realized, and in resolving how and where hierarchies replaced markets. The first British multinational banks were created when the specialized structure of the British banking system had already taken place. The first-mover advantages held by the merchant banks in international banking between Britain, continental Europe, and the United States meant that the attempts to create British multinational banks active in these regions never succeeded. The regulatory context was even more important. The distinctive corporate structure of British multinational banking—of geographically specialized banks with no domestic banking business—was to a large part due to British regulations during the first decades of the overseas banks.

The reasons for the prominence of British multinational banks in the nineteenth century have been explored using Porter's diamond of national competitive advantage. Virtually all aspects of the diamond were favourable for British banks. Factor conditions included access to the world's largest capital markets and a supply of trained personnel. Demand conditions included a unique core market stemming from the importance of British business in the world economy. World trade grew rapidly in the nineteenth century, and British goods accounted for a remarkable share of that trade. The agglomeration of financial services in the City of London provided a powerful cluster of related industries that were internationally competitive. The use of sterling to finance two-thirds of world trade by the late nineteenth century, and the prominence of the bill on London in international trade, gave British banks considerable advantages in their central activities of trade finance and exchange. The overseas banks grew by exploiting these competitive advantages through foreign direct investment.

Despite such formidable country-specific advantages, however, it has been argued that a key determinant of success of the British multinational banks lay in firm strategy and structure. The organizational capability of the British banks was high. They had effective governance structures which were ideal for the finance of international trade. Difficult agent–principal problems were resolved by effective socialization strategies, as well as by more formal hierarchical policies. The banks acquired a reputation for honesty, integrity, and stability which served as a long-term competitive advantage. The presence of groups of competing British banks specializing in particular regions provided a powerful external competitive spur.

The nineteenth-century British multinational banks were not mere 'free-riders' on British economic and political power. The combination of entrepreneurial strategies and high organizational capability within the banks was also a critical factor. As a result, although many speculative or ill-designed banks collapsed, especially in the 1860s, a large number of stable institutions were created and survived. Indeed, the longevity of many of the banks founded in the nineteenth century is one of their most striking features. They were able, for the most part, to survive the major banking crises such as that of the early 1890s, as well as, later, the world financial crisis in 1931.

Effective governance structures also permitted the British banks to pursue flexible business strategies. Beginning with the areas of British colonial settlement, which had the greatest cultural and legal similarities to the United Kingdom, the British banks moved from trade and exchange into domestic and retail banking. By the beginning of the twentieth century such diversification was also evident in British banks in Latin America and Asia. The skilful use of intermediaries and strategies of risk-minimization by on-lending to locally owned financial intermediaries enabled the British banks to diversify beyond British-owned business. From Brazil to China, profitable niche markets were established with indigenous entrepreneurs and traders. As a result, multinational service banks evolved into multinational retail banks.

Public policy played an important, if limited, role in enhancing the competitive advantages of the British banks in the nineteenth century. British government regulations reinforced the geographical and functional specialization of the banks—almost certainly enhancing their stability in the process—but otherwise left them free to pursue their ambitions. British policy stood in contrast to that of the United States, where multinational banking was virtually illegal. British colonial governments also sometimes provided banks with lucrative business. The support of the British Foreign Office was important for the loan issue activity of the Hongkong Bank and the Imperial Bank of Persia.

The absence of strict banking and financial regulation in much of the world beyond Europe and the United States was an important prerequisite for the success of the British banks. There were few restrictions anywhere against foreign banks. There were no exchange controls to handicap foreign exchange business or prevent the investment of 'surplus' deposits on London's money markets. Non-existent or weak regulation enhanced the competitive advantages of the well-managed British banks, for in many regions local banks were (or were believed to be) more prone to fail. Few host governments had liquidity or banking ratios to constrain the strategies of the banks. The result was a most favourable environment for multinational banks.

Multinational banking was a mature industry after the First World War. Products and technologies changed little for the next fifty years. Growth opportunities were limited. World trade growth was very slow in the inter-war years, and even afterwards exchange controls and restrictions on currency convertibility persisted. In many countries locally owned banks were established and flourished, often with official support. The economic performance of the Southern Hemisphere economies weakened, a trend which became most apparent over time in South America. Although many of the host economies of British banks, both in the Southern Hemisphere and Asia, enjoyed some economic growth via import substitution, this was a different kind of activity undertaken by different actors than the trade-related business in which the British banks had excelled.

The original competitive advantages held by the British banks weakened. This was particularly noticeable in demand conditions. The core market for British multinational banks—servicing the requirements of British business overseas—had begun a long-term relative contraction. The United Kingdom missed the era of fast economic growth from the 1950s to 1973, and as a result its economy contracted in international importance. The inter-war years saw the beginning of a shift into US dollars in trade finance. The competitive advantages of being a sterling bank with a head office in London faltered in the inter-war years. After 1945 a sterling capital base became a competitive disadvantage. Regulatory changes limited the former ability of the British banks to move funds internationally.

In the face of a difficult environment and declining competitive advantages, the performance of British multinational banks can be regarded as a considerable success. While the banking systems of much of Europe as well as the United States came under great pressure in the inter-war years, the

British banks were skilled at crisis management and were able to survive both the world wars and the world financial crisis of 1931. The collapse of the Anglo-South American Bank, the largest British bank by asset size, was the one major exception.

The British banks began to be criticized for conservatism in this period, but such criticism can only be partly justified. There was some product and geographical diversification. Even in the inter-war years lending strategies and employment policies were modified. Especially in the late 1940s and 1950s, British banks also pioneered modern banking in 'new' territories in the Arab world and in Africa. In a number of regions, such as Australia and Latin America, their market share of domestic banking stagnated or fell, but given the disadvantages of foreign banks *vis-à-vis* local competitors, it was perhaps more remarkable that the British banks were able to retain their positions at all.

A number of factors helped the British banks to retain market share, and contributed to their continued prominence in multinational banking. Competition from other multinational banks remained muted. American multinational banking remained modest until the late 1950s. The development of German multinational banking, which had posed a considerable threat to British banks in parts of Latin America and Asia before 1914, was stunted by the First World War, and was not to be resumed on a large scale until the 1970s. British banks faced serious competition from local banks in particular markets, but they did not encounter substantial challenges from other multinational banks.

First-mover advantages were also important. By 1914 the British banks had established excellent franchises in many regions in which they operated, and these were not easily overturned, except by aggressive host government action. The banks possessed extensive physical assets in the shape of networks of branches—some of which were imposing buildings in their local contexts. Their intangible assets were even more powerful, especially their reputations for honesty, stability, and efficiency. Although British banking orthodoxies together with real or imagined racial biases in lending policies were criticized, the fact that British banks did not go bankrupt, that their managers were honest, and that customer information really was confidential continued to be powerful advantages in much of Asia, Africa, and Latin America.

In some regions, cross-subsidization explains the survival of the British branch networks in the difficult inter-war period. One of the main functions of the Barclays (DCO) organization in the inter-war years was to use the rising profits from South Africa to subsidize the losses or poor returns achieved in the large branch network covering the West Indies and North, West and East Africa. The branch networks in Latin America and continental Europe were not financially viable for all or part of the inter-war years and would not have survived without the support of their clearing bank owners.

Despite this relatively optimistic assessment of their overall performance, the competitive advantages held by the British banks in their strategies and structures were not so apparent as before the First World War. There were a number of constraints on change which worked to limit their flexibility to respond to a changing environment. The administrative heritage, ideal for trade banks, had less economic rationality for multinational retail banks. The London-based boards could not assess domestic banking risks as well as indigenous banks. They were prone to be conservative and to give a higher priority to the foreign exchange and treasury operations of their banks. The evolution of the banks from trade banks into institutions offering a wider bundle of financial services to indigenous economies ensured their survival after the First World War as British trade began to decline, but paradoxically their organizational structure handicapped them in exploiting the new business to the full. Significantly, the Hongkong Bank, the most dynamic of the British banks after 1945, had its board and chief executive officer in Hong Kong, its core market, where they were better placed to judge lending opportunities. The socialization strategy also acted as a constraint on change. The corporate culture which had worked so well in the nineteenth century, based on the recruitment of public school boys, lifelong employment, and on-the-job training, generated skills that were region- and product-specific. The upshot was that the structures of British multinational banking worked to limit changes in business strategy.

The inherited structure of geographical and functional specialization caused particular problems. The 'free-standing' organization of the banks left them with a weak domestic British client base, while banks which had specialized in the finance of a few commodities produced by a few countries felt a need to diversify their risks. Yet the struggle to integrate domestic and overseas banking and form multi-regional banks proved a prolonged one. The entry of domestic banks into multinational banking around the First World War and the creation of Barclays (DCO) in 1926 as a multiregional bank with close ties to a leading British domestic bank were considerable innovations. However, they were also a false dawn. Although Lloyds Bank acquired substantial shareholdings in overseas banks, it failed for fifty years to achieve any co-ordination between them or with its domestic banking business. The other three of the 'Big Five' domestic banks had extremely modest or no multinational ambitions. During the 1950s and 1960s attempts to overcome the specialized structure of British multinational banking continued by mergers between overseas banks. Grand designs were discussed at length, but it was not until the end of the 1960s that a large-scale reorganization took place.

The slow pace of corporate change can be explained in several ways. The distinctive corporate cultures of the banks may have been a source of strength, but were also an obstacle to mergers, as was made clear by several instances in the 1940s and 1950s when CEOs opposed merger proposals by their own directors. There was limited external threat of competition. The British banks had carved the world out between them and there was little domestic rivalry. Collusive agreements were widespread. The competitive struggle between British banks for good accounts never ceased, but overall the sector was rarely fiercely competitive.

The public policy environment provided further obstacles to corporate reorganization, or any other innovation. The Bank of England resolutely, if unsuccessfully, attempted to prevent the integration of overseas and domestic banking from the 1920s until the 1950s. In the 1950s and 1960s it allowed the various merger schemes to proceed at their leisurely paces, while preventing any kind of hostile take-over threat from either another British bank or a foreign institution. The banks were as constrained by governments in most of their host economies, where regulatory controls severely inhibited the freedom of manœuvre of all banks.

The British multinational banks, therefore, survived the traumatic political and economic events between 1914 and 1945. Their nineteenth-century competitive advantages weakened in this period, but not dramatically, and to a certain extent the banks were able to compensate. They also benefited from first-mover advantages, the absence of other multinational banks, and the willingness of clearing bank shareholders to subsidize loss-making foreign branches. Structure had lagged behind strategy, but multinational banking was a mature industry in which opportunities for radical innovation were in any case limited.

This situation changed in the new era of global banking from the 1960s. Some elements of the diamond moved sharply against British multinational banks. The continued weakness of the British economy affected the demand for their services. British exports continued their relative decline in importance in world trade. British manufacturing industry weakened so much that the United Kingdom's domestic market was increasingly supplied by foreign imports, or by British subsidiaries of foreign multinationals. Sterling's role as a world currency disintegrated. The sun set on the remainder of the British Empire, with the exception of a handful of special cases, such as Hong Kong and the Falkland Islands.

This deterioration in the country-specific sources of competitive advantage subjected the residual of the free-standing form of organization in British multinational banking to great strain. Many of the advantages of possessing a British headquarters to manage a network of overseas branches had disappeared. In the 1960s the surviving free-standing banks had sought refuge in multi-regional mergers, and in equity links with stronger American or British clearing banks. In the following decade ANZ's shift of domicile to Australia was a recognition that the advantages of being a British-based bank were outweighed by the costs.

It would be tempting to explain the problems of British multinational banks as the inevitable consequence of British economic decline, but this is no more satisfactory than a sole explanation of their pre-eminence in the nineteenth century in terms of the strength of the British economy. There has been an evident historical correlation between the extent of a country's multinational banking activity and the overall size of its economy and its position as a capital-exporter, although both regulatory and institutional factors have made the correlation less direct than might have been anticipated. However, to some extent British multinational banks had their competitive advantages renewed. London was reborn as the world's leading international financial centre. American and other banks regarded the opening of a London branch as their first priority—British banks had London as their home base. The new Euromarkets broke the link between the currency of lending and the location of the lending, and as a result liberated British banks to some extent from the decline of sterling. The first era of multinational banking had also left British banks with substantial advantages. Apart from bases in the City of London, British institutions had a uniquely rich experience of international activity and retail deposit bases in a range of countries, including such leading financial centres as Singapore and Hong Kong.

Continued deficiencies in strategy and structure prevented British banks from realizing the full potential of either their inherited franchises or their renewed competitive advantage. The painfully slow merger negotiations during the 1960s coincided with the rapid growth of American multinational banks and rapid product innovation. Even after the consolidations around 1970, the organizational capability of the British banks remained weak. The modest levels of formal training within British banks at least until the 1970s provided an insecure basis for success within a rapidly changing industry.

Deficiencies in structure and organizational capability help to explain the ineffective or ill-advised strategies pursued by British banks in this period. In the 1960s and early 1970s there was a clear preference for strategies which left existing structures and managements in place. This was the period of attempting to use minority shareholdings as a strategic tool to upgrade competitive advantage, and of widespread interest in consortium banking. Such arrangements could have provided useful means to learn new techniques and develop new lines of business, but the limited organizational capability of the British banks restricted their ability to learn. The minority shareholdings in overseas banks by American money centre banks led to little transfer of management techniques, while some

British banks remained attached to the consortium bank concept for some time after its value was questioned by others.

The worst strategic failings, however, were committed in the decade or so after the mid-1970s. Managements often neglected their established—and sometimes potentially valuable—franchises in Asia and Africa, as they sought to emulate the American fashion for diversification into more fashionable countries and activities. As British banks lacked the professional and trained management of the kind employed by American banks, the consequences were often even worse than those experienced by the Americans. Different banks pursued different foibles, but the collective record was of ill-advised and ill-prepared diversification into sovereign lending, consumer finance, and American banking.

By 1990 the managements of most British banks had relearned the reasons why their nineteenth-century predecessors—and their Treasury regulators—had restricted their activities to certain types of business in particular regions. Successful banking demands knowledge of customers and of products. The diversifications of the 1970s and 1980s took the banks into businesses they did not understand. British banks were emulators rather than leaders in these trends, and were far from alone in their sins. A hundred years of multinational banking, however, might have suggested that they would have escaped some of the pitfalls of newcomers into the industry.

It is not too absurd to suggest a more satisfactory outcome for British multinational banking. This would have involved the creation, ideally in the early 1960s, rather than a decade later, of a number of banking groups combining overseas banks with clearing banks. Barclays' and Lloyds' interests provided an obvious basis for two such groups. A merger between Standard and Chartered and one of the remaining clearing banks, possibly Midland, could have provided a third group. These groups would have developed—as Bolsa had attempted to do—a prominent role in the London-based Eurodollar and Eurobond markets. They would have exploited existing overseas franchises more effectively, actively developing third-country business to compensate for declining British business activity, and effectively marketing their multi-regional branch operations as a global franchise. Accumulated historical experience could have been used—as in fact it was in the Hongkong Bank and Standard Chartered—to caution against following the American banks into excessive syndicated lending to the Third World. Such expertise could also have been used to avoid multinational retail strategies in the United States in favour of establishing a limited number of branches performing wholesale and corporate banking in major United States financial and business centres. The recruitment of more formally educated staff and the earlier introduction of extensive training schemes would have provided the organizational capabilities to make the proposed strategies fully effective.

The nineteenth-century legacy weighed heavily against such an outcome. The traditional weak ties between overseas and domestic banking; the strong individualistic corporate cultures and socialization strategies of control; the product- and region-specific skills within the British overseas banks—all helped to provide obstacles to rapid change. Effective entrepreneurship was needed to overcome such obstacles. Both George Bolton and Cyril Hawker deserve credit in the 1960s for their attempts to rearrange the pieces of British multinational banking in a more effective pattern. For the most part, however, the number of men with entrepreneurial vision and/or management skills in the senior ranks of British banking appear to have been few.

## 11.3. Performance and Impact

The British overseas banks founded in the nineteenth century pass the first test of any successful business organization—survival. A few banks active today are direct descendants of banks founded between the 1830s and 1860s. Most of their nineteenth-century contemporaries merged or amalgamated into larger groups in time, but usually by choice rather than because of failure. The banks which lasted more than five years after their foundation survived for a considerable period.

The reasons for such longevity have already been explored. The managerial structures established in the nineteenth century were effective in controlling risks and in securing corporate survival. They were sufficiently flexible to adjust to host economy environments, but took care that flexibility rarely translated into really serious bad debts, or into dishonesty on the part of their staff. Their business organization was not well equipped for responding to radical environmental changes, but this was not a problem until the 1960s.

There were spectacular failures, but the striking thing was their limited number. In the nineteenth century there were the collapses of Agra and Masterman's in 1866 and the Oriental Bank Corporation in 1884. These banks had been the global enterprises of their generations, operating extraordinary branch networks spread over continents.

The failure of the Anglo-South American Bank in the inter-war years was another catastrophe. This bank grew quickly through acquisition, through penetration of new banking markets in Latin America and beyond, and through more flexible lending policies than its staid competitor the Bank of London and South America. For a time, Anglo-South appeared to be developing as a multi-regional bank broadly similar to Barclays (DCO), but the Chilean nitrate crisis overwhelmed it.

A further catastrophe was Midland Bank's purchase of Crocker National in California in the 1980s. Midland had been the largest bank in the world by the end of the First World War, but declined in importance subsequently, even in its domestic market. The acquisition of Crocker National appeared a dramatic sign of corporate renewal. The loss of over £1 billion in the subsequent five years was probably the single most costly failure ever undertaken in the history of multinational banking, even when adjustment is made for price changes, although Midland's core domestic business meant that the bank's survival was never in doubt.

Despite the idiosyncratic factors at work in these cases of corporate failure, some common points are discernible. They centre on the problems faced by multinational banks when they lack knowledge about their market. Oriental's multi-regional branch network gave it insufficient knowledge of local lending conditions, which resulted in bad debts and a portfolio of repossessed coffee and sugar estates. Anglo-South's rapid growth into new markets, often by acquisition, caused serious difficulties even before the nitrate crisis. Midland's background in domestic British banking rendered its management innocent of the dangers of Californian real estate and other areas of that market. Management failure and inadequate organizational capability exacerbated the inherent problems involved in banking in unfamiliar territories.

The evidence presented here suggests that any view that multinational banks perform better than domestic ones because they can escape the systematic risk of any one national market needs qualification. In some multinational banking activities, diversification increases risk. Successful retail and service banking has always required a close knowledge of customers. As a result, operating in a number of markets raises risk rather than reducing it. Barclays (DCO) was able to function effectively as a multi-regional retail bank in part because it was formed out of long-established British or colonial banks which knew their markets well, and whose managements were left in place by Barclays. In contrast, the large British acquisitions of American banks during the 1970s and 1980s were a more risky strategy, for the British banks acquired managements with different traditions active in a very alien market about which they knew little, except that a position in them was apparently *de rigueur* for a serious bank.

The examination of the financial performance of a sample of British multinational banks between 1890 and 1975 has revealed a number of conclusions. British multinational banks performed better in some periods than in others. The early 1890s and the 1930s were particularly poor years, when the shareholders in a majority of the sample banks would have done better to invest in British government stock—Consols—rather than bank shares. Conversely, the banks performed much better in the eras of fast world growth in the decades before the First World War and in the 1950s and 1960s. The sample banks, as a group, did comparatively well in both world wars, unless their overseas branches were actually occupied by the enemy.

Over the long term, domestic banking was a more profitable activity than multinational banking, especially for the half-century after 1914, when the British banking market was essentially an oligopolistic cartel. Such a generalization, however, disguised a range of individual outcomes. Multinational banking was more risky than domestic banking, a situation which brought rewards as well as risks. Shareholders could earn substantially more from holding the equity of 'successful' multinational banks, but they could also fare much worse if they chose a poorly performing institution.

It is evident that British multinational banks performed much better than their published figures showed. Before the 1970s—and in the case of the Hongkong Bank for much later—they made regular transfers to inner reserves before publishing their profits. In periods of difficulty, these inner reserves were used to retain the confidence of depositors as well as shareholders by smoothing the published figures. The value of such a strategy was evident during the world economic crisis of the early 1930s, when several of the sample banks were able to disguise the extent of their 'real' losses by drawing on inner reserves. There was in part a conflict of interest between stakeholders in this matter. The diversion of a portion of profits into inner reserves meant that shareholders received fewer dividends than they might have expected. On the other hand, managements and staff helped to ensure the long-term survival of their banks by accumulating inner reserves which were used as an effective tool of crisis management. Depositors also benefited from stability, which was one reason why British banks in many countries tended to attract funds in periods of crisis.

It is evident that there were wide variations in the performance of British multinational banks, both from the point of view of shareholders and in their overall profitability. The Eastern Exchange banks appear to have been the most successful group of banks over the long-term, although this generalization may break down in inter-war years, when the banks active in Southern Africa appear to have been the best performing. The health of the host regional economy and the kind of business undertaken help to explain this pattern. The provision of trade finance from a modest number of branches in ports and business centres was, generally speaking, a more profitable business than running extensive branch networks providing retail business. Parts of the Asian economy engaged in international trade flourished before 1914, and again from the 1950s. In contrast, the Southern Hemisphere economies offered less good prospects for the British banks. Their primary-commodity-based economies experienced long-term relative decline after the First World War. South Africa offers a partial exception to this pattern. There, the British banks retained from the 1920s to the 1970s a comfortable duopoly in a country with considerable mineral resources which could be exploited by a large pool of cheap, Black, labour.

There were discernible differences of performance between different banks active even in the same region. The Hongkong Bank, most notably, was usually the 'star' of the Eastern Exchange banks. Host economy factors again provide an important part of the reasons for such differences. After the Second World War, the banks which did well were those with good deposit bases in expanding economies with low taxation and light regulation, with no discrimination against foreign banks. The Hongkong Bank was ideally placed in this respect.

Entrepreneurial perception of profitable opportunities was also important. Banks differed in their ability to perceive opportunities. There were missed opportunities in inter-war Australia when the two largest Anglo-Australian banks failed to move quickly enough to position themselves in the industrial and suburban areas of New South Wales. Almost certainly, the location of Hongkong Bank's board and CEO in Hong Kong rather than London was a source of competitive advantage in this respect. Its decision-makers had access to more information, and more up-to-date information, about the markets they served, and were perhaps more able as a result to take risks to exploit them.

It is a more complex matter to move from the performance of the banks as institutions to their performance as contributors to overall economic welfare, especially as there are likely to have been a considerable range of outcomes in different countries at different times. Nevertheless, a number of general observations can be made.

Some of the wilder caricatures of British multinational banks are evidently misplaced. Their absolute level of real profits and of inner reserves was never enormous, for example, and would not support any view that the British banks extracted large sums of money from host economies, and hid the process in their balance sheets. The banks did not, as institutions, speculate in foreign exchanges. Their lending policies were rarely as 'orthodox'—or as racially biased—as either their public statements or their critics maintained. Even before 1914, they seldom confined their business to expatriate interests in Asia and other developing regions.

None of this should be taken to suggest that the banks were other than capitalist institutions. They sought profits for shareholders, and long-term corporate survival. The banks pursued these goals in a tradition of banking broadly based on British principles, and in the context of political, social, and racial ideas prevailing in each generation. As a result, the banks minimized risks by employing British nationals in management positions, and by using intermediaries when undertaking business with unfamiliar cultures. They preferred short-term trade finance, and did not regard it as prudent to finance peasant farmers or make long-term loans to industries.

When higher and safer returns could be earned from London money markets than from lending in their host economies, they collected deposits from overseas and transferred them to Britain. All these policies had welfare costs, but they must be understood as part of a whole system which also gave benefits.

Many of the benefits stemmed from the innovations introduced by British banks when they first entered markets. Naturally these were at their greatest before the First World War. In the Australian colonies and elsewhere they introduced branch banking, and later they brought modern banking to large areas of the developing world. Even in the 1980s, British, along with other foreign, banks influenced the American banking system, through, for example, increasing the pressures for interstate banking. If British banks seldom remained at the forefront of innovation over the long term, such later conservatism should not disguise their initial innovatory impact. Again, in nineteenth-century Latin America, South Africa, and elsewhere, the British banks provided stable and honest financial institutions at a time when local banking structures were undeveloped. The contribution did not end with the First World War. In some countries British banks had acted as quasi-central banks before such entities existed, and played an important role in creating stable monetary institutions.

In some respects, the competitive problems of British overseas banks stemmed partly from their successful diffusion of modern banking methods in many countries in which they operated. The result was, over time, that indigenous institutions copied the British banks, and innovated, drawing on their greater knowledge of local markets.

The British overseas banks had been one of the most extraordinary aspects of nineteenth-century multinational business. The creation of viable banking organizations running branch networks thousands of miles from Britain, and which survived well into the next century, was a triumph of entrepreneurship and of management skills. The shrinking in importance of British multinational banking in the age of global banking from the 1960s was in part an inevitable result of the relative failure of the British economy as a whole. In part it was an illustration of how the competitive advantages of the past can become the competitive disadvantages of the present.

# British Multinational Banks: Total Assets, Market Capitalization, and Foreign Branches and Affiliates

This appendix lists British-owned multinational banks active at the bench-mark dates of 1860, 1890, 1913, 1928, 1938, 1955, 1970, and 1990. Banks which were born and disappeared between bench-mark dates are perforce excluded. A considerable number of the short-lived banks created during nineteenth-century banking manias are therefore missed in the lists, but they do include a very high percentage of those banks which reached the stage of creating and staffing an overseas branch and opening for business. A brief biography of each bank listed at the bench-mark dates is given in Appendix 2. As these tables provide the basis for many of the generalizations given in the text, it is necessary to be explicit about the criterion for inclusion and exclusion.

The primary grounds for inclusion are that a bank should be owned by United Kingdom nationals, ultimately controlled from the United Kingdom, and engage in foreign direct investment, i.e. own and control at least one branch or affiliate outside the United Kingdom. The latter criterion is the most clear-cut. It excludes British banks which engaged in international banking solely through their British offices, or through foreign partnerships or correspondent networks. It also excludes banks whose overseas presence was confined to representative offices. It includes as branches wholly owned 'agencies' which performed some banking functions but not others. Except in the special cases noted below, banks locally incorporated in the British Empire and with their head offices in the colonies are excluded. The tables also exclude the considerable number of British-registered and London-based banks which were affiliates of foreign banks. An early example of such a bank was the German Bank of London, a British-registered bank established in 1871 and largely owned by the Deutsche Bank and other German banks.

The main definitional problem has arisen in the cases of certain banks which were registered outside the United Kingdom but contained a substantial 'British' element. Such banks are given in the tables in italics. The most important of these institutions was the Hongkong Bank, which, for reasons made clear in the text, it would be absurd to exclude from the category of a British bank. The foreign-registered subsidiaries of British clearing banks have also been included in this category up to 1970. They were distinctive banks from their parents, and clearly British-controlled. The National Bank of Egypt and the National Bank of Turkey are also included. Although the former was a quasi-state bank before the Second World War, it had a substantial British private shareholding, and British nationals provided most of its management. Moreover, between its foundation in 1898 and 1940 the bank had three resident directors in London and a powerful London

Committee with influence over important strategic matters. Similarly, the National Bank of Turkey appears in the 1913 list as this bank had a London Committee with substantial influence as well as considerable British equity.

A number of banks were considered for inclusion in the tables but ultimately excluded. The Bank of New Zealand was established in 1862 as an explicitly locally owned and operated bank in New Zealand, but between 1890 and 1894 its head office moved to London. Its inclusion in the 1890 list would have placed it—with total assets of nearly £11.5 million—among the ten largest overseas banks. But it was never truly a 'British' bank except, briefly, in a technical sense.

There was a substantial 'British' influence in the banking system of British India, beyond the Exchange banks included in these lists. At least two Indian-registered domestic banks in the nineteenth century—the Allahabad and the Alliance Bank of Simla—were widely regarded as 'British'. Their management was in British hands, and probably much of their shareholding was controlled by Europeans resident in India. However, there was no 'control' from the United Kingdom, and no element of multinational behaviour as their branch networks were confined to India. As a result, they have been excluded from the lists, although the Allahabad Bank makes an entry as an affiliate following its acquisition by the P & O Banking Corporation in 1920. Similar considerations led to the exclusion of the Presidency banks and their successor, the Imperial Bank of India. The Banks of Bengal, Bombay, and Madras were private sector institutions after 1876, although they retained their quasi-government bank functions. Their directors were largely drawn from British business interests active in India; their managers were recruited in the United Kingdom; and resident Europeans probably formed much of their shareholding. However, although these banks had an overwhelmingly British character, there was no control from the United Kingdom. Moreover, as their branches were confined to India, they were not multinational banks. A full account of the Presidency banks is available in A. K. Bagchi's book, *The Presidency Banks and the Indian Economy, 1876–1914.*

Some banks had a mixed or fluctuating ownership. The Ottoman Bank has been included in 1860 because at that time it was still a British bank incorporated under Royal Charter. It was reconstituted as the Imperial Ottoman Bank under Ottoman law in 1863, and thereafter it had mixed British, French, and Ottoman shareholding and executive. At some periods there was a substantial British influence, but the bank never really functioned as a British bank, and it is excluded from the tables after 1860. The Anglo-Austrian Bank was also under fluctuating British control. It was founded in 1863 as a British bank, but by the next bench-mark date control had passed to Austrian hands. Another period of British control between 1922 and 1926 also fell between bench-mark dates.

The 1990 list differs substantially from that for earlier years, largely because of the integration of most specialist multinational banks into their domestic banking parents, and because of the proliferation of locally registered subsidiaries. It simply provides, for reference purposes, the assets and market capitalization of the principal British banks engaged in multinational banking in that year.

TABLE A1.1. *British multinational banks: total assets, market capitalization, and non-UK branches, 1860*

| Bank | Total assets (£) | Market capitalization (£) | Non-UK branches |
|---|---|---|---|
| Oriental Bank Corporation | 12,697,538 | 2,412,500 | 14 |
| Union Bank of Australia | 6,559,102 | 1,720,000 | 23 |
| Chartered Mercantile Bank of India | 4,489,117 | 700,000 | 10 |
| Bank of Australasia | 4,449,150 | 1,636,875 | 17 |
| Agra and United Service Bank | 3,304,702 | 1,650,000 | 7 |
| Bank of British North America | 2,417,021 | 1,085,000 | 12 |
| Colonial Bank | 2,361,731 | 805,000 | 14 |
| Chartered Bank of India, Australia and China | 2,289,477 | 711,218 | 5 |
| London Chartered Bank of Australia | 2,144,118 | 892,500 | 9 |
| English, Scottish & Australian Chartered Bank | 1,280,189 | 381,250 | 4 |
| Ottoman Bank | 1,058,865 | 475,000 | 4 |
| Bank of South Australia | 1,052,342 | 484,000 | 3 |
| Bank of Egypt | 503,592 | 217,500 | 2 |
| Ionian Bank | n.a. | n.q. | 5 |
| London and South African Bank | 200,000 | n.q. | 3 |
| TOTAL all banks | | | 132 |

*Note*: n.a. = not available, n.q. = not quoted.

TABLE A1.2. *British multinational banks: total assets, market capitalization, and foreign branches and affiliates, 1890*

| Bank | Total assets (£) | Market capitalization (£) | Non-UK branches | Foreign affiliates |
|---|---|---|---|---|
| *Hongkong Bank*[a] | 25,571,439 | 5,480,000 | 22 | |
| Bank of Australasia | 19,251,209 | 4,000,000 | 149 | |
| Union Bank of Australia | 19,174,585 | 4,020,000 | 90 | |
| Chartered Bank of India, Australia and China | 15,923,197 | 1,080,000 | 17 | |
| Standard Bank of South Africa | 13,608,196 | 2,080,000 | 71 | |
| London and River Plate Bank | 12,361,335 | 1,800,000 | 4 | |
| London and Brazilian Bank | 12,119,225 | 1,250,000 | 14 | |
| English Bank of the River Plate | 10,983,039 | 1,050,000 | 5 | |
| Chartered Mercantile Bank | 10,593,188 | 750,000 | 13 | |
| New Oriental Bank Corporation | 10,573,541 | 575,000 | 20 | |
| English Bank of Rio de Janeiro | 10,410,555 | 650,000 | 9 | |
| London Chartered Bank of Australia | 8,999,346 | 1,475,000 | 61 | |
| English, Scottish & Australian Chartered Bank | 8,680,098 | 1,575,000 | 92 | |
| Agra Bank | 6,992,789 | 900,000 | 8 | |
| National Bank of India | 6,858,295 | 466,500 | 8 | |
| Bank of British North America | 5,168,351 | 1,520,000 | 18 | |
| Colonial Bank | 4,865,415 | 1,080,000 | 14 | |
| Bank of South Australia | 4,758,182 | 800,000 | 27 | |
| Bank of Africa | 3,368,230 | 360,000 | 19 | |

TABLE A1.2. (*Cont.*).

| Bank | Total assets (£) | Market capitalization (£) | Non-UK branches | Foreign affiliates |
|---|---|---|---|---|
| Bank of British Columbia | 3,208,695 | 1,140,000 | 9 | |
| National Bank of New Zealand | 2,690,122 | 175,000 | 31 | |
| Anglo-Egyptian Bank | 2,573,135 | 400,000 | 5 | |
| Anglo-Californian Bank | 2,215,644 | 464,535 | 1 | |
| Imperial Bank of Persia | 1,789,427 | 1,100,000 | 5 | |
| Delhi and London Bank | 1,683,037 | 146,867 | 5 | |
| London, Paris and American Bank | 1,598,870 | 600,000 | 1 | |
| London and San Francisco Bank | 1,560,275 | 420,000 | 3 | |
| London Bank of Mexico and South America | 1,513,314 | 350,000 | 1 | 1 |
| Bank of Tarapaca and London | 1,205,865 | 550,000 | 3 | |
| Ionian Bank | 1,149,096 | 239,780 | 5 | |
| Anglo-Argentine Bank | 922,178 | 200,000 | 2 | |
| Union Bank of Spain and England | 905,896 | 174,825 | 5 | |
| Bank of Egypt | 844,280 | 370,000 | 2 | |
| TOTAL UK-registered | | | 717 | 1 |
| TOTAL all banks | | | 739 | 1 |

*Notes*: Banks listed in italics were registered outside the United Kingdom but contained a substantial 'British' element.

[a] Hongkong Bank total assets were $HK149,686,477 and capitalization $HK32,078,049.

TABLE A1.3. *British multinational banks: total assets, market capitalization, and foreign branches and affiliates, 1913*

| Bank | Total assets (£) | Market capitalization (£) | Non-UK branches | Foreign affiliates |
|------|------|------|------|------|
| London and River Plate Bank | 39,829,819 | 5,880,000 | 30 | |
| *Hongkong Bank*[a] | 39,466,404 | 9,540,000 | 32 | |
| Standard Bank of South Africa | 29,626,461 | 3,484,181 | 218 | |
| Chartered Bank of India, Australia and China | 27,243,396 | 3,570,000 | 36 | |
| Union Bank of Australia | 27,228,975 | 3,360,000 | 182 | |
| Bank of Australasia | 25,916,790 | 5,850,000 | 204 | |
| London and Brazilian Bank | 22,312,586 | 3,625,000 | 16 | |
| National Bank of India | 19,817,803 | 3,200,000 | 25 | |
| British Bank of South America | 19,449,679 | 2,400,000 | 13 | |
| Anglo-South American Bank | 19,017,495 | 4,106,250 | 21 | |
| Bank of British North America | 12,872,238 | 1,480,000 | 98 | |
| *National Bank of Egypt* | 12,153,229 | 4,725,000 | 20 | 2 |
| English, Scottish & Australian Bank | 10,146,153 | 582,593 | 133 | |
| Mercantile Bank of India | 8,187,487 | 975,000 | 17 | |
| London Bank of Australia | 7,332,891 | 492,338 | 91 | |
| National Bank of New Zealand | 6,976,044 | 1,500,000 | 50 | |
| African Banking Corporation | 6,612,795 | 480,000 | 45 | |
| Anglo-Egyptian Bank | 5,467,877 | 1,175,000 | 11 | |
| Cox & Co. | 4,673,327 | n.q. | 6 | |
| Colonial Bank | 3,578,878 | 600,000 | 20 | |
| Eastern Bank | 3,299,295 | 525,000 | 3 | |
| Imperial Bank of Persia | 3,305,029 | 712,500 | 17 | |
| Bank of British West Africa | 3,150,842 | 675,000 | 61 | |
| Ionian Bank | 3,062,842 | 388,464 | 15 | |
| Delhi and London Bank | 2,281,342 | 229,585 | 7 | |

TABLE A1.3. (*Cont.*)

| Bank | Total assets (£) | Market capitalization (£) | Non-UK branches | Foreign affiliates |
|---|---|---|---|---|
| Lloyds Bank (France) | 1,558,921[b] | n.q. | 1 | |
| *National Bank of Turkey* | 1,050,340 | *n.q.* | 1 | |
| Bank of Mauritius | 599,298 | 169,493 | 2 | |
| Commercial Bank of Spanish America | 394,853 | n.q. | 9 | |
| Grindlay and Company | n.a. | n.q. | 3 | |
| London, County and Westminster Bank (Paris) | n.a. | n.q. | 1 | |
| TOTAL UK-registered | | | 1334 | — |
| TOTAL all banks | | | 1387 | 2 |

*Notes*: Banks listed in italics were registered outside the United Kingdom but contained a substantial 'British' element; n.a. = not available, n.q. = not quoted.

[a] Hongkong Bank total assets were $HK408,554,906 and capitalization $HK98,757,764.
[b] Estimated.

TABLE A1.4. *British multinational banks: total assets, market capitalization, and foreign branches and affiliates, 1928*

| Bank | Total assets (£) | Market capitalization (£) | Non-UK branches | Foreign affiliates |
|------|------|------|------|------|
| Anglo-South American Bank[a] | 76,449,705 | 6,823,953 | 39 | 3 |
| *Hongkong Bank*[b] | 71,791,858 | 22,480,000 | 40 | |
| Barclays Bank (DCO) | 71,680,929 | 7,353,994 | 455 | |
| Standard Bank of South Africa | 67,356,854 | 7,625,000 | 310 | |
| Bank of London and South America | 65,144,927 | 7,699,500 | 55 | |
| Chartered Bank of India, Australia and China | 60,991,370 | 13,200,000 | 47 | |
| Bank of Australasia | 47,618,928 | 12,937,500 | 237 | |
| Union Bank of Australia | 47,144,289 | 12,300,000 | 214 | |
| *National Bank of Egypt* | 45,027,709 | 10,800,000 | 35 | 2 |
| English, Scottish & Australian Bank | 44,512,778 | 7,687,500 | 451 | |
| National Bank of India | 41,639,338 | 8,400,000 | 29 | |
| Mercantile Bank of India | 18,989,409 | 2,940,000 | 23 | |
| National Bank of New Zealand | 18,809,388 | 5,850,000 | 95 | |
| P & O Banking Corporation | 14,979,222 | 2,399,598 | 9 | 1 |
| Westminster Foreign Bank | 13,396,955 | n.q. | 7 | |
| Imperial Bank of Persia | 13,103,068 | 1,100,000 | 30 | |
| Lloyds and National Provincial Foreign Bank | 12,981,650 | n.q. | 20 | |
| Eastern Bank | 11,601,892 | 1,387,500 | 12 | |
| British Bank of South America[a] | 11,601,339 | n.q. | 7 | |
| Anglo-International Bank | 10,402,499 | 1,715,007 | 3 | |
| Bank of British West Africa | 10,378,153 | 1,425,000 | 54 | |
| Barclays Bank (France) | 9,103,915 | n.q. | 15 | |
| British Italian Banking Corporation | 8,863,772 | n.q. | 1 | |

TABLE A1.4. (*Cont.*)

| Bank | Total assets (£) | Market capitalization (£) | Non-UK branches | Foreign affiliates |
|---|---|---|---|---|
| Ionian Bank | 6,028,832 | 960,000 | 45 | |
| Grindlay and Company | 2,936,596 | n.q. | 5 | |
| Commercial Bank of Spanish America[a] | 582,506 | n.q. | — | |
| Barclays Bank SAI | n.a. | n.q. | 2 | |
| TOTAL UK-registered[c] | | | 2,176 | 4 |
| TOTAL all banks | | | 2,253 | 6 |

*Notes*: Banks listed in italics were registered outside the United Kingdom but contained a substantial 'British' element; n.a. = not available, n.q. = not quoted.

  [a] The Anglo-South American Bank owned almost 100 per cent of the British Bank of South America and the Commercial Bank of Spanish America. Their accounts were not consolidated into the parent bank.

  [b] Hongkong Bank total assets were $HK710,810,474 and capitalization $HK222,574,257.

  [c] This includes the 13 South Asian branches owned by Lloyds Bank and managed by their Eastern department.

TABLE A1.5. *British multinational banks: total assets, market capitalization, and foreign branches and affiliates, 1938*

| Bank | Total assets (£) | Market capitalization (£) | Non-UK branches | Foreign affiliates |
|---|---|---|---|---|
| Barclays Bank (DCO) | 112,873,412 | 9,841,175 | 506 | |
| Standard Bank of South Africa | 86,120,381 | 7,625,000 | 384 | |
| *Hongkong Bank*[a] | 77,738,160 | 12,720,000 | 40 | |
| Bank of London and South America | 76,361,018 | 3,838,000 | 76 | 1 |
| Chartered Bank of India, Australia and China | 60,552,110 | 5,550,000 | 42 | |
| Bank of Australasia | 54,801,223 | 6,525,000 | 248 | |
| Union Bank of Australia | 47,658,188 | 4,600,000 | 231 | |
| English, Scottish & Australian Bank | 46,643,085 | 4,375,000 | 406 | |
| National Bank of India | 33,395,019 | 5,280,000 | 29 | |
| *National Bank of Egypt* | 31,557,160 | 9,150,000 | 45 | |
| Mercantile Bank of India | 18,400,660 | 2,295,000 | 24 | |
| National Bank of New Zealand | 18,275,130 | 1,200,000 | 90 | |
| P & O Banking Corporation[b] | 17,018,614 | 2,594,160 | 10 | 1 |
| Lloyds and National Provincial Foreign Bank | 15,189,264 | n.q. | 12 | |
| Westminster Foreign Bank | 12,753,123 | n.q. | 7 | |
| Eastern Bank | 11,521,445 | 1,250,000 | 12 | |
| Bank of British West Africa | 9,860,306 | 1,200,000 | 37 | |
| Imperial Bank of Iran | 7,735,514 | 1,200,000 | 15 | |
| Barclays Bank (France) | 7,042,935 | n.q. | 15 | |
| *E. D. Sassoon Banking Company* | 5,814,081 | n.q. | 2 | |
| Ionian Bank | 4,989,845 | 195,000 | 51 | |
| Grindlay and Company | 4,138,537 | n.q. | 12 | |
| *Barclays Bank SAI* | n.a. | n.q. | 1 | |
| *Barclays Bank of Canada*[c] | 2,600,000 | n.q. | 2 | |
| TOTAL UK-registered[d] | | | 2,225 | 2 |
| TOTAL all banks | | | 2,315 | 2 |

*Notes:* Banks listed in italics were registered outside the United Kingdom but contained a substantial 'British' element; n.a. = not available, n.q. = not quoted.

[a] Hongkong Bank total assets were $HK1,254m. and capitalization $HK872m.
[b] 1937 figures.
[c] 1934 figures: Barclays Bank of Canada total assets were $C13m. in that year.
[d] This includes the 18 South Asian branches owned by Lloyds Bank and managed by their Eastern department.

TABLE A1.6. *British multinational banks: total assets, market capitalization, and foreign branches and affiliates, 1955*

| Bank | Total assets (£) | Market capitalization (£) | Non-UK branches | Foreign affiliates |
|------|------|------|------|------|
| Barclays Bank (DCO) | 574,398,931 | 21,661,519 | 997 | |
| Standard Bank of South Africa | 340,392,541 | 16,875,000 | 680 | |
| Australia and New Zealand Bank | 339,227,987 | 17,850,000 | 854 | 1 |
| Chartered Bank of India, Australia and China | 223,968,987 | 7,437,500 | 65 | 1 |
| *Hongkong Bank*[a] | 214,199,992 | 19,300,000 | 40 | 1 |
| National Bank of India | 168,653,013 | 4,790,625 | 61 | |
| Bank of London and South America | 140,219,664 | 5,176,250 | 60 | 1 |
| English, Scottish & Australian Bank | 121,113,121 | 6,125,000 | 467 | 1 |
| Bank of British West Africa | 85,827,019 | 4,312,500 | 69 | |
| British Bank of the Middle East | 72,423,492 | 2,587,500 | 23 | |
| Mercantile Bank of India | 72,065,153 | 2,610,000 | 28 | |
| National Bank of New Zealand | 65,015,121 | 3,480,000 | 140 | |
| Eastern Bank | 43,558,711 | 1,650,000 | 23 | |
| Lloyds Bank (Foreign) | 27,654,951 | n.q. | 8 | |
| Grindlays Bank | 26,378,449 | n.q. | 20 | |
| Westminster Foreign Bank | 19,815,089 | n.q. | 7 | |
| Ionian Bank | 16,695,546 | 720,000 | 38 | |
| Barclays Bank (France)[b] | 15,000,000 | n.q. | 12 | |
| TOTAL UK-registered[c] | | | 3,572 | 4 |
| TOTAL all banks | | | 3,612 | 5 |

*Notes*: Banks listed in italics were registered outside the United Kingdom but contained a substantial 'British' element; n.q. = not quoted.

[a] Hongkong Bank total assets were $HK3,428m. and capitalization $HK309m.

[b] This is an estimated figure. The nearest surviving balance sheet is for Barclays Bank (France) for 1951, when the subsidiary had total assets of £12,334,271.

[c] This includes the 20 South Asian branches owned by Lloyds Bank and managed by their Eastern department.

TABLE A1.7. *British multinational banks: total assets, market capitalization, and foreign branches and affiliates, 1970*

| Bank | Total assets (£000) | Market capitalization (£000) | Non-UK branches | Foreign affiliates |
|---|---|---|---|---|
| Standard and Chartered Banking Group | 2,524,509 | 105,432 | 400 | 9 |
| Barclays Bank (DCO) | 2,405,503 | 106,000 | 1,312 | 6 |
| *Hongkong Bank*[a] | 1,809,056 | 160,685 | 118 | 4 |
| Australia and New Zealand Banking Group | 1,773,902 | 82,333 | 1,549 | 2 |
| Bank of London and South America | 932,227 | 50,076 | 86 | 1 |
| Westminster Foreign Bank | 906,907 | n.q | 9 | |
| National and Grindlays | 869,333 | 29,672 | 117 | 3 |
| Lloyds Bank Europe | 612,585 | n.q. | 17 | |
| National Bank of New Zealand | 174,089 | n.q. | 218 | |
| TOTAL UK-registered | | | 3,708 | 21 |
| TOTAL all banks | | | 3,826 | 25 |

*Notes*: Banks listed in italics were registered outside the United Kingdom but contained a substantial 'British' element; n.q. = not quoted.

[a] Hongkong Bank total assets were HK$26,294m. and capitalization HK$2,335m.

TABLE A1.8. *Principal British commercial banks: total assets and market capitalization, 1990*

| Bank | Total assets (£m.) | Market capitalization (£m.) |
|---|---|---|
| Barclays Bank | 134,887 | 5,709.6 |
| National Westminster Bank | 121,100 | 4,341.7 |
| *Hongkong Bank*[a] | 77,372 | 2,023.5 |
| Midland Bank | 59,636 | 1,521.0 |
| Lloyds Bank | 55,202 | 3,698.2 |
| Royal Bank of Scotland | 24,864 | 1,202.0 |
| Standard Chartered | 22,141 | 607.1 |
| Bank of Scotland | 18,395 | 858.8 |

*Notes*: Banks listed in italics were registered outside the United Kingdom but contained a substantial 'British' element.

[a] Hongkong Bank total assets were $HK1,158,256m. and capitalization $HK30,352.5m.

# Corporate Biographies

This appendix contains brief corporate biographies of each bank listed in Appendix 1. The region of operation given is that of the main operating area(s) only. No region is given for the banks active in 1990 or for multi-regional banks such as Barclays (DCO), for which information is given in the text. Individual countries are identified if the bank was almost completely specialized on them.

*African Banking Corporation.* Registered in 1890 as a limited company, and established in 1891 with its head office in London. Took over much of the business of the Cape of Good Hope Bank and the National Bank of the South African Republic. During 1891–2 it absorbed the following local South African banks: the Western Province Bank, the Kaffrarian Colonial Bank, and the Worcester Commercial Bank. Went into voluntary liquidation in 1920 in order to amalgamate with Standard Bank of South Africa (q.v.). Region: Southern Africa.

*Agra and United Service Bank.* Incorporated in 1833 as an Indian bank, and in 1857 as a British bank with its head office in London. In 1864, its name changed to Agra and Masterman's Bank as a result of merger with the London private bankers Masterman, Peters, Mildred and Company. Its operations were suspended in June 1866, but in 1867 it was reconstituted under the name of Agra Bank (q.v.). It went into voluntary liquidation in 1900. Region: South and South-East Asia.

*Agra Bank. See* Agra and United Service Bank.

*Anglo-Argentine Bank.* Registered in 1889 as London and Argentine Bank, but changed its name almost immediately. It went into voluntary liquidation in 1900, prior to its absorption by Bank of Tarapaca and London (q.v.) under the title of Bank of Tarapaca and Argentina (later Anglo-South American Bank, q.v.). Region: Latin America.

*Anglo-Californian Bank.* Founded in 1873. It went into voluntary liquidation in 1909 and was absorbed by the London-Paris National Bank of San Francisco, which then became the Anglo and London-Paris National Bank of San Francisco. Region: United States.

*Anglo-Egyptian Bank.* Established in 1864 as Anglo-Egyptian Banking Company, it acquired its current title at the time of its reconstruction in 1887. Over 90 per cent of its shares were acquired by Barclays Bank (q.v.) in 1920, and in 1925 it became a constituent part of the newly formed Barclays Bank (Dominion, Colonial and Overseas) (q.v.). Region: Egypt, Middle East.

*Anglo-International Bank.* Registered in 1926 with a London head office, to take over and amalgamate the undertakings and assets of the former Anglo-Austrian Bank, reconstituted as a British-based bank with branches in Central Europe in 1922, and the British Trade Corporation, created in 1916 by the British government and granted a Royal Charter in 1917 in order to facilitate British trade abroad. Current banking business was transferred to Glyn, Mills in 1944 and Anglo-International Bank went into voluntary liquidation in 1951. Region: continental Europe.

*Anglo-South American Bank.* Established in 1888 as Bank of Tarapaca and London (q.v.). Its name was changed to Bank of Tarapaca and Argentina in 1900, when it acquired the Anglo-Argentine Bank (q.v.). Took the title of Anglo-South American Bank in 1907. Absorbed London Bank of Mexico and South America (q.v.) in 1912, and purchased the bulk of the capital of Commercial Bank of Spanish America (q.v.) in 1918, and of British Bank of South America (q.v.) and the private Banco Edwards y Cia of Chile in 1920. Nearly collapsed in 1931 and went into voluntary liquidation in 1936, at which date its liabilities and assets were transferred to the Bank of London and South America (q.v.). Region: Latin America.

*Australia and New Zealand Bank.* Incorporated in 1951 as Australia and New Zealand Bank to take over the amalgamated undertakings of Union Bank of Australia (q.v.) and Bank of Australasia (q.v.). Merged with English, Scottish & Australian Bank in 1969, and became integrated into the Australia and New Zealand Banking Group in October 1970. Its domicile moved to Australia in 1976. Region: Australasia.

*Bank of Africa.* Launched in London in 1879, it acquired the South African business of Oriental Bank Corporation. Absorbed by the locally based National Bank of South Africa in 1912. Region: Southern Africa.

*Bank of Australasia.* Incorporated in London by Royal Charter in 1835. It absorbed the locally based Cornwall Bank of Tasmania in 1836 and the Bank of Western Australia in 1841. Merged with Union Bank of Australia (q.v.) in 1951 under the title of Australia and New Zealand bank (q.v.). Region: Australasia.

*Bank of British Columbia.* Incorporated in London by Royal Charter in 1862. Absorbed by the Canadian Bank of Commerce in 1900. Region: Canada.

*Bank of British North America.* Incorporated in London as a joint stock company in 1836, it received a Royal Charter in 1840. In 1918 it went into voluntary liquidation, in order that its undertaking and assets might be taken over by the Bank of Montreal. Region: Canada.

*Bank of British West Africa.* Registered in London as a limited company in 1894 to operate principally in West Africa. Until 1910, when it moved to London, the bank's head office was in Liverpool. Absorbed Bank of Nigeria (founded in 1899 as the Anglo African Bank) in 1912. From 1920, a majority of its shares were owned by Lloyds Bank (q.v.), Westminster Bank (see National Westminster Bank), and Standard Bank of South Africa (q.v.). Changed name to Bank of West Africa in 1957, and in 1965 merged with the Standard Bank of South Africa (q.v.), being known from November 1966 as Standard Bank of West Africa. Region: West Africa.

*Bank of Egypt.* Incorporated in 1856 by Royal Charter. In 1911, it was forced to suspend business and was wound up in 1912. Region: Egypt.

*Bank of London and South America.* Established in London under the title of London, Buenos Aires and River Plate Bank in August 1862, it was known as

London and River Plate Bank (q.v.) until it merged with London and Brazilian Bank (q.v.) in 1923 under the title of Bank of London and South America (Bolsa). Lloyds Bank (q.v.) acquired some 99 per cent of its shares in 1918. On its amalgamation with London and Brazilian Bank, Lloyds' interest fell to 57 per cent. In 1936, it acquired the remaining assets and liabilities of the Anglo-South American Bank (q.v.). In 1970 it merged with Lloyds Bank Europe (see Lloyds and National Provincial Foreign Bank), under the title of Lloyds and Bolsa International Bank (registered as a public company in 1971) in which Lloyds Bank had a 55 per cent interest. In December 1973, Lloyds and Bolsa International became a wholly owned subsidiary of Lloyds and took over most of the parent bank's overseas interests. It was renamed Lloyds Bank International in 1974, and on 1 January 1986 it was merged with Lloyds Bank PLC. Region: Latin America.

*Bank of Mauritius.* Registered in London in 1894, to take over the Mauritian business of New Oriental Bank Corporation (q.v.). Went into voluntary liquidation in 1916, at which time the assets were acquired by Mercantile Bank of India (q.v.). Region: Mauritius.

*Bank of Scotland PLC.* Established 1695 by Act of the Scots Parliament. Its international division was established in 1975, and its first non-UK branch was opened in Hong Kong in 1979.

*Bank of South Australia.* Started business in 1836 as the South Australia Banking Company. Chartered in 1841 in its own right as a bank, and incorporated by Royal Charter in 1847. Registered in 1884 as a limited liability company (at which time it lost its Royal Charter). Certain assets were acquired by Union Bank of Australia (q.v.). Went into voluntary liquidation in 1892, when it was amalgamated with Union Bank of Australia. Region: Australasia.

*Bank of Tarapaca and London.* Founded in 1888. Absorbed Anglo-Argentine Bank (q.v.) in 1900. Was renamed Anglo-South American Bank in 1907 (q.v.). Region: Latin America.

*Barclays Bank (Canada).* Established in 1929 under Canadian law. Amalgamated with Imperial Bank of Canada in 1955. Region: Canada.

*Barclays Bank (DCO).* A reconstitution of Colonial Bank (q.v.), in which Barclays (see Barclays Bank PLC) had a shareholding. In 1925, National Bank of South Africa (locally incorporated in South Africa in 1891) and Anglo-Egyptian Bank (q.v.), wholly owned by Barclays since 1920, were merged with Colonial Bank, which had been renamed Barclays (Dominion, Colonial and Overseas). Barclays Bank held a majority interest in the new bank. In 1954, the bank's name was changed to Barclays Bank DCO. In 1971, Barclays DCO's South African business was repatriated under the title of Barclays National Bank, and the remaining overseas business was absorbed into the parent Barclays Group. Together with the international division of the parent bank, it became a wholly owned subsidiary entitled Barclays Bank International. In 1984, this subsidiary was completely absorbed by Barclays Bank PLC.

*Barclays Bank (France).* Originally incorporated in 1915 as Cox & Co. (France), when it was under the joint ownership of Cox & Co. (q.v.) and London and South Western Bank. When Barclays merged with the latter in 1918, it acquired a half share in Cox & Co. (France). In 1922, the business was completely taken over by Barclays, which formed Barclays Bank (Overseas), renamed Barclays Bank (France) in 1926. In 1968 the name was changed to Barclays Bank (London and International). It became the basis of Barclays Merchant Bank in January 1976, the latter becoming Barclays de Zoete Wedd in 1986. Region: continental Europe.

*Barclays Bank PLC.* Established as a private bank prior to 1694. In 1896, as Barclay, Bevan, Tritton, Ransom, Bouverie and Company it was incorporated with nineteen other banks as Barclay and Company. In 1917, its name was changed to Barclays Bank. It was reregistered as a public limited company under the title of Barclays Bank PLC by the Barclays Bank Act of 1984.

*Barclays Bank SAI.* Established as a wholly owned subsidiary of Barclays Bank (see Barclays Bank PLC) in 1925. Sold 1950. Region: continental Europe.

*British Bank of the Middle East (The).* Incorporated under Royal Charter in 1889 as the Imperial Bank of Persia. Acquired in 1890 the assets and business of New Oriental Bank Corporation (q.v.) in Persia. Operated as the *de facto* state bank of Persia until 1928. Name changed successively to Imperial Bank of Iran (1935), the British Bank of Iran and the Middle East (1949), and the British Bank of the Middle East (1952). Taken over by Hongkong Bank (see Hongkong and Shanghai Banking Corporation) in 1960. Region: Middle East.

*British Bank of South America.* Registered in 1863 as Brazilian and Portuguese Bank. Name changed to English Bank of Rio de Janeiro (q.v.) in 1866. Renamed British Bank of South America in 1891. In 1920 over 99 per cent of its shares were acquired by Anglo-South American Bank (q.v.). It was wound up in 1936. Region: Latin America.

*British Italian Banking Corporation.* Founded in 1916, at the instigation of the British government, by a group of twenty-three prominent British banks led by Lloyds, the National Provincial, and the Westminster. In the mid-1920s its wholly owned subsidiary, Banca Italo-Britannica, suffered large losses, and in 1930 it was sold to Bank of America. Region: continental Europe.

*Chartered Bank of India, Australia and China (The).* Incorporated by Royal Charter in 1853, but did not start business overseas until 1858. Acquired a majority interest in P & O Banking Corporation (q.v.) in 1927. With effect from February 1939, it absorbed P & O completely, taking over, as a result, the latter's interest (more than 90 per cent) in Allahabad Bank (see P & O Banking Corporation). Acquired the Cyprus business of Ionian Bank (q.v.) in 1957, and took over the Eastern Bank (q.v.) in the same year. Under the terms of a supplemental charter of 1956, its name was shortened to the Chartered Bank. In 1969, it merged with Standard Bank (q.v.), the capital of the two banks being acquired in 1970 by a holding company entitled Standard and Chartered Banking Group (q.v.). Region: South, South-east, and East Asia.

*Chartered Mercantile Bank of India, London and China.* Originally established in India in 1853 as Mercantile Bank of Bombay, and almost immediately renamed Mercantile Bank of India, London and China. It attempted to amalgamate with Chartered Bank of Asia (chartered in 1853) in order to benefit from the latter's

Royal Charter. When this proved legally impossible, Chartered Bank of Asia went into voluntary liquidation, and Mercantile Bank secured its own Royal Charter in 1857. Suspended payments in 1892, but was reconstructed later the same year as Mercantile Bank of India (q.v.). Region: South, South-east, and East Asia.

*Colonial Bank*. Incorporated by Royal Charter in 1836. In 1925, it was reincorporated by Private Act as Barclays Bank (Dominion, Colonial and Overseas) (q.v.). Region: West Indies, West Africa (from 1917).

*Commercial Bank of Spanish America*. Registered in 1904 as Cortés Commercial and Banking Company to unite the businesses of London Bank of Central America and Cortés and Company in Colombia, Nicaragua, and San Salvador. In 1910, Anglo-South American Bank (q.v.) purchased a minority interest in it, and in 1911 its name was changed to Commercial Bank of Spanish America. In 1918, Anglo-South American Bank increased its shareholding to some 92 per cent. The bank went into liquidation in 1934. Region: Latin America.

*Cox & Co.* Originated in 1758 and developed pre-eminently as agents and bankers to the British Army. Began direct branch banking overseas in 1905 when its first Indian branch was opened in Bombay. Absorbed the business of Henry S. King with its Indian affiliations and branches in 1922. In 1923, Cox & Co. and its affiliate were absorbed by Lloyds Bank (q.v.). Region: South Asia.

*Delhi and London Bank*. Incorporated in India as the Delhi Banking Corporation in 1844. In 1865 it was registered as a London bank under the title of Delhi and London Bank. Its head office moved to London the following year. In 1916 its business was divided, the Indian business and six Indian branches going to Alliance Bank of Simla (established in 1874 as an Indian joint stock bank with predominantly British management), and the English business going to Boulton Brothers of London. Went into voluntary liquidation in 1924, in the wake of the failure of Boulton Brothers and Alliance Bank of Simla. Region: South Asia.

*Eastern Bank*. Founded in London at the end of 1909. In 1957, it became a wholly owned subsidiary of the Chartered Bank (q.v.), but remained an autonomous entity until its total absorption in 1971. Region: South and East Asia, Middle East.

*English Bank of the River Plate*. Established 1881. Forced to suspend payments in 1891. Reconstructed in 1892 as New English Bank of the River Plate, but went into permanent liquidation in 1894. Region: Latin America.

*English Bank of Rio de Janeiro*. See British Bank of South America.

*English, Scottish & Australian Bank*. Incorporated by Royal Charter as English, Scottish & Australian Chartered Bank in 1852, and started operations in Australia in 1853. Suspended payments in 1893, whereupon it was reconstructed as a limited company under the title of English, Scottish & Australian Bank. Absorbed Commercial Bank of Tasmania and London Bank of Australia in 1921, and Royal Bank of Australia in 1927. Merged with Australia and New Zealand Bank (q.v.) in 1969 and became integrated into the Australia and New Zealand Banking Group in 1970. Region: Australasia.

*Grindlays Bank*. As Grindlay and Company acted as agents and bankers to the Indian Army from the mid-nineteenth century. From 1908, it directly operated branches in India from its London base. Acquired by National Provincial Bank in 1924. National Provincial's shareholding in Grindlays Bank was transferred to National Bank of India (q.v.) in 1948, its business being merged with the latter in 1958. Region: South Asia, Southern Africa (from 1953).

*Grindlay and Company. See* Grindlays Bank.

*Hongkong and Shanghai Banking Corporation (The).* Founded in Hong Kong in 1865 as the Hongkong and Shanghai Banking Company under a Hong Kong Government Banking Ordinance. Its name was changed to the Hongkong and Shanghai Banking Corporation in 1867 after the British government accorded its sanction to the Ordinance. In 1959 it acquired Mercantile Bank (q.v.), in 1960 the British Bank of the Middle East (q.v.), and in 1965 a controlling interest in Hang Seng Bank. In 1980 it acquired 51 per cent of Marine Midland Banks Inc. of New York State (100 per cent in 1987), and in 1984 29.9 per cent of James Capel and Company, the London brokers (100 per cent in 1986). In 1991 the Hongkong Bank Group was reorganized under a new holding company, HSBC Holdings PLC, incorporated in London. In April 1992 the bank made an agreed take-over bid for the Midland Bank, which was acquired in the following June.

*Imperial Bank of Iran. See* British Bank of the Middle East.

*Imperial Bank of Persia. See* British Bank of the Middle East.

*Ionian Bank.* Founded in London in 1839, it received a charter from the United States of the Ionian Islands, a British protectorate, later the same year. In 1844, it also received a Royal Charter. When the Ionian Islands were transferred to the kingdom of Greece in 1864, Ionian Bank was granted a fresh charter under which it became a Société Anonyme in Greece. In 1883, Ionian Bank surrendered its Royal Charter and was registered as a limited liability company in Britain. In Greece it remained a 'privileged' bank of issue on terms of equality with National Bank of Greece until 1920, at which date this privilege lapsed and was transferred to the National Bank. Its Egyptian business was nationalized in 1956. In 1957 its Cyprus business was sold to the Chartered Bank (q.v.) and its Greek business to Commercial Bank of Greece. Thereafter, it continued to operate in London as a small merchant bank. Region: Greece, Egypt (from 1907), Cyprus (from 1926).

*Lloyds and National Provincial Foreign Bank.* Established as Lloyds Bank (France) in 1911, on the basis of Lloyds Bank's (q.v.) acquisition of the business of Armstrong and Company of Paris. In 1917, National Provincial Bank acquired a half-share in the bank and it was renamed Lloyds Bank (France) and National Provincial (France) Bank changing its name two years later to Lloyds and National Provincial Foreign Bank. In 1954, National Provincial sold its share back to Lloyds, and the bank, under the new name of Lloyds Bank (Foreign), became a wholly owned subsidiary of Lloyds Bank. Its name was changed again in 1964 to Lloyds Bank Europe. In 1970, the latter was merged with Bank of London and South America (q.v.), becoming, successively, part of Lloyds and Bolsa International Bank from 1971 and of Lloyds Bank International from 1974 (see Bank of London and South America). Region: continental Europe.

*Lloyds Bank Europe. See* Lloyds and National Provincial Foreign Bank.

*Lloyds Bank (Foreign). See* Lloyds and National Provincial Foreign Bank.

*Lloyds Bank (France). See* Lloyds and National Provincial Foreign Bank.

*Lloyds Bank PLC.* Established originally in 1756, in 1853 its name changed to Lloyds and Company. Incorporated as a joint stock company in 1865, and thereafter absorbed more than fifty private and joint stock banks. In 1889, its name changed to Lloyds Bank. Current name adopted as a result of the 1980 Companies Act. First direct foreign investment made in 1911 when Lloyds Bank (France) was established (see Lloyds and National Provincial Foreign Bank). Acquired 99 per cent of the shareholding of London and River Plate Bank (see Bank of London and South America) in 1918. On the latter's merger with London and Brazilian Bank (q.v.) in 1923, had a 57 per cent interest in the newly amalgamated Bank of London and South America (q.v.), this shareholding falling to 47 per cent when Bolsa absorbed the remaining assets and liabilities of Anglo-South American Bank (q.v.) in 1936. In 1923. Lloyds acquired Cox & Co. (q.v.). The South Asian branches thus acquired were managed by the Eastern Department of Lloyds Bank until 1960, when they were sold to National and Grindlays Bank (q.v.) in return for 25 per cent of the latter's equity. This shareholding was retained until National and Grindlays was sold to the Australia and New Zealand Banking Group (see Australia and New Zealand Bank) in 1984. In 1965, Lloyds acquired total ownership of National Bank of New Zealand (q.v.) in which it had had a minority interest since 1919. From 1974 most overseas interests were concentrated in Lloyds Bank International, which had become a wholly owned subsidiary in December 1973 (see Bank of London and South America). Lloyds Bank California was established in 1974 and sold in 1986. On 1 January 1986, Lloyds Bank International was merged with the parent bank.

*London and Brazilian.* Founded in 1862, in the same year it absorbed Anglo-Portuguese Bank, which had also just been established. In 1871 its name was changed to the New London and Brazilian Bank, but it reverted to its original title in 1885. In 1923, its undertaking and assets were acquired by London and River Plate Bank (see Bank of London and South America), and the newly amalgamated bank became known as Bank of London and South America (q.v.). Region: Latin America.

*London and River Plate Bank. See* Bank of London and South America.

*London and San Francisco Bank.* Established in 1865. In 1871, it absorbed the private banking business in California of Parrot and Company. It was acquired by the Bank of California in 1905. Region: United States.

*London and South African Bank.* Established in 1860, and incorporated under Royal Charter the following year, to operate in the Western Cape province of South Africa. It was absorbed by Standard Bank of South Africa (q.v.) in 1877. Region: South Africa.

*London Bank of Australia.* Incorporated in 1852 by Royal Charter under the title of London Chartered Bank of Australia (q.v.) and began operations in Australia in 1853. Forced to suspend business in 1893, but was reconstructed in the same year as a limited company named London Bank of Australia. Went into voluntary liquidation in 1921 as a result of being absorbed by English, Scottish & Australian Bank (q.v.). Region: Australasia.

*London Bank of Mexico and South America.* Originally established in Peru in 1863 as London and South American Bank, it was amalgamated with a British bank in Mexico (formed in 1864 expressly for this purpose) and renamed London Bank of Mexico and South America. In the mid-1880s, its Mexican business was sold to a locally incorporated institution, El Banco de Londres y Mejico, in which the British bank owned two-thirds of the capital. Subsequently, the London office of the bank was operated as a holding company for locally incorporated banks abroad. At the time of its absorption by Anglo-South American Bank (q.v.) in 1912, the London Bank had holdings in a range of such banks. Region: Latin America.

*London Chartered Bank of Australia.* See London Bank of Australia.

*London County and Westminster Bank (Paris).* See Westminster Foreign Bank.

*London, Paris and American Bank.* Originally an agency in California of Lazard Frères, it was reorganized as a British limited company entitled London, Paris and American Bank in 1884. Thereafter, it became the largest dealer in the international exchange market of the Pacific Coast. In 1908, a Californian group assumed control and it was reorganized as the London-Paris National Bank of San Francisco, and subsequently merged with Anglo-Californian Bank (q.v.) as the Anglo and London-Paris National Bank of San Francisco. Region: United States.

*Mercantile Bank of India.* A reconstruction in 1892 as a limited liability company of the former Chartered Mercantile Bank of India, London and China (q.v.). It acquired the locally incorporated Bank of Calcutta in 1906, and Bank of Mauritius (q.v.) in 1916. In January 1958, its name was changed to Mercantile Bank, and in 1959 it was acquired by Hongkong Bank (see Hongkong and Shanghai Banking Corporation), becoming a wholly owned subsidiary. In 1966, its head office transferred to Hong Kong. In July 1984 the bank's remaining activities were sold after a transition period during which the bulk of its business was absorbed by the Hongkong Bank. Region: South, South-east, and East Asia.

*Midland Bank PLC.* Established in 1836 as the Birmingham and Midland Bank. Reregistered with limited liability in 1880. After a series of acquisitions and name changes, it adopted the title of Midland Bank in 1923. Acquired its current name as a result of the 1980 Companies Act. Took the lead in establishing Midland and International Banks in 1964. In 1974 an international division was created. Acquired 51 per cent of Crocker National Bank of California in 1980 and 100 per cent in 1985, but sold this bank in 1986. In 1987, Hongkong Bank (see Hongkong and Shanghai Banking Corporation) acquired 14.9 per cent of Midland's equity and it secured 100 per cent ownership in 1992.

*National and Grindlays Bank.* A merger of the National Bank of India (q.v.) and its wholly owned subsidiary Grindlays Bank (q.v.) in 1958 under the title of National Overseas and Grindlays Bank, the name being shortened a year later to National and Grindlays Bank. Acquired Lloyds Bank (q.v.) Eastern branches (ex Cox's and King's) in 1960, and the London business and Cyprus, Middle Eastern, and East African branches of Ottoman Bank in 1969. In 1960 25 per cent of its equity was acquired by Lloyds Bank, and in 1968 40 per cent by Citibank. Name changed in January 1974 to Grindlays Bank. Taken over by Australia and New Zealand Banking Group (see Australia and New Zealand Bank) in 1984. Region:

South Asia, East Africa (from 1890s), Southern Africa (from 1953), Middle East (from 1969).

*National Bank of Egypt.* Incorporated in Egypt by Khedivial Decree in 1898. Head office and seat of the board of directors was in Cairo, but there were three directors resident in London. Founded, in conjunction with the Egyptian government, the Agricultural Bank of Egypt in 1902 (established by Khedivial Decree); and, under a concession and charter granted by the Emperor Menelik, the Bank of Abyssinia in 1905 (established by Khedivial Decree as a Société Anonyme Egyptienne). The Bank of Abyssinia's concession was cancelled in 1931 and its business taken over by the new State Bank of Ethiopia, and the Agricultural Bank of Egypt was voluntarily wound up in 1936. National Bank of Egypt became an entirely Egyptian concern in 1948. Region: Egypt.

*National Bank of India.* Founded in Calcutta in 1863 as Calcutta City Banking Corporation, its name was changed to National Bank of India in 1864. Domicile and head office transferred to London in 1866. Absorbed Indo-Egyptian and London Bank in 1865. Acquired ownership of Grindlays Bank (q.v.) in 1948. In 1958, the business of the two banks was merged under the title of National Overseas and Grindlays Bank (see National and Grindlays Bank). Region: South Asia, East Africa (from 1890s).

*National Bank of New Zealand.* Established in 1872 under British joint stock legislation. Absorbed the locally based Bank of Otago in 1874. Forced to write down its capital in 1891. Lloyds Bank (q.v.) purchased a minority shareholding in 1919. At the end of 1965, it became a wholly owned subsidiary of Lloyds. In 1978 its domicile was moved from London to New Zealand. Region: Australasia.

*National Bank of Turkey.* Established by Imperial Ottoman decree in 1909. Its head office was in Constantinople (Istanbul), but six of its directors were British and sat in London as a Special Committee. The bulk of its capital was acquired by the British Trade Corporation (see Anglo-International Bank) in 1919, but it was almost totally moribund by 1922. Finally liquidated in 1931. Region: Turkey.

*National Westminster Bank PLC.* Established 1968 when the boards of the National Provincial (founded 1833) and Westminster (founded 1834 as the London and Westminster) Banks decided to merge. Reregistered as National Westminster Bank PLC as a result of the 1980 Companies Act. For its earliest direct foreign investments, see Westminster Foreign Bank and Lloyds and National Provincial Foreign Bank. New York Agency established in 1969 and became a branch in 1970. International Banking Division established in 1970. In 1973 Westminster Foreign Bank (q.v.) was renamed International Westminster Bank, the latter being fully merged into National Westminster in 1985. National Bank of North America was acquired in 1979 and was renamed National Westminster Bank USA in 1983. In 1988, National Westminster Bancorp Inc. was formed as an American holding company for National Westminster Bank USA and National Westminster Bancorp NJ.

*New Oriental Bank Corporation.* Registered in 1884 as a reconstruction of the Oriental Bank Corporation (q.v.). Failed in 1892 and went into voluntary liquidation a year later. Region: Asia, Middle East, Australasia.

*Oriental Bank Corporation.* Originated in Bombay in 1842 as Bank of Western India. Moved its domicile from Bombay to London in 1845 under the title of Oriental Bank. In 1849, it took over Bank of Ceylon, which had been founded in 1840 and granted a charter two years later. The combined institution, under the name of Oriental Bank Corporation, was given a new Royal Charter in 1851. Failed in 1884. It was reconstructed as a limited liability company, New Oriental Bank Corporation (q.v.), in the same year. Region: Asia, Australasia, South Africa.

*Ottoman Bank.* Incorporated by Royal Charter in 1856 to operate a banking business in the Ottoman Empire. Reincorporated as Imperial Ottoman Bank in 1863, under the protection of the Sultan and his government, with its domicile in Constantinople. Region: Ottoman Empire.

*P & O Banking Corporation.* Incorporated in 1920 as a limited company with its registered office in London, it was sponsored by the P & O Steam Navigation Company in collaboration with Lloyds (q.v.), and National Provincial and Westminster (see National Westminster). In 1920 it acquired a controlling interest in the Indian-registered Allahabad Bank (established in 1865). In 1927, the Chartered Bank (q.v.) bought a controlling interest in P & O Bank, absorbing it completely at the beginning of 1939. At the same time, P & O's controlling interest in Allahabad Bank was acquired, but the latter remained an autonomous entity until its nationalization by the Indian government in 1969. Region: South Asia.

*Royal Bank of Scotland PLC.* Established in 1727 by Royal Charter. In April 1969 it merged with National Commercial Bank of Scotland as a member of the National Commercial Banking Group, whose title was changed to Royal Bank of Scotland. Incorporated as Royal Bank of Scotland PLC in 1984 to effect its merger with Williams & Glyn's Bank, which took place in September 1985. No direct international representation until the 1970s. An international division was created in 1977, and the first overseas branch, in New York, was opened in 1978. Branches in Hong Kong and Singapore followed in 1979 and 1984. In 1988 Citizens Financial Bank of Rhode Island was acquired.

*Sassoon Banking Company (E.D.).* Registered in Hong Kong in 1930 to take over the banking interests in London, Manchester, and Hong Kong of the E. D. Sassoon merchant company. In 1952, a new private E. D. Sassoon Banking Company was registered in the Bahamas, to take over all the assets and liabilities of the Hong Kong concern. In 1963, E. D. Sassoon Banking Company was established as a merchant bank, acquiring in 1967 the Bahamas-incorporated E. D. Sassoon Banking International (formerly E. D. Sassoon Banking Company). In 1972 its capital was acquired by Wallace Brothers and Company (Holdings), and its operations were merged with Wallace Brothers under the title of Wallace Brothers Sassoon Bank. Renamed Wallace Brothers Bank in 1974, it was taken over in 1976 by Standard Chartered Bank (see Standard and Chartered Banking Group). Region: South and East Asia.

*Standard Bank of South Africa.* Originally projected in South Africa in 1857 as Standard Bank of Port Elizabeth, it was finally incorporated as Standard Bank of British South Africa in London in 1862. Renamed Standard Bank of South Africa in 1883. It began operations in South Africa in 1863, absorbing four local banks that year, and one in 1864. Took over five more local banks and London and

South African Bank (q.v.) during the 1870s. Acquired African Banking Corporation (q.v.) in 1920. In 1962, the South African business was split off from the rest of the bank, becoming a wholly owned subsidiary incorporated in South Africa, and the name of the London-based bank was shortened to Standard Bank. It merged with Bank of West Africa (see Bank of British West Africa) in 1965; and with the Chartered Bank (q.v.) in 1969. In February 1970 it became a wholly owned subsidiary of the newly incorporated Standard and Chartered Banking Group (q.v.). Name changed to Standard Chartered Bank Africa PLC in January 1985, a wholly owned subsidiary of Standard Chartered PLC. Divested completely from South Africa in 1987. Region: Southern Africa, Central Africa (from 1890s), East Africa (from 1911), West Africa (from 1965).

*Standard and Chartered Banking Group.* A holding company set up with effect from 1 January 1970 to take over the capital of Standard Bank (see Standard Bank of South Africa) and the Chartered Bank (q.v.), which had decided to merge in 1969 and which thus became wholly owned subsidiaries of the new institution. As from 1971, the business of the Eastern Bank was fully integrated with that of the Chartered Bank. In October 1975, in a move towards total merger, the UK business of both subsidiary banks was transferred to Standard and Chartered Banking Group, which was renamed Standard Chartered. The latter's name was changed to Standard Chartered PLC in February 1980 as a result of the Companies Act of that year. In January 1985, the name was changed again to Standard Chartered Bank, which became, along with Standard Chartered Bank Africa PLC (see Standard Bank of South Africa), a wholly owned subsidiary of a new holding company, Standard Chartered PLC. Acquired Union Bank of California in 1979, and United Bank of Arizona in 1987, but both these subsidiaries were sold in 1988.

*Standard Chartered PLC. See* Standard and Chartered Banking Group.

*Union Bank of Australia.* Established in 1837 in London, it started operations in Australia in 1838. Almost immediately it acquired the locally incorporated Tamar Bank of Tasmania and the Bathurst Bank, followed by Archers Gilles and Company in 1840. It did not have a Royal Charter, setting up instead as a banking co-partnership. However, by 1840 Acts in its favour had been passed by the Colonial Legislatures which put it on an equal legal footing with the chartered banks. Registered as a limited company in 1880. Took over Bank of South Australia (q.v.) in 1892. Merged with Bank of Australasia (q.v.) in 1951, under the title of Australia and New Zealand Bank (q.v.). Region: Australasia.

*Union Bank of Spain and England.* Established in 1881 as a British-registered bank. Ceased operating in 1896 and went into voluntary liquidation a year later. Region: continental Europe.

*Westminster Foreign Bank.* Originated as a wholly owned subsidiary of the London, County and Westminster Bank, under the title of London, County and Westminster Bank (Paris) in 1913. In April 1920, its name changed to London, County Westminster and Parr's Foreign Bank, and in 1923 to Westminster Foreign Bank. In January 1973, it became International Westminster Bank, a subsidiary of National Westminster Bank (q.v.), which was finally merged with the parent bank in 1985. Region: continental Europe.

# Geographical Distribution of Branches of British Multinational Banks, 1860–1970

This table gives the distribution of branches by primary geographical region. The sub-totals give branch numbers for the main countries/regions within each of these primary regions. They do not necessarily add up to the total for each primary region.

TABLE A3.1. *Geographical distribution of foreign branches and affiliates of British multinational banks, 1860–1970*

| Region[a] | 1860 | | 1890 | | | 1913 | | |
|---|---|---|---|---|---|---|---|---|
| | Branches | % | Branches | % | Affiliates | Branches | % | Affiliates |
| Australasia | 60 | 46 | 452 | 61 | | 660 | 47 | |
| *Australia* | 51 | 39 | 378 | 51 | | 521 | 37 | |
| *New Zealand* | 9 | 7 | 73 | 10 | | 138 | 10 | |
| North America | 12 | 9 | 33 | 5 | | 109 | 8 | |
| *USA* | — | — | 12 | 2 | | 13 | 1 | |
| *Canada* | 12 | 9 | 21 | 3 | | 96 | 7 | |
| Rest of Americas | 14 | 11 | 48 | 6 | 1 | 97 | 7 | |
| *W. Indies* | 14 | 11 | 14 | 2 | | 19 | 1 | |
| *Brazil* | — | — | 16 | 2 | | 23 | 2 | |
| *Argentina* | — | — | 8 | 1 | | 29 | 2 | |
| Southern Africa | 3 | 2 | 90 | 12 | | 256 | 19 | |
| *South Africa* | 3 | 2 | 90 | 12 | | 234 | 17 | |
| Rest of Africa | 2 | 1 | 4 | — | | 71 | 5 | |
| *West Africa* | — | — | — | — | | 58 | 4 | |
| *East Africa* | — | — | — | — | | 11 | 1 | |
| Middle East/North Africa | 6 | 5 | 10 | 1 | | 55 | 4 | 2 |
| South Asia | 18 | 14 | 42 | 6 | | 56 | 4 | |
| South-east Asia | 4 | 3 | 19 | 3 | | 32 | 2 | |
| East Asia | 8 | 6 | 22 | 3 | | 25 | 2 | |
| Europe (except UK) | 5 | 3 | 19 | 3 | | 26 | 2 | |
| *Western* | — | — | 4 | 1 | | 15 | 1 | |
| *Southern* | 5 | 3 | 14 | 2 | | 11 | 1 | |
| TOTAL | 132 | | 739 | | 1 | 1,387 | | 2 |
| No. of banks | 15 | | 33 | | | 31 | | |

[a] The following regional definitions have been used: Australasia comprises Australia, New Zealand, and Pacific countries; North America comprises the United States and Canada; rest of Americas comprises Central and South America, and the West Indies; Southern Africa comprises South Africa, and the countries comprising the modern states of Zimbabwe and Zambia (Southern and Northern Rhodesia), Malawi (formerly Nyasaland), Botswana (Bechuanaland), Swaziland, Lesotho, Angola, and Mozambique; rest of Africa excludes Southern Africa and North Africa, but includes West and East Africa, Mauritius, and the Seychelles. In the sub-totals, West and East Africa have been broadly defined, and there is no category for Central Africa; Middle East and North Africa includes Sudan, Israel (Palestine), and Turkey; South Asia comprises the former region of British India (India, Pakistan, Bangladesh, Burma and Sri Lanka); South-east Asia comprises the modern states of Singapore, Malaysia, Indonesia, Philippines, Thailand and Brunei; East Asia includes China, Hong Kong, Japan, Vietnam and Cambodia; Europe includes all of continental Europe; Western Europe includes France, Germany, Benelux, Switzerland, and Scandinavia; southern Europe includes all Mediterranean countries (except France), Cyprus, Malta, and Portugal.

[b] The Eastern department of Lloyds Bank has not been counted as a bank, but its South Asian branches have been included in the analysis.

| 1928 | | | 1938 | | | 1955 | | | 1970 | | |
|---|---|---|---|---|---|---|---|---|---|---|---|
| Branches | % | Affiliates | Branches | % | Affiliates | Branches | % | Affiliates | Branches | % | Affiliates |
| 997 | 45 | | 975 | 42 | | 1,461 | 40 | 2 | 1,767 | 46 | 2 |
| 804 | 36 | | 795 | 34 | | 1,149 | 32 | 2 | 1,334 | 35 | 2 |
| 193 | 9 | | 180 | 8 | | 307 | 8 | | 419 | 11 | |
| 6 | — | 1 | 8 | — | | 6 | — | 1 | 11 | — | 4 |
| 6 | — | 1 | 6 | — | | 6 | — | 1 | 11 | — | 4 |
| — | — | — | 2 | — | | — | — | — | | | |
| 111 | 5 | | 86 | 4 | 1 | 118 | 3 | 1 | 228 | 6 | 1 |
| 19 | 1 | | 19 | 1 | | 19 | 1 | | 115 | 3 | |
| 24 | 1 | | 16 | 1 | | 12 | — | | 14 | | |
| 29 | 1 | | 25 | 1 | | 22 | 1 | | 31 | | |
| 659 | 29 | | 756 | 32 | | 1,326 | 37 | | 1,168 | 31 | 1 |
| 590 | 26 | | 660 | 29 | | 1,082 | 30 | | 823 | 21 | 1 |
| 106 | 5 | | 103 | 5 | | 268 | 7 | | 127 | 3 | 10 |
| 65 | 3 | | 52 | 2 | | 140 | 4 | | — | — | 6 |
| 40 | 2 | | 50 | 2 | | 133 | 3 | | 113 | 3 | 4 |
| 123 | 5 | 2 | 126 | 5 | | 136 | 4 | | 74 | 2 | 2 |
| 73 | 3 | 1 | 84 | 3 | 1 | 100 | 3 | 1 | 113 | 3 | |
| 41 | 2 | | 41 | 2 | | 71 | 2 | | 104 | 3 | — |
| 38 | 2 | | 38 | 2 | | 23 | 1 | | 116 | 3 | 3 |
| 99 | 4 | 2 | 98 | 4 | | 103 | 3 | | 118 | 3 | 2 |
| 50 | 2 | 1 | 39 | 1 | | 32 | 1 | | 34 | 1 | 2 |
| 46 | 2 | 1 | 59 | 3 | | 71 | 2 | | 84 | 2 | |
| 2,253 | | 6 | 2,315 | — | 2 | 3,612 | | 5 | 3,826 | | 25 |
| 27[b] | | | 24[b] | | | 18[b] | | | 9 | | |

# Geographical Distribution of Total Assets of British Multinational Banks, 1860–1990

## 4.1. 1860–1970

Banks did not break down the geographical distribution of their assets in this period, and such data cannot be readily reconstructed from even unpublished data. This table has been compiled by the simple expedient of allotting a bank to a single region (or several regions) and regarding its total assets as allocated to that region. In practice, a proportion of each bank's assets would have been in the United Kingdom. This method probably provides a satisfactory proxy for asset distribution by region before the First World War, given the geographical specialization of the banks, but is not meant to give firm estimates of the absolute level of assets held in each region. Thereafter, the growth of multi-regional banks diminishes the reliability of the data. The assets of multi-regional banks have been allocated to different regions in accordance with the number of their branches and with a subjective assessment of the importance of different regions to the overall business of each bank.

TABLE A4.1. *Geographical distribution of total assets of British multinational banks, 1860–1970 (%)*

| Region | 1860 | 1890 | 1913 | 1928 | 1938 | 1955 | 1970 |
|---|---|---|---|---|---|---|---|
| Australasia | 35 | 27 | 21 | 20 | 22 | 20 | 16 |
| North America | 5 | 6 | 4 | — | — | — | — |
| Rest of Americas | 5 | 23 | 29 | 20 | 12 | 7 | 9 |
| Southern Africa | — | 7 | 10 | 15 | 22 | 29 | 25 |
| Rest of Africa | — | — | 2 | 5 | 6 | 12 | 7 |
| Middle East/North Africa | 4 | 2 | 6 | 8 | 6 | 4 | 3 |
| Asia | 51 | 34 | 27 | 25 | 27 | 25 | 27 |
| Europe (except UK) | — | 1 | 1 | 7 | 5 | 3 | 13 |
| TOTAL ASSETS (£m.) | 45 | 236 | 366 | 803 | 767 | 2,567 | 12,007 |
| No. of banks | 15[a] | 33 | 29[b] | 26[c] | 23[d] | 18[e] | 9 |

[a] Excludes Ionian Bank.
[b] Excludes London County and Westminster Bank (Paris) and Grindlay and Company.
[c] Excludes Barclays Bank SAI and Lloyds Bank Eastern department.
[d] Excludes Barclays Bank SAI and Lloyds Bank Eastern department.
[e] Excludes Lloyds Bank Eastern department.

*4.2. 1990*

The following table is compiled from the Annual Report and Accounts for the banks supplemented by their Annual Report on Form 20-F to the Securities and Exchange Commission, in both cases for 1990. Unfortunately, the banks do not break down their assets by identical geographical regions, and the following table needs to be read in conjunction with the notes. The statistics for Barclays, National Westminster, and Midland are broadly compatible, but those for the other banks are not. Note in particular Standard Chartered and Hongkong Bank's inclusion of the United Kingdom within 'Europe'.

TABLE A4.2. *Geographical distribution of total assets of British multinational banks, 1990*

| Bank | Total assets (£m.) | Foreign assets | | | | | | | | | |
|---|---|---|---|---|---|---|---|---|---|---|---|
| | | Total | | UK-based | | US | | Other Europe | | Rest of the world | |
| | | £m. | % | £m. | % | £m. | % | £m. | % | £m. | % |
| Barclays PLC[a] | 134,887 | 49,214 | 36 | 9,061 | 7 | 15,620 | 12 | 15,310 | 11 | 9,061 | 7 |
| Nat West PLC[b] | 121,000 | 53,065 | 44 | 19,102 | 16 | 15,785 | 13 | n.a. | | 18,178 | 15 |
| Midland PLC | 59,636 | 23,554 | 39 | 13,188 | 22 | 1,843 | 3 | 7,100 | 12 | 1,423 | 2 |
| Lloyds PLC[c] | 55,202 | 9,936 | 18 | n.a. | | n.a. | | 2,760 | 5 | 7,176 | 13 |
| Standard Chartered PLC[d] | 22,141 | n.a. | | n.a. | | 1,039 | 5 | 8,036 | 38 | 12,245 | 37 |
| Hongkong Bank[e] | 77,372 | n.a. | | n.a. | | 20,349 | 26 | 15,629 | 20 | 41,394 | 54 |

*Notes*: n.a. = not available.

[a] The Barclays data for 'other Europe' is for the EC (excluding UK) only.

[b] National Westminster provides an asset breakdown by UK, US, and rest of the world only. No other country has more than 10 per cent of total assets.

[c] Lloyds does not break down domestic UK assets from UK-based foreign assets. As a result, the 18 per cent figure for foreign assets is not compatible with those of Barclays, Nat West, and Midland.

[d] Standard Chartered does not separate the UK from the rest of Europe, and the figure of £8,036 m. is for both. The £1,039m. allocated to the United States is for North America as a whole. The bank had £10,031m. (47%) in Asia-Pacific, £1,052m. (5%) in Africa, £930m. (4%) in Middle East/South Asia, and £232m. (1%) in Australia.

[e] Hongkong Bank does not separate UK from the rest of Europe, and the figure of £15,629m. is for both. The £20,349m. for the United States is for the Americas. In addition, Hongkong Bank had £39,305m. (51%) in Asia-Pacific and £2,089m. (3%) in the Middle East. During the 1992 takeover of Midland Bank the Hongkong Bank revealed further details of its asset distribution in 1990. It had 39.5% in Hong Kong, 11.3% in the rest of Asia-Pacific, 26.3% in the Americas, 20.2% in the UK, 0% in Continental Europe, and 2.7% in Middle East/India.

# Performance, Profitability, and Worth of a Sample of British Multinational Banks, 1890–1975

## 5.1. Methodology and Data

A sample of British multinational banks was selected for systematic analysis. The sample includes at least 60 per cent of the banks active in each period, and after the First World War well over 70 per cent. It is well distributed by size and by geographical area of specialization. Each region is represented. The number of banks included is broadly in accordance with the geographical distribution of assets and branches for all banks. Comparative figures were also calculated for two of the large English clearing banks. The Midland Bank had no multinational operations until the early 1970s. In contrast, Lloyds Bank was the owner, in whole or in part, of several of the overseas banks in the sample. It was decided to focus the study on a core period of 1890 to 1975. For much of the nineteenth century data on off-balance sheet items such as 'real' profits are non-existent, while even balance sheet and share price information is difficult to locate. After 1975 the integration of British domestic and overseas banking had proceeded to the extent that the study would have lost any real meaning. The overall period was broken down into a series of sub-periods, which were related to general exogenous circumstances such as world wars.

Table A5.1 gives selected balance sheet and off-balance sheet data for the sample overseas banks. The fact that different banks had different accounting year-ends is a complication. The following rule was adopted. Year-ends from January to May reverted to the previous year, while those from June to December were counted as the same year. For a bank which reported in April, therefore, the 1900 balance sheet figures given here are for April 1901. For a few banks with different shareholding categories, the market values were determined by the appropriate weighting. Hongkong Bank was the only sample bank which reported in a currency other than sterling, although its dividend was declared in sterling until 1971, and part of its published reserve was held in London and shown in sterling. All other data for that bank were converted into sterling from Hong Kong dollars using prevailing exchange rates.

Most of the headings are straightforward. Retained profits is the net balance carried forward as the result of each year's working. The most contentious items are for real profits and inner reserves. Banks used these terms in different ways. Often inner reserves were held in several different accounts. Thus, although every attempt has been made to standardize this information, the figures need to be treated with caution. There is a particular problem that banks often included in the inner reserve figures contingencies made for identified bad debts and other specific needs. The data given here are, as far as was possible to determine, for the 'free' inner reserves—reserves held off-balance sheet which were not against any known contingency. E, S & A's figure, however, is definitely for total rather than simply free inner reserves, and calculations using them must be treated accordingly. A further problem is that banks often kept contingency reserves at branches. It is usually hard to ascertain the sums involved, and they are in most cases excluded from the data given here. On occasion transfers from branch reserves to central inner reserves result in a misleading impression that the bank's overall reserve has increased. The most serious instance appears to be the Colonial Bank in 1908, when such a manœuvre led to an apparent rapid rise in inner reserves at a time when its overall performance was weak. The concept of real—or true—profits is also a nebulous one. It is used here to mean net published profits before transfers to or from inner reserves. Published profits would normally equal real profits plus or minus such transfers.

The balance sheets of the Anglo-South American Bank and the Lloyds and National Provincial Foreign Bank have been partially reconstructed for the early 1930s. Both banks received large off-balance sheet transfers in this period. These transfers have been incorporated into the data, and used in performance calculations, on the basis of heroic assumptions.

The data on real profits and inner reserves have been largely collected from bank archives. The main sources were as follows, although it should be noted that problems of conflicting data and of gaps in series were often resolved by reference to information scattered more generally in corporate archives. Data on Colonial Bank and Barclays (DCO) were obtained from Barclays Bank Archives, files 38/97 and 38/251. Data on the Bank of Mauritius and Mercantile Bank of India were obtained from Hongkong Bank Group Archives, files MB1191 and MB2371, 2374 and 2397. Data on the Ionian Bank were obtained from Ionian Bank Archives, London School of Economics, Yearly Accounting Ledgers. Data on the London and River Plate Bank and Bolsa were obtained from Lloyds Bank Archives, Green Book, Profit and Loss Books, and Bolsa balance sheets. Data on Lloyds and National Provincial Foreign Bank were largely obtained from National Westminster Bank Archives, file NW4252. Data on Chartered Bank, Standard Bank, Eastern Bank, and the Bank of British West Africa were obtained from Standard Chartered Bank Archives, files SC228, 259–61; P25, P/34, P76; R/21; R/29. Data on the English, Scottish & Australian Bank inner reserves were derived from E, S & A Ledgers and E, S & A Balance Book, 1895–1941, ANZ Archives, as reported in D. Merrett to G. Jones, 29 August 1989. Data on the Imperial Bank of Persia and its successors are published in Geoffrey Jones, *Banking and Empire in Iran* and *Banking and Oil*. Data on the Hongkong Bank are taken from F. H. H. King, *The History of The Hongkong and Shanghai Banking Corporation*, iii. 193 and iv. 200.

Share price data were derived from the *Bankers' Magazine* supplemented by the *Financial Times, Investors' Monthly Manual*, and the *Stock Exchange Ten Year Record*. The share price taken has been for the third week of each December. When such data were unavailable—as between 1942 and 1945, for example—the mean of the annual high–low share price was taken.

Tables A5.2–4 contain an analysis of the profitability and performance of the sample banks from various perspectives. A larger analysis supported by a technical explanation has been deposited with the Economic and Social Research Council Data Archive held at the University of Essex, Colchester, United Kingdom. The data set is entitled Profitability and Worth of British Overseas Banking between 1890 and 1970 (March 1990). This will be referred to as ESRC Report in the following discussion.

The performance measures in this appendix are all in constant prices. The index used is that prepared by Forrest Capie and Allan Webber in *A Monetary History of the United Kingdom, 1870–1982* (London: Allen and Unwin, 1985), vol. 1, table 3(12), col. III GNP Deflator, extended by data from the CSO Blue Books. The price of Consols was also derived from the CSO Blue Books. 1913 has been used as the base year. The ESRC Report gives the various calculations in both prevailing and constant prices.

Table A5.2 gives a calculation of Net Present Value (NPV) and average dividend and yield ratios in constant prices (1913 base). Banks are ranked according to the size of their NPV. The NPV calculation assesses the performance of the sample banks from a shareholder's standpoint. The NPV is the present value of future cash flows over a discrete period of time, discounted at predetermined rates. It is assumed that all the shares of a bank are purchased at their market value at the beginning of a period and sold at a predetermined date, again at market value. In the interim, dividends are paid and the bank retains shareholder funds for various provisions. The ESRC Report measures NPVs on these bases, but Table A5.2 confines itself to the NPV calculated on the basis of dividends paid out. The discount rates have been calculated from the rate of return yielded by an investment in British government Consols over the same discrete time periods. A negative NPV result indicates that investors would have done better to invest in Consols. A ranking of banks according to their NPVs would be misleading as the initial investment in each bank was different. The NPV formula has, therefore, been refined to express for each bank the NPV per £100 unit of investment at the beginning of each discrete period, discounted by the relevant rate.

The NPV data presented here should be used with caution by those unfamiliar with this form of analysis. Non-specialists should note that the NPV has been calculated as a measure of whether a predetermined investment rate of return over a specified period, in the context of each bank's individual dividend-flow profile, has been achieved. Non-specialists should also note the element of hypothesis involved in the notion of buying all the capital at the beginning of a period and selling it at the end, at the relevant market values. For example, the dates of buying and selling have not been adjusted for particular performance characteristics: neither for those relating on the one hand to such bank-related events as the announcement of results, when an unwanted share price movement might be expected, nor for those relating on the other hand to such exogenous events as a declaration of war. A specific point in time has been taken as being representative, no trend analysis or adjustment having been done. The periodization chosen and the assumptions used have a critical influence on the results generated, and these have to be treated accordingly.

The ESRC Report contains other measures of performance from the shareholders' perspective. In all, four Internal Rates of Return measures were calculated, along with four NPV measures with no adjustment for different scales of operation. The NPV per £100 invested measure, on the basis of dividends paid out, has been selected for this book on the grounds that it is the most appropriate comparative measure of performance. The various complications inherent in calculating IRRs are well known (see, for example, S. Lumby, *Investment Appraisal and Related Decisions* (London: Nelson, 1981), 41 ff.) The IRR results of the banks are useful for determining whether or not they were good investments for their shareholders when compared with the alternative investment in Consols, but, taken in isolation, they do not automatically indicate a preferred option. The NPV formula has this relative preference aspect built in, since a positive result indicates a 'good' investment, and a negative result a 'bad' one, suggesting at once that Consols would have been a better investment.

Average dividend and yield ratios are also included in Table A5.2. They were averaged over the same time periods as for the NPV measures. The average dividend is the ratio of gross dividends to paid-up capital. This describes the shareholders' earnings on the nominal capital invested by them. The average dividend payout per share is the gross dividend divided by the number of shares. The yield is the dividend per share divided by the share price.

It should be observed that the fact that dividends were shown in sterling on the Hongkong Bank's otherwise dollar balance sheet has an impact on its dividend/capital ratio. From 1890 to the 1930s, Hongkong Bank's dividend/capital ratio has to be looked at in context of the falling trend of silver prices, and therefore of the value of the Hong Kong dollar against sterling. In general the dollar fell in value until the mid-1930s, when China went off silver and Hong Kong followed. The effect of the depreciation of the Hong Kong dollar is to increase the bank's dividend/capital ratio as calculated here.

Table A5.3 contains the ratio of published profits to shareholder funds, which is a basic measure of profitability, and of capital to deposits. A number of alternative profitability ratios were calculated and are available in the ESRC Report.

Table A5.4 contains a refinement of the profitability ratio by utilizing the available data on real profits and inner reserves. Only the banks for which such data exist are included. In several cases the information is not available over the whole length of each discrete time period. The ratio of published profits to shareholder funds contained in Table A5.3 has therefore been recalculated for the period for which real data exist for each bank in order to make it directly comparable. Where these dates do not coincide with the period dates, the actual dates are inserted with the bank's name. Three new ratios are calculated. These are the ratio of published profits to shareholder funds and inner reserves, and the ratios of real profits to shareholder funds and to shareholder funds and inner reserves. These data provide some indication how far the true profitability and, by implication, balance sheet of the banks differed from their published situation.

An obvious hypothesis to be tested was whether geographical location had an impact on the performance of British multinational banks. The ESRC Report, therefore, allocated the banks to geographical regions and explored the aggregate performance of each regional grouping. The data generated in this exercise were felt to be so potentially misleading that they have not been reproduced here. The allocation of the sample banks to particular regions became arbitrary once multi-regional banks appeared. Moreover, the data analysis was not weighted to take account of the disparity in individual bank size or in the numbers of banks in each region.

The two graphs A5.1 and A5.2 compare the aggregate annual profitability of the sample overseas banks with the published profitability of English and Welsh joint stock banks for the period 1890 to 1939, and the profitability of the English and Welsh joint stock banks with the profitability of the 'best' and 'worst' five overseas banks in each year. The profitability curves are derived from annual percentages of net published profits to published shareholder funds (i.e. paid-up capital plus published reserves plus retained profits). The annual figures are aggregated. In the case of the overseas banks, the percentages used for Graph A5.1 have been derived by aggregating the relevant figures for all the overseas banks in the sample. In the case of Graph A5.2, the percentages have been derived by aggregating the annual figures of the 'best' five and the 'worst' five overseas banks respectively. The profitability ratios for the English and Welsh joint stock banks have been taken from Forrest Capie, 'Structure and Performance in British Banking, 1870–1939', 82–3, table 3.2. The profitability ratios for the British overseas banks have been derived from the annual published balance sheets of the sample banks.

The analysis in this appendix was undertaken by Frankie Bostock and Mark Bostock.

ANGLO-EGYTIAN BANK

| Years | Published net profits | Real profits | Dividends paid (gross) | Paid-up capital | Market value: capital | Published reserves | Retained profits | Inner reserves | Deposits | Total balance sheet |
|---|---|---|---|---|---|---|---|---|---|---|
| 1890 | 45,620 | n.a. | 30,000 | 400,000 | 400,000 | 0 | 14,768 | n.a. | 934,132 | 2,573,135 |
| 1891 | 40,437 | n.a. | 20,000 | 400,000 | 340,000 | 0 | 35,704 | n.a. | 966,494 | 2,696,848 |
| 1892 | 36,151 | n.a. | 24,000 | 400,000 | 320,000 | 0 | 47,855 | n.a. | 637,614 | 2,453,781 |
| 1893 | 37,715 | n.a. | 24,000 | 400,000 | 360,000 | 0 | 60,000 | n.a. | 695,316 | 2,347,452 |
| 1894 | 40,094 | n.a. | 24,000 | 400,000 | 360,000 | 0 | 75,000 | n.a. | 743,787 | 2,516,993 |
| 1895 | 39,611 | n.a. | 24,000 | 400,000 | 380,000 | 0 | 90,000 | n.a. | 796,850 | 3,025,748 |
| 1896 | 40,476 | n.a. | 24,000 | 400,000 | 400,000 | 100,000 | 6,000 | n.a. | 758,562 | 2,769,219 |
| 1897 | 52,783 | n.a. | 28,000 | 400,000 | 440,000 | 125,000 | 5,000 | n.a. | 910,320 | 3,078,142 |
| 1898 | 57,810 | n.a. | 32,000 | 400,000 | 540,000 | 150,000 | 5,000 | n.a. | 1,373,322 | 4,446,307 |
| 1899 | 59,659 | n.a. | 32,000 | 400,000 | 620,000 | 175,000 | 7,000 | n.a. | 1,440,021 | 4,697,340 |
| 1900 | 83,994 | n.a. | 40,000 | 400,000 | 720,000 | 215,000 | 10,000 | n.a. | 1,640,360 | 4,823,955 |
| 1901 | 81,301 | n.a. | 40,000 | 400,000 | 700,000 | 250,000 | 15,000 | n.a. | 1,666,508 | 5,541,117 |
| 1902 | 91,336 | n.a. | 40,000 | 400,000 | 880,000 | 300,000 | 15,000 | n.a. | 2,009,641 | 5,198,234 |
| 1903 | 93,174 | n.a. | 40,000 | 400,000 | 960,000 | 350,000 | 17,000 | n.a. | 2,461,814 | 6,392,484 |
| 1904 | 99,431 | n.a. | 50,000 | 400,000 | 980,000 | 400,000 | 15,000 | n.a. | 2,777,209 | 6,953,625 |
| 1905 | 115,018 | n.a. | 62,500 | 500,000 | 1,375,000 | 450,000 | 36,000 | n.a. | 3,274,364 | 8,570,322 |
| 1906 | 129,893 | n.a. | 75,000 | 500,000 | 1,375,000 | 550,000 | 29,000 | n.a. | 3,122,534 | 6,431,711 |
| 1907 | 133,012 | n.a. | 75,000 | 500,000 | 1,300,000 | 590,000 | 35,000 | n.a. | 2,586,265 | 5,257,870 |
| 1908 | 105,212 | n.a. | 75,000 | 500,000 | 1,350,000 | 600,000 | 43,000 | n.a. | 2,762,258 | 5,412,376 |
| 1909 | 105,162 | n.a. | 75,000 | 500,000 | 1,375,000 | 610,000 | 46,000 | n.a. | 2,985,182 | 5,680,056 |
| 1910 | 104,254 | n.a. | 75,000 | 500,000 | 1,325,000 | 620,000 | 48,000 | n.a. | 2,760,654 | 5,191,700 |
| 1911 | 114,905 | n.a. | 75,000 | 500,000 | 1,200,000 | 640,000 | 50,000 | n.a. | 3,349,013 | 6,929,107 |
| 1912 | 107,905 | n.a. | 75,000 | 500,000 | 1,225,000 | 660,000 | 52,000 | n.a. | 3,001,501 | 5,495,718 |
| 1913 | 108,026 | n.a. | 75,000 | 500,000 | 1,175,000 | 680,000 | 52,000 | n.a. | 2,943,374 | 5,467,877 |
| 1914 | 102,591 | n.a. | 75,000 | 500,000 | 1,200,000 | 680,000 | 77,000 | n.a. | 3,045,867 | 5,461,757 |
| 1915 | 102,299 | n.a. | 75,000 | 500,000 | 937,500 | 680,000 | 50,000 | n.a. | 5,145,305 | 7,196,161 |
| 1916 | 112,825 | n.a. | 87,500 | 500,000 | 1,175,000 | 690,000 | 52,000 | n.a. | 7,495,125 | 9,492,835 |
| 1917 | 144,347 | n.a. | 87,500 | 500,000 | 1,400,000 | 710,000 | 67,000 | n.a. | 9,057,654 | 10,989,554 |
| 1918 | 146,038 | n.a. | 75,000 | 500,000 | 1,600,000 | 710,000 | 38,000 | n.a. | 12,544,967 | 14,794,382 |
| 1919 | 142,980 | n.a. | 105,000 | 600,000 | 1,980,000 | 720,000 | 40,000 | n.a. | 17,113,477 | 19,567,202 |
| 1920 | 133,406 | n.a. | 105,000 | 600,000 | 4,050,000 | 720,000 | 50,000 | n.a. | 15,542,208 | 18,401,562 |

*Notes*: September financial year-end. Controlling interest acquired by Barclays Bank in 1920 (from 1925 part of Barclays (DCO)). n.a. = not available in case of real profits, and not applicable in the case of published reserves.

BANK OF AUSTRALASIA

| Years | Published net profits | Real profits | Dividends paid (gross) | Paid-up capital | Market value: capital | Published reserves | Retained profits | Inner reserves | Deposits | Total balance sheet |
|---|---|---|---|---|---|---|---|---|---|---|
| 1890 | 224,495 | n.a. | 224,000 | 1,600,000 | 4,000,000 | 800,000 | 15,098 | n.a. | 13,657,509 | 19,251,209 |
| 1891 | 211,929 | n.a. | 212,000 | 1,600,000 | 3,800,000 | 800,000 | 15,027 | n.a. | 13,855,142 | 19,318,088 |
| 1892 | 174,960 | n.a. | 180,000 | 1,600,000 | 3,400,000 | 800,000 | 9,986 | n.a. | 15,127,807 | 19,890,696 |
| 1893 | 121,349 | n.a. | 120,000 | 1,600,000 | 2,600,000 | 800,000 | 11,335 | n.a. | 13,060,845 | 17,816,681 |
| 1894 | 94,306 | n.a. | 96,000 | 1,600,000 | 2,200,000 | 800,000 | 9,641 | n.a. | 12,706,772 | 17,424,247 |
| 1895 | 82,013 | n.a. | 80,000 | 1,600,000 | 2,120,000 | 800,000 | 11,654 | n.a. | 13,079,365 | 17,574,519 |
| 1896 | 80,968 | n.a. | 80,000 | 1,600,000 | 2,000,000 | 800,000 | 12,622 | n.a. | 13,695,370 | 18,587,791 |
| 1897 | 85,654 | n.a. | 80,000 | 1,600,000 | 2,120,000 | 800,000 | 18,276 | n.a. | 12,860,664 | 17,765,169 |
| 1898 | 102,694 | n.a. | 96,000 | 1,600,000 | 2,080,000 | 800,000 | 9,970 | n.a. | 12,456,004 | 17,728,077 |
| 1899 | 176,183 | n.a. | 120,000 | 1,600,000 | 2,560,000 | 835,000 | 11,153 | n.a. | 13,646,325 | 19,657,991 |
| 1900 | 299,888 | n.a. | 152,000 | 1,600,000 | 3,160,000 | 925,000 | 14,041 | n.a. | 13,650,832 | 19,471,223 |
| 1901 | 285,196 | n.a. | 160,000 | 1,600,000 | 3,160,000 | 994,000 | 14,237 | n.a. | 13,878,371 | 19,425,453 |
| 1902 | 296,553 | n.a. | 176,000 | 1,600,000 | 3,200,000 | 1,070,000 | 14,648 | n.a. | 14,313,893 | 19,882,524 |
| 1903 | 309,303 | n.a. | 192,000 | 1,600,000 | 3,360,000 | 1,130,000 | 16,952 | n.a. | 14,662,650 | 20,082,628 |
| 1904 | 290,999 | n.a. | 192,000 | 1,600,000 | 3,580,000 | 1,190,000 | 16,951 | n.a. | 15,186,395 | 20,572,520 |
| 1905 | 273,604 | n.a. | 192,000 | 1,600,000 | 3,660,000 | 1,250,000 | 17,555 | n.a. | 16,329,565 | 22,063,673 |
| 1906 | 308,307 | n.a. | 208,000 | 1,600,000 | 3,840,000 | 1,310,000 | 16,862 | n.a. | 16,001,835 | 22,164,826 |
| 1907 | 433,213 | n.a. | 224,000 | 1,600,000 | 4,000,000 | 1,470,000 | 16,075 | n.a. | 15,879,335 | 22,444,425 |
| 1908 | 399,720 | n.a. | 224,000 | 1,600,000 | 4,240,000 | 1,610,000 | 16,795 | n.a. | 15,205,569 | 21,513,680 |
| 1909 | 351,676 | n.a. | 224,000 | 1,600,000 | 4,340,000 | 1,710,000 | 17,472 | n.a. | 16,214,618 | 22,429,779 |
| 1910 | 392,253 | n.a. | 256,000 | 1,600,000 | 4,580,000 | 1,810,000 | 15,725 | n.a. | 16,896,476 | 23,838,452 |
| 1911 | 404,349 | n.a. | 264,000 | 1,600,000 | 4,520,000 | 1,910,000 | 16,074 | n.a. | 17,414,474 | 24,058,048 |
| 1912 | 424,475 | n.a. | 272,000 | 1,600,000 | 4,840,000 | 2,010,000 | 28,549 | n.a. | 17,906,493 | 24,587,279 |
| 1913 | 427,620 | n.a. | 306,000 | 2,000,000 | 5,850,000 | 2,690,000 | 30,169 | n.a. | 18,088,955 | 25,916,790 |
| 1914 | 454,406 | n.a. | 340,000 | 2,000,000 | 5,925,000 | 2,710,000 | 114,575 | n.a. | 19,108,792 | 27,202,663 |
| 1915 | 410,521 | n.a. | 340,000 | 2,000,000 | 5,400,000 | 2,780,000 | 115,096 | n.a. | 20,568,326 | 29,148,214 |
| 1916 | 407,568 | n.a. | 340,000 | 2,000,000 | 5,550,000 | 2,840,000 | 122,664 | n.a. | 19,672,174 | 28,284,504 |
| 1917 | 405,645 | n.a. | 340,000 | 2,000,000 | 5,700,000 | 2,905,000 | 123,309 | n.a. | 20,891,101 | 30,061,763 |

| Year | | | | | | | | | | |
|------|-----------|------|---------|-----------|------------|-----------|---------|------|-------------|-------------|
| 1918 | 438,746 | n.a. | 340,000 | 2,000,000 | 6,850,000 | 3,000,000 | 127,055 | n.a. | 21,903,753 | 31,590,944 |
| 1919 | 460,768 | n.a. | 360,000 | 2,000,000 | 6,275,000 | 3,100,000 | 127,823 | n.a. | 24,351,904 | 33,864,081 |
| 1920 | 573,051 | n.a. | 455,000 | 3,500,000 | 7,000,000 | 3,075,000 | 145,874 | n.a. | 27,018,082 | 39,797,964 |
| 1921 | 588,389 | n.a. | 487,500 | 4,000,000 | 8,800,000 | 3,425,000 | 121,763 | n.a. | 25,603,631 | 37,914,315 |
| 1922 | 620,106 | n.a. | 520,000 | 4,000,000 | 10,600,000 | 3,525,000 | 121,869 | n.a. | 25,661,481 | 37,580,814 |
| 1923 | 618,559 | n.a. | 520,000 | 4,000,000 | 10,500,000 | 3,625,000 | 120,428 | n.a. | 27,352,162 | 39,479,749 |
| 1924 | 629,904 | n.a. | 520,000 | 4,000,000 | 11,000,000 | 3,700,000 | 130,332 | n.a. | 28,010,187 | 39,882,923 |
| 1925 | 632,555 | n.a. | 520,000 | 4,000,000 | 10,900,000 | 3,760,000 | 132,887 | n.a. | 28,708,674 | 40,993,316 |
| 1926 | 652,621 | n.a. | 560,000 | 4,000,000 | 11,000,000 | 3,810,000 | 135,508 | n.a. | 29,394,047 | 42,508,631 |
| 1927 | 654,060 | n.a. | 560,000 | 4,000,000 | 11,600,000 | 3,850,000 | 139,568 | n.a. | 31,478,756 | 44,594,860 |
| 1928 | 675,192 | n.a. | 595,000 | 4,500,000 | 12,937,500 | 4,450,000 | 139,760 | n.a. | 33,876,329 | 47,618,928 |
| 1929 | 677,183 | n.a. | 630,000 | 4,500,000 | 10,800,000 | 4,475,000 | 161,943 | n.a. | 34,414,798 | 49,323,597 |
| 1930 | 615,084 | n.a. | 585,000 | 4,500,000 | 7,312,500 | 4,475,000 | 192,027 | n.a. | 34,232,584 | 48,036,386 |
| 1931 | 217,536 | n.a. | 405,000 | 4,500,000 | 7,312,500 | 2,475,000 | 151,063 | n.a. | 36,678,573 | 50,720,919 |
| 1932 | 254,970 | n.a. | 315,000 | 4,500,000 | 6,637,500 | 2,475,000 | 169,783 | n.a. | 38,120,630 | 51,832,563 |
| 1933 | 258,508 | n.a. | 337,500 | 4,500,000 | 8,775,000 | 2,475,000 | 175,166 | n.a. | 37,833,350 | 52,244,203 |
| 1934 | 371,087 | n.a. | 337,500 | 4,500,000 | 8,100,000 | 2,475,000 | 178,690 | n.a. | 39,601,807 | 53,893,799 |
| 1935 | 273,857 | n.a. | 348,750 | 4,500,000 | 8,100,000 | 2,475,000 | 182,266 | n.a. | 37,058,103 | 51,237,369 |
| 1936 | 300,962 | n.a. | 360,000 | 4,500,000 | 8,887,500 | 2,475,000 | 193,329 | n.a. | 37,165,580 | 51,126,418 |
| 1937 | 309,501 | n.a. | 360,000 | 4,500,000 | 7,650,000 | 2,475,000 | 205,830 | n.a. | 40,775,464 | 55,846,939 |
| 1938 | 310,049 | n.a. | 360,000 | 4,500,000 | 6,525,000 | 2,475,000 | 227,879 | n.a. | 39,563,740 | 54,801,223 |
| 1939 | 292,024 | n.a. | 360,000 | 4,500,000 | 6,075,000 | 2,475,000 | 237,106 | n.a. | 40,921,527 | 56,222,871 |
| 1940 | 266,107 | n.a. | 360,000 | 4,500,000 | 5,850,000 | 2,500,000 | 242,213 | n.a. | 44,458,438 | 59,365,947 |
| 1941 | 237,012 | n.a. | 360,000 | 4,500,000 | 5,175,000 | 2,500,000 | 215,600 | n.a. | 46,768,240 | 62,519,256 |
| 1942 | 188,570 | n.a. | 270,000 | 4,500,000 | 4,753,125 | 2,500,000 | 212,358 | n.a. | 51,776,988 | 67,848,658 |
| 1943 | 215,157 | n.a. | 270,000 | 4,500,000 | 5,779,688 | 2,500,000 | 233,265 | n.a. | 56,106,502 | 74,244,914 |
| 1944 | 195,864 | n.a. | 270,000 | 4,500,000 | 6,567,188 | 2,500,000 | 237,504 | n.a. | 64,278,000 | 82,546,211 |
| 1945 | 200,667 | n.a. | 337,500 | 4,500,000 | 5,934,375 | 2,500,000 | 246,921 | n.a. | 69,426,745 | 75,319,044 |
| 1946 | 223,014 | n.a. | 382,500 | 4,500,000 | 9,562,500 | 2,500,000 | 259,560 | n.a. | 75,180,980 | 95,503,869 |
| 1947 | 243,588 | n.a. | 405,000 | 4,500,000 | 8,100,000 | 2,500,000 | 280,398 | n.a. | 77,703,298 | 101,306,979 |
| 1948 | 271,033 | n.a. | 405,000 | 4,500,000 | 9,337,500 | 2,500,000 | 328,681 | n.a. | 92,972,243 | 108,915,385 |
| 1949 | 278,290 | n.a. | 405,000 | 4,500,000 | 8,775,000 | 2,500,000 | 384,221 | n.a. | 110,130,236 | 137,386,516 |
| 1950 | 290,874 | n.a. | 450,000 | 4,500,000 | 9,000,000 | 2,500,000 | 427,595 | n.a. | 134,097,774 | 171,366,772 |

*Notes*: October financial year-end. Amalgamated with Union Bank of Australia in 1951 (thereafter, see ANZ Bank). n.a. = not available.

ANZ BANK

| Years | Published net profits | Real profits | Dividends paid (gross) | Paid-up capital | Market value: capital | Published reserves | Retained profits | Inner reserves | Deposits | Total balance sheet |
|---|---|---|---|---|---|---|---|---|---|---|
| 1951 | 574,844 | n.a. | 850,000 | 8,500,000 | 15,512,500 | 5,750,000 | 893,324 | n.a. | 275,401,947 | 378,718,425 |
| 1952 | 559,050 | n.a. | 850,000 | 8,500,000 | 13,175,000 | 5,750,000 | 1,006,125 | n.a. | 246,298,446 | 303,357,693 |
| 1953 | 597,502 | n.a. | 850,000 | 8,500,000 | 14,662,500 | 6,000,000 | 886,127 | n.a. | 267,358,232 | 331,782,298 |
| 1954 | 732,000 | n.a. | 1,020,000 | 10,200,000 | 18,870,000 | 6,470,000 | 1,057,127 | n.a. | 276,899,322 | 330,305,369 |
| 1955 | 841,442 | n.a. | 1,224,000 | 10,200,000 | 17,850,000 | 6,470,000 | 1,194,769 | n.a. | 277,587,846 | 339,227,987 |
| 1956 | 801,521 | n.a. | 1,224,000 | 10,200,000 | 17,595,000 | 6,470,000 | 1,292,490 | n.a. | 268,398,397 | 321,525,077 |
| 1957 | 814,291 | n.a. | 1,224,000 | 10,200,000 | 17,340,000 | 7,000,000 | 872,981 | n.a. | 287,053,198 | 343,385,912 |
| 1958 | 824,815 | n.a. | 1,224,000 | 10,200,000 | 19,252,500 | 7,000,000 | 993,996 | n.a. | 291,795,327 | 349,928,265 |
| 1959 | 837,219 | n.a. | 1,224,000 | 10,200,000 | 26,010,000 | 7,000,000 | 1,081,516 | n.a. | 300,089,617 | 365,820,434 |
| 1960 | 971,785 | n.a. | 1,224,000 | 10,200,000 | 17,467,500 | 7,350,000 | 1,285,992 | n.a. | 387,883,488 | 465,076,984 |
| 1961 | 1,022,669 | n.a. | 1,224,000 | 10,200,000 | 21,037,500 | 8,000,000 | 1,408,962 | n.a. | 393,870,637 | 463,321,310 |
| 1962 | 1,087,764 | n.a. | 1,320,000 | 11,000,000 | 22,000,000 | 8,150,000 | 1,138,226 | n.a. | 427,032,687 | 501,889,886 |
| 1963 | 1,503,539 | n.a. | 1,680,000 | 14,000,000 | 39,900,000 | 12,024,043 | 1,447,222 | n.a. | 474,347,194 | 566,530,685 |
| 1964 | 1,727,035 | n.a. | 1,680,000 | 14,000,000 | 37,625,000 | 12,450,537 | 1,718,763 | n.a. | 530,352,425 | 626,303,932 |
| 1965 | 2,079,103 | n.a. | 1,848,000 | 15,400,000 | 35,805,000 | 11,789,581 | 1,973,122 | n.a. | 563,294,071 | 666,727,470 |
| 1966 | 2,411,075 | n.a. | 1,848,000 | 15,400,000 | 37,730,000 | 12,318,229 | 1,990,441 | n.a. | 626,722,653 | 746,670,737 |
| 1967 | 2,958,167 | n.a. | 1,848,000 | 15,400,000 | 55,440,000 | 13,117,000 | 2,302,000 | n.a. | 676,117,530 | 814,222,000 |
| 1968 | 4,147,000 | n.a. | 1,848,000 | 15,400,000 | 73,727,500 | 15,524,000 | 2,533,000 | n.a. | 845,911,000 | 1,019,503,000 |
| 1969 | 6,918,000 | n.a. | 3,055,000 | 32,130,000 | 101,611,125 | 20,383,000 | 4,338,000 | n.a. | 1,241,527,000 | 1,579,254,000 |
| 1970 | 7,350,000 | n.a. | 3,213,000 | 32,130,000 | 82,333,125 | 24,534,000 | 4,325,000 | n.a. | 1,328,707,000 | 1,773,902,000 |
| 1971 | 6,362,000 | n.a. | 3,213,000 | 32,130,000 | 87,714,900 | 27,482,000 | 4,525,000 | n.a. | 1,409,830,000 | 1,919,444,000 |
| 1972 | 8,418,000 | n.a. | 3,213,000 | 32,130,000 | 133,339,500 | 32,396,000 | 5,699,000 | n.a. | 1,749,151,000 | 2,312,572,000 |
| 1973 | 13,731,000 | n.a. | 2,362,000 | 32,130,000 | 107,635,500 | 56,801,000 | 6,856,000 | n.a. | 2,823,950,000 | 3,572,204,000 |
| 1974 | 12,702,000 | n.a. | 3,338,000 | 36,720,000 | 59,486,400 | 72,126,000 | 7,244,000 | n.a. | 2,611,739,000 | 3,661,119,000 |
| 1975 | 16,864,000 | n.a. | 3,562,000 | 36,720,000 | 157,896,000 | 91,420,000 | 8,103,000 | n.a. | 3,438,963,000 | 4,618,888,000 |

*Notes:* September financial year-end. Accounts consolidated from 1960. Merged with English, Scottish & Australian Bank in 1969. From 1973, imputed tax on dividends not taken into account. n.a. = not available.

# BANK OF BRITISH NORTH AMERICA

| Years | Published net profits | Real profits | Dividends paid (gross) | Paid-up capital | Market value: capital | Published reserves | Retained profits | Inner reserves | Deposits | Total balance sheet |
|---|---|---|---|---|---|---|---|---|---|---|
| 1890 | 86,742 | n.a. | 75,000 | 1,000,000 | 1,520,000 | 265,000 | 3,818 | n.a. | 1,982,933 | 5,168,351 |
| 1891 | 78,016 | n.a. | 75,000 | 1,000,000 | 1,500,000 | 265,000 | 6,834 | n.a. | 2,186,109 | 5,453,835 |
| 1892 | 86,030 | n.a. | 75,000 | 1,000,000 | 1,440,000 | 275,000 | 15,512 | n.a. | 2,280,277 | 5,552,233 |
| 1893 | 74,755 | n.a. | 75,000 | 1,000,000 | 1,400,000 | 275,000 | 13,233 | n.a. | 2,074,956 | 4,870,804 |
| 1894 | 40,999 | n.a. | 45,000 | 1,000,000 | 1,380,000 | 275,000 | 4,486 | n.a. | 2,032,426 | 4,608,337 |
| 1895 | 42,139 | n.a. | 40,000 | 1,000,000 | 1,120,000 | 275,000 | 6,444 | n.a. | 1,995,665 | 5,047,031 |
| 1896 | 43,690 | n.a. | 40,000 | 1,000,000 | 1,080,000 | 275,000 | 11,270 | n.a. | 2,066,210 | 5,399,239 |
| 1897 | 59,124 | n.a. | 50,000 | 1,000,000 | 1,280,000 | 285,000 | 12,051 | n.a. | 2,310,148 | 5,129,963 |
| 1898 | 67,834 | n.a. | 50,000 | 1,000,000 | 1,220,000 | 300,000 | 12,527 | n.a. | 2,583,244 | 5,638,982 |
| 1899 | 88,016 | n.a. | 55,000 | 1,000,000 | 1,240,000 | 325,000 | 17,189 | n.a. | 2,908,815 | 6,827,321 |
| 1900 | 95,095 | n.a. | 60,000 | 1,000,000 | 1,260,000 | 350,000 | 18,725 | n.a. | 3,124,634 | 7,009,808 |
| 1901 | 71,039 | n.a. | 60,000 | 1,000,000 | 1,320,000 | 365,000 | 13,121 | n.a. | 3,151,128 | 7,724,706 |
| 1902 | 95,211 | n.a. | 60,000 | 1,000,000 | 1,380,000 | 390,000 | 10,040 | n.a. | 3,098,177 | 8,189,206 |
| 1903 | 75,223 | n.a. | 60,000 | 1,000,000 | 1,280,000 | 400,000 | 12,162 | n.a. | 3,364,030 | 8,287,907 |
| 1904 | 91,960 | n.a. | 60,000 | 1,000,000 | 1,310,000 | 420,000 | 12,922 | n.a. | 3,675,556 | 8,024,827 |
| 1905 | 93,091 | n.a. | 60,000 | 1,000,000 | 1,410,000 | 440,000 | 16,758 | n.a. | 4,155,545 | 9,657,835 |
| 1906 | 129,016 | n.a. | 70,000 | 1,000,000 | 1,460,000 | 460,000 | 57,472 | n.a. | 4,744,750 | 10,265,999 |
| 1907 | 122,618 | n.a. | 70,000 | 1,000,000 | 1,380,000 | 480,000 | 60,214 | n.a. | 4,481,038 | 9,335,823 |
| 1908 | 85,823 | n.a. | 70,000 | 1,000,000 | 1,480,000 | 500,000 | 50,597 | n.a. | 5,384,266 | 9,338,116 |
| 1909 | 101,652 | n.a. | 70,000 | 1,000,000 | 1,510,000 | 520,000 | 39,080 | n.a. | 6,258,913 | 10,583,304 |
| 1910 | 114,030 | n.a. | 70,000 | 1,000,000 | 1,530,000 | 545,000 | 47,806 | n.a. | 6,589,777 | 10,965,325 |
| 1911 | 129,887 | n.a. | 80,000 | 1,000,000 | 1,490,000 | 570,000 | 65,082 | n.a. | 7,411,173 | 12,799,008 |
| 1912 | 139,418 | n.a. | 80,000 | 1,000,000 | 1,560,000 | 600,000 | 55,285 | n.a. | 8,106,777 | 13,618,550 |
| 1913 | 141,728 | n.a. | 80,000 | 1,000,000 | 1,480,000 | 620,000 | 22,281 | n.a. | 7,855,670 | 12,872,238 |
| 1914 | 110,256 | n.a. | 80,000 | 1,000,000 | 1,560,000 | 620,000 | 34,332 | n.a. | 8,686,717 | 12,453,081 |
| 1915 | 67,519 | n.a. | 70,000 | 1,000,000 | 1,235,000 | 620,000 | 10,721 | n.a. | 9,088,014 | 12,639,801 |
| 1916 | 112,263 | n.a. | 70,000 | 1,000,000 | 1,190,000 | 620,000 | 21,416 | n.a. | 10,151,694 | 13,928,621 |
| 1917 | 137,261 | n.a. | 80,000 | 1,000,000 | 1,300,000 | 620,000 | 32,118 | n.a. | 12,140,508 | 15,962,228 |

*Notes:* December financial year-end until 1911; November thereafter. Amalgamated with Bank of Montreal in 1918. n.a. = not available.

BANK OF BRITISH WEST AFRICA

| Years | Published net profits | Real profits | Dividends paid (gross) | Paid-up capital | Market value: capital | Published reserves | Retained profits | Inner reserves | Deposits | Total balance sheet |
|---|---|---|---|---|---|---|---|---|---|---|
| 1894 | 318 | n.a. | 0 | 12,000 | 12,000 | 0 | 318 | n.a. | 0 | 104,030 |
| 1895 | 4,358 | n.a. | 960 | 12,000 | 12,000 | 2,000 | 31 | n.a. | 87,666 | 126,368 |
| 1896 | 1,806 | n.a. | 1,553 | 21,940 | 24,425 | 4,285 | 184 | n.a. | 108,263 | 188,146 |
| 1897 | 2,284 | n.a. | 1,794 | 22,892 | 26,969 | 5,000 | 30 | n.a. | 148,134 | 241,056 |
| 1898 | 4,253 | n.a. | 2,064 | 27,240 | 33,505 | 7,500 | 365 | n.a. | 191,282 | 313,553 |
| 1899 | 4,316 | n.a. | 2,327 | 33,560 | 43,091 | 10,000 | 934 | n.a. | 252,491 | 290,923 |
| 1900 | 2,393 | n.a. | 2,926 | 40,000 | 53,088 | 11,610 | 213 | n.a. | 217,092 | 460,110 |
| 1901 | 8,646 | n.a. | 3,553 | 46,720 | 67,160 | 15,000 | 1,221 | n.a. | 360,954 | 654,451 |
| 1902 | 10,760 | n.a. | 3,845 | 47,760 | 68,655 | 20,000 | 1,018 | n.a. | 523,414 | 668,771 |
| 1903 | 8,334 | n.a. | 4,251 | 60,000 | 90,000 | 26,120 | 1,041 | n.a. | 545,919 | 707,627 |
| 1904 | 7,894 | n.a. | 4,800 | 60,000 | 90,000 | 28,000 | 1,255 | n.a. | 549,123 | 785,814 |
| 1905 | 9,118 | n.a. | 4,800 | 60,000 | 82,500 | 30,000 | 1,574 | n.a. | 541,261 | 864,164 |
| 1906 | 13,402 | n.a. | 4,800 | 60,000 | 93,750 | 35,000 | 2,176 | n.a. | 605,174 | 905,038 |
| 1907 | 16,002 | n.a. | 8,400 | 100,000 | 131,250 | 50,000 | 2,278 | n.a. | 659,297 | 1,186,705 |
| 1908 | 10,851 | n.a. | 9,000 | 100,000 | 137,500 | 50,000 | 2,129 | n.a. | 825,477 | 1,274,483 |
| 1909 | 20,568 | n.a. | 11,712 | 200,000 | 287,500 | 80,000 | 2,985 | n.a. | 841,320 | 1,626,198 |
| 1910 | 30,099 | n.a. | 18,000 | 200,000 | 312,500 | 85,000 | 5,084 | n.a. | 1,074,793 | 1,813,984 |
| 1911 | 29,649 | n.a. | 20,000 | 240,000 | 390,000 | 100,000 | 6,053 | n.a. | 1,251,126 | 2,116,456 |
| 1912 | 43,956 | n.a. | 26,280 | 292,000 | 511,000 | 116,000 | 6,729 | n.a. | 1,388,871 | 2,660,232 |
| 1913 | 60,801 | n.a. | 33,680 | 400,000 | 675,000 | 187,000 | 9,600 | n.a. | 1,805,798 | 3,150,842 |
| 1914 | 47,541 | n.a. | 26,000 | 400,000 | 700,000 | 150,000 | 10,141 | n.a. | 2,025,527 | 3,235,250 |
| 1915 | 59,276 | n.a. | 32,000 | 400,000 | 543,750 | 150,000 | 15,417 | n.a. | 2,267,715 | 3,591,040 |
| 1916 | 64,760 | n.a. | 32,000 | 560,000 | 805,000 | 220,000 | 18,177 | n.a. | 2,523,090 | 4,332,306 |

| Year | | | | | | | | | | |
|---|---|---|---|---|---|---|---|---|---|---|
| 1917 | 71,514 | n.a. | 46,078 | 580,000 | 797,500 | 237,500 | 21,613 | n.a. | 3,083,574 | 6,462,157 |
| 1918 | 83,767 | n.a. | 52,200 | 580,000 | 942,500 | 250,000 | 22,680 | n.a. | 4,668,587 | 9,000,018 |
| 1919 | 125,147 | n.a. | 71,200 | 800,000 | 1,400,000 | 400,000 | 30,377 | n.a. | 6,489,248 | 16,500,922 |
| 1920 | 139,803 | n.a. | 80,000 | 1,200,000 | 1,500,000 | 625,000 | 50,180 | n.a. | 11,810,340 | 13,475,637 |
| 1921 | 105,936 | n.a. | 72,000 | 1,200,000 | 1,312,500 | 400,000 | 34,116 | n.a. | 8,018,670 | 12,294,811 |
| 1922 | 100,574 | n.a. | 60,000 | 1,200,000 | 1,312,500 | 400,000 | 34,690 | n.a. | 7,602,564 | 9,273,632 |
| 1923 | 95,990 | n.a. | 60,000 | 1,200,000 | 1,125,000 | 400,000 | 35,680 | n.a. | 5,823,332 | 9,528,493 |
| 1924 | 112,352 | n.a. | 60,000 | 1,200,000 | 1,312,500 | 400,000 | 38,032 | n.a. | 6,540,010 | 10,103,287 |
| 1925 | 114,368 | n.a. | 60,000 | 1,200,000 | 1,237,500 | 400,000 | 42,400 | n.a. | 6,726,491 | 8,957,301 |
| 1926 | 116,930 | n.a. | 60,000 | 1,200,000 | 1,200,000 | 400,000 | 49,330 | n.a. | 6,068,803 | 10,282,982 |
| 1927 | 124,950 | n.a. | 72,000 | 1,200,000 | 1,425,000 | 400,000 | 52,280 | n.a. | 6,975,748 | 9,988,277 |
| 1928 | 128,331 | n.a. | 72,000 | 1,200,000 | 1,200,000 | 400,000 | 53,611 | n.a. | 6,717,224 | 10,378,153 |
| 1929 | 121,822 | n.a. | 72,000 | 1,200,000 | 1,200,000 | 400,000 | 53,433 | n.a. | 6,873,385 | 9,607,378 |
| 1930 | 24,568 | n.a. | 48,000 | 1,200,000 | 1,012,500 | 400,000 | 30,001 | n.a. | 6,549,175 | 8,885,423 |
| 1931 | 59,625 | n.a. | 48,000 | 1,200,000 | 881,250 | 400,000 | 41,626 | n.a. | 5,909,445 | 8,123,887 |
| 1932 | 58,611 | n.a. | 48,000 | 1,200,000 | 825,000 | 400,000 | 52,237 | n.a. | 5,549,759 | 8,773,570 |
| 1933 | 58,766 | n.a. | 48,000 | 1,200,000 | 1,106,250 | 400,000 | 53,003 | n.a. | 6,107,184 | 8,645,450 |
| 1934 | 64,671 | n.a. | 48,000 | 1,200,000 | 1,200,000 | 400,000 | 54,674 | n.a. | 6,134,040 | 9,297,919 |
| 1935 | 85,298 | n.a. | 60,000 | 1,200,000 | 1,218,750 | 400,000 | 54,972 | n.a. | 6,672,668 | 10,031,422 |
| 1936 | 90,636 | 185,636 | 60,000 | 1,200,000 | 1,743,750 | 400,000 | 55,608 | n.a. | 7,372,929 | 11,383,165 |
| 1937 | 60,106 | 60,106 | 60,000 | 1,200,000 | 1,312,500 | 400,000 | 55,714 | n.a. | 8,695,295 | 12,538,551 |
| 1938 | 42,878 | 59,887 | 48,000 | 1,200,000 | 1,200,000 | 400,000 | 50,592 | 558,649 | 9,851,769 | 9,860,306 |
| 1939 | 36,649 | 36,649 | 36,000 | 1,200,000 | 900,000 | 400,000 | 51,241 | 520,488 | 7,280,392 | 9,757,195 |
| 1940 | 58,888 | 74,317 | 48,000 | 1,200,000 | 600,000 | 400,000 | 52,129 | 569,267 | 7,380,582 | 12,588,707 |
| 1941 | 70,942 | 90,942 | 48,000 | 1,200,000 | 975,000 | 400,000 | 55,071 | 605,829 | 9,976,851 | 13,368,931 |
| 1942 | 74,463 | 96,463 | 48,000 | 1,200,000 | 1,096,875 | 400,000 | 56,534 | 744,722 | 11,141,110 | 16,320,919 |
| 1943 | 117,304 | 142,304 | 48,000 | 1,200,000 | 1,462,500 | 500,000 | 55,838 | 742,624 | 14,056,532 | 18,913,396 |
| 1944 | 126,232 | 161,232 | 60,000 | 1,200,000 | 1,567,500 | 600,000 | 62,070 | 747,316 | 16,380,129 | 21,754,148 |
| 1945 | 130,974 | 160,974 | 72,000 | 1,200,000 | 1,809,375 | 700,000 | 64,644 | 672,690 | 19,271,150 | 28,601,627 |

BANK OF BRITISH WEST AFRICA (*Cont.*)

| Years | Published net profits | Real profits | Dividends paid (gross) | Paid-up capital | Market value: capital | Published reserves | Retained profits | Inner reserves | Deposits | Total balance sheet |
|---|---|---|---|---|---|---|---|---|---|---|
| 1946 | 145,582 | 215,582 | 84,000 | 1,200,000 | 2,531,250 | 800,000 | 64,226 | 714,613 | 23,754,810 | 32,935,921 |
| 1947 | 143,472 | 163,472 | 84,000 | 1,200,000 | 2,887,500 | 850,000 | 61,298 | 735,703 | 25,911,207 | 46,443,690 |
| 1948 | 144,932 | 194,932 | 84,000 | 1,200,000 | 2,250,000 | 900,000 | 60,030 | 785,989 | 38,005,629 | 46,967,016 |
| 1949 | 154,268 | 324,268 | 84,000 | 1,200,000 | 1,875,000 | 950,000 | 68,098 | 1,162,662 | 38,060,185 | 52,182,778 |
| 1950 | 283,321 | 315,321 | 108,000 | 1,200,000 | 2,100,000 | 1,000,000 | 93,969 | 1,519,766 | 44,628,715 | 65,595,347 |
| 1951 | 212,029 | 422,029 | 108,000 | 1,200,000 | 2,287,500 | 1,050,000 | 99,298 | 1,915,309 | 52,710,589 | 66,302,651 |
| 1952 | 242,506 | 456,506 | 120,000 | 1,200,000 | 1,950,000 | 1,100,000 | 101,704 | 2,315,547 | 54,566,977 | 68,852,272 |
| 1953 | 244,712 | 565,712 | 120,000 | 1,200,000 | 2,062,500 | 1,200,000 | 105,416 | 2,785,425 | 58,773,777 | 91,633,366 |
| 1954 | 290,374 | 810,374 | 120,000 | 1,200,000 | 3,000,000 | 1,400,000 | 127,690 | 3,426,700 | 79,435,310 | 91,894,218 |
| 1955 | 351,381 | 661,381 | 250,000 | 2,500,000 | 4,312,500 | 1,900,000 | 135,321 | 3,548,806 | 78,823,505 | 85,827,019 |
| 1956 | 387,047 | 637,047 | 300,000 | 2,500,000 | 3,562,500 | 2,000,000 | 149,868 | 4,089,613 | 68,026,583 | 78,274,864 |
| 1957 | 386,044 | 842,544 | 300,000 | 2,500,000 | 3,750,000 | 2,500,000 | 163,412 | 4,955,302 | 61,859,339 | 80,279,882 |
| 1958 | 385,525 | 903,064 | 300,000 | 2,500,000 | 3,812,500 | 2,750,000 | 119,875 | 5,311,302 | 64,473,918 | 85,986,488 |
| 1959 | 403,274 | 1,028,149 | 320,000 | 4,000,000 | 5,900,000 | 2,700,000 | 127,149 | 4,631,354 | 73,144,294 | 82,306,880 |
| 1960 | 445,426 | 837,575 | 360,000 | 4,000,000 | 4,350,000 | 3,300,000 | 152,075 | 4,627,122 | 65,744,778 | 79,194,933 |
| 1961 | 438,294 | 730,369 | 360,000 | 4,000,000 | 4,250,000 | 3,500,000 | 169,869 | 4,644,429 | 62,642,167 | 84,273,929 |
| 1962 | 466,083 | 805,952 | 360,000 | 4,000,000 | 4,700,000 | 3,700,000 | 215,452 | 4,880,280 | 65,691,305 | 93,115,354 |
| 1963 | 535,212 | n.a. | 400,000 | 4,000,000 | 4,800,000 | 4,000,000 | 205,664 | 5,272,010 | 70,242,815 | 97,215,428 |
| 1964 | 611,630 | n.a. | 440,000 | 4,000,000 | 11,600,000 | 4,000,000 | 205,294 | n.a. | 74,722,190 | 108,372,045 |

*Notes:* March financial year-end; i.e. 1920 ends in March 1921. Shares not quoted until 1901; share prices 1894 to 1900 estimated. Merged with Standard Bank in 1965; acquisition price of 58s. per share offered. n.a. = not available.

BANK OF MAURITIUS

| Years | Published net profits | Real profits | Dividends paid (gross) | Paid-up capital | Market value: capital | Published reserves | Retained profits | Inner reserves | Deposits | Total balance sheet |
|---|---|---|---|---|---|---|---|---|---|---|
| 1895 | 14,165 | n.a. | 5,022 | 125,550 | 125,550 | 5,000 | 1,124 | n.a. | 159,490 | 360,402 |
| 1896 | 16,298 | n.a. | 6,278 | 125,550 | 125,550 | 15,000 | 1,144 | n.a. | 205,002 | 420,000 |
| 1897 | 15,176 | n.a. | 6,278 | 125,550 | 125,550 | 15,000 | 10,043 | n.a. | 178,659 | 425,616 |
| 1898 | 4,283 | n.a. | 6,278 | 125,550 | 116,134 | 20,000 | 3,048 | n.a. | 133,849 | 443,773 |
| 1899 | 16,645 | n.a. | 7,533 | 125,550 | 125,550 | 30,000 | 2,160 | n.a. | 130,394 | 395,053 |
| 1900 | 10,187 | n.a. | 7,533 | 125,550 | 128,689 | 30,000 | 1,814 | n.a. | 226,700 | 519,302 |
| 1901 | 10,204 | n.a. | 7,533 | 125,550 | 119,273 | 30,000 | 3,484 | n.a. | 233,629 | 514,264 |
| 1902 | 11,446 | n.a. | 7,533 | 125,550 | 125,550 | 35,000 | 2,397 | n.a. | 183,815 | 458,926 |
| 1903 | 14,258 | 14,295 | 7,533 | 125,550 | 125,550 | 40,000 | 4,122 | n.a. | 229,020 | 574,857 |
| 1904 | 15,436 | 15,637 | 7,533 | 125,550 | 125,550 | 50,000 | 2,026 | n.a. | 185,058 | 504,371 |
| 1905 | 17,135 | 17,135 | 7,533 | 125,550 | 147,521 | 55,000 | 6,628 | n.a. | 195,204 | 487,674 |
| 1906 | 15,774 | 15,973 | 7,533 | 125,550 | 131,828 | 65,000 | 4,869 | n.a. | 206,356 | 573,765 |
| 1907 | 8,237 | 15,236 | 7,533 | 125,550 | 128,689 | 65,000 | 5,573 | 3,000 | 164,872 | 447,232 |
| 1908 | 14,286 | 14,280 | 7,533 | 125,550 | 125,550 | 75,000 | 2,326 | 3,000 | 205,011 | 511,155 |
| 1909 | 16,144 | 16,144 | 8,788 | 125,550 | 150,660 | 80,000 | 3,682 | 3,000 | 219,824 | 492,092 |
| 1910 | 18,818 | 18,818 | 10,044 | 125,550 | 163,215 | 85,000 | 5,956 | 3,000 | 234,781 | 566,647 |
| 1911 | 12,375 | 18,375 | 10,044 | 125,550 | 182,048 | 87,500 | 4,787 | 3,000 | 287,717 | 546,584 |
| 1912 | 15,430 | 17,432 | 10,672 | 125,550 | 169,493 | 90,000 | 5,045 | 5,000 | 287,726 | 578,982 |
| 1913 | 15,127 | 15,627 | 12,555 | 125,550 | 169,493 | 92,000 | 4,117 | 5,500 | 265,612 | 599,298 |
| 1914 | 25,077 | 35,077 | 12,555 | 125,550 | 178,909 | 100,000 | 6,639 | 15,500 | 621,859 | 906,070 |
| 1915 | 8,915 | 33,279 | 12,555 | 125,550 | 227,873 | 100,000 | 2,999 | 15,500 | 509,881 | 790,079 |

*Notes:* December financial year-end. Share prices for 1895 and 1896 not quoted, so taken at par. Taken over by Mercantile Bank in 1916. n.a. = not available.

BARCLAYS BANK (DCO)

| Years | Published net profits | Real profits | Dividends paid (gross) | Paid-up capital | Market value: capital | Published reserves | Retained profits | Inner reserves | Deposits | Total balance sheet |
|---|---|---|---|---|---|---|---|---|---|---|
| 1926 | 637,020 | 947,955 | 238,915 | 4,975,500 | 6,662,581 | 1,100,000 | 114,295 | 668,096 | 51,838,323 | 62,678,816 |
| 1927 | 482,046 | 738,825 | 254,828 | 4,975,500 | 6,906,313 | 1,250,000 | 122,479 | 1,138,715 | 51,770,262 | 63,997,855 |
| 1928 | 494,823 | 812,905 | 270,740 | 4,975,500 | 7,353,994 | 1,400,000 | 130,710 | 1,716,825 | 59,675,657 | 71,680,929 |
| 1929 | 516,594 | 1,003,875 | 286,653 | 4,975,500 | 6,854,988 | 1,550,000 | 137,982 | 2,006,741 | 61,043,263 | 73,098,634 |
| 1930 | 465,070 | 765,664 | 294,609 | 4,975,500 | 6,931,531 | 1,650,000 | 174,731 | 2,497,928 | 62,690,265 | 74,208,905 |
| 1931 | 402,754 | 708,812 | 294,609 | 4,975,500 | 5,694,938 | 1,650,000 | 244,738 | 1,576,563 | 68,462,423 | 79,428,109 |
| 1932 | 372,103 | 1,127,880 | 294,609 | 4,975,500 | 7,613,425 | 1,650,000 | 215,884 | 2,540,261 | 71,621,970 | 82,535,886 |
| 1933 | 371,549 | 736,987 | 294,609 | 4,975,500 | 8,202,863 | 1,650,000 | 216,477 | 3,084,839 | 74,521,924 | 85,225,869 |
| 1934 | 409,827 | 847,993 | 302,565 | 4,975,500 | 9,193,480 | 1,750,000 | 216,816 | 3,636,483 | 82,865,855 | 94,674,005 |
| 1935 | 473,401 | 936,782 | 318,478 | 4,975,500 | 10,732,063 | 1,850,000 | 223,397 | 4,234,468 | 87,781,143 | 99,439,949 |
| 1936 | 401,191 | 792,562 | 318,478 | 4,975,500 | 11,403,300 | 1,925,000 | 128,903 | 4,462,042 | 96,992,504 | 109,770,242 |
| 1937 | 431,209 | 1,011,404 | 334,390 | 4,975,500 | 10,393,638 | 2,025,000 | 134,320 | 4,678,791 | 96,209,544 | 110,006,923 |
| 1938 | 439,245 | 668,631 | 350,303 | 4,975,500 | 9,841,175 | 2,100,000 | 144,595 | 5,084,924 | 99,543,348 | 112,873,412 |
| 1939 | 414,704 | 640,131 | 350,303 | 4,975,500 | 8,866,250 | 2,100,000 | 154,442 | 4,148,588 | 106,638,711 | 120,885,915 |
| 1940 | 423,692 | 1,203,692 | 350,303 | 4,975,500 | 9,089,253 | 2,100,000 | 171,936 | 5,630,583 | 126,500,726 | 141,954,173 |
| 1941 | 399,685 | 511,861 | 350,303 | 4,975,500 | 10,551,640 | 2,600,000 | 196,470 | 5,981,803 | 156,936,261 | 175,856,636 |
| 1942 | 419,612 | 898,514 | 350,303 | 4,975,500 | 10,358,341 | 3,100,000 | 190,931 | 5,963,193 | 190,824,239 | 213,452,018 |
| 1943 | 415,497 | 707,155 | 350,303 | 4,975,500 | 11,980,270 | 3,600,000 | 181,277 | 4,943,436 | 247,773,599 | 272,841,312 |
| 1944 | 448,864 | 831,699 | 350,303 | 4,975,500 | 12,973,541 | 4,100,000 | 179,990 | 5,954,445 | 282,175,976 | 305,429,453 |
| 1945 | 467,491 | 959,828 | 350,303 | 4,975,500 | 14,136,023 | 4,350,000 | 172,330 | 5,746,399 | 321,497,747 | 344,852,958 |
| 1946 | 516,765 | 1,030,379 | 398,040 | 4,975,500 | 18,999,888 | 4,350,000 | 170,173 | 6,001,001 | 353,278,951 | 386,917,591 |

| 1947 | 572,413 | 1,493,966 | 569,720 | 7,121,500 | 10,820,500 | 7,569,000 | 176,452 | 6,056,365 | 356,941,570 | 400,081,967 |
|------|---------|-----------|---------|-----------|------------|-----------|---------|-----------|-------------|-------------|
| 1948 | 649,874 | 1,471,596 | 569,720 | 7,121,500 | 9,070,125 | 7,800,000 | 181,980 | 6,666,604 | 387,136,660 | 429,102,542 |
| 1949 | 666,879 | 1,802,988 | 569,720 | 7,121,500 | 7,399,313 | 8,000,000 | 185,513 | 7,482,146 | 341,439,104 | 383,079,009 |
| 1950 | 683,201 | 1,855,195 | 569,720 | 7,121,500 | 7,160,625 | 8,000,000 | 205,368 | 7,941,579 | 382,484,292 | 434,233,475 |
| 1951 | 769,581 | 2,580,327 | 569,720 | 7,121,500 | 7,001,500 | 8,855,375 | 225,846 | 8,382,294 | 442,893,048 | 504,384,145 |
| 1952 | 879,888 | 3,007,882 | 742,150 | 9,276,875 | 15,074,922 | 7,500,000 | 241,105 | 5,372,222 | 440,858,810 | 499,306,385 |
| 1953 | 869,431 | 2,302,449 | 742,150 | 9,276,875 | 17,626,063 | 8,000,000 | 252,354 | 8,457,421 | 455,527,000 | 510,592,933 |
| 1954 | 939,953 | 2,405,614 | 862,150 | 10,776,875 | 23,170,281 | 10,050,000 | 259,125 | 9,818,566 | 493,509,345 | 552,357,087 |
| 1955 | 1,152,101 | 3,731,349 | 1,034,580 | 12,932,250 | 21,661,519 | 8,500,000 | 247,868 | 6,007,450 | 508,478,781 | 574,398,931 |
| 1956 | 1,261,189 | 3,338,944 | 1,034,580 | 12,932,250 | 21,014,906 | 9,000,000 | 476,420 | 4,393,751 | 537,021,908 | 606,583,431 |
| 1957 | 1,161,473 | 2,865,219 | 1,034,580 | 12,932,250 | 19,075,069 | 9,500,000 | 543,009 | 4,338,186 | 536,797,601 | 605,945,245 |
| 1958 | 1,267,355 | 3,600,927 | 1,163,903 | 12,932,250 | 23,924,663 | 10,000,000 | 641,120 | n.a. | 539,747,221 | 604,484,738 |
| 1959 | 1,218,512 | 3,041,282 | 1,163,903 | 12,932,250 | 31,199,053 | 10,500,000 | 646,742 | n.a. | 602,012,316 | 688,334,936 |
| 1960 | 1,468,809 | 4,017,313 | 1,293,225 | 12,932,250 | 22,793,091 | 11,250,000 | 573,451 | n.a. | 616,296,179 | 698,445,951 |
| 1961 | 1,585,194 | n.a. | 1,700,000 | 17,000,000 | 32,087,500 | 15,154,299 | 813,997 | n.a. | 635,722,380 | 752,705,776 |
| 1962 | 1,715,115 | n.a. | 1,700,000 | 17,000,000 | 32,087,500 | 16,354,871 | 987,902 | n.a. | 729,062,693 | 852,584,572 |
| 1963 | 2,030,041 | n.a. | 1,700,000 | 17,000,000 | 34,212,500 | 17,106,788 | 1,226,693 | n.a. | 826,374,062 | 961,901,910 |
| 1964 | 2,643,021 | n.a. | 2,640,000 | 24,000,000 | 44,100,000 | 20,365,897 | 1,589,511 | n.a. | 934,902,306 | 1,094,328,814 |
| 1965 | 3,078,136 | n.a. | 2,760,000 | 24,000,000 | 48,600,000 | 21,403,494 | 1,996,147 | n.a. | 1,040,729,073 | 1,209,689,296 |
| 1966 | 3,508,102 | n.a. | 2,760,000 | 24,000,000 | 47,250,000 | 22,167,819 | 1,744,249 | n.a. | 1,169,810,874 | 1,371,797,724 |
| 1967 | 3,759,916 | n.a. | 2,760,000 | 24,000,000 | 66,900,000 | 23,384,171 | 1,744,165 | n.a. | 1,276,663,196 | 1,483,188,221 |
| 1968 | 4,532,253 | n.a. | 3,240,000 | 30,000,000 | 114,375,000 | 34,001,337 | 1,757,251 | n.a. | 1,726,521,607 | 1,975,234,083 |
| 1969 | 5,468,032 | n.a. | 3,675,000 | 30,000,000 | 87,375,000 | 35,939,076 | 2,041,672 | n.a. | 1,998,643,283 | 2,310,419,714 |
| 1970 | 14,277,000 | n.a. | 5,200,000 | 40,000,000 | 106,000,000 | 110,651,000 | n.a. | n.a. | 2,236,205,000 | 2,405,503,000 |

*Notes:* September financial year-end; 1926 is a 15-month year. Accounts consolidated in 1961. n.a. = not available except in the case of retained profits in 1970 when it is not applicable (because of full disclosure of accounts).

CHARTERED BANK

| Years | Published net profits | Real profits | Dividends paid (gross) | Paid-up capital | Market value: capital | Published reserves | Retained profits | Inner reserves | Deposits | Total balance sheet |
|---|---|---|---|---|---|---|---|---|---|---|
| 1890 | 113,337 | 113,337 | 64,000 | 800,000 | 1,080,000 | 300,000 | 9,105 | 25,000 | 6,882,216 | 15,923,197 |
| 1891 | 57,143 | 57,143 | 56,000 | 800,000 | 960,000 | 250,000 | 10,248 | 50,000 | 7,728,332 | 13,553,034 |
| 1892 | 61,107 | 61,107 | 56,000 | 800,000 | 840,000 | 250,000 | 15,855 | 10,000 | 6,320,527 | 12,111,575 |
| 1893 | 105,258 | 120,258 | 56,000 | 800,000 | 800,000 | 275,000 | 16,294 | 25,000 | 5,433,497 | 10,892,927 |
| 1894 | 114,607 | 139,607 | 64,000 | 800,000 | 880,000 | 325,000 | 11,901 | 50,000 | 6,433,168 | 11,021,511 |
| 1895 | 90,457 | 105,457 | 64,000 | 800,000 | 1,060,000 | 350,000 | 13,358 | 65,000 | 7,237,200 | 11,768,948 |
| 1896 | 89,320 | 106,320 | 64,000 | 800,000 | 1,060,000 | 375,000 | 13,678 | 82,000 | 7,032,798 | 11,520,272 |
| 1897 | 160,725 | 205,725 | 72,000 | 800,000 | 1,160,000 | 450,000 | 12,403 | 127,000 | 6,456,711 | 11,830,384 |
| 1898 | 156,809 | 191,809 | 80,000 | 800,000 | 1,300,000 | 500,000 | 14,212 | 162,000 | 7,420,564 | 12,499,422 |
| 1899 | 114,073 | 114,073 | 80,000 | 800,000 | 1,480,000 | 525,000 | 13,285 | 160,000 | 8,788,069 | 14,665,552 |
| 1900 | 148,248 | 173,248 | 80,000 | 800,000 | 1,440,000 | 575,000 | 21,533 | 185,000 | 9,175,272 | 14,556,756 |
| 1901 | 208,571 | 273,571 | 80,000 | 800,000 | 1,540,000 | 650,000 | 40,104 | 250,000 | 9,596,535 | 14,892,665 |
| 1902 | 197,689 | 222,689 | 80,000 | 800,000 | 1,660,000 | 725,000 | 47,793 | 275,000 | 9,958,345 | 15,577,652 |
| 1903 | 170,691 | 170,691 | 80,000 | 800,000 | 1,720,000 | 800,000 | 63,484 | 275,000 | 10,240,354 | 16,218,964 |
| 1904 | 239,595 | 289,595 | 88,000 | 800,000 | 1,820,000 | 875,000 | 80,079 | 325,000 | 10,974,739 | 17,549,307 |
| 1905 | 262,033 | 302,033 | 104,000 | 800,000 | 2,280,000 | 975,000 | 86,112 | 365,000 | 11,58,691 | 19,122,248 |
| 1906 | 264,257 | 264,257 | 104,000 | 800,000 | 2,560,000 | 1,075,000 | 93,369 | 365,000 | 13,204,594 | 20,986,217 |
| 1907 | 268,182 | 283,182 | 112,000 | 1,200,000 | 3,120,000 | 1,525,000 | 129,483 | 397,068 | 12,288,731 | 21,075,232 |
| 1908 | 265,695 | 245,695 | 168,000 | 1,200,000 | 3,420,000 | 1,575,000 | 134,178 | 360,000 | 12,409,842 | 19,484,477 |
| 1909 | 182,990 | 182,990 | 168,000 | 1,200,000 | 3,540,000 | 1,600,000 | 124,168 | 323,915 | 13,664,671 | 20,262,294 |
| 1910 | 251,196 | 271,196 | 168,000 | 1,200,000 | 3,420,000 | 1,625,000 | 126,364 | 339,268 | 15,625,288 | 23,000,476 |
| 1911 | 256,088 | 256,088 | 168,000 | 1,200,000 | 3,300,000 | 1,650,000 | 128,452 | 344,510 | 16,371,844 | 25,028,255 |
| 1912 | 325,118 | 375,118 | 198,000 | 1,200,000 | 3,300,000 | 1,700,000 | 132,570 | 419,336 | 18,040,418 | 27,477,478 |
| 1913 | 350,684 | 390,684 | 204,000 | 1,200,000 | 3,570,000 | 1,800,000 | 120,254 | 454,003 | 17,128,434 | 27,243,396 |
| 1914 | 372,080 | 372,080 | 168,000 | 1,200,000 | 3,900,000 | 1,800,000 | 125,334 | 634,204 | 18,617,884 | 26,775,515 |
| 1915 | 382,872 | 419,721 | 168,000 | 1,200,000 | 3,255,000 | 1,800,000 | 130,206 | 799,717 | 21,548,506 | 29,644,856 |
| 1916 | 381,260 | 541,260 | 204,000 | 1,200,000 | 3,360,000 | 1,900,000 | 157,466 | 706,504 | 22,704,095 | 33,390,842 |
| 1917 | 402,795 | 502,795 | 228,000 | 1,200,000 | 5,280,000 | 2,000,000 | 167,261 | 929,161 | 28,042,149 | 36,126,433 |
| 1918 | 409,221 | 409,221 | 243,000 | 1,200,000 | 5,280,000 | 2,100,000 | 168,482 | 954,374 | 33,777,276 | 47,604,548 |
| 1919 | 447,348 | 447,348 | 243,000 | 2,000,000 | 8,100,000 | 3,000,000 | 172,830 | 952,102 | 47,932,170 | 68,741,696 |

| Year | | | | | | | | | | |
|---|---|---|---|---|---|---|---|---|---|---|
| 1920 | 676,771 | 676,771 | 405,000 | 3,000,000 | 7,800,000 | 3,600,000 | 209,601 | 993,753 | 48,702,304 | 70,932,745 |
| 1921 | 788,069 | 788,069 | 607,500 | 3,000,000 | 9,450,000 | 3,700,000 | 215,170 | 1,267,928 | 42,949,360 | 61,767,781 |
| 1922 | 789,531 | 789,531 | 607,500 | 3,000,000 | 10,950,000 | 3,800,000 | 222,201 | 1,228,030 | 42,408,289 | 60,153,373 |
| 1923 | 782,707 | 782,707 | 607,500 | 3,000,000 | 11,850,000 | 3,900,000 | 222,408 | 1,025,940 | 41,590,027 | 58,765,538 |
| 1924 | 770,716 | 800,716 | 607,500 | 3,000,000 | 12,450,000 | 4,000,000 | 210,624 | 1,053,685 | 42,059,313 | 61,849,258 |
| 1925 | 756,154 | 676,318 | 607,500 | 3,000,000 | 12,600,000 | 4,000,000 | 209,278 | 900,747 | 51,134,282 | 70,866,448 |
| 1926 | 778,576 | 778,576 | 607,500 | 3,000,000 | 12,600,000 | 4,000,000 | 215,354 | 1,050,289 | 50,067,105 | 66,645,956 |
| 1927 | 724,263 | 447,586 | 607,500 | 3,000,000 | 12,600,000 | 4,000,000 | 206,893 | 826,473 | 45,121,907 | 64,442,829 |
| 1928 | 627,263 | 471,195 | 607,500 | 3,000,000 | 13,200,000 | 4,000,000 | 186,656 | 728,800 | 44,004,911 | 60,991,370 |
| 1929 | 661,598 | 661,598 | 607,500 | 3,000,000 | 11,025,000 | 4,000,000 | 190,754 | 746,168 | 44,917,491 | 61,081,685 |
| 1930 | 634,343 | 579,764 | 607,500 | 3,000,000 | 10,575,000 | 4,000,000 | 187,597 | 823,038 | 40,833,796 | 54,802,422 |
| 1931 | 381,788 | (715,872) | 420,000 | 3,000,000 | 6,600,000 | 3,000,000 | 149,385 | 742,458 | 38,616,008 | 53,129,794 |
| 1932 | 454,499 | 394,499 | 420,000 | 3,000,000 | 8,025,000 | 3,000,000 | 184,884 | 813,270 | 43,632,955 | 58,724,031 |
| 1933 | 467,467 | 467,467 | 420,000 | 3,000,000 | 8,925,000 | 3,000,000 | 206,351 | 915,578 | 46,605,658 | 60,297,561 |
| 1934 | 466,044 | 866,044 | 420,000 | 3,000,000 | 9,600,000 | 3,000,000 | 177,395 | 1,690,840 | 46,548,424 | 61,650,731 |
| 1935 | 498,643 | 166,803 | 420,000 | 3,000,000 | 7,800,000 | 3,000,000 | 181,038 | 1,080,092 | 45,986,111 | 59,557,929 |
| 1936 | 496,402 | 716,682 | 420,000 | 3,000,000 | 9,450,000 | 3,000,000 | 182,720 | 1,153,252 | 48,184,255 | 64,508,274 |
| 1937 | 491,065 | 734,680 | 420,000 | 3,000,000 | 7,350,000 | 3,000,000 | 178,785 | 797,454 | 49,741,350 | 64,139,098 |
| 1938 | 335,309 | 144,530 | 300,000 | 3,000,000 | 5,550,000 | 3,000,000 | 179,094 | 515,805 | 46,191,968 | 60,522,110 |
| 1939 | 338,349 | 295,348 | 300,000 | 3,000,000 | 4,950,000 | 3,000,000 | 182,443 | 368,305 | 53,662,308 | 67,568,797 |
| 1940 | 400,159 | 938,743 | 300,000 | 3,000,000 | 4,875,000 | 3,000,000 | 182,602 | 1,219,109 | 65,505,296 | 76,114,229 |
| 1941 | 352,865 | 734,865 | 225,000 | 3,000,000 | 4,500,000 | 3,000,000 | 260,468 | 1,262,250 | 77,990,605 | 90,925,553 |
| 1942 | 296,664 | 682,100 | 150,000 | 3,000,000 | 3,984,375 | 3,000,000 | 357,132 | 1,690,522 | 75,593,151 | 85,975,194 |
| 1943 | 314,240 | 632,083 | 150,000 | 3,000,000 | 5,587,500 | 3,000,000 | 371,372 | 1,960,221 | 78,712,262 | 88,918,258 |
| 1944 | 321,000 | 456,108 | 150,000 | 3,000,000 | 6,431,250 | 3,000,000 | 387,372 | 2,323,102 | 86,338,447 | 95,564,109 |
| 1945 | 326,264 | 748,918 | 150,000 | 3,000,000 | 6,806,250 | 3,000,000 | 383,636 | 2,086,681 | 80,334,979 | 90,045,910 |
| 1946 | 378,632 | 533,974 | 300,000 | 3,000,000 | 6,750,000 | 3,000,000 | 387,268 | 3,591,096 | 103,679,751 | 118,174,870 |
| 1947 | 448,058 | 877,111 | 360,000 | 3,000,000 | 6,825,000 | 3,000,000 | 402,326 | 2,464,840 | 110,048,808 | 126,413,799 |
| 1948 | 467,111 | 949,044 | 360,000 | 3,000,000 | 6,825,000 | 3,000,000 | 406,437 | 3,694,251 | 120,410,809 | 138,421,141 |
| 1949 | 515,592 | 1,180,592 | 360,000 | 3,000,000 | 6,150,000 | 3,000,000 | 409,029 | 3,299,514 | 129,479,187 | 151,520,444 |
| 1950 | 632,807 | 1,532,807 | 420,000 | 3,000,000 | 5,700,000 | 4,000,000 | 365,836 | 3,816,413 | 166,243,044 | 193,602,640 |
| 1951 | 697,097 | 1,697,097 | 420,000 | 3,000,000 | 6,375,000 | 4,000,000 | 397,433 | 3,388,237 | 187,750,702 | 213,632,879 |
| 1952 | 698,782 | 1,740,782 | 420,000 | 3,000,000 | 5,925,000 | 5,000,000 | 399,215 | 3,398,459 | 180,088,401 | 208,514,840 |
| 1953 | 693,798 | 1,606,394 | 490,000 | 3,500,000 | 7,437,500 | 5,000,000 | 403,513 | 5,270,682 | 165,037,787 | 186,962,798 |
| 1954 | 723,147 | 1,813,365 | 525,000 | 3,500,000 | 7,980,000 | 5,000,000 | 392,910 | 7,363,930 | 180,134,217 | 203,685,695 |
| 1955 | 759,340 | 1,934,340 | 525,000 | 3,500,000 | 7,437,500 | 5,000,000 | 424,302 | 3,308,178 | 203,092,213 | 223,968,987 |

CHARTERED BANK (*Cont.*)

| Years | Published net profits | Real profits | Dividends paid (gross) | Paid-up capital | Market value: capital | Published reserves | Retained profits | Inner reserves | Deposits | Total balance sheet |
|---|---|---|---|---|---|---|---|---|---|---|
| 1956 | 800,808 | 1,645,706 | 525,000 | 3,500,000 | 5,862,500 | 5,000,000 | 432,068 | 4,200,689 | 197,718,275 | 222,867,566 |
| 1957 | 1,000,890 | 2,076,963 | 660,000 | 4,400,000 | 7,920,000 | 5,700,000 | 438,458 | 4,805,956 | 243,706,126 | 271,898,015 |
| 1958 | 993,590 | 1,959,840 | 750,000 | 5,000,000 | 11,437,500 | 5,500,000 | 481,673 | 8,885,428 | 259,566,496 | 285,430,502 |
| 1959 | 619,696 | 1,659,696 | 750,000 | 5,000,000 | 13,500,000 | 5,500,000 | 491,994 | 10,672,689 | 287,390,136 | 317,021,709 |
| 1960 | 761,916 | 2,284,553 | 825,000 | 5,500,000 | 12,512,500 | 5,750,000 | 506,254 | 9,781,586 | 333,639,529 | 362,759,636 |
| 1961 | 990,238 | 2,367,810 | 990,000 | 6,600,000 | 17,242,500 | 7,250,000 | 540,648 | 11,762,169 | 365,362,905 | 408,097,902 |
| 1062 | 1,076,748 | 2,004,682 | 990,000 | 6,600,000 | 17,407,500 | 7,700,000 | 591,021 | 16,813,486 | 427,621,917 | 468,658,106 |
| 1963 | 1,069,378 | 2,260,368 | 990,000 | 6,600,000 | 19,057,500 | 8,150,000 | 574,024 | 16,800,640 | 462,651,361 | 579,724,854 |
| 1964 | 1,254,778 | 2,315,778 | 1,155,000 | 7,700,000 | 18,095,000 | 9,700,000 | 571,365 | 12,014,805 | 479,654,265 | 600,518,805 |
| 1965 | 1,310,062 | 2,670,062 | 1,270,500 | 8,470,000 | 20,539,750 | 10,589,865 | 595,605 | 12,668,253 | 575,856,415 | 712,672,214 |
| 1966 | 1,886,657 | 3,171,657 | 1,270,500 | 8,470,000 | 22,233,750 | 10,925,200 | 678,619 | 13,749,139 | 570,211,344 | 715,450,145 |
| 1967 | 2,127,379 | 3,977,379 | 1,270,500 | 8,470,000 | 27,315,750 | 11,527,338 | 857,564 | 13,649,454 | 626,569,158 | 801,182,086 |
| 1968 | 2,477,407 | 4,677,407 | 1,270,500 | 8,470,000 | 31,550,750 | 14,644,533 | 989,776 | 13,015,263 | 721,914,090 | 907,783,000 |
| 1969 | 2,960,210 | 5,710,210 | 1,452,000 | 9,680,000 | 41,261,000 | 17,425,993 | 1,045,622 | 14,517,010 | 709,676,569 | 935,214,607 |

*Notes*: December financial year-end. Accounts consolidated from 1956. Merger with Standard Bank end-1969 to create Standard Chartered. See separate bank.

COLONIAL BANK

| Years | Published net profits | Real profits | Dividends paid (gross) | Paid-up capital | Market value: capital | Published reserves | Retained profits | Inner reserves | Deposits | Total balance sheet |
|---|---|---|---|---|---|---|---|---|---|---|
| 1890 | 74,680 | n.a. | 72,000 | 600,000 | 1,080,000 | 150,000 | 5,404 | n.a. | 1,860,088 | 4,865,415 |
| 1891 | 56,137 | 98,637 | 60,000 | 600,000 | 940,000 | 150,000 | 1,541 | 22,500 | 1,822,718 | 4,878,369 |
| 1892 | 60,503 | 116,503 | 60,000 | 600,000 | 780,000 | 150,000 | 2,044 | 28,000 | 1,747,131 | 4,737,708 |
| 1893 | 64,506 | 91,503 | 60,000 | 600,000 | 760,000 | 150,000 | 6,550 | 18,000 | 1,924,532 | 4,939,773 |
| 1894 | 62,084 | 102,084 | 60,000 | 600,000 | 760,000 | 150,000 | 8,634 | 20,000 | 1,721,279 | 4,848,295 |
| 1895 | 59,104 | 78,048 | 60,000 | 600,000 | 650,000 | 150,000 | 7,738 | 7,400 | 1,790,507 | 4,677,964 |
| 1896 | 50,833 | 86,108 | 48,000 | 600,000 | 660,000 | 150,000 | 10,571 | 20,355 | 1,789,008 | 4,315,345 |
| 1897 | 36,604 | 65,800 | 36,000 | 600,000 | 420,000 | 150,000 | 11,175 | 10,709 | 1,535,733 | 3,748,676 |
| 1898 | 33,885 | 57,648 | 36,000 | 600,000 | 375,000 | 150,000 | 9,060 | 8,361 | 1,592,450 | 3,832,251 |
| 1899 | 34,697 | 66,947 | 36,000 | 600,000 | 400,000 | 150,000 | 7,756 | 22,046 | 1,883,022 | 3,791,728 |
| 1900 | 37,005 | 61,502 | 36,000 | 600,000 | 450,000 | 150,000 | 8,761 | 18,687 | 1,893,636 | 3,911,086 |
| 1901 | 37,671 | 60,025 | 36,000 | 600,000 | 475,000 | 150,000 | 10,432 | 21,584 | 1,852,623 | 3,782,068 |
| 1902 | 38,277 | 57,669 | 36,000 | 600,000 | 475,000 | 150,000 | 12,709 | 23,387 | 2,011,298 | 3,884,841 |
| 1903 | 41,483 | 71,866 | 36,000 | 600,000 | 475,000 | 150,000 | 17,374 | 25,571 | 1,886,656 | 3,705,232 |
| 1904 | 47,395 | 67,591 | 42,000 | 600,000 | 650,000 | 150,000 | 22,769 | 35,188 | 1,925,285 | 3,736,634 |
| 1905 | 42,070 | 57,712 | 42,000 | 600,000 | 650,000 | 150,000 | 22,839 | 13,429 | 1,852,395 | 3,678,773 |
| 1906 | 46,776 | 59,521 | 39,000 | 600,000 | 625,000 | 150,000 | 30,615 | 16,163 | 1,921,033 | 3,645,813 |
| 1907 | 42,051 | 76,173 | 36,000 | 600,000 | 550,000 | 150,000 | 31,666 | 23,993 | 1,897,083 | 3,721,830 |
| 1908 | 44,738 | 56,116 | 36,000 | 600,000 | 500,000 | 150,000 | 30,404 | 97,283 | 2,069,815 | 3,691,960 |
| 1909 | 41,121 | 49,648 | 36,000 | 600,000 | 537,500 | 150,000 | 30,525 | 121,138 | 2,133,459 | 3,746,738 |

COLONIAL BANK (Cont.)

| Years | Published net profits | Real profits | Dividends paid (gross) | Paid-up capital | Market value: capital | Published reserves | Retained profits | Inner reserves | Deposits | Total balance sheet |
|---|---|---|---|---|---|---|---|---|---|---|
| 1910 | 47,555 | 61,982 | 36,000 | 600,000 | 550,000 | 150,000 | 32,080 | 120,895 | 2,313,892 | 4,098,346 |
| 1911 | 55,293 | 63,614 | 36,000 | 600,000 | 825,000 | 150,000 | 35,373 | 85,599 | 2,104,481 | 3,752,993 |
| 1912 | 52,908 | 75,707 | 36,000 | 600,000 | 625,000 | 150,000 | 32,281 | 99,824 | 2,037,917 | 3,653,609 |
| 1913 | 54,646 | 85,021 | 36,000 | 600,000 | 600,000 | 150,000 | 30,927 | 140,304 | 2,051,092 | 3,578,878 |
| 1914 | 52,208 | 80,090 | 36,000 | 600,000 | 575,000 | 150,000 | 36,135 | 103,957 | 1,949,983 | 3,462,703 |
| 1915 | 52,825 | 92,084 | 39,000 | 600,000 | 462,500 | 150,000 | 31,110 | 168,017 | 2,119,693 | 4,069,785 |
| 1916 | 58,625 | 99,425 | 42,000 | 600,000 | 600,000 | 200,000 | 11,185 | 162,910 | 3,714,434 | 5,844,991 |
| 1917 | 73,936 | 101,832 | 45,000 | 600,000 | 650,000 | 225,000 | 26,371 | 187,461 | 4,695,936 | 7,462,367 |
| 1918 | 105,772 | 85,772 | 60,000 | 750,000 | 1,050,000 | 350,000 | 25,680 | 193,294 | 5,406,965 | 8,315,860 |
| 1919 | 147,703 | 148,003 | 90,000 | 900,000 | 1,162,500 | 375,000 | 31,609 | 231,682 | 8,508,544 | 13,711,562 |
| 1920 | 175,206 | n.a. | 90,000 | 900,000 | 900,000 | 400,000 | 39,015 | 377,140 | 10,206,697 | 15,243,266 |
| 1921 | 143,151 | n.a. | 81,000 | 900,000 | 956,250 | 400,000 | 31,166 | 243,460 | 6,646,767 | 10,768,881 |
| 1922 | 106,730 | n.a. | 72,000 | 900,000 | 862,500 | 300,000 | 22,740 | 260,740 | -6,266,466 | 9,601,703 |
| 1923 | 94,083 | n.a. | 72,000 | 900,000 | 937,500 | 300,000 | 28,473 | 321,305 | 6,649,042 | 10,294,708 |
| 1924 | 99,598 | n.a. | 72,000 | 900,000 | 993,750 | 300,000 | 27,621 | 313,190 | 6,631,024 | 9,772,807 |
| 1925 | 65,409 | n.a. | 36,000 | 900,000 | 187,500 | 300,000 | 27,330 | n.a. | 6,973,039 | 10,079,143 |

*Notes*: Biannual accounts; December taken as the financial year-end. Bank reconstructed in 1925; see Barclays (DCO). n.a. = not available.

EASTERN BANK

| Years | Published net profits | Real profits | Dividends paid (gross) | Paid-up capital | Market value: capital | Published reserves | Retained profits | Inner reserves | Deposits | Total balance sheet |
|---|---|---|---|---|---|---|---|---|---|---|
| 1910 | 4,762 | n.a. | 0 | 400,000 | 475,000 | 0 | 1,176 | n.a. | 1,166,190 | 2,233,568 |
| 1911 | 23,996 | n.a. | 16,000 | 400,000 | 475,000 | 0 | 9,172 | n.a. | 1,805,776 | 2,940,593 |
| 1912 | 33,826 | n.a. | 20,000 | 400,000 | 625,000 | 15,000 | 7,998 | n.a. | 2,155,212 | 3,566,636 |
| 1913 | 39,154 | n.a. | 24,000 | 400,000 | 525,000 | 30,000 | 8,152 | n.a. | 1,675,266 | 3,299,295 |
| 1914 | 36,971 | n.a. | 23,646 | 598,653 | 750,000 | 55,000 | 6,477 | n.a. | 1,396,021 | 2,746,049 |
| 1915 | 45,183 | n.a | 30,000 | 599,860 | 581,250 | 55,000 | 6,661 | n.a. | 1,915,883 | 3,795,744 |
| 1916 | 53,885 | n.a. | 36,000 | 599,880 | 600,000 | 70,000 | 9,546 | n.a. | 3,099,801 | 5,154,073 |
| 1917 | 68,373 | n.a. | 42,000 | 599,921 | 750,000 | 90,000 | 15,918 | n.a. | 5,049,972 | 6,845,541 |
| 1918 | 68,888 | n.a. | 45,000 | 600,000 | 1,050,000 | 110,000 | 19,806 | n.a. | 5,784,900 | 7,576,973 |
| 1919 | 102,645 | n.a. | 52,500 | 765,242 | 1,521,100 | 219,406 | 29,951 | n.a. | 12,520,390 | 16,676,409 |
| 1920 | 121,363 | n.a. | 80,000 | 995,780 | 900,000 | 266,000 | 31,010 | n.a. | 8,556,281 | 13,050,388 |
| 1921 | 144,171 | n.a. | 90,000 | 999,844 | 950,000 | 300,000 | 31,181 | n.a. | 5,664,034 | 9,712,219 |
| 1922 | 120,320 | n.a. | 90,000 | 1,000,000 | 1,050,000 | 320,000 | 31,501 | n.a. | 5,433,133 | 9,229,824 |
| 1923 | 121,847 | n.a. | 90,000 | 1,000,000 | 1,075,000 | 340,000 | 33,348 | n.a. | 4,942,940 | 9,668,579 |
| 1924 | 122,052 | n.a. | 90,000 | 1,000,000 | 1,212,500 | 360,000 | 35,400 | n.a. | 5,479,060 | 10,388,341 |
| 1925 | 122,503 | n.a. | 90,000 | 1,000,000 | 1,200,000 | 380,000 | 37,903 | n.a. | 5,693,140 | 10,030,267 |
| 1926 | 120,538 | n.a. | 90,000 | 1,000,000 | 1,225,000 | 400,000 | 38,441 | n.a. | 5,989,036 | 10,772,517 |
| 1927 | 121,910 | n.a. | 90,000 | 1,000,000 | 1,275,000 | 425,000 | 40,351 | n.a. | 6,201,584 | 11,801,668 |
| 1928 | 124,119 | n.a. | 90,000 | 1,000,000 | 1,387,500 | 450,000 | 44,470 | n.a. | 6,170,098 | 11,601,892 |
| 1929 | 123,521 | n.a. | 90,000 | 1,000,000 | 1,200,000 | 480,000 | 47,991 | n.a. | 6,223,523 | 11,238,795 |
| 1930 | 116,694 | n.a. | 90,000 | 1,000,000 | 1,150,000 | 480,000 | 49,685 | n.a. | 5,576,820 | 10,574,891 |
| 1931 | 119,607 | 72,444 | 60,000 | 1,000,000 | 800,000 | 500,000 | 34,292 | 197,272 | 5,605,915 | 9,727,371 |
| 1932 | 121,944 | 89,442 | 60,000 | 1,000,000 | 1,025,000 | 500,000 | 41,236 | 182,697 | 6,007,095 | 9,742,786 |
| 1933 | 125,525 | 87,464 | 60,000 | 1,000,000 | 1,150,000 | 500,000 | 51,761 | 182,697 | 5,604,674 | 9,621,731 |
| 1934 | 130,006 | 152,379 | 90,000 | 1,000,000 | 1,375,000 | 500,000 | 51,767 | 245,676 | 6,450,187 | 10,696,198 |
| 1935 | 125,386 | 141,844 | 60,000 | 1,000,000 | 1,300,000 | 500,000 | 62,153 | 323,734 | 6,799,954 | 10,639,067 |

EASTERN BANK (*Cont.*)

| Years | Published net profits | Real profits | Dividends paid (gross) | Paid-up capital | Market value: capital | Published reserves | Retained profits | Inner reserves | Deposits | Total balance sheet |
|---|---|---|---|---|---|---|---|---|---|---|
| 1936 | 131,865 | 153,210 | 70,000 | 1,000,000 | 1,425,000 | 500,000 | 74,018 | 365,395 | 7,771,799 | 11,904,984 |
| 1937 | 127,173 | 61,738 | 70,000 | 1,000,000 | 1,275,000 | 500,000 | 81,191 | 415,395 | 7,717,024 | 11,921,348 |
| 1938 | 111,601 | 158,870 | 70,000 | 1,000,000 | 1,250,000 | 500,000 | 82,792 | 460,395 | 7,499,725 | 11,521,445 |
| 1939 | 104,490 | (26,530) | 60,000 | 1,000,000 | 800,000 | 500,000 | 82,282 | 360,630 | 8,202,492 | 10,884,020 |
| 1940 | 102,390 | 134,015 | 60,000 | 1,000,000 | 825,000 | 500,000 | 84,672 | 354,510 | 8,820,145 | 11,081,589 |
| 1941 | 95,358 | 137,228 | 45,000 | 1,000,000 | 950,000 | 500,000 | 85,030 | 373,569 | 14,307,099 | 16,430,582 |
| 1942 | 95,581 | 204,253 | 50,000 | 1,000,000 | 912,500 | 500,000 | 85,611 | 424,389 | 18,158,589 | 20,225,851 |
| 1943 | 98,560 | 254,298 | 55,000 | 1,000,000 | 1,356,250 | 600,000 | 79,171 | 444,187 | 22,885,363 | 25,030,762 |
| 1944 | 98,705 | 208,396 | 55,000 | 1,000,000 | 1,593,750 | 700,000 | 72,876 | 455,605 | 21,510,196 | 23,760,161 |
| 1945 | 102,042 | 204,253 | 55,000 | 1,000,000 | 1,656,250 | 800,000 | 69,918 | 421,376 | 21,739,252 | 24,393,915 |
| 1946 | 110,917 | 236,000 | 60,000 | 1,000,000 | 1,850,000 | 850,000 | 70,835 | 548,000 | 22,101,958 | 24,974,550 |
| 1947 | 119,357 | 186,000 | 60,000 | 1,000,000 | 1,625,000 | 900,000 | 80,192 | 643,000 | 22,805,579 | 25,795,690 |
| 1948 | 110,998 | 165,000 | 60,000 | 1,000,000 | 1,625,000 | 1,000,000 | 83,190 | 688,000 | 22,123,649 | 25,176,606 |
| 1949 | 118,244 | 140,000 | 60,000 | 1,000,000 | 1,525,000 | 1,000,000 | 88,434 | 798,000 | 20,972,498 | 24,108,046 |
| 1950 | 123,928 | 140,000 | 60,000 | 1,000,000 | 1,325,000 | 1,200,000 | 89,362 | 658,000 | 24,351,579 | 27,659,393 |
| 1951 | 124,763 | 176,000 | 60,000 | 1,000,000 | 1,350,000 | 1,200,000 | 92,625 | 896,000 | 25,968,630 | 29,325,664 |
| 1952 | 126,722 | 247,000 | 70,000 | 1,000,000 | 1,200,000 | 1,250,000 | 102,597 | 952,000 | 28,037,882 | 31,329,045 |
| 1953 | 127,512 | 240,000 | 80,000 | 1,000,000 | 1,475,000 | 1,300,000 | 106,109 | 1,095,000 | 29,067,987 | 32,458,611 |
| 1954 | 129,011 | 283,000 | 80,000 | 1,000,000 | 1,950,000 | 1,500,000 | 111,120 | 1,137,000 | 33,294,778 | 37,352,355 |
| 1955 | 132,536 | (84,000) | 80,000 | 1,000,000 | 1,650,000 | 1,500,000 | 112,656 | 1,005,000 | 38,892,069 | 43,558,711 |
| 1956 | 129,940 | 195,000 | 80,000 | 1,000,000 | 1,400,000 | 1,500,000 | 111,596 | 1,115,000 | 39,771,749 | 44,173,237 |
| 1957 | 127,542 | (149,000) | 80,000 | 1,000,000 | 1,762,500 | 1,500,000 | 113,138 | 958,000 | 40,198,581 | 43,669,887 |

*Notes*: December financial year-end. Taken over by Chartered Bank in 1957. n.a. = not available.

## ENGLISH, SCOTTISH & AUSTRALIAN BANK

| Years | Published net profits | Real profits | Dividends paid (gross) | Paid-up capital | Market value: capital | Published reserves | Retained profits | Inner reserves | Deposits | Total balance sheet |
|---|---|---|---|---|---|---|---|---|---|---|
| 1893/4 | 164,331 | n.a. | 0 | 816,534 | 816,534 | 0 | 10,154 | n.a. | 950,764 | 6,381,081 |
| 1894/5 | 152,254 | n.a. | 0 | 968,055 | n.q. | 0 | (6,279) | 1,057,000 | 1,008,057 | 6,212,779 |
| 1895/6 | 139,813 | n.a. | 0 | 970,987 | n.q. | 0 | 0 | 990,000 | 1,128,613 | 6,263,569 |
| 1896/7 | 130,536 | n.a. | 0 | 970,987 | n.q. | 0 | 10,870 | 962,000 | 1,396,657 | 6,065,976 |
| 1897/8 | 119,560 | n.a. | 0 | 539,437 | n.q. | 10,870 | 6,034 | 1,177,000 | 1,426,278 | 5,576,230 |
| 1898/9 | 126,449 | n.a. | 13,486 | 539,437 | n.q. | 31,904 | 411 | 877,000 | 1,613,924 | 5,793,792 |
| 1899/1900 | 161,459 | n.a. | 18,880 | 539,437 | n.q. | 46,904 | 7,018 | 504,000 | 1,875,513 | 6,233,525 |
| 1900/1 | 156,374 | n.a. | 21,577 | 539,437 | n.q. | 61,904 | 7,627 | 509,000 | 2,071,800 | 6,162,982 |
| 1901/2 | 161,986 | n.a. | 21,577 | 539,437 | n.q. | 76,904 | 161,389 | 515,000 | 2,106,225 | 6,185,302 |
| 1902/3 | 148,485 | n.a. | 21,577 | 539,437 | n.q. | 91,904 | 10,221 | 500,000 | 2,320,029 | 6,153,463 |
| 1903/4 | 152,863 | n.a. | 21,577 | 539,437 | n.q. | 106,904 | 12,036 | 472,000 | 2,358,550 | 6,295,426 |
| 1904/5 | 151,882 | n.a. | 24,275 | 539,437 | n.q. | 121,904 | 16,612 | 467,000 | 2,555,854 | 6,339,734 |
| 1905/6 | 151,663 | n.a. | 26,972 | 539,437 | n.q. | 136,904 | 17,912 | 455,000 | 3,002,692 | 6,927,913 |
| 1906/7 | 167,948 | n.a. | 26,972 | 539,437 | n.q. | 151,904 | 25,274 | 438,000 | 3,374,866 | 7,449,598 |
| 1907/8 | 164,954 | n.a. | 32,366 | 539,437 | n.q. | 166,904 | 26,095 | 440,000 | 3,654,105 | 7,508,398 |
| 1908/9 | 164,937 | n.a. | 32,366 | 539,437 | n.q. | 181,904 | 30,135 | 417,000 | 4,164,250 | 7,990,141 |
| 1909/10 | 174,079 | n.a. | 37,761 | 539,437 | 485,494 | 200,000 | 30,761 | 382,000 | 4,687,119 | 8,713,324 |
| 1910/11 | 184,952 | n.a. | 43,155 | 539,437 | 528,649 | 215,000 | 31,594 | 385,000 | 5,368,629 | 9,576,416 |
| 1911/12 | 197,422 | n.a. | 43,155 | 539,437 | 604,170 | 250,000 | 32,454 | 378,000 | 5,981,583 | 10,026,755 |
| 1912/13 | 217,010 | n.a. | 43,155 | 539,437 | 582,593 | 300,000 | 32,588 | 406,000 | 6,110,487 | 10,146,153 |
| 1913/14 | 220,663 | n.a. | 43,155 | 539,437 | 722,846 | 350,000 | 43,083 | 447,000 | 6,857,928 | 10,959,280 |
| 1914/15 | 197,056 | n.a. | 43,155 | 539,437 | 852,311 | 400,000 | 33,229 | 452,000 | 7,058,797 | 11,163,389 |
| 1915/16 | 110,695 | n.a. | 43,155 | 539,437 | 598,776 | 450,000 | 33,884 | 464,000 | 7,665,487 | 11,893,718 |
| 1916/17 | 110,419 | n.a. | 43,155 | 539,437 | 668,903 | 500,000 | 34,263 | 482,000 | 9,159,320 | 13,793,684 |

ENGLISH, SCOTTISH & AUSTRALIAN BANK (*Cont.*)

| Years | Published net profits | Real profits | Dividends paid (gross) | Paid-up capital | Market value: capital | Published reserves | Retained profits | Inner reserves | Deposits | Total balance sheet |
|---|---|---|---|---|---|---|---|---|---|---|
| 1917/18 | 133,169 | n.a. | 48,549 | 539,437 | 690,480 | 550,000 | 49,700 | 573,000 | 9,388,452 | 13,835,062 |
| 1918/19 | 133,179 | n.a. | 53,943 | 539,437 | 841,523 | 585,000 | 50,954 | 698,000 | 10,848,250 | 15,441,103 |
| 1919/20 | 170,178 | n.a. | 53,943 | 589,177 | 1,466,595 | 635,000 | 94,209 | 662,000 | 12,090,412 | 16,931,747 |
| 1920/1 | 267,975 | n.a. | 128,807 | 1,319,887 | 1,795,047 | 1,300,000 | 102,604 | 1,305,000 | 22,552,725 | 30,785,298 |
| 1921/2 | 345,475 | n.a. | 131,989 | 1,319,887 | 1,953,434 | 1,450,000 | 107,094 | 1,450,000 | 23,773,421 | 30,903,332 |
| 1922/3 | 470,848 | n.a. | 178,494 | 1,500,000 | 2,925,000 | 1,620,000 | 112,600 | 1,490,000 | 25,202,780 | 32,779,687 |
| 1923/4 | 502,502 | n.a. | 187,500 | 1,500,000 | 3,750,000 | 1,820,000 | 130,102 | 1,525,000 | 25,696,754 | 33,644,879 |
| 1924/5 | 515,981 | n.a. | 243,750 | 2,250,000 | 5,343,750 | 1,950,000 | 183,414 | 1,445,000 | 25,729,311 | 34,548,931 |
| 1925/6 | 542,308 | n.a. | 281,250 | 2,250,000 | 5,484,375 | 2,050,000 | 230,722 | 1,413,000 | 27,918,631 | 37,252,627 |
| 1926/7 | 550,988 | n.a. | 295,312 | 2,625,000 | 6,835,938 | 2,550,000 | 277,960 | 1,734,000 | 33,088,509 | 44,154,758 |
| 1927/8 | 598,769 | n.a. | 375,000 | 3,000,000 | 7,687,500 | 3,000,000 | 311,479 | 1,745,000 | 33,391,267 | 44,512,778 |
| 1928/9 | 601,262 | n.a. | 375,000 | 3,000,000 | 8,625,000 | 3,080,000 | 347,741 | 1,749,000 | 33,734,496 | 45,262,611 |
| 1929/30 | 542,736 | n.a. | 375,000 | 3,000,000 | 7,000,000 | 3,160,000 | 305,477 | 1,807,000 | 30,297,775 | 40,859,738 |
| 1930/1 | 266,658 | n.a. | 240,000 | 3,000,000 | 4,250,000 | 1,605,000 | 297,135 | 2,033,000 | 28,522,421 | 38,579,690 |
| 1931/2 | 147,719 | n.a. | 150,000 | 3,000,000 | 4,125,000 | 1,620,000 | 274,854 | 2,020,000 | 29,372,285 | 39,670,045 |
| 1932/3 | 219,327 | n.a. | 150,000 | 3,000,000 | 4,000,000 | 1,635,000 | 274,181 | 1,966,000 | 28,946,769 | 39,020,572 |
| 1933/4 | 221,566 | n.a. | 150,000 | 3,000,000 | 5,187,500 | 1,650,000 | 275,747 | 1,910,000 | 32,031,348 | 42,439,355 |
| 1934/5 | 243,580 | n.a. | 150,000 | 3,000,000 | 4,312,500 | 1,665,000 | 299,327 | 1,974,000 | 32,409,353 | 42,831,337 |
| 1935/6 | 257,460 | n.a. | 150,000 | 3,000,000 | 4,250,000 | 1,680,000 | 306,787 | 2,029,000 | 32,893,249 | 43,535,963 |
| 1936/7 | 276,127 | n.a. | 210,000 | 3,000,000 | 4,750,000 | 1,695,000 | 305,979 | 2,097,000 | 35,282,660 | 46,688,200 |
| 1937/8 | 280,594 | n.a. | 210,000 | 3,000,000 | 4,375,000 | 1,710,000 | 307,697 | 2,180,000 | 35,188,611 | 46,643,085 |
| 1938/9 | 245,294 | n.a. | 210,000 | 3,000,000 | 3,625,000 | 1,725,000 | 304,367 | 2,143,000 | 34,942,476 | 45,253,106 |
| 1939/40 | 210,088 | n.a. | 210,000 | 3,000,000 | 3,500,000 | 1,740,000 | 294,939 | 2,277,000 | 36,959,564 | 47,284,033 |
| 1940/1 | 213,892 | n.a. | 210,000 | 3,000,000 | 3,375,000 | 1,755,000 | 299,706 | 2,425,000 | 40,416,504 | 51,334,554 |

| | | | | | | | | | | |
|---|---|---|---|---|---|---|---|---|---|---|
| 1941/2 | 126,120 | n.a. | 180,000 | 3,000,000 | 2,875,000 | 1,770,000 | 289,450 | n.a. | 47,469,944 | 56,381,497 |
| 1942/3 | 144,355 | n.a. | 180,000 | 3,000,000 | 3,215,000 | 1,785,000 | 287,869 | n.a. | 54,356,988 | 63,344,321 |
| 1943/4 | 148,444 | n.a. | 180,000 | 3,000,000 | 3,606,000 | 1,800,000 | 290,376 | n.a. | 61,334,648 | 70,172,606 |
| 1944/5 | 139,106 | n.a. | 180,000 | 3,000,000 | 3,656,000 | 1,815,000 | 293,545 | n.a. | 66,432,936 | 75,861,563 |
| 1945/6 | 180,326 | n.a. | 275,000 | 3,000,000 | 6,625,000 | 1,815,000 | 297,621 | n.a. | 62,292,261 | 68,792,320 |
| 1946/7 | 225,920 | n.a. | 300,000 | 3,000,000 | 6,625,000 | 1,815,000 | 323,541 | n.a. | 65,007,504 | 71,827,253 |
| 1947/8 | 235,732 | n.a. | 300,000 | 3,000,000 | 5,500,000 | 1,815,000 | 359,273 | n.a. | 84,159,029 | 90,916,572 |
| 1948/9 | 237,965 | n.a. | 300,000 | 3,000,000 | 6,250,000 | 1,815,000 | 397,238 | n.a. | 96,978,131 | 103,908,599 |
| 1949/50 | 259,310 | n.a. | 300,000 | 3,000,000 | 6,000,000 | 1,815,000 | 456,548 | n.a. | 99,291,535 | 109,289,493 |
| 1950/1 | 253,883 | n.a. | 300,000 | 3,000,000 | 6,375,000 | 2,000,000 | 332,931 | n.a. | 120,795,707 | 131,653,358 |
| 1951/2 | 237,520 | n.a. | 300,000 | 3,000,000 | 5,125,000 | 2,000,000 | 367,951 | n.a. | 109,656,423 | 118,275,573 |
| 1952/3 | 253,873 | n.a. | 375,000 | 3,000,000 | 4,875,000 | 3,000,000 | 372,449 | n.a. | 104,810,925 | 113,448,779 |
| 1953/4 | 254,982 | n.a. | 350,000 | 3,000,000 | 5,062,500 | 3,000,000 | 389,931 | n.a. | 110,190,778 | 119,396,519 |
| 1954/5 | 314,359 | n.a. | 350,000 | 3,000,000 | 6,125,000 | 3,000,000 | 458,040 | n.a. | 111,321,101 | 121,113,121 |
| 1955/6 | 307,746 | n.a. | 247,500 | 3,000,000 | 5,125,000 | 3,000,000 | 483,866 | n.a. | 114,073,741 | 121,577,538 |
| 1956/7 | 343,780 | n.a. | 315,000 | 5,000,000 | 7,250,000 | 3,000,000 | 484,771 | n.a. | 123,005,844 | 131,678,286 |
| 1957/8 | 385,461 | n.a. | 450,000 | 5,000,000 | 7,375,000 | 3,000,000 | 809,976 | n.a. | 124,057,267 | 139,633,978 |
| 1958/9 | 414,993 | n.a. | 450,000 | 5,000,000 | 6,750,000 | 3,000,000 | 904,344 | n.a. | 130,287,838 | 137,367,174 |
| 1959/60 | 378,431 | n.a. | 450,000 | 5,000,000 | 8,500,000 | 3,000,000 | 962,150 | n.a. | 133,804,210 | 142,659,088 |
| 1960/1 | 526,789 | n.a. | 450,000 | 5,000,000 | 6,250,000 | 3,000,000 | 1,151,314 | n.a. | 131,820,387 | 140,856,827 |
| 1961/2 | 691,639 | n.a. | 450,000 | 5,000,000 | 8,375,000 | 3,000,000 | 1,035,422 | n.a. | 134,757,429 | 144,869,037 |
| 1962/3 | 956,066 | n.a. | 450,000 | 5,000,000 | 10,062,500 | 3,250,000 | 914,405 | n.a. | 143,297,012 | 153,529,658 |
| 1963/4 | 1,030,741 | n.a. | 700,000 | 7,000,000 | 17,412,500 | 4,650,000 | 842,679 | n.a. | 163,865,288 | 202,188,135 |
| 1964/5 | 1,213,940 | n.a. | 700,000 | 7,000,000 | 14,612,500 | 4,650,000 | 1,079,632 | n.a. | 174,701,887 | 221,646,583 |
| 1965/6 | 1,403,098 | n.a. | 700,000 | 7,000,000 | 14,525,000 | 4,650,000 | 1,286,391 | n.a. | 183,430,057 | 230,962,399 |
| 1966/7 | 1,658,990 | n.a. | 740,000 | 7,000,000 | 15,137,500 | 4,650,000 | 1,435,576 | n.a. | 190,129,504 | 237,298,036 |
| 1967/8 | 2,189,431 | n.a. | 840,000 | 8,400,000 | 40,565,000 | 5,250,000 | 981,257 | n.a. | 242,653,242 | 315,871,346 |

*Notes:* June financial year-end, so 1893/4 means year ends on 30 June 1894. E, S & A reconstructed August 1893, shares not quoted until 1909. Accounts consolidated from 1958. Amalgamated with ANZ Bank in 1969, see ANZ Bank thereafter. Published reserve figures do not include the special reserve, in force between 1931 and 1945, against depreciation of the Australian currency. n.a. = not available; n.q. = not quoted.

HONGKONG & SHANGHAI BANKING CORPORATION

| Years | Published net profits | Real profits | Dividends paid (gross) | Paid-up capital | Market value: capital | Published reserves | Retained profits | Inner reserves | Deposits | Total balance sheet |
|---|---|---|---|---|---|---|---|---|---|---|
| 1890 | 457,162 | n.a. | 352,500 | 1,588,182 | 5,480,000 | 1,162,793 | 20,564 | n.a. | 17,615,054 | 25,571,440 |
| 1891 | 248,689 | n.a. | 238,500 | 1,542,000 | 4,000,000 | 971,460 | 4,780 | n.a. | 17,583,586 | 23,708,888 |
| 1892 | 222,388 | n.a. | 160,000 | 1,365,000 | 2,760,000 | 491,400 | 9,715 | n.a. | 12,282,277 | 17,675,350 |
| 1893 | 237,963 | n.a. | 160,000 | 1,125,000 | 2,400,000 | 472,500 | 12,970 | n.a. | 10,092,114 | 15,074,346 |
| 1894 | 281,908 | n.a. | 180,000 | 1,000,000 | 2,440,000 | 500,000 | 12,967 | n.a. | 10,430,075 | 15,316,639 |
| 1895 | 302,915 | n.a. | 200,000 | 1,068,000 | 3,240,000 | 614,100 | 33,405 | n.a. | 15,318,968 | 19,987,450 |
| 1896 | 276,830 | n.a. | 200,000 | 1,057,000 | 3,360,000 | 687,050 | 32,907 | n.a. | 14,960,645 | 19,461,357 |
| 1897 | 360,011 | n.a. | 200,000 | 985,000 | 3,360,000 | 788,000 | 29,438 | n.a. | 11,923,086 | 16,682,481 |
| 1898 | 626,737 | n.a. | 300,000 | 979,000 | 4,240,000 | 979,000 | 81,711 | n.a. | 12,826,547 | 17,793,830 |
| 1899 | 464,407 | n.a. | 280,000 | 974,000 | 4,800,000 | 1,120,100 | 93,586 | n.a. | 15,247,626 | 20,287,925 |
| 1900 | 492,002 | n.a. | 280,000 | 1,042,000 | 4,720,000 | 1,354,600 | 146,950 | n.a. | 15,707,369 | 22,033,895 |
| 1901 | 413,685 | n.a. | 280,000 | 927,000 | 5,000,000 | 1,320,975 | 133,326 | n.a. | 17,591,867 | 23,066,837 |
| 1902 | 388,330 | n.a. | 280,000 | 792,000 | 4,960,000 | 1,227,600 | 113,689 | n.a. | 17,478,831 | 22,246,142 |
| 1903 | 390,753 | n.a. | 280,000 | 870,000 | 5,120,000 | 1,435,500 | 123,311 | n.a. | 17,454,611 | 23,297,883 |
| 1904 | 525,959 | n.a. | 320,000 | 982,000 | 5,640,000 | 1,767,600 | 146,653 | n.a. | 21,009,846 | 26,984,745 |
| 1905 | 550,304 | n.a. | 360,000 | 1,023,000 | 7,400,000 | 1,994,850 | 173,887 | n.a. | 22,706,011 | 29,749,206 |
| 1906 | 544,205 | n.a. | 360,000 | 1,130,000 | 7,520,000 | 2,373,000 | 194,536 | n.a. | 22,510,717 | 29,843,049 |
| 1907 | 477,414 | n.a. | 360,000 | 1,359,000 | 9,540,000 | 2,582,100 | 181,235 | n.a. | 20,301,391 | 27,130,811 |
| 1908 | 609,123 | n.a. | 510,000 | 1,297,500 | 9,840,000 | 2,551,750 | 173,539 | n.a. | 25,827,058 | 33,218,027 |
| 1909 | 608,683 | n.a. | 510,000 | 1,344,000 | 10,980,000 | 2,732,800 | 181,797 | n.a. | 24,408,872 | 32,232,645 |
| 1910 | 603,419 | n.a. | 510,000 | 1,375,500 | 10,320,000 | 2,865,625 | 186,990 | n.a. | 24,215,095 | 31,758,802 |
| 1911 | 559,483 | n.a. | 510,000 | 1,390,500 | 9,600,000 | 2,943,225 | 181,983 | n.a. | 27,652,121 | 36,568,604 |
| 1912 | 620,260 | n.a. | 510,000 | 1,554,000 | 10,140,000 | 3,335,920 | 208,382 | n.a | 29,882,957 | 39,600,796 |
| 1913 | 610,377 | n.a. | 510,000 | 1,449,000 | 9,540,000 | 3,153,990 | 199,702 | n.a. | 28,805,218 | 39,466,404 |
| 1914 | 644,927 | n.a. | 546,000 | 1,320,000 | 9,600,000 | 2,904,000 | 229,440 | n.a. | 28,979,480 | 38,295,439 |
| 1915 | 657,236 | n.a. | 546,000 | 1,437,000 | 9,090,000 | 3,161,400 | 290,008 | n.a. | 31,582,443 | 41,784,237 |
| 1916 | 855,186 | n.a. | 576,000 | 1,797,000 | 9,120,000 | 4,013,300 | 379,356 | n.a. | 36,307,522 | 48,256,991 |
| 1917 | 998,040 | n.a. | 636,000 | 2,250,000 | 10,080,000 | 5,175,000 | 483,486 | n.a. | 47,104,137 | 62,841,062 |

| Year | | | | | | | | | | |
|---|---|---|---|---|---|---|---|---|---|---|
| 1918 | 1,106,348 | n.a. | 708,000 | 2,515,500 | 11,880,000 | 6,037,200 | 549,991 | 2,364,570 | 57,214,337 | 72,440,374 |
| 1919 | 1,800,917 | n.a. | 960,000 | 3,657,000 | 14,160,000 | 7,107,708 | 795,482 | 3,998,320 | 82,197,189 | 103,802,741 |
| 1920 | 1,399,557 | n.a. | 960,000 | 2,374,500 | 12,540,000 | 5,902,924 | 521,043 | 3,197,660 | 71,418,719 | 87,826,429 |
| 1921 | 1,398,111 | n.a. | 960,000 | 2,584,000 | 15,600,000 | 7,537,361 | 430,466 | 2,596,920 | 62,112,558 | 80,311,324 |
| 1922 | 1,441,963 | n.a. | 1,280,000 | 2,230,000 | 18,720,000 | 7,233,432 | 373,549 | 2,274,600 | 55,988,984 | 70,890,687 |
| 1923 | 1,536,428 | n.a. | 1,280,000 | 2,322,000 | 20,080,000 | 7,458,774 | 392,338 | 2,275,560 | 58,520,771 | 76,860,586 |
| 1924 | 1,503,328 | n.a. | 1,280,000 | 2,312,000 | 22,560,000 | 7,562,427 | 391,943 | 2,265,760 | 60,480,788 | 79,137,987 |
| 1925 | 1,472,355 | n.a. | 1,280,000 | 2,364,000 | 19,600,000 | 7,690,290 | 401,611 | 2,151,240 | 65,107,242 | 83,192,630 |
| 1926 | 1,386,075 | n.a. | 1,280,000 | 1,958,000 | 18,480,000 | 7,320,628 | 332,769 | 1,918,840 | 60,324,065 | 77,229,618 |
| 1927 | 1,446,712 | n.a. | 1,280,000 | 2,032,000 | 19,440,000 | 7,424,615 | 346,601 | 1,930,400 | 56,640,095 | 73,811,501 |
| 1928 | 1,356,436 | n.a. | 1,280,000 | 2,020,000 | 22,480,000 | 7,411,526 | 343,179 | 1,929,100 | 55,370,800 | 71,791,858 |
| 1929 | 1,150,249 | n.a. | 1,120,000 | 1,626,000 | 19,840,000 | 7,276,350 | 275,402 | 1,650,390 | 53,199,755 | 69,335,845 |
| 1930 | 1,133,752 | n.a. | 1,120,000 | 1,094,000 | 16,960,000 | 7,048,212 | 187,571 | 1,165,110 | 50,604,483 | 66,443,101 |
| 1931 | 1,184,154 | n.a. | 960,000 | 1,438,000 | 16,560,000 | 7,221,261 | 246,007 | 1,265,440 | 55,593,975 | 75,488,929 |
| 1932 | 1,055,858 | n.a. | 960,000 | 1,250,000 | 18,560,000 | 7,125,000 | 214,940 | 1,162,500 | 58,227,364 | 77,115,630 |
| 1933 | 1,107,476 | n.a. | 960,000 | 1,448,000 | 21,120,000 | 7,224,374 | 250,702 | 1,455,240 | 63,270,603 | 84,596,083 |
| 1934 | 1,110,601 | n.a. | 880,000 | 1,708,000 | 22,000,000 | 7,352,732 | 281,367 | 1,614,060 | 58,373,532 | 80,955,966 |
| 1935 | 786,984 | n.a. | 880,000 | 1,302,000 | 15,360,000 | 7,150,584 | 216,592 | 1,484,280 | 50,531,233 | 68,452,736 |
| 1936 | 936,645 | n.a. | 880,000 | 1,240,000 | 17,200,000 | 7,122,185 | 207,129 | 1,364,000 | 51,935,062 | 70,101,389 |
| 1937 | 956,804 | n.a. | 880,000 | 1,240,000 | 14,000,000 | 7,122,185 | 209,746 | 1,413,600 | 53,311,972 | 76,404,139 |
| 1938 | 948,391 | n.a. | 880,000 | 1,240,000 | 12,720,000 | 7,122,185 | 210,839 | 1,153,200 | 54,062,681 | 77,738,160 |
| 1939 | 827,946 | n.a. | 800,000 | 1,240,000 | 13,280,000 | 7,122,185 | 211,502 | 1,085,000 | 52,049,862 | 75,978,625 |
| 1940 | 867,992 | n.a. | 800,000 | 1,240,000 | 12,080,000 | 7,122,185 | 212,224 | 1,122,200 | 54,598,759 | 77,252,525 |
| 1941 | 0 | n.a. | 0 | 1,240,000 | 10,080,000 | 7,124,791 | 0 | n.a. | 57,537,996 | 80,059,043 |
| 1942 | 0 | n.a. | 0 | 1,240,000 | 9,360,000 | 7,127,397 | 0 | n.a. | 60,458,880 | 82,865,561 |
| 1943 | 216,149 | n.a. | 0 | 1,240,000 | 11,680,000 | 7,127,397 | 0 | n.a. | 61,123,398 | 86,578,598 |
| 1944 | 214,136 | n.a. | 0 | 1,240,000 | 13,280,000 | 7,127,397 | 0 | n.a. | 63,409,905 | 87,604,828 |
| 1945 | 217,855 | n.a. | 480,000 | 1,250,000 | 14,440,000 | 7,125,000 | 0 | n.a. | 67,653,912 | 94,512,388 |
| 1946 | 593,447 | n.a. | 800,000 | 1,236,000 | 13,600,000 | 5,995,251 | 113,827 | n.a. | 93,277,942 | 126,743,293 |
| 1947 | 1,025,576 | 1,180,380 | 800,000 | 1,236,000 | 19,040,000 | 5,995,251 | 211,440 | n.a. | 103,643,158 | 149,561,008 |
| 1948 | 1,042,742 | 1,161,840 | 800,000 | 1,236,000 | 16,320,000 | 5,995,251 | 264,419 | n.a. | 111,116,676 | 164,703,819 |
| 1949 | 1,110,770 | 1,462,500 | 800,000 | 1,250,000 | 14,640,000 | 6,000,000 | 334,943 | n.a. | 113,781,972 | 169,476,890 |
| 1950 | 1,077,981 | 1,931,250 | 800,000 | 1,250,000 | 13,040,000 | 6,000,000 | 418,702 | n.a. | 159,916,246 | 216,043,257 |
| 1951 | 1,080,229 | 2,618,750 | 800,000 | 1,250,000 | 14,640,000 | 6,000,000 | 504,708 | n.a. | 195,883,504 | 254,628,696 |

HONGKONG & SHANGHAI BANKING CORPORATION (Cont.)

| Years | Published net profits | Real profits | Dividends paid (gross) | Paid-up capital | Market value: capital | Published reserves | Retained profits | Inner reserves | Deposits | Total balance sheet |
|---|---|---|---|---|---|---|---|---|---|---|
| 1952 | 1,082,588 | 2,806,250 | 800,000 | 1,250,000 | 12,720,000 | 6,000,000 | 593,073 | n.a. | 164,957,425 | 221,338,339 |
| 1953 | 1,080,890 | 2,643,750 | 800,000 | 1,250,000 | 15,120,000 | 6,000,000 | 616,221 | n.a. | 164,779,448 | 221,042,920 |
| 1954 | 1,205,653 | 2,537,500 | 800,000 | 1,250,000 | 17,280,000 | 8,000,000 | 638,454 | n.a. | 167,040,036 | 223,199,676 |
| 1955 | 1,286,270 | 3,225,000 | 1,000,000 | 1,562,500 | 19,300,000 | 8,000,000 | 662,918 | n.a. | 159,835,987 | 214,199,992 |
| 1956 | 1,289,714 | 2,918,750 | 1,000,000 | 1,562,500 | 18,500,000 | 8,000,000 | 689,974 | n.a. | 160,267,989 | 214,393,731 |
| 1957 | 1,314,721 | 3,231,250 | 1,050,000 | 3,125,000 | 18,200,000 | 8,000,000 | 128,904 | n.a. | 168,449,043 | 224,987,116 |
| 1958 | 1,466,628 | 2,500,000 | 1,200,000 | 3,125,000 | 18,800,000 | 8,000,000 | 130,342 | n.a. | 179,392,060 | 227,694,709 |
| 1959 | 1,837,656 | 2,862,500 | 1,500,208 | 3,894,461 | 28,040,119 | 10,949,165 | 176,175 | n.a. | 248,879,084 | 315,879,935 |
| 1960 | 2,932,118 | 5,012,500 | 2,372,365 | 4,940,383 | 45,391,848 | 15,000,000 | 202,005 | n.a. | 368,821,982 | 445,021,142 |
| 1961 | 3,077,904 | 4,231,250 | 2,371,384 | 4,940,383 | 55,332,288 | 15,000,000 | 293,590 | n.a. | 400,120,400 | 478,725,883 |
| 1962 | 3,170,189 | n.a. | 2,529,476 | 4,940,383 | 52,960,904 | 15,000,000 | 315,805 | n.a. | 434,491,944 | 602,880,690 |
| 1963 | 3,305,506 | n.a. | 2,529,476 | 4,940,383 | 64,027,361 | 15,000,000 | 490,760 | n.a. | 454,800,771 | 639,681,908 |
| 1964 | 3,713,143 | n.a. | 3,161,845 | 4,940,383 | 69,560,590 | 15,000,000 | 575,078 | n.a. | 483,391,954 | 682,811,440 |
| 1965 | 4,465,389 | n.a. | 3,179,744 | 9,880,766 | 57,703,671 | 16,843,415 | 1,049,802 | n.a. | 574,896,616 | 801,207,664 |
| 1966 | 5,557,952 | n.a. | 3,497,718 | 10,868,842 | 63,908,792 | 17,827,240 | 1,189,271 | n.a. | 637,516,467 | 888,588,892 |
| 1967 | 5,594,111 | n.a. | 3,864,718 | 11,964,421 | 65,647,807 | 20,444,415 | 1,728,239 | n.a. | 754,704,976 | 1,073,364,031 |
| 1968 | 6,611,794 | n.a. | 4,240,447 | 11,964,421 | 88,689,752 | 22,624,541 | 2,232,176 | n.a. | 915,800,606 | 1,259,566,947 |
| 1969 | 8,775,416 | n.a. | 5,003,602 | 13,160,864 | 110,949,143 | 24,788,535 | 2,730,168 | n.a. | 1,091,072,778 | 1,486,168,377 |
| 1970 | 9,920,190 | n.a. | 5,462,253 | 26,321,728 | 160,684,965 | 27,357,923 | 4,412,497 | n.a. | 1,340,201,160 | 1,809,055,741 |
| 1971 | 11,711,382 | n.a. | 6,093,105 | 28,953,900 | 227,254,451 | 32,638,609 | 5,065,484 | n.a. | 1,539,338,833 | 2,041,428,432 |
| 1972 | 16,389,201 | n.a. | 7,668,828 | 34,858,307 | 564,769,385 | 56,439,923 | 7,490,221 | n.a. | 2,112,267,807 | 2,789,117,553 |
| 1973 | 23,775,396 | n.a. | 11,988,722 | 47,713,977 | 560,681,275 | 70,124,471 | 10,528,706 | n.a. | 2,800,448,588 | 3,793,343,888 |
| 1974 | 26,122,282 | n.a. | 15,665,125 | 60,250,479 | 322,076,294 | 88,961,489 | 10,611,237 | n.a. | 3,135,623,800 | 4,295,483,216 |
| 1975 | 32,719,552 | n.a. | 19,767,433 | 85,204,451 | 1,041,194,916 | 92,404,547 | 15,984,137 | n.a. | 4,109,799,818 | 5,678,040,098 |

*Notes*: December financial year-end until 1921; then August year-end until 1935; December year-end from 1936 on. 1922 is thus an 8-month year and 1936 is a 16-month year. Accounts consolidated from 1959. Balance sheet figures have been derived, where relevant, from Hong Kong dollars at exchange rate quoted in the balance sheets. Dividends were declared in sterling until 1972. The 20,000 new shares issued in 1890 have been valued at same price as old shares. Market capitalization has been derived from the British share prices. n.a. = not available.

IMPERIAL BANK OF PERSIA/BRITISH BANK OF THE MIDDLE EAST

| Years | Published net profits | Real profits | Dividends paid (gross) | Paid-up capital | Market value: capital | Published reserves | Retained profits | Inner reserves | Deposits | Total balance sheet |
|---|---|---|---|---|---|---|---|---|---|---|
| 1890 | 62,249 | n.a. | 51,666 | 1,000,000 | 1,100,000 | 150,000 | 10,582 | n.a. | 113,025 | 1,789,427 |
| 1891 | 42,528 | n.a. | 50,000 | 1,000,000 | 725,000 | 150,000 | 3,110 | n.a. | 225,233 | 2,128,441 |
| 1892 | 64,814 | n.a. | 50,000 | 1,000,000 | 575,000 | 100,000 | 17,923 | n.a. | 356,120 | 2,081,234 |
| 1893 | 33,715 | n.a. | 50,000 | 1,000,000 | 425,000 | 100,000 | 1,639 | n.a. | 285,338 | 2,155,398 |
| 1894 | 24,384 | n.a. | 0 | 1,000,000 | 425,000 | 14,485 | 26,022 | n.a. | 269,162 | 1,930,261 |
| 1895 | 24,214 | n.a. | 35,000 | 650,000 | 325,000 | 56,287 | 1,236 | n.a. | 239,165 | 1,402,695 |
| 1896 | 40,616 | n.a. | 35,000 | 650,000 | 400,000 | 70,488 | 1,852 | n.a. | 225,878 | 1,940,021 |
| 1897 | 36,382 | n.a. | 35,000 | 650,000 | 350,000 | 63,494 | 3,234 | n.a. | 216,803 | 1,584,848 |
| 1898 | 33,958 | n.a. | 35,000 | 650,000 | 400,000 | 72,459 | 2,191 | n.a. | 219,677 | 2,035,416 |
| 1899 | 35,307 | n.a. | 35,000 | 650,000 | 400,000 | 72,459 | 2,498 | n.a. | 179,581 | 1,156,648 |
| 1900 | 46,490 | n.a. | 35,000 | 650,000 | 425,000 | 72,459 | 13,987 | n.a. | 280,758 | 1,377,616 |
| 1901 | 37,868 | n.a. | 35,000 | 650,000 | 425,000 | 80,000 | 9,314 | n.a. | 278,265 | 1,421,245 |
| 1902 | 49,138 | n.a. | 35,000 | 650,000 | 450,000 | 100,000 | 3,451 | n.a. | 282,390 | 1,520,174 |
| 1903 | 47,540 | n.a. | 35,000 | 650,000 | 500,000 | 100,000 | 15,992 | n.a. | 225,439 | 1,507,202 |
| 1904 | 49,784 | n.a. | 40,000 | 650,000 | 575,000 | 115,000 | 10,776 | n.a. | 410,519 | 1,897,674 |
| 1905 | 55,248 | n.a. | 40,000 | 650,000 | 675,000 | 130,000 | 11,024 | 15,273 | 426,118 | 1,986,386 |
| 1906 | 59,930 | 49,930 | 40,000 | 650,000 | 675,000 | 150,000 | 10,953 | 9,048 | 527,460 | 2,001,911 |
| 1907 | 67,262 | 92,262 | 40,000 | 650,000 | 625,000 | 175,000 | 12,000 | 36,051 | 549,048 | 2,189,027 |
| 1908 | 55,279 | 65,279 | 40,000 | 650,000 | 600,000 | 185,000 | 16,494 | 46,051 | 607,937 | 2,202,167 |
| 1909 | 47,985 | 45,944 | 40,000 | 650,000 | 625,000 | 185,000 | 24,479 | 48,095 | 686,541 | 2,448,734 |
| 1910 | 58,447 | 110,027 | 45,000 | 650,000 | 687,500 | 200,000 | 22,925 | 94,515 | 746,854 | 2,753,114 |
| 1911 | 64,501 | 86,898 | 50,000 | 650,000 | 700,000 | 210,000 | 27,426 | 118,117 | 775,792 | 3,057,848 |
| 1912 | 53,538 | 63,020 | 50,000 | 650,000 | 675,000 | 210,000 | 30,965 | 128,636 | 725,010 | 3,004,425 |

IMPERIAL BANK OF PERSIA/BRITISH BANK OF THE MIDDLE EAST (Cont.)

| Years | Published net profits | Real profits | Dividends paid (gross) | Paid-up capital | Market value: capital | Published reserves | Retained profits | Inner reserves | Deposits | Total balance sheet |
|---|---|---|---|---|---|---|---|---|---|---|
| 1913 | 51,149 | 52,886 | 50,000 | 650,000 | 712,500 | 210,000 | 32,114 | 127,085 | 905,995 | 3,305,029 |
| 1914 | 31,244 | 54,891 | 40,000 | 650,000 | 737,500 | 210,000 | 23,310 | 143,438 | 695,368 | 3,102,541 |
| 1915 | 25,749 | (98,633) | 30,000 | 650,000 | 518,750 | 150,000 | 19,108 | 70,369 | 703,199 | 2,486,124 |
| 1916 | 50,170 | 53,090 | 35,000 | 650,000 | 662,500 | 160,000 | 24,277 | 67,449 | 727,838 | 2,650,871 |
| 1917 | 79,962 | 105,148 | 40,000 | 650,000 | 775,000 | 190,000 | 24,240 | 92,635 | 1,187,774 | 4,350,337 |
| 1918 | 78,149 | 283,156 | 40,000 | 650,000 | 900,000 | 220,000 | 27,388 | 297,642 | 1,789,369 | 7,716,747 |
| 1919 | 75,421 | 176,221 | 40,000 | 650,000 | 1,075,000 | 250,000 | 27,809 | 245,084 | 2,830,065 | 10,076,809 |
| 1920 | 76,242 | 40,096 | 40,000 | 650,000 | 725,000 | 280,000 | 29,051 | 136,916 | 3,228,336 | 8,260,996 |
| 1921 | 82,904 | 286,754 | 40,000 | 650,000 | 500,000 | 310,000 | 31,955 | 293,777 | 2,805,375 | 7,172,370 |
| 1922 | 86,766 | 332,966 | 45,000 | 650,000 | 650,000 | 340,000 | 33,721 | 526,970 | 3,966,064 | 7,296,687 |
| 1923 | 135,832 | 406,924 | 70,000 | 650,000 | 750,000 | 390,000 | 34,552 | 710,197 | 4,198,905 | 8,348,277 |
| 1924 | 85,014 | 176,014 | 45,000 | 650,000 | 800,000 | 420,000 | 34,566 | 896,313 | 4,165,429 | 8,001,999 |
| 1925 | 129,402 | 273,023 | 50,000 | 650,000 | 900,000 | 470,000 | 33,968 | 755,464 | 3,916,722 | 9,682,404 |
| 1926 | 135,367 | 270,208 | 55,000 | 650,000 | 937,500 | 520,000 | 34,335 | 1,191,953 | 4,842,729 | 12,358,908 |
| 1927 | 135,312 | 140,429 | 55,000 | 650,000 | 1,075,000 | 570,000 | 34,646 | 1,123,464 | 6,483,396 | 14,332,495 |
| 1928 | 125,955 | 432,020 | 55,000 | 650,000 | 1,100,000 | 610,000 | 35,602 | 1,399,627 | 7,804,441 | 13,103,068 |
| 1929 | 124,279 | 160,102 | 65,000 | 650,000 | 975,000 | 650,000 | 44,831 | 1,508,335 | 6,176,015 | 10,244,844 |
| 1930 | 93,013 | 103,348 | 65,000 | 650,000 | 900,000 | 870,000 | 42,893 | 1,509,991 | 4,212,056 | 7,986,062 |
| 1931 | 88,194 | 117,956 | 65,000 | 650,000 | 650,000 | 890,000 | 46,087 | 1,214,304 | 2,895,227 | 7,060,454 |
| 1932 | 85,802 | 215,734 | 65,000 | 650,000 | 1,025,000 | 910,000 | 46,889 | 1,366,234 | 2,555,647 | 6,084,640 |
| 1933 | 77,169 | 140,696 | 65,000 | 650,000 | 1,387,500 | 920,000 | 49,058 | 1,434,773 | 2,730,969 | 6,726,924 |
| 1934 | 75,760 | 64,695 | 65,000 | 650,000 | 1,362,500 | 930,000 | 49,818 | 1,626,523 | 3,128,793 | 7,370,341 |

| Year | | | | | | | | | | |
|---|---|---|---|---|---|---|---|---|---|---|
| 1935 | 75,786 | 75,978 | 65,000 | 650,000 | 1,325,000 | 940,000 | 50,604 | 1,558,714 | 3,065,478 | 8,071,358 |
| 1936 | 77,430 | 74,811 | 65,000 | 1,000,000 | 1,575,000 | 750,000 | 53,034 | 1,411,208 | 3,587,911 | 7,922,584 |
| 1937 | 65,974 | 115,555 | 65,000 | 1,000,000 | 1,475,000 | 750,000 | 54,008 | 1,456,686 | 3,539,235 | 7,822,113 |
| 1938 | 92,922 | 47,783 | 90,000 | 1,000,000 | 1,075,000 | 750,000 | 56,930 | 1,449,995 | 3,740,552 | 7,735,514 |
| 1939 | 98,437 | 153,785 | 90,000 | 1,000,000 | 900,000 | 760,000 | 55,367 | 1,468,190 | 3,355,430 | 9,307,900 |
| 1940 | 97,440 | 128,133 | 90,000 | 1,000,000 | 1,025,000 | 800,000 | 62,807 | 1,471,462 | 4,544,830 | 8,717,329 |
| 1941 | 132,828 | 83,395 | 90,000 | 1,000,000 | 1,196,875 | 850,000 | 65,635 | 1,400,646 | 4,448,313 | 15,736,287 |
| 1942 | 140,500 | 165,742 | 90,000 | 1,000,000 | 1,168,750 | 900,000 | 66,135 | 1,443,233 | 9,507,949 | 23,571,815 |
| 1943 | 141,335 | 162,238 | 90,000 | 1,000,000 | 1,828,125 | 950,000 | 67,470 | 1,443,546 | 16,668,336 | 26,653,230 |
| 1944 | 145,287 | 244,530 | 90,000 | 1,000,000 | 1,757,500 | 980,000 | 72,757 | 1,543,914 | 20,233,362 | 29,692,864 |
| 1945 | 134,023 | 178,154 | 90,000 | 1,000,000 | 1,800,000 | 1,000,000 | 86,780 | 1,574,817 | 22,099,736 | 33,590,360 |
| 1946 | 138,305 | 222,742 | 90,000 | 1,000,000 | 1,575,000 | 1,050,000 | 115,085 | 1,605,700 | 23,728,923 | 36,842,838 |
| 1947 | 100,350 | 158,896 | 90,000 | 1,000,000 | 1,650,000 | 1,100,000 | 115,934 | 1,626,748 | 24,663,245 | 32,577,008 |
| 1948 | 105,411 | 194,502 | 90,000 | 1,000,000 | 1,400,000 | 1,150,000 | 121,845 | 1,682,485 | 23,032,799 | 34,396,659 |
| 1949 | 96,949 | 172,079 | 90,000 | 1,000,000 | 1,300,000 | 1,200,000 | 119,294 | 1,628,045 | 22,297,488 | 38,905,439 |
| 1950 | 108,089 | 108,657 | 90,000 | 1,000,000 | 1,175,000 | 1,250,000 | 129,383 | 1,608,775 | 26,995,960 | 51,541,500 |
| 1951 | 97,773 | 208,262 | 90,000 | 1,000,000 | 1,250,000 | 1,300,000 | 129,906 | 1,090,567 | 33,612,092 | 58,768,036 |
| 1952 | 105,295 | 447,239 | 100,000 | 1,000,000 | 1,650,000 | 1,350,000 | 130,951 | 1,656,261 | 45,765,466 | 49,811,993 |
| 1953 | 113,814 | 223,733 | 112,500 | 1,500,000 | 2,737,500 | 1,400,000 | 132,890 | 1,915,183 | 24,084,694 | 53,649,904 |
| 1954 | 189,380 | 320,380 | 150,000 | 1,500,000 | 2,587,500 | 1,800,000 | 137,520 | 2,102,400 | 43,158,575 | 65,803,314 |
| 1955 | 251,975 | 528,975 | 150,000 | 1,500,000 | 2,250,000 | 1,900,000 | 153,246 | 1,244,335 | 53,346,430 | 72,423,492 |
| 1956 | 254,213 | 759,213 | 150,000 | 1,500,000 | 2,500,000 | 2,100,000 | 171,209 | 1,457,760 | 57,980,118 | 69,815,229 |
| 1957 | 265,675 | 470,675 | 200,000 | 2,000,000 | 4,700,000 | 2,200,000 | 171,884 | 1,606,773 | 54,690,004 | 80,851,100 |
| 1958 | 331,179 | 826,179 | 300,000 | 2,000,000 | 7,800,000 | 2,200,000 | 174,938 | 2,077,115 | 64,170,097 | 93,004,016 |
| 1959 | 332,063 | 793,063 | 300,000 | 2,000,000 | | 2,300,000 | 173,251 | 2,572,861 | 74,079,687 | 92,881,986 |

*Notes*: September financial year-end until 1924. Thereafter, March financial year-end, i.e. 1925 refers to year ending March 1926. 1923 was an 18-month year since it ended in March 1924 instead of September 1923. Taken over by Hongkong and Shanghai Bank in 1960. n.a. = not available.

## IONIAN BANK

| Years | Published net profits | Real profits | Dividends paid (gross) | Paid-up capital | Market value: capital | Published reserves | Retained profits | Inner reserves | Deposits | Total balance sheet |
|---|---|---|---|---|---|---|---|---|---|---|
| 1890 | 18,797 | n.a. | 15,775 | 315,507 | 239,786 | 0 | 23,195 | n.a. | 296,626 | 1,149,096 |
| 1891 | 17,587 | n.a. | 15,775 | 315,507 | 227,165 | 0 | 25,007 | n.a. | 296,712 | 1,059,635 |
| 1892 | 16,287 | n.a. | 15,775 | 315,507 | 220,855 | 0 | 25,519 | n.a. | 208,601 | 984,704 |
| 1893 | 16,278 | n.a. | 15,775 | 315,507 | 145,133 | 0 | 26,022 | n.a. | 272,951 | 967,018 |
| 1894 | 13,194 | n.a. | 12,620 | 315,507 | 176,684 | 0 | 26,596 | n.a. | 247,981 | 897,831 |
| 1895 | 13,350 | n.a. | 12,620 | 315,507 | 164,064 | 0 | 27,326 | n.a. | 276,761 | 923,579 |
| 1896 | 13,586 | n.a. | 12,620 | 315,507 | 195,615 | 0 | 28,292 | n.a. | 279,341 | 949,430 |
| 1897 | 13,643 | n.a. | 12,620 | 315,507 | 189,305 | 0 | 29,315 | n.a. | 312,812 | 1,035,408 |
| 1898 | 13,601 | n.a. | 12,620 | 315,507 | 201,925 | 0 | 30,296 | n.a. | 340,413 | 1,078,449 |
| 1899 | 17,233 | n.a. | 15,775 | 315,507 | 214,545 | 0 | 31,754 | n.a. | 327,694 | 1,044,710 |
| 1900 | 16,926 | n.a. | 15,775 | 315,507 | 227,165 | 0 | 32,905 | 11,500 | 366,374 | 1,080,043 |
| 1901 | 16,698 | 20,144 | 15,775 | 315,507 | 258,716 | 0 | 33,828 | 24,800 | 533,844 | 1,231,328. |
| 1902 | 16,048 | 15,198 | 15,775 | 315,507 | 239,786 | 0 | 34,101 | 21,460 | 544,294 | 1,250,130 |
| 1903 | 16,548 | 24,262 | 15,775 | 315,507 | 277,647 | 0 | 34,874 | 21,483 | 509,604 | 1,153,539 |
| 1904 | 20,028 | 29,607 | 18,931 | 315,510 | 299,735 | 0 | 35,971 | 25,832 | 593,906 | 1,207,090 |
| 1905 | 19,680 | 23,763 | 18,931 | 315,510 | 331,286 | 0 | 36,720 | 22,671 | 667,482 | 1,275,897 |
| 1906 | 22,896 | 45,458 | 18,931 | 315,510 | 331,286 | 0 | 49,685 | 30,406 | 752,880 | 1,382,800 |
| 1907 | 19,871 | 26,019 | 18,931 | 315,510 | 315,510 | 0 | 41,625 | 37,049 | 1,008,541 | 1,703,201 |
| 1908 | 47,113 | 66,322 | 18,931 | 315,510 | 315,510 | 50,000 | 19,808 | 58,151 | 1,317,386 | 2,190,682 |
| 1909 | 38,813 | 58,022 | 18,931 | 315,510 | 331,286 | 100,000 | 10,938 | 65,735 | 1,676,682 | 2,664,400 |
| 1910 | 32,837 | 52,046 | 24,341 | 315,510 | 467,859 | 114,000 | 8,468 | 73,320 | 1,814,423 | 3,030,836 |
| 1911 | 22,942 | 42,151 | 28,568 | 393,552 | 509,859 | 65,000 | 2,842 | 80,904 | 1,910,902 | 2,874,833 |
| 1912 | 25,099 | 42,166 | 24,279 | 485,580 | 388,464 | 65,000 | 3,662 | 88,488 | 1,832,254 | 2,729,204 |
| 1913 | 24,434 | 41,350 | 24,279 | 485,580 | 388,464 | 65,000 | 3,817 | 106,141 | 2,164,602 | 3,062,842 |
| 1914 | 24,700 | 41,839 | 24,279 | 485,580 | 376,325 | 65,000 | 4,238 | 117,004 | 2,871,095 | 2,871,095 |
| 1915 | 25,594 | 66,139 | 24,279 | 485,580 | 339,906 | 65,000 | 5,553 | 132,769 | 3,047,705 | 3,942,684 |
| 1916 | 43,729 | 86,259 | 29,135 | 485,580 | 364,185 | 75,000 | 7,147 | 83,706 | 5,077,428 | 6,028,509 |
| 1917 | 72,885 | 124,435 | 33,991 | 485,580 | 437,022 | 85,000 | 9,134 | 107,142 | 5,936,105 | 9,571,862 |
| 1918 | 79,865 | 128,728 | 33,991 | 485,580 | 582,696 | 120,000 | 11,008 | 159,825 | 6,427,197 | 9,696,179 |
| 1919 | 39,289 | 39,555 | 33,991 | 485,580 | 631,254 | 125,000 | 11,307 | 83,722 | 6,557,284 | 11,977,231 |
| 1920 | 39,433 | 49,216 | 33,991 | 485,580 | 437,022 | 130,000 | 11,750 | 45,472 | 7,087,587 | 11,554,590 |
| 1921 | 59,021 | 116,110 | 33,991 | 485,580 | 388,464 | 150,000 | 11,781 | 204,501 | 9,782,562 | 15,698,413 |
| 1922 | 37,693 | 93,931 | 22,661 | 485,580 | 388,464 | 155,000 | 11,813 | 231,660 | 2,811,793 | 4,524,966 |

| Year | | | | | | | | | |
|---|---|---|---|---|---|---|---|---|---|
| 1923 | 49,644 | 73,493 | 33,991 | 485,580 | 388,464 | 170,000 | 12,467 | 252,656 | 2,783,582 | 5,013,835 |
| 1924 | 63,077 | 123,429 | 38,846 | 485,580 | 534,138 | 190,000 | 12,640 | 236,186 | 3,210,382 | 6,536,314 |
| 1925 | 69,399 | 107,380 | 38,846 | 587,845 | 720,000 | 220,000 | 13,193 | 194,251 | 3,111,725 | 6,111,763 |
| 1926 | 65,059 | 77,800 | 48,000 | 600,000 | 735,000 | 235,000 | 15,252 | 148,480 | 2,954,290 | 5,663,446 |
| 1927 | 61,080 | 72,513 | 48,000 | 600,000 | 810,000 | 250,000 | 13,331 | 142,688 | 3,707,594 | 6,115,400 |
| 1928 | 53,681 | 75,231 | 48,000 | 600,000 | 960,000 | 250,000 | 19,012 | 123,636 | 3,778,866 | 6,028,832 |
| 1929 | 48,046 | 78,276 | 42,000 | 600,000 | 660,000 | 250,000 | 25,058 | 127,620 | 3,849,297 | 5,776,203 |
| 1930 | 39,531 | 103,046 | 36,000 | 600,000 | 435,000 | 250,000 | 28,589 | 153,761 | 3,844,301 | 55,297,736 |
| 1931 | 47,114 | 48,129 | 12,000 | 600,000 | 180,000 | 200,000 | 8,703 | 218,411 | 3,413,071 | 4,908,344 |
| 1932 | 15,092 | 98,760 | 12,000 | 600,000 | 180,000 | 200,000 | 11,795 | 273,582 | 2,629,231 | 4,087,071 |
| 1933 | 14,730 | 33,325 | 12,000 | 600,000 | 240,000 | 200,000 | 14,525 | 234,335 | 2,592,677 | 3,910,412 |
| 1934 | 12,042 | 17,042 | 12,000 | 600,000 | 300,000 | 200,000 | 14,567 | 202,444 | 2,768,933 | 4,468,018 |
| 1935 | 12,079 | 12,682 | 12,000 | 600,000 | 255,000 | 200,000 | 14,646 | 188,640 | 3,269,850 | 4,325,163 |
| 1936 | 21,177 | 67,394 | 18,000 | 600,000 | 285,000 | 200,000 | 7,823 | 191,461 | 3,151,042 | 4,324,575 |
| 1937 | 16,639 | 33,252 | 15,000 | 600,000 | 270,000 | 200,000 | 9,462 | 167,065 | 3,511,320 | 4,601,583 |
| 1938 | 17,473 | 66,067 | 15,000 | 600,000 | 195,000 | 200,000 | 11,935 | 190,015 | 3,958,583 | 4,989,845 |
| 1939 | 19,111 | 68,919 | 18,000 | 600,000 | 210,000 | 200,000 | 13,406 | 156,900 | 3,970,940 | 5,914,237 |
| 1940 | 15,636 | 48,325 | 0 | 600,000 | 180,000 | 260,000 | 13,406 | 90,858 | 1,631,724 | 2,622,907 |
| 1941 | 18,164 | 34,828 | 0 | 600,000 | 187,500 | 260,000 | 13,406 | 106,082 | 2,370,702 | 3,539,036 |
| 1942 | 18,405 | 25,609 | 0 | 600,000 | 198,000 | 260,000 | 13,406 | 118,627 | 2,393,411 | 3,517,930 |
| 1943 | 26,519 | 55,604 | 18,000 | 600,000 | 285,000 | 275,000 | 6,565 | 142,830 | 3,930,602 | 5,138,201 |
| 1944 | 39,761 | 79,397 | 18,000 | 600,000 | 396,000 | 225,000 | 8,326 | 196,848 | 4,606,662 | 5,728,057 |
| 1945 | 43,525 | 74,408 | 18,000 | 600,000 | 426,750 | 225,000 | 8,851 | 112,012 | 5,646,479 | 6,538,444 |
| 1946 | 38,101 | 61,170 | 18,000 | 600,000 | 390,000 | 150,000 | 8,952 | 123,387 | 7,840,320 | 8,821,402 |
| 1947 | 39,470 | 70,331 | 18,000 | 600,000 | 375,000 | 150,000 | 10,422 | 227,007 | 6,996,677 | 8,027,956 |
| 1948 | 40,399 | 104,911 | 18,000 | 600,000 | 345,000 | 170,000 | 12,821 | 243,337 | 7,478,645 | 10,868,267 |
| 1949 | 44,722 | 86,311 | 18,000 | 600,000 | 276,000 | 179,000 | 14,543 | 236,518 | 9,326,873 | 13,556,849 |
| 1950 | 36,329 | 69,508 | 18,000 | 600,000 | 321,000 | 200,000 | 11,422 | 257,097 | 10,743,602 | 15,184,663 |
| 1951 | 35,580 | 64,836 | 18,000 | 600,000 | 339,000 | 200,000 | 12,552 | 294,500 | 12,617,253 | 18,813,514 |
| 1952 | 37,090 | 73,428 | 24,000 | 600,000 | 261,000 | 300,000 | 17,042 | 461,295 | 11,619,056 | 16,232,568 |
| 1953 | 36,335 | 48,389 | 24,000 | 600,000 | 435,000 | 300,000 | 20,177 | 445,258 | 9,810,838 | 13,408,353 |
| 1954 | 37,067 | 38,657 | 24,000 | 600,000 | 450,000 | 400,000 | 19,044 | 357,611 | 10,318,580 | 15,362,374 |
| 1955 | 37,450 | 84,070 | 24,000 | 600,000 | 465,000 | 400,000 | 22,694 | 404,714 | 11,229,695 | 16,695,546 |
| 1956 | 37,664 | 98,438 | 24,000 | 600,000 | 720,000 | 400,000 | 21,558 | 392,409 | 9,566,289 | 13,457,616 |
| 1957 | 40,593 | 85,593 | 27,000 | 600,000 | 1,440,000 | 500,000 | 21,626 | 602,318 | 2,227,022 | 3,412,840 |

*Notes*: Mid-January financial year-end until 1917, i.e. 1917 ends in mid-January 1918. Then, December year-end until 1921; August year-end until 1935 (1922 thus being an 8-month year), December year-end from 1936 on (1936 thus being a 16-month year). Ceased to be an overseas bank in 1957. n.a. = not available for inner reserves and real profits, and not applicable for published reserves.

## LLOYDS & NATIONAL PROVINCIAL FOREIGN BANK

| Years | Published net profits | Real profits | Dividends paid (gross) | Paid-up capital | Market value: capital | Published reserves | Retained profits | Inner reserves | Deposits | Total balance sheet |
|---|---|---|---|---|---|---|---|---|---|---|
| 1917 | 2,707 | 2,707 | 0 | 480,000 | 480,000 | 0 | 1,022 | n.a. | 5,248,437 | 5,860,604 |
| 1918 | 51,427 | 91,849 | 0 | 480,000 | 480,000 | 0 | 11,740 | n.a. | 7,206,601 | 8,077,995 |
| 1919 | 71,119 | 87,119 | 21,903 | 480,000 | 480,000 | 3,010 | 27,485 | n.a. | 21,687,022 | 22,942,153 |
| 1920 | 171,880 | 216,778 | 18,978 | 480,000 | 480,000 | 9,258 | 94,368 | n.a. | 21,193,420 | 22,647,704 |
| 1921 | 79,364 | 105,625 | 16,800 | 480,000 | 480,000 | 115,222 | 42,840 | 44,800 | 16,716,492 | 17,948,756 |
| 1922 | 67,197 | 60,581 | 18,000 | 480,000 | 480,000 | 114,348 | 67,006 | 123,633 | 12,730,261 | 14,172,027 |
| 1923 | 42,599 | 45,137 | 18,600 | 480,000 | 480,000 | 110,757 | 87,352 | 202,465 | 11,126,403 | 12,937,763 |
| 1924 | 102,706 | 118,661 | 18,600 | 480,000 | 480,000 | 161,311 | 70,899 | 15,955 | 9,437,780 | 11,120,914 |
| 1925 | 80,739 | 79,416 | 19,200 | 480,000 | 480,000 | 157,587 | 62,265 | 34,764 | 8,568,125 | 10,146,345 |
| 1926 | 105,034 | 115,034 | 19,200 | 480,000 | 480,000 | 208,052 | 56,673 | 53,573 | 9,665,755 | 11,420,098 |
| 1927 | 29,942 | 120,085 | 19,200 | 480,000 | 480,000 | 207,954 | 55,720 | 72,382 | 10,599,069 | 12,585,319 |
| 1928 | 74,933 | 104,933 | 26,400 | 840,000 | 840,000 | 225,000 | 54,720 | 91,191 | 10,079,165 | 12,981,650 |
| 1929 | 84,898 | 96,142 | 46,200 | 1,200,000 | 1,200,000 | 250,000 | 56,146 | 110,000 | 9,605,767 | 13,095,061 |
| 1930 | (14,655) | (114,655) | 0 | 1,200,000 | 1,200,000 | 150,000 | 28,261 | 90,294 | 10,272,003 | 12,895,646 |
| 1931 | (22,874) | (54,744) | 0 | 1,200,000 | 1,200,000 | 150,000 | 5,387 | 70,587 | 13,108,565 | 15,372,790 |
| 1932 | 17,543 | (11,483) | 0 | 1,200,000 | 1,200,000 | 150,000 | 6,213 | 48,852 | 12,887,668 | 15,154,670 |
| 1933 | 8,244 | 2,833 | 0 | 1,200,000 | 1,200,000 | 150,000 | 14,457 | 50,471 | 11,873,373 | 14,747,664 |
| 1934 | 8,058 | 14,107 | 0 | 1,200,000 | 1,200,000 | 150,000 | 22,514 | 59,571 | 13,000,938 | 15,761,489 |

| Year | | | | | | | | | | |
|------|------|------|------|-----------|-----------|---------|---------|---------|------------|------------|
| 1935 | (15,682) | (165,682) | 0 | 1,200,000 | 1,200,000 | 150,000 | 6,833 | 64,103 | 12,376,664 | 16,333,233 |
| 1936 | 12,101 | 12,101 | (1,500,000) | 1,200,000 | 1,200,000 | 150,000 | 18,934 | 269,803 | 13,772,459 | 17,427,861 |
| 1937 | 6,910 | (50,403) | 0 | 1,200,000 | 1,200,000 | 150,000 | 25,844 | 334,319 | 14,885,387 | 18,158,416 |
| 1938 | 4,117 | 276,225 | 0 | 1,200,000 | 1,200,000 | 150,000 | 29,961 | 410,034 | 11,798,367 | 15,189,264 |
| 1939 | (26,225) | 23,121 | 0 | 1,200,000 | 1,200,000 | 150,000 | 3,736 | 373,940 | 11,904,179 | 14,830,135 |
| 1940 | 8,535 | 23,121 | 0 | 1,200,000 | 1,200,000 | 150,000 | 12,272 | 337,845 | 4,022,537 | 7,250,917 |
| 1941 | 57,979 | 23,121 | 0 | 1,200,000 | 1,200,000 | 150,000 | 70,250 | 335,172 | 4,379,893 | 7,656,625 |
| 1942 | 30,903 | 23,121 | 0 | 1,200,000 | 1,200,000 | 150,000 | 101,153 | 333,172 | 4,272,324 | 7,592,131 |
| 1943 | 50,343 | 23,121 | 0 | 1,200,000 | 1,200,000 | 150,000 | 151,496 | 331,172 | 4,551,553 | 7,956,094 |
| 1944 | 24,270 | 23,121 | 0 | 1,200,000 | 1,200,000 | 150,000 | 175,766 | 329,910 | 4,715,335 | 8,433,164 |
| 1945 | 49,102 | 49,102 | 0 | 1,200,000 | 1,200,000 | 150,000 | 78,792 | 351,871 | 12,514,921 | 14,844,477 |
| 1946 | 19,771 | 85,089 | 30,000 | 1,200,000 | 1,200,000 | 150,000 | 82,563 | 373,831 | 15,831,431 | 19,988,150 |
| 1947 | 15,460 | 80,310 | 0 | 1,200,000 | 1,200,000 | 150,000 | 100,736 | 395,792 | 15,861,937 | 20,189,759 |
| 1948 | 29,037 | 80,372 | 0 | 1,200,000 | 1,200,000 | 150,000 | 129,773 | 417,753 | 15,109,613 | 20,257,992 |
| 1949 | 26,320 | 101,715 | 0 | 1,200,000 | 1,200,000 | 150,000 | 156,093 | 439,714 | 17,738,260 | 24,180,141 |
| 1950 | 27,483 | 65,514 | 0 | 1,200,000 | 1,200,000 | 150,000 | 183,576 | 461,674 | 18,375,630 | 25,029,517 |
| 1951 | 34,556 | 74,427 | 0 | 1,200,000 | 1,200,000 | 150,000 | 218,132 | 483,635 | 20,218,832 | 26,822,446 |
| 1952 | 34,884 | 85,174 | 0 | 1,200,000 | 1,200,000 | 150,000 | 253,016 | 577,423 | 20,069,884 | 24,426,315 |
| 1953 | 28,670 | 41,240 | 0 | 1,200,000 | 1,200,000 | 150,000 | 281,686 | 671,212 | 21,534,734 | 26,246,737 |
| 1954 | 63,662 | 116,430 | 0 | 1,200,000 | 1,200,000 | 150,000 | 145,348 | 765,000 | 21,755,788 | 26,598,949 |
| 1955 | 51,425 | n.a. | 0 | 1,200,000 | 1,200,000 | 212,716 | 134,057 | 382,500 | 22,339,463 | 27,654,951 |

*Notes*: December financial year-end. Shares not traded, so market capitalization is taken at par value of the shares. Some inner reserve figures estimated on basis of neighbouring years. Large negative figure under Dividends for 1936 indicates 'rescue funds' provided by parent. n.a. = not available; n.q. = not quoted.

# LONDON & BRAZILIAN BANK

| Years | Published net profits | Real profits | Dividends paid (gross) | Paid-up capital | Market value: capital | Published reserves | Retained profits | Inner reserves | Deposits | Total balance sheet |
|---|---|---|---|---|---|---|---|---|---|---|
| 1890 | 149,790 | n.a. | 87,500 | 625,000 | 1,250,000 | 360,000 | 29,545 | n.a. | 3,518,032 | 12,119,255 |
| 1891 | 206,712 | n.a. | 98,750 | 750,000 | 1,162,500 | 450,000 | 87,507 | n.a. | 4,176,631 | 10,895,007 |
| 1892 | 168,472 | n.a. | 105,000 | 750,000 | 1,162,500 | 500,000 | 150,979 | n.a. | 3,806,021 | 10,216,543 |
| 1893 | 185,429 | n.a. | 105,000 | 750,000 | 1,087,500 | 500,000 | 231,408 | n.a. | 4,505,619 | 10,344,765 |
| 1894 | 174,006 | n.a. | 105,000 | 750,000 | 1,350,000 | 500,000 | 200,414 | n.a. | 2,352,731 | 8,775,355 |
| 1895 | 134,861 | n.a. | 105,000 | 750,000 | 1,500,000 | 600,000 | 146,941 | n.a. | 2,535,733 | 8,272,898 |
| 1896 | 122,397 | n.a. | 105,000 | 750,000 | 1,387,500 | 600,000 | 164,339 | n.a. | 2,621,276 | 8,597,155 |
| 1897 | 120,450 | n.a. | 75,000 | 750,000 | 1,350,000 | 600,000 | 163,067 | n.a. | 2,267,018 | 8,351,635 |
| 1898 | 105,610 | n.a. | 105,000 | 750,000 | 1,425,000 | 600,000 | 163,676 | n.a. | 2,469,797 | 8,780,174 |
| 1899 | 116,201 | n.a. | 105,000 | 750,000 | 1,425,000 | 600,000 | 164,877 | n.a. | 2,785,912 | 9,436,011 |
| 1900 | 78,894 | n.a. | 105,000 | 750,000 | 1,462,500 | 600,000 | 138,771 | n.a. | 3,706,808 | 10,108,070 |
| 1901 | 36,828 | n.a. | 75,000 | 750,000 | 1,462,500 | 600,000 | 100,599 | n.a. | 4,153,846 | 10,956,502 |
| 1902 | 81,328 | n.a. | 75,000 | 750,000 | 1,275,000 | 600,000 | 100,825 | n.a. | 3,935,982 | 9,753,420 |
| 1903 | 95,941 | n.a. | 75,000 | 750,000 | 1,200,000 | 600,000 | 108,766 | n.a. | 3,860,249 | 10,316,858 |
| 1904 | 135,537 | n.a. | 93,750 | 750,000 | 1,293,750 | 600,000 | 100,553 | n.a. | 3,523,523 | 11,842,144 |

| Year | | | | | | | | | | |
|---|---|---|---|---|---|---|---|---|---|---|
| 1905 | 183,075 | n.a. | 112,500 | 750,000 | 1,612,500 | 650,000 | 100,123 | n.a. | 3,775,800 | 12,046,509 |
| 1906 | 208,738 | n.a. | 112,500 | 750,000 | 1,818,750 | 700,000 | 100,366 | n.a. | 4,723,175 | 13,523,750 |
| 1907 | 240,111 | n.a. | 150,000 | 1,000,000 | 2,150,000 | 760,000 | 100,477 | n.a. | 4,290,029 | 12,247,844 |
| 1908 | 239,075 | n.a. | 150,000 | 1,000,000 | 2,450,000 | 1,000,000 | 150,552 | n.a. | 4,873,913 | 13,187,927 |
| 1909 | 240,019 | n.a. | 150,000 | 1,000,000 | 2,750,000 | 1,000,000 | 209,071 | n.a. | 5,706,836 | 15,791,218 |
| 1910 | 272,688 | n.a. | 170,000 | 1,000,000 | 3,300,000 | 1,000,000 | 269,759 | n.a. | 7,096,954 | 18,355,117 |
| 1911 | 308,219 | n.a. | 220,000 | 1,000,000 | 3,300,000 | 1,000,000 | 269,978 | n.a. | 8,576,019 | 20,440,664 |
| 1912 | 378,615 | n.a. | 250,000 | 1,250,000 | 4,250,000 | 1,050,000 | 273,593 | n.a. | 8,721,511 | 22,307,654 |
| 1913 | 341,562 | n.a. | 250,000 | 1,250,000 | 3,625,000 | 1,400,000 | 290,155 | n.a. | 8,739,248 | 22,312,586 |
| 1914 | 193,785 | n.a. | 187,500 | 1,250,000 | 3,687,500 | 1,400,000 | 296,440 | n.a. | 8,359,736 | 19,507,871 |
| 1915 | 201,131 | n.a. | 200,000 | 1,250,000 | 3,062,500 | 1,400,000 | 297,571 | n.a. | 8,489,897 | 18,840,689 |
| 1916 | 201,279 | n.a. | 200,000 | 1,250,000 | 2,562,500 | 1,400,000 | 298,850 | n.a. | 8,602,124 | 19,233,297 |
| 1917 | 238,536 | n.a. | 200,000 | 1,250,000 | 2,875,000 | 1,400,000 | 300,386 | n.a. | 9,368,265 | 19,227,589 |
| 1918 | 307,172 | n.a. | 225,000 | 1,250,000 | 3,625,000 | 1,400,000 | 332,558 | n.a. | 12,313,674 | 22,837,010 |
| 1919 | 363,061 | n.a. | 270,000 | 1,500,000 | 3,900,000 | 1,400,000 | 505,619 | n.a. | 13,040,959 | 26,660,866 |
| 1920 | 306,028 | n.a. | 270,000 | 1,500,000 | 3,150,000 | 1,500,000 | 511,647 | n.a. | 18,031,324 | 37,976,717 |
| 1921 | 211,976 | n.a. | 210,000 | 1,500,000 | 3,225,000 | 1,500,000 | 498,623 | n.a. | 20,030,777 | 35,143,845 |
| 1922 | 41,353 | n.a. | 150,000 | 1,500,000 | 3,000,000 | 1,500,000 | 189,976 | n.a. | 19,684,399 | 34,655,903 |

*Notes*: January financial year-end, i.e. 1890 ends on 31 January 1891. Amalgamated with London and River Plate Bank in 1923 to form Bank of London and South American (see Bolsa). n.a. = not available.

LONDON & TARAPACA/ANGLO-SOUTH AMERICAN BANK

| Years | Published net profits | Real profits | Dividends paid (gross) | Paid-up capital | Market value: capital | Published reserves | Retained profits | Inner reserves | Deposits | Total balance sheet |
|---|---|---|---|---|---|---|---|---|---|---|
| 1889/90 | 33,905 | n.a. | 25,000 | 500,000 | 550,000 | 10,000 | 1,384 | n.a. | 131,747 | 1,205,865 |
| 1890/1 | (5,914) | n.a. | 0 | 500,000 | 300,000 | 10,000 | (4,530) | n.a. | 376,259 | 1,153,178 |
| 1891/2 | 60,649 | n.a. | 25,000 | 500,000 | 350,000 | 10,000 | 4,198 | n.a. | 392,049 | 1,433,955 |
| 1892/3 | 25,978 | n.a. | 25,000 | 500,000 | 300,000 | 30,000 | 5,176 | n.a. | 429,355 | 1,479,843 |
| 1893/4 | 12,941 | n.a. | 12,500 | 500,000 | 225,000 | 30,000 | 5,618 | n.a. | 736,339 | 2,014,078 |
| 1894/5 | 33,654 | n.a. | 25,000 | 500,000 | 225,000 | 30,000 | 4,272 | n.a. | 680,928 | 2,144,397 |
| 1895/6 | 28,260 | n.a. | 25,000 | 500,000 | 225,000 | 40,000 | 7,531 | n.a. | 696,316 | 2,112,183 |
| 1896/7 | 21,630 | n.a. | 25,000 | 500,000 | 312,500 | 40,000 | 4,160 | n.a. | 596,300 | 1,778,248 |
| 1897/8 | 34,967 | n.a. | 25,000 | 500,000 | 325,000 | 40,000 | 14,126 | n.a. | 743,035 | 2,326,342 |
| 1898/9 | 15,965 | n.a. | 25,000 | 500,000 | 300,000 | 40,000 | 5,091 | n.a. | 1,262,570 | 2,665,760 |
| 1899/1900 | 72,126 | n.a. | 30,000 | 500,000 | 375,000 | 40,000 | 7,217 | n.a. | 1,201,599 | 2,642,243 |
| 1900/1 | 68,080 | n.a. | 48,125 | 750,000 | 750,000 | 135,000 | 9,646 | n.a. | 1,546,811 | 3,804,860 |
| 1901/2 | 77,038 | n.a. | 45,000 | 750,000 | 675,000 | 150,000 | 9,684 | n.a. | 2,085,264 | 4,906,003 |
| 1902/3 | 89,684 | n.a. | 45,000 | 750,000 | 750,000 | 175,000 | 16,559 | n.a. | 2,207,518 | 4,738,854 |
| 1903/4 | 91,773 | n.a. | 45,000 | 750,000 | 731,250 | 200,000 | 10,331 | n.a. | 2,489,532 | 5,031,298 |
| 1904/5 | 111,277 | n.a. | 45,000 | 750,000 | 918,750 | 250,000 | 18,608 | n.a. | 3,561,150 | 7,220,538 |
| 1905/6 | 165,457 | n.a. | 52,500 | 750,000 | 1,143,750 | 300,000 | 27,965 | n.a. | 5,465,062 | 10,637,299 |
| 1906/7 | 278,017 | n.a. | 67,500 | 950,000 | 2,312,500 | 500,000 | 38,193 | n.a. | 5,836,625 | 14,245,011 |
| 1907/8 | 166,146 | n.a. | 112,500 | 1,250,000 | 1,562,500 | 700,000 | 43,505 | n.a. | 4,894,199 | 11,092,991 |
| 1908/9 | 181,559 | n.a. | 118,750 | 1,250,000 | 1,781,250 | 750,000 | 44,299 | n.a. | 5,227,119 | 11,164,846 |
| 1909/10 | 178,563 | n.a. | 125,000 | 1,250,000 | 2,000,000 | 800,000 | 48,479 | n.a. | 5,394,020 | 11,993,277 |
| 1910/11 | 206,728 | n.a. | 125,000 | 1,250,000 | 2,000,000 | 830,000 | 49,117 | n.a. | 6,598,768 | 13,992,984 |

| | | | | | | | | | |
|---|---|---|---|---|---|---|---|---|---|
| 1911/12 | 253,012 | n.a. | 150,000 | 1,250,000 | 2,062,500 | 850,000 | 40,798 | n.a. | 6,397,040 | 14,526,953 |
| 1912/13 | 320,364 | n.a. | 255,600 | 2,130,000 | 4,106,250 | 1,440,000 | 49,001 | n.a. | 7,182,224 | 19,017,495 |
| 1913/14 | 279,055 | n.a. | 225,000 | 2,250,000 | 3,712,500 | 1,400,000 | 110,164 | n.a. | 7,786,613 | 19,829,841 |
| 1914/15 | 269,286 | n.a. | 180,000 | 2,250,000 | 3,262,500 | 1,400,000 | 133,888 | n.a. | 7,956,289 | 16,993,840 |
| 1915/16 | 257,898 | n.a. | 202,500 | 2,250,000 | 2,587,500 | 1,400,000 | 140,786 | n.a. | 9,076,322 | 18,591,832 |
| 1916/17 | 320,031 | n.a. | 225,000 | 2,250,000 | 2,756,250 | 1,400,000 | 154,966 | n.a. | 14,114,982 | 25,659,835 |
| 1917/18 | 451,690 | n.a. | 281,250 | 2,250,000 | 3,318,750 | 1,600,000 | 188,887 | n.a. | 27,275,473 | 42,602,652 |
| 1918/19 | 520,082 | n.a. | 337,500 | 2,250,000 | 4,556,250 | 1,750,000 | 241,619 | n.a. | 41,829,904 | 61,279,123 |
| 1919/20 | 1,024,155 | n.a. | 654,678 | 4,364,520 | 9,601,944 | 3,850,000 | 393,115 | n.a. | 58,458,171 | 98,276,852 |
| 1920/1 | 743,175 | n.a. | 655,005 | 4,366,700 | 7,423,390 | 4,000,000 | 402,785 | n.a. | 49,823,164 | 83,046,572 |
| 1921/2 | 552,268 | n.a. | 524,025 | 4,366,875 | 7,642,031 | 4,000,000 | 256,685 | n.a. | 45,467,069 | 73,434,597 |
| 1922/3 | 436,257 | n.a. | 436,733 | 4,367,330 | 7,096,911 | 4,000,000 | 337,662 | n.a. | 47,809,274 | 76,324,498 |
| 1923/4 | 425,907 | n.a. | 436,733 | 4,367,330 | 6,223,445 | 4,000,000 | 350,100 | n.a. | 45,567,205 | 73,217,108 |
| 1924/5 | 431,022 | n.a. | 436,733 | 4,367,330 | 6,878,545 | 4,000,000 | 414,925 | n.a. | 42,551,755 | 69,258,599 |
| 1925/6 | 471,714 | n.a. | 436,733 | 4,367,330 | 6,278,037 | 4,000,000 | 375,025 | n.a. | 34,824,312 | 61,967,918 |
| 1926/7 | 474,270 | n.a. | 436,733 | 4,367,330 | 6,005,079 | 3,232,309 | 454,810 | n.a. | 39,079,271 | 64,201,505 |
| 1927/8 | 480,440 | n.a. | 436,733 | 4,367,330 | 6,823,953 | 3,256,422 | 507,172 | n.a. | 49,341,126 | 76,449,705 |
| 1928/9 | 480,716 | n.a. | 436,733 | 4,367,330 | 6,987,728 | 3,356,604 | 507,902 | n.a. | 50,363,213 | 79,970,393 |
| 1929/30 | 491,408 | n.a. | 563,267 | 5,632,670 | 6,873,666 | 3,382,412 | 207,150 | n.a. | 49,814,504 | 81,166,390 |
| 1930/1 | 461,384 | n.a. | 337,960 | 5,632,670 | 4,999,030 | 3,408,466 | 153,070 | (4,500,000) | 40,639,615 | 70,707,814 |
| 1931/2 | 465,892 | n.a. | 0 | 6,632,670 | 3,249,370 | 71,713 | 158,962 | n.a. | 25,563,797 | 40,927,878 |
| 1932/3 | 63,362 | n.a. | 0 | 6,632,670 | (125,000) | 95,864 | 158,962 | n.a. | 28,428,725 | 42,360,033 |
| 1933/4 | 60,783 | n.a. | 0 | 6,632,670 | 4,750,000 | 70,065 | 158,962 | n.a. | 24,585,280 | 38,519,012 |
| 1934/5 | 37,018 | n.a. | 0 | 6,632,670 | 0 | 57,946 | 158,962 | n.a. | 22,796,474 | 35,385,135 |

*Notes*: June financial year-end, so 1890/91 ends 30 June 1891. Share price is that of the previous December; i.e. share price for 1890/1 is that for December 1890. The 1930/1 figure for inner reserves (£4,500,000) indicates the amount of the 'rescue fund' provided for the bank by the Bank of England's consortium. Taken over by Bolsa in 1936. n.a. = not available.

LONDON & RIVER PLATE BANK

| Years | Published net profits | Real profits | Dividends paid (gross) | Paid-up capital | Market value: capital | Published reserves | Retained profits | Inner reserves | Deposits | Total balance sheet |
|---|---|---|---|---|---|---|---|---|---|---|
| 1890 | 351,678 | n.a. | 112,500 | 750,000 | 1,800,000 | 600,000 | 33,079 | n.a. | 7,998,678 | 12,361,335 |
| 1891 | 124,657 | n.a. | 82,500 | 900,000 | 1,620,000 | 700,000 | 25,236 | n.a. | 4,937,025 | 8,554,496 |
| 1892 | 167,953 | n.a. | 112,500 | 900,000 | 1,980,000 | 750,000 | 20,689 | n.a. | 8,541,840 | 13,654,353 |
| 1893 | 174,051 | n.a. | 112,500 | 900,000 | 2,016,000 | 800,000 | 32,240 | n.a. | 9,844,699 | 15,924,764 |
| 1894 | 181,521 | n.a. | 135,000 | 900,000 | 2,304,000 | 850,000 | 23,761 | 463,096 | 9,694,605 | 18,007,648 |
| 1895 | 200,916 | 235,195 | 144,000 | 900,000 | 2,700,000 | 900,000 | 24,957 | 302,295 | 9,877,788 | 17,526,321 |
| 1896 | 217,447 | 259,447 | 162,000 | 900,000 | 3,168,000 | 950,000 | 25,404 | 342,437 | 12,154,319 | 19,849,612 |
| 1897 | 210,477 | 243,477 | 180,000 | 900,000 | 3,492,000 | 1,000,000 | 50,881 | 303,469 | 12,131,161 | 20,932,444 |
| 1898 | 197,053 | 252,053 | 180,000 | 900,000 | 3,780,000 | 1,000,000 | 52,934 | 328,934 | 13,056,547 | 21,534,010 |
| 1899 | 197,494 | 242,494 | 180,000 | 900,000 | 3,816,000 | 1,000,000 | 55,428 | 372,760 | 14,702,444 | 23,343,029 |
| 1900 | 197,652 | 227,652 | 180,000 | 900,000 | 3,636,000 | 1,000,000 | 58,081 | 408,512 | 17,837,623 | 28,703,022 |
| 1901 | 168,008 | 208,008 | 180,000 | 900,000 | 3,564,000 | 1,000,000 | 41,089 | 382,183 | 15,179,273 | 24,484,033 |
| 1902 | 161,068 | 188,069 | 162,000 | 900,000 | 3,528,000 | 1,000,000 | 40,157 | 312,726 | 15,781,648 | 24,687,371 |
| 1903 | 164,211 | 199,211 | 162,000 | 900,000 | 3,420,000 | 1,000,000 | 37,368 | 350,670 | 15,617,420 | 24,751,566 |
| 1904 | 182,887 | 242,887 | 171,000 | 900,000 | 3,492,000 | 1,000,000 | 34,225 | 395,376 | 16,829,429 | 25,996,893 |

| | | | | | | | | | |
|---|---|---|---|---|---|---|---|---|---|
| 1905 | 225,070 | 325,069 | 180,000 | 900,000 | 3,816,000 | 1,000,000 | 44,325 | 445,515 | 17,705,670 | 28,091,257 |
| 1906 | 290,619 | 365,619 | 180,000 | 900,000 | 4,536,000 | 1,000,000 | 44,944 | 524,692 | 19,431,126 | 28,582,104 |
| 1907 | 331,637 | 401,637 | 180,000 | 1,200,000 | 4,000,000 | 1,100,000 | 74,497 | 638,705 | 18,052,386 | 28,221,973 |
| 1908 | 368,894 | 428,894 | 240,000 | 1,200,000 | 4,680,000 | 1,200,000 | 78,391 | 638,705 | 16,128,920 | 26,689,016 |
| 1909 | 345,589 | 385,589 | 240,000 | 1,200,000 | 4,880,000 | 1,300,000 | 158,980 | 663,059 | 18,611,671 | 30,937,050 |
| 1910 | 360,773 | 390,772 | 240,000 | 1,200,000 | 4,840,000 | 1,300,000 | 229,753 | 652,059 | 21,144,694 | 35,570,072 |
| 1911 | 391,597 | 421,597 | 240,000 | 1,200,000 | 4,720,000 | 1,300,000 | 231,350 | 714,229 | 21,371,692 | 35,651,052 |
| 1912 | 477,778 | 504,611 | 312,000 | 1,800,000 | 6,480,000 | 2,000,000 | 273,962 | 745,410 | 21,622,723 | 38,193,519 |
| 1913 | 422,227 | 632,226 | 360,000 | 1,800,000 | 5,880,000 | 2,000,000 | 306,189 | 757,970 | 21,977,918 | 39,829,819 |
| 1914 | 238,970 | 464,268 | 270,000 | 1,800,000 | 5,880,000 | 2,000,000 | 275,175 | 484,000 | 19,039,636 | 32,392,385 |
| 1915 | 222,516 | 299,148 | 270,000 | 1,800,000 | 4,410,000 | 2,000,000 | 260,975 | 450,558 | 20,581,475 | 34,183,577 |
| 1916 | 183,782 | 267,777 | 270,000 | 1,800,000 | 4,020,000 | 2,000,000 | 228,758 | 454,265 | 20,369,465 | 33,232,603 |
| 1917 | 334,599 | 334,599 | 270,000 | 1,800,000 | 4,380,000 | 2,000,000 | 293,357 | 461,690 | 24,375,354 | 37,514,307 |
| 1918 | 400,394 | 416,310 | 270,000 | 1,800,000 | 4,560,000 | 2,000,000 | 323,751 | 455,696 | 30,515,335 | 44,040,165 |
| 1919 | 505,574 | 549,301 | 270,000 | 1,800,000 | 4,560,000 | 2,100,000 | 319,325 | 419,509 | 36,823,491 | 53,783,857 |
| 1920 | 534,815 | 650,194 | 306,000 | 2,040,000 | 4,560,000 | 2,100,000 | 318,140 | 629,236 | 37,923,129 | 60,376,460 |
| 1921 | 404,184 | 444,632 | 244,800 | 2,040,000 | 4,560,000 | 2,100,000 | 317,524 | 160,000 | 30,686,098 | 46,854,000 |
| 1922 | 107,468 | 96,730 | 204,000 | 2,040,000 | 4,560,000 | 2,100,000 | 220,992 | n.a. | 27,581,911 | 43,143,143 |
| 1923 | 162,916 | 162,917 | 163,200 | 2,040,000 | 6,000,000 | 2,100,000 | 220,709 | n.a. | 24,906,959 | 43,478,815 |

*Notes*: September financial year-end. No share quotation 1918–23; share prices estimated on basis of share price offered by Lloyds Bank when the bank was taken over by Lloyds in 1918. n.a. = not available.

BOLSA

| Years | Published net profits | Real profits | Dividends paid (gross) | Paid-up capital | Market value: capital | Published reserves | Retained profits | Inner reserves | Deposits | Total balance sheet |
|---|---|---|---|---|---|---|---|---|---|---|
| 1924 | 415,708 | n.a. | 414,000 | 3,540,000 | 6,460,500 | 3,600,000 | 412,393 | 193,352 | 45,002,048 | 79,113,444 |
| 1925 | 454,307 | 914,308 | 389,400 | 3,540,000 | 7,080,000 | 3,600,000 | 411,300 | 413,352 | 46,363,571 | 79,096,487 |
| 1926 | 449,924 | 549,924 | 389,400 | 3,540,000 | 7,080,000 | 3,600,000 | 390,605 | 373,235 | 40,387,433 | 68,953,725 |
| 1927 | 460,025 | 502,304 | 389,400 | 3,540,000 | 7,434,000 | 3,000,000 | 201,231 | 334,235 | 37,956,766 | 64,636,229 |
| 1928 | 456,997 | 456,997 | 389,400 | 3,540,000 | 7,699,500 | 3,000,000 | 208,828 | 417,545 | 38,734,743 | 65,144,927 |
| 1929 | 435,145 | 360,012 | 389,400 | 3,540,000 | 6,460,500 | 3,000,000 | 209,573 | 500,856 | 41,061,295 | 68,862,647 |
| 1930 | 390,472 | 44,174 | 318,600 | 3,540,000 | 4,956,000 | 3,000,000 | 181,445 | 584,166 | 39,431,736 | 62,752,294 |
| 1931 | 331,898 | (713,898) | 177,000 | 3,540,000 | 3,540,000 | 1,500,000 | 186,343 | 2,084,166 | 34,380,596 | 52,252,731 |
| 1932 | 312,108 | (419,839) | 106,200 | 3,540,000 | 2,478,000 | 1,500,000 | 192,251 | 2,284,166 | 41,437,183 | 56,722,692 |
| 1933 | 337,379 | (249,688) | 106,200 | 3,540,000 | 3,186,000 | 1,500,000 | 193,430 | 2,514,166 | 42,807,816 | 57,854,312 |
| 1934 | 276,331 | 457,564 | 106,200 | 3,540,000 | 3,274,500 | 1,500,000 | 163,561 | 2,714,166 | 31,431,704 | 46,865,302 |
| 1935 | 209,913 | 364,608 | 106,200 | 3,540,000 | 3,009,000 | 2,000,000 | 167,274 | 2,014,166 | 28,325,298 | 43,016,447 |
| 1936 | 252,851 | 328,253 | 106,200 | 4,040,000 | 5,757,000 | 2,000,000 | 168,925 | 2,471,549 | 55,505,375 | 74,749,291 |
| 1937 | 462,076 | 797,583 | 202,000 | 4,040,000 | 4,545,000 | 2,000,000 | 169,000 | 2,723,391 | 58,340,328 | 79,678,893 |
| 1938 | 466,477 | 665,604 | 202,000 | 4,040,000 | 3,838,000 | 2,000,000 | 173,476 | 2,723,391 | 56,322,642 | 76,361,018 |
| 1939 | 472,287 | 515,859 | 202,000 | 4,040,000 | 4,242,000 | 2,000,000 | 173,763 | 2,993,391 | 60,531,234 | 81,068,532 |
| 1940 | 535,564 | 910,831 | 202,000 | 4,040,000 | 4,141,000 | 2,000,000 | 177,327 | 3,323,391 | 55,403,249 | 77,718,069 |
| 1941 | 597,286 | 605,875 | 242,400 | 4,040,000 | 4,949,000 | 2,000,000 | 177,213 | 3,678,391 | 60,505,077 | 81,682,731 |
| 1942 | 636,546 | 880,860 | 242,400 | 4,040,000 | 5,681,250 | 2,000,000 | 176,358 | 4,073,391 | 71,955,551 | 92,913,975 |
| 1943 | 655,475 | 943,396 | 242,400 | 4,040,000 | 6,893,250 | 2,000,000 | 179,434 | 4,132,158 | 93,403,904 | 115,174,352 |
| 1944 | 647,108 | 908,968 | 242,400 | 4,040,000 | 6,868,000 | 2,000,000 | 180,141 | 4,190,924 | 108,314,953 | 128,908,865 |
| 1945 | 638,461 | 821,382 | 242,400 | 4,040,000 | 6,893,250 | 2,000,000 | 179,202 | 4,249,691 | 109,774,750 | 132,892,754 |

| Year | | | | | | | | | |
|---|---|---|---|---|---|---|---|---|---|
| 1946 | 341,588 | 426,258 | 242,400 | 4,040,000 | 7,272,000 | 2,000,000 | 179,469 | 4,308,457 | 117,317,535 | 143,100,204 |
| 1947 | 373,902 | 510,902 | 242,400 | 4,040,000 | 5,858,000 | 2,000,000 | 180,051 | 4,367,224 | 114,717,069 | 167,912,203 |
| 1948 | 350,030 | 606,030 | 242,400 | 4,040,000 | 5,555,000 | 2,000,000 | 180,761 | 4,425,990 | 99,697,441 | 156,284,811 |
| 1949 | 313,217 | 602,060 | 242,400 | 4,040,000 | 4,747,000 | 2,000,000 | 180,658 | 4,484,757 | 109,641,522 | 165,852,025 |
| 1950 | 393,208 | 594,043 | 303,000 | 4,040,000 | 5,050,000 | 2,000,000 | 177,216 | 4,543,523 | 126,259,773 | 165,885,093 |
| 1951 | 359,871 | 828,846 | 303,000 | 5,050,000 | 5,050,000 | 3,000,000 | 178,012 | 4,602,290 | 130,535,744 | 170,915,045 |
| 1952 | 361,094 | 692,802 | 303,000 | 5,050,000 | 4,292,500 | 3,000,000 | 180,031 | 4,661,056 | 119,701,304 | 145,695,226 |
| 1953 | 341,778 | (137,834) | 303,000 | 5,050,000 | 5,024,750 | 3,000,000 | 180,159 | 4,719,823 | 131,682,394 | 161,132,751 |
| 1954 | 393,681 | 1,557,572 | 353,500 | 5,050,000 | 5,428,750 | 3,000,000 | 181,161 | 4,778,589 | 106,262,473 | 134,806,292 |
| 1955 | 391,694 | (124,741) | 353,500 | 5,050,000 | 5,176,250 | 3,000,000 | 177,899 | 4,837,356 | 109,820,043 | 140,219,664 |
| 1956 | 560,047 | 1,203,833 | 454,500 | 5,050,000 | 4,797,500 | 3,000,000 | 211,308 | 4,528,852 | 113,351,206 | 151,824,602 |
| 1957 | 682,559 | 1,423,889 | 454,500 | 5,050,000 | 6,438,750 | 4,000,000 | 213,254 | 5,459,996 | 114,433,052 | 146,321,764 |
| 1958 | 649,150 | 1,118,975 | 656,000 | 7,575,000 | 12,309,375 | 5,000,000 | 213,617 | 5,683,563 | 130,513,020 | 163,564,645 |
| 1959 | 747,452 | 1,268,585 | 757,500 | 7,575,000 | 18,653,438 | 5,000,000 | 228,044 | 6,365,103 | 178,106,714 | 205,161,744 |
| 1960 | 756,340 | 1,514,053 | 757,500 | 9,100,000 | 21,840,000 | 7,100,000 | 238,827 | 5,689,159 | 233,654,735 | 262,709,666 |
| 1961 | 972,988 | n.a. | 1,137,500 | 11,375,000 | 25,735,938 | 9,325,000 | 249,049 | n.a. | 252,565,850 | 288,387,815 |
| 1962 | 1,107,772 | n.a. | 1,296,750 | 13,650,000 | 26,105,625 | 8,000,000 | 271,662 | n.a. | 328,747,660 | 363,392,086 |
| 1963 | 1,138,013 | n.a. | 1,365,000 | 13,650,000 | 29,006,250 | 8,000,000 | 273,613 | n.a. | 415,006,146 | 453,963,908 |
| 1964 | 1,353,088 | n.a. | 1,711,710 | 18,018,000 | 31,531,500 | 8,321,270 | 278,279 | n.a. | 409,090,404 | 456,718,744 |
| 1965 | 1,233,440 | n.a. | 1,711,710 | 18,768,000 | 28,855,800 | 8,877,768 | 281,097 | n.a. | 410,620,899 | 461,237,805 |
| 1966 | 2,093,000 | n.a. | 1,836,000 | 20,109,000 | 29,535,094 | 10,318,000 | 301,000 | n.a. | 426,715,000 | 478,620,000 |
| 1967 | 2,414,000 | n.a. | 1,914,000 | 21,018,000 | 46,765,050 | 10,490,000 | 365,000 | n.a. | 482,686,000 | 535,994,000 |
| 1968 | 3,355,000 | n.a. | 2,067,000 | 21,118,000 | 69,953,375 | 10,825,000 | 871,000 | n.a. | 543,779,000 | 606,403,000 |
| 1969 | 2,563,000 | n.a. | 2,076,000 | 21,318,000 | 53,295,000 | 11,457,000 | 808,000 | n.a. | 711,396,000 | 790,311,000 |
| 1970 | 3,855,000 | n.a. | 2,322,000 | 24,577,000 | 50,075,638 | 15,899,000 | 1,130,000 | n.a. | 842,019,000 | 932,227,000 |

*Notes*: September financial year-end until 1950, thereafter December (1950 was a 15-month year). Became Lloyds and Bolsa International in 1971. n.a. = not available.

## MERCANTILE BANK

| Years | Published net profits | Real profits | Dividends paid (gross) | Paid-up capital | Market value: capital | Published reserves | Retained profits | Inner reserves | Deposits | Total balance sheet |
|---|---|---|---|---|---|---|---|---|---|---|
| 1893 | 21,713 | n.a. | 8,744 | 554,907 | n.q. | 0 | 1,050 | n.a. | 1,188,276 | 3,128,187 |
| 1894 | 16,880 | n.a. | 9,375 | 555,937 | n.q. | 0 | 8,555 | n.a. | 1,138,164 | 2,576,359 |
| 1895 | 16,263 | n.a. | 16,771 | 557,312 | n.q. | 0 | 8,047 | n.a. | 1,539,779 | 2,911,383 |
| 1896 | 23,141 | n.a. | 20,625 | 562,500 | 562,500 | 10,000 | 10,563 | n.a. | 1,437,646 | 2,808,384 |
| 1897 | 21,110 | n.a. | 20,625 | 562,500 | 554,464 | 10,000 | 11,049 | n.a. | 1,396,426 | 3,084,384 |
| 1898 | 31,129 | n.a. | 20,625 | 562,500 | 546,429 | 20,000 | 11,553 | n.a. | 1,367,180 | 3,094,443 |
| 1899 | 31,166 | n.a. | 20,625 | 562,500 | 538,393 | 30,000 | 12,094 | n.a. | 1,526,888 | 3,621,689 |
| 1900 | 35,843 | n.a. | 24,375 | 562,500 | 530,357 | 40,000 | 13,562 | 44,675 | 1,614,110 | 3,515,932 |
| 1901 | 36,423 | n.a. | 24,375 | 562,500 | 522,321 | 50,000 | 15,610 | 54,928 | 1,666,012 | 3,780,192 |
| 1902 | 35,008 | n.a. | 24,375 | 562,500 | 514,286 | 60,000 | 16,243 | 48,115 | 2,010,888 | 3,449,292 |
| 1903 | 46,434 | n.a. | 28,125 | 562,500 | 506,250 | 80,000 | 14,552 | 59,961 | 1,902,457 | 4,122,922 |
| 1904 | 60,675 | n.a. | 28,125 | 562,500 | 506,250 | 110,000 | 15,102 | 76,500 | 2,238,727 | 4,386,010 |
| 1905 | 59,461 | n.a. | 28,125 | 562,500 | 506,250 | 135,000 | 19,437 | 87,745 | 3,717,650 | 4,486,098 |
| 1906 | 71,364 | n.a. | 33,750 | 562,500 | 667,500 | 170,000 | 20,051 | 113,051 | 2,655,616 | 5,903,142 |
| 1907 | 80,300 | n.a. | 33,750 | 562,500 | 746,250 | 210,000 | 24,601 | 146,311 | 3,599,818 | 6,156,773 |
| 1908 | 76,528 | n.a. | 33,750 | 562,500 | 761,250 | 250,000 | 25,379 | 138,289 | 3,459,962 | 5,535,657 |
| 1909 | 71,401 | n.a. | 33,750 | 562,500 | 761,250 | 285,000 | 26,030 | 140,822 | 4,401,868 | 6,498,106 |
| 1910 | 82,867 | n.a. | 39,375 | 562,500 | 738,750 | 325,000 | 26,522 | 132,350 | 5,349,908 | 7,587,400 |
| 1911 | 84,993 | n.a. | 39,375 | 562,500 | 862,500 | 365,000 | 29,140 | 142,560 | 5,595,509 | 7,928,013 |
| 1912 | 98,965 | n.a. | 45,000 | 562,500 | 867,188 | 415,000 | 30,105 | 162,046 | 5,625,602 | 8,368,315 |
| 1913 | 111,499 | n.a. | 45,000 | 562,500 | 975,000 | 465,000 | 34,604 | 188,032 | 5,303,064 | 8,187,487 |
| 1914 | 101,620 | n.a. | 45,000 | 562,500 | 1,104,375 | 500,000 | 47,224 | 243,718 | 5,152,746 | 7,901,553 |
| 1915 | 100,328 | n.a. | 56,250 | 562,500 | 900,000 | 550,000 | 31,302 | 214,004 | 6,413,313 | 9,023,778 |
| 1916 | 133,375 | n.a. | 67,500 | 562,500 | 988,125 | 600,000 | 32,177 | 113,976 | 8,558,582 | 11,265,674 |
| 1917 | 176,005 | n.a. | 78,750 | 562,500 | 1,211,250 | 650,000 | 58,432 | 233,963 | 9,812,321 | 12,807,941 |
| 1918 | 181,112 | n.a. | 78,750 | 562,500 | 1,580,625 | 700,000 | 85,794 | 267,969 | 12,370,253 | 15,302,126 |
| 1919 | 215,636 | n.a. | 120,000 | 750,000 | 2,283,750 | 750,000 | 96,430 | 462,963 | 15,706,213 | 22,450,927 |
| 1920 | 260,208 | n.a. | 144,000 | 1,050,000 | 2,662,500 | 1,100,000 | 127,638 | 868,963 | 15,893,766 | 20,157,778 |
| 1921 | 263,033 | n.a. | 168,000 | 1,050,000 | 2,040,000 | 1,150,000 | 137,671 | 868,963 | 12,743,991 | 16,429,435 |
| 1922 | 267,434 | n.a. | 168,000 | 1,050,000 | 2,362,500 | 1,200,000 | 152,105 | 719,054 | 13,112,374 | 16,643,701 |
| 1923 | 258,707 | n.a. | 168,000 | 1,050,000 | 2,542,500 | 1,250,000 | 157,812 | 632,912 | 12,831,536 | 16,599,678 |
| 1924 | 243,410 | n.a. | 168,000 | 1,050,000 | 2,497,500 | 1,300,000 | 158,222 | 565,373 | 12,158,015 | 16,460,755 |

| Year | | | | | | | | | | |
|---|---|---|---|---|---|---|---|---|---|---|
| 1925 | 257,663 | n.a. | 168,000 | 1,050,000 | 2,490,000 | 1,350,000 | 162,885 | 532,470 | 14,717,982 | 18,418,528 |
| 1926 | 250,782 | n.a. | 168,000 | 1,050,000 | 2,700,000 | 1,385,000 | 160,666 | 471,022 | 14,957,987 | 18,800,720 |
| 1927 | 257,180 | n.a. | 168,000 | 1,050,000 | 2,812,500 | 1,420,000 | 164,846 | 470,778 | 14,442,526 | 18,387,226 |
| 1928 | 250,201 | n.a. | 168,000 | 1,050,000 | 2,940,000 | 1,450,000 | 162,047 | 648,372 | 13,493,253 | 18,989,409 |
| 1929 | 257,495 | n.a. | 168,000 | 1,050,000 | 2,670,000 | 1,480,000 | 166,505 | 621,108 | 12,677,951 | 17,857,416 |
| 1930 | 213,340 | n.a. | 168,000 | 1,050,000 | 2,355,000 | 1,500,000 | 166,845 | 603,154 | 13,979,094 | 17,643,624 |
| 1931 | 152,082 | n.a. | 126,000 | 1,050,000 | 1,560,000 | 1,050,000 | 167,927 | 113,905 | 11,220,361 | 14,668,281 |
| 1932 | 170,809 | n.a. | 126,000 | 1,050,000 | 2,130,000 | 1,075,000 | 171,736 | 443,592 | 13,034,773 | 16,211,689 |
| 1933 | 161,697 | n.a. | 126,000 | 1,050,000 | 2,475,000 | 1,075,000 | 172,433 | 455,215 | 12,248,040 | 15,291,862 |
| 1934 | 173,398 | n.a. | 126,000 | 1,050,000 | 2,715,000 | 1,075,000 | 172,831 | 699,568 | 12,974,356 | 16,730,419 |
| 1935 | 174,266 | n.a. | 126,000 | 1,050,000 | 2,535,000 | 1,075,000 | 174,097 | 710,818 | 13,916,615 | 17,160,163 |
| 1936 | 181,732 | n.a. | 126,000 | 1,050,000 | 2,895,000 | 1,075,000 | 172,829 | 803,964 | 14,675,061 | 18,468,464 |
| 1937 | 183,497 | n.a. | 126,000 | 1,050,000 | 2,595,000 | 1,075,000 | 173,327 | 844,855 | 16,025,388 | 19,673,948 |
| 1938 | 192,443 | 267,443 | 126,000 | 1,050,000 | 2,295,000 | 1,075,000 | 177,770 | 970,518 | 14,852,169 | 18,400,660 |
| 1939 | 195,869 | 307,532 | 126,000 | 1,050,000 | 2,085,000 | 1,075,000 | 179,639 | 1,146,188 | 18,077,610 | 22,025,002 |
| 1940 | 196,106 | 200,606 | 126,000 | 1,050,000 | 2,010,000 | 1,075,000 | 181,745 | 1,191,559 | 20,887,358 | 24,923,500 |
| 1941 | 173,023 | 275,403 | 94,500 | 1,050,000 | 2,145,000 | 1,075,000 | 182,268 | 957,199 | 24,783,662 | 28,632,069 |
| 1942 | 131,916 | 149,006 | 63,000 | 1,050,000 | 1,421,250 | 1,075,000 | 183,184 | 1,017,778 | 25,078,653 | 28,318,370 |
| 1943 | 133,239 | 198,739 | 63,000 | 1,050,000 | 1,680,000 | 1,075,000 | 185,423 | 1,216,965 | 27,126,555 | 31,298,482 |
| 1944 | 133,581 | 217,581 | 63,000 | 1,050,000 | 2,036,250 | 1,075,000 | 188,004 | 1,289,671 | 30,063,977 | 33,150,254 |
| 1945 | 132,991 | 194,991 | 63,000 | 1,050,000 | 1,980,000 | 1,075,000 | 164,995 | 1,356,514 | 33,487,896 | 36,701,950 |
| 1946 | 180,837 | 254,837 | 84,000 | 1,050,000 | 1,995,000 | 1,075,000 | 168,832 | 1,453,004 | 40,193,170 | 44,016,133 |
| 1947 | 183,152 | 296,152 | 105,000 | 1,050,000 | 1,785,000 | 1,200,000 | 176,234 | 1,816,747 | 41,281,138 | 45,073,759 |
| 1948 | 189,238 | 255,238 | 126,000 | 1,050,000 | 1,830,000 | 1,200,000 | 178,172 | 1,842,914 | 45,529,030 | 49,550,860 |
| 1949 | 191,805 | 413,805 | 126,000 | 1,050,000 | 1,950,000 | 1,350,000 | 182,677 | 2,479,658 | 49,931,897 | 54,093,343 |
| 1950 | 193,542 | 585,542 | 126,000 | 1,050,000 | 1,950,000 | 1,500,000 | 188,911 | 2,973,853 | 62,018,130 | 67,041,587 |
| 1951 | 195,361 | 878,361 | 126,000 | 1,050,000 | 1,680,000 | 1,500,000 | 200,130 | 3,239,351 | 67,395,576 | 74,153,595 |
| 1952 | 195,188 | 648,688 | 147,000 | 1,050,000 | 1,642,500 | 1,500,000 | 200,143 | 3,677,237 | 68,510,460 | 73,654,579 |
| 1953 | 194,687 | 537,687 | 147,000 | 1,050,000 | 2,025,000 | 1,500,000 | 200,980 | 4,365,152 | 59,381,939 | 63,634,427 |
| 1954 | 194,324 | 510,824 | 205,800 | 1,479,000 | 2,940,000 | 1,750,000 | 200,284 | 4,257,803 | 63,218,637 | 68,594,152 |
| 1955 | 235,423 | 704,423 | 205,800 | 1,470,000 | 2,610,000 | 1,750,000 | 219,372 | 3,992,653 | 66,984,096 | 72,065,153 |
| 1956 | 236,484 | 777,484 | 205,800 | 1,470,000 | 2,226,000 | 2,000,000 | 224,521 | 4,458,872 | 69,440,154 | 74,897,385 |
| 1957 | 331,243 | 685,699 | 367,500 | 2,940,000 | 7,717,500 | 2,100,000 | 231,452 | 3,324,849 | 68,334,824 | 71,001,656 |
| 1958 | 324,267 | 561,267 | 367,500 | 2,940,000 | 6,703,200 | 2,200,000 | 231,407 | 3,983,332 | 63,809,265 | 71,027,431 |
| 1959 | 300,566 | 429,566 | 367,500 | 2,940,000 | 6,468,000 | 2,200,000 | 231,879 | 4,071,583 | 64,882,480 | 71,083,661 |

*Notes:* December financial year-end. Shares not quoted until 1903; share prices estimated, 1896–1902. Market value of capital derived from prices of all classes of shares. Taken over by Hongkong and Shanghai Banking Corporation in 1959. n.a. = not available; n.q. = not quoted.

NATIONAL BANK OF INDIA/NATIONAL & GRINDLAYS

| Years | Published net profits | Real profits | Dividends paid (gross) | Paid-up capital | Market value: capital | Published reserves | Retained profits | Inner reserves | Deposits | Total balance sheet |
|---|---|---|---|---|---|---|---|---|---|---|
| 1890 | 108,359 | n.a. | 27,990 | 466,500 | 466,500 | 100,000 | 11,011 | n.a. | 4,256,262 | 6,858,295 |
| 1891 | 39,132 | n.a. | 27,990 | 500,000 | 500,000 | 100,000 | 22,153 | n.a. | 4,598,892 | 7,295,353 |
| 1892 | 64,459 | n.a. | 30,000 | 500,000 | 500,000 | 100,000 | 16,237 | n.a. | 4,991,882 | 8,182,344 |
| 1893 | 70,100 | n.a. | 30,000 | 500,000 | 500,000 | 120,000 | 18,952 | n.a. | 4,872,118 | 7,573,943 |
| 1894 | 92,563 | n.a. | 35,000 | 500,000 | 500,000 | 160,000 | 17,507 | n.a. | 3,961,219 | 6,277,973 |
| 1895 | 37,704 | n.a. | 35,000 | 500,000 | 653,600 | 160,000 | 18,211 | n.a. | 4,484,920 | 6,419,984 |
| 1896 | 58,587 | n.a. | 35,000 | 500,000 | 645,000 | 180,000 | 19,798 | n.a. | 4,421,579 | 7,018,377 |
| 1897 | 94,440 | n.a. | 40,000 | 500,000 | 685,000 | 230,000 | 22,238 | n.a. | 4,600,485 | 7,668,545 |
| 1898 | 96,103 | n.a. | 40,000 | 500,000 | 750,000 | 280,000 | 26,341 | n.a. | 5,097,179 | 8,275,216 |
| 1899 | 72,503 | n.a. | 49,000 | 500,000 | 800,000 | 310,000 | 26,844 | n.a. | 5,519,610 | 8,650,804 |
| 1900 | 96,988 | n.a. | 50,000 | 500,000 | 865,000 | 350,000 | 31,332 | n.a. | 5,809,751 | 9,718,646 |
| 1901 | 117,471 | n.a. | 50,000 | 500,000 | 980,000 | 400,000 | 36,303 | n.a. | 6,578,098 | 11,189,289 |
| 1902 | 123,745 | n.a. | 50,000 | 500,000 | 1,040,000 | 450,000 | 47,548 | n.a. | 7,823,207 | 10,918,482 |
| 1903 | 125,461 | n.a. | 60,000 | 500,000 | 1,115,000 | 500,000 | 50,509 | n.a. | 8,476,104 | 11,676,571 |
| 1904 | 156,789 | n.a. | 50,000 | 500,000 | 1,240,000 | 500,000 | 43,798 | n.a. | 8,555,886 | 11,869,953 |
| 1905 | 162,267 | n.a. | 72,000 | 600,000 | 1,608,000 | 550,000 | 69,065 | n.a. | 9,197,877 | 12,675,336 |
| 1906 | 192,600 | n.a. | 72,000 | 600,000 | 1,878,000 | 600,000 | 122,165 | n.a. | 9,806,403 | 13,650,411 |
| 1907 | 241,744 | n.a. | 72,000 | 600,000 | 2,028,000 | 600,000 | 71,909 | n.a. | 10,583,705 | 14,376,199 |
| 1908 | 246,933 | n.a. | 96,000 | 800,000 | 2,472,000 | 700,000 | 102,842 | n.a. | 10,856,746 | 13,871,170 |
| 1909 | 221,812 | n.a. | 96,000 | 800,000 | 2,752,000 | 800,000 | 108,654 | n.a. | 12,005,665 | 15,927,172 |
| 1910 | 248,219 | n.a. | 96,000 | 800,000 | 3,008,000 | 800,000 | 40,873 | n.a. | 12,150,682 | 15,505,852 |
| 1911 | 252,496 | n.a. | 120,000 | 1,000,000 | 3,000,000 | 900,000 | 53,369 | n.a. | 13,080,587 | 17,462,779 |
| 1912 | 270,639 | n.a. | 140,000 | 1,000,000 | 2,960,000 | 1,000,000 | 64,008 | n.a. | 13,936,024 | 18,551,215 |
| 1913 | 294,617 | n.a. | 160,000 | 1,000,000 | 3,200,000 | 1,100,000 | 78,625 | n.a. | 14,876,240 | 19,817,803 |
| 1914 | 269,371 | n.a. | 160,000 | 1,000,000 | 3,280,000 | 1,175,000 | 92,996 | n.a. | 14,832,899 | 19,170,678 |
| 1915 | 291,418 | n.a. | 160,000 | 1,000,000 | 2,880,000 | 1,200,000 | 103,140 | n.a. | 16,447,780 | 20,475,501 |
| 1916 | 297,474 | n.a. | 160,000 | 1,000,000 | 3,120,000 | 1,250,000 | 106,690 | n.a. | 19,551,978 | 24,058,457 |
| 1917 | 353,139 | n.a. | 200,000 | 1,000,000 | 3,480,000 | 1,350,000 | 139,829 | n.a. | 24,685,344 | 29,716,621 |

| Year | | | | | | | | | | |
|---|---|---|---|---|---|---|---|---|---|---|
| 1918 | 403,635 | n.a. | 200,000 | 1,000,000 | 5,680,000 | 1,550,000 | 123,464 | n.a. | 27,517,994 | 32,707,668 |
| 1919 | 452,170 | n.a. | 250,000 | 1,500,000 | 6,840,000 | 2,000,000 | 135,634 | n.a. | 35,164,356 | 42,366,948 |
| 1920 | 553,398 | n.a. | 300,000 | 2,000,000 | 6,240,000 | 2,500,000 | 149,032 | n.a. | 45,200,202 | 55,351,510 |
| 1921 | 555,064 | n.a. | 400,000 | 2,000,000 | 6,160,000 | 2,600,000 | 164,096 | n.a. | 34,295,599 | 42,418,027 |
| 1922 | 535,160 | n.a. | 400,000 | 2,000,000 | 6,880,000 | 2,700,000 | 159,256 | n.a. | 32,267,602 | 40,384,019 |
| 1923 | 534,799 | n.a. | 400,000 | 2,000,000 | 6,880,000 | 2,750,000 | 199,055 | n.a. | 31,254,516 | 38,694,524 |
| 1924 | 535,925 | n.a. | 400,000 | 2,000,000 | 7,680,000 | 2,800,000 | 224,980 | n.a. | 32,548,163 | 40,332,356 |
| 1925 | 536,105 | n.a. | 400,000 | 2,000,000 | 7,440,000 | 2,850,000 | 241,085 | n.a. | 33,168,283 | 40,729,048 |
| 1926 | 534,316 | n.a. | 400,000 | 2,000,000 | 7,600,000 | 2,900,000 | 255,401 | n.a. | 31,973,704 | 39,618,234 |
| 1927 | 541,099 | n.a. | 400,000 | 2,000,000 | 8,000,000 | 2,950,000 | 276,500 | n.a. | 33,655,120 | 41,489,781 |
| 1928 | 530,829 | n.a. | 400,000 | 2,000,000 | 8,400,000 | 3,000,000 | 277,329 | n.a. | 34,088,230 | 41,639,338 |
| 1929 | 511,133 | n.a. | 400,000 | 2,000,000 | 7,440,000 | 3,000,000 | 278,462 | n.a. | 31,467,322 | 38,519,027 |
| 1930 | 480,329 | n.a. | 400,000 | 2,000,000 | 6,640,000 | 3,000,000 | 278,791 | n.a. | 30,860,471 | 37,674,730 |
| 1931 | 470,019 | n.a. | 400,000 | 2,000,000 | 4,480,000 | 2,200,000 | 278,810 | n.a. | 27,804,029 | 35,263,577 |
| 1932 | 450,197 | n.a. | 400,000 | 2,000,000 | 6,880,000 | 2,200,000 | 249,007 | n.a. | 30,113,142 | 35,885,793 |
| 1933 | 450,783 | n.a. | 400,000 | 2,000,000 | 7,240,000 | 2,200,000 | 249,790 | n.a. | 29,636,308 | 35,479,912 |
| 1934 | 460,310 | n.a. | 360,000 | 2,000,000 | 6,960,000 | 2,200,000 | 250,100 | n.a. | 28,703,042 | 34,540,488 |
| 1935 | 457,569 | n.a. | 360,000 | 2,000,000 | 6,880,000 | 2,200,000 | 247,669 | n.a. | 29,382,941 | 35,178,978 |
| 1936 | 456,286 | n.a. | 360,000 | 2,000,000 | 7,600,000 | 2,200,000 | 243,955 | n.a. | 30,027,681 | 35,728,311 |
| 1937 | 465,862 | n.a. | 360,000 | 2,000,000 | 6,560,000 | 2,200,000 | 249,817 | n.a. | 30,466,946 | 36,332,028 |
| 1938 | 444,063 | n.a. | 320,000 | 2,000,000 | 5,280,000 | 2,200,000 | 248,880 | n.a. | 27,856,726 | 33,395,019 |
| 1939 | 442,692 | n.a. | 320,000 | 2,000,000 | 4,480,000 | 2,200,000 | 246,572 | n.a. | 29,166,004 | 36,607,102 |
| 1940 | 439,943 | n.a. | 320,000 | 2,000,000 | 5,040,000 | 2,200,000 | 246,515 | n.a. | 34,795,739 | 40,527,837 |
| 1941 | 437,738 | n.a. | 280,000 | 2,000,000 | 5,040,000 | 2,200,000 | 284,253 | n.a. | 39,695,737 | 45,519,512 |
| 1942 | 439,159 | n.a. | 280,000 | 2,000,000 | 4,120,000 | 2,200,000 | 273,412 | n.a. | 48,513,672 | 54,362,609 |
| 1943 | 436,499 | n.a. | 280,000 | 2,000,000 | 5,480,000 | 2,200,000 | 269,911 | n.a. | 56,138,175 | 61,867,358 |
| 1944 | 441,947 | n.a. | 280,000 | 2,000,000 | 6,220,000 | 2,200,000 | 271,858 | n.a. | 61,112,750 | 66,623,503 |
| 1945 | 442,621 | n.a. | 280,000 | 2,000,000 | 6,810,000 | 2,200,000 | 274,479 | n.a. | 61,803,510 | 67,566,994 |
| 1946 | 452,130 | n.a. | 320,000 | 2,000,000 | 5,760,000 | 2,300,000 | 276,609 | n.a. | 62,598,998 | 68,580,650 |
| 1947 | 475,597 | n.a. | 320,000 | 2,000,000 | 5,360,000 | 2,500,000 | 277,206 | n.a. | 70,226,126 | 76,912,228 |
| 1948 | 379,950 | n.a. | 320,000 | 2,000,000 | 6,000,000 | 2,750,000 | 276,156 | n.a. | 97,652,249 | 107,510,614 |
| 1949 | 458,209 | n.a. | 365,000 | 2,281,250 | 6,022,500 | 3,550,000 | 288,615 | n.a. | 106,863,815 | 114,559,065 |
| 1950 | 399,847 | n.a. | 365,000 | 2,281,250 | 5,840,000 | 3,663,892 | 313,820 | n.a. | 124,989,659 | 133,404,121 |

NATIONAL BANK OF INDIA/NATIONAL & GRINDLAYS (Cont.)

| Years | Published net profits | Real profits | Dividends paid (gross) | Paid-up capital | Market value: capital | Published reserves | Retained profits | Inner reserves | Deposits | Total balance sheet |
|---|---|---|---|---|---|---|---|---|---|---|
| 1951 | 441,457 | n.a. | 365,000 | 2,281,250 | 5,383,750 | 3,738,892 | 318,652 | n.a. | 133,030,752 | 147,283,674 |
| 1952 | 411,676 | n.a. | 365,000 | 2,281,250 | 5,018,750 | 3,738,892 | 323,703 | n.a. | 133,596,157 | 143,467,142 |
| 1953 | 387,644 | n.a. | 365,000 | 2,281,250 | 5,931,250 | 3,738,892 | 320,597 | n.a. | 126,619,173 | 136,454,974 |
| 1954 | 385,923 | n.a. | 427,734 | 2,851,563 | 6,159,375 | 3,168,579 | 326,266 | n.a. | 152,716,970 | 162,031,432 |
| 1955 | 421,839 | n.a. | 427,734 | 2,851,563 | 4,790,625 | 3,168,579 | 342,158 | n.a. | 154,012,447 | 168,653,013 |
| 1956 | 432,835 | n.a. | 427,734 | 2,851,563 | 4,676,563 | 3,168,579 | 354,046 | n.a. | 153,776,259 | 163,635,741 |
| 1957 | 427,490 | n.a. | 427,734 | 2,851,563 | 4,676,563 | 3,168,579 | 355,589 | n.a. | 152,520,838 | 162,105,220 |
| 1958 | 371,707 | n.a. | 427,734 | 2,851,563 | 6,444,531 | 3,168,579 | 351,349 | n.a. | 141,782,636 | 151,491,479 |
| 1959 | 404,708 | n.a. | 427,734 | 3,421,875 | 10,322,656 | 3,000,000 | 301,488 | n.a. | 152,647,354 | 163,035,588 |
| 1960 | 479,276 | n.a. | 453,398 | 3,421,875 | 6,957,813 | 3,050,000 | 308,058 | n.a. | 173,848,690 | 181,508,676 |
| 1961 | 644,273 | n.a. | 638,736 | 4,562,400 | 9,733,120 | 4,000,000 | 311,105 | n.a. | 240,804,001 | 251,284,590 |
| 1962 | 714,730 | n.a. | 912,480 | 5,703,000 | 12,071,350 | 5,250,000 | 316,941 | n.a | 264,726,828 | 277,468,847 |
| 1963 | 679,318 | n.a. | 798,420 | 5,703,000 | 12,831,750 | 5,400,000 | 357,227 | n.a. | 283,766,311 | 356,915,796 |
| 1964 | 771,810 | n.a. | 855,450 | 5,703,000 | 12,641,650 | 5,400,000 | 355,074 | n.a. | 316,562,751 | 392,978,515 |
| 1965 | 1,444,109 | n.a. | 969,510 | 5,703,000 | 13,687,200 | 6,901,000 | 369,596 | n.a. | 373,681,089 | 463,618,964 |
| 1966 | 1,293,000 | n.a. | 969,510 | 7,604,000 | 16,253,550 | 5,100,000 | 437,200 | n.a. | 331,414,400 | 424,540,100 |
| 1967 | 1,390,000 | n.a. | 1,027,000 | 7,604,000 | 17,774,350 | 11,592,000 | 550,000 | n.a. | 408,516,000 | 521,516,000 |
| 1968 | 1,502,000 | n.a. | 1,062,000 | 7,604,000 | 28,705,100 | 11,592,000 | 760,000 | n.a. | 466,208,000 | 588,294,000 |
| 1969 | 2,101,000 | n.a. | 1,915,000 | 11,250,000 | 31,640,625 | 17,671,000 | 945,000 | n.a. | 651,737,000 | 819,830,000 |
| 1970 | 4,112,000 | n.a. | 2,137,000 | 11,250,000 | 29,671,875 | 24,854,000 | 1,975,000 | n.a. | 817,150,000 | 869,333,000 |
| 1971 | 2,728,000 | n.a. | 2,137,000 | 11,250,000 | 41,625,000 | 26,710,000 | 591,000 | n.a. | 849,711,000 | 906,488,000 |
| 1972 | 5,274,000 | n.a. | 1,901,000 | 11,250,000 | 17,325,000 | 29,564,000 | 3,373,000 | n.a. | 1,021,679,000 | 1,097,927,000 |
| 1973 | 5,170,000 | n.a. | 1,473,000 | 11,250,000 | 10,462,500 | 37,281,000 | 3,697,000 | n.a. | 1,220,261,000 | 1,416,060,000 |
| 1974 | (9,998,000) | n.a. | 838,125 | 13,410,000 | 4,693,500 | 49,799,000 | (10,836,000) | n.a. | 1,514,434,000 | 1,590,519,000 |
| 1975 | (20,134,000) | n.a. | 0 | 15,776,000 | 5,679,360 | 20,862,000 | (20,134,000) | n.a. | 1,826,725,000 | 1,917,795,000 |

*Notes:* December financial year-end. Took over Grindlays Bank in 1948, absorbed latter's business in 1958. Taken over by ANZ Bank in 1984. From 1973, no account taken of imputed tax on dividends. n.a. = not available.

NATIONAL BANK OF NEW ZEALAND

| Years | Published net profits | Real profits | Dividends paid (gross) | Paid-up capital | Market value: capital | Published reserves | Retained profits | Inner reserves | Deposits | Total balance sheet |
|---|---|---|---|---|---|---|---|---|---|---|
| 1890 | 18,167 | n.a. | 6,250 | 250,000 | 175,000 | 10,000 | 0 | n.a. | 1,941,458 | 2,690,122 |
| 1891 | 19,335 | n.a. | 12,500 | 250,000 | 50,000 | 0 | 6,835 | n.a. | 1,673,609 | 2,576,797 |
| 1892 | 16,343 | n.a. | 12,500 | 250,000 | 125,000 | 0 | 10,678 | n.a. | 1,605,027 | 2,441,043 |
| 1893 | 16,998 | n.a. | 12,500 | 250,000 | 125,000 | 0 | 15,176 | n.a. | 1,434,366 | 2,285,048 |
| 1894 | 16,431 | n.a. | 12,500 | 250,000 | 75,000 | 0 | 19,107 | n.a. | 1,534,641 | 2,184,102 |
| 1895 | 18,089 | n.a. | 12,500 | 250,000 | 100,000 | 20,000 | 4,696 | n.a. | 1,904,179 | 2,524,482 |
| 1896 | 21,461 | n.a. | 12,500 | 250,000 | 175,000 | 30,000 | 3,657 | n.a. | 2,139,227 | 2,925,950 |
| 1897 | 25,538 | n.a. | 15,000 | 250,000 | 225,000 | 40,000 | 4,195 | n.a. | 2,298,927 | 3,009,903 |
| 1898 | 40,966 | n.a. | 17,500 | 250,000 | 225,000 | 60,000 | 5,161 | n.a. | 2,279,181 | 3,065,133 |
| 1899 | 42,348 | n.a. | 20,000 | 250,000 | 275,000 | 80,000 | 7,509 | n.a. | 2,510,755 | 3,551,189 |
| 1900 | 55,785 | n.a. | 25,000 | 250,000 | 350,000 | 180,000 | 8,294 | n.a. | 2,553,255 | 3,677,223 |
| 1901 | 64,933 | n.a. | 25,000 | 250,000 | 350,000 | 150,000 | 8,227 | n.a. | 2,732,951 | 3,742,044 |
| 1902 | 54,534 | n.a. | 25,000 | 250,000 | 400,000 | 180,000 | 7,761 | n.a. | 2,838,524 | 3,854,202 |
| 1903 | 60,643 | n.a. | 30,000 | 250,000 | 425,000 | 210,000 | 8,403 | n.a. | 3,043,440 | 4,171,361 |
| 1904 | 49,907 | n.a. | 30,000 | 250,000 | 500,000 | 230,000 | 8,310 | n.a. | 3,218,481 | 4,386,727 |
| 1905 | 67,857 | n.a. | 30,000 | 250,000 | 550,000 | 250,000 | 9,167 | n.a. | 3,440,456 | 4,753,696 |
| 1906 | 87,401 | n.a. | 38,750 | 375,000 | 787,500 | 325,000 | 10,318 | n.a. | 3,681,399 | 5,201,862 |
| 1907 | 90,545 | n.a. | 45,000 | 375,000 | 787,500 | 350,000 | 11,363 | n.a. | 3,760,526 | 5,251,819 |
| 1908 | 93,423 | n.a. | 48,750 | 375,000 | 768,750 | 375,000 | 13,036 | n.a. | 3,853,871 | 5,433,090 |
| 1909 | 92,874 | n.a. | 45,000 | 375,000 | 918,750 | 347,000 | 17,910 | n.a. | 4,306,295 | 5,931,312 |
| 1910 | 106,095 | n.a. | 57,500 | 500,000 | 1,150,000 | 480,000 | 20,005 | n.a. | 4,296,328 | 6,213,786 |
| 1911 | 120,759 | n.a. | 65,000 | 500,000 | 1,075,000 | 500,000 | 26,264 | n.a. | 4,357,926 | 6,527,809 |
| 1912 | 135,492 | n.a. | 65,000 | 500,000 | 1,175,000 | 520,000 | 36,756 | n.a. | 4,229,440 | 6,641,961 |
| 1913 | 144,896 | n.a. | 94,335 | 750,000 | 1,500,000 | 665,000 | 43,317 | n.a. | 4,304,654 | 6,976,044 |

NATIONAL BANK OF NEW ZEALAND (*Cont.*)

| Years | Published net profits | Real profits | Dividends paid (gross) | Paid-up capital | Market value: capital | Published reserves | Retained profits | Inner reserves | Deposits | Total balance sheet |
|---|---|---|---|---|---|---|---|---|---|---|
| 1914 | 149,763 | n.a. | 97,500 | 750,000 | 1,575,000 | 685,000 | 48,080 | n.a. | 4,740,397 | 7,444,585 |
| 1915 | 143,529 | n.a. | 97,500 | 750,000 | 1,425,000 | 700,000 | 42,109 | n.a. | 5,298,296 | 8,224,126 |
| 1916 | 153,645 | n.a. | 97,500 | 750,000 | 1,462,500 | 715,000 | 42,754 | n.a. | 5,472,552 | 8,786,888 |
| 1917 | 148,996 | n.a. | 97,500 | 750,000 | 1,575,000 | 730,000 | 45,550 | n.a. | 5,656,903 | 9,945,671 |
| 1918 | 186,882 | n.a. | 97,500 | 750,000 | 1,950,000 | 750,000 | 64,932 | n.a. | 6,481,558 | 10,235,155 |
| 1919 | 256,299 | n.a. | 131,658 | 1,000,000 | 2,600,000 | 1,020,000 | 69,573 | n.a. | 8,856,133 | 13,578,444 |
| 1920 | 326,722 | n.a. | 140,000 | 1,000,000 | 2,200,000 | 1,040,000 | 115,895 | n.a. | 8,296,492 | 15,654,581 |
| 1921 | 212,726 | n.a. | 140,000 | 1,000,000 | 2,300,000 | 1,050,000 | 142,121 | n.a. | 8,243,238 | 14,175,380 |
| 1922 | 228,747 | n.a. | 172,700 | 1,250,000 | 3,187,500 | 1,260,000 | 145,567 | n.a. | 9,261,899 | 15,191,651 |
| 1923 | 243,935 | n.a. | 175,000 | 1,250,000 | 3,312,500 | 1,270,000 | 155,558 | n.a. | 11,442,154 | 16,884,510 |
| 1924 | 279,826 | n.a. | 208,687 | 1,500,000 | 4,275,000 | 1,480,000 | 167,698 | n.a. | 10,822,912 | 17,371,872 |
| 1925 | 333,087 | n.a. | 277,741 | 2,000,000 | 5,500,000 | 2,000,000 | 173,044 | n.a. | 10,438,468 | 18,471,719 |
| 1926 | 312,275 | n.a. | 280,000 | 2,000,000 | 5,600,000 | 2,000,000 | 175,769 | n.a. | 11,283,316 | 18,701,309 |
| 1927 | 289,803 | n.a. | 280,000 | 2,000,000 | 5,600,000 | 2,000,000 | 165,572 | n.a. | 12,088,015 | 18,981,716 |
| 1928 | 290,582 | n.a. | 280,000 | 2,000,000 | 5,850,000 | 2,000,000 | 155,154 | n.a. | 10,507,019 | 18,809,388 |
| 1929 | 282,917 | n.a. | 240,000 | 2,000,000 | 5,100,000 | 2,000,000 | 174,171 | n.a. | 12,165,675 | 19,214,575 |
| 1930 | 208,286 | n.a. | 200,000 | 2,000,000 | 4,000,000 | 2,000,000 | 168,457 | n.a. | 11,657,303 | 17,908,777 |
| 1931 | 177,836 | n.a. | 140,000 | 2,000,000 | 2,800,000 | 2,000,000 | 142,294 | n.a. | 12,314,328 | 18,558,582 |
| 1932 | 116,448 | n.a. | 80,000 | 2,000,000 | 2,250,000 | 2,000,000 | 114,742 | n.a. | 13,767,817 | 20,229,079 |
| 1933 | 135,674 | n.a. | 80,000 | 2,000,000 | 2,400,000 | 2,000,000 | 106,416 | n.a. | 15,595,886 | 22,166,932 |
| 1934 | 132,949 | n.a. | 80,000 | 2,000,000 | 2,150,000 | 1,500,000 | 155,366 | n.a. | 13,554,859 | 18,730,841 |
| 1935 | 102,594 | n.a. | 80,000 | 2,000,000 | 2,100,000 | 1,500,000 | 113,959 | n.a. | 13,655,182 | 18,968,774 |
| 1936 | 102,838 | n.a. | 80,000 | 2,000,000 | 2,150,000 | 1,500,000 | 112,797 | n.a. | 13,751,541 | 18,892,983 |
| 1937 | 105,727 | n.a. | 90,000 | 2,000,000 | 1,700,000 | 1,500,000 | 113,691 | n.a. | 13,908,667 | 18,897,361 |

| Year | | | | | | | | | | |
|---|---|---|---|---|---|---|---|---|---|---|
| 1938 | 106,524 | n.a. | 100,000 | 2,000,000 | 1,200,000 | 1,500,000 | 114,131 | n.a. | 13,298,386 | 18,275,130 |
| 1939 | 86,149 | n.a. | 80,000 | 2,000,000 | 1,150,000 | 1,500,000 | 115,363 | n.a. | 14,905,357 | 19,791,663 |
| 1940 | 81,736 | n.a. | 70,000 | 2,000,000 | 1,050,000 | 1,500,000 | 115,849 | n.a. | 15,180,750 | 20,235,401 |
| 1941 | 92,585 | n.a. | 80,000 | 2,000,000 | 1,050,000 | 1,500,000 | 116,184 | n.a. | 16,863,303 | 21,899,833 |
| 1942 | 88,070 | n.a. | 80,000 | 2,000,000 | 1,040,000 | 1,500,000 | 117,882 | n.a. | 20,069,098 | 24,796,210 |
| 1943 | 100,589 | n.a. | 80,000 | 2,000,000 | 1,445,000 | 1,500,000 | 117,887 | n.a. | 21,723,116 | 26,960,909 |
| 1944 | 102,309 | n.a. | 80,000 | 2,000,000 | 1,663,750 | 1,250,000 | 116,741 | n.a. | 18,104,375 | 22,916,637 |
| 1945 | 99,250 | n.a. | 90,000 | 2,000,000 | 1,640,000 | 1,250,000 | 117,731 | n.a. | 21,498,742 | 26,196,352 |
| 1946 | 110,798 | n.a. | 100,000 | 2,000,000 | 2,200,000 | 1,250,000 | 118,092 | n.a. | 26,840,804 | 32,115,207 |
| 1947 | 139,550 | n.a. | 100,000 | 2,000,000 | 2,384,000 | 1,250,000 | 119,280 | n.a. | 31,020,684 | 36,968,582 |
| 1948 | 160,412 | n.a. | 100,000 | 2,000,000 | 2,300,000 | 1,250,000 | 132,460 | n.a. | 36,514,864 | 43,440,424 |
| 1949 | 168,340 | n.a. | 140,000 | 2,000,000 | 2,260,000 | 1,250,000 | 126,794 | n.a. | 39,976,296 | 46,934,595 |
| 1950 | 204,914 | n.a. | 160,000 | 2,000,000 | 2,260,000 | 1,500,000 | 128,005 | n.a. | 49,964,293 | 57,854,605 |
| 1951 | 244,015 | n.a. | 160,000 | 2,000,000 | 2,440,000 | 1,500,000 | 129,827 | n.a. | 59,179,885 | 67,207,267 |
| 1952 | 210,066 | n.a. | 200,000 | 2,000,000 | 2,440,000 | 2,000,000 | 132,393 | n.a. | 50,582,420 | 59,250,869 |
| 1953 | 213,227 | n.a. | 200,000 | 2,000,000 | 2,680,000 | 2,000,000 | 135,620 | n.a. | 54,571,596 | 63,387,460 |
| 1954 | 265,430 | n.a. | 200,000 | 2,400,000 | 4,000,000 | 2,400,000 | 188,050 | n.a. | 60,024,307 | 69,328,183 |
| 1955 | 277,447 | n.a. | 249,000 | 3,000,000 | 3,480,000 | 2,000,000 | 227,497 | n.a. | 60,304,824 | 65,015,121 |
| 1956 | 269,108 | n.a. | 270,000 | 3,000,000 | 4,800,000 | 2,500,000 | 255,155 | n.a. | 58,104,639 | 63,946,044 |
| 1957 | 275,268 | n.a. | 270,000 | 3,500,000 | 3,600,000 | 2,500,000 | 275,173 | n.a. | 62,907,023 | 68,768,446 |
| 1958 | 301,044 | n.a. | 315,000 | 3,500,000 | 4,812,500 | 2,250,000 | 150,030 | n.a. | 60,157,348 | 66,364,565 |
| 1959 | 299,602 | n.a. | 315,000 | 3,500,000 | 7,175,000 | 2,350,000 | 156,695 | n.a. | 70,043,036 | 76,156,918 |
| 1960 | 316,586 | n.a. | 315,000 | 3,500,000 | 5,556,250 | 2,450,000 | 180,344 | n.a. | 78,115,388 | 84,352,919 |
| 1961 | 313,216 | n.a. | 315,000 | 3,500,000 | 5,250,000 | 2,550,000 | 200,623 | n.a. | 70,213,814 | 76,571,624 |
| 1962 | 338,197 | n.a. | 350,000 | 3,500,000 | 5,818,750 | 2,650,000 | 224,445 | n.a. | 69,949,274 | 76,452,344 |
| 1963 | 366,668 | n.a. | 385,000 | 3,500,000 | 7,612,500 | 2,750,000 | 255,301 | n.a. | 79,901,638 | 86,557,001 |
| 1964 | 401,571 | n.a. | 420,000 | 3,500,000 | 6,781,250 | 3,000,000 | 155,747 | n.a. | 82,781,561 | 89,581,246 |

*Notes:* March financial year-end, i.e. 1980 ends in March 1981. Wholly owned by Lloyds Bank from 1965. n.a. = not available.

P & O BANKING CORPORATION

| Years | Published net profits | Real profits | Dividends paid (gross) | Paid-up capital | Market value: capital | Published reserves | Retained profits | Inner reserves | Deposits | Total balance sheet |
|---|---|---|---|---|---|---|---|---|---|---|
| 1920 | 99,725 | n.a. | 125,000 | 2,500,000 | 2,375,000 | 0 | 6,846 | n.a. | 2,662,391 | 6,139,842 |
| 1921 | 159,300 | n.a. | 142,678 | 2,594,160 | 2,983,284 | 90,000 | 14,043 | n.a. | 6,317,930 | 12,909,967 |
| 1922 | 139,388 | n.a. | 142,678 | 2,594,160 | 3,631,824 | 115,000 | 15,180 | n.a. | 10,360,705 | 22,424,585 |
| 1923 | 136,382 | n.a. | 142,678 | 2,594,160 | 3,210,273 | 135,000 | 17,567 | n.a. | 9,491,219 | 20,271,292 |
| 1924 | 136,215 | n.a. | 129,708 | 2,594,160 | 2,821,149 | 160,000 | 17,584 | n.a. | 9,419,041 | 17,156,484 |
| 1925 | 135,780 | n.a. | 129,708 | 2,594,160 | 2,334,744 | 180,000 | 19,042 | n.a. | 8,245,072 | 16,779,431 |
| 1926 | 125,947 | n.a. | 129,708 | 2,594,160 | 2,788,722 | 180,000 | 19,380 | n.a. | 8,627,483 | 16,944,442 |
| 1927 | 107,632 | n.a. | 129,708 | 2,594,160 | 2,723,868 | 180,000 | 20,495 | n.a. | 7,843,865 | 18,552,005 |
| 1928 | 106,917 | n.a. | 129,708 | 2,594,160 | 2,399,598 | 180,000 | 20,625 | n.a. | 7,238,242 | 14,979,222 |
| 1929 | 107,345 | n.a. | 129,708 | 2,594,160 | 2,140,182 | 180,000 | 25,668 | n.a. | 8,094,623 | 18,795,956 |
| 1930 | 108,450 | n.a. | 129,708 | 2,594,160 | 1,771,811 | 180,000 | 31,589 | n.a. | 7,712,779 | 18,685,974 |
| 1931 | 107,265 | n.a. | 129,708 | 2,594,160 | 1,556,496 | 180,000 | 37,855 | n.a. | 6,897,715 | 14,386,537 |
| 1932 | 111,318 | n.a. | 129,708 | 2,594,160 | 1,919,678 | 180,000 | 44,553 | n.a. | 7,071,905 | 13,625,737 |
| 1933 | 112,393 | n.a. | 129,708 | 2,594,160 | 2,407,380 | 180,000 | 52,196 | n.a. | 6,433,239 | 14,959,484 |
| 1934 | 113,443 | n.a. | 129,708 | 2,594,160 | 2,757,592 | 180,000 | 55,143 | n.a. | 7,169,970 | 16,461,810 |
| 1935 | 111,610 | n.a. | 129,708 | 2,594,160 | 2,674,579 | 180,000 | 56,014 | n.a. | 6,818,404 | 14,713,867 |
| 1936 | 102,481 | n.a. | 129,708 | 2,594,160 | 2,529,306 | 180,000 | 52,971 | n.a. | 7,370,489 | 16,093,117 |
| 1937 | 85,228 | n.a. | 103,766 | 2,594,160 | 2,594,160 | 180,000 | 51,915 | n.a. | 6,761,724 | 17,018,614 |

*Notes*: March financial year-end, i.e. 1920 refers to year ending March 1921. Controlling shareholding acquired by Chartered Bank in 1927. Market valuation thereafter based on share price of minority holding, and a mean of the high/low price for the year. Absorbed by Chartered Bank in February 1939 before financial year-end so no figures for 1938. n.a. = not available.

STANDARD BANK OF SOUTH AFRICA

| Years | Published net profits | Real profits | Dividends paid (gross) | Paid-up capital | Market value: capital | Published reserves | Retained profits | Inner reserves | Deposits | Total balance sheet |
|---|---|---|---|---|---|---|---|---|---|---|
| 1890 | 180,200 | n.a. | 140,000 | 1,000,000 | 2,080,000 | 570,000 | 14,275 | n.a. | 8,881,092 | 13,608,196 |
| 1891 | 171,608 | n.a. | 140,000 | 1,000,000 | 2,060,000 | 600,000 | 15,883 | n.a. | 7,743,102 | 11,880,107 |
| 1892 | 169,811 | n.a | 140,000 | 1,000,000 | 2,120,000 | 630,000 | 15,694 | n.a. | 7,740,698 | 12,196,409 |
| 1893 | 172,994 | n.a. | 140,000 | 1,000,000 | 2,060,000 | 660,000 | 18,688 | n.a. | 8,132,831 | 12,565,727 |
| 1894 | 180,476 | n.a. | 140,000 | 1,000,000 | 2,200,000 | 700,000 | 19,164 | n.a. | 9,048,352 | 13,412,879 |
| 1895 | 205,143 | n.a. | 160,000 | 1,000,000 | 2,440,000 | 740,000 | 19,307 | n.a. | 15,246,053 | 19,931,199 |
| 1896 | 204,005 | n.a. | 160,000 | 1,000,000 | 2,360,000 | 780,000 | 18,312 | n.a. | 13,490,121 | 18,422,059 |
| 1897 | 212,197 | n.a. | 160,000 | 1,000,000 | 2,620,000 | 820,000 | 20,509 | n.a. | 11,029,056 | 16,087,335 |
| 1898 | 213,525 | n.a. | 160,000 | 1,000,000 | 2,680,000 | 860,000 | 24,034 | n.a. | 10,549,854 | 16,057,811 |
| 1899 | 229,594 | n.a. | 179,118 | 1,239,850 | 3,074,828 | 1,167,820 | 44,440 | 566,505 | 13,141,423 | 19,473,030 |
| 1900 | 255,786 | 445,786 | 199,188 | 1,250,000 | 3,500,000 | 1,225,000 | 46,038 | 693,644 | 16,931,474 | 23,423,522 |
| 1901 | 262,895 | 486,895 | 200,000 | 1,250,000 | 3,850,000 | 1,275,000 | 48,933 | 818,184 | 18,875,703 | 25,366,418 |
| 1902 | 298,059 | 415,059 | 212,500 | 1,250,000 | 4,150,000 | 1,335,000 | 54,492 | 782,294 | 23,348,242 | 31,303,614 |
| 1903 | 305,439 | 345,439 | 225,000 | 1,548,475 | 4,806,645 | 1,865,700 | 59,931 | 818,757 | 18,357,173 | 28,489,037 |
| 1904 | 292,886 | 317,253 | 278,734 | 1,548,525 | 5,264,985 | 1,997,050 | 33,083 | 821,554 | 19,479,027 | 27,930,084 |
| 1905 | 278,490 | 305,135 | 247,764 | 1,548,525 | 4,831,398 | 1,997,050 | 37,809 | 794,575 | 20,413,041 | 29,249,666 |
| 1906 | 269,873 | 323,082 | 247,764 | 1,548,525 | 4,335,870 | 1,997,050 | 36,918 | 715,454 | 19,133,621 | 28,015,035 |
| 1907 | 235,600 | 250,600 | 232,279 | 1,548,525 | 3,778,401 | 1,900,000 | 40,239 | 697,650 | 18,377,856 | 26,171,558 |
| 1908 | 151,498 | 151,499 | 170,338 | 1,548,525 | 3,933,254 | 1,900,000 | 21,399 | 689,727 | 17,943,768 | 26,040,791 |
| 1909 | 171,278 | 226,278 | 154,852 | 1,548,525 | 4,026,165 | 1,900,000 | 37,825 | 800,943 | 17,282,245 | 25,789,986 |
| 1910 | 260,681 | 340,681 | 193,566 | 1,548,525 | 3,747,431 | 1,920,000 | 44,940 | 880,943 | 17,544,159 | 26,435,741 |
| 1911 | 304,005 | 374,005 | 201,308 | 1,548,525 | 3,499,667 | 1,960,000 | 47,637 | 950,943 | 19,142,055 | 27,367,183 |
| 1912 | 311,653 | 361,653 | 209,051 | 1,548,525 | 3,561,608 | 1,980,000 | 50,239 | 1,000,943 | 20,845,264 | 28,775,102 |
| 1913 | 338,647 | 414,647 | 216,794 | 1,548,525 | 3,484,181 | 2,000,000 | 52,092 | 1,006,897 | 20,900,321 | 29,626,461 |
| 1914 | 315,142 | 345,142 | 216,794 | 1,548,525 | 3,406,755 | 2,000,000 | 100,440 | 1,041,957 | 21,781,982 | 30,163,923 |
| 1915 | 309,386 | 374,286 | 216,794 | 1,548,525 | 3,213,189 | 2,000,000 | 87,032 | 1,012,878 | 24,555,410 | 32,998,471 |

STANDARD BANK OF SOUTH AFRICA (Cont.)

| Years | Published net profits | Real profits | Dividends paid (gross) | Paid-up capital | Market value: capital | Published reserves | Retained profits | Inner reserves | Deposits | Total balance sheet |
|---|---|---|---|---|---|---|---|---|---|---|
| 1916 | 364,824 | 569,824 | 216,794 | 1,548,525 | 3,174,476 | 2,000,000 | 100,062 | 1,077,221 | 25,338,129 | 35,192,009 |
| 1917 | 406,712 | 556,712 | 237,441 | 1,548,525 | 3,251,903 | 2,000,000 | 204,333 | 1,218,181 | 32,981,024 | 44,230,276 |
| 1918 | 540,357 | 690,357 | 255,507 | 1,548,525 | 4,103,591 | 2,200,000 | 199,184 | 1,290,861 | 39,629,892 | 53,640,065 |
| 1919 | 634,075 | 984,075 | 257,813 | 1,562,500 | 4,218,750 | 2,200,000 | 210,446 | 1,482,665 | 52,624,151 | 70,155,611 |
| 1920 | 759,378 | 953,537 | 413,099 | 2,229,165 | 4,235,414 | 2,893,335 | 206,725 | 1,288,553 | 57,285,173 | 77,913,392 |
| 1921 | 502,313 | 502,313 | 367,812 | 2,229,165 | 4,904,163 | 2,893,335 | 191,226 | 999,396 | 52,018,941 | 70,649,377 |
| 1922 | 388,824 | 678,824 | 312,083 | 2,229,165 | 5,349,996 | 2,893,335 | 117,967 | 898,429 | 48,946,880 | 64,254,180 |
| 1923 | 456,397 | 781,397 | 312,083 | 2,229,165 | 4,736,976 | 2,893,335 | 112,281 | 876,771 | 48,518,049 | 62,580,335 |
| 1924 | 508,952 | 751,952 | 312,083 | 2,229,165 | 5,238,538 | 2,893,335 | 109,150 | 1,119,771 | 47,031,133 | 61,381,739 |
| 1925 | 570,988 | 785,988 | 367,812 | 2,229,165 | 5,071,350 | 2,893,335 | 112,326 | 1,589,985 | 49,416,227 | 65,086,464 |
| 1926 | 583,801 | 753,801 | 367,812 | 2,229,165 | 6,074,475 | 2,893,335 | 128,315 | 1,932,985 | 47,629,322 | 64,265,822 |
| 1927 | 596,596 | 696,596 | 367,812 | 2,229,165 | 6,576,037 | 2,893,335 | 132,099 | 2,211,468 | 49,795,263 | 67,356,854 |
| 1928 | 621,466 | 758,966 | 406,041 | 2,500,000 | 7,625,000 | 3,164,170 | 122,524 | 2,478,614 | 51,830,148 | 71,760,150 |
| 1929 | 652,478 | 702,478 | 425,000 | 2,500,000 | 7,312,500 | 3,164,170 | 125,002 | 2,679,670 | 49,565,891 | 68,451,189 |
| 1930 | 567,620 | 567,620 | 375,000 | 2,500,000 | 7,437,500 | 3,164,170 | 142,622 | 2,342,576 | 51,934,061 | 70,409,068 |
| 1931 | 457,442 | 457,442 | 275,000 | 2,500,000 | 5,250,000 | 2,500,000 | 150,064 | 2,247,739 | 52,152,392 | 69,130,918 |
| 1932 | 429,336 | 529,336 | 250,000 | 2,500,000 | 5,437,500 | 2,500,000 | 154,400 | 2,291,047 | 52,960,375 | 66,996,985 |
| 1933 | 433,180 | 608,180 | 250,000 | 2,500,000 | 6,125,000 | 2,500,000 | 162,580 | 2,484,767 | 55,162,977 | 69,398,755 |
| 1934 | 502,589 | 1,062,589 | 300,000 | 2,500,000 | 6,937,500 | 2,500,000 | 165,169 | 3,060,759 | 55,463,478 | 70,901,373 |
| 1935 | 477,536 | 837,536 | 300,000 | 2,500,000 | 7,562,500 | 2,500,000 | 142,705 | 3,381,403 | 57,880,798 | 73,709,555 |
| 1936 | 556,587 | 1,036,587 | 350,000 | 2,500,000 | 8,000,000 | 3,000,000 | 149,292 | 3,498,422 | 65,971,568 | 84,277,804 |
| 1937 | 621,633 | 1,162,633 | 375,000 | 2,500,000 | 7,250,000 | 3,000,000 | 170,925 | 4,122,466 | 65,149,365 | 85,001,578 |
| 1938 | 573,147 | 897,147 | 350,000 | 2,500,000 | 7,625,000 | 3,000,000 | 169,072 | 4,453,105 | 65,974,635 | 86,120,381 |
| 1939 | 563,860 | 751,860 | 350,000 | 2,500,000 | 6,375,000 | 3,000,000 | 157,932 | 4,502,222 | 70,229,165 | 90,298,959 |
| 1940 | 561,837 | 751,837 | 350,000 | 2,500,000 | 6,312,500 | 3,000,000 | 144,769 | 4,801,718 | 87,897,000 | 106,996,439 |
| 1941 | 560,740 | 743,740 | 350,000 | 2,500,000 | 7,375,000 | 3,000,000 | 155,509 | 5,037,400 | 105,494,024 | 125,266,531 |

| Year | | | | | | | | | | |
|---|---|---|---|---|---|---|---|---|---|---|
| 1942 | 568,326 | 765,326 | 350,000 | 2,500,000 | 6,789,063 | 3,000,000 | 173,835 | 5,325,915 | 136,357,457 | 153,271,783 |
| 1943 | 567,351 | 767,351 | 350,000 | 2,500,000 | 7,781,250 | 3,000,000 | 191,187 | 5,619,772 | 156,883,852 | 174,874,411 |
| 1944 | 557,807 | 659,807 | 350,000 | 2,500,000 | 8,671,875 | 3,500,000 | 198,994 | 5,282,000 | 178,311,006 | 197,265,592 |
| 1945 | 661,299 | 993,299 | 425,000 | 2,500,000 | 9,914,063 | 4,000,000 | 185,293 | 5,152,000 | 213,629,957 | 237,324,292 |
| 1946 | 819,014 | 1,680,439 | 500,000 | 2,500,000 | 14,375,000 | 4,000,000 | 179,307 | 5,494,000 | 226,336,829 | 255,420,502 |
| 1947 | 672,691 | 2,284,682 | 500,000 | 2,500,000 | 14,500,000 | 5,000,000 | 201,998 | 6,190,000 | 278,860,229 | 327,774,855 |
| 1948 | 715,834 | 2,300,509 | 500,000 | 2,500,000 | 12,750,000 | 5,000,000 | 192,832 | 4,684,000 | 243,447,780 | 281,085,232 |
| 1949 | 760,692 | 2,220,235 | 500,000 | 5,000,000 | 10,250,000 | 5,000,000 | 178,524 | 4,284,000 | 232,677,245 | 269,712,508 |
| 1950 | 809,224 | 2,221,852 | 500,000 | 5,000,000 | 10,750,000 | 5,000,000 | 170,873 | 5,640,000 | 272,760,089 | 330,275,676 |
| 1951 | 911,999 | 2,813,592 | 500,000 | 5,000,000 | 9,250,000 | 5,000,000 | 220,372 | 4,627,000 | 268,171,701 | 325,645,970 |
| 1952 | 594,762 | 2,104,762 | 562,500 | 5,000,000 | 7,875,000 | 6,000,000 | 310,447 | 4,571,000 | 285,166,557 | 338,020,363 |
| 1953 | 635,811 | 1,520,712 | 787,500 | 7,000,000 | 12,460,000 | 7,000,000 | 338,133 | 5,538,340 | 292,028,425 | 363,643,250 |
| 1954 | 787,945 | 1,837,054 | 875,000 | 7,000,000 | 13,300,000 | 7,000,000 | 581,703 | 6,461,456 | 301,743,703 | 322,283,560 |
| 1955 | 823,359 | 1,806,200 | 1,125,000 | 9,000,000 | 16,875,000 | 8,750,000 | 458,187 | 6,575,470 | 314,669,176 | 340,392,541 |
| 1956 | 815,669 | 1,472,373 | 1,125,000 | 9,000,000 | 15,300,000 | 8,850,000 | 470,854 | 7,162,463 | 332,563,381 | 366,988,042 |
| 1957 | 876,548 | 1,994,161 | 1,145,000 | 9,160,000 | 15,114,000 | 8,850,000 | 479,021 | 8,377,115 | 332,965,240 | 360,426,433 |
| 1958 | 1,080,864 | 1,930,864 | 1,448,000 | 11,000,000 | 21,037,500 | 10,440,000 | 540,160 | 8,673,848 | 333,102,387 | 360,755,389 |
| 1959 | 1,180,968 | 2,055,968 | 1,540,000 | 11,000,000 | 27,637,500 | 10,600,000 | 567,878 | 9,283,718 | 345,489,682 | 373,080,360 |
| 1960 | 1,338,862 | 2,918,862 | 1,650,000 | 11,000,000 | 19,800,000 | 10,850,000 | 596,115 | 10,306,582 | 376,402,196 | 413,090,634 |
| 1961 | 1,306,899 | 3,336,899 | 1,925,000 | 11,000,000 | 22,550,000 | 16,599,328 | 626,329 | 9,663,425 | 374,012,997 | 408,340,627 |
| 1962 | 1,236,223 | 1,722,223 | 1,650,000 | 11,000,000 | 24,337,500 | 16,699,328 | 701,927 | 9,770,672 | 413,371,609 | 457,178,431 |
| 1963 | 1,906,647 | 2,406,647 | 2,038,750 | 11,650,000 | 27,523,125 | 18,349,328 | 832,636 | 9,891,480 | 467,492,938 | 509,234,792 |
| 1964 | 2,333,267 | 2,983,267 | 2,038,750 | 11,650,000 | 32,037,500 | 19,124,328 | 884,791 | 10,956,026 | 548,558,929 | 612,146,704 |
| 1965 | 3,477,071 | 3,503,905 | 3,127,609 | 17,872,050 | 49,371,538 | 28,668,774 | 1,111,892 | 11,668,431 | 716,774,052 | 779,970,025 |
| 1966 | 3,802,242 | 4,382,242 | 3,127,609 | 17,872,050 | 46,690,731 | 29,081,244 | 1,161,247 | 13,582,760 | 826,368,271 | 892,230,167 |
| 1967 | 4,272,195 | 5,655,195 | 3,127,609 | 17,872,050 | 68,472,292 | 33,764,721 | 1,312,664 | n.a. | 1,031,226,266 | 1,220,821,369 |
| 1968 | 4,752,835 | n.a. | 3,216,969 | 26,808,075 | 81,094,427 | 26,347,697 | 1,349,456 | n.a. | 1,304,948,705 | 1,535,464,836 |
| 1969 | 6,390,664 | n.a. | 3,980,808 | 26,808,075 | 70,036,096 | 39,306,168 | 1,589,199 | n.a. | 1,515,457,419 | 1,805,679,067 |

*Notes*: December financial year-end until 1919, subsequently March year-end. Thus 1920 is a 15-month year, ending March 1921. Accounts consolidated from 1961. Merged with Chartered Bank end-1969; see separate Standard Chartered Bank. n.a. = not available.

STANDARD CHARTERED BANK

| Years | Published net profits | Real profits | Dividends paid (gross) | Paid-up capital | Market value: capital | Published reserves | Retained profits | Inner reserves | Deposits | Total balance sheet |
|---|---|---|---|---|---|---|---|---|---|---|
| 1970 | 16,376,000 | n.a. | 7,809,703 | 52,065,000 | 105,431,625 | 103,111,000 | 10,128,000 | n.a. | 2,335,907,000 | 2,524,509,000 |
| 1971 | 18,051,000 | n.a. | 7,289,000 | 52,065,000 | 182,227,500 | 108,983,000 | 19,762,000 | n.a. | 2,422,449,000 | 2,622,235,000 |
| 1972 | 20,621,000 | n.a. | 6,295,000 | 52,065,000 | 283,754,250 | 131,403,000 | 14,326,000 | n.a. | 3,006,541,000 | 3,235,346,000 |
| 1973 | 34,595,000 | n.a. | 7,362,000 | 60,096,000 | 195,312,000 | 168,897,000 | 27,233,000 | n.a. | 4,265,231,000 | 4,578,901,000 |
| 1974 | 25,029,000 | n.a. | 7,989,000 | 60,096,000 | 117,187,200 | 186,186,000 | 17,040,000 | n.a. | 4,968,169,000 | 5,307,300,000 |
| 1975 | 34,463,000 | n.a. | 10,276,000 | 69,110,000 | 331,728,000 | 235,123,000 | 24,187,000 | n.a. | 5,014,996,000 | 6,680,113,000 |

*Notes*: March financial year-end until 1978 (i.e. year-end for 1977 is March 1978). Then December year-end, so 1978 is a 9-month year. From 1972, imputed tax has not been added to dividends—they reflect the amount actually paid out. n.a. = not applicable because consolidated accounts are made up on basis of full disclosure.

TABLE A5.2. *Performance ratios (constant 1913 prices)*

| Bank | NPV per £100 paid out | | Annual average per period | | |
|---|---|---|---|---|---|
| | Discount rate | Dividends paid (gross) | Average dividend | Average yield | Average dividend |
| | % | £ | £/share | % | % |
| **Period 1: 1890–5** | 3.8 | | | | |
| London & River Plate Bank | | 62.15 | 1.99 | 5.6 | 13.3 |
| National Bank of India | | 54.97 | 0.94 | 6.0 | 6.3 |
| London & Brazilian Bank | | 46.08 | 1.66 | 8.1 | 13.9 |
| Standard Bank of South Africa | | 37.53 | 4.29 | 6.6 | 14.3 |
| Anglo-Egyptian Bank | | 14.88 | 0.36 | 6.8 | 6.1 |
| Chartered Bank | | 14.58 | 1.79 | 6.4 | 7.5 |
| Ionian Bank | | −6.71 | 1.39 | 7.5 | 4.7 |
| Bank of British North America | | −12.54 | 3.83 | 4.6 | 6.4 |
| National Bank of New Zealand | | −14.26 | 0.14 | 10.6 | 4.6 |
| Colonial Bank | | −15.73 | 3.70 | 7.5 | 10.3 |
| Hongkong & Shanghai Bank | | −26.14 | 3.21 | 6.4 | 16.8 |
| Bank of Australasia | | −31.73 | 4.53 | 5.0 | 9.5 |
| Tarapaca & London Bank | | −44.34 | 0.22 | 5.8 | 3.8 |
| Imperial Bank of Persia | | −52.38 | 0.47 | 6.6 | 4.2 |
| Midland Bank | | 46.24 | 2.29 | 5.1 | 15.0 |
| Lloyds Bank | | 22.27 | 1.49 | 4.7 | 15.5 |
| **Period 2: 1896–1913** | 0.3 | | | | |
| Bank of British West Africa (1894– ) | | 5,519.75 | 0.35 | 5.3 | 8.1 |
| Tarapaca & London/Anglo-South American Bank | | 1,831.20 | 0.45 | 6.1 | 8.2 |
| National Bank of New Zealand | | 904.55 | 0.31 | 5.9 | 10.9 |
| National Bank of India | | 464.65 | 1.59 | 4.3 | 11.3 |
| Anglo-Egyptian Bank | | 344.61 | 0.68 | 5.5 | 12.1 |
| Chartered Bank | | 334.14 | 2.72 | 5.0 | 12.1 |
| Hongkong & Shanghai Bank | | 291.83 | 4.27 | 5.2 | 31.8 |
| Bank of Australasia | | 276.36 | 5.23 | 5.2 | 11.5 |
| London & Brazilian Bank | | 252.58 | 1.68 | 6.3 | 15.0 |
| Ionian Bank | | 203.81 | 0.43 | 6.1 | 5.3 |
| Imperial Bank of Persia | | 196.95 | 0.45 | 7.2 | 6.1 |
| Bank of Mauritius ( −1915) | | 159.58 | 0.74 | 5.8 | 6.6 |
| Standard Bank of South Africa | | 152.35 | 2.76 | 5.4 | 14.6 |
| London & River Plate Bank | | 147.78 | 2.92 | 4.9 | 19.1 |
| Mercantile Bank | | 119.53 | 0.75 | 4.6 | 5.3 |
| Bank of British North America | | 100.20 | 3.58 | 4.6 | 6.3 |
| Colonial Bank | | 62.33 | 0.47 | 6.9 | 6.3 |
| Eastern Bank (1911– ) | | 13.22 | 0.21 | 3.7 | 5.0 |
| English, Scottish & Australian | | −2.00 | 0.49 | 12.8 | 3.0 |
| Midland Bank | | 488.77 | 2.63 | 4.8 | 17.9 |
| Lloyds Bank | | 261.78 | 1.61 | 4.6 | 17.9 |
| **Period 3: 1914–20** | −12.2 | | | | |
| Anglo-Egyptian Bank | | 253.25 | 0.56 | 5.5 | 16.2 |
| Anglo-South American Bank | | 184.69 | 0.36 | 6.9 | 10.9 |
| Mercantile Bank | | 165.37 | 0.91 | 5.5 | 12.0 |

TABLE A5.2. (*Cont.*)

| Bank | NPV per £100 paid out | | Annual average per period | | |
|---|---|---|---|---|---|
| | Discount rate | Dividends paid (gross) | Average dividend | Average yield | Average dividend |
| | % | £ | £/share | % | % |
| Bank of British West Africa | | 135.24 | 0.19 | 4.9 | 7.4 |
| English, Scottish & Australian | | 122.76 | 0.70 | 5.8 | 8.4 |
| Chartered Bank | | 116.20 | 1.07 | 4.6 | 15.3 |
| National Bank of India | | 108.42 | 1.38 | 4.7 | 16.8 |
| Colonial Bank | | 104.10 | 0.30 | 7.2 | 7.6 |
| London & Brazilian Bank (−1922) | | 75.61 | 1.00 | 6.4 | 15.6 |
| National Bank of New Zealand | | 66.78 | 0.22 | 6.1 | 13.1 |
| Hongkong & Shanghai Bank | | 61.32 | 3.85 | 6.3 | 32.8 |
| Standard Bank of South Africa | | 57.52 | 0.52 | 6.9 | 15.2 |
| Ionian Bank | | 54.07 | 0.21 | 6.8 | 6.0 |
| Bank of Australasia | | 40.88 | 4.48 | 5.9 | 16.6 |
| Eastern Bank | | 40.31 | 0.17 | 4.8 | 6.0 |
| Imperial Bank of Persia | | 15.58 | 0.26 | 5.0 | 5.7 |
| Bank of British North America (−1917) | | −3.76 | 3.29 | 5.6 | 7.5 |
| London & River Plate Bank | | −6.95 | 1.61 | 5.8 | 15.0 |
| Lloyds Bank | | 111.00 | 0.32 | 6.1 | 18.4 |
| Midland Bank | | 110.82 | 0.29 | 5.8 | 18.0 |
| Period 4: 1921–9 | 15.5 | | | | |
| English, Scottish & Australian | | 166.20 | 0.22 | 4.9 | 11.8 |
| National Bank of New Zealand | | 51.89 | 0.20 | 5.0 | 13.7 |
| Imperial Bank of Persia | | 47.99 | 0.31 | 6.2 | 8.3 |
| London & River Plate Bank (−1923) | | 35.51 | 0.86 | 3.9 | 9.8 |
| Ionian Bank | | 33.86 | 0.21 | 6.3 | 7.2 |
| Eastern Bank | | 16.34 | 0.26 | 7.6 | 9.0 |
| Standard Bank of South Africa | | 11.44 | 0.45 | 6.1 | 15.7 |
| Mercantile Bank | | 10.85 | 0.80 | 6.5 | 16.0 |
| Hongkong & Shanghai Bank | | 7.11 | 4.38 | 6.2 | 57.5 |
| Lloyds, National Provincial Foreign | | 3.17 | 0.51 | 3.8 | 3.8 |
| National Bank of India | | −3.11 | 1.42 | 5.4 | 20.0 |
| Bank of Australasia | | −4.78 | 0.38 | 5.0 | 13.3 |
| Chartered Bank | | −5.05 | 0.58 | 5.1 | 20.3 |
| Anglo-South American Bank | | −13.15 | 0.30 | 6.8 | 10.6 |
| Barclays (DCO) (1926– ) | | −14.96 | 0.03 | 3.8 | 5.3 |
| P & O Banking Corporation (1920– ) | | −15.99 | 0.28 | 4.9 | 5.1 |
| Bolsa (1924– ) | | −18.83 | 0.33 | 5.6 | 11.1 |
| Bank of British West Africa | | −23.42 | 0.12 | 5.2 | 5.4 |
| Colonial Bank (−1925) | | −45.91 | 0.24 | 8.5 | 7.3 |
| Midland Bank | | 11.61 | 0.24 | 5.0 | 18.0 |
| Lloyds Bank | | −2.97 | 0.09 | 5.5 | 16.1 |
| Period 5: 1930–8 | 9.7 | | | | |
| P & O Banking Corporation (−1937) | | 22.41 | 0.32 | 5.5 | 4.9 |
| Imperial Bank of Iran | | 13.16 | 0.44 | 5.6 | 8.8 |

TABLE A5.2. (*Cont.*)

| Bank | NPV per £100 paid out | | Annual average per period | | |
|---|---|---|---|---|---|
| | Discount rate % | Dividends paid (gross) £ | Average dividend £/share | Average yield % | Average dividend % |
| Barclays (DCO) | | −1.40 | 0.04 | 3.5 | 6.3 |
| Eastern Bank | | −5.76 | 0.23 | 5.8 | 7.0 |
| Bank of British West Africa | | −7.85 | 0.11 | 4.5 | 4.3 |
| Mercantile Bank | | −13.74 | 0.71 | 5.4 | 12.4 |
| Standard Bank of South Africa | | −20.48 | 0.41 | 4.6 | 12.5 |
| National Bank of India | | −21.09 | 1.52 | 5.7 | 18.7 |
| Bank of Australasia | | −23.49 | 0.27 | 4.9 | 8.4 |
| Hongkong & Shanghai Bank | | −23.82 | 3.80 | 5.4 | 70.0 |
| Bolsa | | −36.96 | 0.14 | 4.1 | 4.2 |
| Chartered Bank | | −42.53 | 0.46 | 5.2 | 14.2 |
| English, Scottish & Australian | | −45.64 | 0.13 | 4.2 | 6.5 |
| Ionian Bank | | −48.02 | 0.09 | 6.1 | 2.6 |
| National Bank of New Zealand | | −61.30 | 0.08 | 4.5 | 5.1 |
| Anglo-South American Bank (−1935) | | −79.48 | 0.09 | 4.4 | 2.3 |
| Lloyds, National Provincial Foreign | | −177.77 | −4.63 | −14.2 | −14.2 |
| Midland Bank | | −15.20 | 0.21 | 4.2 | 16.2 |
| Lloyds Bank | | −26.52 | 0.08 | 4.3 | 11.8 |
| Period 6: 1939–46 | −0.3 | | | | |
| Bank of British West Africa | | 133.38 | 0.09 | 4.1 | 4.5 |
| Eastern Bank | | 104.47 | 0.13 | 4.6 | 5.5 |
| Standard Bank of South Africa | | 93.92 | 0.35 | 4.6 | 15.0 |
| National Bank of New Zealand | | 78.24 | 0.05 | 6.0 | 4.1 |
| Barclays (DCO) | | 74.12 | 0.03 | 3.0 | 7.1 |
| Imperial Bank of Iran | | 69.83 | 0.43 | 6.9 | 9.0 |
| English, Scottish & Australian | | 62.56 | 0.10 | 5.4 | 6.8 |
| Ionian Bank | | 61.77 | 0.04 | 4.0 | 1.8 |
| Bolsa | | 53.59 | 0.14 | 4.0 | 5.7 |
| Bank of Australasia | | 43.68 | 0.17 | 5.3 | 7.3 |
| National Bank of India | | 31.51 | 0.88 | 5.6 | 14.8 |
| Chartered Bank | | 23.00 | 0.17 | 4.1 | 7.4 |
| Mercantile Bank | | −6.68 | 0.35 | 4.6 | 8.4 |
| Hongkong & Shanghai Bank | | −15.22 | 0.86 | 2.4 | 23.5 |
| Lloyds, National Provincial Foreign | | −29.28 | 0.06 | 0.3 | 0.3 |
| Lloyds Bank | | 33.18 | 0.05 | 4.3 | 11.4 |
| Midland Bank | | 27.74 | 0.14 | 4.0 | 16.0 |
| Period 7: 1947–55 | −6.3 | | | | |
| Ionian Bank (−1957) | | 465.55 | 0.05 | 4.5 | 3.5 |
| Barclays (DCO) | | 211.29 | 0.03 | 5.3 | 8.0 |
| British Bank of the Middle East | | 170.28 | 0.06 | 6.3 | 9.1 |
| Mercantile Bank | | 162.11 | 0.14 | 7.1 | 12.6 |
| National Bank of New Zealand | | 144.86 | 0.05 | 5.7 | 7.4 |
| Bank of British West Africa | | 124.36 | 0.06 | 4.6 | 8.8 |
| Chartered Bank | | 95.67 | 0.08 | 6.3 | 13.5 |
| Eastern Bank (−1957) | | 89.67 | 0.10 | 4.5 | 6.9 |

TABLE A5.2. (*Cont.*)

| Bank | NPV per £100 paid out | | Annual average per period | | |
|---|---|---|---|---|---|
| | Discount rate % | Dividends paid (gross) £ | Average dividend £/share | Average yield % | Average dividend % |
| Standard Bank of South Africa | | 86.34 | 0.06 | 5.3 | 12.3 |
| National Bank of India | | 76.74 | 0.10 | 6.5 | 15.8 |
| Hongkong & Shanghai Bank | | 65.18 | 1.52 | 5.2 | 64.2 |
| ANZ (1951– ) | | 62.53 | 0.03 | 6.0 | 10.4 |
| English, Scottish & Australian | | 59.21 | 0.10 | 5.5 | 10.6 |
| Bolsa | | 56.31 | 0.10 | 5.7 | 6.4 |
| Bank of Australasia (−1950) | | 44.23 | 0.16 | 4.6 | 9.2 |
| Lloyds, National Provincial Foreign | | 18.93 | 0.00 | 0.0 | 0.0 |
| Lloyds Bank | | 61.30 | 0.04 | 4.2 | 11.8 |
| Midland Bank | | 26.53 | 0.10 | 4.2 | 16.4 |
| Period 8: 1956–69 | −2.0 | | | | |
| Bolsa (−1970) | | 1,192.00 | 0.02 | 4.6 | 9.3 |
| Chartered Bank | | 761.72 | 0.03 | 5.5 | 15.0 |
| English, Scottish & Australian | | 750.38 | 0.02 | 4.8 | 9.6 |
| National & Grindlays | | 736.03 | 0.02 | 6.1 | 14.7 |
| Hongkong & Shanghai Bank | | 629.79 | 0.15 | 5.1 | 40.2 |
| ANZ | | 539.46 | 0.02 | 4.4 | 11.7 |
| Standard Bank of South Africa | | 503.10 | 0.03 | 6.1 | 15.2 |
| Barclays DCO (−1970) | | 479.91 | 0.02 | 4.7 | 10.5 |
| British Bank of the Middle East (−1959) | | 280.50 | 0.03 | 5.5 | 12.6 |
| Mercantile Bank (−1959) | | 241.87 | 0.03 | 5.7 | 12.7 |
| National Bank of New Zealand (−1964) | | 94.22 | 0.02 | 5.8 | 9.7 |
| Bank of British West Africa (−1964) | | −15.71 | 0.02 | 6.8 | 10.0 |
| Midland Bank | | 482.66 | 0.03 | 4.3 | 15.4 |
| Lloyds Bank | | 481.66 | 0.02 | 4.1 | 11.4 |
| Period 9: 1970–5 | −7.9 | | | | |
| Hongkong & Shanghai Bank | | 471.60 | 0.01 | 2.3 | 23.3 |
| Standard Chartered Bank | | 198.03 | 0.02 | 4.0 | 13.6 |
| ANZ | | 74.24 | 0.01 | 3.1 | 9.4 |
| National & Grindlays | | −62.51 | 0.02 | 7.6 | 13.0 |
| Midland Bank | | 93.55 | 0.01 | 4.0 | 13.1 |
| Lloyds Bank | | 50.96 | 0.01 | 3.9 | 12.5 |

TABLE A5.3. *Profitability and capital ratios* (constant 1913 prices) (%)

| Bank | Ratio: net published profits to shareholder funds | Ratio: paid-up capital to deposits |
|---|---|---|
| **Period 1: 1890–5** | | |
| Hongkong & Shanghai Bank | 14.6 | 9.2 |
| London & Brazilian Bank | 12.5 | 21.0 |
| London & River Plate Bank | 12.0 | 10.3 |
| Standard Bank of South Africa | 10.8 | 10.5 |
| National Bank of India | 10.8 | 10.9 |
| Anglo-Egyptian Bank | 8.8 | 50.3 |
| Colonial Bank | 8.3 | 33.1 |
| Chartered Bank | 8.2 | 12.0 |
| National Bank of New Zealand | 6.6 | 14.9 |
| Bank of Australasia | 6.3 | 11.8 |
| Bank of British North America | 5.3 | 47.8 |
| Tarapaca & London Bank | 5.1 | 108.7 |
| Ionian Bank | 4.7 | 118.4 |
| Imperial Bank of Persia | 4.0 | 378.8 |
| Lloyds Bank | 10.7 | 6.9 |
| Midland Bank | 9.7 | 8.7 |
| **Period 2: 1896–1913** | | |
| English, Scottish & Australian | 21.1 | 21.6 |
| Hongkong & Shanghai Bank | 15.8 | 5.6 |
| National Bank of India | 13.3 | 7.2 |
| National Bank of New Zealand | 11.8 | 10.4 |
| London & River Plate Bank | 11.5 | 6.3 |
| Anglo-Egyptian Bank | 10.5 | 19.5 |
| Chartered Bank | 10.4 | 8.2 |
| London & Brazilian Bank | 10.0 | 18.6 |
| Bank of British West Africa (1894– ) | 9.8 | 16.8 |
| Bank of Australasia | 9.8 | 10.7 |
| Tarapaca & London/Anglo-South American Bank | 9.8 | 25.9 |
| Standard Bank of South Africa | 8.4 | 7.9 |
| Mercantile Bank | 7.7 | 18.8 |
| Bank of Mauritius (–1915) | 7.7 | 53.1 |
| Eastern Bank (1911– ) | 7.6 | 21.3 |
| Bank of British North America | 6.6 | 22.5 |
| Imperial Bank of Persia | 6.2 | 144.4 |
| Colonial Bank | 5.6 | 31.2 |
| Ionian Bank | 5.5 | 37.8 |
| Lloyds Bank | 13.3 | 5.5 |
| Midland Bank | 10.9 | 5.9 |

TABLE A5.3. (Cont.)

| Bank | Ratio: net published profits to shareholder funds | Ratio: paid-up capital to deposits |
|---|---|---|
| Period 3: 1914–20 | | |
| English, Scottish & Australian | 15.2 | 6.1 |
| Hongkong & Shanghai Bank | 13.9 | 4.4 |
| National Bank of India | 12.8 | 4.9 |
| Mercantile Bank | 11.3 | 6.7 |
| Chartered Bank | 11.2 | 5.1 |
| Standard Bank of South Africa | 11.0 | 5.0 |
| National Bank of New Zealand | 11.0 | 13.3 |
| Anglo-Egyptian Bank | 9.5 | 6.1 |
| Anglo-South American Bank | 9.0 | 13.1 |
| Bank of British West Africa | 8.9 | 15.1 |
| Colonial Bank | 8.7 | 15.5 |
| Bank of Australasia | 8.6 | 10.0 |
| Eastern Bank | 8.2 | 12.4 |
| Ionian Bank | 7.5 | 10.2 |
| London & River Plate Bank | 7.5 | 7.3 |
| London & Brazilian Bank (−1922) | 7.1 | 11.2 |
| Bank of British North America (−1917) | 6.3 | 10.2 |
| Imperial Bank of Persia | 6.1 | 50.0 |
| Midland Bank | 16.1 | 2.6 |
| Lloyds Bank | 14.2 | 3.5 |
| Period 4: 1921–9 | | |
| Hongkong & Shanghai Bank | 14.2 | 3.7 |
| English, Scottish & Australian | 11.1 | 7.5 |
| National Bank of India | 10.5 | 6.1 |
| Chartered Bank | 10.3 | 6.7 |
| Standard Bank of South Africa | 10.2 | 4.6 |
| Mercantile Bank | 10.0 | 7.8 |
| Imperial Bank of Persia | 10.0 | 12.9 |
| Lloyds, National Provincial Foreign | 10.0 | 4.8 |
| Eastern Bank | 8.7 | 17.4 |
| Barclays (DCO) (1926– ) | 8.3 | 8.9 |
| Colonial Bank (−1925) | 8.0 | 13.6 |
| Bank of Australasia | 7.9 | 13.9 |
| National Bank of New Zealand | 7.8 | 15.7 |
| Ionian Bank | 7.3 | 14.3 |
| Bank of British West Africa | 6.9 | 17.7 |
| Bolsa (1924–) | 6.2 | 8.5 |
| Anglo-South American Bank | 5.8 | 9.7 |
| London & River Plate Bank (−1923) | 4.9 | 7.4 |
| P & O Banking Corporation (1920– ) | 4.5 | 32.3 |

TABLE A5.3. (*Cont.*)

| Bank | Ratio: net published profits to shareholder funds | Ratio: paid-up capital to deposits |
|---|---|---|
| Midland Bank | 10.2 | 8.9 |
| Lloyds Bank | 9.9 | 4.4 |
| Period 5: 1930–8 | | |
| Hongkong & Shanghai Bank | 11.7 | 2.4 |
| National Bank of India | 10.1 | 6.8 |
| Standard Bank of South Africa | 9.5 | 4.3 |
| Eastern Bank | 7.9 | 15.2 |
| Mercantile Bank | 7.6 | 7.7 |
| Chartered Bank | 7.5 | 6.6 |
| Barclays (DCO) | 6.0 | 6.0 |
| Bolsa | 5.8 | 8.6 |
| English, Scottish & Australian | 5.3 | 9.5 |
| Imperial Bank of Iran | 4.9 | 23.5 |
| Lloyds, National Provincial Foreign | 4.4 | 9.5 |
| Bank of Australasia | 4.4 | 11.9 |
| P & O Banking Corporation (–1937) | 3.8 | 36.9 |
| Bank of British West Africa | 3.7 | 17.2 |
| National Bank of New Zealand | 3.4 | 14.8 |
| Anglo-South American Bank (–1935) | 3.4 | 19.9 |
| Ionian Bank | 2.6 | 18.6 |
| Midland Bank | 8.8 | 6.0 |
| Lloyds Bank | 6.9 | 4.2 |
| Period 6: 1939–46 | | |
| Standard Bank of South Africa | 10.1 | 1.8 |
| National Bank of India | 9.9 | 4.2 |
| Bolsa | 9.1 | 4.9 |
| Mercantile Bank | 7.0 | 3.9 |
| Imperial Bank of Iran | 6.5 | 8.3 |
| Eastern Bank | 6.0 | 5.8 |
| Chartered Bank | 5.4 | 3.9 |
| Barclays (DCO) | 5.2 | 2.2 |
| Bank of British West Africa | 5.1 | 9.2 |
| Hongkong & Shanghai Bank | 4.7 | 2.0 |
| English, Scottish & Australian | 3.6 | 5.9 |
| Bank of Australasia | 3.2 | 8.2 |
| Ionian Bank | 3.1 | 15.4 |
| National Bank of New Zealand | 2.7 | 10.5 |
| Lloyds, National Provincial Foreign | 1.7 | 15.7 |
| Midland Bank | 7.1 | 2.3 |
| Lloyds Bank | 5.6 | 2.4 |

TABLE A5.3. (*Cont.*)

| Bank | Ratio: net published profits to shareholder funds | Ratio: paid-up capital to deposits |
|------|------|------|
| **Period 7: 1947–55** | | |
| Hongkong & Shanghai Bank | 13.6 | 0.9 |
| Bank of British West Africa | 8.8 | 2.6 |
| Chartered Bank | 8.1 | 2.0 |
| Mercantile Bank | 7.2 | 2.0 |
| National Bank of India | 7.1 | 2.0 |
| Standard Bank of South Africa | 6.6 | 1.9 |
| National Bank of New Zealand | 5.5 | 4.2 |
| Eastern Bank (–1957) | 5.3 | 3.4 |
| Bolsa | 5.0 | 3.9 |
| British Bank of the Middle East | 5.0 | 3.5 |
| Barclays (DCO) | 4.6 | 2.0 |
| English, Scottish & Australian | 4.5 | 3.0 |
| Ionian Bank (–1957) | 4.3 | 6.1 |
| ANZ (1951–) | 4.0 | 3.4 |
| Bank of Australasia (–1950) | 3.7 | 4.4 |
| Lloyds, National Provincial Foreign | 2.2 | 6.3 |
| Midland Bank | 7.5 | 2.0 |
| Lloyds Bank | 6.0 | 1.4 |
| **Period 8: 1956–69** | | |
| Hongkong & Shanghai Bank | 16.4 | 1.4 |
| Chartered Bank | 8.4 | 2.1 |
| National & Grindlays | 7.3 | 1.9 |
| ANZ | 7.3 | 2.7 |
| British Bank of the Middle East (–1959) | 7.1 | 3.0 |
| Standard Bank of South Africa | 6.9 | 2.3 |
| Barclays (DCO) (–1970) | 6.8 | 2.0 |
| Bank of British West Africa (–1964) | 6.6 | 5.1 |
| Bolsa (–1970) | 6.6 | 3.9 |
| Mercantile Bank (–1959) | 6.1 | 3.8 |
| National Bank of New Zealand (–1964) | 5.2 | 4.8 |
| English, Scottish & Australian | 4.4 | 3.7 |
| Midland Bank | 10.3 | 2.1 |
| Lloyds Bank | 7.3 | 2.8 |
| **Period 9: 1970–5** | | |
| Hongkong & Shanghai Bank | 17.2 | 1.9 |
| ANZ | 12.0 | 1.6 |
| Standard Chartered Bank | 10.7 | 1.6 |
| National & Grindlays | –1.0 | 1.1 |
| Midland Bank | 11.1 | 1.8 |
| Lloyds Bank | 9.4 | 1.6 |

TABLE A5.4. *Comparative profit ratios* (%)

| Bank | Ratio: published profits to shareholder funds | Ratio: published profits to shareholder funds + inner reserves | Ratio: real profits to shareholder funds | Ratio: real profits to shareholder funds + inner reserves |
|---|---|---|---|---|
| **Period 1: 1890–5** | | | | |
| Chartered Bank | 8.2 | 7.9 | 9.0 | 8.7 |
| Colonial Bank (1891–) | 8.0 | 7.8 | 12.9 | 12.5 |
| **Period 2: 1896–1913** | | | | |
| English, Scottish & Australian Bank | 21.4 | 11.9 | n.a. | n.a. |
| London and River Plate Bank | 11.5 | 9.5 | 13.9 | 11.5 |
| Chartered Bank | 10.4 | 9.2 | 11.9 | 11.3 |
| Mercantile Bank (1900–) | 8.5 | 7.7 | n.a. | n.a. |
| Standard Bank of South Africa | 8.0 | 6.4 | 10.2 | 8.2 |
| Bank of Mauritius (1907–) | 6.9 | 6.7 | 9.5 | 9.2 |
| Imperial Bank of Persia (1906–) | 6.6 | 6.1 | 8.2 | 7.5 |
| Ionian Bank (1901–) | 5.9 | 5.3 | 8.9 | 7.9 |
| Colonial Bank | 5.6 | 5.3 | 8.7 | 8.4 |
| **Period 3: 1914–20** | | | | |
| English, Scottish & Australian Bank | 15.2 | 10.3 | n.a. | n.a. |
| Hongkong Bank (1918–) | 14.4 | 10.9 | n.a. | n.a. |
| Mercantile Bank | 11.3 | 9.3 | n.a. | n.a. |
| Chartered Bank | 11.2 | 9.2 | 11.9 | 9.8 |
| Standard Bank of South Africa | 11.0 | 8.5 | 16.0 | 12.3 |
| Colonial Bank (–1919) | 8.7 | 7.3 | 10.7 | 9.1 |
| Ionian Bank | 7.5 | 6.3 | 13.0 | 11.0 |
| London and River Plate Bank | 7.5 | 6.7 | 10.3 | 9.2 |
| Imperial Bank of Persia | 6.1 | 5.3 | 9.9 | 8.5 |
| **Period 4: 1921–9** | | | | |
| Hongkong Bank | 14.2 | 11.7 | n.a. | n.a. |
| English, Scottish & Australian Bank | 11.1 | 8.3 | n.a. | n.a. |
| Chartered Bank | 10.3 | 9.1 | 9.6 | 8.5 |
| Standard Bank of South Africa | 10.2 | 7.7 | 13.3 | 10.2 |
| Mercantile Bank | 10.0 | 8.1 | n.a. | n.a. |
| Imperial Bank of Persia | 10.0 | 5.5 | 23.7 | 13.1 |
| Lloyds, National Provincial Foreign | 8.9 | 8.1 | 11.3 | 10.2 |
| Barclays (DCO) (1926–) | 8.3 | 6.8 | 13.6 | 11.2 |
| Ionian Bank | 7.3 | 5.9 | 11.8 | 9.5 |
| Bolsa (1925–) | 6.4 | 6.0 | 7.9 | 7.5 |
| **Period 5: 1930–8** | | | | |
| Hongkong Bank | 11.7 | 10.2 | n.a. | n.a. |
| Standard Bank of South Africa | 9.5 | 6.0 | 14.7 | 9.4 |
| Eastern Bank (1931–) | 7.9 | 6.8 | 7.4 | 6.2 |
| Mercantile Bank | 7.6 | 6.0 | n.a. | n.a. |
| Chartered Bank | 7.5 | 6.5 | 5.9 | 5.1 |
| Barclays (DCO) | 6.0 | 4.0 | 12.1 | 8.0 |

TABLE A5.4. (*Cont.*)

| Bank | Ratio: published profits to shareholder funds | Ratio: published profits to shareholder funds + inner reserves | Ratio: real profits to shareholder funds | Ratio: real profits to shareholder funds + inner reserves |
|------|------|------|------|------|
| Bolsa | 5.8 | 4.2 | 2.5 | 1.8 |
| English, Scottish & Australian Bank | 5.3 | 3.8 | n.a. | n.a. |
| Imperial Bank of Iran | 4.9 | 2.6 | 6.4 | 3.4 |
| Ionian Bank | 2.6 | 2.1 | 6.5 | 5.2 |
| Lloyds, National Provincial Foreign | 0.0 | 0.0 | -0.7 | -0.7 |
| **Period 6: 1939–46** | | | | |
| Standard Bank of South Africa | 10.1 | 5.4 | 14.9 | 8.0 |
| Bolsa | 9.1 | 5.6 | 12.1 | 7.5 |
| Mercantile Bank | 7.0 | 4.6 | 9.8 | 6.4 |
| Imperial Bank of Iran | 6.5 | 3.7 | 8.6 | 4.9 |
| Eastern Bank | 6.0 | 4.8 | 10.0 | 8.0 |
| Chartered Bank | 5.4 | 4.3 | 9.9 | 7.7 |
| Barclays (DCO) | 5.2 | 3.1 | 10.0 | 6.1 |
| Bank of British West Africa | 5.1 | 3.7 | 6.6 | 4.8 |
| English, Scottish & Australian Bank (–1941) | 4.4 | 3.0 | n.a. | n.a. |
| Ionian Bank | 3.1 | 2.7 | 6.6 | 5.8 |
| Lloyds, National Provincial Foreign | 1.9 | 1.5 | 2.4 | 1.9 |
| **Period 7: 1947–55** | | | | |
| Hongkong Bank | 13.6 | n.a. | 25.8 | n.a. |
| Bank of British West Africa | 8.8 | 5.0 | 16.3 | 9.3 |
| Chartered Bank | 8.1 | 5.4 | 19.3 | 12.7 |
| Mercantile Bank | 7.2 | 3.4 | 19.4 | 9.0 |
| Standard Bank of South Africa | 6.6 | 4.5 | 18.3 | 12.5 |
| Eastern Bank (–1957) | 5.3 | 3.9 | 5.9 | 4.3 |
| British Bank of the Middle East | 5.0 | 3.0 | 10.2 | 6.2 |
| Bolsa | 5.0 | 3.1 | 7.8 | 4.8 |
| Barclays (DCO) | 4.6 | 3.2 | 13.4 | 9.4 |
| Ionian Bank (–1957) | 4.3 | 3.1 | 8.3 | 5.9 |
| Lloyds, National Provincial Foreign (–1954) | 2.1 | 1.6 | 5.3 | 3.9 |
| **Period 8: 1956–69** | | | | |
| Hongkong Bank (–1961) | 13.5 | n.a. | 23.7 | n.a. |
| Chartered Bank | 8.4 | 4.9 | 17.0 | 9.9 |
| British Bank of the Middle East (–1959) | 7.1 | 4.8 | 17.1 | 11.7 |
| Bank of British West Africa (–1964) | 6.6 | 4.0 | 13.0 | 7.4 |
| Standard Bank (–1966) | 6.1 | 4.5 | 9.0 | 6.7 |
| Mercantile Bank (–1959) | 6.1 | 3.4 | 12.5 | 6.9 |
| Barclays (DCO) (–1960) | 5.4 | n.a. | 14.3 | n.a. |
| Bolsa (–1960) | 5.3 | 3.8 | 11.1 | 7.9 |

*Note*: n.a. = not available.

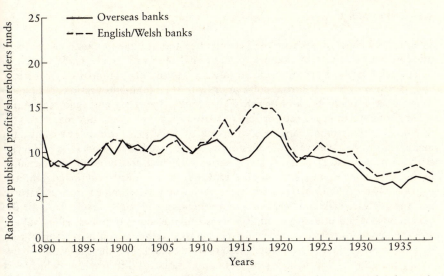

GRAPH A5.1. Comparison of profitability of sample British overseas banks and English and Welsh joint stock banks, 1890–1939

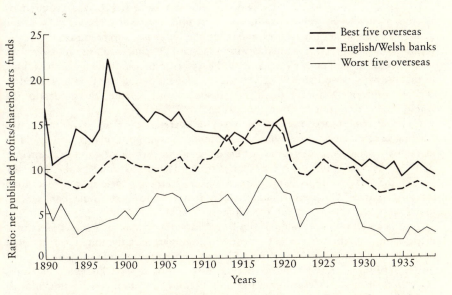

GRAPH A5.2. Comparison of profitability of the best and worst five of the sample overseas banks and English and Welsh joint stock banks, 1890–1939

*5.2. Commentary*

The primary conclusions from the performance and profitability analysis are identified in the main text. A number of additional observations are made here.

The NPV analysis reveals wide variations between institutions in each period,
and at best only a very partial correlation with the profitability ratios. The 'stars'
of most periods—the Bank of British West Africa (1896–1913 and again 1939–46),
or Anglo Egyptian (1914–20) or Ionian Bank (1947–55)—were not major players
in British multinational banking. A ranking by NPV per £100 invested indicates
merely an investor preference; it does not necessarily reflect the underlying financial
strength of a bank. Essentially, any positive NPV indicates a 'good' performance
by a bank when compared with the return from an investment in government
Consols. The NPV measures investment values at predetermined rates of return,
and the key variables in its calculation are the market prices of bank shares at the
beginning and end of each period, hypothesizing the acquisition and selling values,
and the dividends paid out, reflecting income to shareholders. It is evident that an
investor seeking the highest returns was best advised to buy the shares of a bank
which had just started or had gone through a period of difficulty, but which was
about to begin a period of rapid growth, as reflected by a favourable stock market
assessment of its position. Such a description fitted all the banks heading the NPV
ranking for 1896–1913: the Bank of British West Africa, Anglo-South American,
and the National Bank of New Zealand. The problem for individual investors, as
always, was the prediction of growth prospects. The Bank of Mauritius was, like
the Bank of British West Africa, a 'newcomer' in the 1890s, but its dividend
payments and capital growth were never high.

It was also apparent that the shareholders of a bank which was acquired by
another tended to do well, since the take-over price paid was often in excess of the
actual market value of its shares, reflecting the purchaser's expectation of greater
future earnings as a result of amalgamation. Anglo-Egyptian's acquisition by Barclays
was reflected in its high NPV ranking in the 1914–20 period. Ionian's high ranking
in the 1947–55 period and Bolsa's in the subsequent period can also be related to
this phenomenon. Naturally there was no such reward for the shareholders of the
Anglo-South American Bank in the 1930s.

Overseas bank shares were more 'risky' for shareholders than shares in the two
clearing banks included in the analysis. In times of poor performance, shareholders
in the two domestic banks fared better, although in periods of good performance
more spectacular returns were available from the multinational banks. In every
period, the 'best' overseas banks earned higher returns for their shareholders than
the two clearers. Conversely, shareholders in the worse-performing banks fared
much worse than those in the two domestic banks.

The data confirm the image of the British overseas banks as being conservative
institutions. The managements of most banks sought, over the long term, to build
up published reserves and to create additional inner reserves to anticipate risk and
future uncertainty, rather than to increase distribution to shareholders. The banks
built up their inner reserves over time, although the priority they gave this differed
in different periods. In 1913 the inner reserves of nine sample banks amounted to
45 per cent of the level of published reserves. In 1928 the inner reserves of the nine

sample banks for which data exist amounted to 50 per cent of their published reserves and, again, in only two cases were they larger than the published figure. In 1955—when figures are known for ten banks—collective inner reserves were around 95 per cent of published reserves. In four cases inner reserves were larger than published ones.

In the text it has been observed that the published profit ratios suggest that the Eastern Exchange banks were the most profitable group of British overseas banks over the long term. After 1914, except for 1939–46, the Exchange banks supplied at least three of the top five banks with the highest profitability ratio in each period. The surviving 'real' data analysed in Table A5.4 are not able to provide conclusive proof of this interpretation. No information is available for the National Bank of India, and only limited data for the Hongkong Bank. The most consistent data are available for Chartered Bank. These show that its ratio of real profits to shareholder funds was only a little higher than the published figures for 1890–1895, 1896–1913, and 1914–20, and worse for the two inter-war periods. The real performance of certain other banks was noticeably much better. However, the published ratios of Chartered were also sufficient to place it in the 'top five' only twice between 1890 and 1946—namely, for 1914–20 and 1921–9. But, interestingly, the ratio of real profits to shareholder funds of Eastern Bank in 1930–8—when it was one of the 'top five' on published figures—was also lower than its published ratio.

The apparent long-term good performance of the Exchange banks can be explained by several factors discussed in this book. However, one important influence on bank profitability seems to have been the ratio of paid-up capital to deposits, calculated in Table A5.3. In general, and with exceptions, there was a correlation between high profitability and a low capital/deposits ratio. The Exchange banks, with the exception of the 'latecomer' Eastern Bank, had such low ratios. The ratio of paid-up capital to deposits is a measure of whether a bank has the most cost-effective balance of resources, given that the cost involved in the use of capital—dividend payments—was almost always greater than the cost of using deposits—the interest paid to depositors.

Graphs A5.1 and A5.2 reveal the published profitability of the sample overseas banks and the English and Welsh joint stock banks moving in broadly similar patterns between 1890 and 1939. Initially overseas bank profitability exceeded that of domestic banks in some years, but after 1908 this was never the case. The widest divergence in their profitability is revealed as the period of the First World War.

Lance E. Davis and Robert A. Huttenback, in their book *Mammon and the Pursuit of Empire*, 84, 87–9, calculated rates of return of British commercial banks active in the United Kingdom, foreign countries, and the Empire between 1860 and 1912. This calculation is not comparable with either the profitability ratios or the NPV analysis given here. Davis and Huttenback suggest that banks active in foreign countries earned the highest rates between 1880 and 1894, but between then and 1912 banks in the Empire earned more than those in either foreign countries or the United Kingdom. Eleven overseas banks are included in their sample, including the three small Anglo-Californian banks.

No attempt is made here to deal with the idiosyncratic factors which affected

the profitability and performance of individual banks. The data have been generated as part of a comparative examination of a group of businesses, and are not
designed *per se* to provide a self-contained financial history of individual banks.
Anyone seeking to use these data to track the performance of individual banks is
advised to use all the ratios calculated in the appendix—which often illustrate
different elements of each story—and to put the statistical data in the context of
the qualitative discussion given in the main text.

# Select Bibliography

PRIMARY SOURCES

This book has drawn extensively on the confidential records of British multinational banks. With one important exception, every surviving relevant commercial bank archive was examined. The exception was the historical records of the Hongkong Bank, whose history had been thoroughly explored in the four-volume history by F. H. H. King. It should be emphasized, however, that this archival research was not comprehensive. Some archives (notably those of ANZ and Standard Chartered) are enormous, and only a small share of their total holdings could be researched. Conditions of access varied between banks. This circumscribed both the kinds of records consulted and, more frequently, the dates of records which could be researched. References to the specific files consulted in each bank archive are available in the footnotes.

The many mergers and amalgamations among British multinational banks has led to the concentration of their archives in a number of locations. As a result, the following discussion is organized by location of records, rather than by individual bank. All the archives are located in the United Kingdom, apart from those of ANZ and the Hongkong Bank.

The ANZ Group Archives, Melbourne, hold the archives of the Anglo-Australian banks. The records of the Bank of Australasia, the English, Scottish & Australian Bank, and the Union Bank of Australia were consulted, mainly for the inter-war period. ANZ Group Archives also control the surviving archives of the National Bank of India and Grindlays Bank, but at the time of research these were held at the London offices of the bank. Few records of these two banks dating from before the 1970s have survived, but Grindlays board minutes are extant from the 1940s, and were consulted.

At Barclays Bank PLC Archives, the records of Barclays Bank (France), Barclays Bank (DCO), and the Colonial Bank were consulted. Only limited access was possible at the time of research, but the bank is in the process of opening this extensive collection to researchers at an office in Wythenshawe, near Manchester.

At the Hongkong Bank Group Archives, Hong Kong, the records of the Mercantile Bank of India were researched extensively, as were the limited holdings on the Bank of Mauritius. This Archive also holds the records of the British Bank of the Middle East (which were used in the author's two-volume history of that bank) and the Hongkong Bank.

Lloyds Bank Group Archives in London hold the archives of a number of banks, including Lloyds Bank itself, Lloyds and National Provincial Foreign Bank, and Cox & Co. These records were examined. It should be noted that the archives of National Westminster Bank PLC also contain important records of the Lloyds and National Provincial Foreign Bank, which were consulted by the author for an earlier study, published in *Business History*, 24 (1982). At Lloyds, financial data of the National Bank of New Zealand were also consulted. Lloyds also hold part of the surviving historical records of the Bank of London and South America (Bolsa), and its predecessor banks, including the London and River Plate Bank, the London and Brazilian Bank, and the Anglo-South American Bank. The most important records include Bolsa Board Minutes from 1925, and detailed financial information on Bolsa and its predecessors. A limited amount of correspondence has survived and was consulted.

The London School of Economics, British Library of Political and Economic Science, holds the extensive historical records of the Ionian Bank. These were researched in depth.

At the Midland Bank Archives, London, relevant records of the Midland Bank were examined.

At the time of research, Standard Chartered Bank PLC Archives held the historical records of the African Banking Corporation, the Bank of British West Africa, the Chartered Bank of India, Australia and China, Eastern Bank, the P & O Banking Corporation, and Standard Bank of South Africa. These were consulted extensively, but the vast size of the collection meant that only a sample of these archives could be seen. Since completing the research, part of this collection has been transferred to the Guildhall Library, London.

University College, London, D. M. S Watson Library, holds most of the surviving archives of the Bank of London and South America, and its predecessor banks. Most of this collection is correspondence between branches, and between Latin American branches and London, and a sample of this material was consulted.

Two archives in the public domain were of considerable importance for this study. Bank of England archives were used extensively. They hold essential information on the history of British multinational banking after 1914. British government records held at the Public Record Office, London, were also valuable. The main collections consulted were those of the Board of Trade (BT), Colonial Office (CO), Foreign Office (FO), and Treasury (T).

## SECONDARY SOURCES

This bibliography is a guide to the most relevant literature on the history of British multinational banks, and the context in which they operated. It does not list all the sources cited in the text.

*A Bank in Battledress* (London: Barclays Bank (DCO), 1948).

*A Banking Centenary: Barclays Bank (Dominion, Colonial and Overseas), 1836–1936* (London: Barclays, 1936).

Aliber, Robert Z., 'International Banking: A Survey', *Journal of Money, Credit and Banking*, 16(4) (1984), 661–78.

Amphlett, G. T., *History of the Standard Bank of South Africa Ltd., 1862–1913* (Glasgow: Maclehose, 1914).

Appleyard, R. T., and Schedvin, C. B. (eds.), *Australian Financiers* (Melbourne: Macmillan, 1988).

Arndt, H. W., *The Australian Trading Banks* (Melbourne: Cheshire, 1957).

Bagchi, A. K., 'Anglo-Indian Banking in British India: From the Paper Pound to the Gold Standard', *Journal of Imperial and Commonwealth History*, 13(3) (1985), 93–108.

—— *The Evolution of the State of India* (Bombay: Oxford University Press, 1987), parts 1 and 2.

—— *The Presidency Banks and the Indian Economy, 1876–1914* (Calcutta: Oxford University Press, 1989).

Baster, A. S. J., *The Imperial Banks* (London: King, 1929).

—— *The International Banks* (London: King, 1935).

Bird, Graham, *Commercial Bank Lending and Third World Debt* (London: Macmillan, 1989).

Bostock, Frances, 'The British Overseas Banks and Development Finance in Africa after 1945', *Business History*, 33 (1991), 157–76.

—— and Jones, Geoffrey, *Planning and Power in Iran* (London: Cass, 1989).

Burk, Kathleen, *Morgan Grenfell, 1838–1988* (Oxford: Oxford University Press, 1989).

Butlin, S. J., *Australia and New Zealand Bank* (London: Longman, 1961).

—— *The Australian Monetary System, 1851–1914* (Sydney, 1986).

Capie, Forrest, 'The Evolving Regulatory Framework in British Banking', in Martin Chick (ed.), *Governments, Industries and Markets* (Aldershot: Elgar, 1990).

—— 'Structure and Performance in British Banking, 1870–1939', in P. L. Cottrell and D. E. Moggridge (eds.), *Money and Power* (London: Macmillan, 1988).

Carosso, Vincent P., *The Morgans: Private International Bankers, 1854–1913* (Cambridge, Mass.: Harvard University Press, 1987).

Cassis, Youssef, *Les Banquiers de la City à l'époque Edouardienne, 1890–1914* (Geneva: Librairie Droz, 1984).

Casson, Mark, 'Evolution of Multinational Banks: A Theoretical Perspective', in Geoffrey Jones (ed.), *Banks as Multinationals*.

Chandavarkar, 'Money and Credit, 1858–1947', in D. Kumar (ed.), *The Cambridge Economic History of India*, ii (Cambridge: Cambridge University Press, 1983).

Chandler, Alfred D., *Scale and Scope* (Cambridge, Mass.: Harvard University Press, 1990).

—— *Strategy and Structure* (Cambridge, Mass.: MIT Press, 1962).

—— *The Visible Hand* (Cambridge, Mass.: Harvard University Press, 1977).

Channon, Derek F., *British Banking Strategy and the International Challenge* (London: Macmillan, 1977).

—— *Cases in Bank Strategic Management and Marketing* (Chichester: Wiley, 1986).

—— *Global Banking Strategy* (Chichester: Wiley, 1986).

Chapman, Stanley, *The Rise of Merchant Banking* (London: Allen and Unwin, 1984).

Chee Peng Lim, Phang Siew Nooi, and Boh, Margaret, 'The History and Development of the Hongkong and Shanghai Banking Corporation in Peninsular Malaysia', in F. H. H. King (ed.), *Eastern Banking*.

Clay, Christopher, 'The Imperial Ottoman Bank in the Later Nineteenth Century: A Multinational "National" Bank?', in Geoffrey Jones (ed.), *Banks as Multinationals*.

Cleveland, Harold Van B., and Huertas, Thomas F., *Citibank 1812–1970* (Cambridge, Mass.: Harvard University Press, 1985).

Collins, Michael, *Money and Banking in the UK: A History* (Beckenham: Croom Helm, 1988).

Collis, Maurice, *Wayfoong: The Hongkong and Shanghai Banking Corporation* (London: Faber & Faber, 1965).

Cottrell, P. L., 'Aspects of Western Equity Investment in the Banking Systems of East and Central Europe', in Alice Teichova and P. L. Cottrell (eds.), *International Business and Central Europe, 1918–1939* (Leicester: Leicester University Press, 1983).

—— 'The Coalescence of a Cluster of Corporate International Banks, 1855–1875', *Business History*, 33 (1991), 31–52.

—— 'London Financiers and Austria, 1863–1875: The Anglo-Austrian Bank', *Business History*, 11 (1969), 106–19.

Crossley, Sir Julian, and Blandford, John, *The DCO Story* (London: Barclays Bank International Ltd., 1975).

Damanpour, Faramarz, *The Evolution of Foreign Banking Institutions in the United States* (New York: Quorum Books, 1990).

Davenport-Hines, R. P. T., *Dudley Docker* (Cambridge: Cambridge University Press, 1984).

—— and Jones, Geoffrey (eds.), *British Business in Asia since 1860* (Cambridge: Cambridge University Press, 1989).

—— (eds.), *The End of Insularity* (London: Cass, 1988).

Davis, Clarence B., 'Financing Imperialism: British and American Bankers as Vectors of Imperial Expansion in China, 1908–1920', *Business History Review*, 56 (1982), 236–64.

Davis, Lance E., and Huttenback, Robert A., *Mammon and the Pursuit of Empire* (Cambridge: Cambridge University Press, 1986).

Dayer, Roberta Allbert, *Finance and Empire: Sir Charles Addis, 1861–1945* (London: Macmillan, 1988).

Denison, Merrill, *Canada's First Bank: A History of the Bank of Montreal*, 2 vols. (Toronto: Dodd Mead, 1966).

Devlin, Robert, *Debt and Crisis in Latin America* (Princeton, NJ: Princeton University Press, 1989).

Fry, Richard, *Bankers in West Africa* (London: Hutchinson Benham, 1976).

—— (ed.), *A Banker's World* (London: Hutchinson, 1970).

Fulford, Roger, *Glyn's, 1753–1953* (London: Macmillan, 1953).

Gilbert, R. S., 'London Financial Intermediaries and Australian Overseas Borrowing 1900–29', *Australian Economic History Review*, 11 (1971), 39–47.

Goldberg, Lawrence G., and Johnson, Denise, 'The Determinants of US Banking Activity Abroad', *Journal of International Money and Finance*, 9 (1990), 123–37.

Gonjo, Y., 'La Banque coloniale et l'État: la Banque de l'Indochine devant l'interventionnisme, 1917–1931', *Le Mouvement Social*, 142 (1988), 45–74.

Grady, John, and Weale, Martin, *British Banking, 1960–85* (London: Macmillan, 1986).

Graham, Richard, *Britain and the Onset of Modernisation in Brazil 1850–1914* (Cambridge: Cambridge University Press, 1968).

Gray, Jean M., and Gray, Peter H., 'The Multinational Bank: A Financial MNC?', *Journal of Banking and Finance*, 5 (1981), 33–63.

Grubel, H. G., 'A Theory of Multinational Banking', *Banca Nazionale del Lavoro*, 123 (1977), 349–63.

Hall, A. R., *The London Capital Market in Australia, 1870–1914* (Canberra: Australian National University, 1963).

Hawke, G. R., *Between Governments and Banks: A History of the Reserve Bank of New Zealand* (Wellington: Shearer, 1973).

Henry, J. A., *The First Hundred Years of the Standard Bank* (London: Oxford University Press, 1963).

Hertner, Peter, 'German Banks Abroad before 1914', in Geoffrey Jones (ed.), *Banks as Multinationals*.

—— and Jones, Geoffrey (eds.), *Multinationals: Theory and History* (Aldershot: Gower, 1986).

Holder, R. F., *Bank of New South Wales: A History*, i and ii (Sydney: Angus and Robertson, 1970).

Holmes, A. R., and Green, Edwin, *Midland: 150 Years of Banking Business* (London: Batsford, 1986).

Huertas, Thomas F., 'US Multinational Banking: History and Prospects', in Geoffrey Jones (ed.), *Banks as Multinationals*.

*Ionian Bank Ltd.: A History* (London: Ionian Bank, 1953).

Jao, Y. C., 'Financing Hong Kong's Early Postwar Industrialization', in F. H. H. King (ed.), *Eastern Banking*.

—— and King, F. H. H., *Money in Hong Kong* (Hong Kong: Centre of Asian Studies, University of Hong Kong, 1990).

Jones, Charles A., 'Commercial Banks and Mortgage Companies', in Platt (ed.), *Business Imperialism, 1840–1930*.

—— 'The Transfer of Banking Techniques from Britain to Argentina, 1862–1914', *Revue Internationale d'Histoire de la Banque*, 26–7 (1983), 251–64.

Jones, Geoffrey, *Banking and Empire in Iran* (Cambridge: Cambridge University Press, 1986).

—— *Banking and Oil* (Cambridge: Cambridge University Press, 1987).

—— 'The British Government and Foreign Multinationals before 1970', in Martin Chick (ed.), *Governments, Industries and Markets* (Aldershot: Elgar, 1990).

—— 'Competition and Competitiveness in British Banking, 1918–71', in Geoffrey Jones and Maurice Kirby (eds.), *Competitiveness and the State*.

—— 'International Financial Centres in Asia, the Middle East and Australia: A Historical Perspective', in Youssef Cassis (ed.), *Finance and Financiers in European History, 1880–1960* (Cambridge: Cambridge University Press, 1992).

—— 'Lombard Street on the Riviera: The British Clearing Banks and Europe, 1900–1960', *Business History*, 24 (1982), 186–210.

—— (ed.), *Banks as Multinationals* (London: Routledge, 1990).

—— (ed.), *Multinational and International Banking* (Aldershot: Elgar, 1992).

—— and Kirby, Maurice (eds.), *Competitiveness and the State* (Manchester: Manchester University Press, 1991).

Jones, Stuart, 'The Apogee of Imperial Banks in South Africa: Standard and Barclays, 1919–1939', *English Historical Review*, 103 (1988), 892–916.

Jones, Stuart (ed.), *Banking and Business in South Africa* (London: Macmillan, 1988).

Joslin, David, *A Century of Banking in Latin America* (London: Oxford University Press, 1963).

Kent, Marion, 'Agent of Empire? The National Bank of Turkey and British Foreign Policy', *Historical Journal*, 18 (1975), 367–89.

King, David J. S., 'China's First Public Loan: The Hongkong Bank and the Chinese Imperial Government "Foochow" Loan of 1874', in F. H. H. King (ed.), *Eastern Banking*.

—— 'The Hamburg Branch: The German Period, 1889–1920', in F. H. H. King (ed.), *Eastern Banking*.

King, F. H. H., 'Defending the Chinese Currency', in F. H. H. King (ed.), *Eastern Banking*.

—— *The History of the Hongkong and Shanghai Banking Corporation*, i–iv (Cambridge: Cambridge University Press, 1987–91).

—— 'The Mercantile Bank's Royal Charter', in F. H. H. King (ed.), *Asian Policy, History and Development*.

—— 'Structural Alternatives and Constraints in the Evolution of Exchange Banking', in Geoffrey Jones (ed.), *Banks as Multinationals*.

—— (ed.), *Asian Policy, History and Development* (Hong Kong: University of Hong Kong, 1979).

—— (ed.), *Eastern Banking* (London: Athlone, 1983).

Mabin, A., and Conradie, B. (eds.), *The Confidence of the Whole Country* (Johannesburg: Standard Bank Investment Corporation, 1987).

Mackenzie, Compton, *Realms of Silver* (London: Routledge & Kegan Paul, 1954).

Mclean, David, 'International Banking and its Political Implications: The Hongkong and Shanghai Banking Corporation and the Imperial Bank of Persia, 1889–1914', in F. H. H. King (ed.), *Eastern Banking*.

Marichal, Carlos, *A Century of Debt Crises in Latin America* (Princeton, NJ: Princeton University Press, 1989).

Mathur, Rajul, 'The Delay in the Formation of the Reserve Bank of India: The India Office Perspective', *Indian Economic and Social History Review*, 25(2) (1988), 133–69.

Merrett, David, *ANZ Bank* (Sydney: Allen and Unwin, 1985).

—— 'Australian Banking Practice and the Crisis of 1893', *Australian Economic History Review*, 29(1) (1989), 60–85.

—— 'Paradise Lost? British Banks in Australia', in Geoffrey Jones (ed.), *Banks as Multinationals*.

Meuleau, Marc, *Des pionniers en Extrême-Orient* (Paris: Fayard, 1990).

Muirhead, S. W., 'The Mercantile Bank of India on the East Coast of Malaya', in F. H. H. King (ed.), *Eastern Banking*.

*National Bank of Egypt, 1898–1948* (Cairo: National Bank of Egypt, 1948).

Nelson, W. Evan, 'The Hongkong and Shanghai Banking Corporation Factor in the Progress towards a Straits Settlements Government Note Issue, 1881–1889', in F. H. H. King (ed.), *Eastern Banking*.

'The New Oriental Bank Corporation: A Lesson in Bad Banking', *Bankers' Magazine*, 57 (1894), 69–80.

Newlyn, W. T., *Money in an African Context* (Nairobi: Oxford University Press, 1967).

Onoh, J. K., *Money and Banking in Africa* (London: Longman, 1982).

Patrikeef, Felix, 'Prosperity and Collapse: Banking and the Manchurian Economy in the 1920s and 1930s', in F. H. H. King (ed.), *Eastern Banking*.

Phylaktis, Kate, 'Banking in a British Colony: Cyprus, 1878–1959', *Business History*, 30 (1988), 416–31.

Platt, D. C. M. (ed.), *Business Imperialism, 1840–1930* (Oxford: Clarendon Press, 1977).

Pohl, Manfred, *Deutsche Bank Buenos Aires, 1887–1987* (Mainz: Hase & Koehler, 1987).

Porter, Michael, *The Competitive Advantage of Nations* (London: Macmillan, 1990).

Pramuanratkarn, T., 'The Hongkong Bank in Thailand: A Case of a Pioneering Bank', in F. H. H. King (ed.), *Eastern Banking*.

Quigley, Neil C., 'The Bank of Nova Scotia in the Caribbean, 1889–1940: The Establishment and Organisation of an International Branch Banking Network', *Business History Review*, 63 (1989), 797–838.

Redding, S. G., 'Organisational and Structural Change in the Hongkong and Shanghai Banking Corporation, 1950–1980', in F. H. H. King (ed.), *Eastern Banking*.

Republic Bank Ltd., *From Colonial to Republic: One Hundred and Fifty Years of Business in Banking in Trinidad and Tobago, 1837–1987* (Trinidad: Republic Bank, n.d.).

Sayers, R. S., *The Bank of England 1891–1944*, 2 vols. (Cambridge: Cambridge University Press, 1976).

—— *Lloyds Bank in the History of English Banking* (Oxford: Clarendon Press, 1957).

—— (ed.), *Banking in the British Commonwealth* (Oxford: Clarendon Press, 1952).

Segreto, Luciano, 'La City e la "Dolce Vita" romano: la storia della Banca Italo Britannica, 1916–1930', *Passato e Presente*, 13 (1987), 63–95.

Selvaratnam, H. L. D., 'The Guarantee Shroffs, the Chettiars, and the Hongkong Bank in Ceylon', in F. H. H. King (ed.), *Eastern Banking*.

Sit, Victor F. S., 'Branching of the Hongkong and Shanghai Banking Corporation in Hong Kong: A Spatial Analysis', in F. H. H. King (ed.), *Eastern Banking*.

Smith, Carl T., 'Compradores of the Hongkong Bank', in F. H. H. King (ed.), *Eastern Banking*.

*Standard Bank, 1892–1967: Three Quarters of a Century of Banking in Rhodesia* (Salisbury: Standard Bank, 1967).

Standard Chartered Bank, *A Story Brought up to Date* (London: Standard Chartered Bank, 1980).

Tamaki, Norio, 'The Yokohama Specie Bank: A Multinational in the Japanese Interest, 1879–1931', in Geoffrey Jones (ed.), *Banks as Multinationals*.

Teichova, Alice, 'Versailles and the Expansion of the Bank of England into Central Europe', in H. Horn and J. Kocka (eds.), *Law and the Formation of the Big Enterprises in the Nineteenth and Early Twentieth Centuries* (Göttingen: Vandenhoeck and Ruprecht, 1979).

Thane, P., 'Financiers and the British State: The Case of Sir Ernest Cassel', in R. P. T. Davenport-Hines (ed.), *Speculators and Patriots: Essays in Business Biography* (London: Cass, 1986).

Truptil, R. J., *British Banks and the London Money Market* (London: Cape, 1936).

Tschoegl, Adrian E., 'International Retail Banking as a Strategy: An Assessment', *Journal of International Business Studies*, 19(2) (1987), 67–88.

Tuke, A. W., and Gillman, R., *Barclays Bank Limited, 1926–1969* (London: Barclays Bank, 1972).

Tyson, Geoffrey, *100 Years of Banking in Asia and Africa* (London: National and Grindlays, 1963).

White, R. C., *Australian Banking and Monetary Statistics, 1945–1970*, Reserve Bank of Australia, Occasional Paper No. 4B, Sydney, 1973.

Wilkins, Mira, 'Banks over Borders: Some Evidence from their Pre-1914 History', in Geoffrey Jones (ed.), *Banks as Multinationals*.

—— 'Defining a Firm: History and Theory', in Hertner and Jones (eds.), *Multinationals: Theory and History*.

—— 'European and North American Multinationals, 1870–1914: Comparisons and Contrasts', in Davenport-Hines and Jones (eds.), *The End of Insularity*.

—— 'The Free-Standing Company, 1870-1914: An Important Type of British Foreign Direct Investment', *Economic History Review*, 2nd ser., 41 (1988), 259–82.

—— 'The History of European Multinationals: A New Look', *Journal of European Economic History*, 15 (1986), 483–510.

—— *The History of Foreign Investment in the United States to 1914* (Cambridge, Mass.: Harvard University Press, 1989).

—— (ed.), *The Growth of Multinationals* (Aldershot: Elgar, 1991).

Wilson, John Donald, *The Chase* (Boston, Mass.: Harvard Business School Press, 1986).

Wilson, Rodney, 'Financial Development of the Arab Gulf: The Eastern Bank Experience, 1917–1950', *Business History*, 29 (1987), 178–98.

Winton, J. R., *Lloyds Bank, 1918–1969* (Oxford: Oxford University Press, 1982).

## Published Reports

Committee to Review the Functioning of Financial Institutions, *Report and Appendices*, 1980 (Cmnd. 7937).

London Clearing Banks, *Evidence by the Committee of London Clearing Bankers to the Committee to Review the Functioning of Financial Institutions* (London, Nov. 1977).

Monopolies and Mergers Commission, *A Report on the Proposed Mergers of the Hongkong and Shanghai Banking Corporation, Standard Chartered Bank Limited and the Royal Bank of Scotland Group Limited* (London, Jan. 1982).

Monopolies Commission, *Report on the Proposed Merger of Barclays Bank Ltd., Lloyds Bank Ltd., and Martins Bank Ltd.* (London, 1968).

*Report of the Royal Commission Appointed to Inquire into the Monetary and Banking Systems at Present in Operation in Australia* (Melbourne, 1936).

*Report to the Board of Trade by the Committee Appointed to Investigate the Question of Financial Facilities for Trade*, Cd. 8346, 1916.

United Nations Centre on Transnational Corporations, *Transnational Bank Behaviour and the International Debt Crisis* (New York, Sept. 1989).

*Newspapers and Journals*

The following newspapers and journals yielded the most valuable information for this study: *The Banker, Bankers' Magazine, Bank of England Quarterly Bulletin, Economist, Euromoney, Far Eastern Economic Review, Financial Times, Journal of the Institute of Bankers.*


*Unpublished Materials*

Colgate, P., Sheppard, D. K., Guerin, K., and Hawke, G. R., 'A History of the Bank of New Zealand, 1862–1982. Part 1: 1862–1934', Victoria University of Wellington Money and Finance Association, Discussion Paper No. 7, 1990.

Jones, Charles A., 'British Financial Institutions in Argentine, 1860–1914', Ph.D. thesis, Cambridge, 1973.

Hawke, G. R., and Sheppard, D. K., 'The Evolution of New Zealand Trading Banks mostly until 1934', Victoria University of Wellington Working Papers in Economic History, No. 84/2, Mar. 1984.

Merrett, David, 'The 1893 Bank Crashes: The Aftermath', unpublished paper.

—— 'The 1893 Bank Crashes: A Reconsideration', unpublished paper given to Monash Economic History Seminar, 13 Nov. 1987.

—— 'Two Hundred Years of Banking', unpublished paper.

Swanson, J. J., 'History of the Bank in East Africa', Memoirs unpublished MS, June 1954, Standard Chartered Archives.

# Index